TREASURY OF LITERATURE

Components
Grades K-8

Engaging options to help young readers explore their interests, share their experiences, and develop a lifelong love of reading

HARCOURT BRACE

Technology

Big Book Literature Cassette Collection (Grade 1)
Big Book stories recorded for easy listening and to promote fluency.

Literature Cassettes (Grades 1–8)
Delightful recordings of literature selections from the *Student Anthologies*.

Laserdisc and Teacher's Manual (Grades 1–8)
Dynamic full-motion videos and still images that build concepts, illustrate key vocabulary, and stimulate critical thinking—all easily accessed by bar codes.

Reading Software (Grades 3–8)
A reading skills practice program with activities that reinforce vocabulary, comprehension, thinking, study, and language skills (available for use with Apple® IIe, IIc, and IIGS and Macintosh® computers).

Computer Management System (Grades 1–8)
A technology aid for unit reading skills assessment (for use with Apple® IIe, IIc, and IIGS, Macintosh®, and IBM®/MS-DOS® computers).

Holistic Scoring Workshop (Grades 1–8)
Instructional software that supports holistic scoring of students' writing.

Get to Know An Author Videotapes (Grades 1–6)
Favorite authors who love children—and love writing for them—talk about how their ideas originate and how they put their thoughts into words.

Second-Language Support

Alternative Teaching Strategies • Second-Language Support Activities (Grades 1–6)
A valuable teaching resource guide with lesson-by-lesson strategies for helping ESL and less-proficient students of English build language and reading skills—designed specifically for use with *Treasury of Literature*.

Transition for ESL Students, Teacher's Manuals (Grades 1–6)
Useful suggestions and strategies for helping ESL students make a comfortable transition to *Treasury of Literature*.

English as a Second Language Manuals and Posters (Grades 1–5)
Colorful classroom posters and a helpful teacher's manual for developing English language skills, vocabulary, and concepts.

For more information, call 1-800-225-5425.

Copyright © by Harcourt Brace & Company. All rights reserved. Printed in the U.S.A. 9999-55769-4

TREASURY OF LITERATURE

Teacher's Edition

A Place to Dream

SENIOR AUTHORS
ROGER C. FARR
DOROTHY S. STRICKLAND

AUTHORS
RICHARD F. ABRAHAMSON
ELLEN BOOTH CHURCH
BARBARA BOWEN COULTER
BERNICE E. CULLINAN
MARGARET A. GALLEGO
W. DORSEY HAMMOND
JUDITH L. IRVIN
KAREN KUTIPER
DONNA M. OGLE
TIMOTHY SHANAHAN
PATRICIA SMITH
JUNKO YOKOTA
HALLIE KAY YOPP

SENIOR CONSULTANTS
ASA G. HILLIARD III
JUDY M. WALLIS

CONSULTANTS
ALONZO A. CRIM
ROLANDO R. HINOJOSA-SMITH
LEE BENNETT HOPKINS
ROBERT J. STERNBERG

HARCOURT BRACE

Orlando Atlanta Austin Boston San Francisco Chicago Dallas New York
Toronto London

Copyright © 1995 by Harcourt Brace & Company

All rights reserved. No part of this publication may be reproduced or transmitted in any form or by any means, electronic or mechanical, including photocopy, recording, or any information storage and retrieval system.

Permission is hereby granted to reproduce copying masters in this publication in complete pages, with the copyright notice, for instructional use and not for resale, by any teacher using TREASURY OF LITERATURE.

Portions of this work were published in previous editions.

Acknowledgments appear on page R129.

Printed in the United States of America

ISBN 0-15-301241-2

1 2 3 4 5 6 7 8 9 10   030   97 96 95 94

Authors

CLASSROOM MANAGEMENT

❝ Good management grows out of good organization. In literature-based instruction, the needs and interests of students are paramount in determining effective instructional strategies. The related assessment program should help teachers and students understand what a student can do successfully rather than emphasize what a student can't do. ❞

Dr. Roger Farr
Professor of Education and Director of the
Center for Reading and Language Studies,
Indiana University

EMERGENT LITERACY

❝ The principles of emergent literacy recognize that learning to read and write is an ongoing process and that reading and writing develop through active involvement and use. In a classroom that reflects an emergent literacy perspective, both the joy and the functional uses of reading and writing are introduced and supported. ❞

Dr. Dorothy S. Strickland
The State of New Jersey Professor of Reading,
Rutgers University

THE READING OF NONFICTION

❝ Good nonfiction can move us deeply. About half the books students read are nonfiction. Nonfiction plays a powerful role in the reading lives of today's children and young adults—tomorrow's leaders. ❞

Dr. Richard F. Abrahamson
Professor of Education,
University of Houston

MANAGING THE KINDERGARTEN CLASSROOM

❝ One way to do it all is to take the idea of "child-centered" seriously and have the children help you all along the way. ❞

Ellen Booth Church
Early Childhood Educational Consultant

INTEGRATING THE LANGUAGE ARTS

❝ We want children to learn skills at the same time that they are discovering the joy of reading, the power of writing, and the roles that listening and speaking play in those processes. ❞

Dr. Barbara Bowen Coulter
Director, Communication Arts,
Detroit Public School District

AUTHENTIC LITERATURE

❝ Great literature enriches children's lives and makes them aware of the pluralistic nature of our world. It allows children to savor experience and to experience life. ❞

Dr. Bernice E. Cullinan
Professor of Early Childhood and Elementary Education, New York University

SECOND-LANGUAGE SUPPORT

❝ A classroom of diverse students can offer unlimited possibilities for creating a unique community of learners. ❞

Dr. Margaret A. Gallego
Assistant Professor of Education, Michigan State University

COMPREHENSION

❝ The quality of questions teachers ask in order to engage students in their reading directly affects the quality of the students' responses to literature. ❞

Dr. W. Dorsey Hammond
Professor of Education, Oakland University, Rochester, Michigan

MIDDLE SCHOOL

❝ Making connections between subjects can enhance learning for middle-school students. Cross-curricular activities provide scaffolding for a skill that will serve students well throughout their lives. ❞

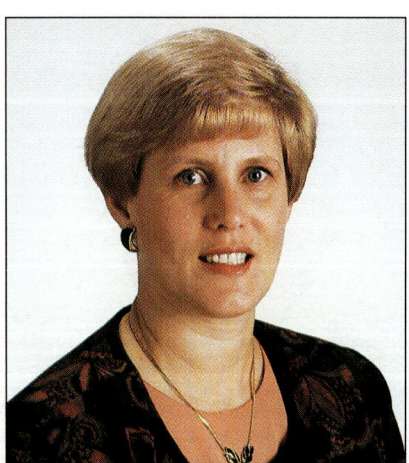

Dr. Judith L. Irvin
Director, Center for the Study of Middle Level Education, Florida State University

READER RESPONSE GROUPS

❝ Children working in response groups bring literature to life, find personal meanings in literature, and share the pleasures of reading. ❞

Dr. Karen Kutiper
Assistant Professor of Education, Southwest Texas State University

STRATEGIC READING

❝ Each reading situation is an encounter between an absent author and a reader who is trying to construct a clear understanding from the available written message. ❞

Dr. Donna M. Ogle
Chair, Reading and Language Arts Department, National-Louis University

WRITING

❝ We must provide children with an abundant heritage of literature while celebrating their voices. Writing, when allied with reading, can become a more powerful avenue to learning. ❞

Dr. Timothy Shanahan
Professor of Urban Education, University of Illinois, Chicago

READING-WRITING CONNECTION

❝ Literature and language are linked together to form an integrated whole for effective reading and writing. ❞

Patricia Smith
Adjunct Professor of Education, University of Houston

MULTICULTURAL LITERATURE

❝ All children are able to develop an understanding of other cultures and see issues from the perspectives of various cultures by having vicarious experiences through multicultural literature. ❞

Dr. Junko Yokota
Assistant Professor, Department of Curriculum and Instruction, University of Northern Iowa

PHONEMIC AWARENESS

❝ Any activity that focuses children's attention on language and encourages experimentation or manipulation of language may be useful in developing phonemic awareness. ❞

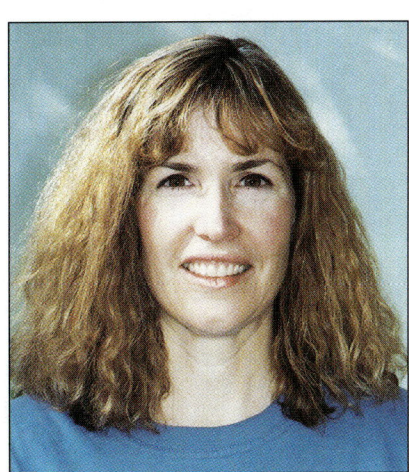

Dr. Hallie Kay Yopp
Associate Professor, Department of Elementary and Bilingual Education, California State University, Fullerton

FROM THE AUTHORS / v

Consultants

MULTICULTURAL INFUSION

❝ The commitment to multicultural infusion is based on the assumption that at one time or another virtually all human groups have played a role in important human events. ❞

Dr. Asa G. Hilliard III
Fuller E. Callaway Professor of Urban Education, Department of Educational Foundations, Georgia State University, Atlanta, Georgia

PREPARING READERS

❝ The reading experiences we create for young people shape the ways in which reading will forever enrich their lives. ❞

Judy Wallis
Coordinator for Elementary Language Arts, Chapter 1, and Pre-Kindergarten and Kindergarten, Alief School District, Alief, Texas

CRITICAL AND CREATIVE THINKING

❝ An ideal reading program offers diversity and challenge, stresses critical and creative thinking, and offers opportunities for students to customize activities that result in concrete accomplishments. ❞

Dr. Robert J. Sternberg
IBM Professor of Psychology and Education, Yale University

MEETING INDIVIDUAL NEEDS

❝ To be effective today, a reading program in a mainstream classroom must meet the needs of *all* students, including those with learning disabilities or other special needs. ❞

Dr. Alonzo A. Crim
Benjamin E. Mays Professor of Urban Educational Leadership, Georgia State University; Professor of Education, Spelman College

POETRY

❝ Poetry should flow freely in the lives of children; it should come to them as naturally as breathing. ❞

Dr. Lee Bennett Hopkins
Poet, Author, Anthologist

WORLD LITERATURE

❝ Reading fine literature set in other countries as well as their own helps children appreciate the uniqueness of various cultures and recognize values and experiences common to many cultures. ❞

Dr. Rolando Hinojosa-Smith
Ellen Clayton Garwood Professor of English and the Mari Sabusawa Michener Chair of Creative Writing, University of Texas

Dear Educator,

TREASURY OF LITERATURE, an integrated reading and language arts program, offers a wealth of literature to touch the hearts and minds of its readers. Readers grow in confidence with the turn of every page because the program is built on the following principles:

Reading is an interactive process of constructing meaning. Good readers are strategic readers. They learn, practice, and apply strategies as part of this dynamic process. Authentic literature provides a richness of opportunities for children to interact with concepts and ideas, setting the foundation for a lifelong love of reading.

Effective instruction is meaning-based and integrates listening, speaking, reading, writing, spelling, and thinking. Integrating language arts instruction across the curriculum enables students to make critical connections to all subject areas.

Emergent literacy activities build upon the language understandings that children bring from home. Immersing children in a print-rich environment allows teachers to capitalize on the children's natural curiosity about print and language.

Meeting individual needs in a classroom means access to a wide variety of instructional activities that provide for different learning modalities, varying language proficiencies, and individual learning styles.

Multicultural literature and activities, infused throughout the curriculum, enable children to appreciate cultural diversity, to grasp the concept that all groups have contributed to society, and to take pride in cultural heritage.

Assessment is an ongoing, natural part of the reading and language process. Whether formal or informal, it should help teachers determine, in a meaningful context, what students know and what they need to learn.

TREASURY OF LITERATURE offers your students a collection of trade books under one cover and sets the foundation for a lifelong love of reading.

Sincerely,
The Authors

CONTENTS

UNIT 1
Being Special

Introducing A Place to Dream / xvi

Unit Opener / T5

Listening to Literature / T10
   Benjamin Banneker's Wooden Clock
   by Margaret Goff Clark   BIOGRAPHY

✓ THEME: **Planting a Seed**

Theme Opener / T12

Managing the Literature-Based Classroom / T14

Miss Rumphius / T15
   written and illustrated by Barbara Cooney   REALISTIC FICTION

Words from the Author and Illustrator:
   Barbara Cooney / T28

A Seed Is a Promise / T43
   by Claire Merrill   NONFICTION

Johnny Appleseed / T49
   retold and illustrated by Steven Kellogg   TALL TALE

Theme Wrap-Up / T79

Writer's Workshop / T80

THEME: Being Different

Theme Opener / T82

Managing the Literature-Based Classroom / T84

The Adventures of Ali Baba Bernstein / T85
   by Johanna Hurwitz   REALISTIC FICTION

Words from the Author: Johanna Hurwitz / T100

Lisa's Fingerprints / T115
   by Mary O'Neill   POEM

Who Am I? / T115
   by Felice Holman   POEM

Theme Wrap-Up / T119

Writer's Workshop / T120

THEME: Listen to This!

Theme Opener / T122

Managing the Literature-Based Classroom / T124

Meet the Orchestra / T125
   by Ann Hayes   NONFICTION

Music, Music for Everyone / T153
   by Vera B. Williams   REALISTIC FICTION

Words from the Author and Illustrator: Vera B. Williams / T172

Theme Wrap-Up / T187

Writer's Workshop / T188

Unit One: Connections / T190

Unit Wrap-Up / T192

Break Time / T194

CONTENTS / ix

CONTENTS

UNIT 2
Friendships

Unit Opener / T195

Listening to Literature / T200
  Good Morning, River! by Lisa Westberg Peters   REALISTIC FICTION

THEME: School Days

Theme Opener / T202

Managing the Literature-Based Classroom / T204

Ramona's Neighborhood / T205

Ramona Quimby, Age 8 / T209
  by Beverly Cleary   REALISTIC FICTION

An Interview with the Author: Beverly Cleary / T221

Theme Wrap-Up / T239

Writer's Workshop / T240

x / A PLACE TO DREAM

THEME: Caring and Sharing

Theme Opener / T242

Managing the Literature-Based Classroom / T244

Through Grandpa's Eyes / T245
  by Patricia MacLachlan   REALISTIC FICTION

Writers / T275
  by Jean Little   POEM

A Gift for Tía Rosa / T277
  by Karen T. Taha   REALISTIC FICTION

Theme Wrap-Up / T305

Writer's Workshop / T306

THEME: Learning About Yourself

Theme Opener / T308

Managing the Literature-Based Classroom / T310

Justin and the Best Biscuits in the World / T311
  by Mildred Pitts Walter   REALISTIC FICTION

Words About the Author: Mildred Pitts Walter / T329

Versos sencillos/Simple Verses / T345
  by José Martí   POEM

Theme Wrap-Up / T347

Writer's Workshop / T348

Unit Two: Connections / T350

Unit Wrap-Up / T352

Break Time / T354

CONTENTS / xi

CONTENTS

UNIT 3
Adventures

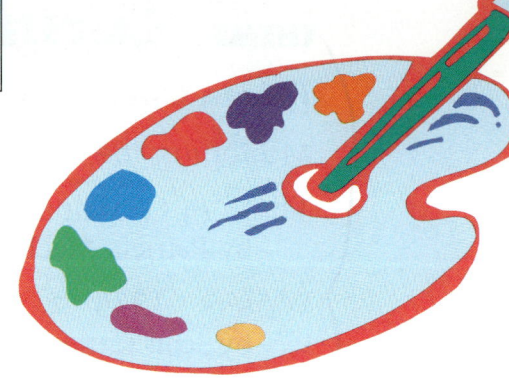

Unit Opener / T355

Listening to Literature / T360
    The Case of the Earthenware Pig by Donald J. Sobol   MYSTERY

THEME: Picture This!

Theme Opener / T362

Managing the Literature-Based Classroom / T364

The Legend of the Indian Paintbrush / T365
    by Tomie dePaola   LEGEND

A Note from the Author: Tomie dePaola / T386

Paddington Paints a Picture / T401
    from *Paddington on Stage*
    adapted by Alfred Bradley and Michael Bond   PLAY

Theme Wrap-Up / T429

Writer's Workshop / T430

THEME: Mysteries to Solve

Theme Opener / T432

Managing the Literature-Based Classroom / T434

Piggins / T435
    written by Jane Yolen
    illustrated by Jane Dyer   MYSTERY

Words from the Author and the Illustrator: Jane Yolen and
    Jane Dyer / T448

xii / A PLACE TO DREAM

Closed, I am a mystery / T465
   by Myra Cohn Livingston   RIDDLE
Hello Book! / T465
   by N. M. Bodecker   POEM
Would you like / T465
   by Lillian Morrison   POEM

Theme Wrap-Up / T469

Writer's Workshop / T470

THEME: **The Great Outdoors**

Theme Opener / T472

Managing the Literature-Based Classroom / T474

The Lost Lake / T475
   written and illustrated by Allen Say   REALISTIC FICTION

Words from the Author and Illustrator: Allen Say / T487

People / T503
   by Charlotte Zolotow   POEM

Some People / T503
   by Rachel Field   POEM

Theme Wrap-Up / T507

Writer's Workshop / T508

Unit Three: Connections / T510

Unit Wrap-Up / T512

Break Time / T514

Introducing the Glossary / T515

Introducing the Index of Titles and Authors / T520

REFERENCE FILE

Reteach Lessons / R1

Kinds of Sentences / R3
Cause and Effect / R4
Active Reading Strategies / R5
Sentence Subject / R6
Following Directions / R7
Structural and Contextual Clues / R8
Predicate / R9
Alphabetical Order / R10
Sources of Information / R11
Common Nouns / R12
Main Idea and Details / R13
Synthesizing Ideas / R14
Test-Taking Strategies / R15
Proper Nouns / R16
Structural Clues / R17
Singular and Plural Nouns / R18
Structural Analysis / R19
Author's Purpose / R20
Plural Nouns / R21
Point of View / R22
Singular Possessive Nouns / R23
Story Elements / R24
Plural Possessive Nouns / R25
Figurative Language / R26
Singular and Plural Pronouns / R27
Making Predictions / R28
Subject Pronouns / R29
Context Clues / R30
Play / R31
Object Pronouns / R32
Fiction and Nonfiction / R33
Adjectives / R34
Synonyms, Antonyms, and Analogies / R35

Harcourt Brace Library and Additional Reading / R37

The Adventures of Ali Baba Bernstein / R39
by Johanna Hurwitz

My Name Is María Isabel / R39
by Alma Flor Ada

Ramona Quimby, Age 8 / R40
by Beverly Cleary

Ty's One Man Band / R40
by Mildred Pitts Walter

Picnic with Piggins / R41
by Jane Yolen

Mush! Across Alaska in the World's Longest Sled-Dog Race / R41
by Patricia Seibert

Animal Fact/Animal Fable / R42
by Seymour Simon

The Stories Julian Tells / R42
by Ann Cameron

Rainy Rainy Saturday / R43
by Jack Prelutsky

The Magic Fan / R43
by Keith Baker

The News About Dinosaurs / R44
by Patricia Lauber

The Keeping Quilt / R44
by Patricia Polacco

Additional Reading / R45

Daily Language Practice / R53

Skills Matrix, Volume 1 / R55
Skills Matrix, Volume 2 / R56
Reproducible Copying Master / R57

UNIT 1: *Being Special*
Planting a Seed / R58
Being Different / R60
Listen to This! / R62

UNIT 2: *Friendships*
School Days / R64
Caring and Sharing / R66
Learning About Yourself / R68

UNIT 3: *Adventures*
Picture This! / R70
Mysteries to Solve / R72
The Great Outdoors / R74

Response Cards / R77

1: Characters / R79
2: Setting / R80
3: Plot / R81
4: Theme/Mood / R82
5: Author's Viewpoint / R83
6: Author's Craft / R84
7: Free Response / R85
8: Written Dialogue / R86
9: Literature Circle / R87
10: How Do I Know What I Know? / R88

Additional Resources / R89

Models of Writing Forms
Personal Narrative / R91
Paragraph of Information / R92
Descriptive Paragraph / R93
Story / R94
How-to Paragraph / R96
Friendly Letter / R97
Persuasive Paragraph / R98
Book Review / R99

Handwriting / R100

Graphic Organizers
Prediction Chart / R102
Knowledge Chart / R103
Predict-o-gram / R104
Story Map / R105
K-W-L Chart / R106
Organizing Ideas (Web) / R107

Independent Reading Masters
Read All About It! / R108
Cover to Cover / R109
Think and Decide / R110
Notes and Quotes / R111

Scope & Sequence and Index / R113

Scope & Sequence / R115
Index / R119
Reviewers: Field Test Sites, Multicultural Advisors, Critical Reviewers / R127
Acknowledgments / R129

A Place to Dream

Previewing the Cover

Invite students to discuss the title and the cover illustration.

Explain that the title of this Student Anthology is *A Place to Dream*. Have students brainstorm what the title might describe. Discuss how the artist, James Ransome, interpreted the title.

You may want to share the following information about James Ransome:

James Ransome is a graduate of Pratt Institute, a prestigious art school in Brooklyn, New York. He also studied at the Art Students League in New York. In 1989, James Ransome received the Society of Illustrators Annual Scholarship Award. His first picture book was called *Do Like Kyla*. Since then he has illustrated many more books and has become well known. James Ransome, who was born in North Carolina, now lives in Jersey City, New Jersey, with his wife, Lesa, and their Dalmatian, Clinton.

Predicting What's Inside

Discuss the letter with the reader.

Direct students' attention to the letter at the beginning of the anthology. Ask them to think about why the authors of their anthology would write a letter to them. Then have students read the letter silently. Ask them to explain in their own words why it is important to have dreams about the future and to work toward achieving those dreams.

Acquaint students with the organization of the book.

Ask students to preview the Contents on pages 4–9. Help them understand the organization of the book by pointing out the unit titles and the three theme titles in each unit. Ask them to use the titles of the selections and the illustrations to make predictions about the stories and poems they will read.

Help students examine end-of-book content.

Have students find the Glossary and the Index of Titles and Authors beginning on page 319 of the Student Anthology. As students locate each section, ask them to tell how they think each of these parts of the book might help them. Pages T515 and T520 contain information about introducing the students to the Glossary and the Index of Titles and Authors.

TREASURY OF LITERATURE

TREASURY OF LITERATURE

A Place to Dream

SENIOR AUTHORS
ROGER C. FARR
DOROTHY S. STRICKLAND

AUTHORS
RICHARD F. ABRAHAMSON
ELLEN BOOTH CHURCH
BARBARA BOWEN COULTER
BERNICE E. CULLINAN
MARGARET A. GALLEGO
W. DORSEY HAMMOND
JUDITH L. IRVIN
KAREN KUTIPER
DONNA M. OGLE
TIMOTHY SHANAHAN
PATRICIA SMITH
JUNKO YOKOTA
HALLIE KAY YOPP

SENIOR CONSULTANTS
ASA G. HILLIARD III
JUDY M. WALLIS

CONSULTANTS
ALONZO A. CRIM
ROLANDO R. HINOJOSA-SMITH
LEE BENNETT HOPKINS
ROBERT J. STERNBERG

HARCOURT BRACE & COMPANY
Orlando Atlanta Austin Boston San Francisco Chicago Dallas New York
Toronto London

Copyright © 1995 by Harcourt Brace & Company

All rights reserved. No part of this publication may be reproduced or transmitted in any form or by any means, electronic or mechanical, including photocopy, recording, or any information storage and retrieval system, without permission in writing from the publisher.

Requests for permission to make copies of any part of the work should be mailed to: Permissions Department, Harcourt Brace & Company, 6277 Sea Harbor Drive, Orlando, Florida 32887-6777.

Portions of this work were published in previous editions.

Printed in the United States of America

ISBN 0-15-301233-1

12345678910 048 97 96 95 94

Acknowledgments
For permission to reprint copyrighted material, grateful acknowledgment is made to the following sources:
Atheneum Publishers, an imprint of Macmillan Publishing Company: Cover illustration by K. Dyble Thompson from *My Name Is Maria Isabel* by Alma Flor Ada. Illustration copyright © 1993 by K. Dyble Thompson.
Bradbury Press, an Affiliate of Macmillan, Inc.: Cover illustration from *Mozart Tonight* by Julie Downing. Copyright © 1991 by Julie Downing.
Carolrhoda Books, Inc., Minneapolis, MN: Cover illustration by Hannu Taina from *Mister King* by Raija Siekkinen, translated by Tim Steffa. Illustration copyright © 1986 by Hannu Taina.
Crown Publishers, Inc.: Cover illustration from *Elaine, Mary Lewis, and the Frogs* by Heidi Chang. Copyright © 1988 by Heidi Chang.
Dillon Press, Inc.: *A Gift for Tía Rosa* by Karen T. Taha. Text © 1986 by Dillon Press, Inc.
Friends of Henry's and Ramona's Neighborhood: "Henry Huggins' Neighborhood" map by Heather Johnson.
Greenwillow Books, a division of William Morrow & Company, Inc.: *Music, Music for Everyone* by Vera B. Williams. Copyright © 1984 by Vera B. Williams.
Harcourt Brace & Company: Cover illustration from *On the Day You Were Born* by Debra Frasier. Copyright © 1991 by Debra Frasier. *Meet the Orchestra* by Ann Hayes, illustrated by Karmen Thompson. Text copyright © 1991 by Ann Hayes; illustrations copyright © 1991 by Karmen Effenberger Thompson. *Piggins* by Jane Yolen, illustrated by Jane Dyer. Text copyright © 1987 by Jane Yolen; illustrations copyright © 1987 by Jane Dyer. Cover illustration by Jane Dyer from *Picnic with Piggins* by Jane Yolen. Illustration copyright © 1988 by Jane Dyer. Pronunciation Key from *HBJ School Dictionary*, Third Edition. Text copyright © 1990 by Harcourt Brace & Company.
HarperCollins Publishers: "Writers" from *Hey World, Here I Am!* by Jean Little. Text copyright © 1986 by Jean Little. *Through Grandpa's Eyes* by Patricia MacLachlan. Text copyright © 1980 by Patricia MacLachlan. Cover illustration by Pat Cummings from *Storm in the Night* by Mary Stolz. Illustration copyright © 1988 by Pat Cummings. "People" from *All that Sunlight* by Charlotte Zolotow. Text copyright © 1967 by Charlotte Zolotow.
HarperCollins Publishers Ltd.: Illustrations by Peggy Fortnum from *Paddington* books by Michael Bond.
Holiday House, Inc.: Cover illustration from *Blast Off To Earth! A Look At Geography* by Loreen Leedy. Copyright © 1992 by Loreen Leedy.
Felice Holman: "Who Am I?" from *At the Top of My Voice and Other Poems* by Felice Holman. Text copyright © 1970 by Felice Holman. Published by Charles Scribner's Sons, 1970.
Henry Holt and Company, Inc.: Cover illustration by Vladimir Radunsky from *Hail To Mail* by Samuel Marshak, translated by Richard Pevear. Illustration © 1990 by Vladimir Radunsky.
Houghton Mifflin Company: From "Paddington Paints a Picture" in *Paddington on Stage* by Michael Bond and Alfred Bradley. Text copyright © 1974 by Alfred Bradley and Michael Bond. Based on the play *The Adventures of Paddington Bear*, published by Samuel French Ltd. All rights reserved. *The Lost Lake* by Allen Say. Copyright © 1989 by Allen Say.
International Creative Management, Inc.: "Lisa's Fingerprints" from *Fingers Are Always Bringing Me News* by Mary O'Neill. Text copyright © 1969 by Mary O'Neill. Published by Doubleday, a division of Bantam Doubleday Dell Publishing Group, Inc.
Lothrop, Lee & Shepard Books, a division of William Morrow & Company, Inc.: From *Justin and the Best Biscuits in the World* by Mildred Pitts Walter. Text copyright © 1986 by Mildred Pitts Walter.
Macmillan Publishing Company, a Division of Macmillan, Inc.: "Some People" from *Poems* by Rachel Field. Published by Macmillan Publishing Company, Inc., 1957. Cover illustration from *I Have Another Language: The Language Is Dance* by Eleanor Schick. Copyright © 1992 by Eleanor Schick.
Morrow Junior Books, a division of William Morrow & Company, Inc.: Illustration by Louis Darling from *Ellen Tebbits* by Beverly Cleary. Copyright © 1951, 1979 by Beverly Cleary. From "Ramona's Book Report" in *Ramona Quimby, Age 8* by Beverly Cleary, illustrated by Alan Tiegreen. Copyright © 1981 by Beverly Cleary. Cover illustration by Alan Tiegreen from *Ramona Forever* by Beverly Cleary. Illustration copyright © 1984 by William Morrow & Company, Inc. Illustrations by Alan Tiegreen from *The Ramona Quimby Diary* by Beverly Cleary. Illustrations copyright © 1984 by William Morrow & Company, Inc. From *The*

continued on page 335

2

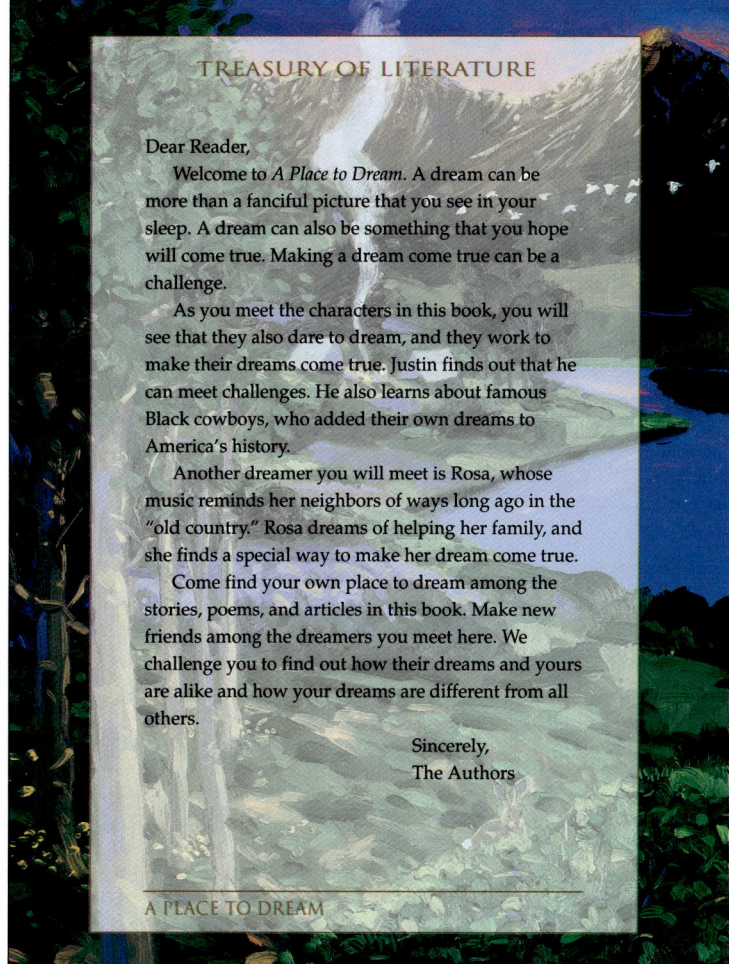

TREASURY OF LITERATURE

Dear Reader,

Welcome to *A Place to Dream*. A dream can be more than a fanciful picture that you see in your sleep. A dream can also be something that you hope will come true. Making a dream come true can be a challenge.

As you meet the characters in this book, you will see that they also dare to dream, and they work to make their dreams come true. Justin finds out that he can meet challenges. He also learns about famous Black cowboys, who added their own dreams to America's history.

Another dreamer you will meet is Rosa, whose music reminds her neighbors of ways long ago in the "old country." Rosa dreams of helping her family, and she finds a special way to make her dream come true.

Come find your own place to dream among the stories, poems, and articles in this book. Make new friends among the dreamers you meet here. We challenge you to find out how their dreams and yours are alike and how your dreams are different from all others.

Sincerely,
The Authors

A PLACE TO DREAM

T1

Unit One
Being Special / 10

Bookshelf / 12

Theme: PLANTING A SEED / 14

Miss Rumphius / 16
written and illustrated by Barbara Cooney
Realistic Fiction

Words from the Author and Illustrator:
Barbara Cooney / 31

A Seed Is a Promise / 32
by Claire Merrill
Nonfiction

Johnny Appleseed / 38
retold and illustrated by Steven Kellogg
Tall Tale

Theme Wrap-Up / 53

Theme: BEING DIFFERENT / 54

The Adventures of Ali Baba Bernstein / 56
by Johanna Hurwitz
Realistic Fiction

Words from the Author:
Johanna Hurwitz / 75

Lisa's Fingerprints / 76
by Mary O'Neill
Poem

Who Am I? / 78
by Felice Holman
Poem

Theme Wrap-Up / 79

Theme: LISTEN TO THIS! / 80

Meet the Orchestra / 82
by Ann Hayes
Nonfiction

Music, Music for Everyone / 94
written and illustrated by Vera B. Williams
Realistic Fiction

Words from the Author and Illustrator:
Vera B. Williams / 120

Theme Wrap-Up / 121

Connections / 122

UNIT TWO
Friendships / 124

Bookshelf / 126

Theme: SCHOOL DAYS / 128

Ramona's Neighborhood / 130
Map

Ramona Quimby, Age 8 / 132
by Beverly Cleary
Realistic Fiction

An Interview with the Author:
Beverly Cleary / 144

Theme Wrap-Up / 147

Theme: CARING AND SHARING / 148

Through Grandpa's Eyes / 150
by Patricia MacLachlan
Realistic Fiction

Writers / 168
by Jean Little
Poem

A Gift for Tía Rosa / 170
by Karen T. Taha
Realistic Fiction

Theme Wrap-Up / 185

Theme: LEARNING ABOUT YOURSELF / 186

Justin and the Best Biscuits
in the World / 188
by Mildred Pitts Walter
Realistic Fiction

Words About the Author:
Mildred Pitts Walter / 212

Versos sencillos/Simple Verses / 214
by José Martí
Poem

Theme Wrap-Up / 215

Connections / 216

Unit Three
Adventures / 218

Bookshelf / 220

Theme: PICTURE THIS! / 222

The Legend of the Indian Paintbrush / 224
retold and illustrated by Tomie dePaola
Legend

A Note from the Author:
Tomie dePaola / 254

Paddington Paints a Picture / 256
adapted by Alfred Bradley and Michael Bond
Play

Theme Wrap-Up / 271

Theme: MYSTERIES TO SOLVE / 272

Piggins / 274
by Jane Yolen
illustrated by Jane Dyer
Mystery

Words from the Author and the Illustrator:
Jane Yolen and Jane Dyer / 289

Closed, I am a mystery / 292
by Myra Cohn Livingston
Riddle

Hello Book! / 293
by N. M. Bodecker
Poem

Would you like / 294
by Lillian Morrison
Poem

Theme Wrap-Up / 295

Theme: THE GREAT OUTDOORS / 296

The Lost Lake / 298
written and illustrated by Allen Say
Realistic Fiction

Words from the Author and Illustrator:
Allen Say / 311

People / 313
by Charlotte Zolotow
Poem

Some People / 314
by Rachel Field
Poem

Theme Wrap-Up / 315

Connections / 316

Glossary / 319

Index of Titles and Authors / 333

UNIT 1
Being Special

THEME:
Planting a Seed
T12–T81

THEME:
Being Different
T82–T121

THEME:
Listen to This!
T122–T189

UNIT 1 OPENER

Planning Center · BEING SPECIAL

What's Ahead in "Being Special"?

PLANTING A SEED: PAGES T12–T81 Challenge your students to think of ways they might beautify the world as they read a realistic story about a woman and a tall tale about a man, both of whom made their world more beautiful.

BEING DIFFERENT: PAGES T82–T121 Being different from everyone else in the world is not as complicated or as difficult as it might seem. Invite your students to read a realistic story and two poems to find out how we are all unique and special.

LISTEN TO THIS!: PAGES T122–T189 Strike up the band! Your students will discover the fun of performing and listening to music as they read a nonfiction selection and a realistic story.

Audiovisual Materials and Software

American Songfest. Weston Woods. Host Robert McCloskey visits four authors and illustrators, including Steven Kellogg. FILM/FILMSTRIP/VIDEO

Big Book Maker: Tall Tales & American Folk Heroes. Pelican, 1990. This program uses art based on traditional folk heroes, including Johnny Appleseed, to develop creative writing skills. COMPUTER SOFTWARE

A Chair for My Mother by Vera Williams. Spoken Arts, 1988. Another touching story by the author of "Music, Music for Everyone." AUDIOCASSETTE

Get Ready, Get Set, Grow! Bullfrog Films/One-Up Productions, 1988. Sequences of young Brooklyn gardeners combine with time-lapse photography to introduce the basics of plant growth. FILM/VIDEO

My First Music Video. Sony Kids' Video, 1993. Step-by-step instructions for making musical instruments from fairly ordinary materials. VIDEO

Out Loud by Eve Merriam. Caedmon, 1988. The poet reads her work about everyday life. AUDIOCASSETTE

Harcourt Brace Literature Cassette

Recordings of some of the selections in "Being Special" may be used for instruction or for students' listening enjoyment:

- "Lisa's Fingerprints"
- "Who Am I?"

Harcourt Brace Big Book
A Chair for My Mother

Daily Language Practice
Proofreading activities for daily use are available on pages R58–R63.

Family Involvement
The *Family Involvement Activities* provide several options for extending each theme and expanding the unit focus. A Read-at-Home piece of literature is also included for family members to read together.

Pacing
This unit is designed to take approximately five or six weeks to complete, depending on your students' needs.

Bulletin Board Idea

Invite students to help create a bulletin board display entitled "Special People." Ask them to think of someone they consider to be special, such as a family member, a friend, a teacher, a local community leader, or someone they have read about or seen in the news. Next, have students write one or two sentences telling who the person is and why he or she is special. Students can then display on the bulletin board a photograph, magazine picture, or drawing of the person along with the sentences.

T6 / A PLACE TO DREAM, UNIT 1

Assessment and Evaluation Options

	READING	INTEGRATED LANGUAGE ARTS	LANGUAGE
Throughout the Unit  *Informal Assessment*	**INFORMAL ASSESSMENT NOTES** Record observations of students, using anecdotal records or behavioral checklists. The symbol at left indicates teachable moments throughout the lessons.	**READING/WRITING PORTFOLIO** Portfolio Assessment combines product and process assessment in a comprehensive, ongoing record of a student's literacy development. Students collect samples of reading and writing activities, including finished work, work-in-progress, and plans/ideas for future work; reading and writing logs; and self-assessment checklists. See the *Portfolio Assessment Teacher's Guide* for implementing a portfolio system.	**STUDENT SELF-ASSESSMENT NOTES** Encourage students to monitor and reflect on their writing so that they can begin to take responsibility for their own improvement. Notes at point of use in the lesson plans may be used to monitor growth.
	STUDENT SELF-ASSESSMENT NOTES Follow point-of-use suggestions in the lesson to have students monitor their own learning, attitudes, and interests.	**PORTFOLIO CONFERENCES** Schedule a conference with each student to learn about the student's reading and writing interests, habits, and attitudes and to help the student reflect on his or her reading and writing.	**WRITTEN RETELLINGS** A student's written retellings can help you analyze how well the student organizes ideas, develops ideas, and applies knowledge of conventions of writing. See the Retelling Analysis Summary form in the *Individual Inventory for Reading and Writing*.
	RUNNING RECORDS Gain insights into students' application of reading strategies by tracking oral reading errors, or miscues. See the *Individual Inventory for Reading and Writing* for administering and interpreting results.	**STUDENT LOGS AND JOURNALS** Encourage students to keep a collection of thoughts, ideas, and opinions to use for reflecting on their reading, writing, and learning.	
	ORAL RETELLINGS Retelling may be used as an alternative to questioning to assess students' comprehension of text: recall of major points and relevant/irrelevant details, what the reader adds to or infers from the text, and insights into how the reader constructs meaning.		
End-of-Unit *Formal Assessment Tools*	**READING SKILLS TEST** Multiple-choice diagnostic tests, to assess mastery of **lesson vocabulary** and **cause and effect**.	**INTEGRATED PERFORMANCE ASSESSMENT** A structured reading-writing task to help you determine whether students can use reading to write and whether they can accomplish a specific writing task.	**LANGUAGE SKILLS AND WRITING TEST** Multiple-choice questions and a writing prompt assess students' knowledge of grammar, mechanics and usage skills (**sentences, subjects and predicates, and common and proper nouns**), and their ability to write a **personal narrative**.
	HOLISTIC READING TEST This test includes theme-related passages accompanied by multiple-choice questions that focus on application of literal, inferential, and critical thinking, major comprehension objectives, and students' ability to construct meaning.		

PLANNING CENTER / T7

PAGES 10–11 Unit Opener

Unit One

Being Special

People find all kinds of ways to be special. A woman in Kenya plants trees to save her country from becoming a desert. A group of friends start a special band to make music and earn money. As you read these selections, think about the ways you can be special.

THEMES

Planting a Seed 14

Being Different 54

Listen to This! 80

Introducing "Being Special"

Invite students to discuss what being special means to them by asking questions such as *Who are some special people?* and *What makes you special?* Next, read with students the unit introduction and the theme titles to help them set a purpose for reading the unit.

Then ask students to name some special people in other cultures they have read about or seen in the news. Encourage them to discuss what they know about the individuals and what makes them special. **CULTURAL AWARENESS**

Writer's Journal pages 4–6: Reading and writing about "Being Special"

T8 / A PLACE TO DREAM, UNIT 1

Unit Opener **PAGES 12–13**

BOOKSHELF

THE ADVENTURES OF ALI BABA BERNSTEIN
by Johanna Hurwitz
David Bernstein thinks his life would be more exciting if he had a different name. He changes it to Ali Baba, and guess what! His life does get more exciting.
Children's Choice
Harcourt Brace Library Book

MY NAME IS MARÍA ISABEL
by Alma Flor Ada
María Isabel is the new girl in her class. When her teacher insists on calling her Mary, María Isabel has to find a way to show her teacher how important a name can be.
Award-Winning Author
Harcourt Brace Library Book

STORM IN THE NIGHT
by Mary Stolz
When the lights go out during a thunderstorm, Thomas learns more about his grandfather— and about himself.
Teachers' Choice, Coretta Scott King Honor

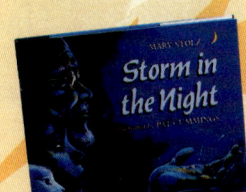

I HAVE ANOTHER LANGUAGE THE LANGUAGE IS DANCE
by Eleanor Schick
This is the story of one day in the life of a young girl who is a dancer. As she prepares for her first performance in front of an audience, she learns a new language. It is the language of dance.

MOZART TONIGHT
by Julie Downing
In this biography, we ride with Amadeus Mozart and his wife, Constanze, as they travel in a carriage to the opera house. Mozart tells of his struggle to become a composer and of his life with Constanze.
Notable Children's Trade Book in Social Studies

From the Harcourt Brace Library

The Adventures of Ali Baba Bernstein tells the story of a curious, adventurous boy named David Bernstein.

- You may want students to first read the beginning of *The Adventures of Ali Baba Bernstein*, which appears in the Student Anthology.
- Have students read *The Adventures of Ali Baba Bernstein* with a partner. Periodically, partners can meet to discuss things they didn't understand.

My Name Is María Isabel describes why María Isabel feels her name makes her special and how she persuades her teacher to use it.

- You may want to have students read *My Name Is María Isabel* after reading "Lisa's Fingerprints" or "Who Am I?" Have students meet in small groups to discuss what they learned about being special.
- Have students compare the problems faced by María Isabel and Rosa (in "Music, Music for Everyone") and the ways the girls solved them.

Harcourt Brace Library Comprehensive lesson plan available for each book.

Bookshelf selections *I Have Another Language: The Language Is Dance* and *Mozart Tonight* are also available as Harcourt Brace PASSPORTS titles.

Listening to Literature

Read aloud to students.

Benjamin Banneker's Wooden Clock

by Margaret Goff Clark

On a winter evening when Benjamin Banneker was twenty-one, he sat down at the kitchen table as soon as the supper dishes were cleared.

In front of him he placed a piece of fine-grained hardwood and a pocket watch that he had borrowed from a friend.

Ben's mother pulled a chair close to the table so she could sew by the light of the candle, and his sister Minta leaned over his shoulder. Minta was a young woman, but she had never before had a chance to look closely at a watch. Few people in the American colonies had a watch or clock.

"How wonderful it would be to own that!" She touched the watch with one slim finger. "I could always know what time it is."

Holding the watch firmly in his left hand, Ben pried it open so he could see the busy wheels inside.

Minta gasped. "Should you do that Benjamin? It isn't your watch."

Ben grinned at her. "Wait till you see what I'm going to do next. I'm going to take it apart. But don't worry. I have permission to do what I wish with the watch, as long as I put it together again."

Ben's father and his sister Molly joined the other members of the family around the table. Only Ben's married sister was missing. Outside, a cold wind whistled around the log cabin. Now and then the howl of a wolf or the cry of a bobcat could be heard. Inside the

Selection Background

During a period in our country when many people of African descent were held in slavery all their lives, Benjamin Banneker began life as a free person. In this story, Banneker borrows a pocket watch, takes it apart, studies the wheels and gears, and then carefully fashions his own wooden clock.

Author **Margaret Goff Clark** began writing books to amuse her children. She has won several awards, including the Book of the Year Award for *The Min-Min*.

Strategies for Listening

LISTENING/THINKING STRATEGY – PROBLEM SOLVING Tell students that to have a greater appreciation of the story, they should listen to discover the character's problem and how he solves it. Explain that listening for these elements will help them understand why a character acts in a certain way.

SET A PURPOSE FOR LISTENING Remind students that the selections in this unit are about "Being Special." Have them listen to this selection to learn about a special man, Benjamin Banneker, and a problem he solved.

T10 / A PLACE TO DREAM, UNIT 1

only sound was the crackling of the fire. One by one, Ben removed the tiny wheels and gears, carefully memorizing their arrangement in the watch as he placed them on the table.

He had forgotten anyone else was in the room with him. When his sister Molly spoke, he was startled.

"Why are you taking all the pieces out of the watch?" she asked.

Ben rubbed the back of his neck where it ached from bending over his work. "I'm going to make a clock," he announced with confidence. "I saw a picture of one in a book. I'm sure I can make one after I study this watch."

"A clock!" Ben's mother let her sewing drop into her lap. "How can you possibly do that? You don't have any metal and you certainly don't have any of the right tools."

Ben put one capable hand on the piece of hardwood that lay on the table. "I have wood and a knife. I'll carve all the parts out of wood."

Several nights passed before he began to carve.

First, he had to measure the wheels. Then he had to figure out the size that each wheel in his clock should be. As he worked at the project, he found he constantly needed to use his knowledge of mathematics.

Every night that winter he worked on his clock. When spring and summer came he had less free time, but whenever he could spare a moment from work on the farm he continued to figure and carve.

Patiently he fashioned the wheels with their toothed edges. Every piece must be exact. Often he would have a wheel almost complete and then a small slip of his knife would ruin it.

He would not use a spring in his clock. A weighted cord wound around a spool would take its place. The clock must have a pendulum, too.

The neighbors for miles around learned of Benjamin's project and came to watch him at work. They knew that he was extremely talented, and as clever with his hands as he was with his mind. He was always making a piece of furniture or a tool. And look at the way he had taught himself to play the violin and the flute! But this time, surely, he was trying to do something that no one could do. To make a clock of wood, without another clock as a pattern, seemed impossible.

Even Benjamin was sometimes discouraged. After months of work he had the carefully carved parts in place. His wooden clock had begun to look like a clock, but a serious problem remained. He could not get the hour and minute hands to move together at the proper rate.

Again and again he studied the mechanism of the watch. Again and again he took his clock apart and put it together. A year had passed since he first started to make it.

"Why don't you give up?" asked his sister Minta. "It's a fine clock. What does it matter if one hand does run a little too fast?"

Benjamin set his lips more firmly together. With great determination he said, "It must keep perfect time."

Several days later he discovered the error in his work and set it right. When at last he saw the hands of the clock working in harmony, he felt at peace.

He enclosed his clock in a neat case and hung it on the wall.

Day after day and year after year people came to see Benjamin Banneker's wooden clock that kept time accurately.

The borrowed watch, unharmed, was again in the pocket of its owner.

Responding to Literature

1. **How would you explain Benjamin Banneker's problem?** (Accept reasonable responses: He wanted to make a clock, but he didn't have metal or the right tools.) INFERENTIAL: SUMMARIZING
2. **The writer says Ben was as clever with his hands as he was with his mind. Why do you think she said that?** (Accept reasonable responses: Ben had to use his mind to make the clock, and then he had to carve each of the pieces.) INFERENTIAL: DRAWING CONCLUSIONS

SPEAKING Have pairs of students improvise the scene in which Ben discovers the error of the clock hands and solves the problem. Invite students to create additional dialogue for Benjamin and Minta. CREATIVE: ORAL COMPOSITION

LISTENING TO LITERATURE / T11

Unit 1 BEING SPECIAL

THEME OPENER

Planting a Seed

Miss Rumphius

T15   A REALISTIC FICTION STORY written and illustrated by Barbara Cooney
As a child, Miss Rumphius declared she would one day go to faraway places, live beside the sea, and do something to make the world more beautiful.

Words from the Author and Illustrator: Barbara Cooney

T28   AN ARTICLE
Barbara Cooney talks about where she got the "seed" for Miss Rumphius.

A Seed Is a Promise

T43   A NONFICTION SELECTION by Claire Merrill
The story of a seed is as amazing as the promise it holds.

Johnny Appleseed

T49   A TALL TALE retold and illustrated by Steven Kellogg
Fact and fancy surrounded folk hero Johnny Appleseed as he headed west planting apple trees for the pioneers who would follow.

For pacing suggestions, see page T14.

Theme Opener: Planting a Seed PAGES 14–15

THEME

Planting a Seed

Have you ever planted a seed and helped it grow? If you have, you have made the world more beautiful. Read the following selections to see what the characters have done to make their world a better place.

CONTENTS

MISS RUMPHIUS
written and illustrated by Barbara Cooney

WORDS FROM THE AUTHOR AND ILLUSTRATOR: BARBARA COONEY

A SEED IS A PROMISE
by Claire Merrill

JOHNNY APPLESEED
retold and illustrated by Steven Kellogg

15

Discussing the Theme

Ask students to look at the illustration and read the paragraph on Student Anthology page 15. Invite them to share the ways in which planting a seed can make the world more beautiful. Then have students read the selection titles and speculate about how the characters improve the world in which they live.

Portfolio Assessment

Tell students to keep their writing responses for the selections in "Planting a Seed" in their portfolios. Remind them also to add to their personal journals thoughts and ideas about books they have read independently.

 As you come across this symbol, you may wish to suggest that students save a piece of their work in their portfolios.

THEME OPENER: PLANTING A SEED / T13

THEME OPENER

Managing the Literature-Based Classroom

Group Discussion Guidelines

Before engaging the whole group in a discussion of the theme, you may want to encourage them to establish informal rules to help discussions run smoothly. Suggestions can be incorporated into a chart to which all can readily refer as needed. In the future, the chart can also serve as a transitional device, its appearance signaling that a group discussion will follow.

Teacher Read-Aloud

Promote interest, fluency, and practice in listening comprehension by reading aloud to your students on a daily basis. Chart the titles, genres, cultures represented, and student reactions to the books read. Use this information to assist in choosing future books. On occasion, decide to read only a portion of a book and then make copies of the book available for student independent reading.

Pacing

This theme has been designed to take about two weeks to complete, depending on your students' needs.

MEETING INDIVIDUAL NEEDS

LOW-ACHIEVING STUDENTS Some students may need to bolster their confidence in their ability to read aloud in group situations. You may want to tell such students in advance which passages they will be asked to read aloud. Students can then use a cassette recorder to practice their reading until they feel satisfied with the results.

GIFTED AND TALENTED After they read and complete all the related activities, challenge pairs of students to role-play Alice Rumphius and Johnny Appleseed, discussing what they think of the world today and what they would do to make it a more beautiful place. *Challenge Cards* provide additional activities to challenge students. Challenge notes throughout the lesson plans suggest additional activities to stimulate critical and creative thinking.

SPECIAL-EDUCATION STUDENTS For students with visual perception problems, you may wish to tape-record the directions for the stages of the writing process and write them on a poster. Students may also want to tape-record their compositions.

STUDENTS ACQUIRING ENGLISH Before students read the selections, pair them with others who are proficient in English to discuss the Key Words. Have partners read the selections cooperatively, helping each other with Key Words and any other words and phrases they find difficult. Second-Language Support notes throughout the lesson plans offer strategies to help students acquiring English to understand the selections.

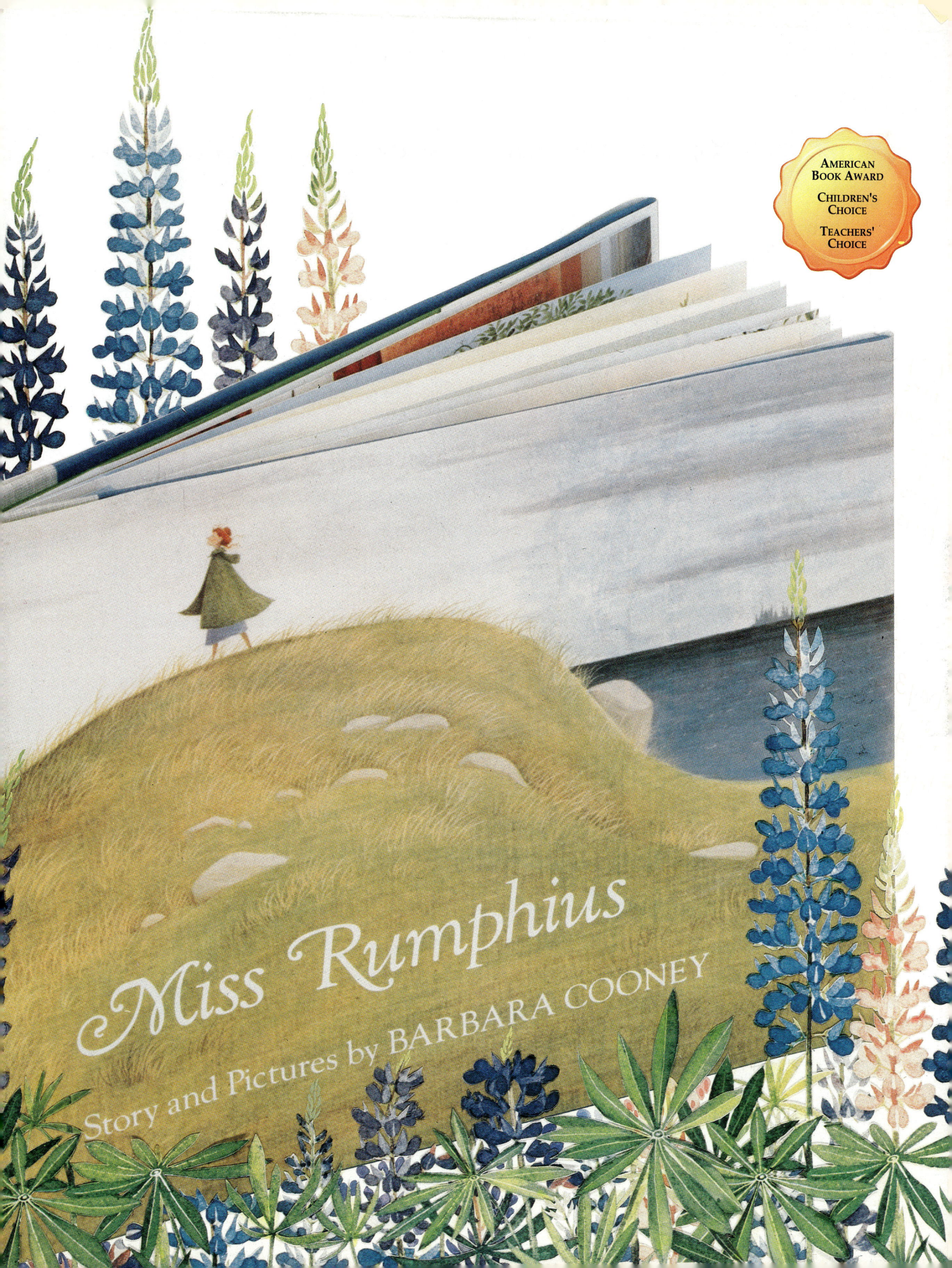

Integrated Lesson Planner

Miss Rumphius
pages 16–30

	READING	LANGUAGE ARTS	CROSS-CURRICULAR CONNECTIONS
PART 1 *Reading the Literature* pages T18–T28 — Day 1	**Building Background** **Vocabulary Strategies** **Prereading Strategies** Preview and Predict Setting a Purpose **Options for Reading**	**Spelling** Pretest Spelling-Vocabulary Connection Generalization: /a/ and /e/ sounds **Grammar Connection** Reviewing Sentences	**Cultural Awareness** The title *Raja* **Social Studies** Beautifying the world
PART 2 *Responding to the Literature* pages T29–T35 — Day 2	**Personal Response** **Cooperative Response** **Summarizing the Literature** — Strong point **Critical Thinking Activity** Speech Balloons **Vocabulary Workshop** Key Words Hyphenated Compound Words	**Language Arts Workshop** **Reading** drama **Writing** letter, anti-boredom lists, ship-related glossary **Listening and Speaking** presentation, hobby sharing **Reviewing Spelling Words** Posttest **Grammar Review** Reviewing Sentences **Grammar Minilesson** Kinds of Sentences	**Social Studies** Writing About the Literature
PART 3 *Learning Through the Literature* pages T36–T42 — Day 3 or Day 4 depending	**Introduce** Comprehension: Cause and Effect (Tested) Comprehension Strategy: Active Reading Strategies	**Reading** It's All for the Better Geographical Facts **Writing** Getting to Know the Kangaroo **Listening and Speaking** Drawing a View	**Science** Getting to Know the Kangaroo **Art** Drawing a View Snapshots of the Imagination **Social Studies** Clothing Around the World It's All for the Better Geographical Facts **Math** Calculating Mileage **Multicultural Perspectives** Making Improvements

may take 3 days to do all parts of parts 1 & 2

OPTIONAL MATERIALS
Charts/Transparencies 1–2
Integrated Spelling pp. 10–13; TE pp. T15–T20
Practice Book pp. 1–6
Writer's Journal pp. 7–8
Alternative Teaching Strategies pp. 2, 34–37
Language Handbook pp. 66–67, 70, 84–89
Grammar Practice pp. 12–13
Family Involvement Activities: Unit 1, pp. 1–4
Response Card 9
Project Cards 3A, 3B, 4A, 4B

MEETING INDIVIDUAL NEEDS
Second-Language Support pp. T19, T20, T24, T35, T37, T39
Mainstreaming p. T20
Reteach pp. T35, T37, T39
Challenge pp. T37, T39

FAMILY INVOLVEMENT Encourage students to work with family members on a beautification project, such as a neighborhood cleanup or a home flower garden. See *Family Involvement Activities*.

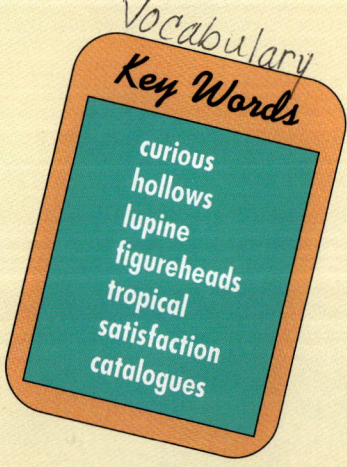

Vocabulary Key Words
curious
hollows
lupine
figureheads
tropical
satisfaction
catalogues

T16 / A PLACE TO DREAM, UNIT 1

Selection Summary

As a little girl, Alice Rumphius told her grandfather that when she grew up she wanted to do two things: visit faraway places and, when she was old, settle by the sea. Her grandfather added that she should also do something to make the world more beautiful. Alice grew up and set out to accomplish these three goals.

One day she injured her back while climbing off a camel and decided it was time to return home and settle down by the sea. But she didn't know how to make the world more beautiful until she discovered a hillside covered with lupines. That gave her the idea to scatter lupine seeds everywhere she went. She came to be known as the Lupine Lady.

Now, Miss Rumphius is very old, and her story is told by her grandniece, Alice, who plans to accomplish the same three goals when she grows up.

About the Author

Barbara Cooney has been a free-lance author and illustrator since 1938 and has illustrated more than one hundred books. Her awards include two Caldecott Medals.

Although Cooney has always drawn pictures, she feels that she had no more artistic talent than any other child. She says, "I started out ruining the wallpaper with crayons, like everybody else, and making eggs with arms and legs. Most children start this way, and most children have the souls of artists. Some of these children stubbornly keep on being children even when they have grown up. Some of these stubborn children get to be artists."

Additional Reading

OTHER BOOKS WRITTEN OR ILLUSTRATED BY BARBARA COONEY

Chanticleer and the Fox, adapted from the Canterbury Tales. HarperCollins, 1982. **CHALLENGING**

*Roxaboxen by Alice McLerran. Lothrop, Lee, & Shepard, 1991. **AVERAGE**

OTHER THEME-RELATED BOOKS

Henry Bear's Park by David McPhail. Little, Brown, 1976. **AVERAGE**

June 29, 1999 by David Weisner. Clarion, 1992. **EASY**

BOOKS FOR APPLYING STRATEGIES: CAUSE AND EFFECT, ACTIVE READING

The Legend of the Bluebonnet by Tomie dePaola. Putnam, 1983. **EASY**

Hattie and the Wild Waves: A Story from Brooklyn by Barbara Cooney. Viking, 1990. **AVERAGE**

Uncle Willie and the Soup Kitchen by Dyanne DeSalvo-Ryan. William Morrow, 1991. **AVERAGE**

*Available as a Harcourt Brace PASSPORTS title

PART 1

Reading the Literature

Building Background

Access prior knowledge and build vocabulary concepts.

Tell students that the story they will read, "Miss Rumphius," is about a woman who wants to improve the world by making it more beautiful.

Have students quickwrite.

Ask students to write a list of things they could do to make the world look more beautiful. Work with students to create a web on the board, using their ideas. The completed web might include some of the following items:

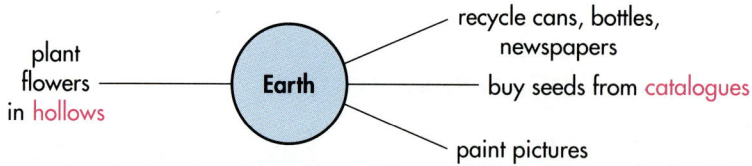

Vocabulary Strategies

Introduce Key Words and strategies.

Display Chart/Transparency 1 or the story on it. Have students read the sentences silently. Model using context clues with structural analysis to decode the underlined words. For example, students might use the context clues *carved* and *decorating the fronts* to determine the meaning of *figureheads*.

Chart/Transparency 1   Key Words

The world is a beautiful place. If you are curious, you'll want to explore it! Climb up high to see mountain wildflowers. Then go down into the hollows to see what kinds of flowers grow in valleys.

By the sea, look for a beautiful rose or lupine growing. You might see sailing ships with carved figureheads decorating the fronts. Maybe you could sail on a ship to a very warm, tropical island.

If you can't get to all those places, you can still find joy and satisfaction from exploring—by reading! Learn about flowers by looking at seed catalogues. Read books about places all over this beautiful world.

Key Words

- curious
- hollows
- lupine
- figureheads
- tropical
- satisfaction
- catalogues

KEY WORDS DEFINED

curious eager to know more

hollows small valleys

lupine a plant that has long spikes of flowers

figureheads carved figures used to decorate the prows, or fronts, of ships

tropical relating to hot, damp parts of the world

satisfaction the condition of fully having what is wanted

catalogues books or pamphlets that show and describe things to buy

---

T18 / A PLACE TO DREAM, UNIT 1

Check all students' understanding.

Create a chart like the one below. Have students work in pairs to classify the new words according to the headings shown. Model the placement of the first word. Then ask pairs to share their completed charts. Discuss students' reasons for placing the words where they did. STRATEGY: CATEGORIZING

People	Plants	Places	Things
curious (satisfaction)	(lupine) (catalogues)	(hollows) (tropical)	(figureheads)

PROPER NOUNS Display the following names and discuss their pronunciations as necessary: *Lupine Lady* [lōō′pin], *Miss Rumphius* [rum′fē·əs], *the Bapa Raja* [bä′pə rä′jə].

Integrate spelling with vocabulary.

SPELLING-VOCABULARY CONNECTION *Integrated Spelling* Lesson 1 reinforces the spellings of words with short *a* and short *e*, such as *back* and *best* found in the selection. In addition, the Words to Explore help reinforce the concept of nature as it relates to the selection.

 **SPELLING PRETEST** You may want to use the Pretest/Posttest Sentences on *Integrated Spelling Teacher's Edition* page T15 to assess students' knowledge of the spelling generalization.

MEETING INDIVIDUAL NEEDS

SECOND-LANGUAGE SUPPORT Have students use the illustration on Student Anthology page 19 as a picture clue for *figureheads* and on page 27 for *lupine*. See also the manual *Alternative Teaching Strategies*, pages 2, 34–37.

OPTIONAL INDEPENDENT PRACTICE

INTEGRATED SPELLING pages 10–13: Words with Short *a* and Short *e*

PRACTICE BOOK page 1: Reinforcing Key Words
NOTE: This page may be completed now or after students have read the story.

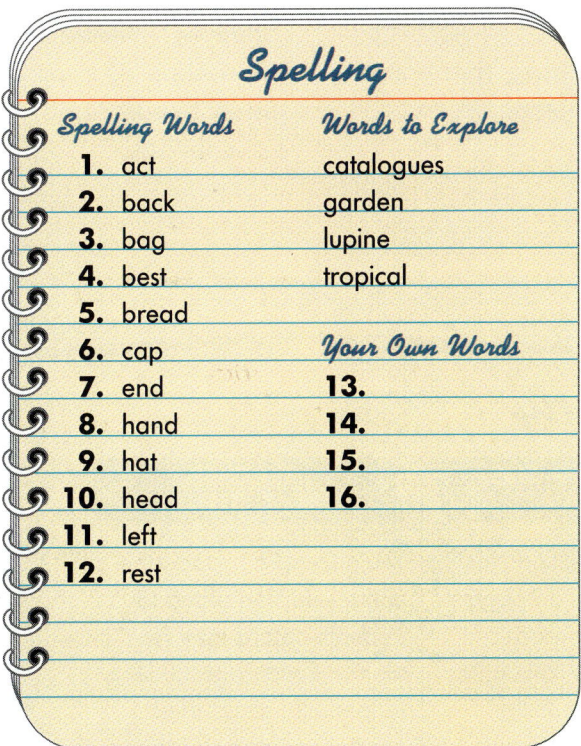

Spelling

Spelling Words
1. act
2. back
3. bag
4. best
5. bread
6. cap
7. end
8. hand
9. hat
10. head
11. left
12. rest

Words to Explore
catalogues
garden
lupine
tropical

Your Own Words
13.
14.
15.
16.

Spelling generalization: /a/ and /e/ sounds

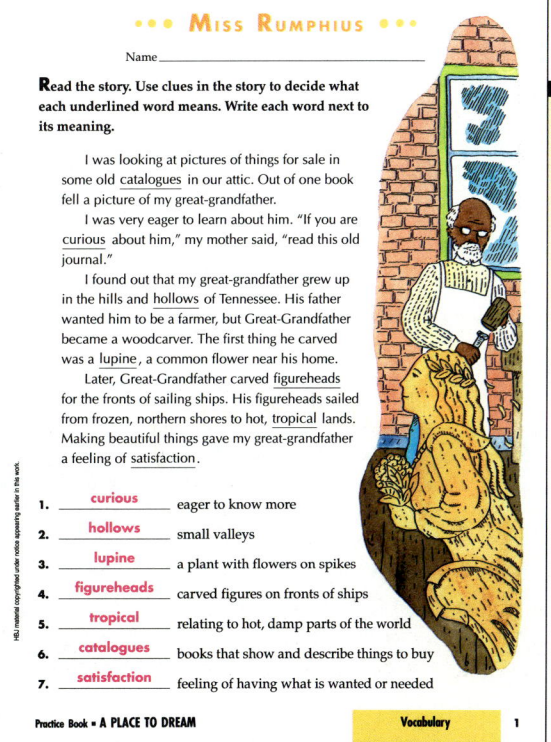

MISS RUMPHIUS / T19

Prereading Strategies

MEETING INDIVIDUAL NEEDS

Preview and Predict

Discuss the preview/predict strategy.

Explain to students that previewing, or looking over a story, will help them predict what the story is about and will also help them decide on a purpose, or reason, for reading it. Then model the strategy:

> First, I read the story title and the first few paragraphs and then I look at the pictures. I learn that the story is about someone named Miss Rumphius, who is called the Lupine Lady. The pictures show a little girl, a young woman, and an old woman, so I predict that the story will be about one woman's life.

Have students preview and predict.

Have students preview the story. Then ask questions, such as the following, to help them consider what might happen in the story:

- Why do you think Miss Rumphius is called the Lupine Lady?
- Who is telling the story? How might Miss Rumphius affect the life of her grandniece?

 **PERSONAL JOURNAL** Have students write their predictions about the story in their personal journals. Ask students to support their predictions.

Setting a Purpose

Encourage students to set purposes.

Tell students that setting a purpose for reading gives them a reason for reading, helps them stay focused on important events as they read, and helps them know what reading rate to choose. Guide students in setting a purpose based on their predictions.

If students have difficulty setting a purpose, offer this suggestion:

> I'm going to read to find out how Miss Rumphius, the Lupine Lady, will affect the life of her grandniece.

SECOND-LANGUAGE SUPPORT Students should pay attention to the pictures as they preview. You may want to have students read with English-fluent partners. See also the manual *Alternative Teaching Strategies,* pages 2, 34–37.

SUPPORT FOR MAINSTREAMING You may need to help students understand the time shifts that occur in the story—from present to past and back to the present.

PERSONAL JOURNALS

Have students begin personal journals in which they can
- record predictions before reading
- confirm predictions after reading
- include ideas discussed in Responding to Literature

Students may use any type of notebook. Encourage them to decorate the covers.

Options for Reading

Guided Reading *1st time they've heard it*

SUSTAINED SILENT READING	STRATEGIC READING	READER RESPONSE GROUPS	TEACHER READ-ALOUD
Have students read the story silently with their purpose for reading in mind. Remind them that they may revise their purpose and their predictions as they read.	To stimulate discussion, use the suggestions that appear on pages T21, T25, and T27.	Follow the suggestions for Literature Circles on page T21. As students read, suggest that they take notes about the setting or the character to discuss with their groups.	You may wish to read the entire selection aloud to students before they read it silently. Encourage students to mentally revise their predictions as they listen.

T20 / *A PLACE TO DREAM,* UNIT 1

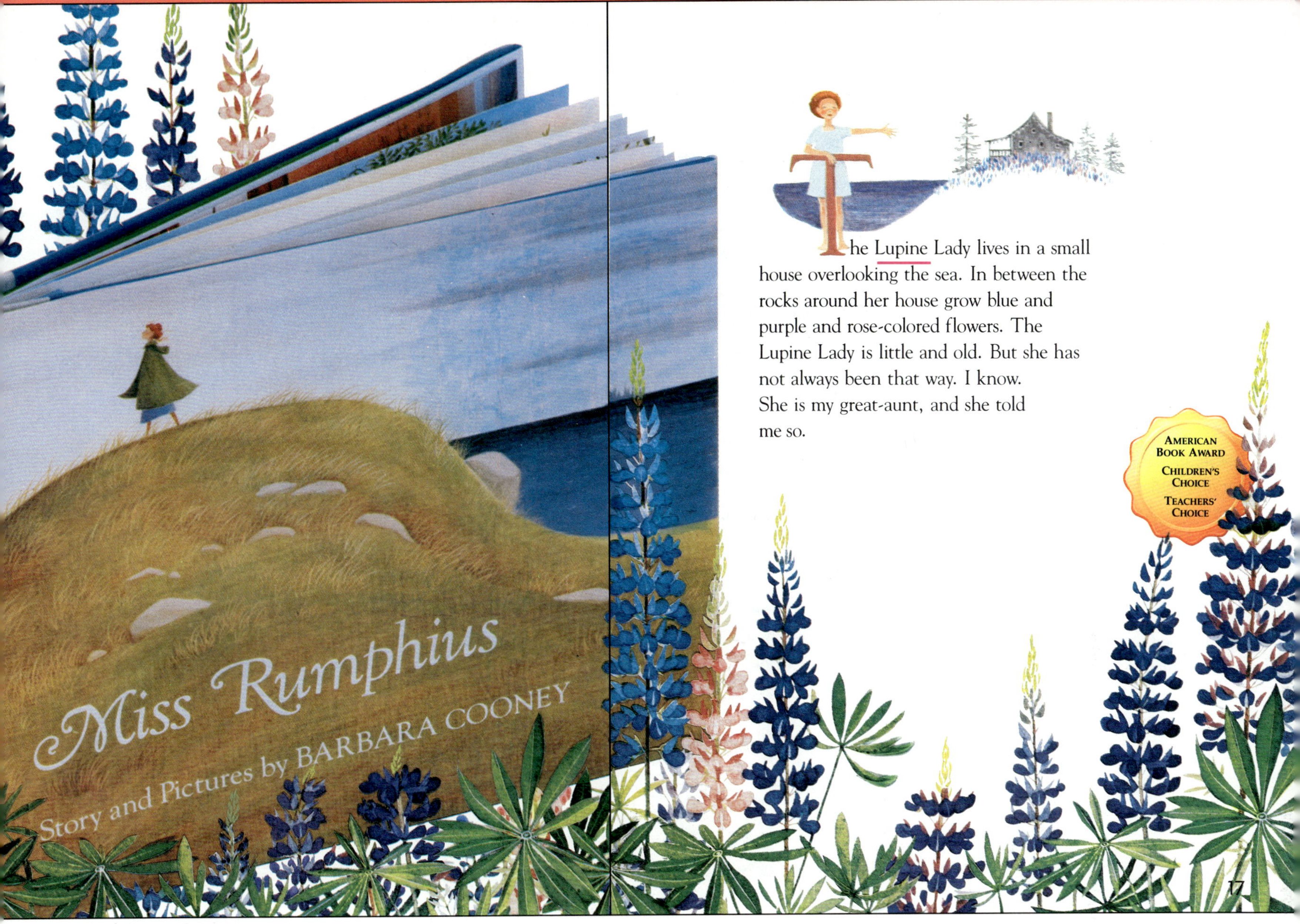

MISS RUMPHIUS   PAGES 16–17

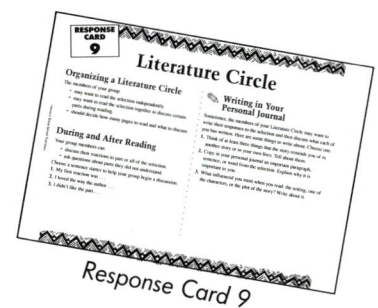

The Lupine Lady lives in a small house overlooking the sea. In between the rocks around her house grow blue and purple and rose-colored flowers. The Lupine Lady is little and old. But she has not always been that way. I know. She is my great-aunt, and she told me so.

Miss Rumphius
Story and Pictures by BARBARA COONEY

AMERICAN BOOK AWARD
CHILDREN'S CHOICE
TEACHERS' CHOICE

Reader Response Groups

LITERATURE CIRCLES Have each group of three to five students read and discuss the selection, pausing after page 25 for a brief discussion. Use Response Card 9 (Literature Circles), found on page R87, or provide discussion questions such as these:

- Think about the three things Miss Rumphius wants to do. Would these be important goals for you? Explain your answer.
- What kind of a person is Miss Rumphius? How do you know?

Response Card 9

Strategic Reading

SET PURPOSE/PREDICT: PAGES 16–25 Have students read through page 25. Ask students what they will be reading to find out.

MISS RUMPHIUS / T21

PAGES 18–19 MISS RUMPHIUS

Once upon a time she was a little girl named Alice, who lived in a city by the sea. From the front stoop she could see the wharves and the bristling masts of tall ships. Many years ago her grandfather had come to America on a large sailing ship.

Now he worked in the shop at the bottom of the house, making figureheads for the prows of ships, and carving Indians out of wood to put in front of cigar stores. For Alice's grandfather was an artist. He painted pictures, too, of sailing ships and places across the sea. When he was very busy, Alice helped him put in the skies.

In the evening Alice sat on her grandfather's knee and listened to his stories of faraway places. When he had finished, Alice would say, "When I grow up, I too will go to faraway places, and when I grow old, I too will live beside the sea."

Expanding the Literature When does the story take place? How do you know? (You can tell that the story takes place sometime in the past by looking carefully at the clothes people are wearing.) INFERENTIAL: AUTHOR'S CRAFT/DETERMINING SETTING

Informal Assessment

CHARACTER TRAITS You can informally assess your students' comprehension as they are reading silently. On occasion, ask students questions such as these:

- What kind of person is Alice?
- How does Alice's life change at different times?

By encouraging students to talk freely about their own thinking, you will get important diagnostic insights into how well they are reading.

MISS RUMPHIUS   PAGES 20–21

"That is all very well, little Alice," said her grandfather, "but there is a third thing you must do."

"What is that?" asked Alice.

"You must do something to make the world more beautiful," said her grandfather.

"All right," said Alice. But she did not know what that could be.

In the meantime Alice got up and washed her face and ate porridge for breakfast. She went to school and came home and did her homework.

And pretty soon she was grown up.

Then my Great-aunt Alice set out to do the three things she had told her grandfather she was going to do. She left home and went to live in another city far from the sea and salt air. There she worked in a library, dusting books and keeping them from getting mixed up, and helping people find the ones they wanted. Some of the books told her about faraway places.

People called her Miss Rumphius now.

20

GRAMMAR CONNECTION

REVIEWING SENTENCES   You may wish to review sentences with students by having them look at the first two paragraphs on page 20. Remind students that a sentence is a complete thought. You might ask students to find a sentence on the page that asks a question. (second paragraph)

Social Studies Connection   Alice's grandfather tells her that she must do something to make the world more beautiful. Do you think this is something everyone can do? Why or why not? (Accept reasonable responses: Yes; everyone has some kind of talent that he or she can use to make the world more beautiful.) CRITICAL: MAKING GENERALIZATIONS

See page T41 for information found on Project Card 4B.

MISS RUMPHIUS / T23

PAGES 22–23 MISS RUMPHIUS

Sometimes she went to the conservatory in the middle of the park. When she stepped inside on a wintry day, the warm moist air wrapped itself around her, and the sweet smell of jasmine filled her nose.

"This is almost like a tropical isle," said Miss Rumphius. "But not quite."

So Miss Rumphius went to a real tropical island, where people kept cockatoos and monkeys as pets. She walked on long beaches, picking up beautiful shells. One day she met the Bapa Raja, king of a fishing village.

"You must be tired," he said. "Come into my house and rest."

So Miss Rumphius went in and met the Bapa Raja's wife. The Bapa Raja himself fetched a green coconut and cut a slice off the top so that Miss Rumphius could drink the coconut water inside. Before she left, the Bapa Raja gave her a beautiful mother-of-pearl shell on which he had painted a bird of paradise and the words, "You will always remain in my heart."

"You will always remain in mine too," said Miss Rumphius.

22

Second-Language Support Students may be unfamiliar with the terms *jasmine*, *bird of paradise*, and *cockatoos*. Explain that jasmine is a plant with white or yellow flowers that have a very sweet smell. Then tell students that a bird of paradise is not a bird, but an orange-and-purple flower. Finally, point out the cockatoo that appears in the picture on page 23, and explain that it is a bird found in tropical parts of the world.

MEETING INDIVIDUAL NEEDS

Cultural Awareness Ask students to use context clues and the illustrations to try to figure out the meaning of *Raja* in the third paragraph. Explain that this title is used in India and certain other eastern countries such as Malaysia. The word comes from the Sanskrit word *rajan*, meaning "king." Sanskrit is an ancient language of India.

T24 / A PLACE TO DREAM, UNIT 1

MISS RUMPHIUS PAGES 24–25

My great-aunt Miss Alice Rumphius climbed tall mountains where the snow never melted. She went through jungles and across deserts. She saw lions playing and kangaroos jumping. And everywhere she made friends she would never forget. Finally she came to the Land of the Lotus-Eaters, and there, getting off a camel, she hurt her back.

"What a foolish thing to do," said Miss Rumphius. "Well, I have certainly seen faraway places. Maybe it is time to find my place by the sea."

And it was, and she did.

From the porch of her new house Miss Rumphius watched the sun come up; she watched it cross the heavens and sparkle on the water; and she saw it set in glory in the evening. She started a little garden among the rocks that surrounded her house, and she planted a few flower seeds in the stony ground. Miss Rumphius was *almost* perfectly happy.

"But there is still one more thing I have to do," she said. "I have to do something to make the world more beautiful."

But what? "The world already is pretty nice," she thought, looking out over the ocean.

Strategic Reading

MODELING A STRATEGY: PAGES 16–25 What have you learned about Miss Rumphius so far?

THINK ALOUD Provide a think-aloud model, if necessary: *I know that Miss Rumphius is the aunt of the girl who is telling the story. When Miss Rumphius was a young girl, her grandfather told her about faraway places. He also told her that she should do something to make the world a more beautiful place. When she grew up, Miss Rumphius began traveling the world, had exciting adventures, and made many friends.* ANALYZING CHARACTERS

SET PURPOSE/PREDICT: PAGES 26–30 Discuss with students the third thing Alice Rumphius wants to do (make the world more beautiful), and ask them to predict whether she will do this, based on what has happened so far in the story. Then have them read the rest of the story to confirm their predictions.

MISS RUMPHIUS / T25

PAGES 26–27 MISS RUMPHIUS

The next spring Miss Rumphius was not very well. Her back was bothering her again, and she had to stay in bed most of the time.

The flowers she had planted the summer before had come up and bloomed in spite of the stony ground. She could see them from her bedroom window, blue and purple and rose-colored.

"Lupines," said Miss Rumphius with satisfaction. "I have always loved lupines the best. I wish I could plant more seeds this summer so that I could have still more flowers next year."

But she was not able to.

After a hard winter spring came. Miss Rumphius was feeling much better. Now she could take walks again. One afternoon she started to go up and over the hill, where she had not been in a long time.

"I don't believe my eyes!" she cried when she got to the top. For there on the other side of the hill was a large patch of blue and purple and rose-colored lupines!

"It was the wind," she said as she knelt in delight. "It was the wind that brought the seeds from my garden here! And the birds must have helped!"

Then Miss Rumphius had a wonderful idea!

26

Vocabulary Strategy Point out the word *hard* on page 26. Remind students that many words have more than one meaning, and explain that in this sentence the word *hard* means "very cold, harsh, stormy." Then ask students to form oral sentences about the story with the word *hard*, using some of its other meanings. ("difficult": *It was hard for little Alice to think of a way to make the world more beautiful;* "firm to the touch": *Alice's grandfather made figureheads from hard wood*) STRATEGY: CONTEXT CLUES

See page T33 for information found on Project Card 3A.

MISS RUMPHIUS PAGES 28–29

he hurried home and got out her seed catalogues.
ent off to the very best seed house for five bushels
ine seed.
All that summer Miss Rumphius, her pockets full of
, wandered over fields and headlands, sowing lupines.
scattered seeds along the highways and down the
try lanes. She flung handfuls of them around the
olhouse and back of the church. She tossed them into
ws and along stone walls.
Her back didn't hurt her any more at all.
Now some people called her That Crazy Old Lady.
The next spring there were lupines everywhere. Fields
hillsides were covered with blue and purple and rose-
ed flowers. They bloomed along the highways and
n the lanes. Bright patches lay around the school-
e and back of the church. Down in the hollows and
g the stone walls grew the beautiful flowers.
Miss Rumphius had done the third, the most difficult
g of all!
My Great-aunt Alice, Miss Rumphius, is very old now.
hair is very white. Every year there are more and more
es. Now they call her the Lupine Lady. Sometimes my
ds stand with me outside her gate, curious to see the
old lady who planted the fields of lupines. When she
es us in, they come slowly. They think she is the oldest
an in the world. Often she tells us stories of faraway places.

Strategic Reading

MODELING A STRATEGY: PAGES 26–30 Have students summarize what they have read on these pages.

THINK ALOUD Provide a think-aloud model, if necessary: *I see that after the wind and birds carry lupine seeds to the other side of a hill, Miss Rumphius decides to scatter seeds everywhere she goes, and she accomplishes her third goal: to make the world more beautiful.*
SUMMARIZING

Returning to the Predictions/Purpose

PREVIEW AND PREDICT Ask students to discuss the predictions that they made before reading the story. Have them explain how they changed their predictions as they read. Encourage volunteers to share their purposes for reading and tell whether their purposes were met.

NOTE: Responses to the questions and support for the Write activity appear on page T29.

PAGES 30–31 MISS RUMPHIUS

"When I grow up," I tell her, "I too will go to faraway places and come home to live by the sea."

"That is all very well, little Alice," says my aunt, "but there is a third thing you must do."

"What is that?" I ask.

"You must do something to make the world more beautiful."

"All right," I say.

But I do not know yet what that can be.

Do you agree with Alice's grandfather that a person should do something to improve the world? Tell why you feel as you do.

Miss Rumphius described her third goal as the most difficult to complete. Why do you think she felt that way?

Besides her grandfather, who or what else was important in Miss Rumphius's life?

WRITE If you could do something to make the world more beautiful, what would it be? Write a journal entry telling how you would make the world a more beautiful place.

30

When I was building a house in Maine, I noticed that we had an abundance of lupines on our land. Where did they all come from, I wondered. One of the workmen said, "There's an old woman down in Christmas Cove who goes around throwing lupine seeds. That's why there are so many flowers." I thought that was a good "seed" for a story.

One day, I sat down and said I would write a fairy tale about a heroine who had to do three things, and the hardest was the third, sowing the lupine seeds. The rest of the story patches together things that happened to me or my family. The story starts off in Brooklyn, where I was born, and the travels are mine, though I took them later in my life. My great-grandfather did carve cigar-store Indians, and my grandfather did help him paint in the skies in his pictures. I have ridden on camels, but I don't like them. It's too hard to get on and off!

Knowing I was going to have lots of lupines in my story, the minute they began to bloom I started drawing and photographing them. I didn't finish the book until much later, after the flowers were gone, but at least I had the drawings and the photos to work with.

When I create a book, I always do the story first. I think it's important to have a good story. The pictures come after the story, like beads on a string.

Words from the Author and Illustrator Barbara Cooney

AWARD-WINNING AUTHOR AND ILLUSTRATOR

Words from the Author and Illustrator

AUTHOR/ILLUSTRATOR'S PURPOSE Invite students to read page 31 to find out how Barbara Cooney came to write "Miss Rumphius." When they have finished reading, ask them to explain what they read in their own words. (Accept reasonable responses: She got the idea for the story when she heard about a woman in Christmas Cove, Maine, who went around scattering lupine seeds; she thought of a fairy-tale heroine who would have to do three things; once she had the idea, she began drawing and photographing lupines.)

T28 / *A PLACE TO DREAM*, UNIT 1

PART 2

Responding to the Literature

Personal Response

Encourage critical thinking.

Do you agree with Alice's grandfather that a person should do something to improve the world? Tell why you feel as you do. (Responses will vary.) CRITICAL: EXPRESSING PERSONAL OPINIONS

Miss Rumphius described her third goal as the most difficult to complete. Why do you think she felt that way? (Accept reasonable responses: The world was already beautiful; she didn't know what she could do to make it more beautiful.)
METACOGNITIVE: DRAWING CONCLUSIONS

Besides her grandfather, who or what else was important in Miss Rumphius's life? (keeping her promise to her grandfather; traveling and exploring faraway places; her house by the sea; her friends; making the world beautiful) INFERENTIAL: DRAWING CONCLUSIONS

Encourage creative written responses.

 **WRITE** If you could do something to make the world more beautiful, what would it be? Write a journal entry telling how you would make the world a more beautiful place. Encourage students to use their imaginations as they consider various ideas. CREATIVE: WRITING A JOURNAL ENTRY

Cooperative Response

Have reader response groups extend their discussions.

LITERATURE CIRCLES Suggest that Literature Circles meet to share their thoughts and feelings about the story. Then have them discuss a question such as this:

If you could visit one of the places that Miss Rumphius visited, which one would you choose, and why?

STRATEGY CONFERENCE

Discuss with students how previewing and making predictions helped them understand and appreciate the selection. (Accept reasonable responses: Previewing and predicting help a reader stay focused on story events and understand them better.)

NOTE

An additional writing activity for this selection appears on page T32.

MISS RUMPHIUS / T29

Summarizing the Literature

Have students retell the story and write a summary.

Guide students in beginning a chart to summarize the story by recalling the different names Miss Rumphius was known by and the important events at each stage of her life. Students can retell the story using their completed charts and can then write a brief summary. See *Practice Book* page 2 below.

	How old she was	Where she lived or traveled	Things she did
Alice	(a child)		
Miss Rumphius	(a young woman)		
That Crazy Old Lady	(an older woman)		
The Lupine Lady	(a very old woman)		

Portfolio

STUDENT SELF-ASSESSMENT

Help students self-assess their summaries of the story by having them draw pictures of Miss Rumphius at different times in the story. Encourage students to add their summaries and their pictures to their portfolios.

Critical Thinking Activity

Have students write three questions.

COMPLETE SPEECH BALLOONS If you could meet Miss Rumphius, what three questions would you ask her? Have students use speech balloons as shown below to write down their questions. You may want to have one student role-play the part of Miss Rumphius and try to answer the questions. **CRITICAL: EXTENDING STORY CONCEPTS**

Writer's Journal

Practice Book

OPTIONAL INDEPENDENT PRACTICE

WRITER'S JOURNAL
page 7: Writing a personal response

PRACTICE BOOK
page 2: Summarizing the selection

T30 / A PLACE TO DREAM, UNIT 1

VOCABULARY WORKSHOP

Reviewing Key Words

Have students write the Key Words on individual slips of paper. After you read aloud each description below, have students hold up the word that matches that description.

1. **The children felt this way when they wondered about Miss Rumphius.** *(curious)*
2. **These are the kinds of carved statues that Miss Rumphius's grandfather made for ships.** *(figureheads)*
3. **This is the flower that Miss Rumphius planted everywhere she went.** *(lupine)*
4. **Miss Rumphius ordered seeds from these.** *(catalogues)*
5. **Miss Rumphius tossed lupine seeds down into these parts of the land.** *(hollows)*
6. **This word describes the hot, moist climate on the island where Miss Rumphius met the Bapa Raja and his wife.** *(tropical)*
7. **This is what Miss Rumphius felt after she had found a way to make the world more beautiful.** *(satisfaction)*

Extending Vocabulary

HYPHENATED COMPOUND WORDS Write the word *grandfather* on the board and have students identify it. Point out that *grandfather* is made up of two smaller words, and ask students to name those words. (*grand* and *father*) Remind students that a word made up of smaller words is called a *compound word*. Encourage them to give examples of other compound words.

Then remind students that the author of "Miss Rumphius" describes some of the lupines as *rose-colored*. Display the word *rose-colored* and point out the hyphen. Explain that a hyphenated word such as *rose-colored* is another type of compound word. Ask students to find other hyphenated words in the story, and write them on the board. (*great-aunt, mother-of-pearl, Lotus-Eaters*)

Draw the following diagram, including the words, on the board. Have students form hyphenated compounds by combining a word from each of the two columns. Then have them think of a noun to follow each hyphenated word. Model creating the phrases *rose-colored glasses* and *Great-uncle Harry*. (Remind students to capitalize *Great-aunt* or *Great-uncle* when it is followed by a name.) Encourage students to come up with as many variations as they can.

| rose
green
brown
great
bright
red | + | haired
colored
uncle
aunt
eyed | = | (rose-colored)
(great-uncle) |

MISS RUMPHIUS / **T31**

Language Arts WORKSHOP

READING

Oral Rereading/Drama

Have students form groups of three and reread the part of the story in which Miss Rumphius meets the Bapa Raja. Ask students to choose the parts of Miss Rumphius, the Bapa Raja, and the narrator, and to begin by silently rereading page 22. Model reading aloud a brief passage, using the appropriate intonation and facial expressions. Give students a chance to rehearse before they present their readings.   LISTENING/READING

SPELLING

Reviewing Spelling Words

SPELLING WORDS: *act, back, bag, best, bread, cap, end, hand, hat, head, left, rest*

WORDS TO EXPLORE: *catalogues, garden, lupine, tropical*

Create a list of words that contain the short *a* and short *e* sounds. Use Spelling Words along with students' own lists that follow the spelling generalization. Write the headings *short a* and *short e* in two columns on one half of the board; do the same on the other half. Arrange two teams of students in lines in front of the two halves of the board. As you call out a word, the first person in line on each team rushes to write the word under the correct heading. The spellers then go to the end of the line, and the game continues.   LISTENING/WRITING/SPELLING

Use *Integrated Spelling* Lesson 1 to reinforce the Spelling Words and the Words to Explore. See pages T15–T20 in *Integrated Spelling Teacher's Edition*.

 **SPELLING POSTTEST** You may want to use the Pretest/Posttest Sentences on *Integrated Spelling Teacher's Edition* page T15 to assess students' knowledge of the spelling generalization.

WRITING

Writing About the Literature

 **WRITE A LETTER** Have each student think of a person he or she admires and then write a letter to that person. Suggest that they write to someone whom they know personally, or someone they know of, such as a famous scientist, writer, or athlete. Encourage students to describe things they would like to do. The frame below may be used for prewriting.

> Dear _____,
>   Things I admire about you:
>   _____
>
>   Things I want to tell you about me:
>   Places I'd like to see _____
>   A job I'd like to have _____
>   Other things about me _____
>   Your friend,
>   _____

Remind students to include their address and the date at the top of the letter. See Writing Model, page R97.
READING/WRITING

GRAMMAR REVIEW: SENTENCES As students revise their letters, remind them to check that their sentences tell a complete thought, and that each begins with a capital letter and ends with an end mark. You may want to have volunteers write sentences on the board and discuss whether each tells a complete thought.

 **LANGUAGE HANDBOOK** *Everyday Writing, pages 66–67, 70; Sentences, pages 84–85*

 **DAILY LANGUAGE PRACTICE** *Oral language exercises are provided on pages R58–R59.*

Language Arts WORKSHOP

WRITING

Never Say "Bored"

Available on Project Card 3A

COOPERATIVE LEARNING Have students recall that when Miss Rumphius hurt her back, she had to stay in bed and was probably bored. Ask students to brainstorm a list of things that people can do so they don't get bored. Have a Recorder write down the ideas. Ideas might include drawing pictures, making paper airplanes, making paper snowflakes, and reading stories. Encourage students to work together to create a book of "anti-boredom" ideas for third graders. Assign two Materials Managers to gather and distribute needed supplies.   LISTENING/SPEAKING/WRITING

LISTENING AND SPEAKING

Describe an Imaginary Land

Invite students to imagine a new land Miss Rumphius or other adventurers could visit. Encourage them to brainstorm descriptive details, using a web like the one below:

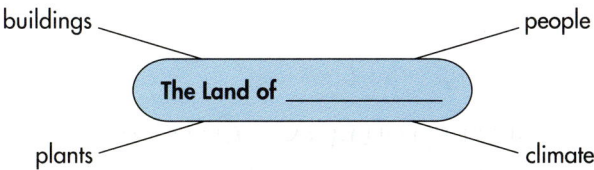

Then have students pretend to be travel agents and make a presentation to a group of classmates encouraging them to take a vacation there.   LISTENING/SPEAKING

LISTENING AND SPEAKING

Show and Tell

Available on Project Card 3B

Remind students that when Miss Rumphius was older, she liked to walk and garden. Ask students to discuss what they like to do in their spare time. Many students may have hobbies, such as drawing, building models, or collecting rocks. Encourage them to bring their collections or creations to class, describe the hobby, and tell why they enjoy it.   LISTENING/SPEAKING/VIEWING

WRITING

Words About Ships

COOPERATIVE LEARNING Write the words *wharves, ships, figureheads, prows,* and *masts* on the board and discuss them with students. Explain that there are many other words that tell about ships and navigation. Have students work in small groups to come up with other words, and list them on the board. Have students create an illustrated glossary of terms related to ships. If necessary, review what a glossary is and how to use it, referring to the Glossary at the back of the Student Anthology. Encourage students to consult a dictionary if they need help with word meaning or spelling. Assign two or more Checkers and Recorders to facilitate the work.   LISTENING/SPEAKING/READING/WRITING

MISS RUMPHIUS / T33

Grammar MINI LESSON

Kinds of Sentences

OBJECTIVES: *To recognize that a sentence tells a complete thought; to recognize that the words in a sentence should be in an order that makes sense and that every sentence begins with a capital letter and ends with an end mark; to distinguish between a statement, a question, an exclamation, and a command*

Oral Warm-Up

Display the following sentences from "Miss Rumphius":

- **What is that?**
- **Come into my house and rest.**
- **You will always remain in my heart.**
- **I don't believe my eyes!**

Read each sentence aloud, using proper inflection. Then ask students questions based on the headings of the chart below. (For example: "Which sentence shows strong feeling?") Record students' responses in the chart.

Simply Tells Something	Asks Something	Shows Strong Feeling	Tells Someone to Do Something
(You will always remain in my heart.)	(What is that?)	(I don't believe my eyes!)	(Come into my house and rest.)

Interactive Teaching

SENTENCES Remind students that a **sentence** must tell a complete thought. Erase the word *You* from the statement in the chart, and ask students why the remaining words are not a sentence. (They don't express a complete thought.) Next, write this scrambled sentence on the board: *My house and rest come into*. Help students understand that this phrase makes no sense because the words are not in the correct order. Have a volunteer rewrite the words in an order that makes sense. Finally, circle the capital letter and the end mark in each sentence in the chart, and tell students that the first word in every sentence begins with a capital letter and that every sentence ends with an end mark.

STATEMENTS AND QUESTIONS Write the following sentence on the board: *Miss Rumphius planted many beautiful flowers.* Explain to students that a sentence that tells something is called a **statement** and that all statements end with a period. Then write another sentence on the board: *How many seeds did Miss Rumphius plant?* Read this sentence aloud, and tell students that a sentence that asks something is called a **question** and ends with a question mark. Ask volunteers to write on the board statements and questions using the words *travel, climb,* and *bloom*.

COMMANDS AND EXCLAMATIONS Tell students that a sentence that gives an order or a direction is called a **command**. Explain that a sentence that shows strong feeling is an **exclamation**. Write the following sentences on the board:

- **Send me five bushels of lupine seeds.**
- **Those are the most beautiful flowers I've ever seen!**

Ask volunteers to indicate which sentence is an exclamation and which is a command. Then explain to students that exclamations end with an exclamation point and that commands usually end with a period. Tell students that a command sometimes ends with an exclamation point when the sentence shows strong feeling. You may want to illustrate this point with the examples *Hurry up!* and *Look out!*

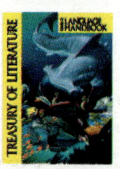 **LANGUAGE HANDBOOK** *Kinds of Sentences,* pages 84–89

Practice Activities

Alice's Continuing Adventures

COOPERATIVE LEARNING Write the following sentences on the board: *Alice Rumphius went on an adventure in India. She met a famous gardener.* Have students work in groups of four to create a journal entry about Miss Rumphius and the gardener. Tell groups to use at least one example of each of the sentence types. When the Recorders have finished writing, have groups exchange entries and check the word order, the end marks, and the capitalization in each other's work. Then have volunteers from each group read the journal entries aloud. **AUDITORY**

Comic Strip Sentences

Have students work in pairs to write four or five sentences, using at least one example of each of the sentence types. Then have partners work together to create a comic strip using their sentences. Tell students to add the sentences to the bottom of each frame in the comic strip or write the sentences in speech balloons to accompany the illustrations. When partners have finished, have them exchange their comic strips with another pair of students, and check each other's end marks, word order, and capitalization of sentences. Some students may want to act out their comic strips. Have students compile their work to create a class comic book.

VISUAL/KINESTHETIC

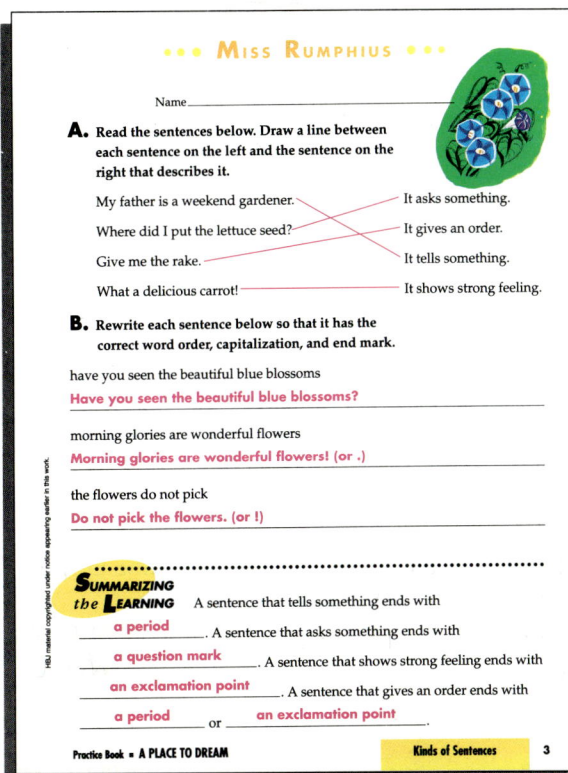

Practice Book

MEETING INDIVIDUAL NEEDS

SECOND-LANGUAGE SUPPORT Remind students whose first language is Spanish that in English, exclamation points and question marks are used only at the end of a sentence, not at the beginning.

RETEACH Follow the visual, auditory, and kinesthetic/motor models on page R3.

OPTIONAL INDEPENDENT PRACTICE

PRACTICE BOOK
page 3: Identifying and using kinds of sentences

GRAMMAR PRACTICE
pages 12–13: Reinforcing kinds of sentences

PART 3

Learning through the Literature

COMPREHENSION
INTRODUCE

Cause and Effect

OBJECTIVE: *To determine cause-and-effect relationships*

Interactive Teaching

Focus on "Miss Rumphius."

LITERATURE CONNECTION Ask students why Miss Rumphius went to a tropical island. (She wanted to visit faraway places.) Explain that why something happens is the *cause* and that what happens is the *effect*. Point out that recognizing causes and effects will help students understand what they read.

Model the thinking.

DISCUSS SELF-QUESTIONING Tell students that to understand causes and effects, they can ask themselves "What happened?" and "Why did it happen?" Have students reread the last three paragraphs on page 26. Have them tell what caused the lupines to grow on the hillside. If necessary, use this think-aloud to model how to recognize an effect with more than one cause:

> I read that lupines grew on the side of the hill. I ask myself, "Why did this happen?" There are two causes: The wind blew some seeds there; birds carried others. So, lupines grew on the hillside because the wind and birds carried seeds there. The word *because* signals a cause.

Discuss unstated and stated causes and effects.

FIND CAUSES AND EFFECTS Explain that sometimes readers must figure out causes and effects on their own. Sometimes authors will use clue words such as *because*, *so*, and *as a result* to signal causes and effects. Display Chart/Transparency 2 or the diagram on it. Complete it with students. Then help them combine the sentences using clue words.

ADDITIONAL BOOKS FOR APPLYING CAUSE AND EFFECT

The Legend of the Bluebonnet by Tomie dePaola. Putnam, 1983.   EASY

Hattie and the Wild Waves: A Story from Brooklyn by Barbara Cooney. Viking, 1990.   AVERAGE

Chart/Transparency 2 Cause and Effect	
More Than One Cause	**One Effect**
The wind blew seeds. → (The birds carried seeds.) →	Lupines grew on the other side of the hill.
One Cause (not stated)	**One Effect**
(She was ill.) →	She couldn't plant.

T36 / A PLACE TO DREAM, UNIT 1

Practice Activity

Cause or Effect?

Have students write cause-effect sentences.

On the board, write phrases about Miss Rumphius:

Miss Rumphius

went to the jungle   scattered seeds
wanted to travel   made the world beautiful

Have pairs of students choose phrases to make into pairs of sentences stating a cause and an effect. Examples: *Miss Rumphius wanted to travel.* (cause) *Miss Rumphius went to the jungle.* (effect)   VISUAL

Performance Assessment

Have students read aloud the pairs of sentences they wrote for the Cause or Effect? activity. Classmates should tell which one states a cause and which one states an effect. For evaluation guidelines, see *Staff Development Guide*.

Reader ↔ Writer Connection
Cause and Effect

WRITERS need to plan stories so that causes and effects make sense.

READERS need to know why things happen in a story in order to understand it better.

WRITE A STORY   Have students write a story that is a chain of cause-and-effect events.

Writer's Journal

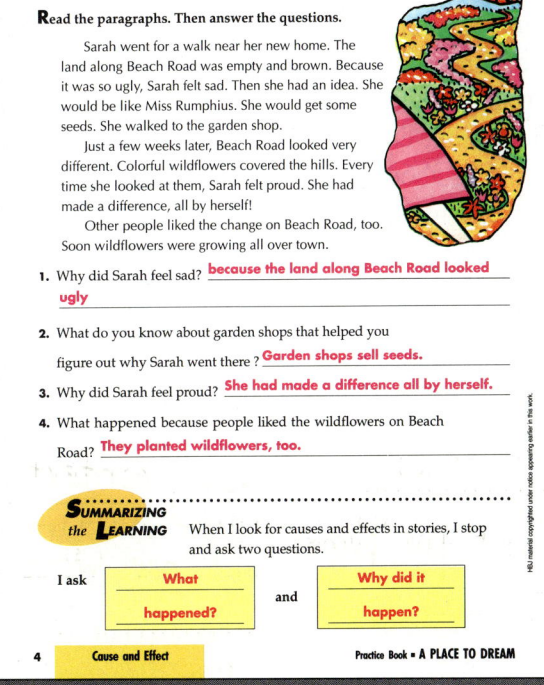

Practice Book

MEETING INDIVIDUAL NEEDS

RETEACH   Follow the visual, auditory, and kinesthetic/motor models on page R4.

CHALLENGE   Ask students to make up events that happened during Miss Rumphius's travels and that include cause-and-effect relationships. Have students include at least one effect that has more than one cause.

SECOND-LANGUAGE SUPPORT   Students can draw and explain a comic strip that shows how one event from the story caused another event to happen. See also the manual *Alternative Teaching Strategies*, pages 2, 34–37.

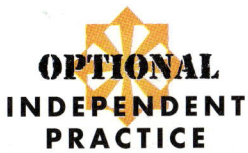

OPTIONAL INDEPENDENT PRACTICE

WRITER'S JOURNAL
page 8: Finishing a story using cause and effect

PRACTICE BOOK
page 4: Identifying cause and effect

MISS RUMPHIUS / **T37**

> COMPREHENSION STRATEGY
> **INTRODUCE**

Active Reading Strategies

OBJECTIVE: *To apply reading-process strategies to gain meaning*

Interactive Teaching

Use reading strategies with "Miss Rumphius."

LITERATURE CONNECTION Discuss with students the different things they did before, during, and after reading "Miss Rumphius." (Accept reasonable responses: previewed the story, made predictions, compared predictions with what happened, summarized.) Explain to students that the things they described are called *strategies*, and that strategies are plans to help them understand, enjoy, and remember what they read.

Ask questions that focus on strategies.

DISCUSS WHEN TO USE STRATEGIES To help students understand during-reading and after-reading strategies, ask these questions:

- Did you find you needed to change your prediction as you learned more about Miss Rumphius?
- Did you come to any word you didn't know as you were reading? If you did, what did you do?
- Was there any time when you didn't understand what you were reading? What did you do?
- What was your purpose for reading "Miss Rumphius"? Was the purpose met? Explain your answer.
- What did you do to sum up, or summarize, the story?

Model how to classify strategies.

CHART STRATEGIES Write headings like the ones below on the board. Model the thinking:

> At different times in the reading process, I use different strategies. For example, I preview *before* reading to help me think about what might happen in the story.

Then read aloud the following strategies and have students list each under the appropriate category: using context clues to figure out a new word; previewing; setting a purpose; summarizing; predicting; changing a prediction; confirming a prediction; thinking about the purpose for reading; deciding whether the purpose for reading was met; deciding whether you liked the story. Point out that some strategies may be used at several different times.

Before Reading	During Reading	After Reading
(previewing)	(changing a prediction)	(summarizing)
- previewing	- using context clues to figure out new word	summarizing
- predicting	- changing a prediction	- confirming a prediction
- thinking about the purpose for reading		- was purpose for reading met
		- did you like the story?

AN ADDITIONAL BOOK FOR APPLYING ACTIVE READING STRATEGIES

Uncle Willie and the Soup Kitchen by Anne DiSalvo-Ryan. Morrow, 1991. AVERAGE

Practice Activity

Match Me

Have students play a game.

COOPERATIVE LEARNING Have groups of three or four students play Match Me. Before they begin, have students write the names of these reading strategies on individual index cards: Preview, Make Predictions, Set a Purpose, Use Context Clues, Change Predictions, Confirm Predictions, Summarize, Decide if Purpose Was Met. Have a Facilitator in each group mix up the cards and place them face down. In turn, players pick a strategy and tell whether it should be used before, during, or after reading. Explain that some strategies can be used at more than one time. Players should give reasons to support their matches. Checkers can help settle disagreements. **KINESTHETIC**

Performance Assessment

To assess how students matched reading strategies in the Match Me activity, ask them to show you some cards they matched and explain why they matched them. For evaluation guidelines, see *Staff Development Guide*.

MEETING INDIVIDUAL NEEDS

RETEACH Follow the visual, auditory, and kinesthetic/motor models on page R5.

CHALLENGE Have students apply strategies they can use before, during, and after reading a library book.

SECOND-LANGUAGE SUPPORT Students can demonstrate their understanding of this skill by orally identifying one strategy they can use before, one they can use during, and one they can use after reading a story. See also the manual *Alternative Teaching Strategies*, pages 2, 34–37.

OPTIONAL INDEPENDENT PRACTICE

PRACTICE BOOK
pages 5–6: Applying active reading strategies

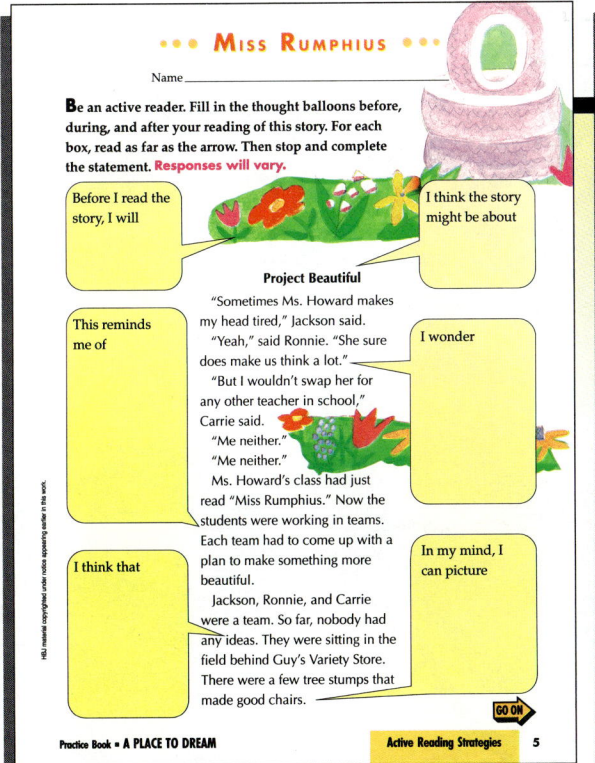

Practice Book

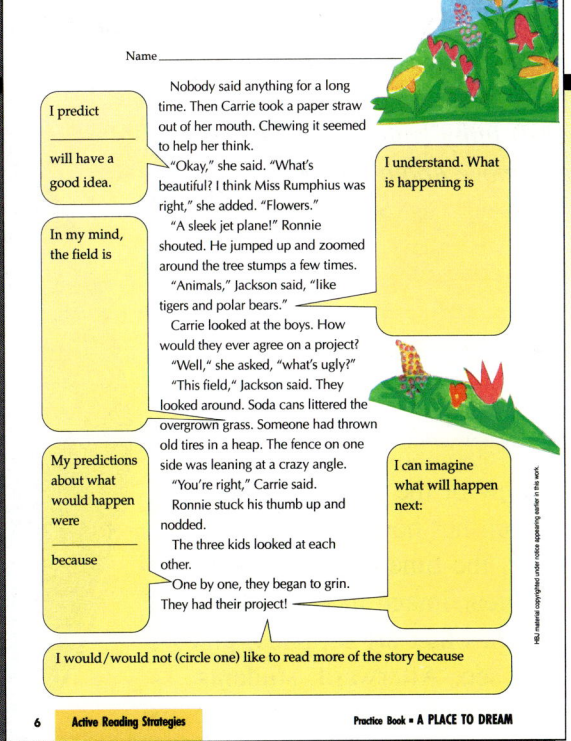

Practice Book

MISS RUMPHIUS / T39

Integrated CURRICULUM

SCIENCE

Getting to Know the Kangaroo

USE REFERENCE SOURCES Students may be interested in finding out more about kangaroos, one of the animals Miss Rumphius saw during her travels. Have them put together a brief report about kangaroos. To guide their research, suggest that they go to the school library to find the answers to these and other questions: *In what part of the world do kangaroos live? What is a baby kangaroo called? Where does a baby kangaroo live after it is born? How do kangaroos move about?* Students may wish to illustrate their reports. **READING/WRITING**

ART

Drawing a View

Ask students to visualize the view of the garden and the sea that Miss Rumphius had from her house. Encourage them to think about the weather, the time of day, and the season. When students have a clear image in their mind, provide them with watercolors (or other art supplies) and ask them to illustrate what they see. Afterward, students can compare their scenes and discuss how the scenes are alike and different. **LISTENING/SPEAKING/VIEWING**

SOCIAL STUDIES

Clothing Around the World

CULTURAL AWARENESS Have students look at the picture of the Bapa Raja on page 23. Ask them to describe what he is wearing. Then explain to students that although many people around the world wear Western-style clothing as most Americans do, some people may wear the traditional clothing of their country, especially on special occasions. Help students name some of these kinds of clothing. (saris, kimonos, Scottish kilts, sarongs, *charro* suits) Have students form pairs. Assign one kind of traditional dress to each pair, or allow students to select their own if they wish. Provide students with books to which they can refer. Have them draw a picture of the traditional or ceremonial dress and write two or three sentences about it. When the pictures are ready, display them on a bulletin board. **LISTENING/SPEAKING/READING/WRITING**

T40 / A PLACE TO DREAM, UNIT 1

ART

Snapshots of the Imagination

Available on Project Card 4A

Have students create a "photo album" of Miss Rumphius's travels. Ask students to visualize and then draw some of the things Miss Rumphius might have seen. Then ask them to write a caption under each picture. ("The Bapa Raja and his wife," "Me on a camel in the Land of the Lotus-Eaters," "A sunset on the tropical island") Put all the pictures together in a class binder. WRITING/VIEWING

SOCIAL STUDIES

It's All for the Better

Available on Project Card 4B

CULTURAL AWARENESS Ask students to think of famous people around the world who have made the world more beautiful or who have improved it in some other way. Then encourage them to choose one person and find out more about what he or she has done. Students' choices could range from poets and painters (Emily Dickinson, Langston Hughes, Georgia O'Keeffe, Diego Rivera) to inventors and scientists (Jonas Salk, Marie Curie, Thomas Edison, Garrett Morgan, Louis Braille). Have students write brief reports about their findings. READING/WRITING

MATH

Calculating Mileage

Show students a table of highway mileage between major cities in your part of the United States and explain how to read the table. Ask pairs of students to pick two of the places listed that they would like to visit. Then have them use the table to figure out how far they would have to travel from their home to both of these places and then back home again. Suggest that students present their results in the form of a diagram, a chart, or a map. READING/WRITING

SOCIAL STUDIES

Geographical Facts

USE AN ALMANAC AND AN ATLAS Have students create a game of facts about islands, jungles, deserts, and mountains—all places that Miss Rumphius visited. Give each student two blank cards. On one side of each card, have students write a question related to a geographical place; on the other side, they should write the answer. Provide this example: *Which is the tallest mountain in the world?* (Mount Everest) Students should refer to a science or social studies book, or to an almanac or an atlas to prepare the game. When students are ready, have them place all the cards in one pile, with the answers face down. Students take turns picking a card from the pile. If a student can answer a question correctly, he or she keeps the card. Otherwise, it must be placed at the bottom of the pile. Students get a point for each card they collect. LISTENING/SPEAKING/READING/WRITING

BOOKS TO SHARE

SCIENCE *My First Garden Book: A Life-Size Guide to Growing Things at Home* by Angela Wilkes. Alfred A. Knopf, 1994. AVERAGE

SOCIAL STUDIES *John Muir: Man of the Wild Places* by Carol Greene. Childrens Press, 1991. EASY

MULTICULTURAL PERSPECTIVES

Making Improvements

DISCUSSION STARTER

How can people make the world a better or more beautiful place?

READ ALOUD

Some people have improved the world through science. Take, for example, Benjamin Franklin. His many inventions include the Franklin stove and bifocal glasses, eyeglasses with two-part lenses: one part for seeing objects that are close up and the other part for seeing objects that are far away.

Another important early American scientist was Benjamin Banneker, whose father was of African descent. Banneker was a brilliant mathematician and an astronomer, a person who studies the planets and stars. Banneker wrote almanacs for the years 1792–1803. His almanac was an important reference book in the households of the time and contained many facts, including the time of sunrise and sunset for each day of the year, dates and times of eclipses, tide tables, dates of phases of the moon, and dates of holidays. In 1753 he completed a wooden clock—the first clock made in America. He also helped survey the land and helped draw the plans for the new nation's capital—Washington, D.C.

Today people working to improve the world may use one invention to produce another. Martine Kempf, who came to the United States from France, used her home computer to design a voice-controlled wheelchair. Her invention allows people who are paralyzed to move their wheelchairs by speaking commands into a microphone.

ACTIVITY CORNER

● Have students research the lives of Benjamin Franklin and Benjamin Banneker and make time lines of the major events in their lives. Some students may wish to illustrate their findings.

● Assign groups of students a common household object that an African American has invented or helped to perfect. Have them explain how the object works and who the inventor was. Encourage students to add drawings to their explanations. Possible objects include the ironing board (Sarah Boone), range (T. A. Carrington), kitchen table (H. A. Jackson), and eggbeater (W. Long).

Martine Kempf in the wheelchair she designed.

Benjamin Banneker made all the mathematical calculations that were included in his farmer's almanac.

T42 / A PLACE TO DREAM, UNIT 1

NONFICTION

A Seed Is a Promise

SELECTION SUMMARY This informational selection compares a seed to a promise because there is the promise of a new plant contained within every seed. Using text and illustrations, the selection explains how seeds form, how they grow, and what conditions are necessary in order for them to "keep their promise."

Building Background

Have students begin a K-W-L chart about seeds.

On the board, draw a K-W-L chart such as the one below and have students copy it onto a sheet of paper. Model for students how to fill in the first column with what they know about seeds:

To fill in the first column of the chart, I ask myself what I already know about seeds. I know that they need soil, water, and sunlight to grow. I also know that fruits have seeds in them. I'll write this information in the first column of my chart.

What I Know	What I Want to Know	What I Learned
Seeds need soil, water, and sunlight to grow. Fruits have seeds in them.		

Strategic Reading

Help students write questions in their K-W-L charts.

SETTING A PURPOSE Have students write in the second column of their K-W-L charts questions they hope will be answered by the selection. The chart below shows some examples. Tell students to use the questions to set a purpose for reading the selection. Suggest that they add other questions to the chart as they read. Have students read the selection with their purposes for reading in mind.

What I Know	What I Want to Know	What I Learned
Seeds need soil, water, and sunlight to grow. Fruits have seeds in them.	Why does the author call a seed "a promise"? If you keep seeds a long time before planting them, will they still grow?	

MEETING INDIVIDUAL NEEDS

SECOND-LANGUAGE SUPPORT Students will benefit from a discussion about seeds, flowers, and plants. Encourage students to share what they know about seeds and to name several foods that contain seeds, especially those that may be unfamiliar to some students. Incorporate into the discussion the names of a variety of foods, plants, and flowers. See also the manual *Alternative Teaching Strategies,* pages 3–4, 38–39.

PAGES 32–33 A SEED IS A PROMISE

A SEED IS A PROMISE

BY CLAIRE MERRILL

You know a lot about seeds.

When you eat an orange, you see little white seeds inside.

You've seen the seeds of other fruits, too—apples, pears, melons, grapes.

Have you eaten peas or lima beans for dinner? Peas and lima beans are seeds. They are the seeds of vegetables.

Have you ever bought flower seed packets in the store? Or fed grass seed to a pet bird?

Have you ever worn maple tree seeds on your nose? Or played tea party with the seeds of an oak tree?

Do you know where all these seeds come from? All seeds come from plants.

And in every seed there is a promise, the promise that a new plant will grow.

If you know what kind of plant a seed comes from, you know what it will grow into.

ILLUSTRATED BY ANDREA EBERBACH

A bean seed will grow into a bean plant. An orange seed will grow into an orange tree. But an orange seed will never grow into a lemon tree.

How are seeds made? Most seeds begin inside flowers. Look at the center part of the flower. This is called the pistil. At the bottom of the pistil there are tiny egg cells.

Now look at the parts around the pistil. These are the stamens. They make a yellow powder called pollen.

A grain of pollen must reach an egg cell to make a seed.

32

Teaching Tip For students who are unfamiliar with maple trees, you may wish to explain that the fruit of a maple tree, called a *key,* consists of a pair of seeds with green "wings" that enable the seeds to "fly" down from the tree. As it floats down, the key whirls around like a miniature propeller until it comes to rest on the ground, where it can take root. The part of the fruit between the wings is sticky. When the fruit is green, some children stick keys on their noses. Some also use the little cup- or saucer-shaped caps on oak seeds, called *acorns,* as tiny toy teacups.

Vocabulary Strategy Ask how students might visualize *a grain of pollen*. (Accept reasonable responses: They might use phrases they have heard before, such as "a grain of sand" and "a grain of rice," to figure out that a *grain* is one particle of a substance. Then they might use the phrase *a yellow powder called pollen* to figure out that pollen, which is a powder, must have even tinier grains than sand, since sand is coarser than powder.) **STRATEGY: PRIOR KNOWLEDGE/CONTEXT CLUES**

T44 / A PLACE TO DREAM, UNIT 1

Some flowers use their own pollen to make seeds. But most flowers use the pollen of other flowers.

Bees and other insects carry pollen from flower to flower. Wind blows pollen through the air.

A grain of pollen lands on the pistil of a flower. The pollen grain grows a long tube down into the pistil and joins an egg cell. A seed begins.

Soon the flower starts to die. Its petals dry and fall. The flower dies, but inside the pistil new seeds are growing.

As the seeds grow, a pod or a fruit grows around them. The fruit protects the seeds. The fruit gets bigger and bigger. It gets riper and riper.

The fruit breaks open. The seeds are ready to start new plants.

Some seeds fall to the ground right next to the plant that made them.

Other seeds travel.

The seeds of violets and pansies shoot into the air.

Milkweed and dandelion seeds ride silken strands into the wind.

Some seeds have sturdy wings that let them glide on the wind or float on the water.

Some seeds travel with your help or even with your dog's. Their sharp little burrs hook on to clothing or fur.

Not all of these seeds will grow into plants. Many things may go wrong.

A seed may not land on good earth. It may land on a rock, or in your house. A hungry bird or squirrel may eat it.

But almost every seed starts out with a chance to grow. You can find out why.

Soak a lima bean in water overnight. In the morning, let your mother or father help you cut the seed in half.

Inside you will see a tiny baby plant.

There is a tiny baby plant curled up tight in every seed. This tiny plant can grow into a big plant.

And as long as the tiny plant stays alive, there is a chance that the seed can keep its promise—even after a very long time.

Expanding the Literature   How might the fruit that protects seeds break open? (Accept reasonable responses: People or animals might cut or bite open the fruit and discard the seeds; some fruit might fall from trees and break open when it rots.) CRITICAL: SPECULATING

Science Connection   Point out that bees collect nectar and pollen from flowers. They use the nectar to make honey, and they eat the pollen, which they carry home to their hive in special cavities in their hind legs. However, extra pollen sticks to the bee's body. When it flies to other flowers, some of this extra pollen may rub off the bee and *cross-pollinate* flowers of the same species.

Second-Language Support   Point out to students the phrase *keep its promise* on the last line of page 35. Cup your hands and place them together to pantomime keeping something precious. Explain that when people keep promises, they remember things they said they would do and then do those things. Make sure students understand the difference between *making* a promise and *keeping* one.

MEETING INDIVIDUAL NEEDS

PAGES 36–37 A SEED IS A PROMISE

Here is a true story about some seeds that grew after a *very, very* long time.

One day in the cold north country of Canada a miner was digging in the frozen earth.

Deep down, he found some old animal burrows. Inside the burrows were some animal bones. Next to the bones were tiny seeds.

The miner took the bones and seeds. He showed them to some scientists.

The scientists found out that the bones were the bones of little animals called lemmings. The bones were very, very old.

Thousands and thousands of years ago, in prehistoric times, the lemmings must have stored the seeds for food.

Everyone wondered, could such old seeds still grow? Had the earth acted like the freezer in your refrigerator? Had it kept the seeds from spoiling?

The scientists put the seeds on special wet paper and waited.

Two days later, this is what they saw. Some of the seeds had kept their promise. They had sprouted after thousands and thousands of years.

In time the seeds grew into healthy plants. The plants grew flowers. The flowers made new seeds—each with a promise of its own.

What did you learn by reading "A Seed Is a Promise"?

In what ways is a seed like a promise?

WRITE   Write a description of a flower. Try to add details in your description that will help your reader to see it.

Science Connection   Have students speculate about methods the scientists used to find out how old the bones and seeds found by the miner were. Explain that they might have figured out the age by determining the age of the rock layer nearest to the lemmings' burrow. Or they could have tested chemicals in the bones or compared them to other fossilized bones of ancient lemmings.

Returning to the Predictions/Purpose   Invite students to tell what they learned about seeds and whether their questions were answered. Have students complete the third column of their K-W-L charts with information they learned about seeds. The chart shown gives examples.
NOTE: Responses to the questions and support for the Write activity appear on page T47.

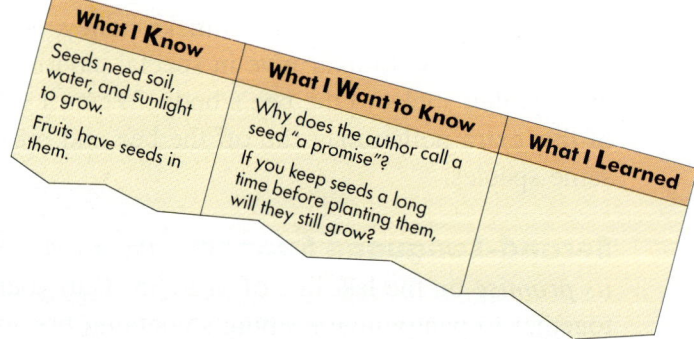

Personal Response

Encourage critical thinking.

What did you learn by reading "A Seed Is a Promise"? (Encourage students to refer to their K-W-L charts. They might mention the following: Parts of a flower include the pistil, which holds egg cells, and the stamens, which make pollen. When pollen reaches an egg cell, it forms a seed. Some flowers use their own pollen to make seeds, while others use other flowers' pollen.) INFERENTIAL: SUMMARIZING

In what ways is a seed like a promise? (Accept reasonable responses: Within every seed is the "promise" that a new plant will grow.) INFERENTIAL: MAKING COMPARISONS

Encourage creative written responses.

WRITE Write a description of a flower. Try to add details in your description that will help your reader to see it. If possible, have students each bring to class a flower to describe. Alternatively, direct them to encyclopedias and books on flowers such as field guides. Encourage them to choose unusual flowers to describe, such as the Venus's-flytrap, which consumes flies, or the rafflesia, the world's largest flower (up to three feet across) CREATIVE: WRITING A DESCRIPTION

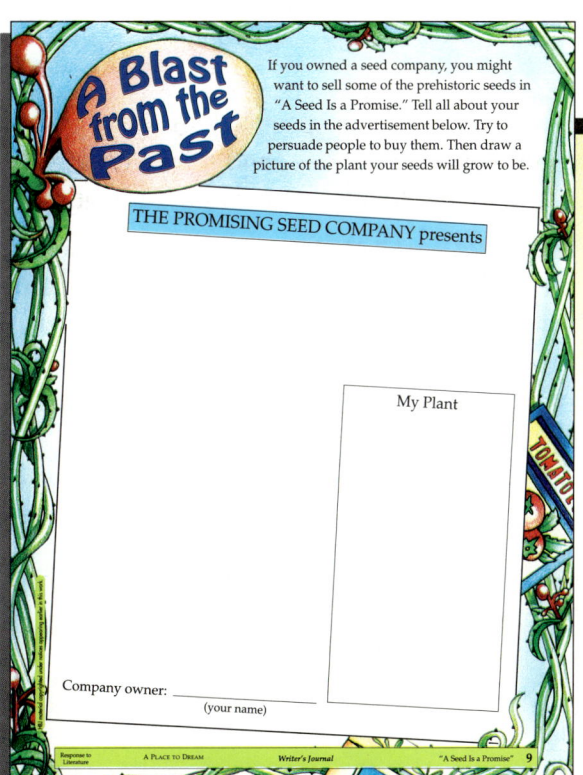

Writer's Journal

INFORMAL ASSESSMENT

When students use the information in a text to write, the product reveals how well students understood the article. It will show whether students recognize important details and understand main ideas.

OPTIONAL INDEPENDENT PRACTICE

WRITER'S JOURNAL
page 9: Writing a personal response

A SEED IS A PROMISE / T47

Appreciating Literature

Encourage students to relate personal experiences.

Have students work in small groups to discuss the selection. Provide questions such as the following to help the groups begin:

Have you ever grown plants from seeds? What did you need to do to help the seeds grow?

 **PERSONAL JOURNAL** Have students use their personal journals to write about ideas discussed in the groups.

Critical Thinking Activities

Encourage both cooperative and individual responses.

HAVE A DISCUSSION **Why is it important for seeds to keep their promise?** Have small groups of students discuss possible answers to this question. CRITICAL: SPECULATING

KEEP A RECORD **How do seeds become plants?** Have students carry out the seed experiment described on page 37 in the selection to see how seeds keep their promise. Have them wet a paper towel, and line a glass jar with it; place some lima beans between the glass and the damp paper towel; and keep the paper towel moist. Have students check the seeds each day and record any changes on a chart such as the one below. When the seeds sprout, students may plant them in soil in the bottom portion of a clean milk carton. CREATIVE: EXPANDING UPON IDEAS IN THE SELECTION

	M	T	W	Th	F	Sat	Sun
Make sure towel is moist							
How many lima beans have sprouted?							

WRITE PARAGRAPHS Many of the foods we eat begin as seeds. **What is your favorite food that comes from seeds?** Ask students to write one or two paragraphs that tell why this food is their favorite. Then have students draw pictures of their favorite foods. CREATIVE: ILLUSTRATING PARAGRAPHS

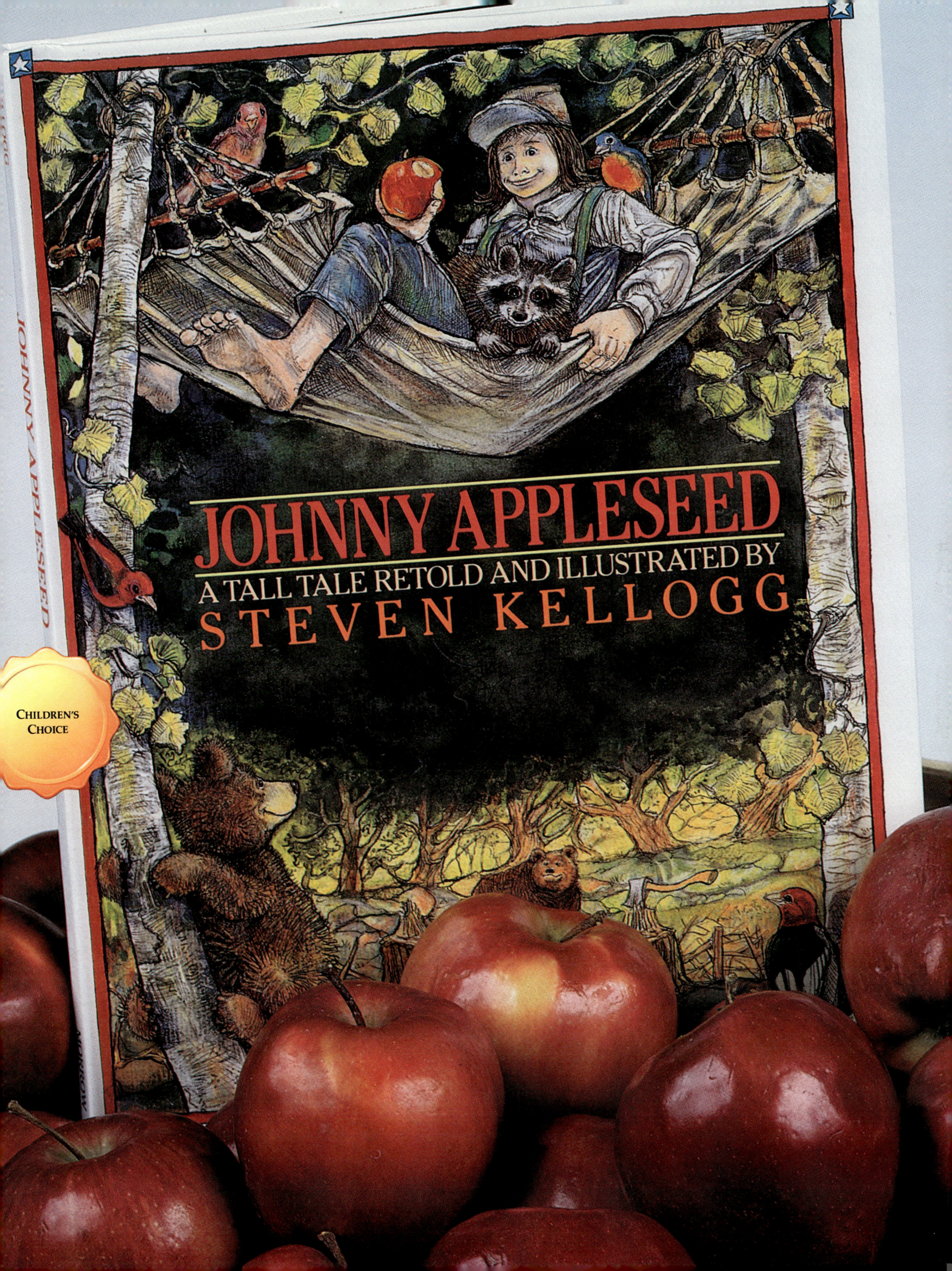

Integrated Lesson Planner

Johnny Appleseed
pages 38–52

	READING	**LANGUAGE ARTS**	**CROSS-CURRICULAR CONNECTIONS**
PART 1 *Reading the Literature* pages T52–T62	**Building Background** **Vocabulary Strategies** **Prereading Strategies** K-W-L Chart Setting a Purpose **Options for Reading**	**Spelling** Pretest Spelling-Vocabulary Connection Generalization: /i/, /o/, /u/ **Grammar Connection** Reviewing Sentence Types	**Cultural Awareness** History of apples **Social Studies** Pioneers moving west People who have brightened the world
PART 2 *Responding to the Literature* pages T63–T69	**Personal Response** **Cooperative Response** **Summarizing the Literature** **Critical Thinking Activity** Picture **Vocabulary Workshop** Key Words Compound Words	**Language Arts Workshop** **Reading** oral rereading **Writing** tall tale, expressions **Listening and Speaking** summarize an article, discuss tall tales **Reviewing Spelling Words** Posttest **Grammar Review** Sentence Types **Grammar Minilesson** Sentence Parts: Subject	**Social Studies** Improving the World Today **Music** Believing Tall Tales
PART 3 *Learning Through the Literature* pages T70–T78	**Introduce** Study Skills: Following Directions (Tested) Vocabulary Strategies: Structural and Contextual Clues **Review** Comprehension: Cause and Effect (Tested) Comprehension Strategies: Active Reading Strategies	**Reading** Apple Everything **Writing** Heroes in the Community Garden Journals **Listening and Speaking** Traditional Foods Go West	**Art** Making Mosaics **Social Studies** Heroes in the Community Traditional Foods Go West **Math** Apple Math **Health** Apple Everything **Science** Garden Journals **Multicultural Perspectives** Blazing Trails

OPTIONAL MATERIALS
Charts/Transparencies 3–4
Integrated Spelling pp. 14–17; TE pp. 21–26
Practice Book pp. 7–16
Writer's Journal pp. 10–11
Alternative Teaching Strategies pp. 3–4, 40–43
Language Handbook pp. 36–39, 86–90
Grammar Practice pp. 14–15
Family Involvement Activities: Unit 1, pp. 1–4
Response Card 2
Project Cards 5A, 5B, 6A, 6B

 **MEETING INDIVIDUAL NEEDS**
Second-Language Support pp. T53, T54, T59, T69, T71, T73
Mainstreaming p. T54
Reteach pp. T69, T71, T73
Challenge pp. T71, T73, T74, T75

FAMILY INVOLVEMENT Have students work with family members to learn more about apples. See *Family Involvement Activities*.

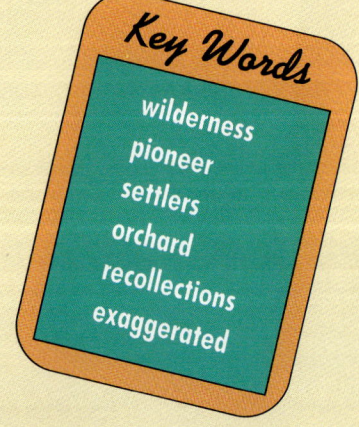

Key Words
wilderness
pioneer
settlers
orchard
recollections
exaggerated

T50 / A PLACE TO DREAM, UNIT 1

Selection Summary

This selection tells the story of John Chapman, better known as Johnny Appleseed. Chapman was born in Massachusetts in 1774. He understood the usefulness of the apple orchard near his home.

He left home to cross the Allegheny Mountains, through Pennsylvania and Ohio, clearing land and planting apple orchards for the pioneers he knew would follow. He became well known for his tree-planting efforts.

People loved John and told tall tales about him. John continued to plant apple orchards until he grew too old. He died in 1845, after falling ill while traveling in a snowstorm. The legend of Johnny Appleseed was carried westward by the pioneers and remains with us today.

Johnny Appleseed was selected as a Children's Choice in 1989.

About the Author and Illustrator

Steven Kellogg has written and illustrated twenty-four books and illustrated forty-nine others. A number of his books have been made into filmstrips and have won awards. When he was young, he used to illustrate stories invented by his sisters and himself. He loved drawing animals and once assigned himself the project of drawing every creature in the encyclopedia. He covered his bedroom with illustrations. "I think to this day my parents will always remember that project. The walls were ruined by hundreds of thumbtack holes," Kellogg says.

Kellogg says he sometimes finds himself working late into the night when he gets caught up in a story idea. "I just try to let my mind drift and then, as the story starts to suggest a direction, I write and draw in response to that," he says.

Additional Reading

OTHER BOOKS BY STEVEN KELLOGG

The Island of the Skog. Dial, 1976.   AVERAGE

Pinkerton, Behave! Dial, 1982.   AVERAGE

Prehistoric Pinkerton. Puffin, 1991.   AVERAGE

OTHER THEME-RELATED BOOKS

Frederick by Leo Lionni. Alfred A. Knopf, 1987.   EASY

The Tree of Here by Chaim Potok. Alfred A. Knopf, 1993.   AVERAGE

BOOKS FOR APPLYING STRATEGIES: FOLLOWING DIRECTIONS, STRUCTURAL AND CONTEXTUAL CLUES

Greening the City Streets by Barbara A. Huff. Clarion, 1990.   CHALLENGING

Just a Dream by Chris Van Allsburg. Houghton Mifflin, 1990.   AVERAGE

The Life and Times of the Apple by Charles Micucci. Orchard Books, 1992.   AVERAGE

PART 1

Reading the Literature

Building Background

Access prior knowledge and build vocabulary concepts.

Explain to students that Johnny Appleseed was a real person who lived about two hundred years ago, when much of the United States was wilderness. Discuss with students how having an apple orchard might have helped a family of pioneers.

Have students quickwrite a K-W-L chart.

Refer students to *Practice Book* page 8 (on T64), or draw a K-W-L chart on the board, such as the one shown below. Have students copy it on a sheet of paper and write in the first column what they know about Johnny Appleseed.

What I **K**now	What I **W**ant to Know	What I **L**earned
(He improved the world.) (He planted apple trees.)		

Vocabulary Strategies

Introduce Key Words and strategies.

Display Chart/Transparency 3 or the story on it. Have students read the story silently. Model using context clues and phonetic and structural analysis to figure out the meanings of the underlined words. For example, explain that *who traveled into this new land* is a clue to the meaning of *pioneer*.

Chart/Transparency 3   Key Words

Two hundred years ago, most of the United States was a wilderness of forests and wide-open spaces. Each pioneer who traveled into this new land faced many challenges. Settlers cleared the land and built homes. Families sometimes planted an orchard of apple trees.

The pioneers told stories about fighting bears and snakes. Over time, some of these recollections became tall tales. In telling tall tales, storytellers exaggerated the truth. One small bear becomes ten huge bears. These stories help us understand how the pioneers felt.

CULTURAL AWARENESS

You may want to explain to students that apples have been eaten since ancient times. Apples are described in early writings of the Greeks, the Egyptians, and the Chinese.

Key Words

wilderness
pioneer
settlers
orchard
recollections
exaggerated

KEY WORDS DEFINED

wilderness   region that remains wild, with no crops

pioneer   one of the first people exploring or making a home in a new place

settlers   people who make a home in a new place

orchard   group of trees planted for their fruit or nuts

recollections   memories

exaggerated   made to appear greater than is really true

T52 / A PLACE TO DREAM, UNIT 1

Check all students' understanding.

Display the Key Words. Ask students to predict how the author will use each Key Word in the selection by thinking about whether the word has to do with the people, the places, or the events in the life of Johnny Appleseed. Guide them in using the Key Words to complete this predict-o-gram. Explain that after reading they will come back to the predict-o-gram and think about how these words are used in the selection. **STRATEGY: CLASSIFYING**

PREDICT-O-GRAM

People	Places	Events
pioneer	wilderness	recollections
settlers	orchard	exaggerated

PROPER NOUNS Display the following words, and model their pronunciations as necessary: *Massachusetts, Allegheny Mountains, Pennsylvania,* and *Ohio.*

Integrate spelling with vocabulary.

SPELLING-VOCABULARY CONNECTION *Integrated Spelling* Lesson 2 reinforces the spelling of words with short *i*, short *o*, or short *u* sounds, such as *hunt* found in the selection. In addition, the Words to Explore help reinforce concepts about apples related to the selection.

SPELLING PRETEST You may want to use the Pretest/Posttest Sentences on page T22 in *Integrated Spelling Teacher's Edition* to assess students' knowledge of the spelling generalization.

Spelling

Spelling Words	Words to Explore
1. block	cider
2. clock	orchard
3. club	pioneer
4. drop	wilderness
5. hunt	
6. milk	*Your Own Words*
7. pick	13.
8. sick	14.
9. spot	15.
10. such	16.
11. think	
12. truck	

Spelling generalization: /i/, /o/, /u/

Practice Book

MEETING INDIVIDUAL NEEDS

SECOND-LANGUAGE SUPPORT Discuss with students the concept of westward expansion by pioneers, using a map of the United States as a visual aid. Incorporate the words *pioneer, wilderness, orchard,* and *settlers.* See also the manual *Alternative Teaching Strategies,* pages 3–4, 40–43.

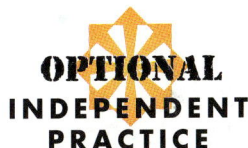

OPTIONAL INDEPENDENT PRACTICE

INTEGRATED SPELLING pages 14–17: Words with Short *i*, Short *o*, or Short *u*

PRACTICE BOOK page 7: Reinforcing Key Words

NOTE: This page may be completed now or after students have read the selection.

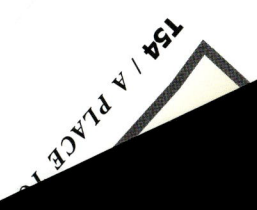

Prereading Strategies

K-W-L Chart

Have students preview and predict.

Have students preview the selection by reading the title and the first two pages and by examining the illustrations. Ask students to take out the K-W-L charts they began in Building Background. Remind them that in the first column they wrote what they already know about Johnny Appleseed. Have students fill in the second column with questions they hope "Johnny Appleseed" will answer.

Model forming questions, if necessary.

If students have difficulty thinking of questions they would like answered, offer the examples now shown in the middle column of the K-W-L chart:

What I **K**now	What I **W**ant to Know	What I **L**earned
(He improved the world.) (He planted apple trees.)	(What kind of person was Johnny Appleseed?) (What were some of the important events in his life?)	

Have students use their K-W-L charts to predict what might happen and then add their predictions to their personal journals.

Setting a Purpose

Encourage students to set purposes.

Have students set a purpose for reading the selection, based on the questions from the second column of their K-W-L charts. Encourage them to read to try to find the answers to their questions.

If students have difficulty setting a purpose, offer this suggestion:

I'm going to read to find out what some of the important events in Johnny Appleseed's life were.

MEETING INDIVIDUAL NEEDS

SECOND-LANGUAGE SUPPORT Students may benefit from the Strategic Reading activities and the additional guidance under the Student Anthology pages. See also the manual *Alternative Teaching Strategies*, pages 3–4, 40–43.

SUPPORT FOR MAINSTREAMING Point out to students that Johnny Appleseed and the pioneers of his day lived off the land. Ask students if they have ever gone camping, hiking, or adventuring in the wilderness. Ask them if they would like to have lived like Johnny Appleseed.

Options for Reading

SUSTAINED SILENT READING
After students finish reading, encourage them to discuss the questions at the end of the selection with another student who has read independently.

STRATEGIC READING
To stimulate discussion, use the suggestions that appear on pages T55, T57, and T62.

READER RESPONSE GROUPS
Follow the suggestions for Literature Circles on page T55. As students read, they should note any questions or comments about the selection that they would like to discuss with the group.

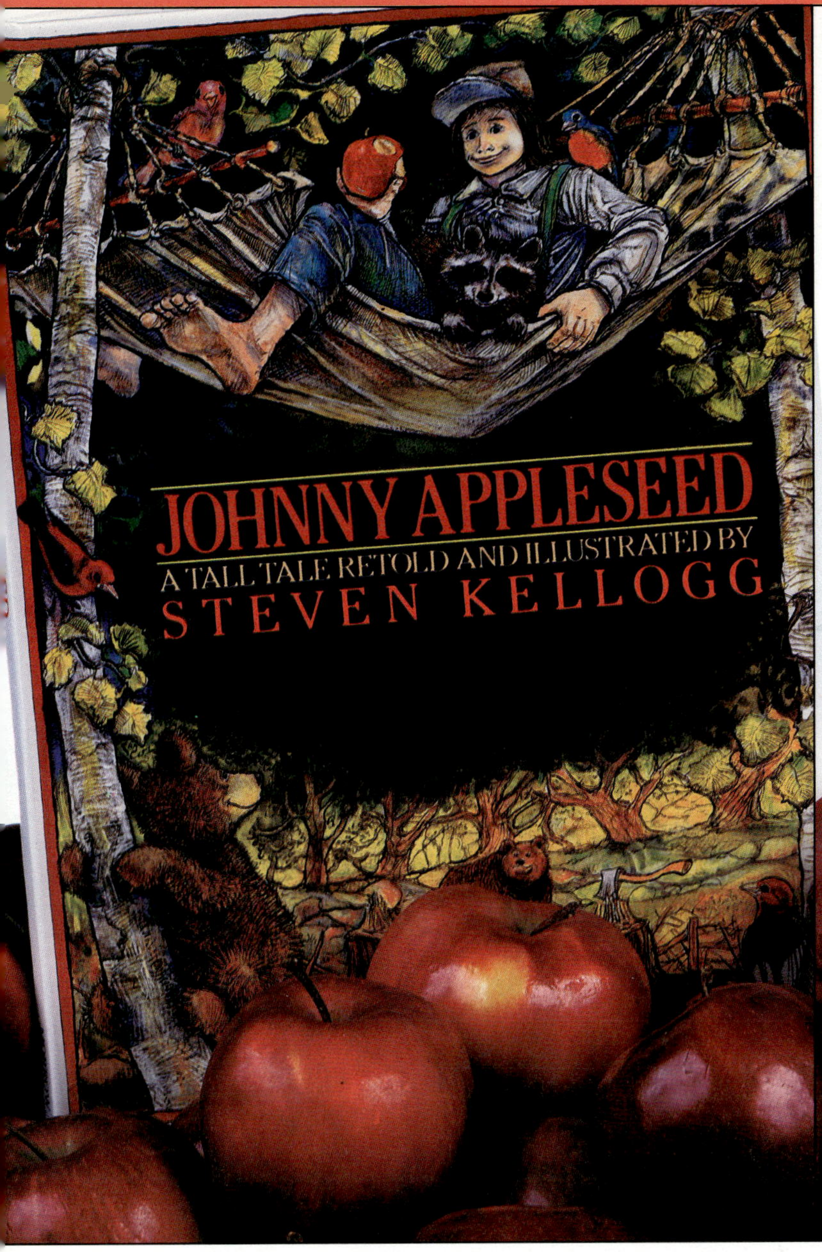

JOHNNY APPLESEED   PAGES 38–39

CHILDREN'S CHOICE

John Chapman, who later became known as Johnny Appleseed, was born on September 26, 1774, when the apples on the trees surrounding his home in Leominster, Massachusetts, were as red as the autumn leaves.

John's first years were hard. His father left the family to fight in the Revolutionary War, and his mother and his baby brother both died before his second birthday.

By the time John turned six, his father had remarried and settled in Longmeadow, Massachusetts. Within a decade their little house was overflowing with ten more children.

Nearby was an apple <u>orchard</u>. Like most early American families, the Chapmans picked their apples in the fall, stored them in the cellar for winter eating, and used them to make sauces, cider, vinegar, and apple butter. John loved to watch spring blossoms slowly turn into the glowing fruit of autumn.

39

Reader Response Groups

LITERATURE CIRCLES   Have each group of three to five students read the selection silently, stopping at page 43 for a brief discussion. You may want to distribute Response Card 2 (Setting), found on page R76, for possible discussion questions or provide the following questions:

- How would you describe the time and place in which John Chapman lived?
- How might the time and place have affected John's actions?

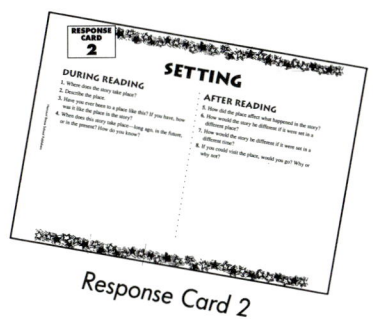

Response Card 2

Strategic Reading

SET PURPOSE/PREDICT: PAGES 38–43   Have students read through page 43. Encourage them to use the questions in the second column of their K-W-L charts to decide what they will be reading to find out.

JOHNNY APPLESEED / T55

PAGES 40–41 JOHNNY APPLESEED

Watching the apples grow inspired in John a love of all of nature. He often escaped from his boisterous household to the tranquil woods. The animals sensed his gentleness and trusted him.

40

As soon as John was old enough to leave home, he set out to explore the vast <u>wilderness</u> to the west. When he reached the Allegheny Mountains, he cleared a plot of land and planted a small orchard with the pouch of apple seeds he had carried with him.

Social Studies Connection On a map of the United States, help students locate the Allegheny Mountains. Ask them to name the states through which these mountains extend. (Pennsylvania, Maryland, West Virginia, and Virginia) **How do you think the mountains might have affected pioneers who wanted to travel west?** (Accept reasonable responses: The mountains would make traveling difficult, dangerous, and challenging. Some pioneers had to find alternate routes.) INFERENTIAL: DETERMINING CAUSE/EFFECT

See page T77 for information found on Project Card 6B.

Project Card 6B

T56 / A PLACE TO DREAM, UNIT 1

JOHNNY APPLESEED   PAGES 42–43

John walked hundreds of miles through the Pennsylvania forest, living like the Indians he befriended on the trail. As he traveled, he cleared the land for many more orchards. He was sure the pioneer families would be arriving before long, and he looked forward to supplying them with apple trees.

When a storm struck, he found shelter in a hollow log or built a lean-to. On clear nights he stretched out under the stars.

Over the next few years, John continued to visit and care for his new orchards. The winters slowed him down, but he survived happily on a diet of butternuts.

One spring he met a band of men who boasted that they could lick their weight in wildcats. They were amazed to hear that John wouldn't hurt an animal and had no use for a gun.

They challenged John to compete at wrestling, the favorite frontier sport. He suggested a more practical contest—a tree-chopping match. The woodsmen eagerly agreed.

43

Strategic Reading

MODELING A STRATEGY: PAGES 38–43   What have you learned about John Chapman?

THINK ALOUD   You may want to model analyzing characters: *I wanted to find out what kind of person John Chapman was. By thinking about what he said, thought, and did, I can tell that he knew about nature and loved being outdoors; he knew how to survive in winter; he made friends with Native Americans; he was practical and was interested in helping people.*
ANALYZING CHARACTERS

SET PURPOSE/PREDICT: PAGES 44–52   Have students predict what other things John might have done during his life. Then have them read the rest of the selection to confirm their predictions.

JOHNNY APPLESEED / T57

PAGES 44–45 JOHNNY APPLESEED

Expanding the Literature Ask students to describe the picture on pages 44–45, giving as many details as possible. Then ask them to summarize their description in one sentence. (Example: All the people in the tree-chopping contest chopped as fast and as hard as they could.)
INFERENTIAL: SUMMARIZING

In what way is John's work different from that of the woodsmen?
(He plants trees as well as chops them down.)   INFERENTIAL: COMPARING AND CONTRASTING

When the sawdust settled, there was no question about who had come out on top.

John was pleased that the land for his largest orchard had been so quickly cleared. He thanked the exhausted woodsmen for their help and began planting.

During the next few years, John continued to move westward. Whenever he ran out of apple seeds, he hiked to the eastern cider presses to replenish his supply. Before long, John's plantings were spread across the state of Ohio.

Meanwhile, pioneer families were arriving in search of homesites and farmland. John had located his orchards on the routes he thought they'd be traveling. As he had hoped, the settlers were eager to buy his young trees.

John went out of his way to lend a helping hand to his new neighbors. Often he would give his trees away. People affectionately called him Johnny Appleseed, and he began using that name.

He particularly enjoyed entertaining children with tales of his wilderness adventures and stories from the Bible.

In 1812 the British incited the Indians to join them in another war against the Americans. The settlers feared that Ohio would be invaded from Lake Erie.

It grieved Johnny that his friends were fighting each other. But when he saw the smoke of burning cabins, he ran through the night, shouting a warning at every door.

Second-Language Support The concept of westward expansion may be unfamiliar to students. Using a map of the United States to illustrate, offer this explanation: The first people to arrive in the United States from Europe settled along the East Coast. Eventually settlers moved westward in search of new land to farm. Explain to students that John Chapman helped the pioneers by planting apple trees.

MEETING INDIVIDUAL NEEDS

Vocabulary Strategy Write the terms *ran out* and *replenish* on the board. **The selection says that whenever John ran out of apple seeds, he hiked east to replenish his supply. What do you think *replenish* means?** ("get more") **What clues can you use to figure out the word?** Help students see that *ran out* and *replenish* are opposites; knowing that *ran out* means "had no more" can help readers figure out that *replenish* means "get more." STRATEGY: CONTEXT CLUES/ANTONYMS

PAGES 48–49 JOHNNY APPLESEED

After the war, people urged Johnny to build a house and settle down. He replied that he lived like a king in his wilderness home, and he returned to the forest he loved.

During his long absences, folks enjoyed sharing their <u>recollections</u> of Johnny. They retold his stories and sometimes they even <u>exaggerated</u> them a bit.

Informal Assessment

CAUSE AND EFFECT To assess whether students can identify cause and effect, ask questions like these:

- Why did Johnny return to the forest instead of building a house and settling down? (He felt comfortable living in the wilderness; he wanted to keep planting apple trees.)
- What might have happened as a result of his decision? (More pioneers might have been able to enjoy the trees.)

A review lesson on **cause and effect** appears on page T74.

Social Studies Connection
Why did people enjoy talking about Johnny Appleseed? (Accept reasonable responses: Johnny helped brighten their world by planting trees.) Point out to students that there are many people they can read about who have also brightened the world.

See page T67 for information found on Project Card 5B.

Project Card 5B

T60 / A PLACE TO DREAM, UNIT 1

Some recalled Johnny sleeping in a treetop hammock and chatting with the birds.

Others remembered that a rattlesnake had attacked his foot. Fortunately, Johnny's feet were as tough as elephant's hide, so the fangs didn't penetrate.

It was said that Johnny had once tended a wounded wolf and then kept him for a pet.

An old hunter swore he'd seen Johnny frolicking with a bear family.

The storytellers outdid each other with tall tales about his feats of survival in the untamed wilderness.

As the years passed, Ohio became too crowded for Johnny. He moved to the wilds of Indiana, where he continued to clear land for his orchards.

When the settlers began arriving, Johnny recognized some of the children who had listened to his stories. Now they had children of their own.

It made Johnny's old heart glad when they welcomed him as a beloved friend and asked to hear his tales again.

When Johnny passed seventy, it became difficult for him to keep up with his work. Then, in March of 1845, while trudging through a snowstorm near Fort Wayne, Indiana, he became ill for the first time in his life.

Johnny asked for shelter in a settler's cabin, and a few days later he died there.

Expanding the Literature Do you think all the stories people told about Johnny Appleseed really could have happened? (no) Which ones could not have happened? (Johnny couldn't have frolicked with bears. It's also unlikely that a rattlesnake bite wouldn't have hurt him.) What do you call tales like these that exaggerate facts? (tall tales) Explain to students that unlike lies, tall tales are not intended to deceive; they are told and written down to entertain people. CRITICAL: AUTHOR'S CRAFT/IDENTIFYING GENRE

GRAMMAR CONNECTION

REVIEWING TYPES OF SENTENCES Review with students the four types of sentences: statements, questions, exclamations, and commands. Ask students what type of sentence the author uses to describe the tales people told about Johnny. (a statement)

Curiously, Johnny's stories continued to move westward without him. Folks maintained that they'd seen him in Illinois or that he'd greeted them in Missouri, Arkansas, or Texas. Others were certain that he'd planted trees on the slopes of the Rocky Mountains or in California's distant valleys.

Even today people still claim they've seen Johnny Appleseed.

Are you like Johnny Appleseed in any way? Why or why not?

How did Johnny Appleseed help to settle the West?

A folk hero is an everyday person who becomes famous. How does Johnny Appleseed fit that description?

WRITE Imagine you are Johnny Appleseed, moving from place to place planting apples. Write a newspaper story about your travels. Begin when you first leave home, and stop when you leave Ohio.

Strategic Reading

MODELING A STRATEGY: PAGES 44–52 Ask students if what they read on pages 44–52 matched their predictions.

THINK ALOUD You may want to model confirming predictions: *I predicted that Johnny would win the tree-chopping match and would continue planting trees. I based my predictions on what I know about Johnny's skills, his love of the outdoors, and his desire to help pioneers.* CONFIRMING PREDICTIONS

Returning to the Predictions/Purpose

K-W-L CHART Ask students to share the questions they wrote in the second column of their K-W-L charts. Discuss whether their questions were answered and how they might find answers to any unanswered questions.

NOTE: Responses to the questions and support for the Write activity appear on page T63.

What I Know	What I Want to Know	What I Learned
(He improved the world.) (He planted apple trees.)	(What kind of person was Johnny Appleseed?) (What were some of the important events in his life?)	

PART 2

Responding to the Literature

Personal Response

Encourage critical thinking.

Are you like Johnny Appleseed in any way? Why or why not? (Responses will vary.) CRITICAL: EXPRESSING PERSONAL OPINIONS

How did Johnny Appleseed help to settle the West? (He traveled west through Pennsylvania, Ohio, and Indiana, clearing land that had been wilderness. He planted many apple trees to provide food for pioneer families.) INFERENTIAL: SYNTHESIZING

A folk hero is an everyday person who becomes famous. How does Johnny Appleseed fit that description? (Accept reasonable responses: He just traveled around the country planting apple trees, but many people loved him and told tall tales about him; we talk about him even today.) CRITICAL: CLASSIFYING

Encourage creative written responses.

WRITE Imagine you are Johnny Appleseed, moving from place to place planting apples. Write a newspaper story about your travels. Begin when you first leave home, and stop when you leave Ohio. Encourage students to think about what Johnny Appleseed may have seen, heard, touched, and smelled during his travels. Remind them to base their stories on the events described in the selection. CREATIVE: WRITING A NEWS STORY

Cooperative Response

Have reader response groups extend their discussions.

LITERATURE CIRCLES Encourage Literature Circles to discuss their reactions to the selection. They might begin by sharing questions they have about the selection. Then have them discuss a question such as this one:

If Johnny Appleseed were alive today, how might he help American families?

STRATEGY CONFERENCE

Discuss with students how using the K-W-L strategy helped them understand, remember, and appreciate the selection. Invite students to share other reading strategies, such as visualizing, that helped them understand what they read.

NOTE

An additional writing activity for this selection appears on page T66.

JOHNNY APPLESEED / **T63**

Summarizing the Literature

Have students retell the story and write a summary.

Have students complete the K-W-L charts they started earlier by filling in the third column of the chart. Students can use the completed chart to retell the story and write a brief summary. See *Practice Book* page 8.

What I **K**now	What I **W**ant to Know	What I **L**earned
(He improved the world.) (He planted apple trees.)	(What kind of person was Johnny Appleseed?) (What were some of the important events in his life?)	(Johnny Appleseed was kind, practical, and resourceful.) (He left home at a young age to explore the wilderness. He planted trees to help pioneer families.)

Critical Thinking Activity

Describe a favorite quiet place.

DRAW A PICTURE John Chapman liked to visit the woods when his noisy household became too much for him. What do you do when you want some peace and quiet? Have students draw a picture of themselves in a favorite quiet place and then write a few sentences describing the place and what they like about it. Invite volunteers to read their descriptions aloud.
CRITICAL: AUTHOR'S CRAFT/IDENTIFYING WITH CHARACTERS

Writer's Journal

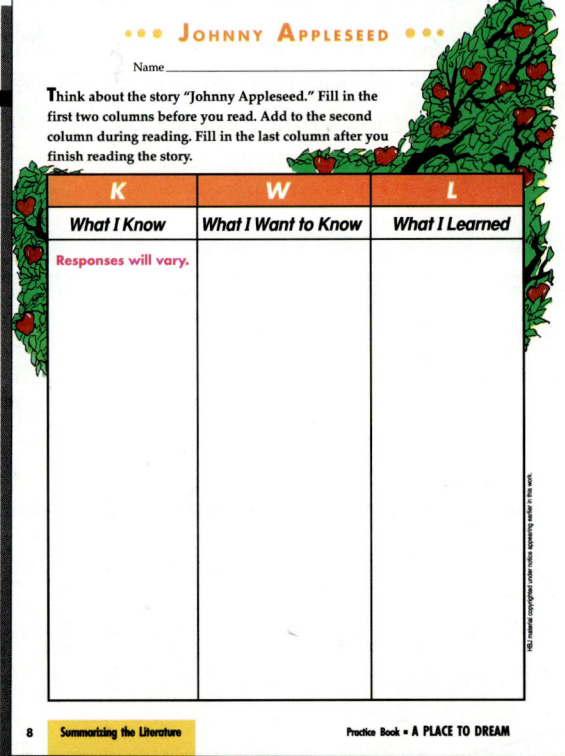
Practice Book

T64 / A PLACE TO DREAM, UNIT 1

Portfolio

STUDENT SELF-ASSESSMENT

Help students self-assess their summaries by asking them to write what they included that they think is the most informative. Encourage students to add their statements to their portfolios.

OPTIONAL INDEPENDENT PRACTICE

WRITER'S JOURNAL
page 10: Writing a personal response

PRACTICE BOOK
page 8: Summarizing the selection

VOCABULARY WORKSHOP

Reviewing Key Words

To review Key Words, display the vocabulary predict-o-gram (shown below) that students completed before reading. Have students tell, orally or in writing, how each word is used in the selection. Possible responses are given here:

PREDICT-O-GRAM

People	Places	Events
pioneer	wilderness	recollections
settlers	orchard	exaggerated

An *orchard* is where Johnny Appleseed planted apple trees.

The *settlers* bought the young apple trees that grew from the seeds Johnny planted.

Wilderness is the wild land where Johnny lived and worked during his life.

The word *pioneer* is a name for a person who settled in the wilderness.

Recollections are the memories people had of Johnny. Their recollections became the stories we still tell about him today.

People *exaggerated* when they stretched the truth about things Johnny did. Tall tales about him were created in this way.

Extending Vocabulary

COMPOUND WORDS Write the word *household* on the board. Explain that this is a *compound word*, or word that is made by putting two words together. Then draw diagrams like these:

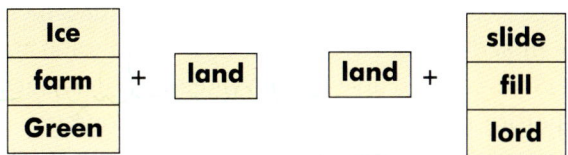

Have students combine two base words to make new compound words. Ask students to suggest other words that could be added to the diagrams that could be used to make compound words.

PRACTICE BOOK
page 9: Using compound words

Practice Book

JOHNNY APPLESEED / T65

Language Arts WORKSHOP

READING

Oral Rereading

Have students form groups of three. Each student should select a passage that tells about an important event in Johnny's life. Have students in each group read their passages in sequence. Model reading a paragraph in an expressive voice. Have students read the passages silently before reading them aloud, and encourage students to practice before presenting their readings.
LISTENING/SPEAKING/READING

SPELLING

Reviewing Spelling Words

SPELLING WORDS: *block, clock, club, drop, hunt, milk, pick, sick, spot, such, think, truck*

WORDS TO EXPLORE: *cider, orchard, pioneer, wilderness*

Play a game of "Twenty Questions" with students. First, prepare a list of words with short *i*, short *o*, or short *u* sounds. Include words from students' own lists. Write each word on a slip of paper, and put the slips into a hat.

Group students into two teams. Ask each team to draw a word and then take turns attempting to guess the other team's word by asking up to twenty questions about it. To earn a point for a word they guess correctly, the guessing team must spell it correctly. **LISTENING/SPEAKING/SPELLING**

Use *Integrated Spelling* Lesson 2 to reinforce the Spelling Words and Words to Explore. See pages T23–T25 in *Integrated Spelling Teacher's Edition*.

 **SPELLING POSTTEST** You may want to use the Pretest/Posttest Sentences on *Integrated Spelling Teacher's Edition* page T22 to assess students' knowledge of the spelling generalization.

WRITING

Writing About the Literature

 **WRITE A TALL TALE** Remind students that people enjoyed telling stories that exaggerated what Johnny Appleseed really said or did and that such stories are called tall tales. Explain that students are going to create their own tall tales about Johnny Appleseed. Guide students in developing a character tree like the one below. Demonstrate how to select a character trait and then invent an episode that stretches the truth for dramatic effect. See Writing Model, page R94. **LISTENING/SPEAKING/WRITING**

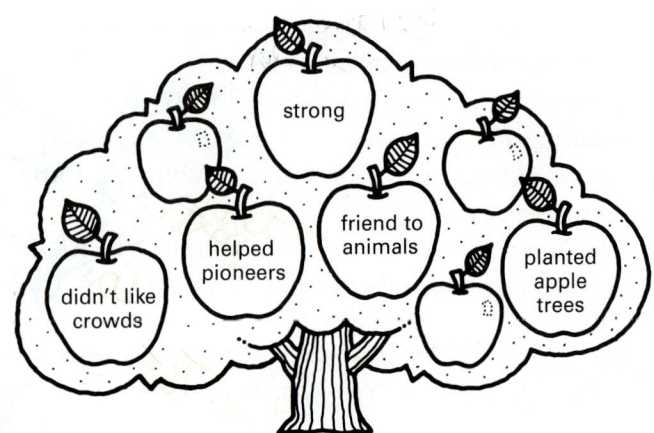

GRAMMAR REVIEW: TYPES OF SENTENCES Suggest that students experiment with different sentence types as they revise their tall tales. For example, they may want to begin their tales with a question to the reader. Have pairs of students exchange final copies of their tall tales and check for correct end punctuation.

 **LANGUAGE HANDBOOK** *Writing to Entertain and Express,* pages 36–37, 38–39; *Types of Sentences,* pages 86–89

 **DAILY LANGUAGE PRACTICE** *Oral language exercises are provided on pages R58–R59.*

T66 / A PLACE TO DREAM, UNIT 1

Language Arts WORKSHOP

WRITING

Say It with Apples

Available on Project Card 5A

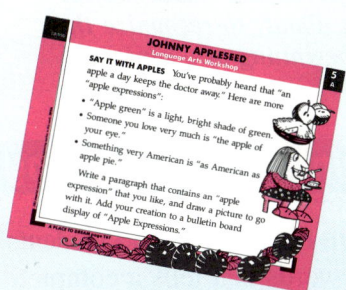

Help students compile a list of terms and expressions that contain the word *apple* or *apples*. The list could include *the apple of my eye, Adam's apple, you're talking apples and oranges, Big Apple, an apple a day helps keep the doctor away,* and *as American as apple pie.* Discuss with students the meanings of these expressions. Then ask them to pick one expression and write a paragraph that includes it. Have students illustrate their paragraphs. Display their drawings and paragraphs on a bulletin board.

SPEAKING/WRITING/VIEWING

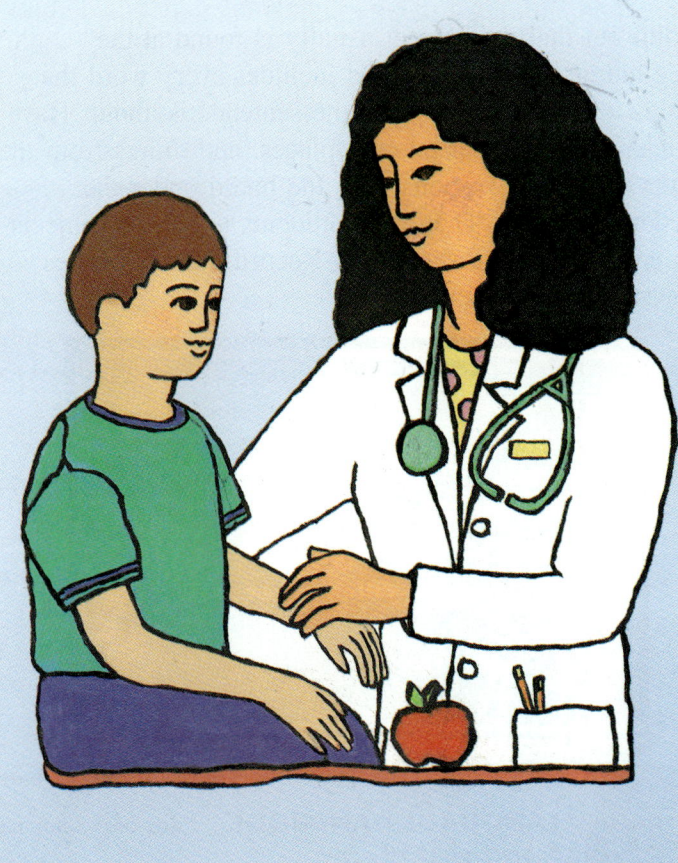

LISTENING AND SPEAKING

Believing Tall Tales

Read aloud a tall tale about another folk hero. You might read one of the many tall tales that James Flora has written for children, or a traditional tall tale about a character such as Paul Bunyan or Pecos Bill. Have students tell which parts of the story could have happened in real life, and which could not. Students might wish to illustrate and display their favorite scenes in the tale. They also might enjoy writing songs that these folk heroes might have sung. Suggest that students make up new words to tunes they already know.

LISTENING/WRITING

LISTENING AND SPEAKING

Improving the World Today

Available on Project Card 5B

Remind students that Johnny Appleseed tried to make the world a better place for pioneers traveling west. Have students work with an older family member to find out about people who are trying to improve the world today. Have students look through newspapers and magazines for articles about people who are doing something to protect the environment or to help others. Ask students to summarize the article for their classmates. **LISTENING/SPEAKING/READING**

JOHNNY APPLESEED / T67

Grammar MINI LESSON

Parts of a Sentence: Subject

OBJECTIVES: *To recognize that every sentence has a subject that tells who or what a sentence is about; to recognize that a subject usually appears at the beginning of a sentence*

Oral Warm-Up

Display and ask volunteers to read aloud the following sentences from "Johnny Appleseed":

- **John loved to watch spring blossoms slowly turn into the glowing fruit of autumn.**
- **The animals sensed his gentleness and trusted him.**
- **The woodsmen eagerly agreed.**
- **The winters slowed him down.**
- **People affectionately called him Johnny Appleseed.**

Have students identify whom or what each sentence is about. Write their responses in apples hanging from an apple tree similar to the one below. (Some responses are shown.)

Interactive Teaching

SUBJECTS Remind students that a sentence is a group of words that tells a complete thought. Explain that every sentence has a **subject,** which is the part that tells who or what the sentence is about. (Point to each apple on the tree on the board.)

Write the following sentences on the board, and ask volunteers to circle each subject.

- **Johnny Appleseed planted many apple orchards.**
- **The apple trees grew tall and strong.**
- **Pioneer families came and settled near the orchards.**
- **Everyone ate the apples.**

Point out that the subject usually is found at the beginning of a sentence and includes every word that helps identify who or what the sentence is about. Have students name other people, places, and things from the story. List their responses on the board under the heading *Subject*. Then have students use these subjects to create complete sentences. Record their sentences next to each subject.

 **LANGUAGE HANDBOOK** *Parts of a Sentence: Subject, page 90*

Practice Activities

Who/Whatdunit?

Ask students a variety of riddles about people and objects in the classroom. For example: "She has glasses and always tells funny stories. Who is she?" Or "What has only one foot but moves around to measure things?" Volunteers should write the answers on the board in a complete sentence. *(Tanda has glasses and always tells funny stories. The ruler has only one foot but moves around to measure things.)* Have each volunteer circle the subject of the sentence and point out the subject in the room. Then have students work in groups of four to challenge each other with similar riddles. Ask them to write their responses on a separate sheet of paper.
VISUAL/KINESTHETIC

Famous or Favorite Subjects

Ask each student to write on a strip of paper a sentence about a favorite or famous person, event, or place. You may need to make sure each sentence has a subject. Encourage students to write their names on their strips. Collect all the strips. Then have volunteers select a strip other than their own, read it aloud, and cut out and display the subject. The rest of the class or group should verify that the subject has been correctly identified. Repeat the procedure until all the sentence strips have been used.
VISUAL/AUDITORY/KINESTHETIC

MEETING INDIVIDUAL NEEDS

SECOND-LANGUAGE SUPPORT Provide students with two sets of index cards, one with subjects (*the girl/boy, a dog/cat, a tree/flower*) and the other with simple predicates (*eats, runs, grows*). Have students combine two cards (one from each set), copy them onto a separate sheet of paper, read the sentence aloud, and then circle the subject.

RETEACH Follow the visual, auditory, and kinesthetic/motor models on page R6.

Practice Book

- **PRACTICE BOOK**
  page 10: Identifying and using subjects

- **GRAMMAR PRACTICE**
  pages 14–15: Writing with simple subjects

JOHNNY APPLESEED / T69

PART 3

Learning through the Literature

STUDY SKILLS
INTRODUCE

Following Directions

OBJECTIVE: *To interpret and follow directions*

Interactive Teaching

Focus on "Johnny Appleseed."

LITERATURE CONNECTION Help students create a list of steps Johnny Appleseed followed as he went about growing apples. Include clearing the land, planting seeds, caring for the trees, and selling them.

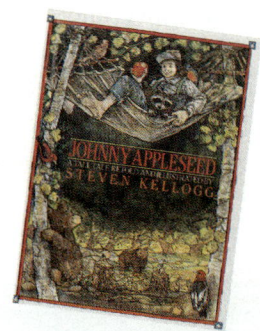

Explain how to follow directions.

Explain to students that they can learn how to do many things by following directions. Ask volunteers to share their own experiences with following directions for making something or for playing a board game. Help them state these points:

- Read or listen carefully to all of the directions.
- Gather all of the tools or materials you will need.
- Ask questions about any part you don't understand.
- Use the pictures or diagrams to follow each step in order.

MODEL FOLLOWING DIRECTIONS Discuss what might happen if you didn't mind these points when planting a tree.

> **If I didn't gather all the materials I would need, I might not be able to dig a hole for planting the tree. If I didn't clear the land *before* planting the tree, other trees might block the sunlight and the tree wouldn't grow.**

Display Chart/Transparency 4 or the directions below. Have students work independently to follow the directions.

ADDITIONAL BOOKS FOR FOLLOWING DIRECTIONS

Greening the City Streets by Barbara A. Huff. Clarion, 1990. CHALLENGING

The Life and Times of the Apple by Charles Micucci. Orchard Books, 1991. AVERAGE

Chart/Transparency 4   Following Directions

```
        B           D
A               C           E
```

1. First, copy the letters above on a sheet of paper. Copy them just as they are shown.
2. Then draw a line from A to B.
3. Draw a line from B to C.
4. Draw a line from C to D.
5. Draw a line from D to E.
6. Next, write the words *Allegheny Mountains* under your picture.
7. Draw a tree on the mountain that has the letter B at the top.

Practice Activities

From Seed to Fruit

Have students write directions for planting an apple tree.

Ask students to imagine that they are writing a step-by-step guide to growing apple trees. Copy the following chart on the board, and have students fill in information under each heading to create an illustrated set of directions. **VISUAL/KINESTHETIC**

HOW TO PLANT AN APPLE TREE		
Materials You Will Need	Steps to Follow	Picture/Diagram
	1.	
	2.	

Learning to Do Something New

Have students use directions to learn something new.

COOPERATIVE LEARNING Have small groups of students brainstorm and list things they would like to learn, such as a craft or a recipe. Encourage each group to choose one thing from the list and to write and then follow directions. Allow students to assign the roles of Facilitator and Recorder. Have students share what they learned. **VISUAL/AUDITORY**

Performance Assessment

Have volunteers explain the steps they followed in writing the directions. Ask students to create a list of writing tips that they can refer to whenever they want to write directions. For evaluation guidelines, see *Staff Development Guide*.

MEETING INDIVIDUAL NEEDS

RETEACH Follow the visual, auditory, and kinesthetic/motor models on page R7.

CHALLENGE Have pairs of students write directions for locating on a map where Johnny Appleseed was born and where he died.

SECOND-LANGUAGE SUPPORT Have students explain how they would follow the directions given in the From Seed to Fruit activity. See also the manual *Alternative Teaching Strategies*, pages 3–4, 40–43.

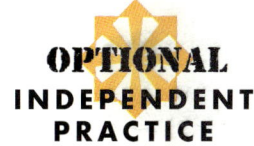

OPTIONAL INDEPENDENT PRACTICE

WRITER'S JOURNAL
page 11: Writing directions

PRACTICE BOOK
page 11: Following directions

Writer's Journal

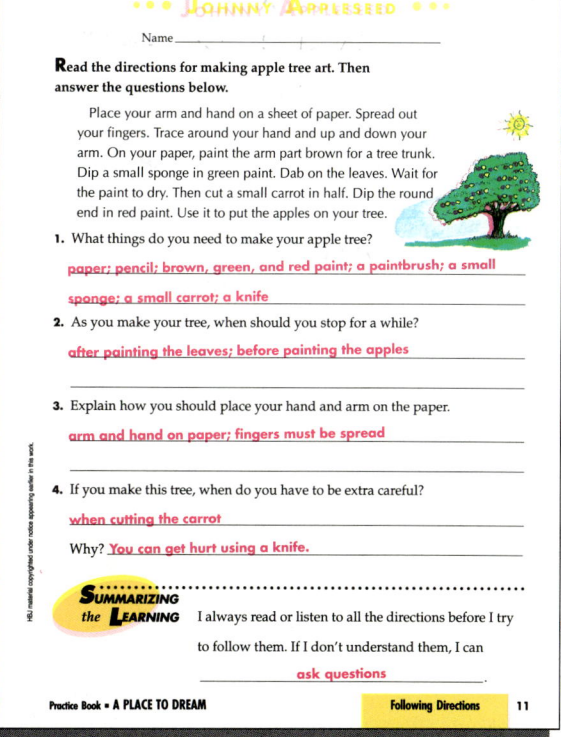

Practice Book

JOHNNY APPLESEED / **T71**

VOCABULARY STRATEGIES

INTRODUCE

Structural and Contextual Clues

OBJECTIVE: *To use structural and contextual clues to determine the meanings of words*

Interactive Teaching

Connect to the literature.

LOOKING FOR CLUES Explain to students that good readers are like detectives—when they come across something they don't understand, they use clues to figure out what it means. Ask volunteers to tell what words in "Johnny Appleseed" were not familiar to them and to explain how they were able to guess the meanings of these words. If students are unable to think of any examples, you may want to discuss these words: *blossoms* (page 39), *inspired* (page 40), *shelter* (page 43).

Teach the strategy.

USING STRUCTURAL AND CONTEXTUAL CLUES Tell students that there are three main strategies to use when figuring out the meanings of unfamiliar words. Write the following on the board:

using context clues
looking at how a word is put together
using a dictionary or a glossary

Model the thinking.

Read aloud the first paragraph on page 47 of "Johnny Appleseed." Model how to use context clues and structural analysis to figure out new words.

> At first I wasn't sure what *woodsmen* means. Then I saw that it's a compound word made up of the two words *woods* and *men*. By thinking about these two words, I was able to guess that *woodsmen* are people who work or live in the forest. I also wondered what *exhausted* means. I asked myself how the woodsmen would feel after a tree-chopping contest. *Exhausted* must mean "very tired."

Strategy: Have students use context clues and word structure.

Write the following sentences on the board:

John's home was usually wild and noisy. John liked to escape from his boisterous household. The animals in the woods sensed his gentleness.

Ask students to figure out the meaning of the word *boisterous* and to explain what helped them understand it. *("noisy, rowdy"; the words wild and noisy in the first sentence)* Then ask how they figured out what *gentleness* means. *(Gentle means "kind"; -ness is a suffix meaning "the quality of being"; therefore gentleness means "the quality of being kind.")*

AN ADDITIONAL BOOK FOR STRUCTURAL AND CONTEXTUAL CLUES

Just a Dream by Chris Van Allsburg. Houghton Mifflin, 1990. AVERAGE

T72 / A PLACE TO DREAM, UNIT 1

Practice Activity

Word Detectives

Have students apply vocabulary strategies.

COOPERATIVE LEARNING Have small groups of students look back through "Johnny Appleseed" for words that might have been unfamiliar to their classmates. Ask students to list five words and the pages on which these appear. Then have groups create a Detectives' Log as shown below.

Detectives' Log for "Johnny Appleseed"			
Detectives on the Case	Word	What It Means	Clues We Used

One student can be the Recorder, and others can be Checkers or Readers. The Summarizer can summarize what the group has learned about figuring out new words.   VISUAL/KINESTHETIC

Performance Assessment

Have volunteers explain how they figured out the meanings of the new words in the Word Detectives activity. Record their responses on the board. Then have students create a class chart that provides strategies for determining the meanings of new words. Encourage students to add to the chart throughout the school year. For evaluation guidelines, see *Staff Development Guide*.

MEETING INDIVIDUAL NEEDS

- **RETEACH** Follow the visual, auditory, and kinesthetic/motor models on page R8.

- **CHALLENGE** Encourage students to write and illustrate five dictionary entry words. Have them choose words from the selection with meanings they have figured out using context clues and structural analysis.

- **SECOND-LANGUAGE SUPPORT** Have students point out an unfamiliar word in the selection and use context clues or structural analysis to figure out its meaning. See also the manual *Alternative Teaching Strategies*, pages 3–4, 40–43.

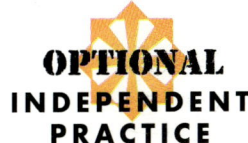

OPTIONAL INDEPENDENT PRACTICE

PRACTICE BOOK
pages 12–13: Using structural and contextual clues

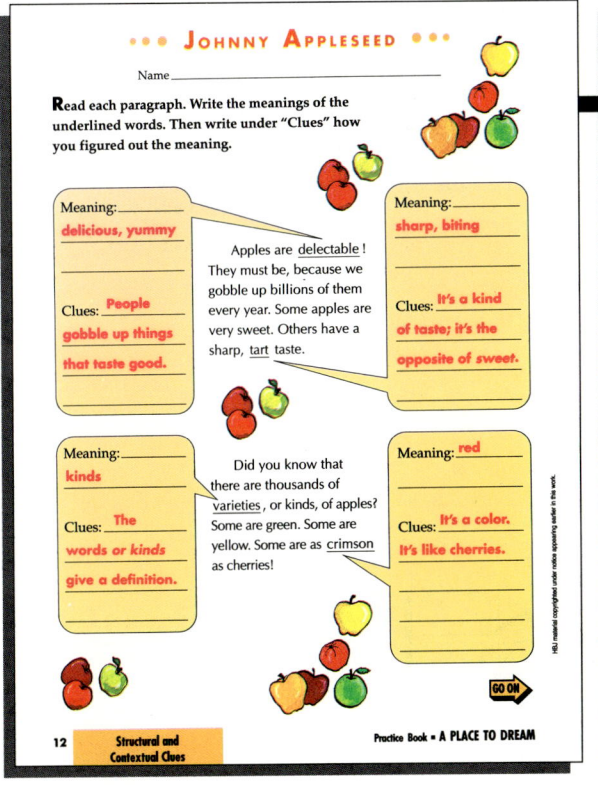

Practice Book

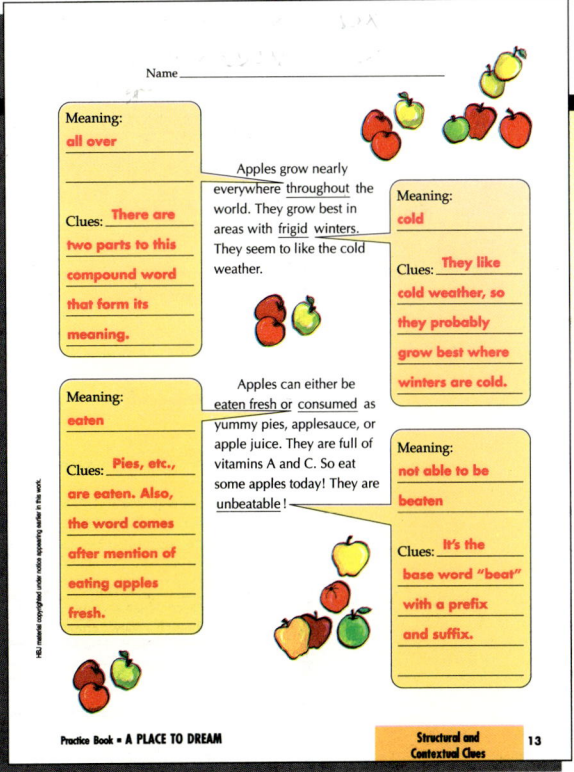

Practice Book

COMPREHENSION
REVIEW

Cause and Effect

OBJECTIVE: *To determine cause-and-effect relationships*

Review

Model multiple causes and one effect.

REVIEW CAUSE-AND-EFFECT RELATIONSHIPS Remind students that authors sometimes directly explain the cause or effect of events with words such as *because* and *therefore*. Point out that one event can have more than one cause. Model using this example from "Johnny Appleseed":

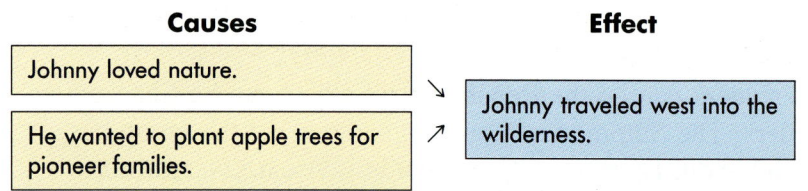

Practice Activity

Why Did It Happen?

Have students look for multiple causes.

Have students expand the cause-and-effect chart with other examples from the selection. Remind them to look for multiple causes. Students also may want to create causal chains by showing how certain effects became causes of other events. Ask students to explain how they figured out the causes and effects they listed, and what clue words were used. VISUAL

MEETING INDIVIDUAL NEEDS

CHALLENGE Ask students to write an account of one of the adventures mentioned in the story, such as Johnny Appleseed's encounter with a rattlesnake. Have them tell what caused the event and what the effects were. Then have students exchange stories and identify causes and effects.

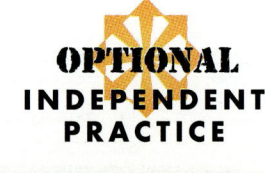

OPTIONAL INDEPENDENT PRACTICE

PRACTICE BOOK
page 14: Understanding cause-and-effect relationships

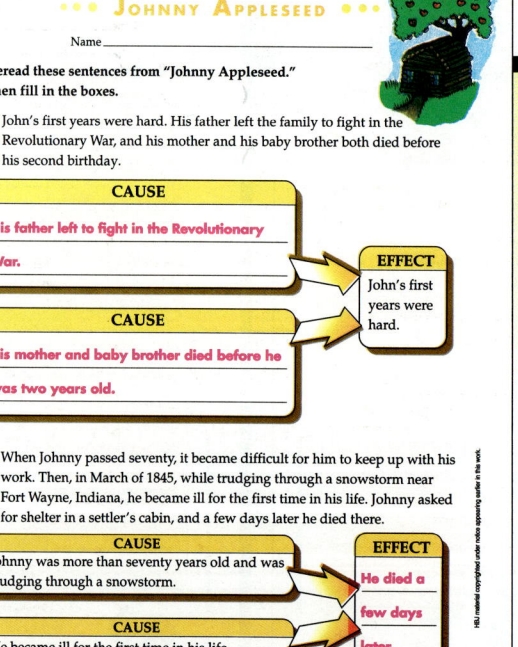

Practice Book

COMPREHENSION STRATEGIES
REVIEW

Active Reading Strategies

OBJECTIVE: *To summarize after reading*

Review

Model the summarizing strategy.

LITERATURE CONNECTION Discuss with students the strategies they can use to help them understand what they read. Remind them that one strategy they can use is summarizing. Model the thinking:

> To summarize "Johnny Appleseed," I ask myself, "Who is this story mostly about?" The answer is Johnny Appleseed. Next I ask, "What important points does the author make about him?" This helps me know what I have read.

Practice Activity

Important Points

Have students summarize the selection.

Ask students to summarize "Johnny Appleseed" by writing down the topic and the most important ideas in the selection. Have volunteers present oral summaries of "Johnny Appleseed" based on the points they wrote. Encourage students to discuss why they included various points. **AUDITORY**

MEETING INDIVIDUAL NEEDS

CHALLENGE Have pairs of students summarize a selection or a book that they have read. Then ask them to present oral summaries to classmates.

OPTIONAL INDEPENDENT PRACTICE

PRACTICE BOOK
pages 15–16: Using active reading strategies

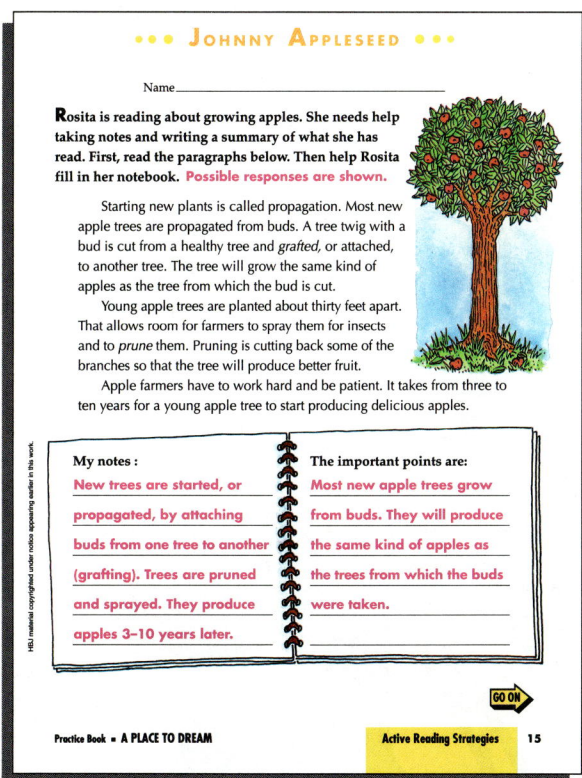

Practice Book

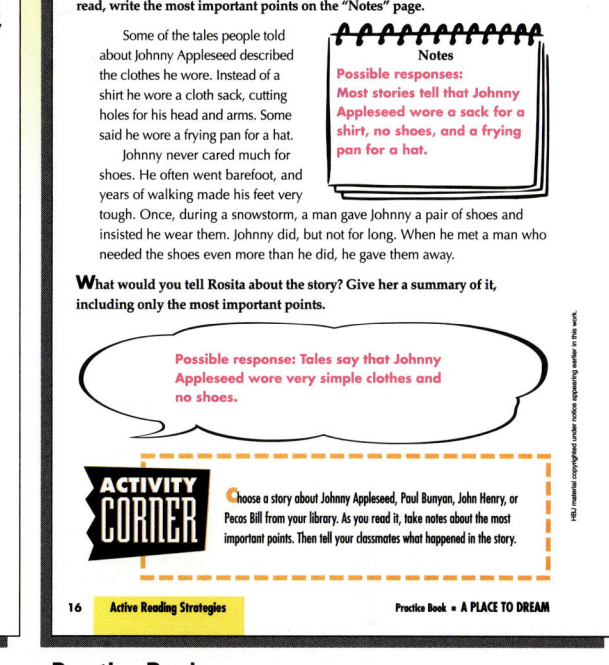

Practice Book

JOHNNY APPLESEED / T75

Integrated CURRICULUM

ART

Making Mosaics

Have students make mosaics from various kinds and sizes of seeds. Popcorn kernels, watermelon or apple seeds, uncooked lentils or lima beans, and pumpkin seeds are all good mosaic materials. Tell students to draw a design or a picture on cardboard in pencil, mark where each kind of seed will go, and then glue on the seeds. Students can use feathers, twigs, and other natural materials for accents. Give students the opportunity to show and describe their mosaics to their classmates.
LISTENING/SPEAKING/VIEWING

SOCIAL STUDIES

Heroes in the Community

Point out that Johnny Appleseed was a kind of hero to the pioneers. Have students write reports about people they feel are heroes in their community. They may write about specific individuals, such as the mayor, or about specific groups of people, such as firefighters. Display students' reports on a bulletin board.   WRITING

SOCIAL STUDIES

Traditional Foods

CULTURAL AWARENESS   Point out to students that foods such as apples, corn, potatoes, and wheat have been a common part of the American diet for hundreds of years. Invite students from various ethnic groups to tell about foods that are a traditional part of their diet. You might suggest that students begin by describing or illustrating a breakfast, lunch, and dinner typical for their culture.   LISTENING/SPEAKING

MATH

Apple Math

Bring a sack of apples to class, and have students use them to illustrate whatever simple math concept they are learning. Students can add, subtract, multiply, divide, and even learn about fractions (by cutting the apples). You may want to direct the activity by putting a math problem on the board and having a volunteer come forward and use apples to solve it. At the end of the activity, slice the apples for a class snack.
LISTENING/SPEAKING

T76 / A PLACE TO DREAM, UNIT 1

HEALTH

Apple Everything

Available on Project Card 6A

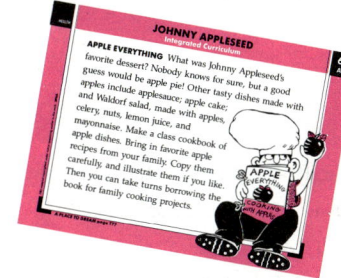

COOPERATIVE LEARNING
Have students bring to class their favorite recipes for dishes made with apples. Possibilities include apple pie, applesauce, Waldorf salad, hot apple cider, apple dumplings, pork chops baked with apples, and apple cake. Have students copy and illustrate the recipes, and then collect them into a class cookbook. Appoint two Recorders, a Facilitator to organize and oversee students' work, and two Checkers to proofread the recipes. Suggest that students take turns borrowing the cookbook for family cooking projects.
READING/WRITING

SCIENCE

Garden Journals

COOPERATIVE LEARNING Have students work in groups to grow plants in containers such as jelly jars, coffee cans, and pie tins. Each group might appoint a Materials Manager and a Reporter. An excellent book for ideas, written at a child's level, is *How to Grow a Jelly Glass Farm* by Kathy Mandry (Pantheon, 1974). Have students start a "garden journal" to keep track of the various steps they must take to help their plants grow.
READING/WRITING

SOCIAL STUDIES

Go West

Available on Project Card 6B

USE REFERENCE SOURCES Students may be interested in finding out more about American pioneers. Encourage each student to choose a different aspect of frontier life, such as the ways pioneers traveled, how they made their homes, or what they wore. Suggest to students that they use a K-W-L chart to organize their information into categories. Then have students research the topic of their choice in the school library, and have them present their findings orally. Encourage them to make their presentations lively by using photographs, drawings, and props. If there is a pioneer landmark or museum in your area, you may wish to have students focus their research on some aspect of it. If possible, visit the site with your students. **LISTENING/SPEAKING/READING/WRITING**

BOOKS TO SHARE

SCIENCE *Green Thumbs Up! The Science of Growing Plants* by Barbara Taylor. Random House Books for Young Readers, 1994.
CHALLENGING

How Trees Help Me by Bobbie Kalman and Janine Schaub. Crabtree, 1992. **AVERAGE**

JOHNNY APPLESEED / T77

MULTICULTURAL PERSPECTIVES

Blazing Trails

DISCUSSION STARTER
Have people always been interested in traveling across America?

READ ALOUD
Johnny Appleseed was just one of many American travelers whose lives were full of adventure. Jean Baptiste Pointe DuSable [zhän ba·tēst′ pwan dyŏŏ·sä′bl] was born in Haiti. His father, a French sea captain, took him to France for schooling. DuSable's later travels took him to New Orleans, up the Mississippi River to St. Louis, and then to the lands of the Potowatomi [pät·ə·wät′ə·mē] and Peoria [pē·ôr′ē·ə] Indians in Illinois. Still restless, DuSable headed for the shores of Lake Michigan, where he established a successful trading post. His log cabin, built in 1779, was the first house on the site of what is now Chicago. As the first settler, DuSable is recognized as the founder of Chicago.

Another traveler who made history was a Shoshone [shō·shō′nē] woman named Sacajawea [sak·ə·jə·wē′ə], a member of the Lewis and Clark expedition in 1804. Lewis and Clark's mission was to explore and map the huge Louisiana Territory. Sacajawea served as both guide and interpreter. Without her, the group would have had great difficulty crossing the Rocky Mountains.

ACTIVITY CORNER

• Have students research additional information about Jean Baptiste Pointe DuSable's life and write a brief story about an adventure he might have had during his travels. Have students explain how the adventure may have affected his life.

• Ask students to think about all the things Lewis and Clark would have had to take with them on their journey. First, have each student make a list on a sheet of paper. Then, help students compile their lists into one. When that list is completed, discuss how the explorers might have transported all their supplies and equipment over rugged land and along rivers.

• Have students write a letter to the DuSable Museum of African American History located in Chicago, Illinois. Have them request a picture and information on the life of Jean Baptiste DuSable. After they read the information, ask students to write about what they felt was the most interesting part of DuSable's life.

Sacajawea's skill as a guide and interpreter was essential to the Lewis and Clark expedition.

Jean Baptiste Pointe DuSable, an African American, is recognized as the founder of Chicago.

THEME WRAP-UP

Discussing the Theme

Remind students that the selections in this theme told about making the world more beautiful.

Discussion Question

PAGE 53 Johnny Appleseed planted apple trees far and wide. Miss Rumphius planted flowers at home. If you wanted to do something to make the world more beautiful, would you start in your own neighborhood? Or would you want to go far from home to begin? Tell why you feel as you do. (Responses will vary.)
CRITICAL: MAKING JUDGMENTS

Theme Wrap-Up

Planting a Seed

Johnny Appleseed planted apple trees far and wide. Miss Rumphius planted flowers at home. If you wanted to do something to make the world more beautiful, would you start in your own neighborhood? Or would you go far from home to begin? Tell why you feel as you do.

WRITER'S WORKSHOP
Think about a time when something you did made someone happy. Write a paragraph describing what you did and how you felt before and after.

Writer's Choice:
You have read about people who did special things. You might want to write about something special you could do. Plan what you will write, and carry out your plan.

53

Writer's Workshop

See pages T80–T81 for suggestions for guiding students through the writing process as they respond to the literature.   **WRITING PROCESS: PERSONAL NARRATIVE**

Writer's Choice
Students may benefit from referring to the *Language Handbook* as they write. Encourage students to create a web as they organize their ideas.

When students are ready to revise and proofread, have them exchange their drafts with partners. Encourage them to help each other identify misspelled words and spell them correctly. Suggest that writing partners use the following guidelines:

- Is it clear to you what the writer is trying to say?
- Are there any details the writer could add to make the point clearer?

Writer's Workshop

Personal Narrative

Theme Wrap-Up

Students write a first-person narrative in which they tell about something they did that made another person happy.

Prepare students for writing personal narratives by reading aloud the first paragraph of "Miss Rumphius," in which the author tells her audience about herself and how she learned a story about her great-aunt. Explain to students that when they write personal narratives, they are telling true stories about themselves.

Use the Writer's Workshop assignment on page 53 as you work through the writing process with students.

ALTERNATIVE TOPICS If you wish, allow students to choose their own topics for writing. Suggest that they refer to the *Language Handbook* for an explanation of the writing process for personal narratives. See Writing Model, page R91.

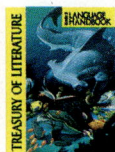

LANGUAGE HANDBOOK *Writing to Inform, pages 48–49; Personal Narrative, page 50*

Prewriting

Before students begin to write, encourage them to discuss what types of experiences they have had that made others happy and that might also interest readers. Suggest that students make a chart like the following one to organize details for their own personal narratives in the order in which they happened.

| **Beginning** | Last summer at camp, I found a lost kitten and wanted to keep it. |

| **Middle** | My camp counselor made me keep the kitten outdoors. I saw a camper crying because she had lost a kitten. |

| **Ending** | I returned kitten to owner and made everyone happy! |

Drafting

Have students draft their personal narratives. Encourage them to

- write a strong beginning sentence, telling who the story is about (themselves) and when and where it happened.
- write what happened in the beginning, the middle, and the ending.
- use the words *I*, *me*, and *my*.

Responding and Revising

Before students share their writing with others, have them ask themselves the following questions:

- Do the sentences tell the order in which the events happened?
- Does the narrative include the words *I*, *me*, and *my*?

Then have students read their work aloud in a peer conference. Have listeners and writers respond to the following questions and complete the following task:

Listener	Writer
Does the personal narrative tell a story about the writer? Does it tell when and where it happens?	When you read your personal narrative aloud, do you feel that you are telling an interesting story? Are some parts stronger than others? Think of two things you can do to improve it.

T80 / A PLACE TO DREAM, UNIT 1

Proofreading

Offer the following tips as students proofread:

- Check for capitalization and punctuation of sentences.
- Check for and correct fragments and run-on sentences.
- Check for words that may be misspelled.

MINI-CONFERENCE STRATEGY For students who are having trouble placing end punctuation correctly in sentences, you might want to make observations such as, "The words have to form a complete sentence or thought. A capital letter and an end mark are not enough to turn words into a sentence."

COMPUTER TIP

PROOFREADING Have students investigate and use the spell-check program that may be available in their computer.

Publishing Options

CLASSROOM BOOKS Suggest that students illustrate their personal narratives and make them into books to display in the classroom library.

ORAL PRESENTATION Have student volunteers read their personal narratives to the class. Suggest that they practice reading their narratives to a classmate before reading them to the rest of the class.

Assessment Options

STUDENT SELF-ASSESSMENT Encourage students to summarize the writing experience by responding to this question in their journals:

- **What was the best tip I received in writing my personal narrative?**

You may also want to have students complete the Self-Assessment Checklist in the *Portfolio Assessment Teacher's Guide*.

WRITING OBSERVATION RECORDS Record students' attempts to revise their writing to improve it.

After students publish, you may want to have them add their personal narratives to their portfolios.

GRAMMAR CONNECTION

Proofreading: Complete Sentences

Using Transparency A, share the examples with students to help them check for and correct sentence fragments and run-on sentences. Remind students that a sentence always expresses a complete thought and begins with a capital letter and ends with an end mark.

> **Transparency A**
> **Bobby's Cold**
>
> **BEFORE**
> Uncle Ted was surprised when he didn't see Bobby I said Bobby had a cold and. Was upstairs sleeping Uncle Ted said. He hoped Bobby would be well soon he wanted. To take Bobby fishing for his birthday.
>
> **AFTER**
> Uncle Ted was surprised when he didn't see Bobby. I said Bobby had a cold and was upstairs sleeping. Uncle Ted said he hoped Bobby would be well soon. He wanted to take Bobby fishing for his birthday.

Have students share their writing in small groups to check that they have corrected sentence fragments and run-on sentences.

LANGUAGE HANDBOOK *Sentences, pages 84–85*

WRITER'S WORKSHOP / T81

Unit 1: BEING SPECIAL

THEME OPENER

Being Different

The Adventures of Ali Baba Bernstein
T85 — A REALISTIC FICTION STORY by Johanna Hurwitz
David "Ali Baba" Bernstein looks for adventure after choosing an exciting new name for himself.

Words from the Author: Johanna Hurwitz
T100 — AN ARTICLE
How does your name make you feel? Johanna Hurwitz tells about her name and the names of her characters.

Lisa's Fingerprints
T115 — A POEM by Mary O'Neill
Lisa is delighted to know that no one else in the world has fingerprints exactly like hers.

Who Am I?
T115 — A POEM by Felice Holman
A child learns from the wind and the rain the answer to the question "Who am I?"

For pacing suggestions, see page T84.

Theme Opener: Being Different PAGES 54–55

THEME

Being Different

Are you glad to be different from everyone else? As you read the following story and poems, think about the ways each person is different and special, even when he or she seems ordinary in other ways.

CONTENTS

THE ADVENTURES OF ALI BABA BERNSTEIN
by Johanna Hurwitz

WORDS FROM THE AUTHOR: JOHANNA HURWITZ

LISA'S FINGERPRINTS
by Mary O'Neill

WHO AM I?
by Felice Holman

55

Discussing the Theme

Ask students to discuss what it means to "stand out in a crowd." Next, ask students if they feel different or special only after doing something different or special. After the discussion, ask students to look at the illustration and read the information and titles on Student Anthology page 55. Encourage them to speculate about how the characters in the story and poems might feel about being different.

Portfolio Assessment

Remind students to keep their writing responses for the selections in "Being Different" in their portfolios. Remind them also to add to their personal journals thoughts and ideas about books they have read independently.

 Whenever you come across this symbol, you may want to encourage students to enter a piece of their work in their portfolios.

THEME OPENER: BEING DIFFERENT / T83

THEME OPENER

Managing the Literature-Based Classroom

Establish Centers

Decide on activities students can accomplish individually or in small groups when they complete assignments. Set up the centers with directions, materials, and motivational signs. Change specific tasks on a regular basis, but consider using permanent center labels, such as *Listening, Writing, Free Reading, Skills, Research,* and *Artistic Response*.

Deck of Student Names

Write each student's name on an index card, and use this deck of cards to select students for such responsibilities as answering questions, performing tasks, becoming a group participant, and so on.

Pacing

This theme has been designed to take about two weeks to complete, depending on your students' needs.

MEETING INDIVIDUAL NEEDS

LOW-ACHIEVING STUDENTS Have students complete the Vocabulary Strategy for "The Adventures of Ali Baba Bernstein" in cooperative groups. Then have the same groups cooperatively read the selection, helping each other with Key Words and any other words they find difficult.

GIFTED AND TALENTED As students complete writing activities such as the Writer's Workshop on Student Anthology page 79, invite them to explore a variety of options for publishing their writing. *Challenge Cards* provide additional activities to challenge students. Challenge notes throughout the lesson plans suggest additional activities to stimulate critical and creative thinking.

SPECIAL-EDUCATION STUDENTS Review your lesson plans with the special-education staff and make any necessary changes to meet the needs of your students.

STUDENTS ACQUIRING ENGLISH Have students work with a partner who speaks English as a first language to discuss answers to the end-of-selection and Theme Wrap-Up questions. Partners should discuss and summarize their answers before sharing their responses with their classmates. Second-Language Support notes throughout the lesson plans offer strategies to help students acquiring English to understand the selection.

Integrated Lesson Planner

The Adventures of Ali Baba Bernstein
pages 56–75

	READING	LANGUAGE ARTS	CROSS-CURRICULAR CONNECTIONS
PART 1 *Reading the Literature* pages T88–T100	**Building Background** **Vocabulary Strategies** **Prereading Strategies** Predict-o-gram Setting a Purpose **Options for Reading**	**Spelling** Pretest Spelling-Vocabulary Connection Generalization: /ō/, /ī/ **Grammar Connection** Reviewing Subjects	**Cultural Awareness** Naming traditions among Spanish-speaking peoples Middle Eastern folktales **Math** Writing large numbers
PART 2 *Responding to the Literature* pages T101–T107	**Personal Response** **Cooperative Response** **Summarizing the Literature** **Critical Thinking Activity** Opinion Chart **Vocabulary Workshop** Key Words Origin of Names	**Language Arts Workshop** **Reading** oral rereading **Writing** journal entry, imaginary adventure **Listening and Speaking** humorous names, book report **Reviewing Spelling Words** Posttest **Grammar Review** Subjects **Grammar Minilesson** Parts of a Sentence: Predicate	**Social Studies** Origin of Names
PART 3 *Learning Through the Literature* pages T108–T114	**Introduce** Study Skills: Alphabetical Order Sources of Information	**Reading** Big Town, Small Town **Listening and Speaking** Presenting My Goldfish—Jaws Opera, Anyone? **Writing** "X" Marks the Spot	**Social Studies** Under One Flag This Place Called Home **Math** How Old Are You Today? Big Town, Small Town **Art** Presenting My Goldfish—Jaws "X" Marks the Spot **Music** Opera, Anyone? **Multicultural Perspectives** Building Better Homes

OPTIONAL MATERIALS
Charts/Transparencies 5–7
Integrated Spelling pp. 18–21; TE pp. T27–T32
Practice Book pp. 17–23
Writer's Journal pp. 12–13
Alternative Teaching Strategies pp. 5, 44–47
Language Handbook pp. 66–68, 90–91
Grammar Practice pp. 16–17
Family Involvement Activities: Unit 1, pp. 1–4
Response Card 1
Project Cards 7A, 7B, 8A, 8B

MEETING INDIVIDUAL NEEDS
Second-Language Support pp. T89, T90, T98, T107, T109, T111
Mainstreaming p. T90
Reteach pp. T107, T109, T111
Challenge pp. T109, T111

FAMILY INVOLVEMENT Encourage students to learn more about the origin and meaning of their own name. Family members might want to work together to create a family tree of names. See *Family Involvement Activities*.

Key Words
adventures
apartment
assigned
treasure
explore
exciting

T86 / A PLACE TO DREAM, UNIT 1

Selection Summary

David Bernstein's third-grade class has four Davids in it. He longs for a unique, exotic name. Discovering that there are at least seventeen other David Bernsteins living in Manhattan makes David even more eager to find a new name. When he reads *The Arabian Nights,* he finds his new name: Ali Baba Bernstein. Unfortunately, David finds that changing his name does not make his life any more exciting—until he finds a trunk full of jewels and gold in the basement of his apartment building! Disappointingly, the treasure turns out to be costume jewelry. But during the course of his investigations, David meets a new friend, Mr. Vivaldi, who introduces David (or Ali Baba) to opera music.

About the Author

Johanna Hurwitz, in addition to writing more than thirty books for children, has been a librarian for many years. She has great respect for children as readers and as humans. She says, "There is an intensity and seriousness about childhood which fascinates me. I can remember my own childhood in great detail and also the childhood of my daughter and son." Many of the episodes she describes in her books are based on her memories and observations of everyday life.

Johanna Hurwitz has won numerous awards and prizes. She has been honored by the states of Florida, New Jersey, Kentucky, West Virginia, and Mississippi as well as by the American Library Association, the International Reading Association, and the Children's Book Council.

Additional Reading

OTHER BOOKS BY JOHANNA HURWITZ

Aldo Peanut Butter. William Morrow, 1990. **CHALLENGING**

Hurray for Ali Baba Bernstein. Scholastic, 1990. **CHALLENGING**

OTHER THEME-RELATED BOOKS

Daddy Has a Pair of Striped Shorts by Mimi Otey. Farrar, Straus & Giroux, 1990. **EASY**

Dancing Teepees: Poems of American Indian Youth, selected by Virginia Driving Hawk Sneve. Holiday House, 1989. **CHALLENGING**

*I Have Another Language: The Language Is Dance by Eleanor Schick. Macmillan, 1992. **EASY**

BOOKS FOR APPLYING STRATEGIES: ALPHABETICAL ORDER, SOURCES OF INFORMATION

A, My Name Is Alice by Jane Bayer. Dial, 1984. **EASY**

I Took My Frog to the Library by Eric Kimmel. Viking, 1990. **EASY**

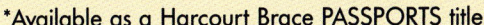

*Available as a Harcourt Brace PASSPORTS title

PART 1

Reading the Literature

Building Background

Access prior knowledge and build vocabulary concepts.

Tell students that the next story, "The Adventures of Ali Baba Bernstein," is about a boy who wishes he had a different name. Discuss with students their ideas about names: Are names important or unimportant? Why do some people have nicknames?

Have students quickwrite.

Encourage students to use their ideas to develop a web on the board similar to the one below:

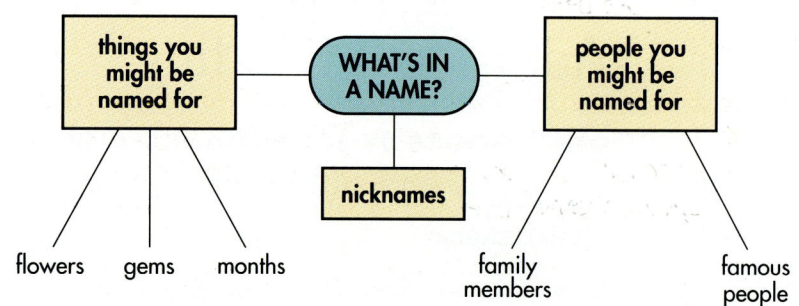

Vocabulary Strategies

Introduce Key Words and strategies.

Display Chart/Transparency 5 or the paragraph on it. Have students read the sentences silently, using context clues along with phonetic and structural analysis to figure out the meanings of the underlined words. For example, students might determine from context that *adventures* are *exciting* rather than boring.

Chart/Transparency 5 Key Words

I am hardly ever bored, because I have lots of <u>adventures</u>. Yesterday, for example, I was headed home to my family's <u>apartment</u>. We live on the fifth floor of a building on Fourth Street. I was thinking about the book report my teacher had <u>assigned</u>. Suddenly I saw something strange on the sidewalk. It was an old box like the kind pirates used for their <u>treasure</u>—their gold and jewels. I wondered what was inside, so I decided to <u>explore</u>. I opened it and found . . . a tiny kitten! My mom let me keep it! What an <u>exciting</u> day!

CULTURAL AWARENESS

Students may be interested to know that different world cultures have their own naming traditions. In many Spanish-speaking countries, a child takes the surnames of both parents. For example, Jaime, the son of Rodrigo Ruíz and Consuelo Chavez, would be called Jaime Ruíz-Chavez. (The father's surname goes first.)

Key Words

adventures
apartment
assigned
treasure
explore
exciting

KEY WORDS DEFINED

adventures unusual or thrilling experiences

apartment a single room or group of rooms rented out as a living space

assigned gave as a task

treasure stored-up and carefully kept valuables such as gold and jewels

explore to look through or examine closely

exciting thrilling

T88 / A PLACE TO DREAM, UNIT 1

Check all students' understanding.

Display the Key Words. On the board, help students develop a chart such as the following in which they associate other words and phrases with the Key Words. Students might suggest synonyms, examples, or qualities of things the Key Words name. Have students tell how each word or phrase they suggest relates to the Key Word. STRATEGY: EXAMPLES/SYNONYMS

Key Word	Related Words
adventures	(journeys, exciting, Robin Hood, heroes, danger, far-off lands)
assigned	(told to do, homework, teacher, book report, semester project)
exciting	(thrilling, adventures, opposite of boring, roller coaster ride)
apartment	(rented, building, elevator, city home)
explore	(look around, discover, far-off lands, wilderness)
treasure	(pirates' gold, jewels, buried, riches)

Integrate spelling with vocabulary.

SPELLING-VOCABULARY CONNECTION *Integrated Spelling* Lesson 3 reinforces the spelling of words with /ō/ and /ī/ sounds, such as *fright* and *soap* found in the selection. In addition, the Words to Explore help reinforce the concept of city living as it relates to the selection.

 **SPELLING PRETEST** You may want to use the Pretest/Posttest Sentences on page T27 in *Integrated Spelling Teacher's Edition* to assess students' knowledge of the spelling generalization.

MEETING INDIVIDUAL NEEDS

SECOND-LANGUAGE SUPPORT Have students retell the paragraph from the Chart/Transparency in their own words, using as many Key Words as possible. Also discuss what life is like in a big, bustling city such as New York. See also the manual *Alternative Teaching Strategies*, pages 5, 44–47.

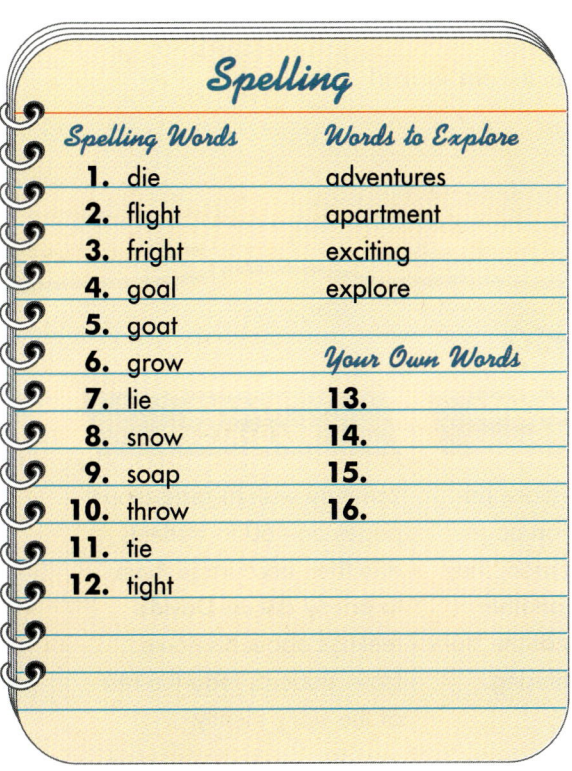

Spelling

Spelling Words	Words to Explore
1. die	adventures
2. flight	apartment
3. fright	exciting
4. goal	explore
5. goat	
6. grow	*Your Own Words*
7. lie	13.
8. snow	14.
9. soap	15.
10. throw	16.
11. tie	
12. tight	

Spelling generalization: /ō/ and /ī/ sounds

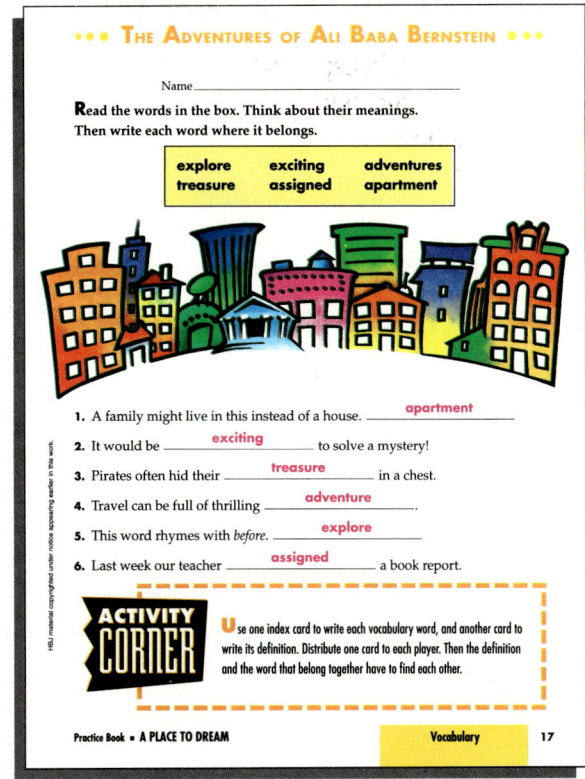

Practice Book

OPTIONAL INDEPENDENT PRACTICE

INTEGRATED SPELLING pages 18–21: Spelling Words with Long Vowels

PRACTICE BOOK page 17: Reinforcing Key Words

NOTE: This page may be completed now or after students have read the selection.

THE ADVENTURES OF ALI BABA BERNSTEIN / **T89**

Prereading Strategies

Predict-o-gram

Have students preview. Have students preview the story by thinking about the title, looking at the illustrations, and reading the first page.

Help students complete a predict-o-gram. Copy the following predict-o-gram on the board, filling in only the left-hand column. Or you may want to distribute copies of the predict-o-gram on page R104. Then read aloud the words and phrases from the right-hand column in a scrambled order. Explain that these words and phrases come from the story. Have volunteers write each one in an appropriate row. Possible placements are shown below.

Characters	(Ali Baba Bernstein; David Bernstein; David's parents; David's teacher; Mr. Vivaldi)
Setting	(school library; apartment building; storage area)
Problem/Events	(wished for an exciting name; exciting adventures; rubies, pearls, and gold chains; a misunderstanding)
Solution	(makes a new friend)

PERSONAL JOURNAL Have students use the predict-o-gram to predict what might happen in "The Adventures of Ali Baba Bernstein." Tell students to write their predictions in their personal journals.

Setting a Purpose

Encourage students to set purposes. Tell students that setting a purpose for reading will help them focus on important story events. Have them use the predict-o-gram to set purposes.

If students have difficulty setting a purpose, offer this suggestion:

I'm going to read to find out who Ali Baba Bernstein is and what kind of adventures he has.

MEETING INDIVIDUAL NEEDS

SECOND-LANGUAGE SUPPORT Students may benefit from the Strategic Reading activities and the additional guidance under the Student Anthology pages. See also the manual *Alternative Teaching Strategies*, pages 5, 44–47.

SUPPORT FOR MAINSTREAMING Some students may be confused when, on page 60, the author begins referring to David as "Ali Baba." You may wish to help them understand that the main character's real name is still David—the author is just being funny when she calls him "Ali Baba."

Options for Reading

SUSTAINED SILENT READING	STRATEGIC READING	READER RESPONSE GROUPS	TEACHER READ-ALOUD
As students read the story, encourage them to record interesting or unfamiliar words in a vocabulary section of their notebooks. Suggest that students look up these words in a dictionary and record the definitions next to the words.	To model strategic reading, use the suggestions that appear on pages T91, T93, T96, and T99.	Follow the suggestions for Partner Reading on page T91. As partners read, they should help one another understand parts of the story that they find confusing.	You may wish to read aloud pages 56–60 to students and then encourage them to briefly discuss David's feelings about his name. Have students read the rest of the story silently.

T90 / A PLACE TO DREAM, UNIT 1

THE ADVENTURES OF ALI BABA BERNSTEIN PAGES 56–57

BY JOHANNA HURWITZ

David Bernstein was eight years, five months, and seventeen days old when he chose his new name.

There were already four Davids in David Bernstein's third-grade class. Every time his teacher, Mrs. Booxbaum, called, "David," all four boys answered. David didn't like that one bit. He wished he had an <u>exciting</u> name like one of the explorers he learned about in social studies—Vasco Da Gama. Once he found two unusual names on a program his parents brought home from a concert—Zubin Mehta and Wolfgang Amadeus Mozart. Now those were names with pizzazz!

David Bernstein might have gone along forever being just another David if it had not been for the book report that his teacher <u>assigned</u>.

"I will give extra credit for fat books," Mrs. Booxbaum told the class.

She didn't realize that all of her students would try to outdo one another. That afternoon when the third grade went to the school library, everyone tried to find the fattest book.

Reader Response Groups

PARTNER READING Have partners read the story silently, stopping at pages 60 and 66 for brief discussions. Or, have partners take turns reading aloud pages of the story to each other. You may want to distribute Response Card 1 (Characters), found on page R79, or provide the following questions for discussion:

- What kind of person is Mr. Vivaldi? Support your answer with information from the story.
- How do you think David feels at the end of the story? Tell why you think so.

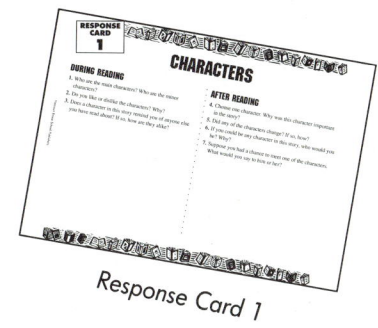

Response Card 1

Strategic Reading

SET PURPOSE/PREDICT: PAGES 56–60 Have students read through page 60. Encourage them to explain what they will be reading to find out.

PAGES 58–59 THE ADVENTURES OF ALI BABA BERNSTEIN

Melanie found a book with eighty pages.
Sam found a book with ninety-seven pages.
Jeffrey found a book with one hundred nineteen pages.

David K. and David S. each took a copy of the same book. It had one hundred forty-five pages.

None of the books were long enough for David Bernstein. He looked at a few that had over one hundred pages. He found one that had two hundred fourteen pages. But he wanted a book that had more pages than the total of all the pages in all the books his classmates were reading. He wanted to be the best student in the class—even in the entire school.

That afternoon he asked his mother what the fattest book was. Mrs. Bernstein thought for a minute. "I guess that would have to be the Manhattan telephone book," she said.

David Bernstein rushed to get the phone book. He lifted it up and opened to the last page. When he saw that it had over 1,578 pages, he was delighted.

He knew that no student in the history of P.S. 35 had ever read such a fat book. Just think how much extra credit he would get! David took the book and began to read name after name after name. After turning through all the *A* pages, he skipped to the name Bernstein. He found the listing for his father, Robert Bernstein. There were fifteen of them. Then he counted the number of David Bernsteins in the telephone book. There were seventeen. There was also a woman named Davida and a man named Davis, but he didn't count them. Right at that moment, David Bernstein decided two things: he would change his name and he would find another book to read.

The next day David went back to the school library. He asked the librarian to help him pick out a very fat book. "But it must be very exciting, too," he told her.

"I know just the thing for you," said the librarian.

She handed David a thick book with a bright

58

Math Connection Explain to students that according to a count done in 1990, 1,487,536 people live in Manhattan, which is why Manhattan's telephone book is so "fat." Use a place value chart (including ones, tens, hundreds, thousands, ten thousands, hundred thousands, millions) to help students visualize the number 1,487,536.

See page T112 for information found on Project Card 8A.

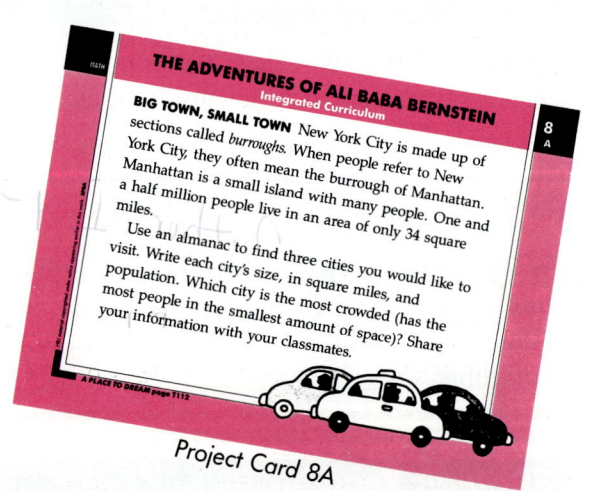

Project Card 8A

THE ADVENTURES OF ALI BABA BERNSTEIN PAGES 60–61

red cover. It was *The Arabian Nights.* It had only three hundred thirty-seven pages, but it looked a lot more interesting than the phone book. David checked the book out of the library and spent the entire evening reading it. When he showed the book to his teacher the next day, she was very pleased.

"That is a good book," she said. "David, you have made a fine choice."

It was at that moment that David Bernstein announced his new name. He had found it in the library book.

"From now on," David said, "I want to be called Ali Baba Bernstein."

Mrs. Booxbaum was surprised. David's parents were even more surprised. "David is a beautiful name," said his mother. "It was my grandfather's name."

"You can't just go around changing your name when you feel like it," his father said. "How will I ever know who I'm talking to?"

"You'll know it's still me," Ali Baba told his parents.

Mr. and Mrs. Bernstein finally agreed, although both of them frequently forgot and called their son David.

So now in Mrs. Booxbaum's class, there were three Davids and one Ali Baba. Ali Baba Bernstein was very happy. He was sure that a boy with an exciting name would have truly exciting adventures.

Only time would tell.

61

Cultural Awareness Explain that *The Arabian Nights* is a collection of more than 200 Middle Eastern folktales. You might also point out that "Ali Baba and the Forty Thieves" is one story within this collection. Ali Baba discovers the treasure cave of forty thieves.

Strategic Reading

MODELING A STRATEGY: PAGES 56–60 What can you do if you don't understand something you are reading?

THINK ALOUD Model using a fix-up strategy if necessary: *I don't understand why David changes his name to Ali Baba. I reread page 60, which tells me that David found his new name in the library book,* The Arabian Nights. *So there must be a character in that book called Ali Baba. Ali Baba must be a character with an exciting life, because that's the kind of life David wants to have.* USING FIX-UP STRATEGIES

SET PURPOSE/PREDICT: PAGES 61–66 Ask students to predict whether David's new name will change his life as he thinks it will. Direct them to read through page 66 to confirm their predictions.

THE ADVENTURES OF ALI BABA BERNSTEIN / T93

PAGES 62–63 THE ADVENTURES OF ALI BABA BERNSTEIN

The first Ali Baba—the one Ali Baba Bernstein had read about in his library book—found a robber's treasure. He knew the magic words to open a secret cave and he knew how to trick the wicked robbers. Nothing like that ever happened to Ali Baba Bernstein. Five days a week he went to school. Third grade was not very different from second grade, even if the work was a little harder. The kids were the same and the games they played at recess or in phys ed were about the same, too.

Sometimes on the weekends Ali Baba rode the subway to his grandparents' house. As the train rumbled along and the lights in the dark tunnel flickered on and off, Ali Baba would pretend the train had crossed onto a secret track. Maybe they were all heading to a mysterious cave deep underground where robbers had hidden gold and jewels. The speeding train would begin to slow down as it approached a station. Ali Baba hoped it would be a station where no train had ever stopped before. But then he looked out the train window. The sign read: SIXTY-SIXTH STREET, where his grandparents lived.

"I thought having a name like Ali Baba would make things pick up around here," Ali Baba complained to his mother. "But I still keep doing David sort of things."

"Changing your name won't make your life any different," Mrs. Bernstein said. "It won't make you grow up any faster. This year you can cross Broadway by yourself," his mother reminded him. "You can walk to Roger Zucker's house all alone. Last year you thought that was a big deal."

It was true. A year ago, crossing Broadway, a two-way street with lots of traffic, *had* seemed like a big

Expanding the Literature Ali Baba's real name is David. Why does the author call him "Ali Baba"? (Accept reasonable responses: to be funny; to show that David thinks of himself as Ali Baba now.)
CRITICAL: APPRECIATING AUTHOR'S CRAFT/DETERMINING AUTHOR'S PURPOSE

GRAMMAR CONNECTION
REVIEWING SENTENCE PARTS: SUBJECT Ask students who or what the following sentence on page 62 is about: "The speeding train would begin to slow down as it approached a station." (It is about the speeding train.) Point out that *The speeding train* is the subject, and remind students that the subject usually comes at the beginning of the sentence.

adventure. Now that he could actually do it, Ali Baba longed for bigger adventures than just crossing the street.

One Saturday morning when Ali Baba Bernstein was eight years, six months, and twenty-three days old, his mother asked him to help her carry the laundry down to the basement of their apartment building, where there were washing machines and dryers. Mrs. Bernstein began to load two of the machines with laundry, but she realized that she'd forgotten the detergent.

"David, will you watch our laundry while I go get the soap?"

"My name is Ali Baba," he corrected her. "Don't worry about the laundry." Who in the world would want to steal their dirty clothes?

Mrs. Bernstein went to the elevator and Ali Baba sat down near the washing machines. But after a moment or two he got up and started to look around. The dim, slightly damp basement was a little like a cave, he thought.

In one corner of the basement was the furnace that heated the building during the winter and made the hot water. Ali Baba could hear the furnace's motor and the whole area around it was hot. It didn't exactly frighten him, but he decided he would rather explore another part of the basement instead. This was where people in the building stored their old furniture, bikes, baby carriages, suitcases, and anything else that they didn't need but didn't want to get rid of.

The storage area was divided into cages with heavy mesh wiring between each cage. Ali Baba had been inside the cage where the Bernsteins kept their castoffs. He peeked in now and tried the door to the cage but it was locked. Through the wire mesh, he could see his old tricycle from when he was little and even his crib, which stood in pieces leaning against someone else's table.

Ali Baba walked down the row of cages, trying each door as he went past. He didn't expect any of the doors to be open, but he tried anyway. At the very end of the row, he found one door that was unlocked. He went inside.

There were old chairs covered with dusty velvet and three big, old-fashioned trunks, like the ones Ali Baba had seen in movies. He didn't know anyone who owned anything like them. It didn't seem like snooping to open them, especially when the lids on the trunks lifted so easily. Ali Baba wrinkled his nose at the odor of mothballs. The first two trunks contained old clothing. He almost didn't open the third trunk. But he knew the first

Vocabulary Strategy Ask how students might figure out what *castoffs* means on page 65. (They might use context to figure out that this word describes "old furniture, bikes, baby carriages, suitcases, and anything else that they didn't need but didn't want to get rid of." Or they might break this compound word into two shorter words, *cast* and *off*, to figure out that castoffs are things people cast, or throw, off.) **STRATEGY:** CONTEXT CLUES/STRUCTURAL ANALYSIS

PAGES 66–67 THE ADVENTURES OF ALI BABA BERNSTEIN

Ali Baba would never leave a trunk unexplored so he decided to take a peek. Even in the dim light, he had no trouble seeing what was in the third trunk. It was filled with sparkling diamonds, rubies, pearls, and gold chains.

Ali Baba could hardly believe his eyes. He closed the lid and read the label with the owner's name: VIVALDI. Who was that?

"David, David," a voice called. It was his mother returning to the basement with the soap. Ali Baba was so stunned by what he had found in the third trunk that he didn't even correct her when she used his old name. All he could think about was the jewels. He was about to tell his mother everything but he stopped just in time. She might say that he had no business poking into other people's trunks.

At lunchtime, Ali Baba was still wondering about the jewels. Why would anyone keep a treasure in the basement? It must be that the owner of the jewels did not want anyone to find them inside his apartment. The more he thought about it, the more certain he was that he had stumbled on a stolen treasure. He wished he could talk about this with his friend Roger Zucker. Maybe the two of them could solve the mystery together. Unfortunately Roger and his family had gone away for the weekend. Ali Baba would have to get to the bottom of this mystery by himself. He would make sure the jewels were returned to their rightful owners. He would be a hero just like the first Ali Baba!

After lunch, Ali Baba's mother asked him to go get the mail. Although there was rarely any mail for him, this was a chore Ali Baba enjoyed. Today he studied all the names on all the other mail boxes in the lobby. Box 4K was labeled VIVALDI. There was no question about it. The thief lived right in this building!

"Did you ever hear the name Vivaldi?" Ali Baba asked his parents when he returned with the mail.

"Of course," said his mother. "He's an Italian composer of baroque music."

"Does he have a police record?" asked Ali Baba.

"Not that I know of. He's been dead at least two hundred years."

66

Strategic Reading

MODELING A STRATEGY: PAGES 61–66 Did you have to change your predictions? If yes, explain why.

THINK ALOUD Provide a think-aloud to model revising predictions: *I predicted that David's new name, Ali Baba Bernstein, would cause him to begin having adventures. But David seems to be having many adventures because he is so curious about things.* REVISING PREDICTIONS

SET PURPOSE/PREDICT: PAGES 67–74 Ask students to predict what David will do about the trunk full of jewels. Encourage them to finish reading the story to confirm their predictions.

T96 / A PLACE TO DREAM, UNIT 1

THE ADVENTURES OF ALI BABA BERNSTEIN   PAGES 68–69

"I don't think we're talking about the same man," said Ali Baba. The jewels in the basement couldn't have been there that long. The building was only fifty years old.

"There's someone named Vivaldi living in this building," said Mr. Bernstein, looking up from the letter he was reading. "I met him at a tenants' meeting. He was worried that he wouldn't be able to buy his apartment if our building was turned into a co-op. I told him that as a senior citizen he couldn't be evicted."

A thief should be evicted, Ali Baba thought darkly. But he didn't say anything.

That afternoon Mrs. Bernstein sent Ali Baba to the store on the corner. She needed eggs for a recipe she wanted to try. Ali Baba was glad to go. On the way back he could check up on Mr. Vivaldi. Ali Baba rode the elevator down to the street and rushed to get the eggs. When he returned to the building, he got off the elevator at the fourth floor.

Even as he was coming out of the elevator, Ali Baba could hear a woman screaming. As he approached the door of 4K, he heard the woman's screams come from inside the apartment. Ali Baba stood frozen. Did Mr. Vivaldi lure women with jewels into his apartment and rob them? The woman screamed again.

Why couldn't any of Mr. Vivaldi's neighbors hear her? The woman shrieked louder. Without thinking, Ali Baba banged on Mr. Vivaldi's door. He didn't have any weapon on him. All he had was a dozen eggs. If he had to, he could throw them at Mr. Vivaldi.

"Open the door!" shouted Ali Baba.

Slowly the apartment door opened. Ali Baba was about to rush inside, but one look at the man in the doorway stopped him.

He had on a helmet, but it didn't look like the kind football players wore. He was holding a shield, and there was a sword hanging from his waist.

The woman shrieked again. Ali Baba remembered why he was there. "I'll save you," Ali Baba cried and pushed

69

Informal Assessment

MAKING INFERENCES To assess students' ability to use details and make inferences to evaluate characters' actions, ask a question such as the following:

- If you were David and you heard screaming inside Mr. Vivaldi's apartment, would you have done the same thing David does, or something different? Use story details to tell why.

Expanding the Literature David lives in an apartment building. What are some examples of apartment living on pages 68 and 69? (David's father talks of a tenants' meeting at which Mr. Vivaldi was worrying about being evicted; David has to take the elevator to get outside.) INFERENTIAL: ANALYZING DETAILS

See page T113 for information found on Project Card 8B.

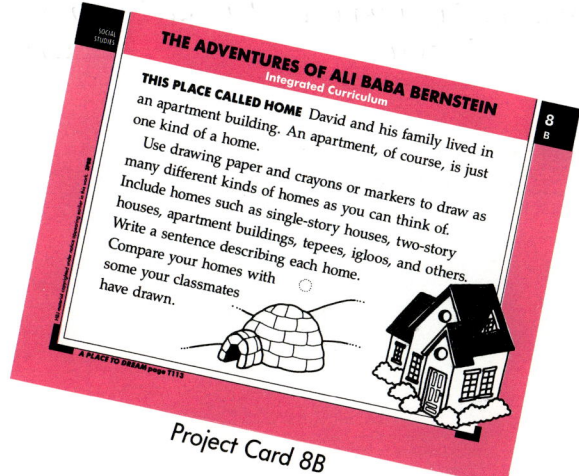

Project Card 8B

THE ADVENTURES OF ALI BABA BERNSTEIN / T97

PAGES 70–71 THE ADVENTURES OF ALI BABA BERNSTEIN

his way into the apartment. He could hear the woman, but he couldn't see her.

"Where did you hide her?" Ali Baba demanded. He pulled the carton of eggs out of the paper bag. If Mr. Vivaldi drew his sword, he would throw it in his face.

"Is she in the bathroom?"

"What's wrong with you, young man?" asked Mr. Vivaldi.

"What's wrong with *me*?" Ali Baba said. "You're the one who steals women's jewels. Shame on you. You should be in jail."

Mr. Vivaldi walked over to his phonograph and turned it off. Suddenly the room was quiet. There was no more shrieking.

"Who are you?" asked the man. "Will you please tell me what this is all about?"

Ali Baba held the carton of eggs ready, just in case. "I heard a woman screaming in here," he said. "I want to know where she is."

"I think you mean *Norma*," said the man.

"Aha!" said Ali Baba. "I knew it. Don't try any of your tricks."

"*Norma* is the name of an opera. The role was sung by Maria Callas."

"Maria?" echoed Ali Baba. "How many women do you have stashed in this apartment?"

"Alas," sighed Mr. Vivaldi. "Maria Callas is dead. It is a great loss to the world."

"You should have thought of that before you killed her," Ali Baba said. "Don't make a move, or I'll throw these eggs at you. I'm going to call the police."

Ali Baba edged toward the telephone. He remembered that the number for emergencies was 911.

"I didn't kill her," said Mr. Vivaldi. "That was a role I never got."

"Then who did?" demanded Ali Baba. "Do you have an accomplice? And where did you get all those jewels I saw in the basement?"

Mr. Vivaldi sat down on his sofa. "I'm sorry. I think there has been a misunderstanding," he said.

"It's too late for excuses, Mr. Vivaldi."

Second-Language Support Help students use context clues to determine the meaning of the idiomatic expression "Shame on you," on page 70. Guide them to understand that David thinks Mr. Vivaldi should feel shame, or anger and embarrassment at himself.

MEETING INDIVIDUAL NEEDS

THE ADVENTURES OF ALI BABA BERNSTEIN   PAGES 72–73

"Please," the man said. "Put down those eggs before you drop them on my carpet. I'll tell you everything."

Reluctantly Ali Baba put down the eggs. If Mr. Vivaldi lunged forward with his sword, Ali Baba would have to move very quickly.

"For many years I sang with the opera," said Mr. Vivaldi. "I had many fine roles. Now I am too old to sing onstage. But I still listen to my operas on the phonograph. I like to pretend that I'm singing before an audience. That's why I've kept my old costumes."

"I didn't think you bought that outfit at a department store," said Ali Baba.

Mr. Vivaldi smiled. "You heard me playing the opera *Norma*. To you, I guess, it did sound like someone screaming. But what you actually heard was the voice of Maria Callas."

"The one who's dead?" asked Ali Baba.

Mr. Vivaldi nodded.

"Then there aren't any women in the apartment with you?" Ali Baba didn't know if he was relieved or disappointed.

"That is correct, young man."

"But what about the jewels?" asked Ali Baba. "I saw them with my own eyes in the trunk in the basement. Who did you steal them from?"

"I think you are referring to the fake jewelry we used on the stage," said Mr. Vivaldi. "Alas, none of it is worth a penny."

"You mean those aren't real diamonds and rubies?"

Mr. Vivaldi shook his head.

"Gee," said Ali Baba. "I never saw so many jewels before. I was sure you were a robber." He looked the old man straight in the eye. "Are you sure you aren't lying to me?"

"Young man," said Mr. Vivaldi, "you flatter me. Imagine thinking I was young enough to be a jewel thief. You make me feel seventy again! And I'm going to be eighty-three on my next birthday."

"Gee," said Ali Baba. "That's really old."

"So it is," said Mr. Vivaldi. "How old are you?"

"Eight years, six months, and twenty-three days," said Ali Baba.

"That's a good age," said Mr. Vivaldi. "What is your name? You never told me."

Strategic Reading

MODELING A STRATEGY: PAGES 67–74 Were your predictions confirmed? Explain how you know.

THINK ALOUD Provide a think-aloud model, if necessary: *I predicted that Ali Baba would try to catch the thief. I based my prediction on the fact that Ali Baba said he wanted to have more adventures like the ones he read about in books. Ali Baba did try to catch the thief, but he also learned that he had jumped to the wrong conclusion about Mr. Vivaldi.* **CONFIRMING PREDICTIONS**

PAGES 74–75 THE ADVENTURES OF ALI BABA BERNSTEIN

"Ali Baba. Ali Baba Bernstein."

"Interesting name. Well, Ali Baba, now that we are properly introduced, come another day if you would like. We can listen to *Carmen* together."

Ali Baba got ready to leave. He knew his mother would be wondering where he was.

As he waited for the elevator, Ali Baba could hear the phonograph playing again in apartment 4K. This time a man was singing. Ali Baba wondered if that was the way Mr. Vivaldi used to sound. He stood listening to the music until the elevator came.

If you could change your name, what name would you choose? Explain why.

How do David's parents feel about him changing his name?

What do you think Ali Baba learns in this story?

WRITE After David changes his name to Ali Baba, he seems to look for adventure. Make a list of how you think your life would change if you had a different name.

74

Words from the Author: Johanna Hurwitz

When I write a book, I seldom think of the title first. With *The Adventures of Ali Baba Bernstein*, it was the name that bounced into my head. I remembered that when my son was young, the name David was very popular, and at one time there were four Davids in his class. I decided to write about a boy who changes his name.

Sometimes I use things that happened to my children as a starting point for a story. When my first book came out, the characters I was writing about, Busybody Nora and her brother, Teddy, were 5 and 3, and my children were 10 and 12. Because Nora and Teddy were so young, my children didn't feel as if I was talking about them.

I always wanted to be a writer, but I never really knew I was a funny writer until after my first book was done. It surprised me. Sometimes I look at my stuff and say, "Hey, I wrote that! It's funny!" I guess the way I write fits in with my philosophy of life—you'd better laugh at things, or otherwise you'll be crying much of the time.

AWARD-WINNING AUTHOR

Returning to the Predictions/Purpose

PREDICT-O-GRAM Have students look over the predict-o-gram they made and filled in before reading. Have them revise the predict-o-gram based on what they learned from reading "The Adventures of Ali Baba Bernstein."

NOTE: Responses to the questions and support for the Write activity appear on page T101.

Words from the Author: Johanna Hurwitz

AUTHOR'S PURPOSE Invite students to read page 75 to find out how Johanna Hurwitz feels about her writing. When they have finished reading, ask volunteers to retell what she has to say in their own words. (She always wanted to be a writer and finds it surprising that she is funny. She loves to write books that make people laugh.)

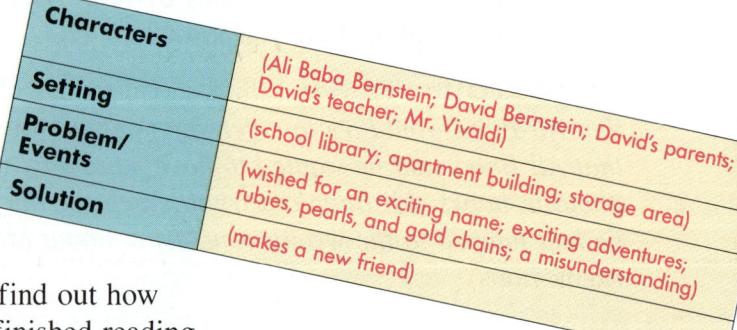

Characters	(Ali Baba Bernstein; David Bernstein; David's parents; David's teacher; Mr. Vivaldi)
Setting	(school library; apartment building; storage area)
Problem/Events	(wished for an exciting name; exciting adventures; rubies, pearls, and gold chains; a misunderstanding)
Solution	(makes a new friend)

T100 / A PLACE TO DREAM, UNIT 1

PART 2

Responding to the Literature

Personal Response

Encourage critical thinking.

If you could change your name, what name would you choose? Explain why. (Responses will vary.) CRITICAL: EXPRESSING PERSONAL OPINIONS

How do David's parents feel about him changing his name? (surprised and a little hurt) INFERENTIAL: DETERMINING CHARACTERS' EMOTIONS

What do you think Ali Baba learns in this story? (Accept reasonable responses: not to jump to conclusions; that changing your name will not change your life.) CRITICAL: SYNTHESIZING

Encourage creative written responses.

 **WRITE** **After David changes his name to Ali Baba, he seems to look for adventure. Make a list of how you think your life would change if you had a different name.** Have students brainstorm a list of names they might change theirs to. Possibilities might include names of story characters, names of people whom students know and respect, or names students invent. Once they have chosen a "new name" they can begin to list ways it might (or might not) change their lives.

Cooperative Response

Have reader response groups extend their discussions.

PARTNER READING Encourage partners to talk about their favorite parts of the story, as well as parts they didn't understand. You may wish to have them discuss questions such as these:

If this story were one episode in a television series, and you were the director, which part would you want the most to dramatize? Explain your answer.

STRATEGY CONFERENCE

Have students explain how completing a predict-o-gram helped them read the story. (Accept reasonable responses: Using this strategy encourages readers to keep reading to see whether their predictions match the actual story.)

NOTE

An additional writing activity for this selection appears on page T104.

THE ADVENTURES OF ALI BABA BERNSTEIN / **T101**

Summarizing the Literature

Have students retell the story and write a summary.

Guide students in completing a story frame. Then have them write a one-sentence summary of "The Adventures of Ali Baba Bernstein." See *Practice Book* page 18 below.

"The Adventures of Ali Baba Bernstein" takes place in the city of __(New York)__. It is about a boy whose real name is __(David)__. He decides to change his name to __(Ali Baba)__, because __(he thinks that this will help him have exciting adventures)__.

Critical Thinking Activity

Examine how opinions change.

CREATE A CHART David learns something that changes his opinion of Mr. Vivaldi. **How has your opinion changed after you found out more about him?** Divide students into small groups and have each member contribute to a chart like the one shown here. When the groups are finished, have them share their charts with the rest of the class and talk about them. CREATIVE: EXPANDING STORY CONCEPTS

Old Opinion	Event or Information That Changed Your Opinion	New Opinion

Portfolio

STUDENT SELF-ASSESSMENT

Encourage students to discuss their story frames in small groups. Ask them to evaluate how well they summarized the story. Explain that it is fine for their responses to vary, but that if they think they can improve their story frames, they should. Have students add their initial and final story frames to their portfolios.

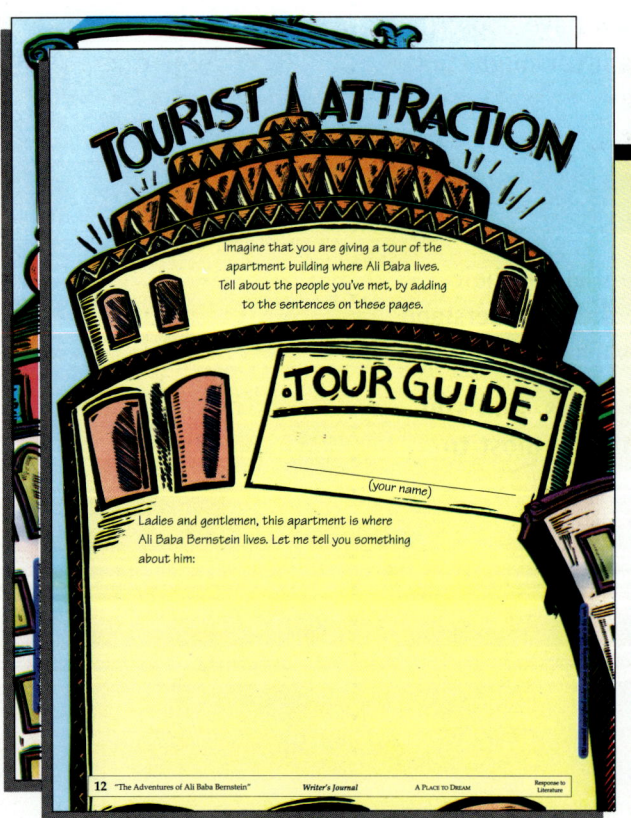

Writer's Journal

Practice Book

OPTIONAL INDEPENDENT PRACTICE

WRITER'S JOURNAL
pages 12–13: Writing a personal response

PRACTICE BOOK
page 18: Summarizing the selection

T102 / A PLACE TO DREAM, UNIT 1

VOCABULARY WORKSHOP

Reviewing Key Words

Copy the two lists below on the board, but omit the lines. Read the following questions. As students answer, have a volunteer draw a line from the character's name in the left-hand column to the Key Word it goes with in the right-hand column. Tell students that a character can be used more than once.

David	explore
Mrs. Booxbaum	assigned
the librarian	exciting
Mr. Vivaldi	adventures
Ali Baba (the character in *The Arabian Nights*)	treasure
	apartment

1. Who longs to have *adventures*? (David)
2. Who *assigned* a book report to David and his classmates? (Mrs. Booxbaum)
3. Who finds David an *exciting* new book to read? (the librarian)
4. Who decides to *explore* the basement of the apartment building? (David)
5. Who lives in *apartment* 4K? (Mr. Vivaldi)
6. Who discovers a robber's *treasure* in a secret cave? (Ali Baba—the character in *The Arabian Nights*)

Extending Vocabulary

ORIGIN OF NAMES Point out to students that many names have meanings. Some first names, such as Hope, say exactly what they mean. The last name Johnson originally meant "son of John." Some last names originally told what a person did for a living, such as Miller, "one who mills." Other names have meanings that are harder to figure out. Draw on the board a chart like the one below, and guide students in adding names they know.

Name	Meaning	Language It Comes From
Peter	"rock"	Greek
Felicidad	"happiness"	Spanish
Amy	"beloved"	French
Rex	"king"	Latin
Domingo	"Sunday"	Spanish
Smith	"one who works with iron"	Old English

Have students form pairs and add more names to the chart. Provide available reference books about names and their meanings and origins. A good source for this information is baby-naming books. When partners have finished, help them compile their work in a classroom chart.

THE ADVENTURES OF ALI BABA BERNSTEIN / T103

Language Arts WORKSHOP

READING

Oral Rereading

Ask students to suggest some words or phrases that describe David Bernstein. **(Examples: wants excitement; wants to be different; brave)** Record their suggestions on the board. Then have volunteers each choose a passage from the story to read aloud that exhibits one or more of the qualities listed on the board. Allow students time to read their passages silently before rehearsing them and presenting them to classmates. You may wish to model selecting your own passage and reading it aloud in an expressive voice. LISTENING/SPEAKING/READING

WRITING

Writing About the Literature

Available on Project Card 7A

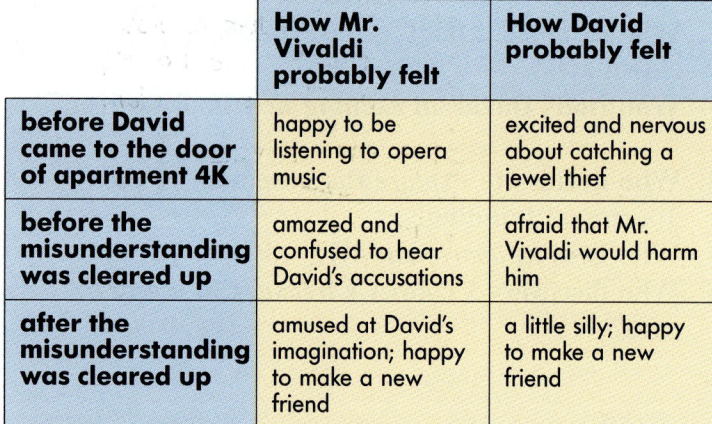

 **WRITE A JOURNAL ENTRY** Have students write a journal entry from the point of view of either David or Mr. Vivaldi that describes the incident in Mr. Vivaldi's apartment. Encourage them to organize their ideas with a chart like the following. WRITING

	How Mr. Vivaldi probably felt	How David probably felt
before David came to the door of apartment 4K	happy to be listening to opera music	excited and nervous about catching a jewel thief
before the misunderstanding was cleared up	amazed and confused to hear David's accusations	afraid that Mr. Vivaldi would harm him
after the misunderstanding was cleared up	amused at David's imagination; happy to make a new friend	a little silly; happy to make a new friend

GRAMMAR REVIEW: SUBJECTS When students revise their journal entries, remind them that each of their sentences should contain a subject. Use the following activity to reinforce this skill: Have students each write a paragraph telling about what David might have done after he left Mr. Vivaldi's apartment. Tell them to circle the subject in each sentence. When they have finished writing, have students exchange and check each other's paragraphs.

 **LANGUAGE HANDBOOK** Everyday Writing, pages 66–68; Sentence Parts: Subject, page 90

 **DAILY LANGUAGE PRACTICE** Oral language exercises are provided on pages R60–R61.

T104 / A PLACE TO DREAM, UNIT 1

Language Arts WORKSHOP

SPELLING

Reviewing Spelling Words

SPELLING WORDS: *die, flight, fright, goal, goat, grow, lie, snow, soap, throw, tie, tight*

WORDS TO EXPLORE: *adventures, apartment, exciting, explore*

Have students challenge a partner to a contest using the Spelling Words and other words with /ī/ and /ō/ sounds. Tell each student to see how many of the words he or she can use in a sentence; for instance, *This bar of soap is as white as snow.* Set a five-minute time limit and ask students to write their sentences on separate sheets of paper. When time is up, have partners compare sentences and check unfamiliar words in a dictionary.
LISTENING/SPEAKING/SPELLING

Use *Integrated Spelling* Lesson 3 to reinforce the Spelling Words and the Words to Explore. See pages T27–T32 in *Integrated Spelling Teacher's Edition*.

 **SPELLING POSTTEST** You may want to use the Pretest/Posttest Sentences on *Integrated Spelling Teacher's Edition* page T27 to assess students' knowledge of the spelling generalization.

WRITING

Expect the Unexpected!

Have students recall that when David rides the subway to his grandparents' house, he imagines that the train is taking him to a cave like the one in *The Arabian Nights*. Have students think of some ordinary activities they do every day. Then have them pick one and write a paragraph or short story describing an imaginary adventure in which the ordinary activity leads to an unexpected place or event. Remind students to add descriptive details to their story to help the reader see, hear, and feel what the character is experiencing. Students may also enjoy illustrating their paragraphs or stories. When they are done, have volunteers read their stories aloud to the class. LISTENING/SPEAKING/WRITING

LISTENING AND SPEAKING

Mrs. Booxbaum and the Reading Explosion

Available on Project Card 7B

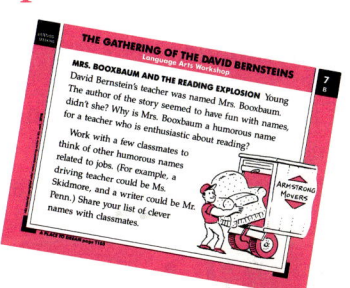

Have students recall the name of David's teacher, Mrs. Booxbaum. Then have students work in small groups to invent humorous names for characters with different professions. Tell them to try to think of names that have something to do with each job (such as Ms. Skidmore for a driving-school teacher, or Mr. Penn for a writer) and list them on a sheet of paper. LISTENING/SPEAKING/WRITING

LISTENING AND SPEAKING

A Book I Liked . . .

Remind students that David enjoys *The Arabian Nights*. Have each student prepare an oral report about a book he or she especially enjoyed reading. Remind students that in a book report, they should include the title of the book, the author's name, a brief summary of the events in the book, and their own opinion of the book. You may want to ask them not to give away the ending. After students present their reports, encourage class members to ask questions. LISTENING/SPEAKING/READING/WRITING

THE ADVENTURES OF ALI BABA BERNSTEIN / T105

Grammar MINI LESSON

Parts of a Sentence: Predicate

OBJECTIVES: *To understand that every sentence has a predicate that tells what the subject of a sentence is or does; to recognize that a predicate usually appears in the last part of a sentence*

Oral Warm-Up

Write the following sentences from "The Adventures of Ali Baba Bernstein" on the board, omitting the circles and lines. Ask students to follow along as you read them aloud.

- (Melanie) found a book with eighty pages.
- (David Bernstein) rushed to get the phone book.
- (Ali Baba Bernstein) was very happy.
- (Ali Baba) wrinkled his nose at the odor of mothballs.

Circle the subject in each sentence. Then have volunteers underline the part of each sentence that tells what the subject is or does. Begin a diagram like this on the board:

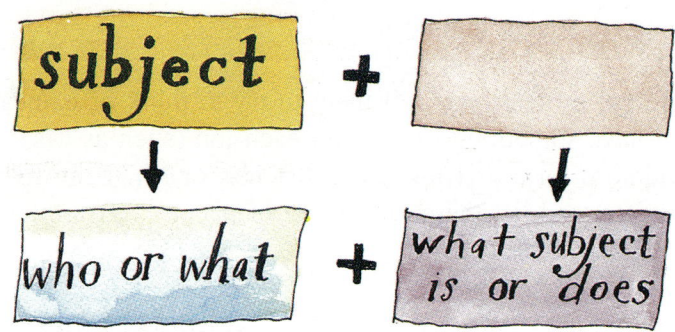

Leave the top right box empty for students to fill in during Interactive Teaching.

Interactive Teaching

PREDICATES Have a volunteer tell what a sentence is. (a group of words that tells a complete thought) Explain that in addition to the subject of a sentence, every sentence has a **predicate,** which is the part that tells what the subject is or does. (Point to the underlined section of each sentence on the board.)

Write the following sentences on the board, and ask volunteers to orally identify the predicate in each one. Correct responses are underlined.

- The phone book <u>is 1,578 pages long.</u>
- Ali Baba <u>had a truly exciting adventure.</u>
- Ali Baba's mother <u>is a good cook.</u>
- Mr. Vivaldi <u>listens to the opera.</u>

Point out that the predicate usually is found in the last part of the sentence and includes every word that helps identify what the subject is or does. Ask a student to write *predicate* in the diagram you began in Oral Warm-Up. Have volunteers write sentences on the board about other events from the story. Have a volunteer underline the predicate in each sentence.

 **LANGUAGE HANDBOOK** Parts of a Sentence: Predicate, page 91

T106 / A PLACE TO DREAM, UNIT 1

Practice Activities

Predicate Treasure

Ask students to think about one thing they would do if they found a hidden treasure. (clap, cheer, jump up and down, and so on) Have volunteers come to the front of the class and pantomime what they would do. Ask the remaining students to write a sentence that describes what each volunteer is doing. Have several students share their sentences by writing them on the board, reading them aloud, and identifying the predicate. VISUAL/AUDITORY/KINESTHETIC

Household Helpers

Remind students that David Bernstein helped his mother with the laundry. Ask each student to write a paragraph that tells about some of the chores and other things he or she does to help out at home. Ask students to exchange their paragraphs with a partner. Partners should read each other's work for correct capitalization and punctuation and then underline the predicate in each sentence. Have volunteers read the paragraphs aloud. VISUAL/AUDITORY

MEETING INDIVIDUAL NEEDS

SECOND-LANGUAGE SUPPORT Write on the board simple sentences. Read each sentence aloud and ask: "What does this sentence tell you about what the subject is or does?" Have students underline the words that answer this question.

RETEACH Follow the visual, auditory, and kinesthetic/motor models on page R9.

OPTIONAL INDEPENDENT PRACTICE

PRACTICE BOOK
page 19: Using predicates

GRAMMAR PRACTICE
pages 16–17: Identifying predicates

Practice Book

THE ADVENTURES OF ALI BABA BERNSTEIN / T107

PART 3

Learning through the Literature

STUDY SKILLS
INTRODUCE

Alphabetical Order

OBJECTIVE: *To alphabetize using the fourth and fifth letters*

Interactive Teaching

Discuss how Ali Baba used the phone book.

LITERATURE CONNECTION Ask students how David located other David Bernsteins in the phone book in "The Adventures of Ali Baba Bernstein." (by finding the last name *Bernstein*) Tell students that alphabetical order will help them find information in reference books.

Have students alphabetize to the fifth letter.

MODEL THE THINKING Display Chart/Transparency 6 or write the columns of names on the board. Use the words in column one to review alphabetical order to the first letter. Use column two to alphabetize words that have the same beginning letter. Then have a volunteer use the words in column three to demonstrate alphabetizing to the third letter.

Chart/Transparency 6		Alphabetical Order	
1	**2**	**3**	**4**
Drake	Carson	Smith	Bergdorf
Mitchell	Cole	Small	Bernini
Arnold	Clemens	Smollen	Berber
Zerner	Crest	Smetler	Bernstein

Use column four to model alphabetizing to the fourth and fifth letters:

> I see that the first three letters in each name are the same—*B, E, R*—so I'll need to look at the fourth letter in each name: *G, N, B,* and *N*. For the two names that have *N* as the fourth letter, I look at the fifth letters.

Also explain how reference books such as telephone books, dictionaries, and encyclopedias use *guide words* to help readers locate the entry they want. Explain that all the entries on a page fall alphabetically between two guide words. Show students the guide words at the top of a two-page spread in the telephone book as an example.

- **AN ADDITIONAL BOOK FOR APPLYING ALPHABETICAL ORDER**

  A, My Name Is Alice by Jane Bayer. Dial, 1984. EASY

T108 / A PLACE TO DREAM, UNIT 1

Practice Activities

Alphabetize the Words

Have students alphabetize words.

Write these words on the board:

credit	running	this	station
classmate	runner	librarian	sign
count	third	liberty	soap

Have students work independently to alphabetize the three words in each column. Then have them think of two guide words that might appear at the top of a two-page spread in a dictionary or glossary containing all of these words. (Example: *class/this*) **VISUAL**

What's the Order?

Have partners alphabetize lists.

Have students work independently to pick ten or twelve different words from the story and list them on separate slips of paper. Tell them that some of their words should have the first two or three letters in common. Then have them trade slips with a partner. Have students alphabetize their partners' slips. **VISUAL/KINESTHETIC**

Performance Assessment

Have students display their alphabetized words from Alphabetize the Words or from What's the Order? Encourage classmates to check the lists to see if they are correct. For evaluation guidelines, see *Staff Development Guide*.

Practice Book

Practice Book

MEETING INDIVIDUAL NEEDS

RETEACH Follow the visual, auditory, and kinesthetic/motor models on page R10.

CHALLENGE Have pairs of students create an alphabetized directory of the students in your classroom. If the list requires more than one page, have students write guide words at the top of each page.

SECOND-LANGUAGE SUPPORT Have students name two classmates whose last names come before theirs in alphabetical order and two whose last names come after theirs. See also the manual *Alternative Teaching Strategies*, pages 5, 44–47.

OPTIONAL INDEPENDENT PRACTICE

PRACTICE BOOK
pages 20–21: Using alphabetical order

STUDY SKILLS
INTRODUCE

Sources of Information

OBJECTIVE: *To locate information in a library*

Interactive Teaching

Focus on the library trip in the story.

LITERATURE CONNECTION Ask students to recall where David Bernstein's third-grade class went to find books for their book reports. (the library) Explain to students that if they understand how a library is organized and how to locate books, they will be able to find the books they need quickly and easily.

Have students use a card catalog.

MODEL USING THE CARD CATALOG Explain to students that they can use the *card catalog* to find books in a library. Tell them that the card catalog is a set of drawers that holds a title card and an author card for every book in the library. Add that nonfiction books also have subject cards. Point out that the cards are arranged in alphabetical order. Explain that some libraries have a computerized card catalog, so that readers can look for information on a computer screen instead of in drawers.

MODEL WHEN TO USE A SUBJECT CARD Provide a think-aloud model for students:

> **I want to find out what my name means, so I'm going to look in the library for a book on the meanings of names. I don't know the titles of any books on this subject, so I'll look in the card catalog under *N* for a subject card on names or naming.**

Display Chart/Transparency 7 or write the information from the transparency on the board. Point out the subject, author, title, call number (on the left-hand side), publisher, and copyright date on the subject card. Explain how you would use the call number to find the book. Tell students that most libraries keep reference books such as telephone books, dictionaries, atlases, and encyclopedias in a special section. Inform them that usually these books can be used in the library reference area, but may not be taken home.

Chart/Transparency 7   Subject Card

NAMES
929.4   Lee, Mary Price.
Your name—all about it/Mary Price Lee.
Philadelphia: Westminster Press, c1980.

AN ADDITIONAL BOOK FOR REINFORCING SOURCES OF INFORMATION

I Took My Frog to the Library by Eric Kimmel. Illustrated by Blanche Sims. Viking, 1990. EASY

Practice Activities

Step by Step

Have students list steps.

COOPERATIVE LEARNING Write the following on the board:

1. another book by Johanna Hurwitz
2. a book titled *How to Change Your Name*
3. a book about Saudi Arabia

Have students work in small groups to list the steps they would take to find each book. Each group should choose a Recorder, a Facilitator, and a Reporter to read the group's list to the class. VISUAL/AUDITORY

Search and Find

Have students find a library book.

Have pairs of students work together to find a book in the school library about a subject that interests them. Tell the pairs they should use the card catalog to find their books. Instruct them to keep a list of all the steps they took. VISUAL/KINESTHETIC

Performance Assessment

As students share their lists from the Step by Step activity, have other students ask questions to clarify things that are unclear. Have pairs explain exactly how they found their books in the Search and Find activity. For evaluation guidelines, see *Staff Development Guide*.

MEETING INDIVIDUAL NEEDS

RETEACH Follow the visual, auditory, and kinesthetic/motor models on page R11.

CHALLENGE Have students think of an idea for a nonfiction book and create an author card, a subject card, and a title card for that book.

SECOND-LANGUAGE SUPPORT Display Chart/Transparency 7 and have students point out the subject, author, title, and call number on the subject card. See also the manual *Alternative Teaching Strategies*, pages 5, 44–47.

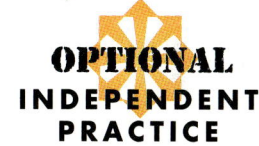

OPTIONAL INDEPENDENT PRACTICE

PRACTICE BOOK

pages 22–23: Using library skills

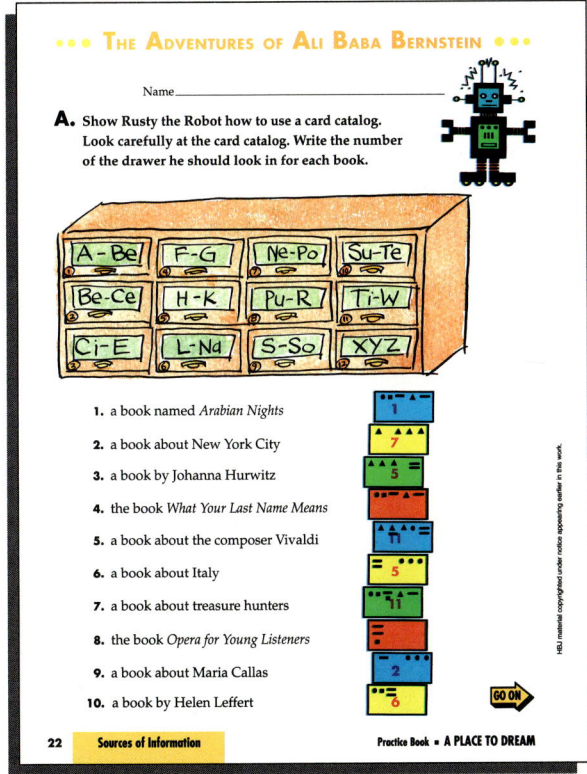

Practice Book

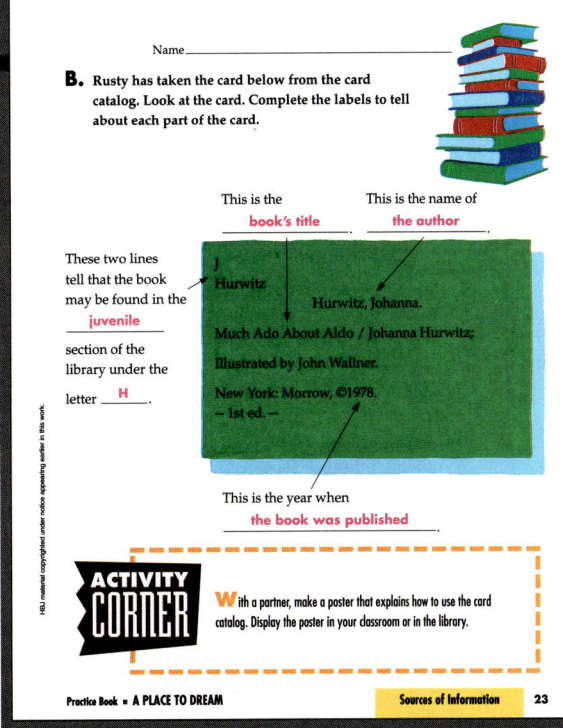

Practice Book

THE ADVENTURES OF ALI BABA BERNSTEIN / T111

Choices

Integrated CURRICULUM

MATH

How Old Are You Today?

Ask students why they think Ali Baba keeps close track of his exact age. (Accept reasonable responses: He is probably interested in mathematical details; he can't wait to turn nine years old.) Have students work independently to figure out exactly how old they are today. Provide a calendar to review the number of days in each month, and remind students to add an extra day for leap years, if necessary. (If they know the time they were born, they can figure out how old they are to the minute!) **WRITING**

SOCIAL STUDIES

Under One Flag

COOPERATIVE LEARNING Remind students that David Bernstein found many other people with the last name Bernstein in the phone book. Explain to students that Bernstein is a common German-Jewish name and that many Jewish people settled in New York City. Have pairs conduct a survey of the ethnic backgrounds of their classmates. Provide a world map on a bulletin board and help students put pushpins in the countries they or their relatives and ancestors come from. **LISTENING/SPEAKING**

MATH

Big Town, Small Town

Available on Project Card 8A

USE AN ALMANAC Point out that Manhattan is home to about one and one-half million people living on an area of only 34 square miles. Have students choose three cities they would like to visit and use an almanac to find each city's size and population. Have them arrange the cities in a certain order, such as smallest city to largest city or greatest population to least population. Then have students present their findings orally. **LISTENING/ SPEAKING/READING/WRITING**

ART

Presenting My Goldfish—Jaws

COOPERATIVE LEARNING Have students work in groups to discuss pets, toys, or other possessions they have named. Encourage them to explain how they decided on a particular name and the feelings they have toward the pet or the object. Some students may wish to draw a picture of the pet or the possession. **LISTENING/ SPEAKING**

T112 / A PLACE TO DREAM, UNIT 1

SOCIAL STUDIES

This Place Called Home

Available on Project Card 8B

Remind students that David and his family live in an apartment building. Tell students that people in crowded cities often live in apartment buildings because there is not enough land on which to build a separate house for each family. Give students paper and colored markers or crayons and have them draw as many different types of homes as they can. They might include traditional American houses, apartment buildings, igloos, dome homes, cabins, and houses built on stilts or made of thatch. Encourage students to write a sentence about each home.   WRITING

MUSIC

Opera, Anyone?

Have students recall that the woman Ali Baba hears "screaming" in Mr. Vivaldi's apartment turns out to be the late opera singer Maria Callas. Tell students that Maria Callas was a famous American opera singer who was born in New York City of Greek parents. Ask students if they have ever heard live or recorded opera music. Invite volunteers to tell about their experiences. If possible, bring in a recording of Bellini's *Norma*, as sung by Maria Callas, and play it for students. Alternatively, you might play them portions of an operetta such as Gilbert and Sullivan's *H.M.S. Pinafore*. After they listen, ask students to give their opinions about what they heard.   LISTENING/SPEAKING

ART

"X" Marks the Spot

Remind students that Ali Baba Bernstein finds a mysterious trunk full of "treasure" in the basement of his apartment building. Have students work in small groups to create maps leading to imaginary hidden treasure. Suggest that they first decide where their treasure will be, and then draw and write out directions leading to it. The treasure might be hidden in their homes, in their neighborhoods, or at school. Provide students with paper and colored markers. You might also want to show them how to make their treasure maps look old by rubbing wet coffee grounds into the paper. When students are finished, display their maps in the classroom.   WRITING

BOOKS TO SHARE

SOCIAL STUDIES   *Emily* by Michael Bedard. Doubleday, 1993.   AVERAGE

Loving by Ann Morris. Lothrop, Lee & Shepard, 1990.   EASY

Walden. Text selected by Steve Lowe. Philomel, 1990.   AVERAGE

THE ADVENTURES OF ALI BABA BERNSTEIN / T113

MULTICULTURAL PERSPECTIVES

Building Better Homes

DISCUSSION STARTER

New York City was built by immigrants. How have people from other countries contributed to your community?

READ ALOUD

One hundred years ago, the poorest immigrants often ended up living in tiny rooms in crowded apartment buildings with little fresh air or sunlight. Danish-born reporter Jacob Riis wanted to show all Americans how bad the living conditions were for these immigrants. His book *How the Other Half Lives* led to many improvements in housing.

Robert Weaver spent his whole career searching for solutions. His first government job was as advisor to the Secretary of the Interior, Harold Ickes, in 1933. He later became an expert on how to improve housing for poor people. President Lyndon Johnson chose him to be the first head of the Department of Housing and Urban Development. He was the first African American to hold this position.

I. M. Pei, one of the most famous architects in the world, also worked to improve housing. Though he could have worked on almost any project he chose, he designed low-cost apartment buildings. Pei, who came to the United States from China, enjoyed the challenge of designing apartments that were comfortable and attractive but still affordable.

ACTIVITY CORNER

- Help students think about how abandoned buildings might be "recycled." To begin, you may want to find out how the following individuals reshaped urban environments and share your findings with students: Fernando Juarez (architect), Scott Lee (developer), or Alice Callaghan (community housing preservationist).

- Have groups of students use balsa wood, blocks, or other materials to construct a model of a building in which people could live in your neighborhood. Individual responsibilities might include choosing the building, planning the project, and building it.

American architect Ieoh Ming Pei.

President Johnson congratulates Robert C. Weaver after Weaver is sworn in as Secretary of Housing and Urban Development.

T114 / A PLACE TO DREAM, UNIT 1

POEMS

Lisa's Fingerprints
Who Am I?

Felice Holman

ABOUT THE POETS Mary O'Neill is perhaps best known for *Hailstones and Halibut Bones,* selected as one of the best one hundred children's books of the year by *The New York Times Book Review.* Felice Holman's work has been honored with commendations such as the ALA Notable Book and the Lewis Carroll Shelf Award.

ABOUT THE POEMS "Lisa's Fingerprints" is from *Fingers Are Always Bringing Me News.* Written from a child's point of view, the poem tells what makes Lisa unique. "Who Am I?" is about a child's conversation with the elements of nature.

Reading the Poems

Help students set a purpose for reading.

Remind students that David Bernstein wanted to be different from the other Davids. Then ask students if they have ever been told how much they look like other members of their family. Discuss how this makes them feel.

Ask students to predict what, according to the poets, can make children feel different and special. Then have them listen to or read the poems.

Responding to the Poems

Return to the purpose for reading.

Ask students whether their predictions were confirmed. Discuss what makes the child in each poem unique. Read the poems aloud to students. Then invite them to read the poems with you.

Encourage students to respond creatively.

You may wish to use the following activity for responding to the poems:

DISCUSSING DIFFERENCES Have students make thumbprints, fingerprints, or handprints, using washable ink or watercolor paint. Then ask pairs of students to examine and compare their prints, using a magnifying glass. Elicit from students that although there may be similarities, each person's prints are unique. **LISTENING/SPEAKING**

TEACHING TIP

You may want to read the poems aloud before students read them independently so that they may hear the rhythm.

MEETING INDIVIDUAL NEEDS

SECOND-LANGUAGE SUPPORT Students may need help understanding references to *wing, paw, hoof,* and *fin* in the last line of "Lisa's Fingerprints." Define the words, and explain that each represents a different kind of animal.

LISA'S FINGERPRINTS/WHO AM I? / **T115**

PAGES 76–77 LISA'S FINGERPRINTS/WHO AM I?

Lisa's Fingerprints

by Mary O'Neill

Some say I have my mother's nose,
My father's eyes, my uncle's toes,
And so I think it is just fine
My fingerprints are only mine.
Not my father, or my mother,
Or my sister or my brother,
Those now, before, or after me
Will lack this nonconformity.
No set of prints whose every line
Matches yours, or matches mine.
Is this distinction true within
The world of wing, paw, hoof, and fin?

Expanding the Poems Why do you think Lisa says "And so I think it is just fine/My fingerprints are only mine"? (Accept reasonable responses: Lisa probably does not like being compared to her mother, her father, and her uncle, so having fingerprints that are unlike anyone else's makes her happy.) INFERENTIAL: DRAWING CONCLUSIONS

The last line of the poem refers to animal prints. Do you think animals are unique and as different as people are? (Responses will vary.) CRITICAL: EXPRESSING PERSONAL OPINIONS

Who Am I?
by Felice Holman
illustrated by Karen Barbour

The trees ask me,
And the sky,
And the sea asks me
　Who am I?

The grass asks me,
And the sand,
And the rocks ask me
　Who I am.

The wind tells me
At nightfall,
And the rain tells me
　Someone small.

Someone small
Someone small
　But a piece
　　of
　　it
　　all.

Expanding the Poems What is talking to the child in the poem? (trees, sky, sea, grass, sand, rocks, wind, rain) **What does this tell you about the poem?** (It is a fantasy.) CRITICAL: DISTINGUISHING BETWEEN FANTASY AND REALITY

Appreciating Literature

Have students share personal responses.

Have students work in small groups to discuss the poems. Provide a general question such as the following to help the groups begin:

The child asks the wind and the rain "Who am I?" Do you think the answer, "Someone small, but a piece of it all," is a good one? Why or why not?

 **PERSONAL JOURNAL** Have students use their personal journals to write about ideas and feelings discussed in the groups.

Writer's Journal

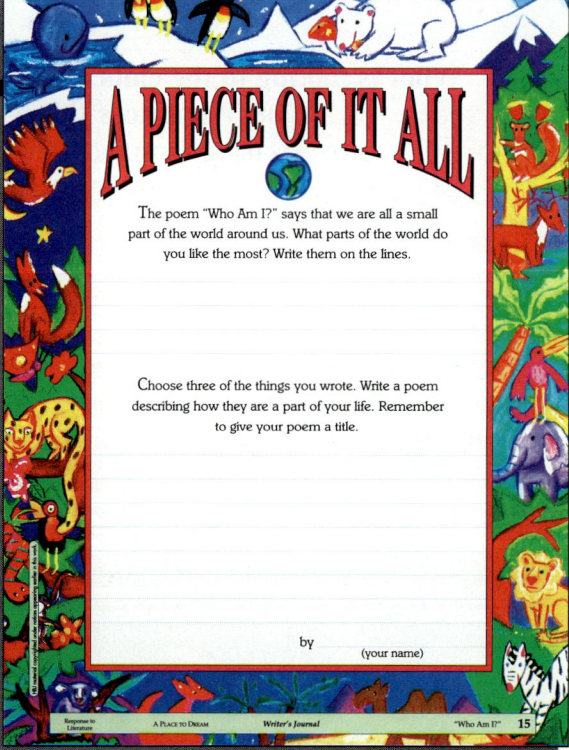

Writer's Journal

OPTIONAL INDEPENDENT PRACTICE

WRITER'S JOURNAL
pages 14–15: Writing a creative response

T118 / *A PLACE TO DREAM*, UNIT 1

THEME WRAP-UP

Discussing the Theme

Remind students that the selections in this theme showed how people are different and special.

Discussion Question

PAGE 79 Ali Baba Bernstein, Lisa, and the author of "Who Am I?" all want you to see just how different they are. Ali Baba has even changed his name to be different. Do you think a new name or a nickname could make you act a certain way? Explain why you think as you do. (Responses will vary.) CRITICAL: EXPRESSING PERSONAL OPINIONS

Theme Wrap-Up

Being Different

Ali Baba Bernstein, Lisa, and the author of "Who Am I?" all want you to see just how different they are. Ali Baba even changes his name to be different. Do you think a new name or a nickname could make you act a certain way? Explain why you think as you do.

WRITER'S WORKSHOP

Write a paragraph about yourself. Give details that tell how you are special.

Writer's Choice: You might want to write about the ways in which people are the same instead of how they are different. Choose an idea, and write about it. Share your idea.

79

Writer's Workshop

See pages T120–T121 for suggestions for guiding students through the writing process as they respond to the literature. WRITING PROCESS: AN INFORMATIONAL PARAGRAPH

Writer's Choice
Students may need help deciding what form of writing to use. Suggest that they look through the table of contents in their Student Anthology to help them think about forms. You may also want to have students refer to the *Language Handbook* for help.

Encourage students to share their work in a special way, such as creating a booklet with other students, organizing a read-aloud, or framing their work inside a collage.

THEME WRAP-UP / T119

Writer's Workshop

Paragraph of Information

Theme Wrap-Up

Students write a paragraph of information about themselves, telling how they are special and different from everyone else.

To prepare students for writing a paragraph of information, ask them to recall details about how David Bernstein was special in "Ali Baba Bernstein." List the details on the board. Then ask students if they think they could use these details to write about David Bernstein in a paragraph. Tell students that a paragraph in which the detail sentences tell facts about the topic or main idea is called a paragraph of information.

Use the Writer's Workshop assignment on page 79 as you work through the writing process with students.

ALTERNATIVE TOPICS If you wish, allow students to choose their own topics for writing. Suggest to students that they refer to the *Language Handbook* for an explanation of the writing process for paragraphs of information. See Writing Model, page R92.

LANGUAGE HANDBOOK Writing to Inform, pages 48–49; Paragraph of Information, page 51

Prewriting

Suggest that students gather information about themselves by brainstorming details in a list, looking in their journals, or making and filling in a chart similar to this one.

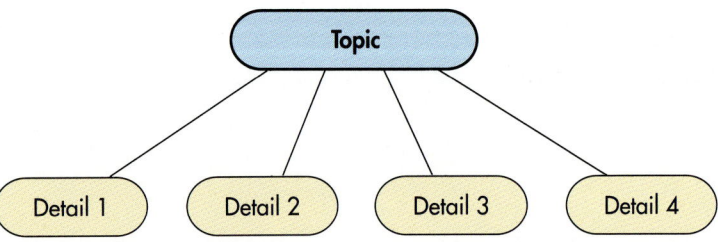

Drafting

Have students write a draft of their paragraphs of information. Remind them to

- write a strong beginning sentence that tells the topic of the information paragraph.
- refer to their prewriting notes or charts for details.

In this case, you might suggest that they freewrite without worrying about order, grammar, spelling, or mechanics. Remind students that they can revise later.

Responding and Revising

Before students share their paragraphs of information with partners, suggest that they

- highlight the topic sentence and underline the detail sentences.
- delete any sentences that don't give information about the topic.
- add any details that are missing.

Then have student writers read their work aloud in a peer conference. Have writers and listeners answer the following questions and complete the following task:

Listener	Writer
Does the paragraph of information have a topic sentence that tells the main idea of the paragraph? Do any details seem to be missing? Is the paragraph written in a clear and interesting way?	When you read your paragraph of information aloud, do you notice any details missing? Are some parts better than others? Jot down thoughts about improvements.

COMPUTER TIP

REVISING Word processing programs on computers make it easy to combine subjects or predicates in sentences. Have students explore the cut-and-paste function for this purpose.

Proofreading

Offer the following tips as students proofread:

- Check that verb tenses are consistent.
- Make sure the paragraph is indented.
- Correct misspelled words.

MINI-CONFERENCE STRATEGY Help students locate verb-tense errors by directing their attention to any shifts in time with observations such as "In this sentence you use *run*, while in the next sentence you use *ran*."

Publishing Options

ALI BABA DAY Tell students to prepare their paragraphs for a special "Ali Baba Day." Have them make a bulletin board display honoring Ali Baba Bernstein. Then have students make a neat copy of their paragraphs of information but leave off their names. If students like, they can sign the work with a fanciful new name. Have students post their paragraphs. Encourage other students to guess who wrote the paragraphs.

ORAL PRESENTATION Students may volunteer to read their paragraphs aloud to their classmates. Suggest that they first practice reading aloud, using clear pronunciation.

Assessment Options

STUDENT SELF-ASSESSMENT Encourage students to summarize the writing experience by responding to this question in their journals:

- **How did the prewriting information help once you began drafting your paragraph?**

You may also want to have students complete the Self-Assessment Checklist in the *Portfolio Assessment Teacher's Guide*.

WRITING OBSERVATION RECORDS Note students' return to an earlier stage in the writing process, demonstrating an understanding of the recursiveness of the process.

After students publish, you may want to have them add their paragraphs of information to their portfolios.

GRAMMAR CONNECTION

Revising: Combining Sentences

Using Transparency B, share the examples with students to help them see how combining subjects or predicates helps them avoid short, choppy sentences and adds variety to their writing. Point out that combining the subjects or predicates of two sentences also avoids repeating words.

> **Transparency B**
> **David's Choices**
>
> **BEFORE**
> David loves to read books. He enjoys <u>reading about baseball</u>. He enjoys <u>reading about weather</u>. <u>His father</u> goes with him to the library each weekend. <u>His sister</u> goes with him to the library each weekend, too.
>
> **AFTER**
> David loves to read books. He enjoys reading about <u>baseball and weather</u>. <u>His father and sister</u> go with him to the library each weekend.

Have students work in small groups to share their writing and to check for places where subjects or predicates can be combined.

LANGUAGE HANDBOOK *Expanding Your Writing, page 23; Subject, page 176; Predicate, page 178*

WRITER'S WORKSHOP / T121

Unit 1 • BEING SPECIAL

THEME OPENER

Listen to This!

Meet the Orchestra

T125   A NONFICTION SELECTION by Ann Hayes
Which orchestral instruments sound like the color blue? Which are triumphant and gallant? Which crash like thunder?

Music, Music for Everyone

T153   A REALISTIC FICTION STORY by Vera B. Williams
The money jar has been empty ever since Grandma became sick. Will the Oak Street Band be able to fill it again?

Words from the Author: Vera B. Williams

T172   A LETTER
Vera B. Williams describes for readers the time and energy that went into creating Music, Music for Everyone.

For pacing suggestions, see page T124.

THEME

Listen to This!

You can enjoy music by making music. You can also enjoy music by being part of the audience. In the following selections, you'll read about the instruments that make up a symphony orchestra. You'll also meet four friends who form a neighborhood band.

CONTENTS

MEET THE ORCHESTRA
by Ann Hayes

MUSIC, MUSIC FOR EVERYONE
written and illustrated by Vera B. Williams

WORDS FROM THE AUTHOR AND ILLUSTRATOR: VERA B. WILLIAMS

Discussing the Theme

Ask students to look at the illustration on Student Anthology page 80 and read the information on page 81. Then have them speculate about what kind of music they will read about and what they will learn about music.

Portfolio Assessment

Remind students to keep their writing responses for the selections in "Listen to This!" in their portfolios. Remind them also to add thoughts to their personal journals about books they have read independently.

 This symbol is a reminder that you might want to encourage students to save their work in their portfolios.

Harcourt Brace Big Book

A Chair for My Mother, another story written and illustrated by Vera B. Williams, may be shared at appropriate times throughout the unit.

THEME OPENER

Managing the Literature-Based Classroom

Encourage Involvement

To encourage students to participate in discussions with the whole class, you may want to vary seating arrangements. For greater informality, have students draw their chairs into a circle. Or have them set their chairs close together in two or three rows to make a mini-auditorium. While a student is speaking, he or she sits in a special chair facing the group.

Reading Corner

A comfortable reading corner is an ideal place for individual students to spend time between scheduled activities or after finishing assigned work. You may wish to feature books and magazines that relate to the theme.

Pacing

This theme has been designed to take about two weeks to complete, depending on your students' needs.

MEETING INDIVIDUAL NEEDS

LOW-ACHIEVING STUDENTS Encourage students to share their own experiences related to the theme and the selections. If you determine that their personal experiences are somewhat limited, provide additional background information, using filmstrips, pictures, magazines, and maps.

GIFTED AND TALENTED After students have finished reading and discussing "Meet the Orchestra" and "Music, Music for Everyone," encourage partners to imagine what a musician from the orchestra and a musician from the Oak Street Band might talk about. Encourage students to role-play the two musicians having a conversation about performing or about their instruments' voices. *Challenge Cards* provide additional activities to challenge students. Challenge notes throughout the lesson plans suggest additional activities to stimulate critical and creative thinking.

SPECIAL-EDUCATION STUDENTS Some students may benefit from using a graphic organizer to record details as they read. Students can then refer to it during group or class discussions about the selection.

STUDENTS ACQUIRING ENGLISH You may wish to record the selections, or passages from each, and have students listen as they read along. Second-Language Support notes throughout the lesson plans offer strategies to help students acquiring English to understand the selection.

Meet the Orchestra

written by Ann Hayes
illustrated by Karmen Thompson

Meet the Orchestra
pages 82–93

	READING	LANGUAGE ARTS	CROSS-CURRICULAR CONNECTIONS
PART 1 *Reading the Literature* pages T128–T136	**Building Background** **Vocabulary Strategies** **Prereading Strategies** K-W-L Chart Setting a Purpose **Options for Reading**	**Spelling** Pretest Spelling-Vocabulary Connection Generalization: Long Vowel Sounds **Grammar Connection** Reviewing Predicates	**Cultural Awareness** Indonesian orchestras **Social Studies** Yoruba language
PART 2 *Responding to the Literature* pages T137–T143	**Personal Response** **Cooperative Response** **Summarizing the Literature** **Critical Thinking Activity** Opinion Web **Vocabulary Workshop** Key Words Pronunciation Key	**Language Arts Workshop** **Reading** Readers Theatre, ancient instruments **Writing** paragraph of information **Listening and Speaking** symphony **Reviewing Spelling Words** Posttest **Grammar Review** Predicates **Grammar Minilesson** Common Nouns	**Social Studies** Flute-Playing at the Pyramids **Music** *Peter and the Wolf*
PART 3 *Learning Through the Literature* pages T144–T152	**Introduce** Comprehension: Main Idea and Details (Tested) Comprehension Strategy: Synthesizing Ideas Study Skills: Test Taking	**Reading** Sound Waves in Motion **Writing** Great Band and Orchestra Leaders **Listening and Speaking** A Band of Our Own Jump-Rope Contest	**Science** Sound Waves in Motion **Art/Music** A Band of Our Own **Social Studies** Great Band and Orchestra Leaders **Health** Jump-Rope Contest **Multicultural Perspectives** Leaders of the Band

OPTIONAL MATERIALS
Charts/Transparencies 8–11
Integrated Spelling pp. 22–25; TE pp. T33–T38
Practice Book pp. 24–31
Writer's Journal pp. 16–17
Alternative Teaching Strategies pp. 6, 48–51
Language Handbook pp. 48–49, 51, 91, 93
Grammar Practice pp. 18–19
Family Involvement Activities: Unit 1, pp. 1–4
Response Card 10
Project Cards 9A, 9B, 10A, 10B, 11

MEETING INDIVIDUAL NEEDS
Second-Language Support pp. T129, T130, T134, T143, T145, T147, T149
Mainstreaming p. T130
Reteach pp. T143, T145, T147, T149
Challenge pp. T145, T147, T149

FAMILY INVOLVEMENT Encourage family members to play their favorite musical recordings for one another and then talk about this music. See *Family Involvement Activities.*

Key Words
orchestra
instruments
musicians
shrill
audience
rhythm
chords

T126 / A PLACE TO DREAM, UNIT 1

Selection Summary

In this nonfiction selection, Ann Hayes describes instruments found in the string, woodwind, brass, and percussion sections of a symphony orchestra. Instruments with strings can be plucked or bowed; musicians play woodwinds and brass instruments by blowing air into them. Percussion instruments are struck to produce booms, bangs, dings, pings, and crashes. Hayes uses figurative language and colorful descriptions to portray the sounds of sixteen instruments. The text is accompanied by humorous illustrations of formally attired animal musicians. The conductor, portrayed by a lion with an artistic-looking mane, is introduced at the end.

About the Author

Ann Hayes loves attending orchestra performances. She is an artist as well as a writer and has written and illustrated several activity books for children. An avid cross-country skier, Hayes lives in Boulder, Colorado. Her idea for *Meet the Orchestra* grew from her interest in the Colorado Music Festival Orchestra.

Additional Reading

OTHER THEME-RELATED BOOKS

*Mozart Tonight by Julie Downing. Bradbury, 1991. AVERAGE

Caribbean Carnival: Songs of the West Indies by Irving Burgie. Tambourine Books, 1992. EASY

The Musical Life of Gustave Mole by Katherine Meyrick. Child's Play, 1990. AVERAGE

Peter and the Wolf retold by Selina Hastings. Henry Holt, 1990. AVERAGE

BOOKS FOR APPLYING STRATEGIES: MAIN IDEA AND DETAILS, SYNTHESIZING IDEAS

Fishy Facts by Ivan Chermayeff. Harcourt Brace, 1994. EASY

A Very Young Musician by Jill Krementz. Simon and Schuster, 1991. AVERAGE

Alligators and Music by Donald Elliott. Gambit, 1976. AVERAGE

*Available as a Harcourt Brace PASSPORTS title

PART 1

Reading the Literature

Building Background

Access prior knowledge and build vocabulary concepts.

Tell students that "Meet the Orchestra" describes different instruments found in orchestras. Ask volunteers to tell what an orchestra is and to name some of the instruments played in an orchestra. Encourage them to tell what each sounds like and how it is played. Record their responses on the board.

Have students quickwrite in a K-W-L chart.

Distribute the K-W-L chart on page R106, or draw a K-W-L chart on the board and have students copy it. Model for students how to fill in the first column with what they know about orchestras.

What I **K**now	What I **W**ant to Know	What I **L**earned
Orchestras include violins, horns, and drums. A conductor helps the musicians play together.		

Vocabulary Strategies

Introduce Key Words and strategies.

Display Chart/Transparency 8 or the paragraphs on it. Have students read the sentences silently. Encourage them to use phonetic and structural analysis along with context clues. For example, students might see that *musicians* is based on the word *music*.

Chart/Transparency 8   Key Words

Jody tried out for the school orchestra today. Of all the instruments in the orchestra, he chose to play the violin. He has been playing the violin for six months. Like many other beginning musicians, Jody used to sound shrill and screechy. But he always believed that someday he would be good enough to play for a large audience.

Jody's friend Lauren plays the kettledrums in the rhythm section. The kettledrum never plays chords, or combinations of two or more notes. The violin seldom does. But each takes skill and talent to play.

CULTURAL AWARENESS

Explain that instruments found in orchestras throughout the world can vary widely. For instance, an Indonesian orchestra, called a *gamelan*, includes gongs and *gambangs*, which are similar to xylophones.

Key Words

orchestra
instruments
musicians
shrill
audience
rhythm
chords

KEY WORDS DEFINED

orchestra group that plays music together

instruments devices used to make musical sounds

musicians people who are skilled in music

shrill high-pitched, piercing

audience group of listeners, as at a concert

rhythm repetition of a sound; a type of instrument that repeats a sound

chords combinations of two or more musical tones sounded together

T128 / A PLACE TO DREAM, UNIT 1

Check all students' understanding.

Invite students to play "Probable Sentences" with the Key Words. Display a chart like the following, and have volunteers fill in the second column with sentences that they think could appear in the selection. Then have other volunteers read aloud each sentence, and conduct an all-student vote on whether each new word is used correctly. Call on students to support their votes. You may wish to keep the chart to return to after reading. STRATEGY: EXAMPLES

PROBABLE SENTENCES

Word	Sentence
orchestra	
instruments	
musicians	
shrill	
audience	
rhythm	
chords	

Integrate spelling with vocabulary.

SPELLING-VOCABULARY CONNECTION *Integrated Spelling* Lesson 4 reinforces the spelling of words with long vowel sounds, such as *meet* and *beat* from the selection. In addition to these words, the Words to Explore help reinforce the concept of orchestras as it relates to the selection.

SPELLING PRETEST You may want to use the Pretest/Posttest Sentences on page T33 in *Integrated Spelling Teacher's Edition* to assess students' knowledge of the spelling generalization.

Spelling

Spelling Words	Words to Explore
1. beat	audience
2. clay	instruments
3. clean	musicians
4. hay	orchestra
5. main	
6. meet	*Your Own Words*
7. paid	13.
8. raise	14.
9. sleep	15.
10. teach	16.
11. three	
12. tree	

Spelling generalization: long vowel sounds

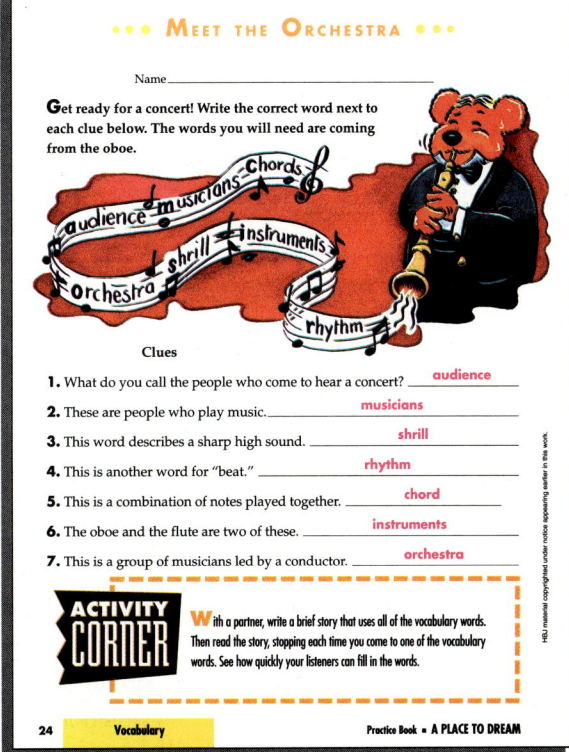

Practice Book

MEETING INDIVIDUAL NEEDS

SECOND-LANGUAGE SUPPORT Provide students with a photograph or an illustration of an orchestra from an encyclopedia or a book about music. Have each student work with a partner proficient in English to describe the orchestra, using as many of the Key Words as possible. See also the manual *Alternative Teaching Strategies*, pages 6, 48–51.

OPTIONAL INDEPENDENT PRACTICE

INTEGRATED SPELLING
pages 22–25: More Words with Long Vowels

PRACTICE BOOK
page 24: Reinforcing Key Words
NOTE: This page may be completed now or after students have read the story.

MEET THE ORCHESTRA / T129

Prereading Strategies

K-W-L Chart

Discuss nonfiction, and have students preview the selection.

Tell students that "Meet the Orchestra" is a nonfiction selection. Discuss with students the purpose of nonfiction. (to give readers information about real-life topics) Explain that in "Meet the Orchestra," they will learn facts about orchestra instruments.

Have students preview the selection by thinking about the title, reading the first two pages, and looking at the illustrations. Ask what is *not* realistic about the illustrations. (Animals do not wear clothes or play in orchestras.)

Encourage students to make predictions.

Use the K-W-L charts students began in the Building Background activity. Tell students to fill in the second column with questions they would like answered.

Model forming questions, if necessary.

If students need help thinking of questions that they would like answered, offer some examples:

What I **K**now	What I **W**ant to Know	What I **L**earned
Orchestras include violins, horns, and drums. A conductor helps the musicians play together.	What are some percussion instruments? How are woodwinds different from brass instruments?	

Setting a Purpose

Encourage students to set purposes.

Have students set a purpose for reading, using the questions in the second column of their K-W-L charts.

If students have difficulty setting a purpose, offer this suggestion:

I'm going to read to find out the differences among string, woodwind, brass, and percussion instruments.

MEETING INDIVIDUAL NEEDS

SECOND-LANGUAGE SUPPORT Remind students to use picture clues to help them understand the selection. See also the manual *Alternative Teaching Strategies*, pages 6, 48–51.

SUPPORT FOR MAINSTREAMING Build students' motivation for reading by having them briefly discuss the types of music they like. If students are interested in popular music like rock and roll, point out that some of the greatest popular musicians first learned their trade by playing classical or traditional music.

Options for Reading

SUSTAINED SILENT READING	STRATEGIC READING	READER RESPONSE GROUPS	TEACHER READ-ALOUD
After students finish reading, encourage them to discuss the questions at the end of the selection with another student who has read independently.	To stimulate discussion, use the suggestions that appear on pages T131, T133, and T136.	Follow the suggestions for Literature Circles on page T131. While reading, students should note questions and comments about the selection that they would like to discuss with their group.	You may want to read aloud the first four pages of the selection. Point out that instruments are categorized by family, and each instrument within that family is described under its own heading.

MEET THE ORCHESTRA PAGES 82–83

Meet the Orchestra

written by Ann Hayes
illustrated by Karmen Thompson

The orchestra plays tonight. The audience has arrived. The musicians are coming on stage with their instruments. What a lot of different kinds they play—strings, woodwinds, brass, and percussion.

Violin

Players with like instruments sit together in "families." The violin belongs to the string family, along with the viola, the cello, and the big string bass. You play all of these with a bow or pluck them with your fingers. The violin is the smallest of the string instruments. Its song can be bright as laughter, light as air, soft as a whisper, or sad as a tear.

Viola

As instruments get bigger, their voices get lower. The viola looks and sounds like a big brother to the violin. It has a deeper tone, reminding you of evening shadows, cloudy skies, and the color blue.

Reader Response Groups

LITERATURE CIRCLES Have groups of three to five students read silently up to page 87. Then they should pause briefly to discuss what they learned about the instruments. You may want to distribute Response Card 10 (How Do I Know What I Know?), found on page R88, or provide the following questions for discussion:

- What do you know so far about families of instruments? How do the illustrations help you know this?
- What questions do you have that are still not answered?

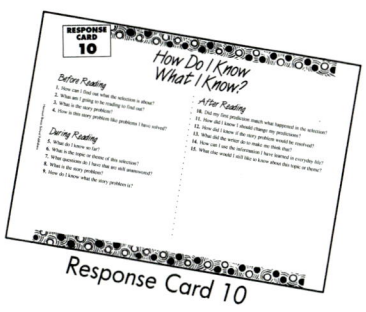

Response Card 10

Strategic Reading

SET PURPOSE/PREDICT: PAGES 82–87 Have students read through page 87. Encourage them to use the questions in the second column of their K-W-L charts to tell what they will be reading to find out.

MEET THE ORCHESTRA / T131

PAGES 84–85 MEET THE ORCHESTRA

Cello
You can't tuck a cello under your chin the way you do a violin or viola. It is so big you must rest it on the floor. The cello's rich, mellow voice speaks of deep feelings like joy and sadness. It can remind you of the calm beauty of a drifting swan and of the color purple.

String Bass
The string bass is the grandpapa of the string family. It is so tall that you must stand up or sit on a high stool to play it. When bowed, its low notes moan and groan. When plucked, its booming sound helps other musicians to keep the beat.

Flute
The flute belongs to the woodwind family, along with the piccolo, oboe, bassoon, and clarinet. You blow into these instruments to play them. At one time, all of them were made of wood; today the flute is often made of silver or even of gold. To play the flute, you hold it sideways, tighten your lips, and blow across the air hole. With practice, you can trill like a bird or play slow, quivering notes as cool as a mountain stream.

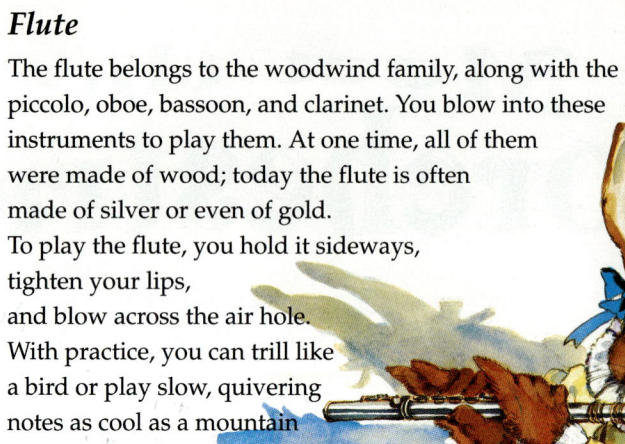

Piccolo
The piccolo, little sister to the flute, loves attention and always gets it. This tiny flute is so shrill you can't help hearing it. Its high notes almost pierce your eardrums. Yet everyone loves the piccolo because it has such a great sense of fun.

84

GRAMMAR CONNECTION
REVIEWING PREDICATES   Point out the sentence on page 85 that begins *You blow into these instruments . . .* Have a volunteer name the subject of the sentence. *(You)* Have another volunteer identify the predicate. *(blow into these instruments to play them)* Remind students that every sentence they write needs both a subject and a predicate.

Vocabulary Strategy   Point out the word *woodwind* on page 85. Ask students how they might figure out its meaning. (Use context clues such as *At one time, all of them were made of wood* to figure out that *woodwind* describes a group of similar instruments.)   **STRATEGY: CONTEXT CLUES**

T132 / A PLACE TO DREAM, UNIT 1

MEET THE ORCHESTRA PAGES 86–87

Oboe

The oboe has a mouthpiece made of reed. The reed can be fussy and troublesome. Then it honks like a goose with a bad cold.

But usually the oboe can be trusted. The oboe plays that single note to which the whole orchestra tunes just before the concert begins. Its voice may remind you of faraway castles at sunset, autumn leaves, and the sadness of saying good-bye to someone you love.

Bassoon

The bassoon is like a large, folded oboe. It also has a reed mouthpiece. Its voice, like its name, has a kind of loneliness. Yet the bassoon can also be playful. It chats and chuckles with the other instruments. You often hear it chugging along like a tough little engine. Can't you almost see puffs of smoke coming out the top?

Clarinet

Here are two different clarinets. The straight one is nimble and quick. It tootles up and down the scale, never tripping over a note. Its cool tones melt in your ears just like ice cream melts in your mouth.

This very long clarinet is bent at both ends so that it doesn't touch the floor when played. Its low, slow notes may remind you of clouds drifting across the moon or a snake swaying to a snake charmer's music.

B-flat clarinet   *bass clarinet*

87

Strategic Reading

MODELING A STRATEGY: PAGES 82–87   Ask students to name any instruments whose sounds they had difficulty imagining as they read pages 82–87.

THINK ALOUD   You may want to model a visualizing strategy with this think-aloud: *I don't understand how a cello's voice could make someone think of "the calm beauty of a drifting swan." I reread page 84, which says that the cello has a "rich, mellow voice." Then I try to form a picture in my mind of a swan floating on a peaceful lake. I understand now that the cello's voice is deep, soothing, and graceful.*   USING FIX-UP STRATEGIES/ VISUALIZING

SET PURPOSE/PREDICT: PAGES 88–93   Invite students to predict what instruments or other topics they will learn about in the selection. Encourage them to confirm their predictions as they read the rest of the selection.

MEET THE ORCHESTRA / **T133**

PAGES 88–89 MEET THE ORCHESTRA

French Horn

Make way for the brass family, the powerhouse of the orchestra! Even when they play softly, you can sense a huge cat crouched to spring.

The brass do not have reed mouthpieces. Your lips buzzing against the metal mouthpiece produce the sound. The tubes of the horns magnify it, as a bullhorn magnifies an announcer's voice.

The French horn is like a big, bright bell at the end of a long, thin tube. The tube is coiled, so the horn can be played with one hand on the valves and the other inside the bell. The hand inside softens the sound. (Uncoiled, the French horn would reach all the way across a very large room. Someone would surely trip over it.)

The French horn has many voices. It can calm you with its gentle tones or thrill you with its gallant hunting call.

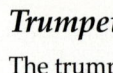

Trumpet

The trumpet's shorter tube makes it look easier to play than some of the fancier brass. But is it? No, say the trumpeters. You must work just as hard to learn it.

The trumpet's call is noble and exciting. It can remind you of flags flying, soldiers marching, and royal persons entering a great hall.

Tuba

The tuba has a huge bell and a very long tube. Do you remember that the bigger strings have deeper voices? The same is true of the horns. The bigger ones make lower sounds.

The tuba seldom carries a tune. It is more of a rhythm instrument. Its "umpahs" help the brass to keep the beat, just as the thump of the bass does for the strings.

 Informal Assessment

VOCABULARY STRATEGY To assess how effectively students use vocabulary strategies as they read, ask questions such as these:

- Are there words in this selection that are new to you? Point out one. (Possible examples on page 88: *powerhouse, crouched, magnify*)
- How can you figure out what this word means?
- Do you have to know this word's meaning to understand what you are reading? If not, what should you do? (Read on. After reading, you might look up this word in a dictionary.)

Second-Language Support Point out the phrases *flags flying* and *carries a tune* on page 89. If possible, wave a flag to show students how flags look when they are flying. Explain that the expression *carries a tune* means "sings the notes of a song."

MEETING INDIVIDUAL NEEDS

T134 / A PLACE TO DREAM, UNIT 1

Timpani or Kettledrums

The big kettledrums sit in the "kitchen," or percussion section of the orchestra. Everything that is beaten, banged, dinged, or pinged belongs there.

Have you ever heard the orchestra rumble with the sound of distant thunder? Suddenly it explodes with a "BOOM-BOOM-BOOM!" That is the timpani. They look like big kettles sitting side by side. Each has a slightly different pitch. You beat rapidly from one to another, making the thunder crash and roll.

Cymbals

The cymbals look like a pair of pot lids. When banged together, they crash with the fury of an electric storm. If the kettledrums give you the roll of thunder, the cymbals give you the flash of lightning. Hear them ring out just when the music reaches a peak of excitement. This is a proud moment for the whole orchestra!

Piano

When you sit down at the piano, the black and white keys make your fingers want to dance. From the center you can play them all—the high ones on your right and the low ones on your left.

When you hear a murmur of notes burst into thundering chords, then fade into silence, it is probably the voice of the piano. When it is over, you may want to clap—or perhaps even cry.

Conductor

Now, meet the conductor. He is often called "maestro," which means master of the orchestra. That he is, for he leads the musicians at all times. He does it mostly by talking with his hands! In his right hand he holds a small stick—the baton. With it he beats time. His left hand motions, "You play now!" "Be quick!" "Livelier!" "Louder!" "Softer!" "Ah, that's perfect!" A raised eyebrow says, "You're playing off key!"

Social Studies Connection Point out the illustration of kettledrums on page 90. Tell students that Yoruba drummers of western Africa often play the *iya-ilu*, or talking drum, to communicate with one another. The Yoruba language is based on tones, and a word spoken in a high voice may have a different meaning from the same word spoken in a low voice. The *iya-ilu* has leather thongs stretched lengthwise around it. To change tones, the drummer presses the thongs while striking the drum. The drum can produce sounds very similar to Yoruba words. Skillful drummers use this drum to recite poetry.

See page T141 for information found on Project Card 9B.

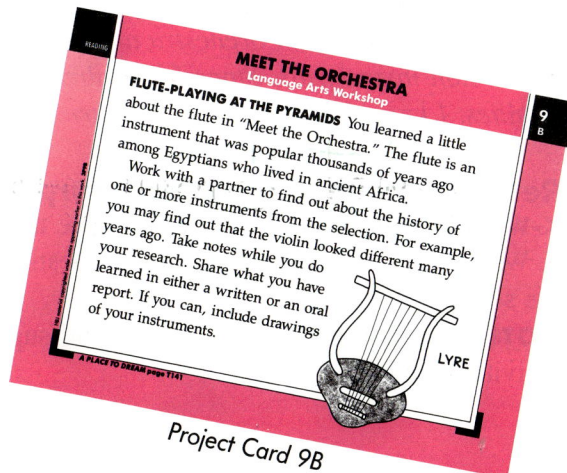

Project Card 9B

PAGES 92–93 MEET THE ORCHESTRA

The musicians have taken their places. The strings, who are by far the largest group of players, sit in front, almost filling the stage. The woodwinds sit close together at the center. The brass and percussion are in back.

The conductor strides on stage in front of the orchestra, raises his baton . . .

Let the music start!

The orchestra played tonight. Now it is time to go home. Like the voices of their instruments, the musicians drift off into the night.

What instrument would you want to play in an orchestra? Tell why.

Which instruments probably make the softest sounds? Which probably make the loudest sounds? How do you know?

In the story, the conductor is a lion. Why is a lion a good animal to cast as the conductor?

WRITE   Think about a song or a kind of music you enjoy. Write three sentences that tell what you like about this music.

92

Strategic Reading

MODELING A STRATEGY: PAGES 88–93   Did what you read on pages 88–93 match your predictions?

THINK ALOUD   You may want to model confirming predictions: *I predicted I would learn about the brass and the percussion families—and I did. I based my prediction on what the author wrote at the beginning: The four families in an orchestra are the string, woodwind, brass, and percussion instruments. Since I had already learned about two of these families, I knew I had two more to learn about.*   CONFIRMING PREDICTIONS

Returning to the Predictions/Purpose
K-W-L CHART   Have students complete the third column of their K-W-L charts, and tell whether their questions were answered by the selection.

NOTE: Responses to the questions and support for the Write activity appear on page T137.

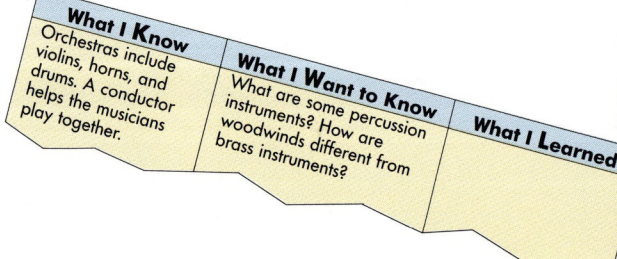

T136 / A PLACE TO DREAM, UNIT 1

PART 2

Responding to the Literature

Personal Response

Encourage critical thinking.

What instrument would you want to play in an orchestra? Tell why. (Responses will vary.) CRITICAL: EXPRESSING PERSONAL OPINIONS

Which instruments probably make the softest sounds? Which probably make the loudest sounds? How do you know? (Accept reasonable responses: The softest instruments might be the violin, which sounds "as soft as air," and the French horn, which can have "gentle tones." The loudest instruments might be the timpani, which sounds "like thunder"; the cymbals, which "crash"; and the piano, which can make "thundering chords.") INFERENTIAL: COMPARING AND CONTRASTING

In the story, the conductor is a lion. Why is a lion a good animal to cast as the conductor? (Accept reasonable responses: The lion is often called the king of the jungle, and the conductor is the master of an orchestra.) CRITICAL: MAKING JUDGMENTS

Encourage creative written responses.

WRITE Think about a song or a kind of music you enjoy. Write three sentences that tell what you like about the music. Encourage students to support their opinions with specific examples. CREATIVE: WRITING PERSONAL OPINIONS

Cooperative Response

Have reader response groups extend their discussions.

LITERATURE CIRCLES Encourage groups to discuss the most interesting facts they learned in "Meet the Orchestra." You may also want to have them discuss questions such as the following:

How has this book changed the way you understand the members and the instruments of an orchestra?

STRATEGY CONFERENCE

Discuss with students how completing the K-W-L chart helped them understand this nonfiction selection. Have students compare what they learned with what they knew before reading.

NOTE

An additional writing activity for this selection appears on page T140.

MEET THE ORCHESTRA / T137

Summarizing the Literature

Have students retell the selection and write a summary.

Help students fill in instrument webs like the one below for the string, brass, woodwind, and percussion families. Then have them retell the selection and write a short summary. See *Practice Book* page 25 below.

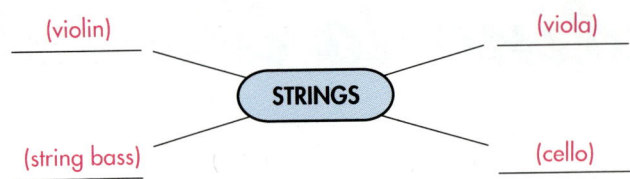

Critical Thinking Activity

Evaluate types of music.

BUILD AN OPINION WEB Suppose the author of "Meet the Orchestra" wanted to persuade people to listen to orchestral music. She could use her colorful descriptions of the different instruments to help convince others that orchestral music is beautiful and interesting. *What would you say to convince people to listen to your favorite kind of music?* Have students who like the same kind of music work in small groups to create a web with words and pictures that express the good points of the music. CRITICAL: EXPRESSING PERSONAL OPINIONS

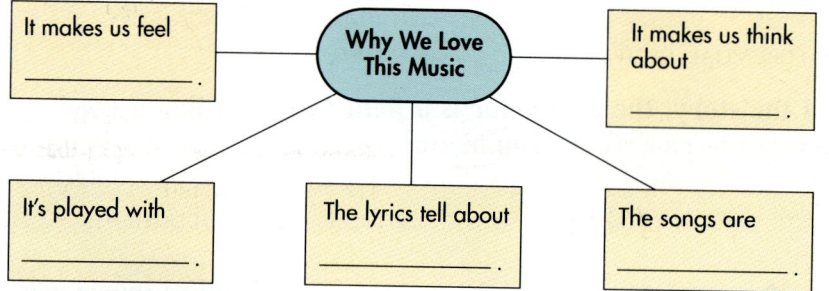

Writer's Journal

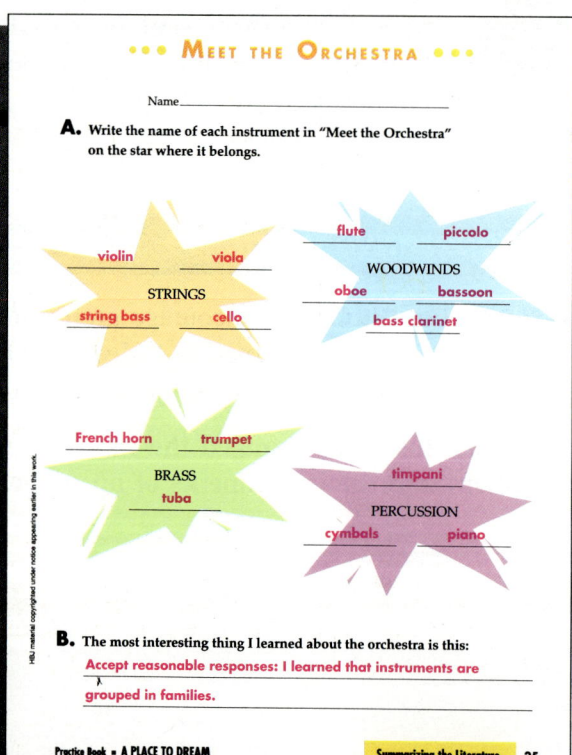

Practice Book

T138 / A PLACE TO DREAM, UNIT 1

Portfolio

STUDENT SELF-ASSESSMENT

Ask students how an instrument web can help them remember what they read. (Accept reasonable responses: The web shows how the instruments are grouped into families.) Encourage students to add their webs and their summaries to their portfolios.

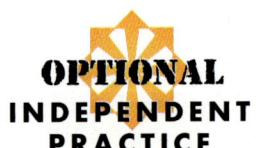

OPTIONAL INDEPENDENT PRACTICE

WRITER'S JOURNAL
page 16: Writing a personal response

PRACTICE BOOK
page 25: Summarizing the selection

VOCABULARY WORKSHOP

Reviewing Key Words

Display the Key Words, and then copy the following chart. Omit the words in parentheses. Tell students to copy the chart and then fill in the empty space above each set of clues with the correct Key Word.

(orchestra)	(instruments)	(musicians)	(shrill)
many people	French horns, trumpets, or tubas	play instruments well	piercing; high-pitched; screechy
(audience)	**(rhythm)**		**(chords)**
listens, watches, applauds	by helping to keep the beat		by playing two or more notes at the same time

OPTIONAL INDEPENDENT PRACTICE

PRACTICE BOOK page 26: Using a pronunciation key

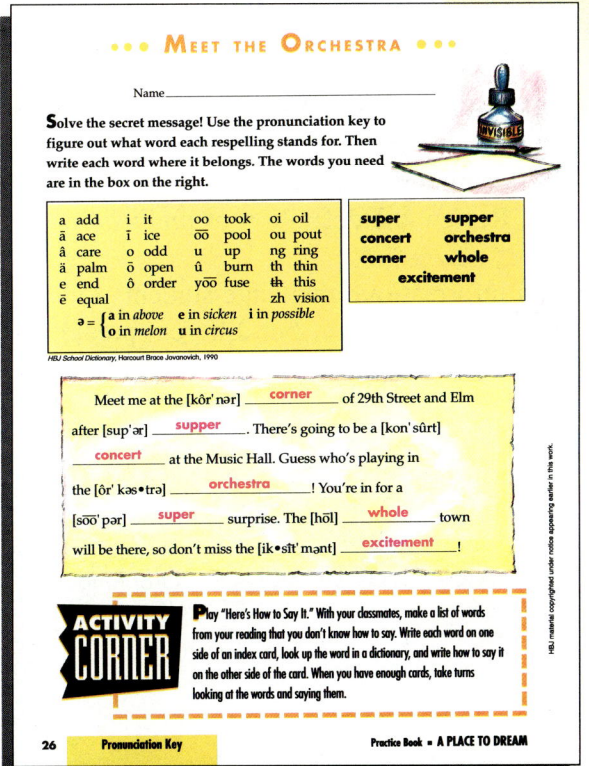

Extending Vocabulary

PRONUNCIATION KEY/MULTIPLE-MEANING WORDS

Write these three sentences on the board: *Jenny and her father fished for bass in the river. Chris's voice was too high to sing bass notes. Rich brought his big string bass to the rehearsal.* Have volunteers read the sentences aloud; help them with pronunciation as needed. Point out that *bass* can have different meanings and pronunciations. Have volunteers look up this word in a dictionary and identify the meaning used in each sentence on the board. If necessary, model using context clues to figure out word meaning. Explain that dictionaries provide respellings of words and a *key*, or guide, to help readers figure out how to pronounce them. Have students find two pronunciations for *bass* in the dictionary and identify which to use in each sentence.

On the board, make a chart like the following. Invite students to work in pairs to find two pronunciations and meanings for *tear* and to use each in a sentence. Challenge students to add *bow* and *wind* to the chart.

Word	Pronunciation	Meaning	Sentence
tear	(1. tir)	(a drop of clear salty water from the eye)	(The child wiped a tear from his eye.)
	(2. târ)	(to pull apart)	(George will tear the movie ticket for you.)

MEET THE ORCHESTRA / T139

Language Arts WORKSHOP

READING

Oral Rereading/Readers Theatre

COOPERATIVE LEARNING Have students form groups of six to eight. Group members should sign up to read the part of the narrator, the description of one of the sixteen instruments, or the description of the conductor. Each student will need to read two parts, and some students may need to read three. Remind students to read nonfiction slowly so that listeners will have time to understand the information. Tell students to read their passages silently before reading them aloud. An Encourager in each group can help individuals rehearse and encourage them to speak clearly and expressively. Students should practice with their groups before presenting their readings to the class. **LISTENING/SPEAKING/READING**

WRITING

Writing About the Literature

Available on Project Card 9A

 **WRITE A PARAGRAPH OF INFORMATION**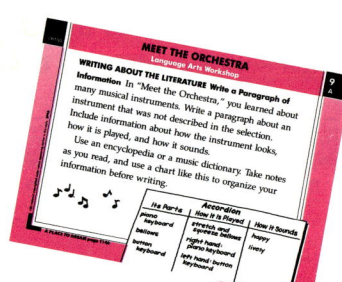
Remind students that the nonfiction selection they have just read describes sixteen instruments. Have each student think of another instrument that is not described in the selection and write a paragraph explaining how it looks and sounds, and how it is played. If students do not know, direct them to encyclopedias, music dictionaries, and other resource books. See Writing Model, page R92. **READING/WRITING**

Accordion		
Its Parts	**How It Is Played**	**How It Sounds**
piano keyboard, bellows, button keyboard	stretch and squeeze bellows; right hand plays piano keyboard; left hand plays button keyboard	happy, lively

GRAMMAR REVIEW: PREDICATES As students revise their paragraphs, remind them that each sentence must tell a complete thought. Each sentence needs a subject *and* a predicate. Review the definition of *predicate*. (the part of a sentence that tells what the subject is or does) To reinforce this information, challenge students to write sentences using the same subject but different predicates.

 **LANGUAGE HANDBOOK** Writing to Inform, pages 48–49, 51; Parts of a Sentence: Predicate, page 91

 **DAILY LANGUAGE PRACTICE** Oral language exercises are provided on pages R62–R63.

Language Arts WORKSHOP

READING

Flute-Playing at the Pyramids
Available on Project Card 9B

CULTURAL AWARENESS Some of the instruments described in "Meet the Orchestra" are similar to those that were played thousands of years ago. Tell students that an early form of flute, for example, was popular among Egyptians in ancient Africa. Have pairs of students find out about the history of other instruments described in the selection. Tell them to take notes as they read. When they finish their research, they can share it orally or in writing. Suggest that students also make drawings of the instruments they research. SPEAKING/READING/WRITING/VIEWING

LISTENING AND SPEAKING

Peter and the Wolf

Tell students that Russian composer Sergei Prokofiev (ser·gā′ prô·kôf′yif) wrote a classical music piece especially for children. In 1936, he wrote the story and music for *Peter and the Wolf*. Have students listen to a recording of this work and take notes on what they hear. You may want to play for them the version by Leonard Bernstein and the New York Philharmonic on Columbia Masterworks, 1973, CBS, Inc.—part of *The Sound of Genius Masterworks Library* series. Have students compare what they learn from listening to *Peter and the Wolf* with what they learned from reading "Meet the Orchestra." LISTENING/SPEAKING

SPELLING

Reviewing Spelling Words

SPELLING WORDS: *beat, clay, clean, hay, main, meet, paid, raise, sleep, teach, three, tree*

WORDS TO EXPLORE: *audience, instruments, musicians, orchestra*

Write the Spelling Words on a list visible only to you. Then have students form two teams. Read a word to a student on Team A, and ask that student to spell the word. If the speller answers correctly, cross the word off your list, and have the speller write it on the board under the heading *Team A*. If the speller answers incorrectly, the word remains on your list. When all the words have been crossed off your list, the team with the most correctly spelled words wins. LISTENING/SPEAKING/SPELLING

Use *Integrated Spelling* Lesson 4 to reinforce the Spelling Words and the Words to Explore. See pages T33–T38 in *Integrated Spelling Teacher's Edition*.

SPELLING POSTTEST You may want to use the Pretest/Posttest Sentences on *Integrated Spelling Teacher's Edition* page T33 to assess students' knowledge of the spelling generalization.

MEET THE ORCHESTRA / T141

Grammar MINI LESSON

Common Nouns

OBJECTIVE: *To understand that a common noun names any person, place, or thing and that all common nouns begin with a lowercase letter*

Oral Warm-Up

Write on the board the following sentences from "Meet the Orchestra." Call on volunteers to pantomime the words you have underlined.

- You play all of these with a <u>bow</u> or pluck them with your <u>fingers</u>.
- As <u>instruments</u> get bigger, their <u>voices</u> get lower.
- The big <u>kettledrums</u> sit in the "<u>kitchen</u>," or percussion section of the orchestra.
- They look like big <u>kettles</u> sitting side by side.

Discuss with students the idea that all these words name things or places. Then ask students to name some jobs that people might do if their careers are in music. (composer, player, teacher, singer)

Draw a chart on the board like the one below, and work with students to categorize each word they pantomimed or listed.

	Nouns
People	(composer) (player) (teacher) (singer)
Places	(kitchen)
Things	(instruments) (bow) (fingers) (voices) (kettledrums) (kettles)

Interactive Teaching

COMMON NOUNS Explain to students that the words on the chart which name people, places, or things are called **common nouns.** Point out that common nouns begin with a lowercase letter.

Work together to find more common nouns in various passages in the book. Have a volunteer copy a passage about a musical instrument onto the board, and allow students to work together to find the common nouns. "Cello" and "String Bass" (both on page 84) are two passages from the selection that lend themselves to this activity.

You may wish to extend the activity by having students brainstorm other musical instruments, such as saxophone, harmonica, koto, mandolin, and kalimba. Encourage them to help you compose a paragraph about one of the instruments. Have a volunteer write the paragraph on the board, and have other volunteers identify the common nouns in it.

LANGUAGE HANDBOOK
Common nouns, page 93

T142 / A PLACE TO DREAM, UNIT 1

Practice Activities

Nouns in an Interview

Assign each student a partner. Then ask partners to choose a particular instrument and research it. For their reference material, encourage students to go to the library to find books and encyclopedia articles about the instrument or to interview a student or a teacher who plays the instrument. (If the school has a music department, refer students there for firsthand access to the instrument.) After students have finished doing research about their instrument, have them plan an interview. Let one student be the interviewer, and the other, the interviewee. Partners should collaborate to write interview questions. Each question must contain at least one common noun. Encourage students' creativity by having them make props to hold and to wear, and encourage them to make their interviews humorous as well as factual. Designate a "Meet the Orchestra" day on which pairs of students present their interviews to the class. **VISUAL/AUDITORY/KINESTHETIC**

Performance Nouns

Have students write a paragraph about a musical performance they attended or about one they would like to attend. Encourage them to use common nouns to describe the people, places, and things they saw or would expect to see. Then have students exchange their work with a partner. Ask partners to read each other's paragraphs, place a check above all the common nouns, and make sure each one begins with a lowercase letter. Ask volunteers to read aloud and display the finished paragraphs.
VISUAL

MEETING INDIVIDUAL NEEDS

SECOND-LANGUAGE SUPPORT To provide extra practice, hold up objects and ask students to name each one. Write the nouns on the board. Then ask volunteers to choose a word from the list, read it aloud, and locate the object.

RETEACH Follow the visual, auditory, and kinesthetic/motor models on page R12.

OPTIONAL INDEPENDENT PRACTICE

PRACTICE BOOK
page 27: Identifying and using common nouns

GRAMMAR PRACTICE
pages 18–19: Using common nouns

Practice Book

MEET THE ORCHESTRA / T143

PART 3

Learning through the Literature

COMPREHENSION	
INTRODUCE	**Main Idea and Details**

OBJECTIVE: *To understand how details in a paragraph or passage support a stated or an unstated main idea*

Interactive Teaching

Focus on important points in the selection.

LITERATURE CONNECTION Ask volunteers to tell the most important points in "Meet the Orchestra." (Possible responses: Each instrument has a unique sound. The instruments are grouped in families. The voices of the instruments can remind listeners of different colors and feelings.) Explain that knowing how to recognize the main points in a selection can help students understand what they read.

Teach stated and unstated main idea.

MODEL FINDING MAIN IDEAS AND DETAILS Tell students that a main idea is the idea that the paragraph or passage is about. Supporting details give more information about the main idea. Sometimes the main idea is stated in a sentence. Other times it is unstated, and readers must think about the important details to figure out the author's main idea. Have students reread the section "Conductor" on page 91. Display Chart/Transparency 9, or copy the chart on the board. Model how to find a main idea.

AN ADDITIONAL BOOK FOR APPLYING MAIN IDEA AND DETAILS

Fishy Facts by Ivan Chermayeff. Harcourt Brace, 1994. EASY

Chart/Transparency 9 Main Idea and Details		
Main Idea		
The conductor leads the musicians at all times.		
Details		
The conductor beats time with a baton held in the right hand.	The conductor motions with the left hand.	The conductor raises an eyebrow to show that a musician is playing off key.

From this paragraph, I learn that the conductor beats time, gives directions, and lets musicians know when they are playing off key. I think about these details and decide that the main idea is stated in the third sentence: "He [the conductor] leads the musicians at all times."

T144 / A PLACE TO DREAM, UNIT 1

Practice Activity

Movers and Shakers and Pottery Makers

Have students write details and infer main ideas.

Have each student choose his or her favorite kind of art and write a paragraph about why this art form is fun to see, hear, or create—without naming the form. When students finish, have them exchange papers and guess each other's art forms. Students can give each other clues by pantomiming.   **KINESTHETIC**

Performance Assessment

Have volunteers explain how they found the main ideas and details in the Movers and Shakers activity. Record their responses on the board. Then have small groups list guidelines for finding main ideas and supporting details. Tell students they can refer to the information on the board as they write their lists. For evaluation guidelines, see *Staff Development Guide*.

Reader ↔ Writer Connection
Main Idea and Details

WRITERS include details to support their main ideas.

READERS look for important details in order to understand main ideas and to find exact information.

WRITE A PARAGRAPH   Have students write a paragraph about a photograph, beginning with the main idea and then adding at least three details.

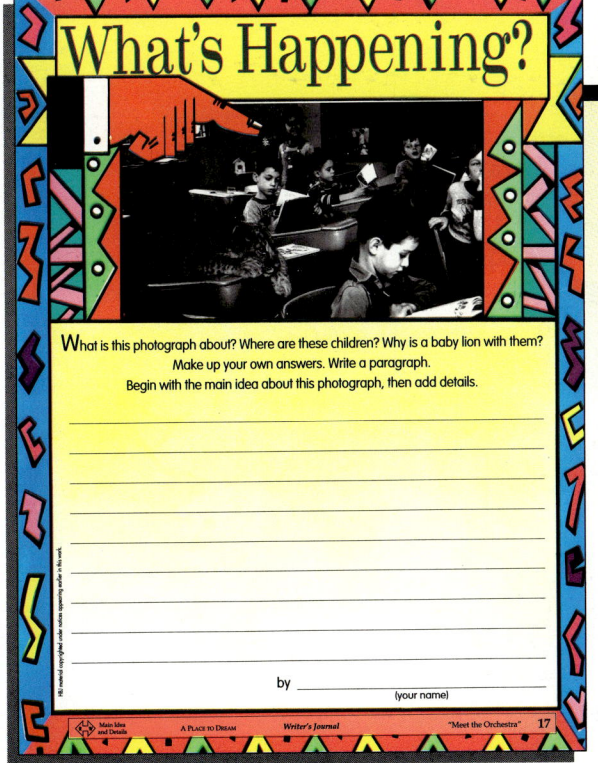
Writer's Journal

Practice Book

MEETING INDIVIDUAL NEEDS

RETEACH Follow the visual, auditory, and kinesthetic/motor models on page R13.

CHALLENGE Have students write a paragraph with an unstated main idea. Then have them exchange papers and identify each other's main ideas.

SECOND-LANGUAGE SUPPORT Choose a paragraph from "Meet the Orchestra," and have students work in pairs to identify its main idea and the details that support this main idea. See also the manual *Alternative Teaching Strategies*, pages 6, 48–51.

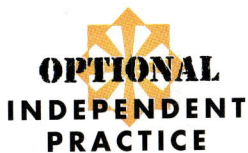

OPTIONAL INDEPENDENT PRACTICE

WRITER'S JOURNAL
page 17: Writing a paragraph

PRACTICE BOOK
page 28: Reinforcing main idea and details

MEET THE ORCHESTRA / T145

COMPREHENSION STRATEGY

INTRODUCE

Synthesizing Ideas

OBJECTIVE: *To combine important parts of a story or an article to determine its overall, or global, meaning*

Interactive Teaching

Focus on combining ideas from the selection.

LITERATURE CONNECTION Write on the board the following statement: *Every instrument adds something important to the orchestra.* Have students identify parts of "Meet the Orchestra" that support this statement. Record their responses on the board. Explain that stories and articles are made up of many separate parts and ideas. *Synthesizing* means combining important ideas into one central idea. Explain that synthesizing can help readers understand and summarize what they read.

Teach and model.

MODEL SYNTHESIZING Have students reread pages 83–84. Tell them that as they read, they should think about the overall message that the author wants them to understand. Model how to use questions to get at the whole meaning:

> After I read a section of "Meet the Orchestra," I ask myself, "What is this section about?" To clarify this question further, I ask, "What are the *most* important ideas in this section?"

Display Chart/Transparency 10 or copy the chart on the board. Have students use the Chart/Transparency to discuss synthesizing ideas.

Chart/Transparency 10 Synthesizing Ideas

Important Ideas

- The violin can have a bright or a sorrowful voice.
- The viola has a lower, deeper tone.
- The cello has a deep, emotional voice.
- The string bass has a booming sound.

Summary

The sounds of string instruments can make listeners become aware of deep feelings.

ADDITIONAL BOOKS FOR APPLYING SYNTHESIZING IDEAS

Alligators and Music by Donald Elliott. Gambit, 1976. **AVERAGE**

A Very Young Musician by Jill Krementz. Simon & Schuster, 1991. **AVERAGE**

Practice Activities

Symphony Synthesis

Have students use synthesizing to look closely at other parts of the selection.

COOPERATIVE LEARNING Have students reread sections of "Meet the Orchestra" and work in groups to complete a diagram similar to the one on Chart/Transparency 10 for each section they reread. A Facilitator can help group members decide whether each idea really belongs in the diagram, and a Reporter can present the group's diagram to the class. **VISUAL/AUDITORY**

Synthesizing Sounds

Have students synthesize one another's writing.

Tell each student to write a paragraph that describes sounds heard at a beach, in a schoolyard, or on a city street. Remind them to keep in mind a central place that all the sentences tell about. When they finish, have students read their paragraphs aloud. Other students can develop a statement that synthesizes the ideas and identifies the place. **AUDITORY**

Performance Assessment

Have students discuss any difficulties they had synthesizing ideas while participating in the activities. Also encourage students to share synthesizing tips they found helpful. For evaluation guidelines, see *Staff Development Guide*.

MEETING INDIVIDUAL NEEDS

RETEACH Follow the visual, auditory, and kinesthetic/motor models on page R14.

CHALLENGE Have students write four sentences about an orchestra. Tell them to choose four ideas that synthesize the most important information in the selection.

SECOND-LANGUAGE SUPPORT Encourage students to express important selection ideas orally and then to locate supporting information physically, by pointing at passages and illustrations. See also the manual *Alternative Teaching Strategies,* pages 6, 48–51.

OPTIONAL INDEPENDENT PRACTICE

PRACTICE BOOK
pages 29–30: Synthesizing ideas

Practice Book

Practice Book

STUDY SKILLS

INTRODUCE

Test Taking

OBJECTIVE: *To develop test-taking strategies*

Interactive Teaching

Focus on facts in "Meet the Orchestra."

LITERATURE CONNECTION Remind students that they read about a real-life topic in "Meet the Orchestra." Have students imagine that they are going to take a test on some of the facts they learned from the selection. Point out that learning ways to take tests can help students succeed in school and show how much they have learned.

Discuss and teach test-taking strategies.

MODEL PREPARING FOR A TEST Ask volunteers to explain how they prepare for tests. (Accept reasonable responses: by reviewing notes and rereading information, by having a classmate quiz them on the material) Explain that, if possible, before beginning a test, students should read the entire test and make a plan. Display Chart/Transparency 11 or write the test on the board. Model scanning and developing a plan:

> First, I scan the entire test. I see that Part 1 contains multiple-choice questions and Part 2 contains fill-in-the-blank questions. In Part 1, I need to circle the correct answer. In Part 2, I need to complete the sentences by writing on the lines. I need to remember not to spend too much time on one question. I'll also look for clue words, like *what* and *why,* to help me understand and correctly answer each question.

Chart/Transparency 11   Test Items

Part 1
Circle the letter for the correct answer.
1. Why are some instruments grouped in families?
   (A) They have similar shapes and sounds.
   (B) They are made by the same person.
   (C) They look and sound exactly the same.

2. What is difficult about playing the oboe?
   (A) The metal mouthpiece can make an unpleasant buzz.
   (B) The reed can be troublesome to use.
   (C) It is so large that it has to rest on the floor.

Part 2
Write the answer on the line.
3. Three instruments in the string family are
   _____.

4. You play the flute by
   _____.

T148 / A PLACE TO DREAM, UNIT 1

Practice Activities

MEETING INDIVIDUAL NEEDS

The Quiz Wiz

Have students develop test-taking strategies.

Tell students to imagine that they have fifteen minutes in which to take the test on Chart/Transparency 11. Help them identify the clue words *why* in the first question and *what* in the second. Then have students read the fill-in-the-blank questions, tell in what order they would tackle the questions, and name any clue words they see. **(three, string family; play, flute)** VISUAL/AUDITORY

Tips for Taking Tests

Have students create a strategies poster.

COOPERATIVE LEARNING Have small groups of students work together to create a poster of tips for taking tests. Before they begin, they can brainstorm strategies from their own test-taking experience. Groups can appoint a Facilitator to organize the steps and a Materials Manager to keep track of the art supplies. AUDITORY/KINESTHETIC

Performance Assessment

Have volunteers explain how the test-taking strategies they discussed in The Quiz Wiz and Tips for Taking Tests can help them take tests. Ask them to describe new strategies that they learned while completing the activities. For evaluation guidelines, see *Staff Development Guide*.

RETEACH Follow the visual, auditory, and kinesthetic/motor models on page R15.

CHALLENGE Suggest that students make up their own tests using key facts from "Meet the Orchestra." Encourage them to include several types of questions.

SECOND-LANGUAGE SUPPORT Help students create test-taking-strategies bookmarks that include what they should do first **(scan the test)**, next **(decide which questions to answer first)**, and last **(decide how much time to allow for each question)**. See also the manual *Alternative Teaching Strategies*, pages 6, 48–51.

OPTIONAL INDEPENDENT PRACTICE

PRACTICE BOOK
page 31: Test-taking strategies

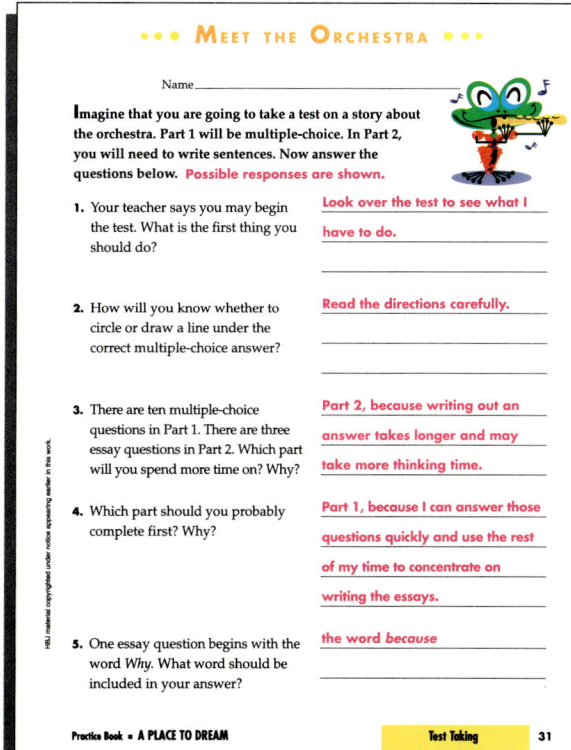

Practice Book

Integrated CURRICULUM

SCIENCE

Sound Waves in Motion

COOPERATIVE LEARNING Explain that sounds are made when an object vibrates. For example, bees make a buzzing sound when their wings vibrate in air. Then have small groups of students research a topic related to sound. Before groups begin their research, have members brainstorm sound-related topics and vote on the one they would like to investigate. Possible topics include how the human voice produces sound, how animals produce sound, how instruments produce sound, what noise pollution is, and how sound travels. Suggest that groups choose a Recorder, a Facilitator, and an Encourager to make the project go smoothly.
READING/WRITING

ART/MUSIC

A Band of Our Own

Available on Project Card 10A

Encourage students to recall times when they have played music using ordinary objects. Perhaps they have banged wooden spoons on cooking pots or made "trumpet" sounds through long cardboard tubes. Direct students to books that tell how to make simple musical instruments. You may want to share the following ideas: Students can make drums out of empty cylindrical oatmeal containers, blow across the tops of different-size bottles, or create papier-mâché maracas from balloon molds filled with dried beans. Encourage students to decorate their instruments. When students' instruments are ready, have them perform some familiar songs together.   **LISTENING/SPEAKING**

T150 / A PLACE TO DREAM, UNIT 1

SOCIAL STUDIES

Great Band and Orchestra Leaders

Available on Project Card 10B

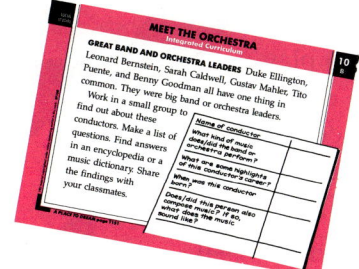

COOPERATIVE LEARNING
Encourage students to learn about distinguished band and orchestra leaders such as Duke Ellington, Leonard Bernstein, Sarah Caldwell, Gustav Mahler, Tito Puente, or Benny Goodman. Have students work in small groups to discover why these leaders are admired. Suggest that before they begin, they make a list of questions that they want to have answered and organize them in a chart like this:

Name of Conductor	
What kind of music does/did his or her band or orchestra perform?	
What are some highlights of this conductor's career?	
When was this conductor born?	
Does/did this person also compose music? If so, what does the music sound like?	

Have groups appoint a Recorder, a Facilitator, and a Reporter. Encourage students to find recorded performances by the conductor and his or her band or orchestra, or recordings of the conductor's compositions performed by others. Students can play the recordings as part of their reports.   LISTENING/SPEAKING/WRITING

HEALTH

Jump-Rope Contest

Ask students why it is important in jumping rope for the jumper to keep the beat. (If a jumper doesn't jump to a regular rhythm, he or she may trip on the rope and lose a turn.) Tell students that jump-rope rhymes are not only fun to recite but also help the players keep a steady rhythm. Have students list their favorite jump-rope rhymes and games and teach them to others. If possible, allow students to hold a jump-rope demonstration or contest.   LISTENING/SPEAKING

BOOKS TO SHARE

SOCIAL STUDIES *Gonna Sing My Head Off!: American Folk Songs for Children*, collected and arranged by Kathleen Krull. Alfred A. Knopf, 1992.   AVERAGE

MUSIC *What Instrument Is This?* by Rosemarie Hausherr. Scholastic, 1992.   AVERAGE

MULTICULTURAL PERSPECTIVES

Leaders of the Band

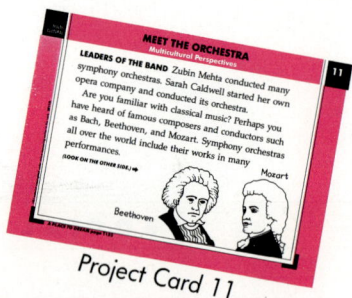

Project Card 11

DISCUSSION STARTER
What does it take to be a good orchestra conductor?

READ ALOUD
Conducting an orchestra takes a lot of hard work and musical talent. One famous conductor is Zubin Mehta. He was born in Bombay, India. At the age of 18, Mehta traveled to Vienna, Austria. There he studied conducting for six years. Teachers recognized his special ability to lead an orchestra. Later, Mehta became the conductor of orchestras in Montreal, Los Angeles, New York, and Israel.

Another well-known conductor is Sarah Caldwell. In 1957 she began her own opera company in Boston, Massachusetts, and conducted its orchestra. Later, she became the first woman to conduct at the Metropolitan Opera House in New York City.

Seiji Ozawa is another talented orchestra conductor. He was born in a region of China called Manchuria. After studying conducting in Germany, Ozawa was asked by many orchestras to be their leader. Ozawa conducted in New York, Toronto, and San Francisco. He is known for conducting many different kinds of music, including music written by modern Japanese composers.

Conductors such as Zubin Mehta, Sarah Caldwell, and Seiji Ozawa use their special musical gifts to lead orchestras.

ACTIVITY CORNER
● Invite students who play a musical instrument to demonstrate for the class. Also, encourage them to share their techniques with classmates, one-on-one, offering brief lessons on how to play each instrument. Encourage students to tell what they enjoy about playing their instruments.

Available on Project Card 11
● Have students close their eyes and listen as you play a piece of classical music in the classroom. Later, invite students to tell what they liked or didn't like about the music. Also, encourage them to describe how the music made them feel.

T152 / *A PLACE TO DREAM,* UNIT 1

Music, Music for Everyone
pages 94–120

	READING	LANGUAGE ARTS	CROSS-CURRICULAR CONNECTIONS
PART 1 *Reading the Literature* pages T156–T172	**Building Background** **Vocabulary Strategies** **Prereading Strategies** Prediction Diagram Setting a Purpose **Options for Reading**	**Spelling** Pretest Spelling-Vocabulary Connection Generalization: One-Syllable Words with Long Vowels **Grammar Connection** Reviewing Common Nouns	**Cultural Awareness** Asian music scales Accordions and ethnic music **Music** Playing an accordion
PART 2 *Responding to the Literature* pages T173–T179	**Personal Response** **Cooperative Response** **Summarizing the Literature** **Critical Thinking Activity** Brainstorm Ideas **Vocabulary Workshop** Key Words Alliteration	**Language Arts Workshop** **Reading** drama, research **Writing** book review, business letter **Listening and Speaking** musical sounds **Reviewing Spelling Words** Posttest **Grammar Review** Common Nouns **Grammar Minilesson** Proper Nouns	**Music** The Sounds of Music
PART 3 *Learning Through the Literature* pages T180–T186	**Introduce** Decoding Strategy: Structural Clues **Review** Study Skills: Following Directions (Tested) Comprehension: Cause and Effect (Tested)	**Reading** Instruments Around the World Effects of Music **Listening and Speaking** Music Makes Me Feel . . . Move Your Feet to the Beat! **Writing** Instruments Around the World Effects of Music	**Social Studies** Instruments Around the World **Art** Music Makes Me Feel . . . **Math** What's My Share? **Science** Effects of Music **Physical Education** Move Your Feet to the Beat! **Multicultural Perspectives** Young and Gifted Musicians

OPTIONAL MATERIALS
Charts/Transparencies 12–13
Integrated Spelling pp. 26–29; TE pp. T39–T44
Practice Book pp. 32–38
Writer's Journal pp. 18–19
Alternative Teaching Strategies pp. 7–8, 52–55
Language Handbook pp. 60–61, 63, 93–94
Grammar Practice pp. 20–21
Family Involvement Activities: Unit 1, pp. 1–4
Response Card 1
Project Cards 12A, 12B, 13A, 13B, 14

 **MEETING INDIVIDUAL NEEDS**
Second-Language Support pp. T157, T158, T164, T179, T181
Mainstreaming p. T158
Reteach pp. T179, T181
Challenge pp. T181, T182, T183

FAMILY INVOLVEMENT Encourage family members to discuss with students the different kinds of music they especially enjoy. See *Family Involvement Activities.*

Key Words

assembly
anniversary
accordion
empty
single

Selection Summary

When Rosa's grandmother gets sick, the big chair in the living room as well as the money jar used for saving spare change remain empty. All of the family's savings must be used to help take care of Rosa's grandmother. After school, Rosa and her friends Leora, Mae, and Jenny sometimes play their musical instruments for Grandma. One day, Rosa gets an idea. Soon, she and her friends have formed the Oak Street Band and are practicing hard to earn money by playing for special occasions. Leora's mother gives the band its first job. At a huge celebration, the Oak Street Band plays while the guests dance. Their music is a great success, and the girls earn their fee, which they divide equally. Rosa knows what she will do with her share of the money—she puts it into the family's big money jar.

Music, Music for Everyone was listed by the American Library Association and the School Library Journal as a notable book for children in 1984.

About the Author and Illustrator

Vera B. Williams graduated from Black Mountain College, North Carolina, where she majored in graphic art. Since then, she has worked for peace, taught school, and raised three children. She is also the author and illustrator of many award-winning books for children, including *Something Special for Me* and *A Chair for My Mother*, which was a Caldecott Honor Book and the winner of the *Boston Globe–Horn Book* Award for outstanding illustration in 1983. These two titles are the first in a series about Rosa and her family. *Music, Music for Everyone* is the third title.

Additional Reading

OTHER BOOKS BY VERA B. WILLIAMS

A Chair for My Mother. William Morrow, 1988.   AVERAGE

Something Special for Me. William Morrow, 1986.   AVERAGE

OTHER THEME-RELATED BOOKS

Grandpa's Song by Tony Johnston. Dial, 1991.   AVERAGE

*Mozart Tonight by Julie Downing. Bradbury, 1991.   AVERAGE

Red Dancing Shoes by Denise Lewis Patrick. William Morrow, 1993.   EASY

*Available as a Harcourt Brace PASSPORTS title

PART 1

Reading the Literature

Building Background

Access prior knowledge and build vocabulary concepts.

Tell students that the next story, "Music, Music for Everyone," is about a young girl who finds a wonderful use for her musical talents. Invite students to share experiences they have had playing or listening to a musical instrument.

Have students quickwrite.

Have students work in groups to make a chart that shows other talents they have and how they might use them to help someone. The completed charts might include the following:

Talent	Ways to Help Someone
reading	share books with younger family members
singing	entertain others; make money

Vocabulary Strategies

Introduce Key Words and strategies.

Display Chart/Transparency 12, or the paragraphs on it. Invite students to read the paragraphs silently, using context clues to figure out the meaning of each underlined word. For example, students can use the context clue "meeting that brings everyone together" to figure out what *assembly* means.

Chart/Transparency 12 Key Words

Our school has a weekly <u>assembly</u>, a meeting that brings everyone together for a special program. This week our school is twenty-five years old, and we are celebrating its <u>anniversary</u>. I have been asked to play my <u>accordion</u>.

As I stand on the stage and press the buttons and the keys of my instrument, practicing the song I am going to play, I stare out at the <u>empty</u> chairs. I dream about how I will play when every <u>single</u> chair is filled.

CULTURAL AWARENESS

Students may be interested to know that Asian music sounds different from Western music not only because different instruments are used but also because the musical scales are different. For example, the Indian scale has 22 steps to an octave, compared to the 12 steps used in Western music.

Key Words

assembly
anniversary
accordion
empty
single

KEY WORDS DEFINED

assembly group of people gathered together for some purpose

anniversary yearly return of a special date

accordion musical wind instrument with bellows, reeds, keys, and buttons

empty with nothing or no one in it

single separate from others

T156 / A PLACE TO DREAM, UNIT 1

Check all students' understanding. List the Key Words and their meanings in random order on the board, as shown below. Have each student number a sheet of paper from one to five and then write the Key Word that matches each meaning. Have volunteers write the answers on the board.
STRATEGY: DEFINITIONS

Key Words	Meanings
assembly (3)	1. special yearly date
anniversary (1)	2. separate from others
accordion (4)	3. large gathering
empty (5)	4. musical instrument
single (2)	5. with nothing in it

Integrate spelling with vocabulary. **SPELLING-VOCABULARY CONNECTION** *Integrated Spelling* Lesson 5 reinforces the spellings of one-syllable words with long vowel sounds, such as *rose* found in the selection. In addition, the Words to Explore help reinforce the concept of celebration as it relates to the selection.

 **SPELLING PRETEST** You may want to use the Pretest/Posttest Sentences on page T39 in *Integrated Spelling Teacher's Edition* to assess students' knowledge of the spelling generalization.

Spelling

Spelling Words	Words to Explore
1. bike	anniversary
2. cake	assembly
3. drove	company
4. face	empty
5. fine	
6. ice	Your Own Words
7. rose	13.
8. same	14.
9. smoke	15.
10. spoke	16.
11. stone	
12. these	

Spelling generalization:
one-syllable words with long vowel sounds

Practice Book

MEETING INDIVIDUAL NEEDS

SECOND-LANGUAGE SUPPORT As you read aloud the story on Chart/Transparency 12, have students pantomime each word. For example, students could hold up their fingers to show twenty-five years and act out playing an accordion. See also the manual *Alternative Teaching Strategies,* pages 7–8, 52–55.

OPTIONAL INDEPENDENT PRACTICE

INTEGRATED SPELLING pages 26–29: Words like *bike* and *face*

PRACTICE BOOK page 32: Reinforcing Key Words
NOTE: This page may be completed now or after students have read the story.

MUSIC, MUSIC FOR EVERYONE / **T157**

Prereading Strategies

Prediction Diagram

Help students preview the story. Help students find "Music, Music for Everyone" in the table of contents. Ask students to name the author and to tell the page on which the story begins. Review the steps involved in previewing a story before it is read. Encourage students to read the title, look at the illustrations, and read the first page.

Have students make predictions. Help students make predictions about what might happen in the story by having them begin a diagram like the one below:

Story Information		What I Already Know
Rosa's after-school routine has changed because Grandma is sick.	+	People who are sick need special attention.

My Predictions	What Actually Happens
Rosa will do something nice for Grandma.	

 **PERSONAL JOURNAL** Have students add their predictions about the story to their personal journals. Ask students to support their predictions.

Setting a Purpose

Encourage students to set purposes. Have students use the predictions they wrote in their prediction diagrams to set a purpose for reading.

If students have difficulty setting a purpose for reading, offer this suggestion:

I'm going to read to find out how Rosa will help her grandmother.

MEETING INDIVIDUAL NEEDS

SECOND-LANGUAGE SUPPORT Tell students that idioms are phrases that have meanings different from the meanings of the words in the phrases. As they read the story, explain any idiomatic expressions they come across. See also the manual *Alternative Teaching Strategies,* pages 7–8, 52–55.

SUPPORT FOR MAINSTREAMING Help students make personal connections to the story by discussing ways that they could use their own talents to help a sick person feel better.

Options for Reading

SUSTAINED SILENT READING	STRATEGIC READING	READER RESPONSE GROUPS
Encourage students to change their predictions as they read and acquire new information.	Use the questions that appear on pages T159, T162, T167, and T171 to stimulate discussion.	Follow the suggestions for Literature Circles on page T159. Have students note in their journals their thoughts and feelings about the characters and situations.

T158 / A PLACE TO DREAM, UNIT 1

MUSIC, MUSIC FOR EVERYONE   PAGES 94–95

Our big chair often sits in our living room empty now.

When I first got my accordion, Grandma and Mama used to sit in that chair together to listen to me practice. And every day after school while Mama was at her job at the diner, Grandma would be sitting in the chair by the window. Even if it was snowing big flakes down on her hair, she would lean way out to call, "Hurry up, Pussycat. I've got something nice for you."

But now Grandma is sick. She has to stay upstairs in the big bed in Aunt Ida and Uncle Sandy's extra room. Mama and Aunt Ida and Uncle Sandy and I take turns taking care of her.

When I come home from school, I run right upstairs to ask Grandma if she wants anything.

Reader Response Groups

LITERATURE CIRCLES Have groups of three to five students read the selection silently, stopping at pages 101 and 111 for a brief discussion. You may want to distribute Response Card 1 (Characters), found on page R79, or provide the following questions:

- What do you think of Rosa? Tell how you feel about her.
- Are you like Rosa in any way? Explain your answer.

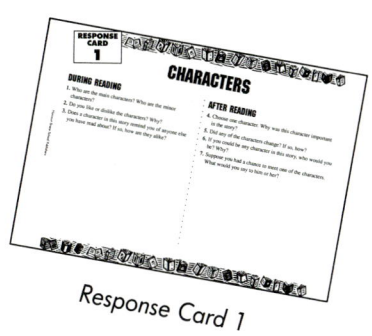

Response Card 1

Strategic Reading

SET PURPOSE/PREDICT: PAGES 95–101 Have students read through page 101. Encourage them to tell what they will be reading to find out.

MUSIC, MUSIC FOR EVERYONE / T159

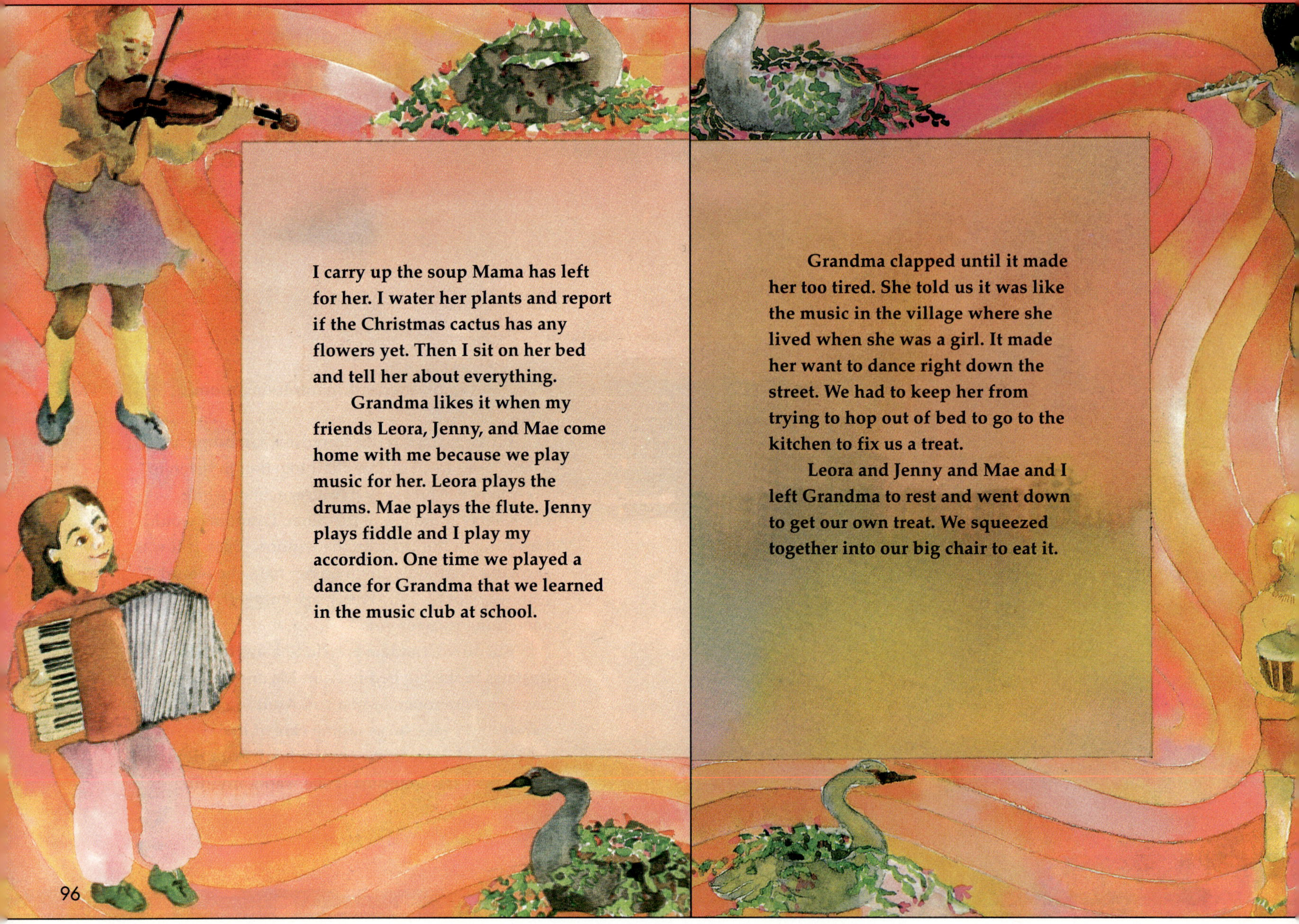

I carry up the soup Mama has left for her. I water her plants and report if the Christmas cactus has any flowers yet. Then I sit on her bed and tell her about everything.

Grandma likes it when my friends Leora, Jenny, and Mae come home with me because we play music for her. Leora plays the drums. Mae plays the flute. Jenny plays fiddle and I play my accordion. One time we played a dance for Grandma that we learned in the music club at school.

96

Grandma clapped until it made her too tired. She told us it was like the music in the village where she lived when she was a girl. It made her want to dance right down the street. We had to keep her from trying to hop out of bed to go to the kitchen to fix us a treat.

Leora and Jenny and Mae and I left Grandma to rest and went down to get our own treat. We squeezed together into our big chair to eat it.

Music Connection Point out the narrator's accordion in the picture on page 96. Explain that an accordion player plays the piano-like keys with the right hand and the buttons with the left. The accordion player also squeezes and pulls apart the accordion's folded *bellows* (the middle part) to make the sound. Also explain that *fiddle* is another name for a violin.

Teaching Tip Discuss with students that authors of trade books, such as Vera B. Williams, write and sometimes illustrate only the story. Explain that the publisher of an anthology, such as this one, adds the discussion questions and the questions that appear in the Student Anthology. Students will read a letter from the author on page 120.

See page T184 for information found on Project Card 13A.

ART

MUSIC, MUSIC FOR EVERYONE
Integrated Curriculum

13 A

MUSIC MAKES ME FEEL . . . When Rosa and her friends played music, Grandma felt like dancing and remembered when she was a girl. Does some music make you feel happy?

Listen to three or four musical recordings with a partner. After you hear each piece, describe to your partner how the music made you feel.

Use drawing paper and crayons, pencils, or markers to draw pictures to show how the music made you feel.

After you have made a drawing for each recording, display your work, and explain it.

A PLACE TO DREAM page T184

Project Card 13A

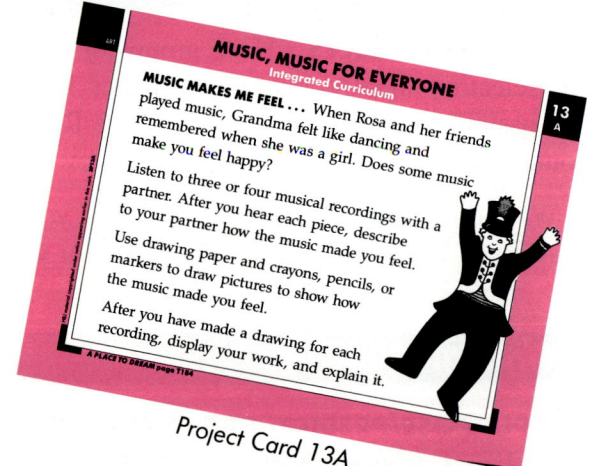

MUSIC, MUSIC FOR EVERYONE PAGES 98–99

"It feels sad down here without your grandma," Leora said. "Even your big money jar up there looks sad and empty."

"Remember how it was full to the top and I couldn't even lift it when we bought the chair for my mother?" I said.

"And remember how it was more than half full when you got your accordion?" Jenny said.

"I bet it's empty now because your mother has to spend all her money to take care of your grandma till she gets better. That's how it was when my father had his accident and couldn't go to work for a long time," Mae said.

Mae had a dime in her pocket and she dropped it into the jar. "That will make it look a little fuller anyway," she said as she went home.

 Informal Assessment

CAUSE AND EFFECT To assess whether students understand the story situation, you might ask questions such as these:

- Why does Leora say the room "feels sad"? (Grandma is not there.)
- What caused the money jar to be empty? (Rosa's mother spends all her money to take care of Grandma.)

A review lesson on **cause and effect** appears later in this lesson, on page T183.

PAGES 100–101   MUSIC, MUSIC FOR EVERYONE

But after Jenny and Leora and Mae went home, our jar looked even emptier to me. I wondered how we would ever be able to fill it up again while Grandma was sick. I wondered when Grandma would be able to come downstairs again. Even our beautiful chair with roses all over it seemed empty with just me in the corner of it. The whole house seemed so empty and so quiet.

Strategic Reading

MODELING A STRATEGY: PAGES 95–101   Invite students to summarize the story's mood so far and the details the author provides to create this mood.

THINK ALOUD   Provide a think-aloud model, if necessary: *I think that so far, this story has a sad mood. The author uses two things in particular, the big chair and the money jar, to show sadness and how much things have changed since Grandma got sick. Now the chair where Grandma used to sit seems empty and the money jar really is empty.*   **SUMMARIZING**

SET PURPOSE/PREDICT: PAGES 102–111   Invite students to predict what the narrator might do to make things more cheerful for herself and her family. Encourage them to read through page 111, changing their predictions as they read if necessary.

T162 / A PLACE TO DREAM, UNIT 1

MUSIC, MUSIC FOR EVERYONE   PAGES 102–103

I got out my accordion and I started to play. The notes sounded beautiful in the empty room. One song that is an old tune sounded so pretty I played it over and over. I remembered what my mother had told me about my other grandma and how she used to play the accordion. Even when she was a girl not much bigger than I, she would get up and play at a party or a wedding so the company could dance and sing. Then people would stamp their feet and yell, "More, more!" When they went home, they would leave money on the table for her.

That's how I got an idea for how I could help fill up the jar again. I ran right upstairs. "Grandma," I whispered. "Grandma?"

"Is that you, Pussycat?" she answered in a sleepy voice. "I was just having such a nice dream about you. Then I woke up and heard you playing that beautiful old song. Come. Sit here and brush my hair."

I brushed Grandma's hair and told her my whole idea. She thought it was a great idea. "But tell the truth, Grandma," I begged her. "Do you think kids could really do that?"

103

Expanding the Literature   Invite students to briefly discuss the illustration on page 102. Ask them what mood the picture expresses. **How do you think Rosa feels in this picture? What is she thinking about?** (Accept reasonable responses: dreamy, thoughtful; remembering her grandmother's stories and making plans.)   CRITICAL: APPRECIATING

ILLUSTRATOR'S CRAFT

MUSIC, MUSIC FOR EVERYONE / **T163**

PAGES 104–105 MUSIC, MUSIC FOR EVERYONE

"I think you and Jenny and Leora and Mae could do it. No question. No question at all," she answered. "Only don't wait a minute to talk to them about it. Go call and ask them now."

And that was how the Oak Street Band got started.

Our music teachers helped us pick out pieces we could all play together. Aunt Ida, who plays guitar, helped us practice. We practiced on our back porch. One day our neighbor leaned out his window in his pajamas and yelled, "Listen, kids, you sound great but give me a break. I work at night. I've got to get some sleep in the daytime." After that we practiced inside. Grandma said it was helping her get better faster than anything.

At last my accordion teacher said we sounded very good. Uncle Sandy said so too. Aunt Ida and Grandma said we were terrific. Mama said she thought anyone would be glad to have us play for them.

GRAMMAR CONNECTION

REVIEWING COMMON NOUNS Point out the name *Oak Street Band* in the second paragraph on page 105. Write this sentence on the board: *Our band is called the Oak Street Band.* Ask why the first *band* in the sentence isn't capitalized like the second one. (The first *band* is not the name of a particular band.)

Second-Language Support Explain to students that to *take a break* means to stop what you are doing and take a rest (as in taking a break from your work). So when the neighbor man asks the girls to "give [him] a break," he is asking them to help him out by giving him a rest from their music.

MEETING INDIVIDUAL NEEDS

T164 / A PLACE TO DREAM, UNIT 1

MUSIC, MUSIC FOR EVERYONE   PAGES 106–107

It was Leora's mother who gave us our first job. She asked us to come and play at a party for Leora's great-grandmother and great-grandfather. It was going to be a special <u>anniversary</u> for them. It was fifty years ago on that day they first opened their market on our corner. Now Leora's mother takes care of the market. She always plays the radio loud while she works. But for the party she said there just had to be live music.

Vocabulary Strategy   Ask how students might figure out the meanings of the words *great-grandmother* and *great-grandfather* on page 107. (Accept reasonable responses: They might break each of these words into two parts—*great* and *grandmother; great* and *grandfather;* then they might use one meaning of *great,* "of a large size or number," to figure out that a great-grandparent has lived for a greater number of years than a grandparent.) Clarify for students that a great-grandparent is a grandparent's parent.   STRATEGY: CONTEXT CLUES/STRUCTURAL ANALYSIS

PAGES 108–109 MUSIC, MUSIC FOR EVERYONE

All of Leora's aunts and uncles and cousins came to the party. Lots of people from our block came too. Mama and Aunt Ida and Uncle Sandy walked down from our house very slowly with Grandma. It was Grandma's first big day out.

There was a long table in the backyard made from little tables all pushed together. It was covered with so many big dishes of food you could hardly see the tablecloth. But I was too excited to eat anything.

Expanding the Literature Why do you think the author-illustrator used two pages instead of one to create this illustration? Encourage students to name some interesting details in the picture. (Accept reasonable responses: to show how long the table full of food is and how delicious the food looks.) CRITICAL: APPRECIATING ILLUSTRATOR'S CRAFT

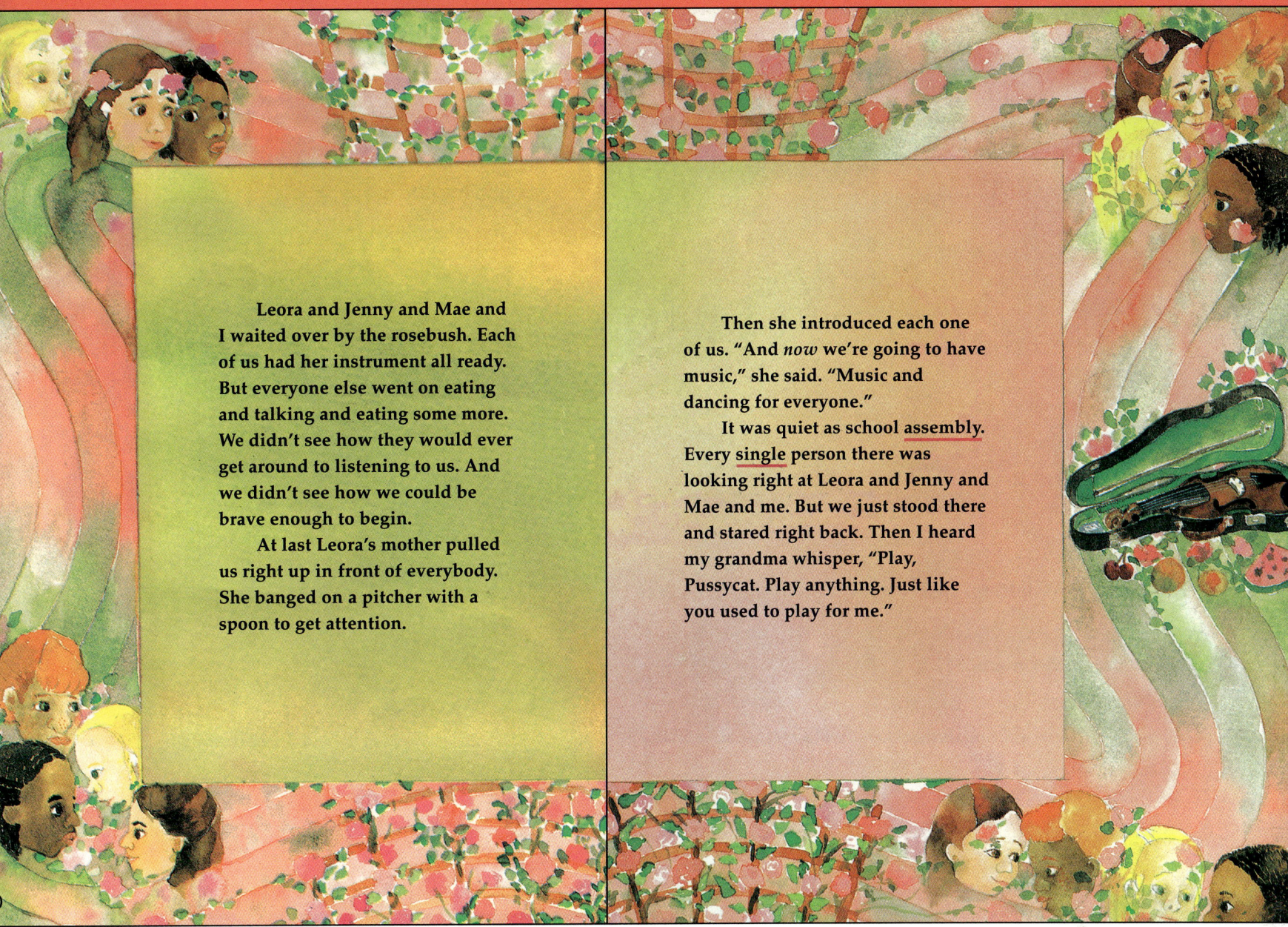

MUSIC, MUSIC FOR EVERYONE PAGES 110–111

Leora and Jenny and Mae and I waited over by the rosebush. Each of us had her instrument all ready. But everyone else went on eating and talking and eating some more. We didn't see how they would ever get around to listening to us. And we didn't see how we could be brave enough to begin.

At last Leora's mother pulled us right up in front of everybody. She banged on a pitcher with a spoon to get attention.

Then she introduced each one of us. "And *now* we're going to have music," she said. "Music and dancing for everyone."

It was quiet as school assembly. Every single person there was looking right at Leora and Jenny and Mae and me. But we just stood there and stared right back. Then I heard my grandma whisper, "Play, Pussycat. Play anything. Just like you used to play for me."

Strategic Reading

MODELING A STRATEGY: PAGES 102–111 Were your predictions about the story confirmed? Explain how you know.

THINK ALOUD You may wish to model confirming predictions: *I predicted that the narrator would do something involving music to help her grandmother and the rest of her family—and I was right. I based my prediction on the story title, "Music, Music for Everyone." I also remembered that Grandma felt better when the narrator and her friends played for her.* CONFIRMING PREDICTIONS

SET PURPOSE/PREDICT: PAGES 112–119 Invite students to predict how the girls' band will sound, and whether their playing will help the narrator's family. Encourage students to read the rest of the story to confirm their predictions.

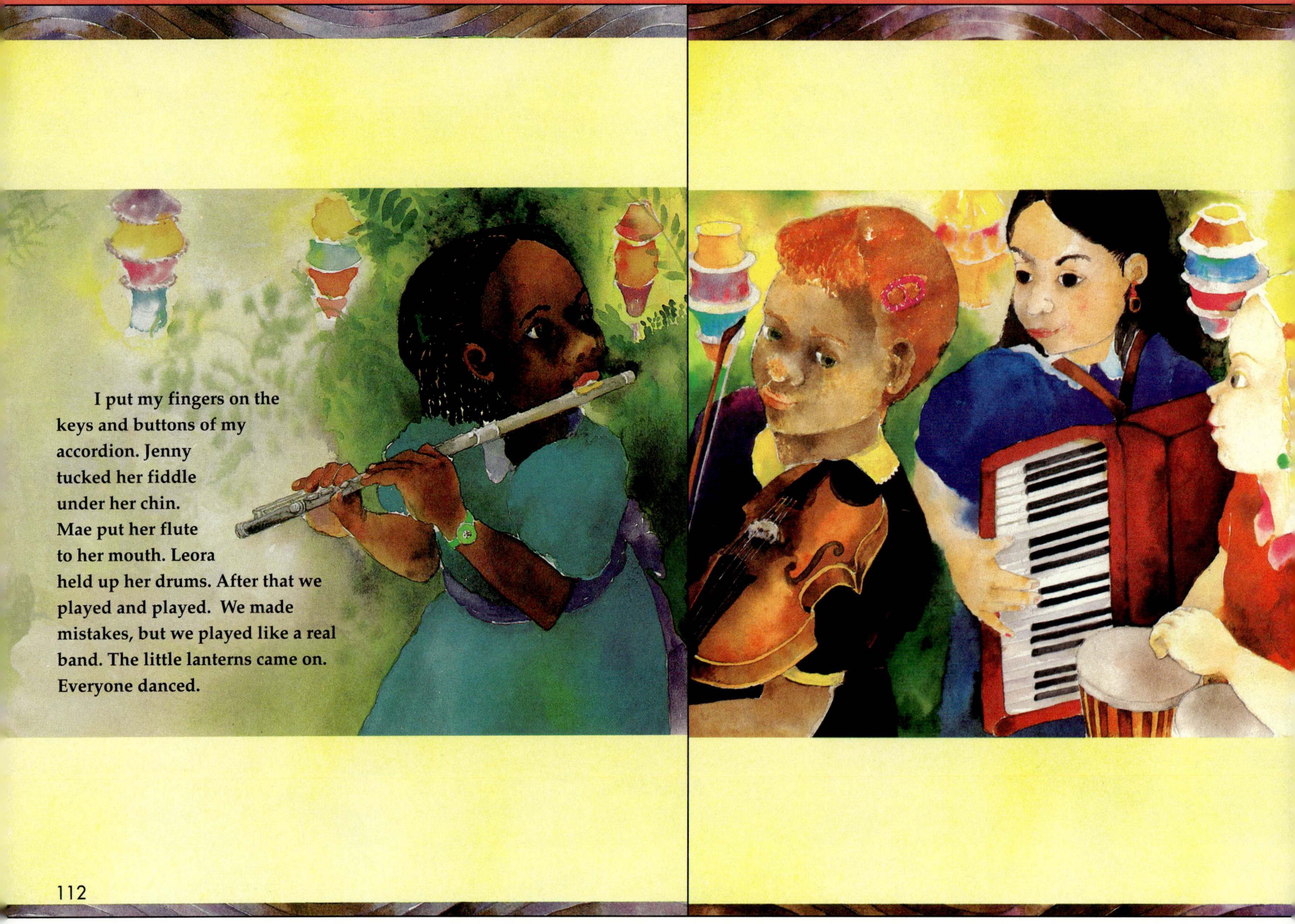
I put my fingers on the keys and buttons of my accordion. Jenny tucked her fiddle under her chin. Mae put her flute to her mouth. Leora held up her drums. After that we played and played. We made mistakes, but we played like a real band. The little lanterns came on. Everyone danced.
112

Cultural Awareness Explain that many cultures have developed types of music that feature the accordion. For instance, the band of the television host Lawrence Welk, who was of German heritage, played polkas and waltzes and featured the accordion as the lead instrument. *Zydeco* music developed by African Americans living in southern Louisiana features the accordion, too. A musical style of South Texas known as *conjunto* also uses the accordion as the lead instrument. This instrument is important in the folk music of many other cultures, including Italian, French, Polish, and Czech cultures.

See page T185 for information found on Project Card 13B.

PHYSICAL EDUCATION
MUSIC, MUSIC FOR EVERYONE
Integrated Curriculum
13 B
MOVE YOUR FEET TO THE BEAT! The Oak Street Band played dance music. Different kinds of dances have developed for different kinds of music.
Listen to the music for three or four different dances. Then choose one kind of dance. Use encyclopedias or other reference books about music or dance to research the steps of your dance and its origin.
Square dancing
A PLACE TO DREAM page T185

Project Card 13B

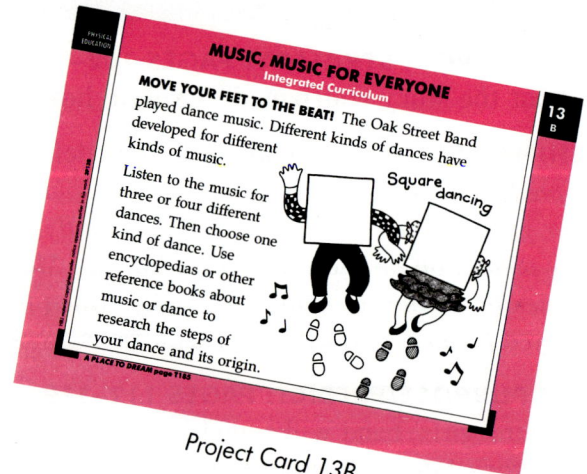

MUSIC, MUSIC FOR EVERYONE   PAGES 114–115

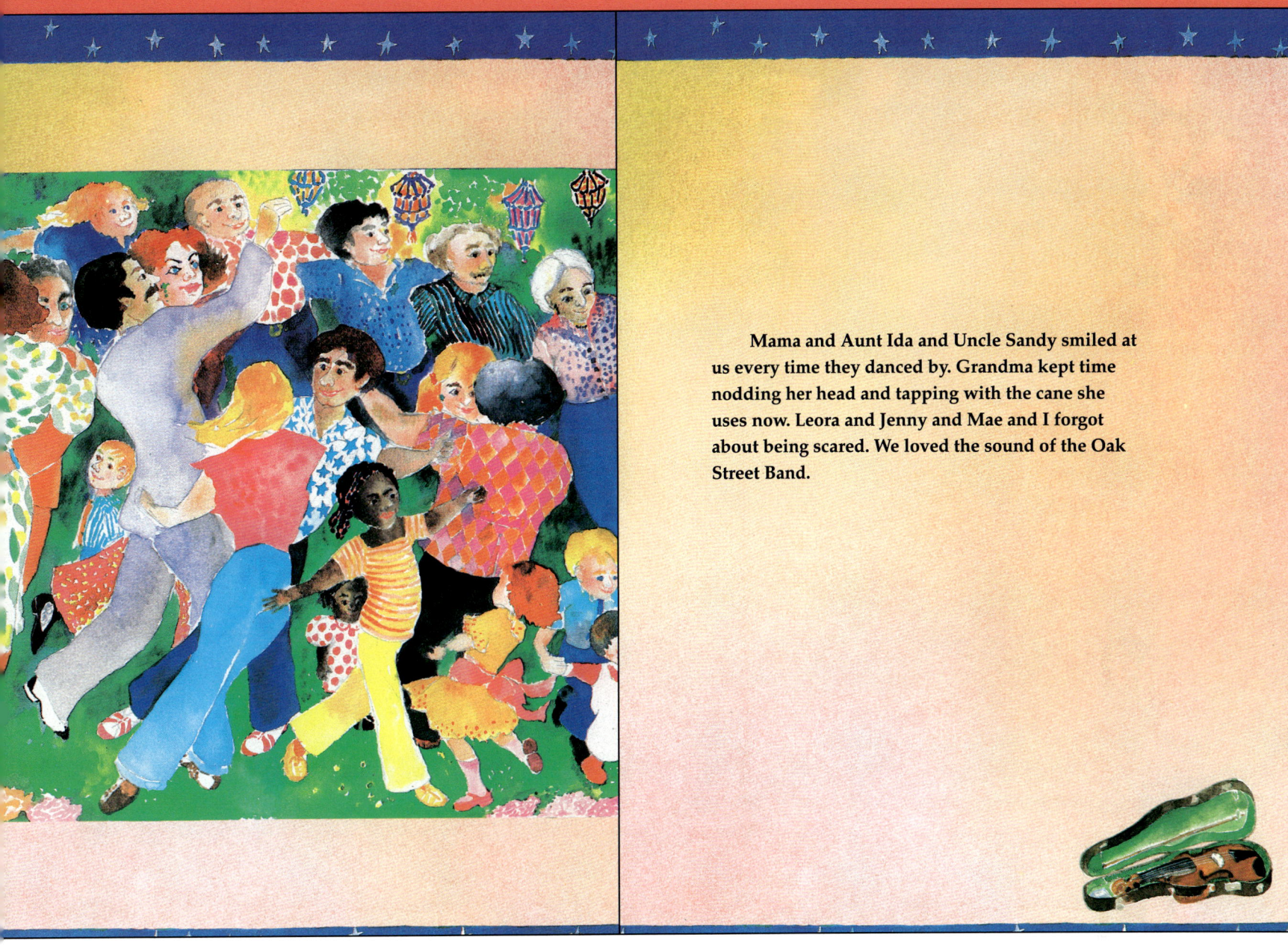

Mama and Aunt Ida and Uncle Sandy smiled at us every time they danced by. Grandma kept time nodding her head and tapping with the cane she uses now. Leora and Jenny and Mae and I forgot about being scared. We loved the sound of the Oak Street Band.

Expanding the Literature   How has the mood of the story changed? Explain how you know. (Accept reasonable responses: The story is much happier now; I can tell because everyone is dancing and smiling.)   METACOGNITIVE: DETERMINING MOOD

MUSIC, MUSIC FOR EVERYONE / T169

PAGES 116–117 MUSIC, MUSIC FOR EVERYONE

And afterward everybody clapped and shouted. Leora's great-grandfather and great-grandmother thanked us. They said we had made their party something they would always remember. Leora's father piled up plates of food for us. My mama arranged for Leora, Jenny, and Mae to stay over at our house. And when we finally all went out the gate together, late at night, Leora's mother tucked an envelope with our money into Leora's pocket.

Expanding the Literature Use details on pages 116 and 117 to explain how you might feel if you were a member of the Oak Street Band. (Accept reasonable responses: I would probably feel proud and happy, and glad to have made everyone else happy. I might feel a little relieved that the performance was over so I could enjoy the food and the party. I would probably feel tired after all the excitement.) INFERENTIAL: IDENTIFYING WITH CHARACTERS

MUSIC, MUSIC FOR EVERYONE   PAGES 118–119

As soon as we got home, we piled into my bed to divide the money. We made four equal shares. Leora said she was going to save up for a bigger drum. Mae wasn't sure what she would do with her share. Jenny fell asleep before she could tell us. But I couldn't even lie down until I climbed up and put mine right into our big jar on the shelf near our chair.

Think about the part of the story that meant the most to you. Use your own words to retell your favorite part of the story to a friend.

Rosa, the main character, uses her music to help her family. What could you imagine doing to help other people who are having troubles?

WRITE   In this story, Rosa worries about her sick grandma and the empty money jar. Write your opinions about happy stories and sad stories and which you'd rather read. Tell about different stories you remember or tell one from your own life that would make a good book.

119

Strategic Reading

MODELING A STRATEGY: PAGES 112–119   What was your purpose for reading the whole story? Did you learn what you wanted to learn?

THINK ALOUD   If necessary, provide a think-aloud model: *I wanted to find out how Rosa, the narrator, would help her grandmother. I found out that she helped her grandmother by playing music at a party with her friends. Hearing her granddaughter play made Grandma happy. Rosa also helped her whole family by contributing her share of the money the band was paid to the family's savings.*   RETURNING TO THE PURPOSE

Returning to the Predictions/Purpose

PREDICTION DIAGRAM   Have students look over the prediction diagrams they filled in before reading. Have them revise their diagrams on the basis of the events in "Music, Music for Everyone."

NOTE: Responses to the questions and support for the Write activity appear on page T173.

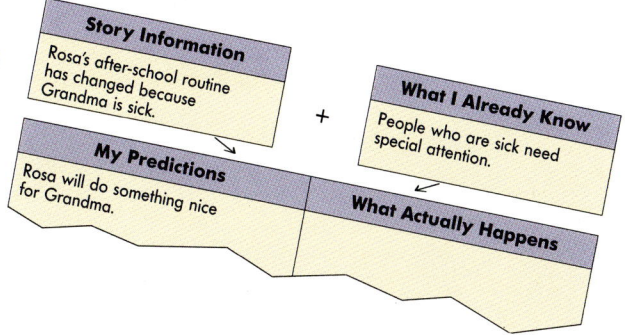

MUSIC, MUSIC FOR EVERYONE / T171

Words from the Author and Illustrator

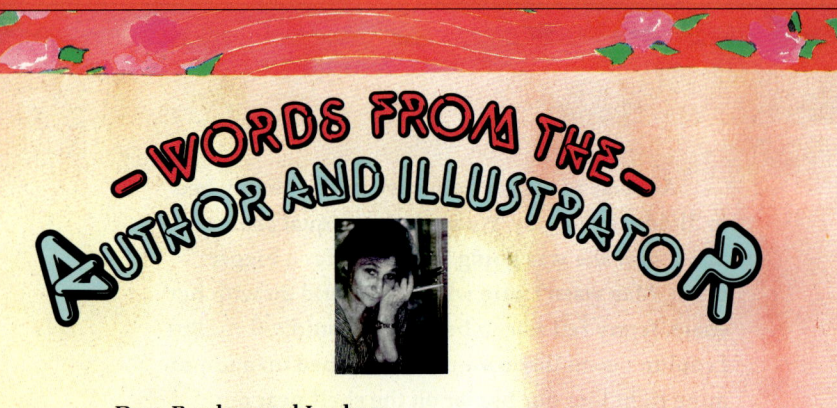

Dear Readers and Lookers,

I'm glad you've had a chance to read my story in this collection. The complete story is printed here just as I wrote it. But it wasn't possible to put in all the pictures and borders and backgrounds.

I'd like you to see my whole book in a library or bookstore sometime because I planned *Music, Music for Everyone* from the very front cover to the back cover. I painted all the borders and the watercolored backgrounds. I even picked out the kind of alphabet letters to use from the hundreds of kinds that the printing company has.

First I wrote the story. It took about a month till I got it just right. After that I made a sample book of the right size and glued in copies of the paragraphs and sketches. I tried different arrangements for the pages. When I made the paintings I had to imagine how everyone should look and all the rooms and all the food. Everything. That's the most exciting part for me.

While I worked I had the radio on. I listened to all kinds of music, and I think that music is in the colors and wave shapes of the borders now for everyone to see.

Vera B. Williams

AWARD-WINNING AUTHOR

Words from the Author and Illustrator

AUTHOR/ILLUSTRATOR'S CRAFT Invite students to read page 120 to find out about the process Vera B. Williams went through when she was writing and illustrating this story. Ask them to explain this process in their own words. (Accept reasonable responses: First she wrote the story. Then she made a model of the book that was the same size the real book would be. To figure out how the book would look, she glued in copies of the paragraphs and sketches of the pictures. As she worked, she listened to music, which helped give a musical feel to the pictures.)

• LANGUAGE ARTS • CROSS-CURRICULAR CONNECTIONS • READING • LANGUA   IONS READING • LANGUAGE ARTS • CROSS-CURRICULAR CONNECTIONS • READING • LA

PART 2

Responding to the Literature

Personal Response

Encourage critical thinking.

Think about the part of the story that meant the most to you. Use your own words to retell your favorite part of the story to a friend. (Responses will vary.) CRITICAL: EXPRESSING PERSONAL OPINIONS

Rosa, the main character, uses her music to help her family. What could you imagine doing to help other people who are having troubles? (Responses will vary.) CREATIVE: SOLVING PROBLEMS

Encourage creative written responses.

WRITE In this story, Rosa worries about her sick grandma and the empty money jar. Write your opinions about happy stories and sad stories and which you'd rather read. Tell about different stories you remember or tell one from your own life that would make a good book. You may want to offer students the choice of responding to just one part of the writing prompt: they can write *either* about happy stories and sad stories *or* about a story that would make a good book. CRITICAL: MAKING JUDGMENTS/ STORYTELLING

Cooperative Response

Have reader response groups extend their discussions.

LITERATURE CIRCLES Encourage the Literature Circles to share their reactions to the story. Suggest that they discuss any questions or comments they wrote down as they read. Then have students discuss a question such as the following:

What kind of person is Rosa? Use examples from the story to support your answer.

STRATEGY CONFERENCE

Ask students how the prediction diagram helped them understand and enjoy the story. (Accept reasonable responses: This strategy helped me focus on the important story events.)

NOTE

An additional writing activity for this story appears on page T176.

STUDENT SELF-ASSESSMENT

To help students self-assess their listening, write a list of good listening skills on the board:

A good listener:
- does not interrupt
- thinks about other people's ideas
- adds ideas to what others have to say

MUSIC, MUSIC FOR EVERYONE / T173

Summarizing the Literature

Have students retell the story and write a summary. Encourage students to summarize the story by recalling key story events. Guide them in beginning the story steps below (starting at the bottom), and have them finish independently. Students may use their completed steps to retell the story and to write a brief summary. See *Practice Book* page 33 below.

At the end of the story, the girls feel (happy) because (they had fun; they earned money).

The people at the party think the Oak Street Band plays (very well).

The Oak Street Band gets this job: (playing at a party for Leora's great-grandmother and great-grandfather).

Grandmother says (it is a good idea).

She tells her grandmother this idea: (She and three friends will make money by playing their musical instruments).

The main character sees her family's money jar and notices (it is empty).

Critical Thinking Activity

Solve problems through discussion.

BRAINSTORM IDEAS What are some other ways in which Rosa and her friends could earn money?

Suggest students brainstorm ways their talents could be used to make money. CRITICAL: SOLVING PROBLEMS

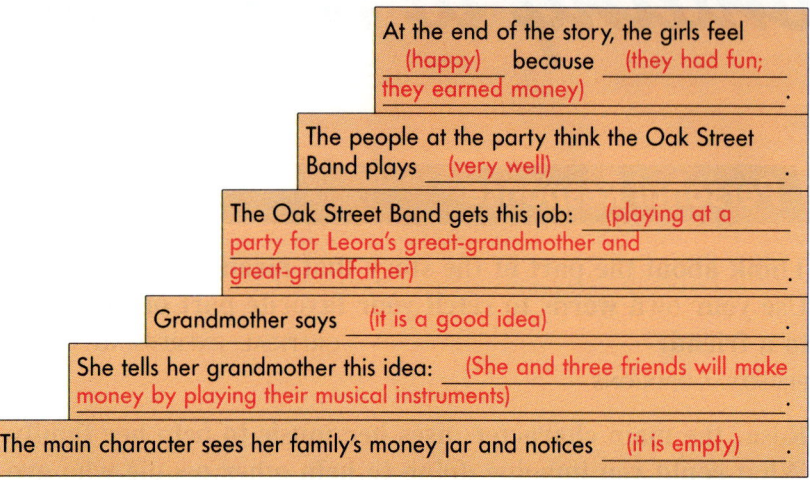

tutoring — Earning Money — raking leaves
pet sitting — recycling

Writer's Journal

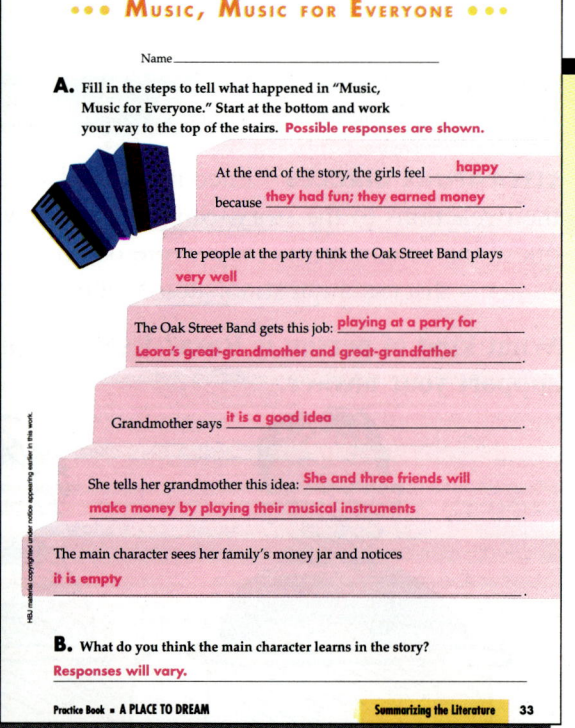

Practice Book

OPTIONAL INDEPENDENT PRACTICE

WRITER'S JOURNAL
pages 18–19: Writing a personal response

PRACTICE BOOK
page 33: Summarizing the selection

T174 / A PLACE TO DREAM, UNIT 1

VOCABULARY WORKSHOP

Reviewing Key Words

Write the following words on the board, and have students copy them on index cards or slips of paper.

- instrument
- gathering
- year
- one
- full

Read aloud the first part of each analogy below, and discuss the relationship between the two words. Then read the third word aloud, and ask students which word on their cards goes with the third word in the same way. Have students hold up that card. Repeat the activity if necessary.

- broccoli : vegetable :: accordion : (instrument)
- Sunday : week :: anniversary : (year)
- hot : cold :: empty : (full)
- quiet : silent :: assembly : (gathering)
- several : many :: single : (one)

Extending Vocabulary

ALLITERATION   Ask students what beginning letter is repeated in the title "Music, Music for Everyone." (m) Explain that when an author uses words that have the same beginning letter or sound, the author is using *alliteration*. Recite the following line from a Mother Goose rhyme:

Peter Piper picked a peck of pickled peppers.

Ask students to identify the repeated sound. (/p/) Then repeat the activity with these rhymes:

- **Baa, baa, black sheep**
- **Peter, Peter, pumpkin-eater**

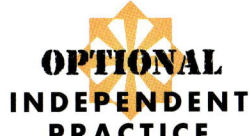

PRACTICE BOOK
page 34: Writing with alliteration

Practice Book

MUSIC, MUSIC FOR EVERYONE / T175

Language Arts WORKSHOP

READING

Oral Rereading/Drama

Recall with students that Rosa is a very resourceful character. Invite students to locate a passage in the story that shows how resourceful Rosa is. Have them read the passage silently first, and then encourage several students to read aloud the passage they selected. After they finish reading, ask students how the passage they chose demonstrates Rosa's resourcefulness. LISTENING/SPEAKING/READING

SPELLING

Reviewing Spelling Words

SPELLING WORDS: *bike, cake, drove, face, fine, ice, rose, same, smoke, spoke, stone, these*

WORDS TO EXPLORE: *anniversary, assembly, company, empty*

Have students form small groups. Assign each group at least four Spelling Words, and have them list words that follow the same spelling generalization (e.g., for *bike*, words might be *hike* and *like*). When groups are finished, have them pantomime the words they listed. Remind students who are guessing that the words being pantomimed rhyme with a certain Spelling Word.
LISTENING/SPEAKING/WRITING/SPELLING

Use *Integrated Spelling* Lesson 5 to reinforce the Spelling Words and the Words to Explore. See pages T39–T44 in *Integrated Spelling Teacher's Edition*.

 **SPELLING POSTTEST** You may want to use the Pretest/Posttest Sentences on *Integrated Spelling Teacher's Edition* page T39 to assess students' knowledge of the spelling generalization.

WRITING

Writing About the Literature

Available on Project Card 12A

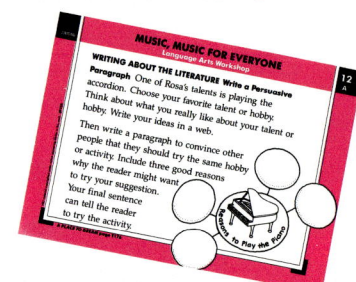

WRITE A BOOK REVIEW Ask students to be book critics and write a review of "Music, Music for Everyone." Have students use the following diagram to organize information for their review. Provide time for students to share their work. See Writing Model, page R99.
LISTENING/SPEAKING/READING/WRITING

> Begin with the book title and the author's name.

> Next, briefly tell what the book is about.

> Then tell what you liked and didn't like about the book.

> Finally, tell whether you would recommend the book to your friends.

GRAMMAR REVIEW: COMMON NOUNS When students revise their book reviews, remind them to check their use of common nouns. They should be sure that common nouns, which name any person, place, or thing, begin with a lowercase letter. To reinforce the skill, have students work in pairs to find and list common nouns from the story.

 **LANGUAGE HANDBOOK** *Writing to Persuade, pages 60–61, 63; Common Nouns, page 93*

 **DAILY LANGUAGE PRACTICE** *Oral language exercises are provided on pages R62–R63.*

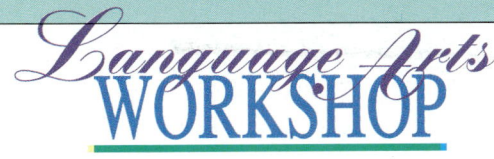

WRITING

A Business Letter

Invite students to imagine that Rosa wants to buy special sheet music for the Oak Street Band. Ask them how she could go about doing this. (She could call music companies or write them letters asking about the music she wants.) Encourage students to write a letter for Rosa to the Kramer Music Company. You may wish to display an actual business letter and encourage students to copy its format, including its heading, greeting, body, closing, and signature. When the letters are finished, encourage volunteers to read them aloud. LISTENING/READING/WRITING

READING

Learn All About It!

Take students to the school library, and have them borrow books about something they would like to learn how to do. For instance, some students might like to learn how to read music. Have students read their books, take notes, and then present brief oral reports describing the information they learned. LISTENING/SPEAKING/READING/WRITING

LISTENING AND SPEAKING

The Sounds of Music

Available on Project Card 12B

For a week, have students keep a daily record of the musical sounds they hear. Suggest that students develop a chart like the one below in which they include each type of sound, a musical instrument that makes a similar sound, and a description of the sound. At the end of the week, encourage students to share their charts with others. LISTENING/SPEAKING/WRITING

Musical Sounds		
Type of Sound	**Instrument**	**Description**
birds chirping	flute	sweet, quick notes
train whistle	trumpet	shrill blast

MUSIC, MUSIC FOR EVERYONE / T177

Grammar MINILESSON

Proper Nouns

OBJECTIVE: *To understand that a proper noun names a particular person, place, or thing and that all important words in proper nouns begin with a capital letter*

Oral Warm-Up

Write on the board the following sentences from "Music, Music for Everyone," without underlining the nouns.

- <u>Leora</u> plays the <u>drums</u>. <u>Mae</u> plays the <u>flute</u>.
- And that was how the <u>Oak Street Band</u> got started.
- <u>Aunt Ida</u> and <u>Grandma</u> said we were terrific.

Have students identify the words that name a person, place, or thing. Underline the nouns as students name them. Then have a volunteer circle each noun that names a particular person, place, or thing. **(Leora, Mae, Oak Street Band, Aunt Ida, Grandma)**

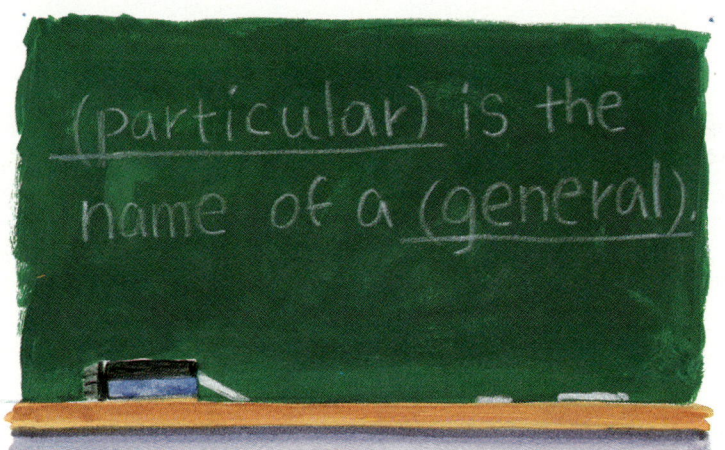

Have volunteers name particular and general things in a format like the following. **(Accept reasonable responses: Pittsburgh, city; Ford, car; Jack, person; and so on.)**

Interactive Teaching

PROPER NOUNS Explain that a noun that names a *particular* person, place, or thing is a **proper noun.** Write on the board a sentence that identifies your school and the city where it is located. Use the full name of the school. Underline the proper nouns, and explain that proper nouns begin with a capital letter. Explain also that if a proper noun contains more than one word, the first letter in each important word is capitalized. Provide students with several examples. **(Main Street, Library of Congress, Smithfield Mall)** Next, ask students to come up with sentences that tell about their favorite musical performer or group or about a place they have gone or would like to go to listen to music. Write their sentences on the board. Then have volunteers circle the proper nouns in each sentence.

With students, fill in a chart like the following to show various types of proper nouns:

person's name	(Tabitha, Frank)
person's title	(Dr., Ms., Miss)
street name	
city name	
school name	
holiday	
day of week	
month	

LANGUAGE HANDBOOK
Proper Nouns, page 94

T178 / A PLACE TO DREAM, UNIT 1

Practice Activities

Proper Cards

Provide each student with a piece of construction paper. Have students fold their paper in half and use the inside of the folded paper to write a greeting card to a grandparent, another older relative, or a friend. Encourage them to tell the person about what they and their friends like to do and where they like to go. Tell them to name several particular people, places, and things in their message. Have students exchange their cards with a partner to check each other's capitalization of proper nouns. Then let students decorate their cards. If possible, have them mail or deliver their cards.   VISUAL

Race for Nouns

COOPERATIVE LEARNING   Divide the group into four teams. Provide each team with a copy of the same passage that contains numerous proper nouns. Have one member of each team act as a Recorder. At your signal, the other members of the team should scan or read the passage, identify each proper noun, and tell it to the Recorder. Give each group one minute to come up with as many proper nouns as possible. Then collect each group's list. Review the passage with students, having volunteers identify each proper noun. Have a member of each group review another group's list for correct word selection and capitalization. The team with the most correct words wins.   VISUAL

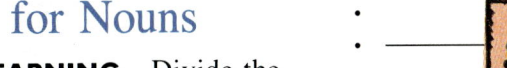

Practice Book

MEETING INDIVIDUAL NEEDS

SECOND-LANGUAGE SUPPORT   Have students work in pairs to reread a page from a story the class has read together and to copy all the proper nouns onto a separate sheet of paper.

RETEACH   Follow the visual, auditory, and kinesthetic/motor models on page R16.

OPTIONAL INDEPENDENT PRACTICE

- **PRACTICE BOOK**
  page 35: Identifying and using proper nouns
- **GRAMMAR PRACTICE**
  pages 20–21: Reinforcing proper nouns

MUSIC, MUSIC FOR EVERYONE / T179

PART 3

Learning through the Literature

DECODING STRATEGY
INTRODUCE

Structural Clues

OBJECTIVE: *To use structural analysis for the independent decoding of words*

Interactive Teaching

Focus on words in "Music, Music for Everyone."

LITERATURE CONNECTION Recall with students that "Music, Music for Everyone" probably contained a few words they did not recognize. Have volunteers point out such words. Tell students that sometimes, looking at the smaller parts, or syllables, in a word can help them pronounce it. Explain that once they can pronounce a word, they may discover that they have heard it before and know what it means.

Strategy: Have students examine words with word parts.

MODEL USING STRUCTURAL CLUES Write *unsuccessful* on the board. Tell students that *un-* is a *prefix*, a group of letters added to the beginning of a word, and can mean "not." Then explain that *-ful* is a *suffix*, a group of letters added to the end of a word, and can mean "full of." Tell students that prefixes change the meanings of the words and that suffixes change the meanings and how the words are used.

Display Chart/Transparency 13 or the following sentences. Have students use structural clues to figure out the pronunciations and meanings of the underlined words.

Chart/Transparency 13   Structural Clues

1. Rosa was <u>careful</u> when she took down the money jar.
2. The jar looked <u>fuller</u> after Mae put a dime in it.
3. Leora's mother would be <u>unhappy</u> if there was no music at the party.
4. The people at the party thought the Oak Street Band was <u>wonderful</u>.

T180 / A PLACE TO DREAM, UNIT 1

Practice Activities

What's That Word?

Have students use structural clues.

Have students complete the chart shown below, using structural clues to help them decode the words. Encourage students to use a dictionary to help them write meanings. Then have them exchange charts with a partner and compare the meanings they wrote for the unfamiliar words.   VISUAL

Word	Clue	Meaning
careful	care + -ful	("done with care")
fuller	full + -er	("more full than before")
unhappy	un- + happy	("not happy")
wonderful	wonder + -ful	("full of wonder," "very good")

More Clues

Extend the lesson by having students look at another story.

Encourage students to list unfamiliar words they come across and write them down. Have them tell when they used structural clues to figure out the meaning of a word.   AUDITORY

Performance Assessment

Have volunteers explain how they used structural clues to figure out unfamiliar words in the What's That Word? and More Clues activities. Then ask students to make a poster that lists these prefixes and suffixes and their meanings. Suggest that students add other suffixes and prefixes to the chart as they learn them. For evaluation guidelines, see *Staff Development Guide*.

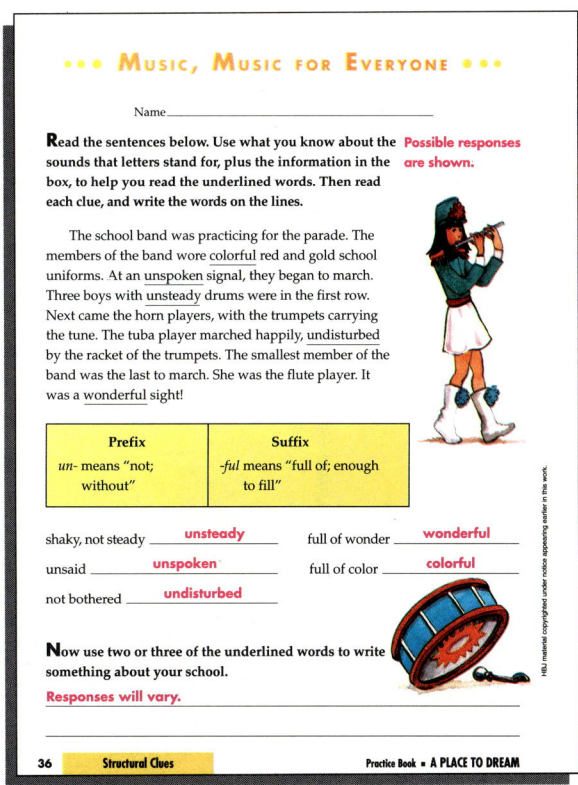

Practice Book

MEETING INDIVIDUAL NEEDS

RETEACH Follow the visual, auditory, and kinesthetic/motor models on R17.

CHALLENGE Have students write a paragraph about a time when they sang, danced, or played an instrument for someone. Challenge them to include words with prefixes and suffixes.

SECOND-LANGUAGE SUPPORT Write on the board two sentences using the words *beautiful* and *unhappy*. Have students identify the prefix or suffix in each of the words. See also the manual *Alternative Teaching Strategies,* pages 7–8, 52–55.

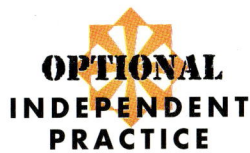

OPTIONAL INDEPENDENT PRACTICE

PRACTICE BOOK

page 36: Using structural analysis to decode words

MUSIC, MUSIC FOR EVERYONE / T181

STUDY SKILLS
REVIEW

Following Directions

OBJECTIVE: *To follow and give oral and written directions*

Review

Have students analyze directions.

REVIEW FOLLOWING AND GIVING DIRECTIONS Invite students to share experiences when they have not given or followed directions correctly. Then, together, create a set of tips such as those below for giving and following directions:

Giving Directions	Following Directions
1. Speak or write clearly. 2. Give steps in order, using time-order words or numbers.	1. Listen or look for key words. 2. Recall the steps in order. 3. Imagine doing each step.

Practice Activity

Follow the Leader

Have students write directions. Have students write a set of directions for something that they know how to do well and that can be easily completed in class. Then have them cut apart the directions, mix them up, and have a partner try to put them in the correct order. Partners should take turns reading aloud their directions, explaining how they decided on the order as they read.   VISUAL/KINESTHETIC

MEETING INDIVIDUAL NEEDS

CHALLENGE Provide paper and crayons to pairs of students, and have them sit so they cannot see one another. Have one partner create a pattern and then explain to the other partner how to duplicate the pattern. Ask partners to compare their patterns and discuss how the directions might have been clearer. Have partners reverse roles.

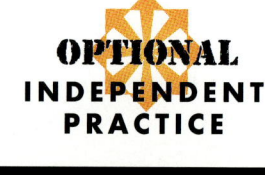

OPTIONAL INDEPENDENT PRACTICE

PRACTICE BOOK

page 37: Following directions

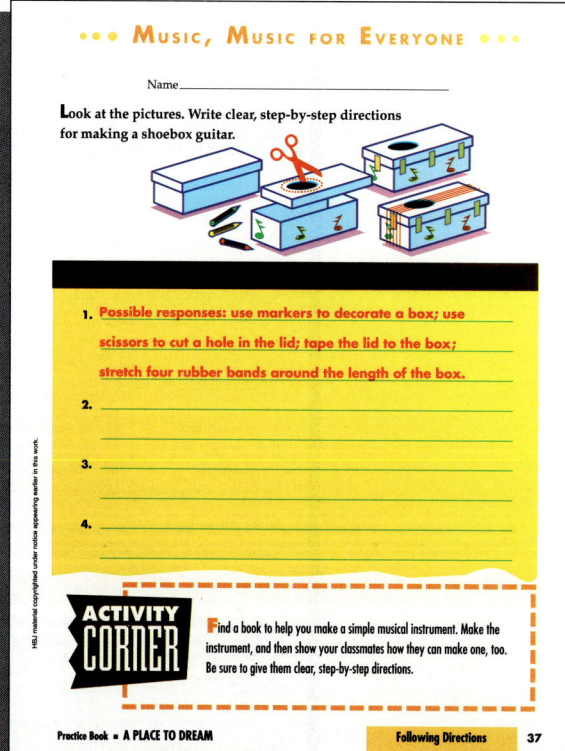

Practice Book

T182 / A PLACE TO DREAM, UNIT 1

COMPREHENSION REVIEW

Cause and Effect

OBJECTIVE: *To recognize cause-and-effect relationships*

Review

Discuss probable causes and effects.

USE STORY EVIDENCE PLUS PRIOR KNOWLEDGE Remind students that sometimes an author tells readers when one thing causes another thing, and other times the reader must figure out causes and effects. Discuss how to determine cause and effect. (Use story information plus prior knowledge.) Model the strategy by using the following chart:

Effect	Story Information	Prior Knowledge	Probable Cause
The money jar is empty.	Grandma is sick.	Being sick can be costly.	The money was used to care for Grandma.

Practice Activity

Why Did It Happen?

Have students chart cause and effect.

Have groups of students make their own charts to show other cause-and-effect relationships in the story. Suggest that groups share and discuss their charts with another group.   VISUAL

MEETING INDIVIDUAL NEEDS

CHALLENGE Have students write a short paragraph in which they tell something that happened (the effect) but not why it happened (the cause). Ask students to exchange papers and try to determine the probable cause or causes. Encourage students to use a cause-and-effect chart.

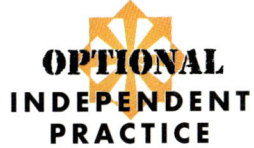

OPTIONAL INDEPENDENT PRACTICE

PRACTICE BOOK
page 38: Recognizing cause-and-effect relationships

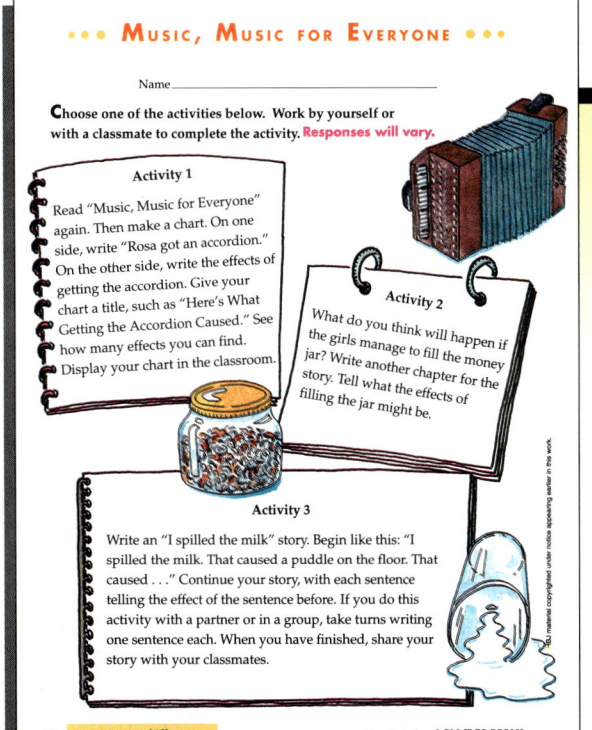

Practice Book

MUSIC, MUSIC FOR EVERYONE / **T183**

Integrated CURRICULUM

SOCIAL STUDIES

Instruments Around the World

CULTURAL AWARENESS Recall with students that each member of the Oak Street Band plays a different instrument. Explain to students that some instruments, like drums, are common to many cultures; others, such as Scottish or Irish bagpipes or the Japanese samisen, were developed in a particular culture. Invite students to work in small groups to research an instrument and to discover if it is specific to a particular culture or if it is found in many cultures. Students in each group should work together to make a poster showing people playing the instrument and a map of where it was developed and to tell something about how the instrument is played. When students have completed their research, invite groups to explain their poster to classmates. LISTENING/SPEAKING/READING/WRITING/VIEWING

ART

Music Makes Me Feel . . .

Available on Project Card 13A

Play a variety of musical recordings for students. After each piece, encourage students to describe how the music makes them feel. Next, provide drawing paper and crayons. Play additional recordings, and invite students to express in drawings how the music makes them feel. After students have completed three or four drawings, invite them to display their work and to explain what they have drawn. LISTENING/SPEAKING/VIEWING

MATH

What's My Share?

Recall with students that the members of the Oak Street Band divided the money they earned into four equal parts. Ask students how much money each member would get if the total payment were $24.00, $40.00, or $80.00. ($6.00, $10.00, or $20.00) Then ask students to imagine that the Oak Street Band becomes so popular that its members decide to add another musician. Ask students how much each person in the band would receive if the band's fee were $25.00, $50.00, or $100.00. ($5.00, $10.00, or $20.00) LISTENING/SPEAKING

T184 / A PLACE TO DREAM, UNIT 1

SCIENCE

Effects of Music

USE REFERENCE SOURCES Write the following saying on the board: *Music has charms to soothe.* Invite students to share their opinions as to the meaning of this saying. Then ask students to work in groups to find out what effect music has on animals or people, according to research. Suggest that students try to locate information in science encyclopedias and other reference books. If students cannot find information, you may wish to have them write letters to organizations that work with animals. Have students share their findings with classmates. LISTENING/SPEAKING/READING/WRITING

PHYSICAL EDUCATION

Move Your Feet to the Beat!

Available on Project Card 13B

Explain to students that many types of dance—for example, the tango, square dancing, clogging, waltz, and many rock-and-roll and contemporary dances—have been developed in response to different kinds of music. If possible, play a variety of recordings to share the music that usually accompanies specific dances. Then invite students to select one kind of dance and to research its origin and how the dance is done. Invite volunteers to teach the dance they learned to classmates. LISTENING/SPEAKING/READING

BOOKS TO SHARE

SOCIAL STUDIES *Cynthia Gregory Dances Swan Lake* by Cynthia Gregory. Simon & Schuster, 1990. AVERAGE

Chin Chiang and the Dragon's Dance by Ian Wallace. Macmillan, 1984. CHALLENGING

MULTICULTURAL PERSPECTIVES

Young and Gifted Musicians

DISCUSSION STARTER
How old do you think a person has to be to become a great musician?

READ ALOUD
Many successful musicians reveal their talent at a young age. Yo-Yo Ma is a case in point. He played his cello in concert for the first time when he was just five years old. He owes a lot to his father, who was a music professor in China. But it is Yo-Yo Ma's special gift, along with a lot of hard work, that has made him a brilliant and respected musician.

Itzhak Perlman, too, is brilliant and respected. Born in Israel, he says he always wanted to play the violin. Indeed, he was only four when his parents bought him his first violin. Something else happened that year. Perlman came down with polio. That did not stop him from practicing, but it did mean he would always walk with leg braces and crutches. At the age of thirteen, he came to the United States to appear on television's *Ed Sullivan Show*. From that day on, Americans never stopped applauding this virtuoso violinist.

Another talented violinist, Chouhei Min, began violin lessons at the age of five. She was just nine years old when she first played with the Seoul Philharmonic Orchestra in Korea. After studying in Boston, she joined first the Dallas Symphony Orchestra and later the Minnesota Orchestra.

ACTIVITY CORNER
Available on Project Card 14
● Have groups of students research other famous child prodigies, such as Shirley Temple and Andre Watts, and prepare biographies. Encourage groups to give oral presentations, having each student tell about a certain aspect of the person's life. If students locate photographs, they should share them with classmates.

● Arrange for students to listen to a recording by one of the musicians discussed here. Afterward, encourage them to write a paragraph explaining how the music made them feel and what they liked or did not like about it.

Yo-Yo Ma and Itzhak Perlman showed a talent for their instruments when they were still quite young.

T186 / A PLACE TO DREAM, UNIT 1

THEME WRAP-UP

Discussing the Theme

Remind students that the selections in this theme show that you can enjoy music by making music or by being part of the audience.

Discussion Question

PAGE 121 As you read these selections, you learned about musical instruments and about how music can make people happy. Can you think of something other than music that can make you happy? (Responses will vary.)
CREATIVE: EXPRESSING PERSONAL OPINIONS

Theme Wrap-Up

Listen to This!

As you read these selections, you learned about musical instruments and about how music can make people happy. Can you think of something other than music that can make you happy?

WRITER'S WORKSHOP
Think about your favorite music. Then write a paragraph that describes how that music sounds and how it makes you feel.

Writer's Choice:
You might decide to write about an instrument you would like to play. Or you might invent an instrument and write a description of it. Plan what you would like to write and how you will share it.

121

Writer's Workshop

See pages T188–T189 for suggestions for guiding students through the writing process as they respond to the literature.   WRITING PROCESS: DESCRIPTIVE PARAGRAPH

Writer's Choice
You may want to have students refer to the *Language Handbook* as they write. Have them choose a writing form and refer to the guidelines for writing that particular form. Encourage students to use descriptive words and phrases, as well as vivid verbs, to help make their writing more interesting.

After students revise and proofread, you may want to ask volunteers to read their work aloud. Encourage students who are listening to notice words and phrases that help them "see" or "hear" the descriptions.

Writer's Workshop

Descriptive Paragraph

Theme Wrap-Up

Students write a descriptive paragraph telling how a favorite piece of music sounds and makes them feel.

To prepare students for the writing task and form, review the vivid descriptions of instruments and music given in "Meet the Orchestra." Discuss the images the descriptions bring to mind. Tell students that in writing good description they should use vivid words that let the reader see, hear, feel, and—whenever possible—taste and smell what is being described.

Use the Writer's Workshop assignment on page 121 as you work through the writing process with students.

ALTERNATIVE TOPICS If you wish, allow students to choose their own topics for writing. Suggest to students that they refer to the *Language Handbook* for an explanation of the writing process for descriptive paragraphs. See Writing Model, page R93.

 **LANGUAGE HANDBOOK** *Writing to Describe,* pages 44–45; Descriptive Paragraph, page 46

Prewriting

Have students meet with partners to brainstorm favorite music that they would like to describe. Suggest that students list sensory details in a chart like the one below to help them create a vivid picture. Suggest also that students use the word *like* or *as* to tell how their favorite music is like something else.

My Favorite Electric Guitar Music	
sounds loud	has energy like a rocket
makes strong vibrations	makes me feel happy

Drafting

Have students draft their descriptive paragraphs. Remind them to

- write a strong beginning sentence that tells what they are going to describe.
- refer to their prewriting notes for ideas and sensory words to describe the music.
- use vivid describing words and exact nouns as they write.

If some students have trouble getting started, have them draw a picture of what they want to describe before writing about it.

Responding and Revising

Before students get together for peer conferences, suggest that they

- check that their sentences give a vivid picture of the music.
- check that they included comparisons using *like* or *as*.
- make sure that they used exact nouns.

Then have students read their work aloud in a peer conference and answer the following questions and complete the following task:

Listener	Writer
Does the descriptive paragraph give you a vivid feeling about how the music might sound? Does the writer tell what the music is like? Do the sentences make sense?	When you read your descriptive paragraph aloud, do some parts seem stronger than other parts? Could you use more or better sensory details? If some parts are weak, think of ways you can make them stronger.

COMPUTER TIP

 **REVISING** Students might use the thesaurus provided with many word processing programs to help them find exact nouns.

Proofreading

Offer the following tips for students as they proofread:

- Check that any proper nouns are capitalized.
- Check that the paragraph is indented.
- Circle words that may be misspelled, and check them in a dictionary.

MINI-CONFERENCE STRATEGY Help students locate instances in which they have lowercased proper nouns or capitalized common nouns with observations such as "Is *the boston symphony* a specific symphony somewhere, or does it mean any symphony?"

Publishing Options

SCHOOL DISPLAYS Encourage students to create music collages to go with their descriptions. The collages can show visually how the music makes them feel and what they would compare its sounds to. Arrange their descriptions and collages on a school bulletin board.

ORAL-AURAL PRESENTATIONS Have students bring in recordings of the music they have described from home or the library. Volunteers can play the music for classmates and then read their descriptions aloud.

Assessment Options

 STUDENT SELF-ASSESSMENT Encourage students to summarize the writing experience by responding to this question in their journals:

What did I learn about describing something that can't actually be seen or touched?

You may also want to have students complete the Self-Assessment Checklist in the *Portfolio Assessment Teacher's Guide*.

WRITING OBSERVATION RECORDS Record instances in which students use dictionaries, thesauruses, and other resources such as books on music as evidence of curiosity about language and the assignment.

 After students publish, you may want to have them add their descriptive paragraphs to their portfolios.

GRAMMAR CONNECTION

Revising: Exact Nouns

Use Transparency C to share with students ways to use exact nouns to make their writing more vivid.

> **Transparency C**
> **Birds and Thunder**
>
> **BEFORE**
> Some parts of the music sound like <u>birds</u> singing in tiny but high <u>sounds</u>. Those <u>parts</u> seem like a sour <u>fruit</u> to <u>me</u>. Later in the music, a loud <u>sound</u> is like thunder in my <u>head</u>.
>
> **AFTER**
> Some parts of the music sound like <u>hummingbirds</u> singing in tiny but high <u>voices</u>. Those parts seem like a sour <u>lemon</u> to me. Later in the music, a loud <u>boom</u> is like thunder in my <u>ears</u>.

Have small groups of students share their writing to check that it includes a variety of exact nouns.

 **LANGUAGE HANDBOOK** *Using Vivid Words,* page 25; Nouns, pages 92–94

UNIT 1

CONNECTIONS

The Connections activities on Student Anthology pages 122–123 guide students to link multicultural and content-area information to the unit theme. Have students identify their favorite selections from the unit and suggest why they think each was included in a unit called "Being Special."

To prepare students for the Multicultural Connection, ask whether they have heard of the country called Kenya. Have a volunteer locate Kenya on a map or globe. Then invite students to share what they know about the country. You may wish to record their responses on the board.

Tell students that if they traveled along the coast of Kenya, they would see beaches, lagoons, swamps, and some rain forests. Traveling farther inland, they would come to a vast plain that covers almost three-fourths of the country. This area has a very dry climate and poor soil. Point out, however, that in the southwest there is a highland with enough rain and fertile soil for farming. This is where most of the people in Kenya live. Further explain that most Kenyans are Africans. Students may also find it interesting to know that many kinds of animals, including elephants, giraffes, zebras, rhinoceroses, and lions, live in Kenya. Explain that Kenya, like every other nation in the world, faces environmental problems, such as endangered wildlife.

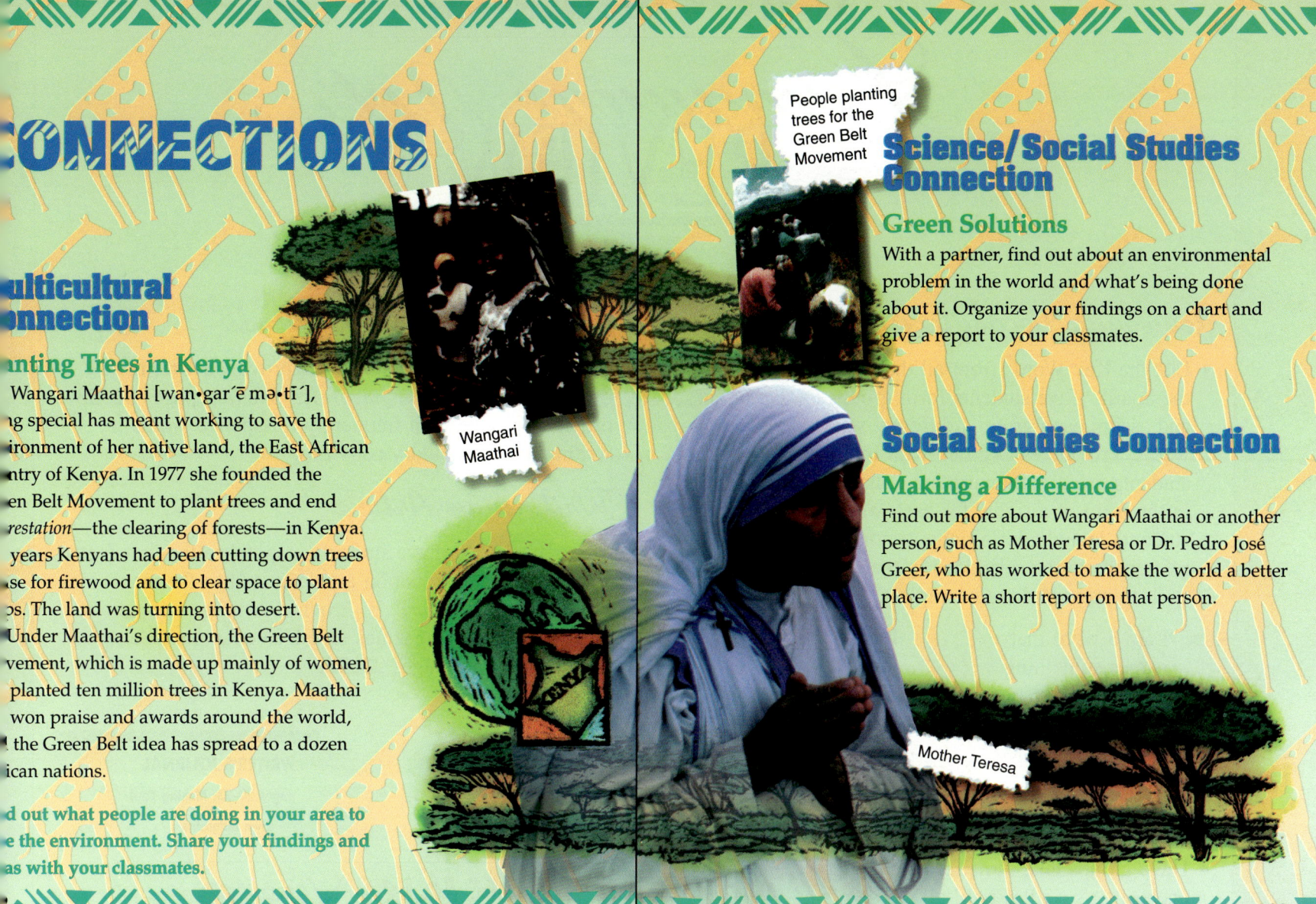

CONNECTIONS

Multicultural Connection

Planting Trees in Kenya

For Wangari Maathai [wan•gar´ē mə•tī´], doing special has meant working to save the environment of her native land, the East African country of Kenya. In 1977 she founded the Green Belt Movement to plant trees and end deforestation—the clearing of forests—in Kenya. For years Kenyans had been cutting down trees to use for firewood and to clear space to plant crops. The land was turning into desert.

Under Maathai's direction, the Green Belt Movement, which is made up mainly of women, has planted ten million trees in Kenya. Maathai has won praise and awards around the world, and the Green Belt idea has spread to a dozen African nations.

Find out what people are doing in your area to save the environment. Share your findings and ideas with your classmates.

Wangari Maathai

People planting trees for the Green Belt Movement

Science/Social Studies Connection

Green Solutions

With a partner, find out about an environmental problem in the world and what's being done about it. Organize your findings on a chart and give a report to your classmates.

Social Studies Connection

Making a Difference

Find out more about Wangari Maathai or another person, such as Mother Teresa or Dr. Pedro José Greer, who has worked to make the world a better place. Write a short report on that person.

Mother Teresa

Multicultural Connection

PLANTING TREES IN KENYA Provide students with materials concerning state and local environmental issues and problems. Help them find the names, telephone numbers, and addresses of local, state, and federal environmental organizations. Then have students form groups, choose an organization, and write a letter to request information about a problem or issue.

Science/Social Studies Connection

GREEN SOLUTIONS Have students make a list of environmental problems they are aware of. Then have pairs of students choose a problem, note what they know about it, and determine what they need to find out. With the help of the librarian, students should use reference books, magazines, and newspapers to find information to complete the chart.

Social Studies Connection

MAKE A DIFFERENCE Check with the school librarian to be sure materials are available on Wangari Maathai, Mother Teresa, and Martin Luther King, Jr., who all worked to improve the world. Invite students to read aloud their reports to classmates.

UNIT 1 WRAP-UP

Language Arts REVIEW

Reviewing Vocabulary

- List the Key Words from all the selections in Unit 1 on the board. Have students form groups of five or six, and assign each group a different set of six or ten words. Provide each group with index cards. Have students use a dictionary and a thesaurus to write clues in the form of a riddle for each word. Suggest that students include definitions, synonyms, antonyms, and references to the selections in their clues. You may wish to provide these examples:

  I am a word that names something you can use to make musical sounds. A violin is a good example of me. Which word am I? *(instrument)*

  I am a word that describes. I am how a piccolo can sound when it's high-pitched and screechy. *(shrill)*

- Have groups take turns reading aloud and answering each other's riddles until all the words have been guessed.

Reviewing Grammar

Have students write common and proper nouns on index cards and place them in a jar or box. Then ask them to pick two cards and create a sentence using the nouns shown. Encourage each student to create each of the following sentence types:

1. statement
2. question
3. command
4. exclamation

After a student writes a sentence, have other players check the capitalization and punctuation. Allow students to share humorous or interesting sentences by reading them aloud.

Reviewing Spelling Words

Integrated Spelling pages 30–31 provide a Unit review of the Spelling Words. *Integrated Spelling* pages 32–33 provide practice with frequently misspelled words in writing and vocabulary activities.

Writing an Article

You may wish to have students respond to the unit focus by writing an information article to add to the magazines in their *Writer's Journals*. Provide them with copies of articles from magazines to use as examples. See *Writer's Journal* pages 20–23.

WRITER'S JOURNAL
pages 20–23: Making Your Own Magazine

Writer's Journal

UNIT 1 WRAP-UP

Assessment Options

Informal Assessment

The suggestions below can help you informally assess students' progress in Unit 1.

INFORMAL ASSESSMENT NOTES AND CHECKLISTS If you used the informal assessment notes in the lesson plans, you may now want to summarize your Running Records. You may also want to administer Oral Retellings with individual students. If they have not done so, encourage students to complete the Self-Assessment Checklist in the *Portfolio Assessment Teacher's Guide*.

PORTFOLIO CONFERENCE A Portfolio Conference offers you a chance to learn about each student's

- interest in reading realistic fiction as one type of genre.
- general writing development.
- awareness of cause and effect.

Discuss the realistic fiction stories that were read in Unit 1, focusing on whether the students enjoyed them and why. Ask each student to name similar stories she or he has read.

Then ask the student to choose a favorite piece of writing from the portfolio. The student may want to share the journal entry he or she wrote in response to "Miss Rumphius," telling how to make the world a more beautiful place, or the invitation to a party, written in response to "Music, Music for Everyone." Ask the student to describe what he or she liked about the piece. Provide positive feedback and encouragement.

Formal Assessment

Select from the following assessment tools to meet your assessment needs.

UNIT READING SKILLS ASSESSMENT The *Unit Reading Skills Assessment* for Unit 1 provides feedback about students' mastery of the specific skills and strategies taught in Learning Through the Literature. The skill tested in this unit is Cause and Effect. If students had difficulty, refer to the lessons in the Reteach section for visual, auditory, and kinesthetic/motor models that can be used to reteach the tested skill.

UNIT HOLISTIC READING ASSESSMENT The *Unit Holistic Reading Assessment* for Unit 1 may be used to assess a student's ability to understand passages written at the same level as the selections in the Student Anthology. If students have difficulty, use the Reteach Lesson for Active Reading Strategies. Use the modeling suggestions found throughout the *Teacher's Edition* to support students as they read the selections in Unit 2.

UNIT INTEGRATED PERFORMANCE ASSESSMENT The *Unit Integrated Performance Assessment* for Unit 1 gives you a profile of how well each student uses reading, writing, listening, and speaking strategies to read and respond to a piece of literature. Assessment results reflect how well students make use of the strategies modeled and practiced in the classroom.

UNIT LANGUAGE AND WRITING ASSESSMENT The *Unit Language and Writing Assessment* for Unit 1 includes a Skills Inventory to assess students' knowledge of sentences (definition, word order, capital letters, end marks), subjects and predicates, and common and proper nouns, and a Writing Test, which contains a writing prompt, evaluation rubrics, and scoring guidelines for personal narratives. Corresponding lessons and practice in the *Language Handbook* may be used with students who have difficulty on the assessment instrument.

Break Time!

ENCOURAGING ENVIRONMENTAL AWARENESS

Teachers and students alike are concerned about conserving natural resources and cleaning up the environment. Through various projects, students can examine the impact on the school environment of food services, paper products, and graffiti. Such projects not only improve the environment but also teach students research and problem-solving strategies. Here are some tips for your budding environmental activists:

1. *Choose a topic.* Brainstorm topic ideas:
   - Is this problem important and interesting?
2. *Make predictions.* Once the topic is chosen, make predictions:
   - What do we expect to learn?
3. *Devise procedures.* Develop an organizational plan:
   - What course of action seems most likely to succeed?
4. *Collect data.* Use your information and observations to form a plan:
   - How will we learn what we need to know?
5. *Analyze the data.* Make connections with what you already know:
   - What patterns can we see?
6. *Make evaluations.* Think about the value of your project:
   - Was this a worthwhile topic?
   - How would we do it differently another time?

Use materials from the following sources to help students get started:

Center for Environmental Education
1725 DeSales Street NW, Suite 500
Washington, D.C. 20036

National Wildlife Federation
8925 Leesburg Pike
Vienna, VA 22184

JOSHUA'S STRUGGLE

Joshua Lee was diagnosed as having visual and perceptual problems when he was eight years old. As a sophomore in college, Joshua wrote about his early school experiences:

"Reading was extremely hard....It wasn't easy to watch others reading when I couldn't. What I didn't realize at the time was that I could do things they couldn't....As far back as I can remember, I was the one who stopped fights, made game rules, and generally tried to advise others with problems....I overcame whatever self-doubts I acquired with my learning disabilities because I was always surrounded by people whose support of me was unflagging."

Clearly, special needs can also bring special rewards to those who struggle and to those who support that struggle.

"Isn't it astonishing that no two of us are exactly alike?"

UNIT 2

Friendships

THEME: **School Days**
T202–T241

THEME: **Caring and Sharing**
T242–T307

THEME: **Learning About Yourself**
T308–T349

UNIT 2 OPENER

Planning Center · FRIENDSHIPS

What's Ahead in "Friendships"?

SCHOOL DAYS: PAGES T202–T241 Meet author Beverly Cleary and eight-year-old Ramona Quimby, the character she created. Students will enjoy reading about Ramona's humorous adventures as a third grader.

CARING AND SHARING: PAGES T242–T307 Invite your students to discover the significance of caring and sharing as they read the stories and poem about three very special relationships between friends and family members and between older and younger people.

LEARNING ABOUT YOURSELF: PAGES T308–T349 Your students may learn new things about themselves when they read a story about a city boy on his grandpa's ranch, an article about the author, and a poem about friendship.

Audiovisual Materials and Software

Big Book Maker: Feeling Good About Yourself! Pelican. This program is designed to motivate self-expression through writing and illustrating books. COMPUTER SOFTWARE

A Kid's Guide to Good School Behavior. Learning Tree, 1993. Cartoons, music, and narration help students understand what is expected of them in school. FILMSTRIP

Meet the Newbery Author: Beverly Cleary. Random House. This is an inside look at the life of the author of the Ramona stories and other popular titles. FILMSTRIP

Ramona by Beverly Cleary. Warner Home Video, 1988. Ramona and her family come to life in this series of thirteen live-action episodes from Beverly Cleary's Ramona books. VIDEO

Through Grandpa's Eyes by Patricia MacLachlan. Barr, 1987. Grandpa has his own special way of "seeing" even though he is blind. FILM/VIDEO

Ty's Homemade Band. Phoenix/BFA, 1983. Based on the book *Ty's One-Man Band* by Mildred Pitts Walter, this video features Taj Mahal as the wandering minstrel. VIDEO

Harcourt Brace Literature Cassette

Recordings of some of the selections for "Friendships" may be used for instruction or for students' listening enjoyment:

- "Writers"
- "A Gift for Tía Rosa"

Harcourt Brace Big Book
Best Friends

Daily Language Practice
Proofreading activities for daily use are available on pages R64–R69.

Family Involvement
The *Family Involvement Activities* offer several possibilities for extending each theme and expanding the unit focus. A Read-at-Home piece of literature is also included for family members to enjoy together.

Pacing
This unit is designed to take approximately five or six weeks to complete, depending on your students' needs.

Bulletin Board Idea

Write the phrase "Friendship is . . ." in the center of a bulletin board. Then ask students to think about what friendship means to them. Invite students to help create a bulletin board display about friendship by writing or finding poems about friendship; drawing, painting, or cutting out magazine pictures that demonstrate friendship; or writing their own definitions of friendship. Encourage students to share and discuss their contributions and to add to the display as they get new ideas from reading the selections in Unit 2.

Assessment and Evaluation Options

Throughout the Unit — Informal Assessment

READING

INFORMAL ASSESSMENT NOTES
Record observations of students, using anecdotal records or behavioral checklists. The symbol at left indicates teachable moments throughout the lessons.

STUDENT SELF-ASSESSMENT NOTES
Follow point-of-use suggestions in the lesson to have students monitor their own learning, attitudes, and interests.

RUNNING RECORDS
Gain insights into students' application of reading strategies by tracking oral reading errors, or miscues. See the *Individual Inventory for Reading and Writing* for administering and interpreting results.

ORAL RETELLINGS
Retelling may be used as an alternative to questioning to assess students' comprehension of text: recall of major points and relevant/irrelevant details, what the reader adds to or infers from the text, insights into how the reader constructs meaning.

INTEGRATED LANGUAGE ARTS

READING/WRITING PORTFOLIO
Portfolio Assessment combines product and process assessment in a comprehensive, ongoing record of a student's literacy development. Students collect samples of reading and writing activities, including finished work, work-in-progress, and plans/ideas for future work; reading and writing logs; and self-assessment checklists. See the *Portfolio Assessment Teacher's Guide* for implementing a portfolio system.

PORTFOLIO CONFERENCES
Schedule a conference with each student to learn about the student's reading and writing interests, habits, and attitudes and to help the student reflect on his or her reading and writing.

STUDENT LOGS AND JOURNALS
Encourage students to keep a collection of thoughts, ideas, and opinions to use for reflecting on their reading, writing, and learning.

LANGUAGE

STUDENT SELF-ASSESSMENT NOTES
Encourage students to monitor and reflect on their writing so that they can begin to take responsibility for their own improvement. Notes at point of use in the lesson plans, plus checklists in the *Language Handbook* and the *Portfolio Assessment Teacher's Guide,* may be used to monitor growth.

WRITTEN RETELLINGS
A student's written retellings can help you analyze how well the student organizes ideas, develops ideas, and applies knowledge of conventions of writing. See the Retelling Analysis Summary form in the *Individual Inventory for Reading and Writing*.

End-of-Unit — Formal Assessment Tools

READING SKILLS TEST
Multiple-choice diagnostic tests to assess mastery of **lesson vocabulary, main idea and details, following directions,** and **structural analysis.**

HOLISTIC READING TEST
This test includes theme-related passages accompanied by multiple-choice questions that focus on application of literal, inferential, and critical thinking, major comprehension objectives, and students' ability to construct meaning.

INTEGRATED PERFORMANCE ASSESSMENT
A structured reading-writing task to help you determine whether students can use reading to write and whether they can accomplish a specific writing task.

LANGUAGE SKILLS AND WRITING TEST
Multiple-choice questions and a writing prompt assess students' knowledge of **singular and plural nouns, irregular plural nouns,** and **possessive nouns** and their ability to write a **how-to paragraph.**

PLANNING CENTER / T197

PAGES 124–125 *Unit Opener*

Unit Two
Friendships

*We're not a bit the same and yet,
We're closer than most people get.*

    Jean Little

Some friends you see every day, and some friends you may never meet. But how can someone you have never met be a friend? In a way, Antonia Novello was a friend to everyone in the United States, because she was the doctor in charge of our nation's public health program. In what other ways can someone be a friend? Think about this question as you read the next selections.

THEMES

School Days 128

Caring and Sharing 148

Learning About Yourself 186

Introducing "Friendships"

Invite students to share their ideas about how they feel when they are with a friend and why they think friendship is important. Then ask students to read the unit introduction and the theme titles to help them set a purpose for reading the unit.

Ask students how they might develop a friendship with someone from another culture. Encourage students to speculate on the types of things each person might learn from the relationship. **CULTURAL AWARENESS**

Writer's Journal pages 24–26: Reading and writing about "Friendships"

T198 / A PLACE TO DREAM, UNIT 2

BOOKSHELF

RAMONA QUIMBY, AGE 8
by Beverly Cleary

Ramona Quimby is having a little trouble adjusting to third grade. She wants to be a good student and a help to her family, but sometimes just being Ramona is hard enough.
Newbery Honor Book
Harcourt Brace Library Book

TY'S ONE-MAN BAND
by Mildred Pitts Walter

This original American folktale, created by the author, tells about a peg-legged man named Andro who entertains others as a one-man band. One summer he brings joy to Ty's town through the music he makes.
Award-Winning Author
Harcourt Brace Library Book

ELAINE, MARY LEWIS, AND THE FROGS
by Heidi Chang

Elaine Chow is very unhappy after moving to a small town in Iowa, until she shares a new friendship and a science project with Mary Lewis, a girl very interested in frogs. Elaine's father teaches them both something about his hobby, which helps them with their project and becomes a symbol of their friendship.

MISTER KING
by Raija Siekkinen

A lonely king who has no subjects is paid a visit by a very unusual cat. The cat brings about many surprises, and the king's life changes in several ways.
Award-Winning Author

JULIAN'S GLORIOUS SUMMER
by Ann Cameron

Julian is afraid of bicycles, but he has trouble showing his fear to his friend Gloria, who can ride a bike with no hands. Julian goes to amazing lengths to keep bicycles out of his life.
ALA Notable Book

From the Harcourt Brace Library

Ramona Quimby, Age 8 follows Ramona's developing relationships with her family, her teacher, and her friends as she enters the third grade.

- You may wish to have students read *Ramona Quimby, Age 8* independently after reading the selection in the Student Anthology. Then have them discuss story elements such as plot, characters, and setting.
- Students can read *Ramona Quimby, Age 8* before reading the selection in the Student Anthology. While reading, they might focus on a specific element, such as the author's use of humor.

Ty's One-Man Band is an unusual tale about a boy named Ty and a man who brings special music to Ty's neighborhood.

- You may want to have students read the book before reading the selections in this unit. Before reading, encourage them to discuss activities friends can share.

Harcourt Brace Library Comprehensive lesson plan available for each book.

Bookshelf selections *Mister King* and *Julian's Glorious Summer* are also available as Harcourt Brace PASSPORTS titles.

Listening to Literature

Read aloud to students.

Good Morning, River!

by Lisa Westberg Peters

"Good morning!"

Katherine heard the old man's voice boom out across the broad river valley. A softer voice called back, "Good morning . . . good morning. . . ."

The old man was Carl. He was Katherine's friend. He always told Katherine that the softer voice was the river talking back to him.

"That's silly," Katherine would say. "The river can't talk." Then she would shout in a squeaky voice, "Good morning!" No voice ever called back.

"See?" Katherine would say. "The river doesn't talk to me."

"Maybe someday it will," he'd say.

After breakfast, Katherine ran to Carl's house. It was time to check the river's ice. They climbed down the bluff and saw thick slabs of ice curled over the shore as if they had frozen in the middle of a wave. Carl walked out and bounced a few times.

Then Katherine stepped out. Crunch, one foot. Crunch, the other foot.

They crouched down and brushed away the white snow. Dark ice, full of ripples, bubbles, and cracks, lay beneath.

"How can you tell it's safe to walk on?" Katherine asked.

The ice rumbled gently. "The river tells me," Carl said with a wink. Katherine listened again, but she heard nothing.

The winter passed. The river was swollen with snow melt and rain. Floodwater rose to the limbs of the trees, and everywhere was the sweet smell of rotting leaves.

Carl marked Katherine's height on his wooden cane and said, "You're a half inch taller, Miss Katherine. That's big enough for a jungle ride."

They climbed into the red canoe. Carl pretended he was dizzy with jungle fever, and Katherine pretended she was sweaty in the steamy rain.

"Watch out for alligators and snakes," she warned. He paddled around them.

Katherine listened for jungle sounds and heard a soft chuckle. "It's a monkey!" she cried. But when she looked for it, all she saw was the river rushing past their canoe.

Spring turned to summer, and the floodwater drew back. The river sparkled in hot white sunlight, and shimmery heat rose from the sand.

One afternoon, Katherine lost her first tooth. Carl reached into his pocket and gave her two nickels—a shiny one as old as she, and a smooth one as old as he.

"Been saving these for you," he said. "You're growing up. In fact, I'll bet you can swim all the way to the dock this year."

"I don't want to," she said. "I might bump into a turtle."

"I used to swim underwater with my eyes wide open," Carl said. "Never bumped into a thing."

Katherine decided to try. She held her breath, opened her eyes, and stared into the watery darkness. "Hello!"

Selection Background

Katherine wishes that the river would talk to her as it talks to Carl, her friend. Every day, Carl calls to the river, "Good morning!" and the river answers. Carl shares with Katherine his love and knowledge of the river as it changes through the seasons, until one day, she, too, can speak to it—and it answers her!

Author **Lisa Westberg Peters** spent her childhood summers on the St. Croix River. She loved the river so much that she decided to write a story that would make rivers seem less scary to children.

Strategies for Listening

LISTENING/THINKING STRATEGY—MOOD Tell students that the mood of a story is the feeling that the story conveys to the listener.

SET A PURPOSE FOR LISTENING Remind students that this unit is called "Friendships." Ask students to pay close attention to the descriptive details used by the author to tell how things look, feel, and sound in the river valley. Also tell students to listen for examples of the friendship Katherine and Carl share.

she shouted, but the word bubbled up to the surface and popped.

After her swim, she sat on the beach with Carl and sang her favorite songs. The river answered with its own music—a steady slap . . . slap . . . slap of the evening ripples. Carl didn't sing. He was asleep.

In the fall, a steady wind began to blow across the river. It whipped the waves into gray peaks and tossed their foamy caps into the air.

One morning, Katherine didn't hear Carl's booming voice, just the dry scratch of branches against the glass. She left her breakfast and ran through the woods to his house. Carl sat rocking in his favorite wicker chair.

"I had a pretty bad night, Katherine," he said, patting his chest. "My sister is coming from town to fetch me. She says I need a good rest."

"When will you come back?" Katherine asked.

"After a while," he said. "And then we'll chase around some more."

Katherine stayed until Carl's sister came. The car disappeared in the dust of the gravel road.

All that fall, the cold drizzle chilled the chickadees into silence. The river was silent, too.

It froze over one day with a thin skin of ice. No ripples, no bubbles, no cracks. That was the day Carl came home.

Katherine saw the smoke from his chimney and raced to see him. There he was, rocking in his wicker chair, but something was different. His booming voice was gone. "I don't think I can say good morning to the river today," he whispered.

Katherine hesitated. "Maybe I can," she said.

She turned to face the broad valley, stood tall, and held her hands around her mouth. As loudly as she could, Katherine yelled, "Good morning!"

And she heard the river answer. A softer voice called back, "Good morning . . . good morning. . . ."

Responding to Literature

1. **What mood or feeling does this story give you? What words does the author use to make you feel that way?** (Accept reasonable responses: The mood is peaceful or happy; *the softer voice was the river* and *the river sparkled in hot white sunlight*.)
   INFERENTIAL: AUTHOR'S CRAFT/APPRECIATING LANGUAGE

2. **Why do you think Katherine chose Carl to be her friend?** (Accept reasonable responses: He was kind; he taught Katherine about the river.) CRITICAL: DRAWING CONCLUSIONS

SPEAKING Have each student draw a picture of his or her favorite season in the river valley as it is described in the story. Then have volunteers describe their pictures. Encourage them to use colorful language. CREATIVE: ORAL COMPOSITION

TEACHING TIP In "Good Morning, River," you can help establish the mood of the story by using appropriate pace, pitch, and volume.

LISTENING TO LITERATURE / T201

Unit 2 FRIENDSHIPS

THEME OPENER

School Days

Ramona's Neighborhood

T205 A MAP
Although Beverly Cleary's characters Henry and Ramona are fictional, the places she writes about in Portland, Oregon, are real.

Ramona Quimby, Age 8

T209 A REALISTIC FICTION STORY by Beverly Cleary
Ramona has a great idea for making her book report special, but she worries that her teacher will think she is showing off.

An Interview with the Author: Beverly Cleary

T221 AN INTERVIEW
Is Beverly Cleary anything like her characters? She answers that question and others during an informative interview.

For pacing suggestions, see page T204.

Theme Opener: School Days   PAGES 128–129

THEME

School Days

While growing up, people often have some funny experiences mixed in with their everyday school activities. You are going to read about a funny character and about the author who created her—Beverly Cleary.

CONTENTS

RAMONA'S NEIGHBORHOOD

RAMONA QUIMBY, AGE 8
by Beverly Cleary

AN INTERVIEW WITH THE AUTHOR: BEVERLY CLEARY

129

Discussing the Theme

Ask students to look at the illustration and discuss how it relates to the theme "School Days." Next, ask students to read the paragraph on Student Anthology page 129 and to share some of their own funny experiences in school. Then have students read the selection titles and speculate about the kind of experience Ramona might have.

Portfolio Assessment

Tell students to keep their writing responses for the selections in "School Days" in their portfolios. Remind them also to add to their personal journals thoughts and ideas about books they have read independently.

 As you come across this symbol, you might encourage students to save a sample of their work in their portfolios.

THEME OPENER: SCHOOL DAYS / T203

THEME OPENER

Managing the Literature-Based Classroom

Publishing Center

A publishing center, equipped with a computer or a typewriter, paper, and art materials, can be used to great advantage by small groups of students. Encourage them to combine their ideas and their writing and artistic skills to make maximum use of the publishing center. You may want to post a schedule so groups and individuals can sign up for specified blocks of time.

Reader's Response Sheet

To help students be more positive and effective when responding to or reviewing their classmates' writing for the Writer's Workshop, you may wish to provide a "Reader's Response Sheet" with specific instructions.

Reader's Response Sheet

Name _____ Date _____

- Underline a sentence that captured your interest.
- Circle interesting descriptive words and time-order words.
- Write a positive comment.
  _____
- Identify any part that is unclear to you.
  _____
- Make suggestions for improvement.

Pacing

This theme has been designed to take about two weeks to complete, depending on your students' needs.

MEETING INDIVIDUAL NEEDS

LOW-ACHIEVING STUDENTS You may wish to provide additional background information about the selection setting by locating Portland, Oregon, on a map of the United States and displaying pictures of the city or showing a filmstrip or travel video about the city.

GIFTED AND TALENTED Remind students that "Ramona Quimby, Age 8" is an excerpt from a book of the same title. Encourage students to read the book as well as others from the Ramona series, and then have a group discussion in which students who have read the book share their opinions about it. *Challenge Cards* provide additional activities to challenge students. Challenge notes throughout the lesson plans suggest additional activities to stimulate critical and creative thinking.

SPECIAL-EDUCATION STUDENTS When reading "An Interview with the Author," you may wish to have students with visual perception problems use small self-stick notes of two different colors to distinguish between the interviewer's questions and Beverly Cleary's responses.

STUDENTS ACQUIRING ENGLISH When writing their new story endings for the Writer's Workshop activity, students may find it helpful to first sketch the events and then arrange the pictures in order before writing a draft. Second-Language Support notes throughout the lesson plans offer strategies to help students acquiring English to understand the selection.

MAP

Ramona's Neighborhood

ABOUT THE ILLUSTRATOR Alan Tiegreen is an artist and an illustrator of books for children. As a child, he was interested in both art and music, but he says his interest in art prevailed because he "did not have enough patience to practice" his music. He has illustrated many children's books, including four books by Beverly Cleary.

SELECTION SUMMARY On this map of a Portland, Oregon, neighborhood, five places from Beverly Cleary's books are indicated. A group of readers of Cleary's books used clues in the stories to identify places on the map.

Building Background

Provide background and access prior knowledge about maps.

Point out to students that in the next selection they will meet Ramona Quimby. Invite students to share what they may already know about Beverly Cleary's "Ramona" books. Explain that the map titled "Ramona's Neighborhood" shows a real neighborhood in Portland, Oregon, where Beverly Cleary grew up and which is the setting for her Ramona stories. Have students list different kinds of maps, and ways in which a map is useful. Then use their ideas to develop a web on the board like the one below:

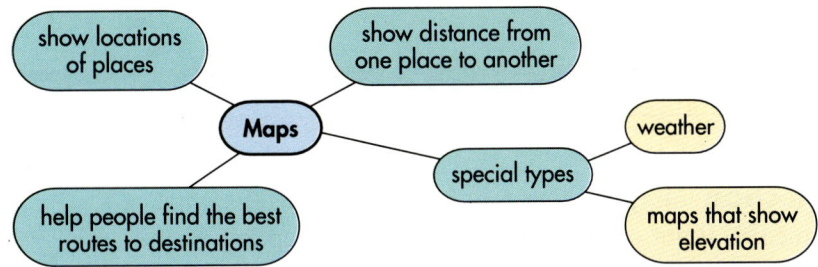

Strategic Reading

Help students make predictions and set a purpose.

Ask students to look at the map key. Point out the book titles in parentheses. Have students predict what else the map will tell them.

SETTING A PURPOSE Help students use their predictions to set a purpose for reading the map "Ramona's Neighborhood." Offer the following suggestion if students have difficulty setting a purpose independently:

I'm going to study the map to find out how it relates to the events in stories about Ramona.

TEACHING TIP

Point out that even though the map depicts a real place, it is meant to show how the neighborhood relates to the Ramona stories. Therefore, it is not an exact street map, and it shows some things that usually would not be on a map of a real place.

MEETING INDIVIDUAL NEEDS

SECOND-LANGUAGE SUPPORT Show students a simple road map or street map. Ask them to tell what the map shows, and have them point to and name some of the places they see. See also the manual *Alternative Teaching Strategies*, pages 9, 56–57.

PAGES 130–131   RAMONA'S NEIGHBORHOOD

RAMONA'S Neighborhood

Beverly Cleary was born, attended school, and grew up in Oregon. This walking map of the northeast section of Portland, Oregon, identifies landmarks from some of her books. The places shown on the map were suggested by people who read books in the Henry and Ramona series and searched for clues in them that referred to Portland landmarks. When they found clues, they described what happened there. Even though Beverly Cleary's characters are fictional, Ramona's neighborhood is a real place.

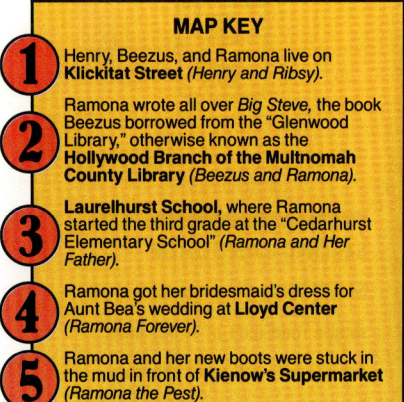

MAP KEY

1. Henry, Beezus, and Ramona live on **Klickitat Street** (Henry and Ribsy).
2. Ramona wrote all over Big Steve, the book Beezus borrowed from the "Glenwood Library," otherwise known as the **Hollywood Branch of the Multnomah County Library** (Beezus and Ramona).
3. **Laurelhurst School,** where Ramona started the third grade at the "Cedarhurst Elementary School" (Ramona and Her Father).
4. Ramona got her bridesmaid's dress for Aunt Bea's wedding at **Lloyd Center** (Ramona Forever).
5. Ramona and her new boots were stuck in the mud in front of **Kienow's Supermarket** (Ramona the Pest).

Social Studies Connection   Explain that a map key usually tells what each symbol on a map means. Point out that, in this case, the map key explains the numbers on the map. Have students point to the number 1 on the map and to the corresponding number on the map key. Explain that Klickitat Street is a real street in Portland, Oregon, and that in Beverly Cleary's books it is also the name of the street where Ramona lives.

Returning to the Predictions/Purpose   Encourage students to tell whether their predictions changed as they studied the map. Discuss with students how the places identified on the map are supposed to relate to events in the stories about Ramona. (Each one corresponds to a place named in the stories; the specific books in which these places are named are listed in the map key.)

Personal Response

Encourage critical thinking.

Do you think Ramona's neighborhood would be a good place for a child to live? Tell why you think as you do. (Accept reasonable responses: Yes, there seem to be many places to go and things to do.) CRITICAL: EXPRESSING PERSONAL OPINIONS

What are some kinds of things in Ramona's neighborhood that are also in your neighborhood? (Accept reasonable responses: parks, shopping center, school, library.) CRITICAL: COMPARING AND CONTRASTING

Encourage creative written responses.

WRITE What is your favorite place to go in your neighborhood? Write directions for how to get there from your home or school. Suggest that students think about the way they would go. If necessary, use a local map to help them recall the names of the streets. CREATIVE: WRITING DIRECTIONS

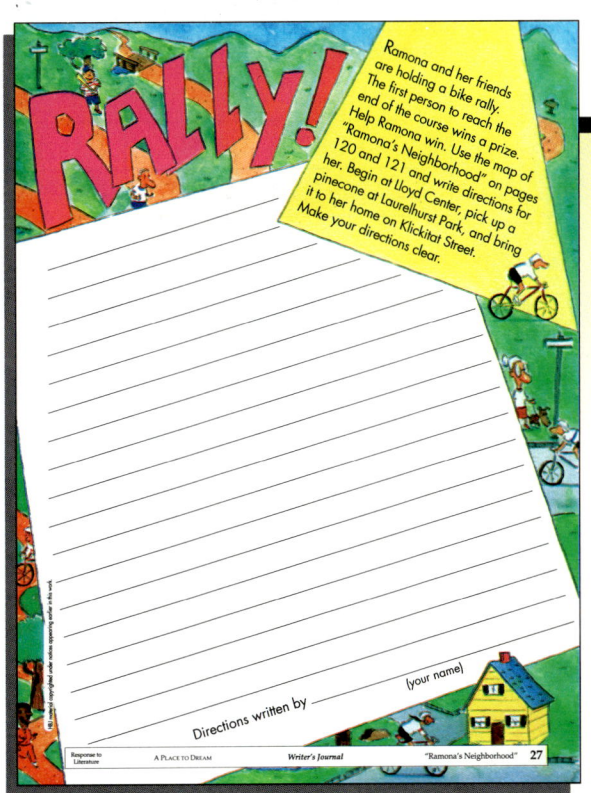

Writer's Journal

INFORMAL ASSESSMENT

Asking students to use the information in a text to write about something related can reveal clearly how well students understand the information.

OPTIONAL INDEPENDENT PRACTICE

WRITER'S JOURNAL

page 27: Writing a personal response

Appreciating Literature

Have students work in small groups to discuss the map. Provide a question such as the following to help the groups begin:

If you wrote realistic stories like Beverly Cleary's, where would your stories take place? What would you name the streets, schools, parks, and shopping centers?

 **PERSONAL JOURNAL** Have students use their personal journals to write about ideas discussed in the groups.

Critical Thinking Activities

Encourage both cooperative and individual responses.

GIVE DIRECTIONS **How would Ramona get from her house to the library? Describe the shortest route she might take.** Have students study the map and name the streets and turns she would follow to get from Klickitat Street to the library on the corner of Tillamook Street and N.E. 39th Ave. (number 2 on the map). CREATIVE: VISUALIZING

DRAW A MAP **If a story were written about you, your classmates, and your neighborhood, what places do you think would appear on a map about the story?** Invite students to work in small groups. Suggest that they list the names of places in their neighborhood and then think of events that could happen there that might be part of the story. Then have students draw a neighborhood map, number the places, and create a key to explain each number. Students may want to organize their ideas in a chart such as the one below. CRITICAL: MAKING JUDGMENTS

Place	Event
post office	class field trip
(Main Street)	(July 4 street fair)
(Central Park)	(bicycle race)
(Northgate Shopping Center)	(getting lost)

T208 / A PLACE TO DREAM, UNIT 2

Ramona Quimby, AGE 8

by **Beverly Cleary**
illustrated by **Alan Tiegreen**

Integrated Lesson Planner

Ramona Quimby, Age 8
pages 132–146

	READING	**LANGUAGE ARTS**	**CROSS-CURRICULAR CONNECTIONS**
PART 1 *Reading the Literature* pages T212–T222	**Building Background** **Vocabulary Strategies** **Prereading Strategies** Story Map Setting a Purpose **Options for Reading**	**Spelling** Pretest Spelling-Vocabulary Connection Generalization: *kn, wr, gh, ph* **Grammar Connection** Reviewing Proper Nouns	**Cultural Awareness** Egypt, birthplace of the book **Math Connection** Number sentences
PART 2 *Responding to the Literature* pages T223–T229	**Personal Response** **Cooperative Response** **Summarizing the Literature** **Critical Thinking Activity** Role-Play **Vocabulary Workshop** Key Words Homophones	**Language Arts Workshop** **Reading** Readers Theatre **Reviewing Spelling Words** Posttest **Writing** paragraph of information, a school assignment **Listening and Speaking** improvisation, TV jingle, public address **Grammar Review** Proper Nouns **Grammar Minilesson** Singular and Plural Nouns	**Science** Writing About the Literature
PART 3 *Learning Through the Literature* pages T230–T238	**Introduce** Decoding: Structural Analysis (Tested) Comprehension: Author's Purpose **Review** Comprehension: Main Idea and Details (Tested) Vocabulary Strategy: Contextual and Structural Clues	**Reading** All About Cats **Writing** Masks Around the World **Listening and Speaking** Careers in Public Speaking	**Social Studies** Careers in Public Speaking **Science** About Your Memory All About Cats **Art** Masks Around the World **Math** Picture This **Multicultural Perspectives** An Education for All

OPTIONAL MATERIALS
Charts/Transparencies 14–16
Integrated Spelling pp. 34–37; TE pp. T51–T56
Practice Book pp. 39–45
Writer's Journal pp. 28–29
Alternative Teaching Strategies pp. 9, 58–61
Language Handbook pp. 51, 96–99
Grammar Practice pp. 28–29
Family Involvement Activities: Unit 2, pp. 1–4
Response Card 9
Project Cards 17A, 17B, 18A, 18B, 19

MEETING INDIVIDUAL NEEDS
Second-Language Support pp. T213, T214, T216, T229, T231, T233
Mainstreaming p. T214
Reteach pp. T229, T231, T233
Challenge pp. T231, T233, T234, T235

FAMILY INVOLVEMENT Encourage family members to discuss and categorize their favorite television commercials with descriptions such as "funny" or "good use of music." See *Family Involvement Activities*.

Key Words
accuracy
commercials
entertainment
chorus
nuisance
giggle
performance
memorizing

T210 / A PLACE TO DREAM, UNIT 2

Selection Summary

In an introduction to this excerpt from *Ramona Quimby, Age 8,* we learn that Ramona thinks her teacher, Mrs. Whaley, doesn't like her. As the excerpt begins, Ramona is preparing a report on *The Left-Behind Cat,* a book Mrs. Whaley has assigned to her. She writes her report in the style of a TV commercial, using cat masks for herself and for her backup kitty chorus. Her presentation goes well until she gets distracted by a classmate and forgets her lines. She finally blurts out the only thing she can think of: "I can't believe I read the whole thing!" Everyone bursts out laughing, including Mrs. Whaley; and when Ramona talks with her afterward, she learns that Mrs. Whaley does like her very much, and that Ramona's fears were based on a misunderstanding.

Ramona Quimby, Age 8 was a Newbery Honor Book in 1982.

About the Author

Beverly Cleary did not always love reading and writing. She recalls, "As a child I had difficulty learning to read. The discovery, when I was about eight years old, that I could actually read, and read with pleasure, was one of the most exciting moments of my life. . . . The stories I write are the stories I wanted to read as a child, and the experience I hope to share with children is the discovery that reading is one of the pleasures of life and not just something one must do in school."

For her work Beverly Cleary has won numerous awards which include the following: the American Library Association's Laura Ingalls Wilder Medal for her collected works; the Golden Kite Award of the Society of Children's Book Writers for her novel *Ralph S. Mouse;* and both the Christopher Award and the Newbery Medal for her book *Dear Mr. Henshaw.*

Additional Reading

OTHER BOOKS BY BEVERLY CLEARY

Henry and the Paper Route. William Morrow, 1957. CHALLENGING

Muggie Maggie. Avon, 1991. AVERAGE

*Ramona Forever. William Morrow, 1984. CHALLENGING

OTHER THEME-RELATED BOOKS

The Candy Corn Contest by Patricia Reilly Giff. Dell, 1984. EASY

The Math Wiz by Betsy Duffey. Puffin, 1993. AVERAGE

BOOKS FOR APPLYING STRATEGIES: AUTHOR'S PURPOSE

Best Friends by Steven Kellogg. Dial, 1986. EASY

Chicken Sunday by Patricia Polacco. Philomel, 1992. AVERAGE

The Hot and Cold Summer by Johanna Hurwitz. Scholastic, 1985. CHALLENGING

*Available as a Harcourt Brace PASSPORTS title

PART 1

Reading the Literature

Building Background

Access prior knowledge and build vocabulary concepts.

Explain that in "Ramona Quimby, Age 8," Ramona's assignment is to "sell" the book she's read. Have students brainstorm different ways to report on a book and the information that should be included in these reports.

Have students quickwrite.

Have students write a list of the information they would expect to find included in a book report. The completed list might include the following items:

> **Book Report**
> 1. Title
> 2. Author and illustrator
> 3. Where and when the story takes place
> 4. Characters
> 5. What the book is about
> 6. Problems and how they are solved

Vocabulary Strategies

Introduce Key Words and strategies.

Display Chart/Transparency 14 or the story on it. Have students read the paragraph silently, using context clues to figure out the meanings of the underlined words. For example, students might use the clue *always gets the channel she wants* to determine the meaning of *accuracy*.

> **Chart/Transparency 14   Key Words**
>
> My sister has amazing <u>accuracy</u> with a remote-control TV channel changer. She always gets the channel she wants. She changes the channel when <u>commercials</u> interrupt a show. She switches to the <u>entertainment</u> shows, especially the ones with a <u>chorus</u> of singers.
>
> At times she can be a <u>nuisance</u> as she jumps from channel to channel. She gets so pleased with herself she begins to <u>giggle</u>. She pushes all the buttons. I think she enjoys giving a <u>performance</u> to show how well she is doing. She has even been <u>memorizing</u> the keys so she can switch stations without looking.
>
>

CULTURAL AWARENESS

Students may be interested to learn that Egypt is probably the birthplace of the book. Ancient Egyptians recorded their words on long sheets of papyrus, a paperlike material made from plants.

Key Words

accuracy
commercials
entertainment
chorus
nuisance
giggle
performance
memorizing

KEY WORDS DEFINED

accuracy   freedom from mistakes; correctness

commercials   paid ads on TV or radio

entertainment   something that entertains or amuses

chorus   group of singers or dancers

nuisance   something that annoys or irritates

giggle   to laugh in a silly or nervous way

performance   show or presentation

memorizing   learning by heart

Check all students' understanding.

Draw on the board the web shown below, omitting the Key Words. Have students use the Key Words to add to the web. (Placement of words may vary.) Encourage students to give reasons to support the placement of each word. This activity might be done in pairs, after which students can compare and discuss their word placements.   STRATEGY: CATEGORIZING

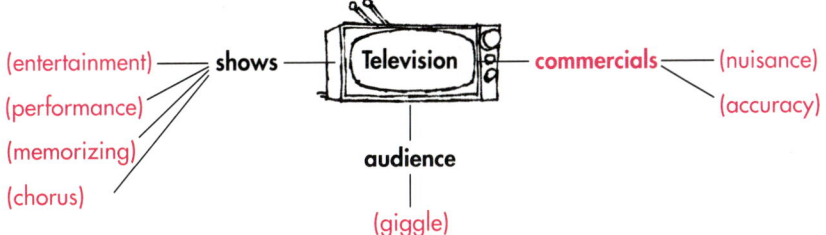

PROPER NOUNS Display the following words, and discuss their pronunciations as necessary: *Yard Ape, Lefty, Mrs. Whaley, Mrs. Larson.*

Integrate spelling with vocabulary.

SPELLING-VOCABULARY CONNECTION *Integrated Spelling* Lesson 7 reinforces spelling of words with *kn, wr, gh,* and *ph* found in the selection, such as *know, write, laugh,* and *phone.* In addition, the Words to Explore reinforce the concept of television as it relates to the selection.

 **SPELLING PRETEST** You may want to use the Pretest/Posttest Sentences on page T51 in *Integrated Spelling Teacher's Edition* to assess student's knowledge of the spelling generalization.

MEETING INDIVIDUAL NEEDS

SECOND-LANGUAGE SUPPORT Students can demonstrate their understanding of the Key Words by naming several items that relate to each word. For example, have students identify three of their favorite *commercials.* See also the manual *Alternative Teaching Strategies,* pages 9, 58–61.

OPTIONAL INDEPENDENT PRACTICE

INTEGRATED SPELLING
pages 34–37: Words with *kn, wr, gh,* and *ph*

PRACTICE BOOK
page 39: Reinforcing Key Words

NOTE: This page may be completed now or after students have read the story.

Spelling

Spelling Words	Words to Explore
1. knee	chorus
2. knife	commercials
3. knock	entertainment
4. know	performance
5. known	
6. laugh	*Your Own Words*
7. laughing	13.
8. phone	14.
9. telephone	15.
10. write	16.
11. wrong	
12. wrote	

Spelling generalization: words with *kn, wr, gh,* and *ph*

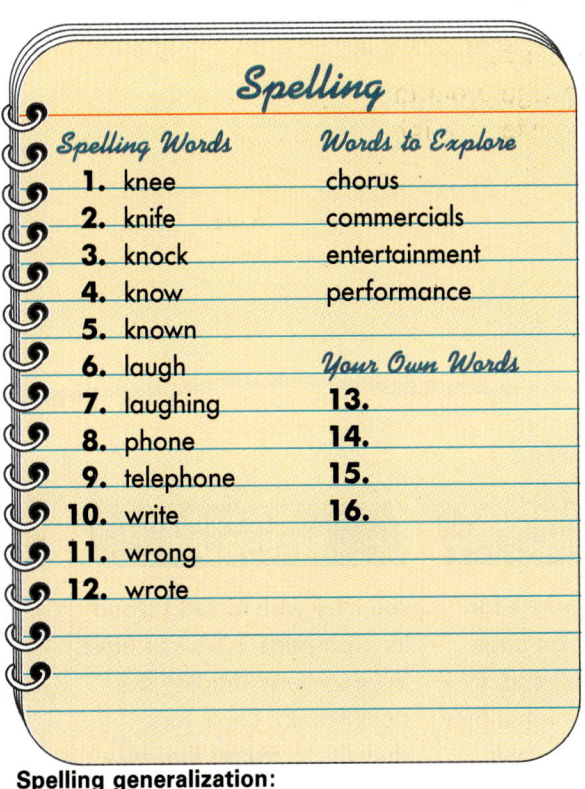

Practice Book

RAMONA QUIMBY, AGE 8 / T213

Prereading Strategies

MEETING INDIVIDUAL NEEDS

Story Map

Have students preview the literature.

Have students read the title and the introduction on page 132 and then preview through page 134. Allow time for them to preview all of the illustrations.

Help students begin a story map.

On the board, create a story map similar to the one below. You may want to distribute copies of the map found on page R105. Begin the map by having students fill in the characters, settings, and problem.

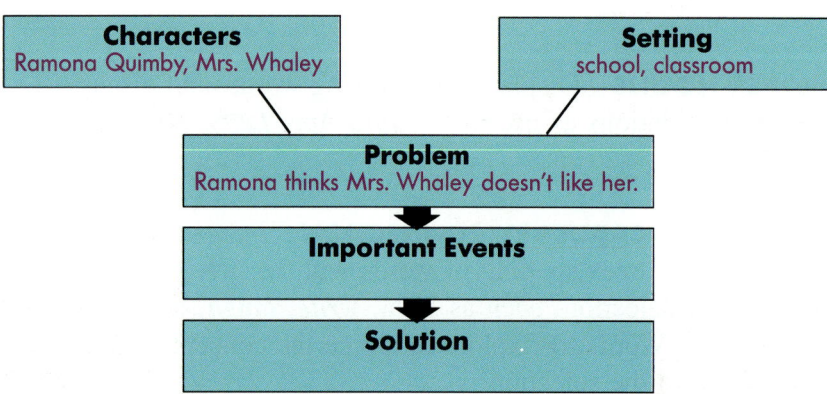

 **PERSONAL JOURNAL** Have students use their maps to predict what might happen and then add their predictions to their personal journals.

Setting a Purpose

Encourage students to set purposes.

Remind students that setting a purpose for reading helps them focus on important ideas. Have students use their predictions to set a purpose for reading.

If students have difficulty setting a purpose, offer this suggestion:

I'm going to read to find out what Mrs. Whaley *really* thinks of Ramona.

SECOND-LANGUAGE SUPPORT Explain any idiomatic expressions students might come across as they read, such as *to pass the time, jump in a lake,* and *odds and ends.* You may wish to have an Idiom Board on which the expressions and their meanings are posted. See also the manual *Alternative Teaching Strategies,* pages 9, 58–61.

SUPPORT FOR MAINSTREAMING Review the parts of the story map, making sure students understand the terms *setting, characters, problem, important events,* and *solution.*

Options for Reading

SUSTAINED SILENT READING	STRATEGIC READING	READER RESPONSE GROUPS	TEACHER READ-ALOUD
Encourage students who are reading independently to pause after several pages to make new predictions.	To stimulate discussion, use the suggestions that appear on pages T215, T217, and T220.	Follow the suggestions for Literature Circles on page T215. As students read, they can write questions that they wish to discuss with their groups.	You may wish to read aloud through page 137, and have students finish reading the story silently. Encourage students to discuss the story with a partner.

T214 / A PLACE TO DREAM, UNIT 2

RAMONA QUIMBY, AGE 8   PAGES 132–133

Ramona Quimby, AGE 8

by **Beverly Cleary**
illustrated by **Alan Tiegreen**

Ramona enjoys third grade, but she is often teased by a boy nicknamed Yard Ape, and she thinks her teacher, Mrs. Whaley, doesn't like her. When Ramona breaks a raw egg instead of a boiled egg on her head, she overhears Mrs. Whaley calling her a show-off and really thinks of herself as a nuisance.

After Ramona stays home from school for a few days because she is sick, she decides to begin working on a book report.

The book, *The Left-Behind Cat*, which Mrs. Whaley had sent home for Ramona to read for her report, was divided into chapters but used babyish words. The story was about a cat that was left behind when a family moved away and about its adventures with a dog, another cat, and some children before it finally found a home with a nice old couple who gave it a saucer of cream and named it Lefty because its left paw was white and because it had been left behind. Medium-boring, thought Ramona, good enough to pass the time on the bus, but not good enough to read during Sustained Silent Reading. Besides, cream cost too much to give to a cat. The most the old people would give a cat was half-and-half, she thought. Ramona required accuracy from books as well as from people.

NEWBERY HONOR
ALA NOTABLE BOOK
CHILDREN'S CHOICE

Reader Response Groups

LITERATURE CIRCLES   Have each group of students decide whether they will read the story together or whether they will read independently before coming to the group. You may want to distribute to students Response Card 9 (Literature Circles), found on page R87, or provide the following questions for discussion:

- Were there any words, events, or ideas you did not understand? Discuss them with the group.
- Did you enjoy this story? Tell what you did or did not like.

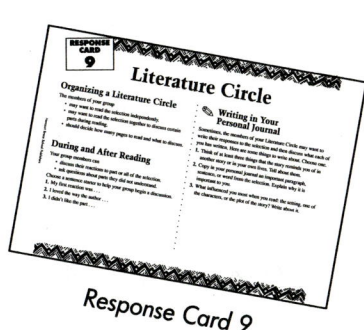

Response Card 9

Strategic Reading

SET PURPOSE/PREDICT: PAGES 132–137   Have students read through page 137. Remind them to think about what they learned when they previewed the story. Then ask them what they will be reading these pages to find out.

PAGES 134–135 RAMONA QUIMBY, AGE 8

"Daddy, how do you sell something?" Ramona interrupted her father, who was studying, even though she knew she should not. However, her need for an answer was urgent.

Mr. Quimby did not look up from his book. "You ought to know. You see enough commercials on television."

Ramona considered his answer. She had always looked upon commercials as entertainment, but now she thought about some of her favorites—the cats that danced back and forth, the dog that pushed away brand-X dog food with his paw, the man who ate a pizza, got indigestion, and groaned that he couldn't believe he ate the *whole* thing, the six horses that pulled the Wells Fargo bank's stagecoach across deserts and over mountains.

"Do you mean I should do a book report like a T.V. commercial?" Ramona asked.

"Why not?" Mr. Quimby answered in an absent-minded way.

"I don't want my teacher to say I'm a nuisance," said Ramona, needing assurance from a grown-up.

This time Mr. Quimby lifted his eyes from his book. "Look," he said, "she told you to pretend you're selling the book, so sell it. What better way than a T.V. commercial? You aren't being a nuisance if you do what your teacher asks." He looked at Ramona a moment and said, "Why do you worry she'd think you're a nuisance?"

Ramona stared at the carpet, wiggled her toes inside her shoes, and finally said, "I squeaked my shoes the first day of school."

"That's not being much of a nuisance," said Mr. Quimby.

"And when I got egg in my hair, Mrs. Whaley said I was a nuisance," confessed Ramona, "and then I threw up in school."

"But you didn't do those things on purpose," her father pointed out. "Now run along. I have studying to do."

Ramona thought this answer over and decided that since her parents agreed, they must be right. Well, Mrs. Whaley could just go jump in a lake, even though her teacher had written, without wasting words, that she missed her. Ramona was going to give her book report any way she wanted. So there, Mrs. Whaley.

134

Teaching Tip Explain that at the time the author wrote the book from which this selection was taken, two TV commercials were very popular. One was a cat-food commercial that included dancing cats. The other was an advertisement for a product to relieve upset stomachs due to overeating. These are the two ads Ramona incorporates into her book report.

Second-Language Support Students may need help understanding the phrase *go jump in a lake*. Rephrase this part of the sentence, using simple, literal language. (It doesn't matter what Mrs. Whaley thinks; I'm going to do my book report the way I like.) Ask students to use context clues and what they have learned about Ramona to confirm their understanding of this phrase.

MEETING INDIVIDUAL NEEDS

T216 / A PLACE TO DREAM, UNIT 2

RAMONA QUIMBY, AGE 8 PAGES 136–137

Ramona went to her room and looked at her table, which the family called "Ramona's studio," because it was a clutter of crayons, different kinds of paper, Scotch tape, bits of yarn, and odds and ends that Ramona used for amusing herself. Then Ramona thought a moment, and suddenly, filled with inspiration, she went to work. She knew exactly what she wanted to do and set about doing it. She worked with paper, crayons, Scotch tape, and rubber bands. She worked so hard and with such pleasure that her cheeks grew pink. Nothing in the whole world felt as good as being able to make something from a sudden idea.

Finally, with a big sigh of relief, Ramona leaned back in her chair to admire her work: three cat masks with holes for eyes and mouths, masks that could be worn by hooking rubber bands over ears. But Ramona did not stop there. With pencil and paper, she began to write out what she would say. She was so full of ideas that she printed rather than waste time in cursive writing. Next she phoned Sara and Janet, keeping her voice low and trying not to giggle so she wouldn't disturb her father any more than necessary, and explained her plan to them. Both her friends giggled and agreed to take part in the book report. Ramona spent the rest of the evening memorizing what she was going to say.

Strategic Reading

MODELING A STRATEGY: PAGES 132–137 What words would you use to describe Ramona? Why?

THINK ALOUD Provide a think-aloud model, if necessary: *I think Ramona is honest, self-confident, and creative. Telling her father about being a nuisance shows her honesty. Her determination to give her book report the way she wants shows her self-confidence, and the book report plan and the masks she makes show her creativity.* **ANALYZING CHARACTERS**

SET PURPOSE/PREDICT: PAGES 138–143 Encourage students to predict whether Ramona's book report will be as successful as she hopes. Have students read the rest of the story to confirm their predictions.

RAMONA QUIMBY, AGE 8 / T217

PAGES 138–139 RAMONA QUIMBY, AGE 8

The next morning on the bus and at school, no one even mentioned Ramona's throwing up. She had braced herself for some remark from Yard Ape, but all he said was, "Hi, Superfoot." When school started, Ramona slipped cat masks to Sara and Janet, handed her written excuse for her absence to Mrs. Whaley, and waited, fanning away escaped fruit flies, for book reports to begin.

After arithmetic, Mrs. Whaley called on several people to come to the front of the room to pretend they were selling books to the class. Most of the reports began, "This is a book about . . ." and many, as Beezus had predicted, ended with ". . . if you want to find out what happens next, read the book."

Then Mrs. Whaley said, "We have time for one more report before lunch. Who wants to be next?"

Ramona waved her hand, and Mrs. Whaley nodded.

Ramona beckoned to Sara and Janet, who giggled in an embarrassed way but joined Ramona, standing behind her and off to one side. All three girls slipped on their cat masks and giggled again. Ramona took a deep breath as Sara and Janet began to chant, "*Meow, meow, meow, meow. Meow, meow, meow, meow,*" and danced back and forth like the cats they had seen in the cat-food commercial on television.

138

Informal Assessment

CONTEXTUAL AND STRUCTURAL CLUES To assess whether students need instruction in this vocabulary strategy, read the first sentence in the last paragraph on page 138. Then ask students these questions:

- What clue helps you figure out the meaning of the word *beckoned*? (The sentence says that when Ramona did this, Sara and Janet went to join her.)
- What does *beckoned* mean? ("waved" or "signaled")

A review lesson on **contextual and structural clues** appears on page T235.

See page T227 for information found on Project Card 17B.

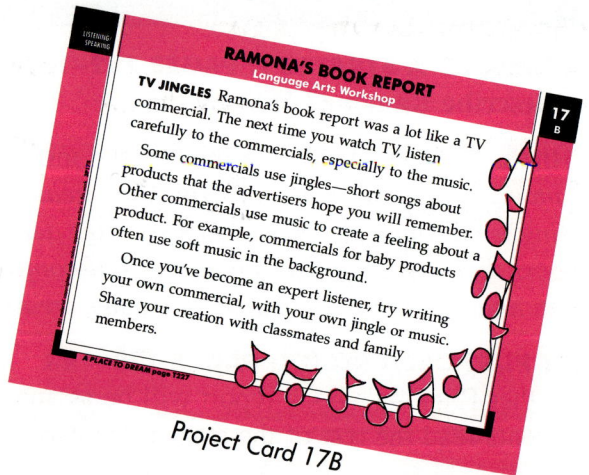

Project Card 17B

T218 / A PLACE TO DREAM, UNIT 2

"*Left-Behind Cat* gives kids something to smile about," said Ramona in a loud clear voice, while her chorus meowed softly behind her. She wasn't sure that what she said was exactly true, but neither were the commercials that showed cats eating dry cat food without making any noise. "Kids who have tried *Left-Behind Cat* are all smiles, smiles, smiles. *Left-Behind Cat* is the book kids ask for by name. Kids can read it every day and thrive on it. The happiest kids read *Left-Behind Cat*. *Left-Behind Cat* contains cats, dogs, people—" Here Ramona caught sight of Yard Ape leaning back in his seat, grinning in the way that always flustered her. She could not help interrupting herself with a giggle, and after suppressing it she tried not to look at Yard Ape and to take up where she had left off. ". . . cats, dogs, people—" The giggle came back, and Ramona was lost. She could not remember what came next. ". . . cats, dogs, people," she repeated, trying to start and failing.

Mrs. Whaley and the class waited. Yard Ape grinned. Ramona's loyal chorus meowed and danced. This performance could not go on all morning. Ramona had to say something, anything to end the waiting, the meowing, her book report. She tried desperately to recall a cat-food commercial, any cat-food commercial, and could not. All she could remember was the man on television who ate the pizza, and so she blurted out the only sentence she could think of, "I can't believe I read the *whole* thing!"

Mrs. Whaley's laugh rang out above the laughter of the class. Ramona felt her face turn red behind her mask, and her ears, visible to the class, turned red as well.

"Thank you, Ramona," said Mrs. Whaley. "That was most entertaining. Class, you are excused for lunch."

Ramona felt brave behind her cat mask. "Mrs. Whaley," she said, as the class pushed back chairs and gathered up lunch boxes, "that wasn't the way my report was supposed to end."

"Did you like the book?" asked Mrs. Whaley.

"Not really," confessed Ramona.

"Then I think it was a good way to end your report," said the teacher. "Asking the class to sell books they really don't like isn't fair, now that I stop to think about it. I was only trying to make book reports a little livelier."

Encouraged by this confession and still safe behind her mask, Ramona had the boldness to speak up. "Mrs. Whaley," she said with her heart pounding, "you told Mrs. Larson that I'm a nuisance, and I don't think I am."

141

GRAMMAR CONNECTION

REVIEWING PROPER NOUNS You may wish to point out the words *Cat* and *cats* in the middle of the first paragraph on page 140. Ask students why the word *Cat* is capitalized but *cats* is not. Remind students that words that name particular things, such as book titles, are called proper nouns and that proper nouns should be capitalized.

See page T236 for information found on Project Card 18A.

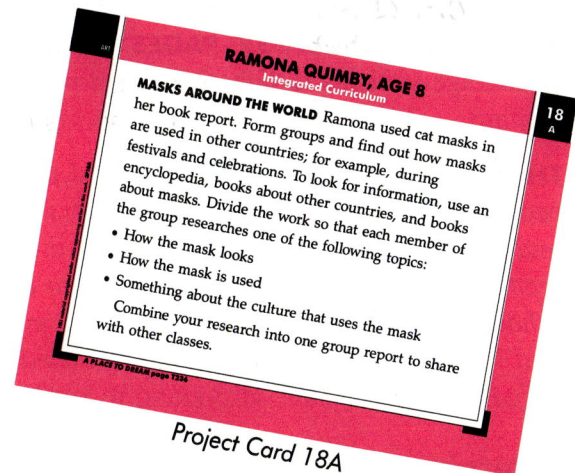

Project Card 18A

PAGES 142–143 RAMONA QUIMBY, AGE 8

Mrs. Whaley looked astonished. "When did I say that?"

"The day I got egg in my hair," said Ramona. "You called me a show-off and said I was a nuisance."

Mrs. Whaley frowned, thinking. "Why, Ramona, I can recall saying something about my little show-off, but I meant it affectionately, and I'm sure I never called you a nuisance."

"Yes, you did," insisted Ramona. "You said I was a show-off, and then you said, 'What a nuisance.'" Ramona could never forget those exact words.

Mrs. Whaley, who had looked worried, smiled in relief. "Oh, Ramona, you misunderstood," she said. "I meant that trying to wash egg out of your hair was a nuisance for Mrs. Larson. I didn't mean that you personally were a nuisance."

Ramona felt a little better, enough to come out from under her mask to say, "I wasn't showing off. I was just trying to crack an egg on my head like everyone else."

Mrs. Whaley's smile was mischievous. "Tell me, Ramona," she said, "don't you ever try to show off?"

Ramona was embarrassed. "Well . . . maybe . . . sometimes, a little," she admitted. Then she added positively, "But I wasn't showing off that day. How could I be showing off when I was doing what everyone else was doing?"

142

"You've convinced me," said Mrs. Whaley with a big smile. "Now run along and eat your lunch."

Ramona snatched up her lunch box and went jumping down the stairs to the cafeteria. She laughed to herself because she knew exactly what all the boys and girls from her class would say when they finished their lunches. She knew because she planned to say it herself. "I can't believe I ate the *whole* thing!"

If you were Mrs. Whaley, what grade would you give Ramona on her book report? Explain why.

Ramona doesn't remove her mask when she talks to Mrs. Whaley after the commercial. Why do you think she leaves the mask on?

"Ramona is a show-off." Explain why you agree or disagree with the statement.

WRITE If you had to present a book report as an advertisement, what kind of advertisement would you use? Choose a book you've enjoyed reading, and write the advertisement you would use for it.

Strategic Reading

MODELING A STRATEGY: PAGES 138–143
Encourage students to talk about their purpose for reading.

THINK ALOUD Provide a think-aloud model, if necessary: *I wanted to find out what Mrs. Whaley really thinks of Ramona. I learned that the book report does help change the way Ramona and Mrs. Whaley feel about each other. Ramona's misunderstanding of some things that Mrs. Whaley had said are straightened out when the two of them talk about the assignment.* RETURNING TO THE PURPOSE

Returning to the Predictions/Purpose
STORY MAP Have students review the story maps they made before reading and revise them as necessary. Encourage volunteers to share their purposes for reading and what they enjoyed about the story.
NOTE: Responses to the questions and support for the Write activity appear on page T223.

Characters
Ramona Quimby, Mrs. Whaley

Setting
school, classroom

Problem
Ramona thinks Mrs. Whaley doesn't like her.

Important Events

Solution

BEVERLY CLEARY PAGES 144–145

INTERVIEW WITH THE AUTHOR: Beverly Cleary

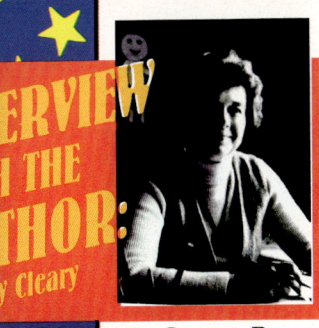

Writer Ilene Cooper spoke with Beverly Cleary to find out how she creates the characters in her books. This interview tells where Ms. Cleary gets the ideas for her characters. It also tells how she became interested in reading and writing.

Ms. COOPER: Ramona is so funny, and she comes up with all kinds of interesting ideas, such as the way she did her book report. Were you at all like Ramona when you were a child?

Ms. CLEARY: I think I was like Ramona until I started school. I lived on a farm where I was wild and free and could use my imagination. I was allowed to do almost anything I wanted to do as long as it was safe. When I began school, I became much more like Ellen Tebbits, another character.

Ms. COOPER: What did you like to read when you were a third and fourth grader?

Ms. CLEARY: Well, I read the complete fairy tale section of our branch library. I did have a couple of favorite books when I was in the third and fourth grades—one favorite, but it's out of print now.

Ms. COOPER: Did you always like to read?

Ms. CLEARY: Oh, no.

Ms. COOPER: But you made the change from somebody who didn't like to read to a reader—a real reader.

Ms. CLEARY: Yes, in the third grade.

Ms. COOPER: What happened then?

Ms. CLEARY: The right book. It was *The Dutch Twins* by Lucy Fitch Perkins. I started to look at the pictures because I was bored, and I discovered that I was reading it and enjoying it!

Ms. COOPER: Did you write at all when you were that age?

Ms. CLEARY: No.

Ms. COOPER: You just did school writing?

Ms. CLEARY: Just school assignments. But compositions were always my favorite assignments.

Ms. COOPER: What advice would you give to young people who want to write?

Ms. CLEARY: Writing doesn't have to be a story. Why not write a page of dialogue, such as a quarrel between a brother and sister? Be original and don't copy. Don't use characters from other people's books or television shows. Look around you and find your own characters. Good writing is original and comes from within the writer.

Ms. COOPER: What do you think about keeping a diary, or notebook?

Ms. CLEARY: I think keeping a diary is useful.

Ms. COOPER: What do you think is the hardest thing about writing, and what do you think is the easiest thing about writing?

Ms. CLEARY: The hardest thing about writing is pushing through to the end of the story. The easiest thing is revising. I think all writers do some revising. That's when I cross out a lot and reduce a page to one paragraph. It's necessary because in my first draft I tend to put in

AWARD-WINNING AUTHOR

An Interview with the Author: Beverly Cleary

AUTHOR'S PURPOSE Invite students to read pages 144–146 to find out how Beverly Cleary writes about Ramona Quimby. When students have finished reading, ask volunteers to tell what advice Ms. Cleary gives young writers. (She tells them to be original and not copy others. They should choose from their own experiences and write about them.) Have students share other things they learned about Beverly Cleary from reading the interview. Encourage volunteers to share questions they would like to ask Ms. Cleary.

extra material as it comes to mind. And then when I finish I realize that some of it wasn't needed.

Ms. Cooper: When you start a book, do you know how it's going to end?

Ms. Cleary: No I don't, and I don't always write stories in order. In *Ramona and Her Father,* I wrote the last chapter first. I begin with the characters and something they would do and just let the story work itself out.

Ms. Cooper: That's interesting. You start in the middle and maybe one day you feel like writing about what happened before the incident, and then the next day . . .

Ms. Cleary: I write everything that's vivid to me. And it usually all fits together.

Ms. Cooper: Some of the vivid incidents—for example, Ramona breaking the egg over her head—did those things really happen, or did you just make them up?

Ms. Cleary: Well, both. I happened to hear about the egg incident when a group of teachers were talking. Sometimes I write about things that happened in my own childhood, but I change them. Sometimes I want to write about something, and it won't fit into the story. I wanted to write about the time my cat ate my jack-o'-lantern. And it took me about 20 years before that would work into a story.

Ms. Cooper: So sometimes you just put an idea into the back of your mind and save it?

Ms. Cleary: Yes, I've had characters wandering about in the back of my mind who will not come into books.

Ms. Cooper: They're just waiting for their own stories.

Ms. Cleary: Yes.

Expanding the Interview If you asked Beverly Cleary, "What steps should I follow to write a story?" what do you think she would say? (Accept reasonable responses: "It depends on you as a writer; you should start wherever you feel comfortable.") INFERENTIAL: SPECULATING

PART 2

Responding to the Literature

Personal Response

Encourage critical thinking.

If you were Mrs. Whaley, what grade would you give Ramona on her book report? Explain why. (Responses will vary.)
CRITICAL: EXPRESSING PERSONAL OPINIONS

Ramona doesn't remove her mask when she talks to Mrs. Whaley after the commercial. Why do you think she leaves the mask on? (Accept reasonable responses: Wearing the mask makes Ramona feel brave; she feels safe; the mask gives her confidence.) METACOGNITIVE: RECOGNIZING CHARACTERS' EMOTIONS

"Ramona is a show-off." Explain why you agree or disagree with the statement. (Responses will vary.) CRITICAL: EXPRESSING PERSONAL OPINIONS

Encourage creative written responses.

 **WRITE** If you had to present a book report as an advertisement, what kind of advertisement would you use? Choose a book you've enjoyed reading, and write the advertisement you would use for it.
Remind students that a book report should give information about a book but should not give away the ending. CREATIVE: WRITING AN ADVERTISEMENT

Cooperative Response

Have reader response groups extend their discussions.

LITERATURE CIRCLES Have Literature Circles discuss their feelings about the story. You may want to offer the following question:

Ramona thought of a clever way to present her book report. What are some other creative but informative ways to give book reports?

STRATEGY CONFERENCE

Discuss with students how completing a story map helped them understand the selection. (Accept reasonable responses: It helps readers pay attention to important story details.)

NOTE

An additional writing activity for this selection appears on page T226.

RAMONA QUIMBY, AGE 8 / T223

Summarizing the Literature

Have students retell the story and write a summary. Encourage students to summarize the story by recalling key story events. Guide them in beginning the sequence chain below. Then have them use their completed chains to retell the story and write a brief summary statement. See *Practice Book* page 40 below.

Title: Ramona Quimby, Age 8

First, Ramona reads the book for her report. → Next, → Then,
↓
After That, → Then, → Finally,

Critical Thinking Activity

Encourage students to offer solutions. **ROLE-PLAY** Ramona was troubled by a mistaken idea she had about her teacher. How would you have advised Ramona to handle a situation like this? Have students role-play scenes.
CREATIVE: INVENTING NEW SCENES

INFORMAL ASSESSMENT

The details in a reading selection that a student chooses to think critically about are a clear indication of whether their importance to main ideas and themes has been well understood.

OPTIONAL INDEPENDENT PRACTICE

WRITER'S JOURNAL
- page 28: Writing a personal response

PRACTICE BOOK
- page 40: Summarizing the literature

Writer's Journal

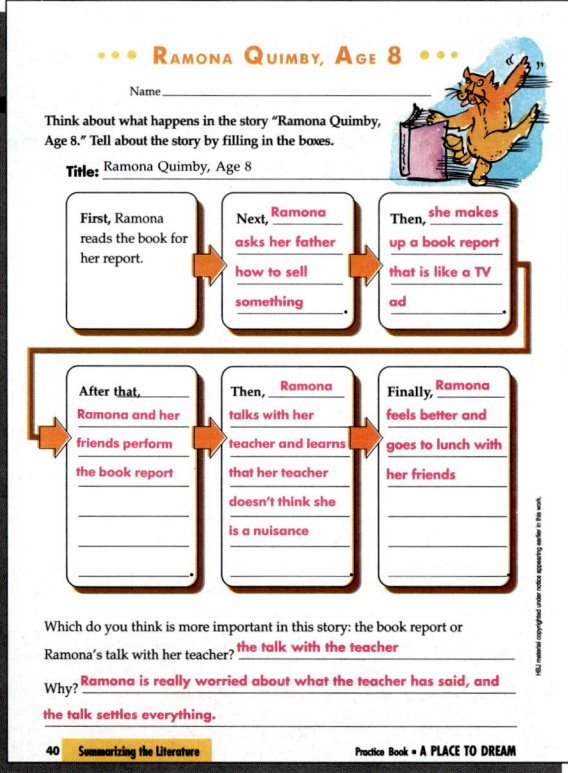

Practice Book

T224 / A PLACE TO DREAM, UNIT 2

VOCABULARY WORKSHOP

Reviewing Key Words

Display the Key Words, and read aloud each set of words below. Have students name the Key Word that goes with each set of words.

1. laugh, snicker, _____ (giggle)
2. truth, correctness, _____ (accuracy)
3. pest, pain, _____ (nuisance)
4. ads, advertisements, _____ (commercials)
5. learning, studying, _____ (memorizing)
6. shows, fun, _____ (entertainment)
7. singing group, dancing group _____ (chorus)
8. presentation, show, _____ (performance)

Extending Vocabulary

HOMOPHONES Point out that one of the commercials the author referred to in her selection was about a man who groaned that he couldn't believe he *ate* the *whole* thing. Write the words *ate, eight, whole,* and *hole* on the board. Explain that these words are called *homophones,* words that are pronounced alike but are spelled differently and have different meanings. Remind students that context clues will help them determine the correct spelling and meaning of a homophone.

Have students complete the following chart.

flour	(flower)
raise	(rays)
right	(write)

Then ask them to use the homophones listed on the chart to complete the following advertising slogans:

(flower, flour) Bake your bread with Daisy! It's the ____(flour)____ that's fresh as a daisy—or any other ____(flower)____ !

(rays, raise) Catch some ____(rays)____ when you ____(raise)____ your Dandy Window Shades!

(right, write) Spiff ball-point pens ____(write)____ only ____(right)____ answers!

Encourage students to illustrate one of the advertising slogans.

OPTIONAL INDEPENDENT PRACTICE

PRACTICE BOOK page 41: Writing homophones

Practice Book

RAMONA QUIMBY, AGE 8 / T225

Language Arts WORKSHOP

READING

Oral Rereading/Readers Theatre

Have students perform a Readers Theatre. Ask each group of students to choose a passage in the story that includes dialogue. Ask one member of each group to be the narrator. You may wish to model how to read the narrator's lines along with the dialogue. Challenge students to read aloud their parts as if they were actually the characters. Allow time for students to rehearse their scenes before presenting them to the others. In Readers Theatre, students do not memorize lines, but rather read the dialogue from the story. **LISTENING/READING**

SPELLING

Reviewing Spelling Words

SPELLING WORDS: knee, knife, knock, know, known, laugh, laughing, phone, telephone, write, wrong, wrote

WORDS TO EXPLORE: chorus, commercials, entertainment, performance

"Auction off" Spelling Words to students. Write each Spelling Word on a separate card. Then on other cards, misspell each word by changing *ph* and *gh* to *f* and by removing the silent letters *k* and *w*. Distribute about 50 tokens to each student. Hold up one card at a time, and have students "bid" on each word, with the card going to the highest bidder. The object is to acquire only correctly spelled words. Award to bidders 3 points for each correctly spelled word, and subtract 5 points for each misspelled word. **LISTENING/SPEAKING/SPELLING**

Use *Integrated Spelling* Lesson 7 to reinforce the Spelling Words and the Words to Explore. See pages T51–T56 in *Integrated Spelling Teacher's Edition*.

 **SPELLING POSTTEST** You may want to use the Pretest/Posttest Sentences on *Integrated Spelling Teacher's Edition* page T51 to assess students' knowledge of the spelling generalization.

WRITING

Writing About the Literature

Available on Project Card 17A

 **WRITE AN INFORMATION PARAGRAPH**

Have students write an informational paragraph about caring for a pet cat or another animal. To help them get started, have students complete a web like the one shown below. Ask them to brainstorm interesting details to tell about the main idea, caring for a pet cat. Remind students to include only details that tell about their main idea. Ask volunteers to share their completed paragraphs with their classmates. See Writing Model, page R92. **LISTENING/SPEAKING/WRITING**

GRAMMAR REVIEW: PROPER NOUNS When students revise their informational paragraphs, remind them to make sure that they have correctly capitalized any proper nouns they have used. Have each student write on individual slips of paper two common nouns from their paragraphs and two proper nouns. Gather the slips, and place them in a container. Have students take turns drawing a word and taping it on one of two charts you create: one labeled *Common Nouns* and the other labeled *Proper Nouns*.

 **LANGUAGE HANDBOOK** *Expository Writing, pages 48–49, 51; Proper Nouns, page 94*

 **DAILY LANGUAGE PRACTICE** *Oral language exercises are provided on pages R64–R65.*

T226 / A PLACE TO DREAM, UNIT 2

Language Arts WORKSHOP

LISTENING AND SPEAKING

TV Jingles

Available on Project Card 17B

Have students listen to several television commercials. Ask them to pay close attention to the music. Discuss with students how the music helps create a particular mood or feeling that conveys a message about the product or service. Encourage students to identify important "feeling" words and then combine these with their own music to create musical commercials.
LISTENING/SPEAKING

LISTENING AND SPEAKING

And So I Said . . .

COOPERATIVE LEARNING Remind students that Ramona forgot the script she had memorized and that she finished her report by improvising—by thinking of something to say "on the spot." Have cooperative groups develop a list of common classroom situations. A Recorder in each group can write down the ideas. When they have finished, have Readers read aloud their lists. Ask them to select one situation and improvise what they might say. For example, "You just walked into your classroom and realize you forgot your lunch money. What would you say to your teacher?"
LISTENING/SPEAKING

WRITING

Lively Assignments

Remind students that Ramona's teacher is trying to make book reports a little more exciting. List with students some of the various activities you and they do with books. Ask each student to choose a favorite activity and write a few sentences about why they enjoy it. Students' responses can give you helpful insights ino their interests.   LISTENING/SPEAKING/WRITING

✓ LISTENING AND SPEAKING

Public Address

Have students offer guidelines for giving speeches. Guide students to understand that good posture, eye contact, tone of voice, and rate of speech can be almost as important as what the speaker is saying. Ask volunteers to demonstrate examples of good speech presentations, while others watch, listen, take notes, and ask questions afterward.   LISTENING/SPEAKING/WRITING

RAMONA QUIMBY, AGE 8 / T227

Grammar MINI LESSON

Singular and Plural Nouns

OBJECTIVES: *To recognize that a singular noun names one person, animal, place, or thing and that a plural noun names more than one; to recognize that most nouns add -s or -es to form the plural; to form singular and plural nouns correctly*

Oral Warm-Up

Display and read aloud the following sentences from "Ramona Quimby, Age 8":

- Besides, cream cost too much to give to a <u>cat</u>.
- The next morning on the <u>bus</u> and at <u>school</u>, no one even mentioned Ramona's throwing up.
- She laughed to herself because she knew exactly what all the <u>boys</u> and <u>girls</u> from her class would say when they finished their <u>lunches</u>.

Write the following diagram on the board, omitting the lines. Ask students to decide whether the displayed sentences tell about *one* or *more than one* of each item in the right-hand column. Have students draw a line from each item to the answer in the left-hand column.

How Many?	
One	cat, bus, school
More than one	boy, girl, lunch

Interactive Teaching

SINGULAR NOUNS Draw the following chart on the board. Ask students to look at the diagram from the Oral Warm-Up, and then identify whether each names a person, an animal, a place, or a thing. Have volunteers write each noun under the appropriate heading.

Person	Animal	Place	Thing
boy girl	cat	school	bus lunch

Tell students that a word that names only one person, animal, place, or thing is called a **singular noun**. Have students suggest several more singular nouns for each of the four categories.

PLURAL NOUNS Tell students that a word that names more than one person, animal, place, or thing is called a **plural noun**. Explain that to make most singular nouns into plural nouns, *-s* or *-es* is added to the singular noun. Point out to students that *-es* must be added to singular nouns ending in *s, x, ch,* or *sh* to make them into plural nouns.

Distribute index cards to students, and have them write the letter *s* on one side and the letters *es* on the other. Write the following nouns on the board: *box, book, sandwich,* and *teacher.* Then point to each noun, and ask students to hold up their index cards to show the ending needed to make the correct plural form of the noun. Have a volunteer come to the board to add the correct ending to the word. Repeat the procedure, using words that students supply.

LANGUAGE HANDBOOK
Singular and Plural Nouns, pages 96–97

T228 / A PLACE TO DREAM, UNIT 2

Practice Activities

I Spy

Have students form small groups. Tell students in each group to take turns pointing to an item in the classroom and naming the item by saying, "I spy a(n) . . . ." The other students in the group should write down the name of the item and then write next to it the plural form of the word. Have students continue until each person in the group has named one item. Then have group members share their lists of words and check each other's spelling. Have students play several rounds.
VISUAL/AUDITORY

Have I Got a Noun for You!

Remind students that Ramona prepared a commercial for a book she liked. Have students work in pairs to make posters advertising a product of their choice. You may want to provide students with advertisements from magazines to use as models. Tell partners to think of an item they want to try to sell and to come up with several reasons why someone should buy it. You may want to provide partners with sentence frames to use in their ads, such as "Buy this (these) _____ and you'll feel great!" Encourage students to decorate their posters. When students are finished, display their posters around the room. Then have volunteers identify all the nouns that appear on a poster and classify each one as singular or plural. **VISUAL**

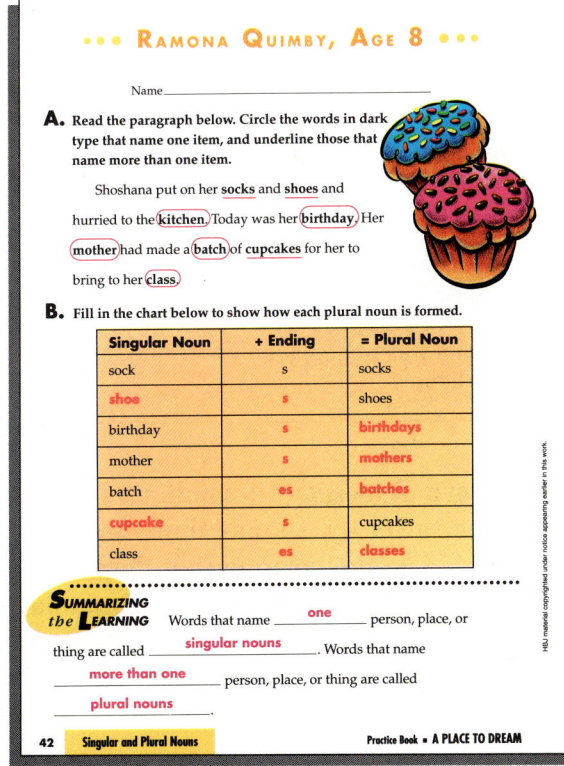

Practice Book

MEETING INDIVIDUAL NEEDS

SECOND-LANGUAGE SUPPORT Demonstrate that the article *the* in English does not indicate whether the noun it precedes is singular or plural. Write the following examples on the board:

el gato—los gatos

the cat—the cats

Ask students how they know a noun is plural in English. (Most plural nouns end in *-s* or *-es*.)

RETEACH Follow the visual, auditory, and kinesthetic/motor models on page R18.

OPTIONAL INDEPENDENT PRACTICE

PRACTICE BOOK
page 42: Writing singular and plural nouns

GRAMMAR PRACTICE
pages 28–29: Singular and Plural Nouns

RAMONA QUIMBY, AGE 8 / T229

PART 3

Learning through the Literature

DECODING
INTRODUCE

Structural Analysis

OBJECTIVE: *To use prefixes, base words, and suffixes to decode words*

Interactive Teaching

Focus on words from the selection.

LITERATURE CONNECTION Tell students that some words are made up of a base word and one or more other word parts. Have students reread the first sentence on page 140. Point out the word *softly,* and have students identify the base word and the ending. Tell students that a word part at the beginning of a word is called a *prefix* and that a word part at the end of a word is called a *suffix.* Have students demonstrate their understanding of *softly* by acting out what the chorus did.

Strategy: Have students examine word parts.

MODEL THE STRATEGY Display Chart/Transparency 15 or the sentences on it. Have a volunteer read aloud the first sentence. Then model the process of using structural analysis to determine the meaning of the underlined word:

> **Chart/Transparency 15   Prefixes and Suffixes**
>
> 1. Ramona tried <u>desperately</u> to recall the cat-food commercial.
> 2. Ramona tried to <u>recall</u> the cat-food commercial. ("call again")
> 3. Ramona knew <u>exactly</u> what everyone would say at lunch. ("in an exact way")
> 4. Ramona was <u>careful</u> when she cut out the cat masks. ("full of care")
> 5. Ramona felt <u>helpless</u> when she couldn't remember what came next. ("without help")
> 6. Ramona was <u>unhappy</u> about writing the book report. ("not happy")

The word *desperately* is made up of the base word *desperate* and the suffix *-ly*. I know that *-ly* often means "in a way that is." I can determine that *desperately* means "in a way that is desperate or hopeless." Ramona is trying very, very hard to remember the commercial, but she cannot.

Encourage students to think aloud as they decode the other underlined words.

T230 / A PLACE TO DREAM, UNIT 2

Practice Activities

Word Parts and Meanings

Have students identify word parts.

Have students work in pairs to find words with prefixes or suffixes in "Ramona Quimby, Age 8" or in another selection. Ask students to make a list, circle each base word, and give the word's meaning. **KINESTHETIC**

Mix and Match

Have students create words.

COOPERATIVE LEARNING Display a chart similar to the one below. Encourage groups to make as many words as they can by adding prefixes and/or suffixes to the base words. *(unhappily, unsuccessful, playfully, and so on)* Have Recorders keep track of the words. Have a Reporter from each group list the words on the board. Then discuss the meanings of the words, and have students use them in sentences. **VISUAL/AUDITORY**

Prefix	Base Word		Suffix
un-	happy	cover	-ly
re-	help	success	-ful
	play	care	-less

Performance Assessment

Have students each choose two words with affixes from the activities above. Ask them to write two or three things they could do to figure out the meaning of each word as they are reading. For evaluation guidelines, see *Staff Development Guide*.

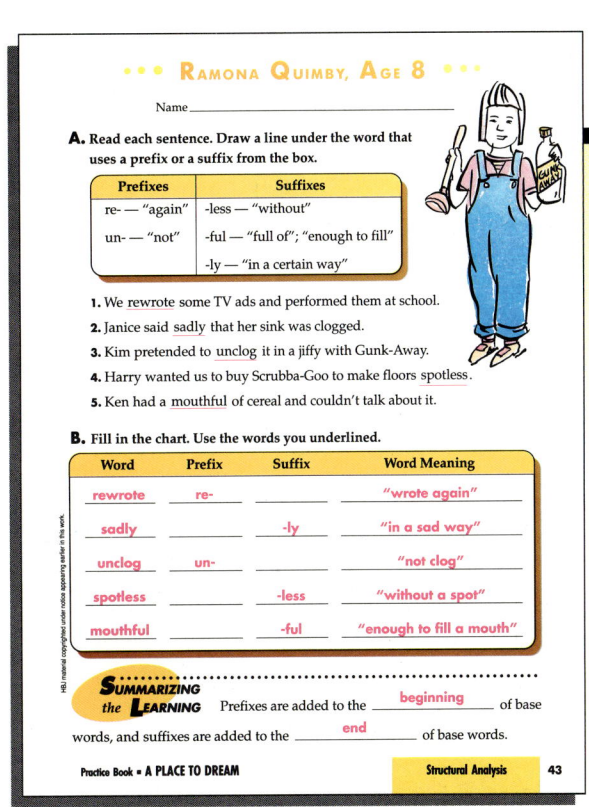

Practice Book

MEETING INDIVIDUAL NEEDS

RETEACH Follow the visual, auditory, and kinesthetic/motor models on page R19.

CHALLENGE Have students make and use their own charts for the Mix and Match activity.

SECOND-LANGUAGE SUPPORT Help students identify the base word and the prefix or the suffix in the words *sadly, rebuild, untrue, careless,* and *joyful*. See also the manual *Alternative Teaching Strategies,* pages 9, 58–61.

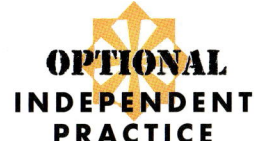

OPTIONAL INDEPENDENT PRACTICE

PRACTICE BOOK
page 43: Using prefixes and suffixes

RAMONA QUIMBY, AGE 8 / T231

COMPREHENSION
INTRODUCE

Author's Purpose

OBJECTIVE: *To identify an author's main purpose for writing*

Interactive Teaching

Discuss "Ramona Quimby, Age 8."

LITERATURE CONNECTION Ask students what they enjoyed about "Ramona Quimby, Age 8." Explain that authors write books and stories for several reasons. Point out that identifying an author's purpose can help students better understand and enjoy what they read.

Discuss the author's purpose.

MODEL THE THINKING Tell students that authors may write to inform, to entertain, or to provide directions. Reread aloud the last seven lines on page 140 and the first seven lines on page 141. Use that passage to model identifying the author's purpose:

> **The author provides information about Ramona and what she is going through while she gives her book report. But the author's humorous way of describing the scene makes me realize that her main purpose is to entertain readers.**

Have students build a think-aloud web.

Work with students as a group to create a web like the one on Chart/Transparency 16 that gives reasons why authors write.

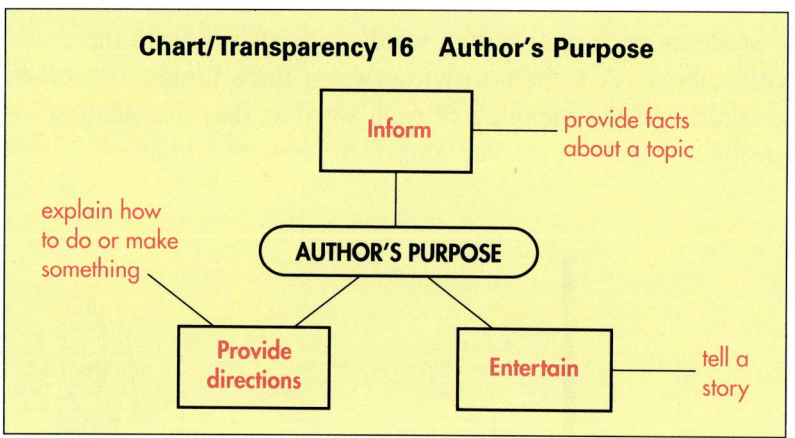

Explain to students that they may be able to identify the author's purpose when they preview. Point out that nonfiction selections may have subheadings, photographs, or illustrations. Then explain that if they think the author's purpose is to inform, they should adjust their reading rate and read more slowly to understand new facts and unfamiliar vocabulary.

ADDITIONAL BOOKS FOR APPLYING AUTHOR'S PURPOSE

Best Friends by Steven Kellogg. Dial, 1986. **EASY**

Chicken Sunday by Patricia Polacco. Philomel, 1992. **AVERAGE**

The Hot and Cold Summer by Johanna Hurwitz. Scholastic, 1985. **CHALLENGING**

Practice Activity

What's the Purpose?

Have students determine purposes.

COOPERATIVE LEARNING Have students work in small groups to determine the author's purpose in previously read selections. Encourage students to use the web they created to help them. Reporters can present their group's conclusions. VISUAL/AUDITORY

Performance Assessment

After Reporters have presented the conclusions from the What's the Purpose? activity, have each group cite examples from the selections they chose to explain how they determined each author's purpose. For evaluation guidelines, see *Staff Development Guide*.

Reader ↔ Writer Connection
Author's Purpose

WRITERS choose a format and content that is best for their purpose for writing.

READERS identify an author's purpose to help them understand and enjoy what they read.

WRITE A STORY Have students write about a breakfast cereal. First, they should try to persuade readers to buy it. Then they should tell a humorous story about it.

Writer's Journal

MEETING INDIVIDUAL NEEDS

RETEACH Follow the visual, auditory, and kinesthetic/motor models on page R20.

CHALLENGE Have students recall the major purposes for writing. (to inform, to entertain, to provide directions) Ask students to write three sentences, one for each purpose.

SECOND-LANGUAGE SUPPORT Have students complete the following statements orally: When authors tell a story, they are usually writing to (entertain). When authors provide information about a topic, they are writing to (inform). See also the manual *Alternative Teaching Strategies*, pages 9, 58–61.

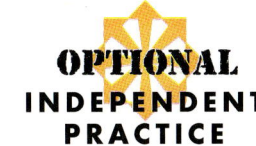

OPTIONAL INDEPENDENT PRACTICE

WRITER'S JOURNAL
page 29: Writing for different purposes

RAMONA QUIMBY, AGE 8 / **T233**

COMPREHENSION REVIEW

Main Idea and Details

OBJECTIVE: *To identify main idea and details*

Review

Have students identify the main idea.

REVIEW FINDING MAIN IDEA AND DETAILS Ask students what they can do to figure out the main idea of a paragraph or group of paragraphs. (look for important details) Use page 136 of the story to model asking and answering questions *(Who? What? Where? Why? How?)* to help find important details. Then have students identify the main idea. (Ramona thinks she has a good idea.)

Who?	Ramona
What?	She looks at her table cluttered with crayons, paper, and other things.
Where?	She is in her room at her "studio."
Why?	She needs to prepare a book report.
How?	She starts working with paper, crayons, tape, and rubber bands.

Practice Activity

What's the Idea?

Have students write paragraphs.

Have students work in pairs, each writing a paragraph with a main idea and supporting details. Have them exchange paragraphs and underline the main idea in the partner's paragraph. **KINESTHETIC**

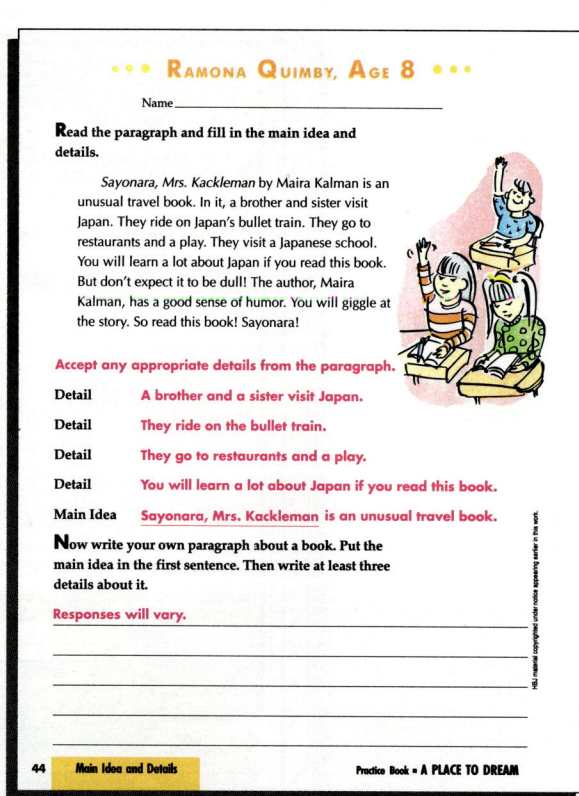

Practice Book

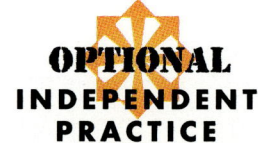

MEETING INDIVIDUAL NEEDS

CHALLENGE Encourage students to choose a fiction book they've read and make a chart listing the details and main idea of the book.

OPTIONAL INDEPENDENT PRACTICE

PRACTICE BOOK
page 44: Identifying main idea and details

T234 / A PLACE TO DREAM, UNIT 2

VOCABULARY STRATEGY
REVIEW

Contextual and Structural Clues

OBJECTIVE: *To use context clues and structural analysis to determine meanings of unfamiliar words*

Review

Review vocabulary strategies.

HAVE A VOLUNTEER THINK ALOUD Ask students what vocabulary strategies they used to figure out unfamiliar words in "Ramona Quimby, Age 8." (context clues, word parts) Have a volunteer use this sentence to model how to determine the meaning of *indigestion*: *The man ate a pizza, got indigestion, and groaned that he couldn't believe he ate the whole thing.*

Practice Activity

Use the Clues

Have students determine word meanings.

Ask pairs of students to find these words in the story and to use the strategies to figure out their meanings: *babyish* ("like a baby"), *encouraged* ("given courage"), and *misunderstood* ("did not understand"). **VISUAL**

MEETING INDIVIDUAL NEEDS

CHALLENGE Encourage students to use vocabulary strategies to determine the meanings of unfamiliar words in a newspaper article. Ask students to make a chart listing several words and their meanings.

OPTIONAL INDEPENDENT PRACTICE

PRACTICE BOOK
page 45: Using context clues and structural analysis

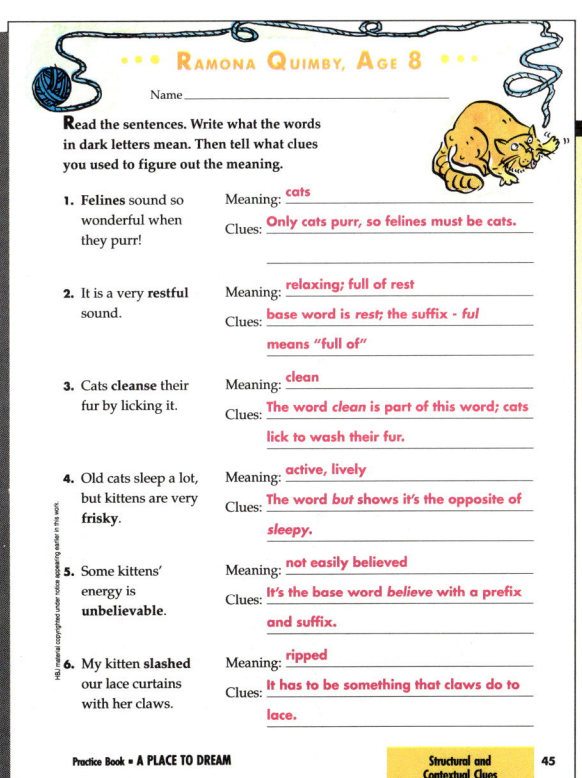

Practice Book

RAMONA QUIMBY, AGE 8 / **T235**

Integrated CURRICULUM

SOCIAL STUDIES

Careers in Public Speaking

Point out that Ramona might have used her book report as an opportunity to "show off." Ask students to brainstorm different purposes for public speaking. Guide them in a discussion of careers in which the ability to speak in public is essential. Ask students to identify their favorite announcers, newscasters, or performers from radio and television. Encourage students to write a personal letter to someone they admire, asking that person for some tips about public speaking.   LISTENING/SPEAKING/WRITING

SCIENCE

About Your Memory

COOPERATIVE LEARNING   Have students recall that Ramona tries to memorize what she plans to say in her book report. Ask them to brainstorm different tricks they might use to remember important information. Record their suggestions on a chart.

You may wish to research the topic of memory and share some memory techniques with students. Invite cooperative groups to combine their memory tips into a handbook that can be shared by everyone. As a final project, have students form groups, and let each group select a poem or a story to memorize and recite. Have Materials Managers gather needed supplies and locate poems and stories from which to choose.   LISTENING/SPEAKING/READING/WRITING

ART

Masks Around the World

Available on Project Card 18A

CULTURAL AWARENESS   Remind students that Ramona uses masks in her presentation. Discuss other ways masks are used. (drama, festivals, holidays) Encourage cooperative groups to investigate mask making by people in different cultures. Students may divide the research tasks into distinct objectives: description of what the mask looks like, directions for making the mask, description of the culture or country, and description of how the mask is used. Students should combine their research to create one report with illustrations for the group. Encourage groups to share what they learned.
LISTENING/SPEAKING/READING/WRITING

MATH

Picture This

Available on Project Card 18B

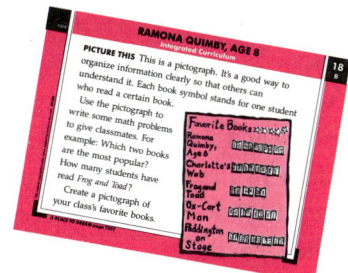

Provide students with the following pictograph. Tell them that a pictograph is one way to organize information so that it can be read and understood easily. Remind them that a pictograph uses symbols to represent information. Tell students that in this pictograph each book symbol represents one time that one of the students has read a particular book. Ask them to write math story problems based on the information contained in the pictograph; for example: Which two books are the most popular?

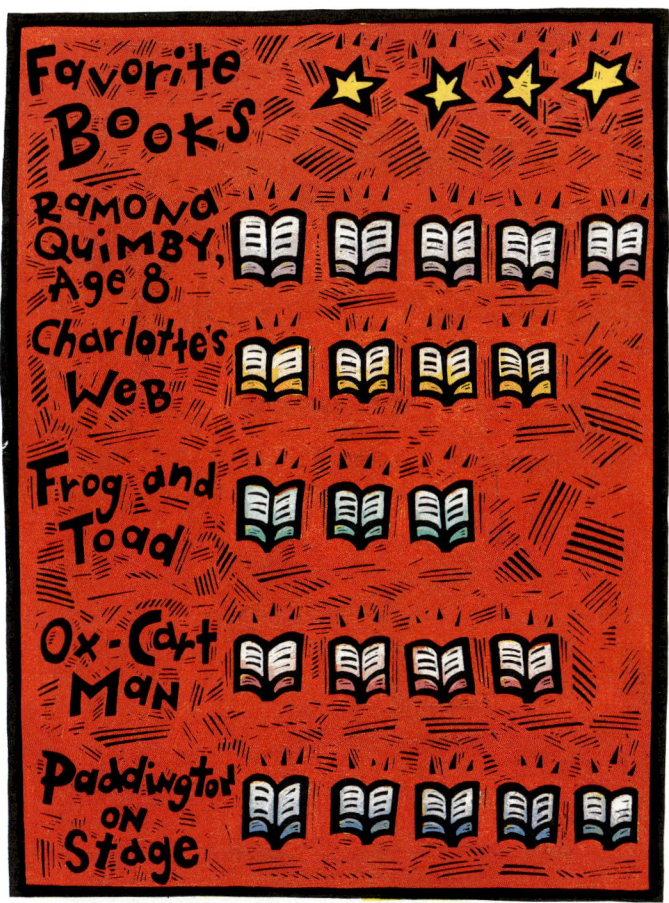

Invite volunteers to share their math problems. Some students may wish to use this activity as a model to develop a pictograph representing their own classroom favorites. **LISTENING/SPEAKING/WRITING/VIEWING**

SCIENCE

All About Cats

USE REFERENCE SOURCES Encourage students to look through picture books to find different members of the cat family. Students should group the cats they find into two "CATegories"—wild and domesticated. Some students might be interested in learning where different species of cats originated. Others may wish to ask pet-store owners or veterinarians about the basics of cat care—including the best kind of food! Have students orally share the information they find. **LISTENING/SPEAKING/READING/WRITING**

BOOKS TO SHARE

MATHEMATICS *Anno's Math Games* by Mitsumasa Anno. Philomel, 1987. AVERAGE

SCIENCE *I Can Be a Biologist* by Paul P. Sipiera. Childrens Press, 1992. AVERAGE

SOCIAL STUDIES *How a Book Is Made* by Aliki. HarperCollins, 1988. AVERAGE

RAMONA QUIMBY, AGE 8 / T237

MULTICULTURAL PERSPECTIVES

An Education for All

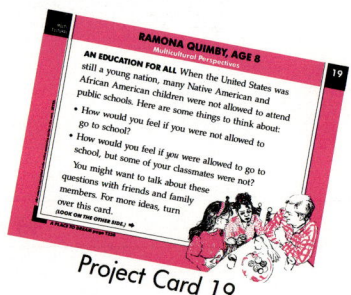

Project Card 19

DISCUSSION STARTER
How would you feel if you had to go to work every day instead of to school? What kind of future do you think you'd have?

READ ALOUD
Education has not always been available to all children in our country, as it is today. When the United States was a young nation, many children were unable to go to school. Some had to work on the family farm. Others worked in factories.

Many public schools were not open to Native Americans, most of whom were confined to reservations after 1871. Some Native American nations—such as the Cherokee, Seminole, and Choctaw—opened their own schools and sent a number of their graduates to colleges in the East.

African Americans, even after the Civil War, were often prevented from going to school at all. Dedicated educators such as Mary McLeod Bethune helped change that. Bethune attended an elementary school for African American children near her home in South Carolina. She put herself through college and later began her own school, Bethune-Cookman College in Florida. For her devotion to education, President Franklin Roosevelt chose her as an adviser, and in 1942 she received the Thomas Jefferson Medal as the "outstanding woman of the year."

ACTIVITY CORNER
Available on Project Card 19

• Ask how students would feel if they, like Native American and African American children in the past, were not allowed to attend school. Then ask how they would feel if they could go to school but some of their classmates were excluded. Would they feel comfortable with that situation? If not, what actions could they take to try to change things? Suggestions might include talking to parents or writing letters to newspapers or school officials.

• Have students find out information about their school. They might determine when it was built, for whom it was named, and where students went to school before the present school was built. Also ask students to identify schools in their city named after an African American and a woman. Invite students to share their findings with their classmates.

American Indian nations such as the Cherokee, Seminole, and Choctaw, opened their own schools and sent a number of their graduates to college.

Thanks to determined educators like Mary McLeod Bethune, all American children today can go to school.

THEME WRAP-UP

Discussing the Theme

Remind students that the selections in this theme focused on the school experiences of a fictional character and on the author who created her.

Discussion Questions

PAGE 147 In this theme you read about the school experiences of two girls—Ramona Quimby, a fictional character, and Beverly Cleary, an author. How is the author like the character she created? How is she different? (Accept reasonable responses: Beverly Cleary and Ramona are both creative; Cleary says she was a lot like Ramona until she started school.)
CRITICAL: COMPARING AND CONTRASTING/IDENTIFYING WITH CHARACTERS

Theme Wrap-Up

School Days

In this theme you read about the school experiences of two girls—Ramona Quimby, a fictional character, and Beverly Cleary, an author. How is the author like the character she created? How is she different?

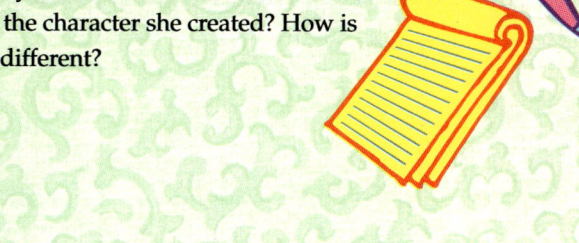

WRITER'S WORKSHOP
Ramona did a book report on a story she did not especially like. Choose a story you did not especially like and write a new ending for it.

Writer's Choice:
Writing does not always have to be a story. Write an imaginary conversation between two people. Or write a commercial for a book. Plan what you will write and how you will share it.

147

Writer's Workshop

See pages T240–T241 for suggestions for guiding students through the writing process as they respond to the literature. **WRITING PROCESS: STORY ENDING**

Writer's Choice
Have students work with partners to brainstorm ideas. You may want to suggest that if they choose to write a conversation they should refer to the *Language Handbook*, page 40, for rules about writing dialogue correctly.

When students are ready to publish their work, you may wish to suggest that they share it with their classmates. Let students decide if they want to share it orally or simply display it.

Writer's Workshop
Story Ending

Theme Wrap-Up

Students choose a story that they have read and did not especially like and write a new ending for it.

To prepare students for the writing task and form, ask them if they have ever had an experience like Ramona had in "Ramona Quimby, Age 8," in which she didn't care for a particular story at all. Help them understand that the ending of a story tells how the main problem in the story is solved.

Use the Writer's Workshop assignment on page 147 as you work through the writing process with students.

ALTERNATIVE TOPICS If you wish, allow students to choose their own topics for writing. Suggest that they refer to the *Language Handbook* for an explanation of the writing process for stories and their endings. See Writing Model, page R94.

LANGUAGE HANDBOOK *Writing to Entertain and Express, pages 36–37; Story, pages 38–39*

Prewriting

Have students work with partners or in small groups to brainstorm stories they have recently read. Then have students select the story they want to write a new ending for. Encourage students to prepare a story map such as the following one for the whole story and add the new ending.

	Characters	Setting	What Happens
Beginning			
Middle			
Ending			
New Ending			

Drafting

Have students draft their story ending. Suggest that they

- try to write a believable first sentence of the new ending so that there is a smooth transition from the middle of the story.
- refer to their prewriting story maps for details about the characters, setting, and actions.

Responding and Revising

Before students read their story ending to a partner, have them ask themselves these questions:

- Does the new ending begin with a sentence that makes sense with the information that came before?
- Does the new ending include dialogue as well as narration?
- Does the new ending solve the problem of the story?

Then have student writers read their work aloud in a peer conference. Have listeners and writers respond to the following questions:

Listener	Writer
Does the new ending make sense? Is it believable with what happened before in the story? Has the writer left out important characters? Is the new ending as interesting as the old one?	When you read your new ending aloud, are some parts stronger than others? Can you make the sentences in the new ending read more smoothly? If the new ending seems weak in some ways, think of ways you can make it stronger.

COMPUTER TIP

REVISING Encourage students to take advantage of the Move, Insert, and Delete functions on a computer to revise and improve their story endings.

Proofreading

Offer these tips for students to use as they proofread:

- Check for correct capitalization.
- Check that apostrophes are used correctly in contractions.
- Circle words that need to be checked for spelling.

MINI-CONFERENCE STRATEGY In writing a new story ending, students might use contractions to match what was done in the beginning and middle of the story. Use the occasion to help students locate errors in placing the apostrophe by making observations such as, "You wrote *are'nt* in this sentence, but shouldn't the apostrophe be placed where the missing letter in *not* is?"

Publishing Options

CLASSROOM BOOKS Have students gather copies of different endings to one particular story and bind them into a classroom book. Have students with other endings combine their writing in a class book that contains a table of contents of new endings.

ORAL SUMMARIES Suggest that individual volunteers summarize for classmates the original story and then read aloud their new ending. Encourage students to work with partners to practice reading their endings aloud.

Assessment Options

STUDENT SELF-ASSESSMENT Encourage students to summarize the writing experience by responding in their journals to this question:

- **How did I think of a story ending that I believe is better than or as good as the author's?**

You may also want to have students complete the Self-Assessment Checklist in the *Portfolio Assessment Teacher's Guide*.

WRITING OBSERVATION RECORDS Record instances during drafting or revising in which students stopped erasing mistakes and began crossing them out instead as an indication of their acceptance that a draft does not have to look like a clean copy of the final product.

After students publish, you may want to have them add their story endings to their portfolios.

GRAMMAR CONNECTION

Proofreading: Proper Nouns

Using Transparency D, show students how to check for correct capitalization of proper nouns that they have used in their story endings.

> **Transparency D**
> **Winter Party**
>
> **BEFORE**
> Tracy laughed as she skated up to mary lee in central park.
> "Thank you for such a great Party in the middle of winter in new york!"
> Mary Lee smiled back at her best Friend.
> "I bet you never thought a cold, cloudy saturday could be like this," she said.
>
> **AFTER**
> Tracy laughed as she skated up to Mary Lee in Central Park.
> "Thank you for such a great party in the middle of winter in New York!"
> Mary Lee smiled back at her best friend.
> "I bet you never thought a cold, cloudy Saturday could be like this," she said.

Have small groups of students share their writing to check for correct capitalization of proper nouns.

LANGUAGE HANDBOOK *Proper Nouns, page 94*

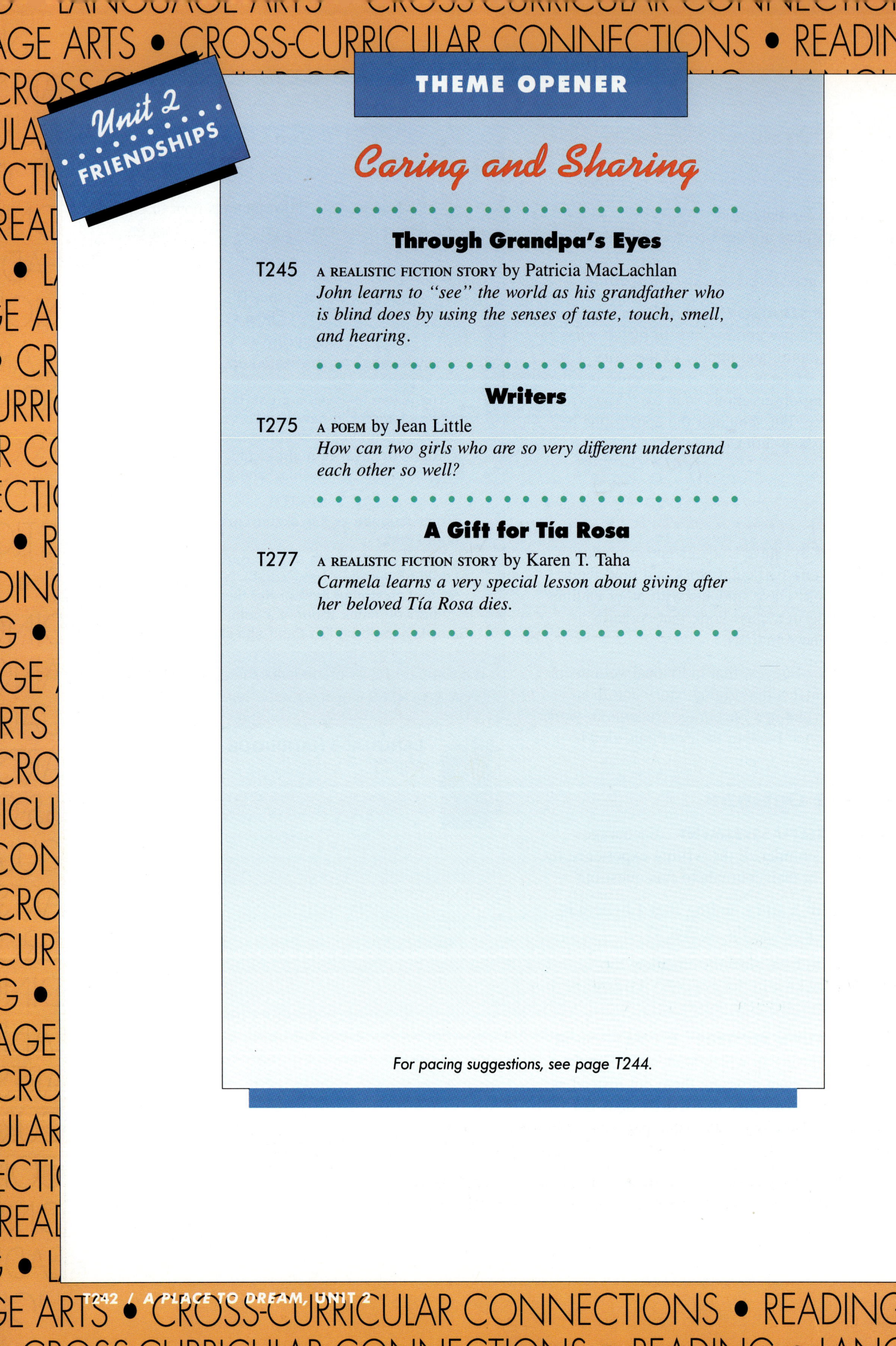

Unit 2 FRIENDSHIPS

THEME OPENER

Caring and Sharing

Through Grandpa's Eyes

T245   A REALISTIC FICTION STORY by Patricia MacLachlan
John learns to "see" the world as his grandfather who is blind does by using the senses of taste, touch, smell, and hearing.

Writers

T275   A POEM by Jean Little
How can two girls who are so very different understand each other so well?

A Gift for Tía Rosa

T277   A REALISTIC FICTION STORY by Karen T. Taha
Carmela learns a very special lesson about giving after her beloved Tía Rosa dies.

For pacing suggestions, see page T244.

Theme Opener: Caring and Sharing PAGES 148–149

THEME

Caring and Sharing

Giving of yourself — your time and your friendship — is a special way of sharing with others. The following stories and poem tell about some special ways that people show they care.

CONTENTS

THROUGH GRANDPA'S EYES
by Patricia MacLachlan

WRITERS
by Jean Little

A GIFT FOR TÍA ROSA
by Karen T. Taha

149

Discussing the Theme

Read aloud the theme title, "Caring and Sharing," and ask students to explain what it means to them and to give examples of caring and sharing. Next, have students read the paragraph on Student Anthology page 149 and tell how they think it relates to the illustration. Then encourage students to speculate, based on the selection titles and the discussion, what the characters in the selections might share and how they might show that they care about one another.

Portfolio Assessment

Remind students to keep their writing responses for the selections in "Caring and Sharing" in their portfolios. Also, remind them to add to their personal journals thoughts about books they have read independently.

 Whenever you see this symbol, you may provide students the opportunity to save some of their work in their portfolios.

THEME OPENER: CARING AND SHARING / T243

THEME OPENER

Managing the Literature-Based Classroom

Paired Reading

The theme "Caring and Sharing" is an excellent one with which to initiate a paired reading program. Students may enjoy reading and discussing the selections with a partner. You may wish to emphasize the element of caring, as well as the ways that reading partners can share, in preparing students for the experience. The paired reading program and variations on it can continue as appropriate throughout the school year.

Providing Options

Because paired reading naturally generates a noise level that may interfere with other students' ability to read silently, you may want to provide drawing materials for those students not participating in paired reading on a particular day. Students can work on creating cartoons or posters about the theme to share with their partners at their next paired reading session.

Pacing

This theme has been designed to take about two weeks to complete, depending on your students' needs.

MEETING INDIVIDUAL NEEDS

LOW-ACHIEVING STUDENTS If students feel apprehensive about paired reading, make arrangements for them to read with an older student. Suggest that they prepare by reading the first paragraph of the selection and previewing the remaining pages. Offer to help students with ideas or words that need further discussion, and point out that they will have the opportunity to work with their partners in the same way.

GIFTED AND TALENTED After students finish reading "Through Grandpa's Eyes" and/or "A Gift for Tía Rosa," suggest that they create a diagram to analyze the story structure. Encourage students to share their diagrams with students who may need additional help. *Challenge Cards* provide additional activities to challenge students. Challenge notes throughout the lesson plans suggest additional activities to stimulate critical and creative thinking.

SPECIAL-EDUCATION STUDENTS For students who are easily distracted:

- Provide headsets to block out noises.
- Designate a quiet area in the room.
- Make a privacy screen using three sides of a cardboard box to place around the edge of a student's desk or table.

STUDENTS ACQUIRING ENGLISH Create a map or diagram that follows the structure of the Writer's Workshop assignment—directions for showing how something is done—and encourage students to use the diagram when writing their draft. You may also wish to provide a variety of samples for students to study. Second-Language Support notes throughout the lesson plans offer strategies to help students acquiring English to understand the selection.

THROUGH GRANDPA'S EYES

by Patricia MacLachlan

illustrated by Greg Shed

AWARD-WINNING AUTHOR

Integrated Lesson Planner

Through Grandpa's Eyes
pages 150–167

	READING	LANGUAGE ARTS	CROSS-CURRICULAR CONNECTIONS
PART 1 *Reading the Literature* pages T248–T259	**Building Background** **Vocabulary Strategies** **Prereading Strategies** Prediction Chart Setting a Purpose **Options for Reading**	**Spelling** Pretest Spelling-Vocabulary Connection Generalization: *sh, ch, str, wh* **Grammar Connection** Reviewing Singular and Plural Nouns	**Cultural Awareness** French contributions to nonvisual education **Social Studies** Sculpture of the past **Science** Migratory geese
PART 2 *Responding to the Literature* pages T260–T267	**Personal Response** **Cooperative Response** **Summarizing the Literature** **Critical Thinking Activity** Chart **Vocabulary Workshop** Key Words Inflected Ending *-ing*	**Language Arts Workshop** **Reading** drama **Writing** description, Braille messages, characteristics **Listening and Speaking** using senses, role-play, guessing game **Reviewing Spelling Words** Posttest **Grammar Review** Singular and Plural Nouns **Grammar Minilesson** More Plural Nouns	**Social Studies** Understanding Braille
PART 3 *Learning Through the Literature* pages T268–T274	**Introduce** Literary Appreciation: Point of View **Review** Comprehension: Author's Purpose Comprehension Strategy: Active Reading Strategies	**Reading** Was That a Bird I Heard? **Writing** Labeling Flowers **Listening and Speaking** Sculpt a Gift Make a Musical Instrument	**Art** Sculpt a Gift **Science** Was That a Bird I Heard? Labeling Flowers **Social Studies** Mapping from Memory **Math** Determine Time **Music** Make a Musical Instrument **Multicultural Perspectives** Overcoming Challenges

OPTIONAL MATERIALS
Chart/Transparency 17
Integrated Spelling pp. 38–41; TE pp. T57–T62
Practice Book pp. 46–51
Writer's Journal pp. 30–31
Alternative Teaching Strategies pp. 10, 62–65
Language Handbook pp. 44–46, 96–97, 98–101
Grammar Practice pp. 24–25
Family Involvement Activities: Unit 2, pp. 1–4
Response Card 4
Project Cards 20A, 20B, 21A, 21B, 22

MEETING INDIVIDUAL NEEDS
Second-Language Support pp. T249, T250, T254, T267, T269
Mainstreaming p. T250
Reteach pp. T267, T269
Challenge pp. T269, T270, T271

FAMILY INVOLVEMENT Suggest that family members talk about time spent with older relatives. See *Family Involvement Activities.*

Key Words
promptly
exercises
Braille
sculpt
imitating
dollop
marigolds
sternly

T246 / *A PLACE TO DREAM*, UNIT 2

Selection Summary

When John visits his grandparents, he learns to use his senses of taste, touch, smell, and hearing to "see" the world as his blind grandfather does. John closes his eyes to learn what it is like to do familiar activities, such as exercising, identifying foods being cooked, and playing the cello, without being able to see. He also discovers how extraordinarily sharp his grandfather's senses are as he and his grandfather take a walk in the country, listen to bird calls, wash dishes, read, and relax after a full, rich day together.

About the Author

Patricia MacLachlan has written many award-winning books for young readers. Family life is a recurring theme in her work. She was born in Cheyenne, Wyoming and now lives in Massachusetts.

Through Grandpa's Eyes was named a Notable Children's Trade Book in Social Studies in 1980. *Sarah, Plain and Tall* was awarded the Newbery Medal in 1986; *Arthur, for the Very First Time* won the Golden Kite Award for Fiction in 1980; and *Unclaimed Treasures* was named a *Boston Globe–Horn Book* Award Honor Book in 1984.

Patricia MacLachlan is a neighbor to Jane Yolen, author of *Owl Moon*. Jane credits Patricia with being a fine response partner who helped her find the right wording for the *Owl Moon* lead.

Additional Reading

OTHER BOOKS BY PATRICIA MACLACHLAN

Mama One, Mama Two. HarperCollins, 1982. EASY

Three Names. HarperCollins, 1991. AVERAGE

OTHER THEME-RELATED BOOKS

The First Strawberries: A Cherokee Story retold by Joseph Bruchac. Dial, 1993. EASY

Mister King by Raija Siekkinen. Carolrhoda Books, 1986. AVERAGE

BOOKS FOR APPLYING STRATEGIES: POINT OF VIEW

Happy Birthday, Grampie by Susan Pearson. Dial, 1987. EASY

The True Story of the Three Little Pigs by Jon Scieszka. Viking, 1989. EASY

*Available as a Harcourt Brace PASSPORTS title

PART 1

Reading the Literature

Building Background

Access prior knowledge and build vocabulary concepts.

Tell students that a main character in the next story, "Through Grandpa's Eyes," is blind. Explain that people who are blind must rely on senses other than sight. Ask students to name the five senses and then name some objects they would be able to identify by feeling (piece of paper), smelling (soap), tasting (orange), and hearing (whistle). Then have them choose one of the senses and create a web, such as the one below, listing things that could be identified with that sense.

Have students quickwrite.

Have students write one or two sentences about using one or more of their senses to do something.

Vocabulary Strategies

Introduce Key Words and strategies.

Display Chart/Transparency 17, or write the story on the board. Have students read the story silently, using context clues to figure out the meanings of the underlined words. For example, students can use the phrase *or carve* to figure out what *sculpt* means.

Chart/Transparency 17   Key Words

Miguel is blind, but that doesn't slow him down. As soon as he wakes up every day, he promptly starts his exercises to stay fit. He reads books in Braille by touching the raised dots that stand for the letters. He can sculpt, or carve, statues by touch alone. He learned to do these things, not by watching and imitating others, but by hearing and touching.

Miguel can put a dollop of honey in his tea to add a little sweetness. He smells flowers from across the yard and says it is easy to know they are marigolds because of their strong smell. One day Miguel heard a boy tease a dog and spoke sternly to him. But my friend Miguel always speaks kindly to me.

CULTURAL AWARENESS

You might tell students that the French have done much to help blind people. In the late 1700s, the first school for the blind was opened in Paris. Later Louis Braille, a blind French boy of fifteen, created a way of writing for those without sight.

Key Words

promptly
exercises
Braille
sculpt
imitating
dollop
marigolds
sternly

KEY WORDS DEFINED

promptly   quickly; right away

exercises   a series of movements to build strength

Braille   a system of writing designed for blind people

sculpt   to carve shapes from wood, clay, or stone

imitating   mimicking

dollop   small portion

marigolds   yellow flowers that have a strong smell

sternly   firmly

Check all students' understanding. Display a chart like the one below, listing each Key Word and an example of a related word. Ask students to suggest other words that are either synonyms for the Key Words or examples of things that are related in some way to the Key Words. Ask students to explain why they made their suggestions. **STRATEGY: PRIOR KNOWLEDGE**

Key Words	Related Words
promptly	quickly (on time)
exercises	jumping jacks (healthy)
Braille	raised dots (blindness, read books)
sculpt	clay (marble, art, statue)
imitating	mimicking (watching, acting)
dollop	jam (honey, spoonful)
marigolds	flowers (smell, yellow)
sternly	seriously (firmly)

Integrate spelling with vocabulary. **SPELLING-VOCABULARY CONNECTION** *Integrated Spelling* Lesson 8 reinforces the spelling of words with digraphs and clusters, such as *sharp*, found in the selection. In addition, the Words to Explore help reinforce the concept of words that tell *how* as it relates to the selection.

 **SPELLING PRETEST** You may want to use the Pretest/Posttest Sentences on page T57 in *Integrated Spelling Teacher's Edition* to assess students' knowledge of the spelling generalization.

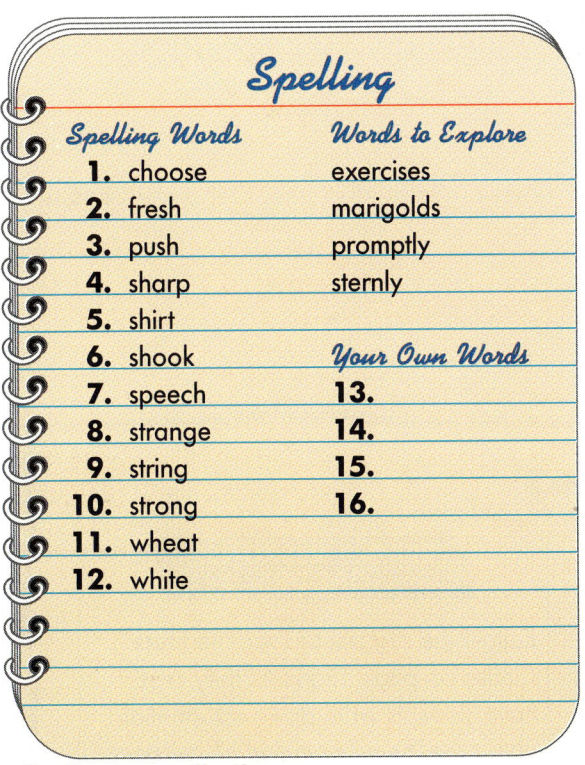

Spelling generalization: digraphs and clusters *sh, ch, str, wh*

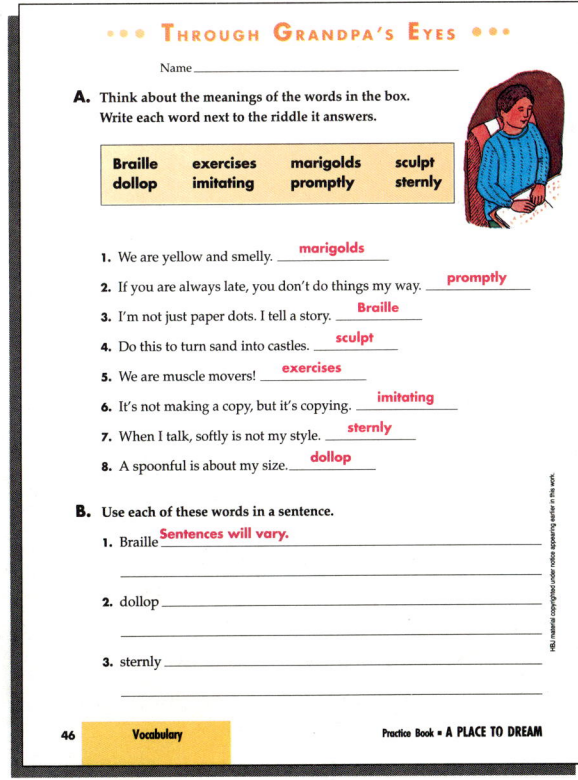

Practice Book

MEETING INDIVIDUAL NEEDS

SECOND-LANGUAGE SUPPORT Pair students and have them retell in their own words the story on Chart/Transparency 17. Have one student describe some of the things Miguel can do while the second student pantomimes the actions. See also the manual *Alternative Teaching Strategies*, pages 10, 62–65.

OPTIONAL INDEPENDENT PRACTICE

INTEGRATED SPELLING pages 38–41: Words with *sh, ch, str,* and *wh*

PRACTICE BOOK page 46: Reinforcing Key Words

NOTE: This page may be completed now or after students have read the selection.

THROUGH GRANDPA'S EYES / T249

Prereading Strategies

Prediction Chart

Have students preview the literature.

Remind students that previewing a story before they read helps prepare them for what they are going to read. Have students preview "Through Grandpa's Eyes" by reading to the end of the fourth paragraph on page 152 and looking at the illustrations.

Have students begin a prediction chart.

Write the following chart on the board. Begin by having students fill in the first two boxes.

Information from the Story	What I Already Know
John's favorite house is his grandpa's house. His grandpa is blind.	Grandparents often teach their grandchildren things. Blind people cannot see.

Prediction
John's grandfather will teach him how to do things without seeing.

What Happens

 **PERSONAL JOURNAL** Have students use the information in the first two boxes to predict what might happen. Suggest that they add their predictions to the chart and their personal journals.

Setting a Purpose

Have students set purposes.

Ask students to set a purpose for reading based on their preview, what they already know, and their predictions.

If students have trouble setting a purpose, offer this suggestion:

I want to read to find out what John learns from his grandfather.

MEETING INDIVIDUAL NEEDS

SECOND-LANGUAGE SUPPORT Students will benefit from a brief comparison of grandparents and grandchildren, and a more detailed preview in which characters are introduced. See also the manual *Alternative Teaching Strategies*, pages 10, 62–65.

SUPPORT FOR MAINSTREAMING Ask students to sit quietly with their eyes closed. Encourage them to tell about what they can hear, smell, and feel around them. Tell students to draw upon this experience as they read the story.

Options for Reading

SUSTAINED SILENT READING
Remind students who are reading independently to revise their predictions as they find out new story information.

STRATEGIC READING
To stimulate discussion, use the suggestions that appear on pages T251, T256, and T259.

READER RESPONSE GROUPS
Follow the suggestions for Literature Circles on page T251. As they read, have students write down information about the theme or mood of the story to discuss with their group.

THROUGH GRANDPA'S EYES   PAGES 150–151

THROUGH GRANDPA'S EYES

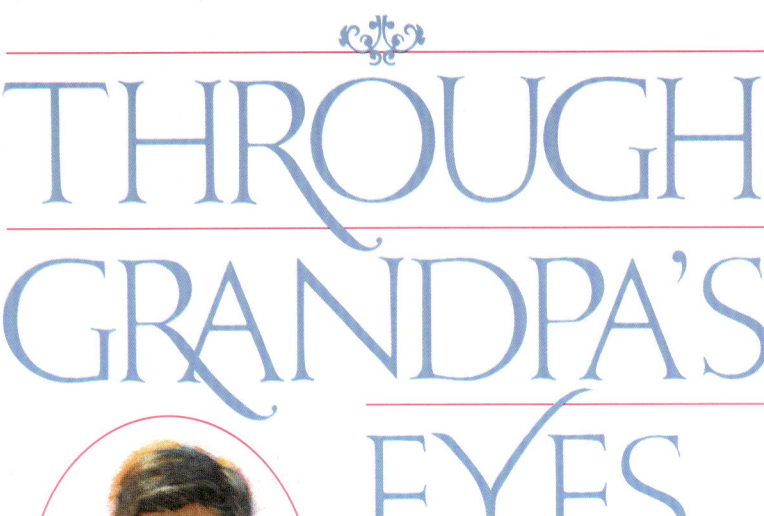

by Patricia MacLachlan

illustrated by Greg Shed

Of all the houses that I know, I like my grandpa's best. My friend Peter has a new glass house with pebble-path gardens that go nowhere. And Maggie lives next door in an old wooden house with rooms behind rooms, all with carved doors and brass doorknobs. They are fine houses. But Grandpa's house is my favorite. Because I see it through Grandpa's eyes.

151

Reader Response Groups

LITERATURE CIRCLES Have groups of three to five students read the selection silently, stopping at page 161 for a brief discussion. You may want to distribute Response Card 4 (Theme/Mood), found on page R82, for possible discussion questions or provide the following questions:

- From the title of the story, what did you think this story would be about?
- How do you feel about what you have read? Why?

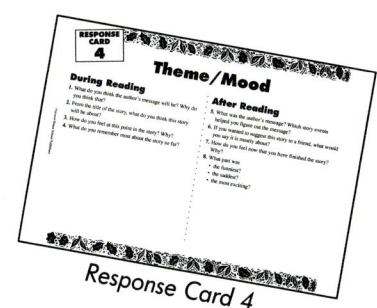

Response Card 4

Strategic Reading

SET PURPOSE/PREDICT: PAGES 150–161 Have students read through page 161. Ask students what they will be reading to find out.

THROUGH GRANDPA'S EYES / T251

PAGES 152–153 THROUGH GRANDPA'S EYES

Grandpa is blind. He doesn't see the house the way I do. He has his own way of seeing.

In the morning, the sun pushes through the curtains into my eyes. I burrow down into the covers to get away, but the light follows me. I give up, throw back the covers, and run to Grandpa's room.

The sun wakes Grandpa differently from the way it wakes me. He says it touches him, *warming* him awake. When I peek around the door, Grandpa is already up and doing his morning exercises. Bending and stretching by the bed. He stops and smiles because he hears me.

"Good morning, John."

"Where's Nana?" I ask him.

"Don't you know?" he says, bending and stretching. "Close your eyes, John, and look through my eyes."

I close my eyes. Down below, I hear the banging of pots and the sound of water running that I didn't hear before.

"Nana is in the kitchen, making breakfast," I say.

When I open my eyes again, I can see Grandpa nodding at me. He is tall with dark gray hair. And his eyes are sharp blue even though they are not sharp seeing.

I exercise with Grandpa. Up and down. Then I try to exercise with my eyes closed.

"One, two," says Grandpa, "three, four."

152

 Informal Assessment

ACTIVE READING STRATEGIES To informally assess whether students use active reading strategies as they read, ask questions like these:

- How do you picture Nana and what she is doing?
- What details does the author give to help you form this mental picture?
- What do you know from real life that helps you visualize Nana and her actions?

A review lesson on **active reading strategies** appears on page T271.

See page T272 for information found on Project Card 21B.

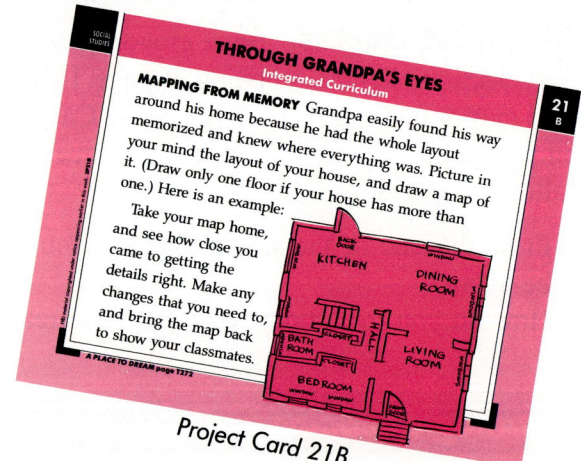

Project Card 21B

T252 / A PLACE TO DREAM, UNIT 2

THROUGH GRANDPA'S EYES PAGES 154–155

"Wait!" I cry. I am still on one, two when Grandpa is on three, four.

I fall sideways. Three times. Grandpa laughs as he hears my thumps on the carpet.

"Breakfast!" calls Nana from downstairs.

"I smell eggs frying," says Grandpa. He bends his head close to mine. "And buttered toast."

The wooden banister on the stairway has been worn smooth from Grandpa running his fingers up and down. I walk behind him, my fingers following Grandpa's smooth path.

We go into the kitchen.

"I smell flowers," says Grandpa.

"What flowers?" I ask.

He smiles. He loves guessing games.

"Not violets, John, not peonies . . ."

"Carnations!" I cry. *I love guessing games.*

"Silly." Grandpa laughs. "Marigolds. Right, Nana?" Nana laughs, too.

"That's too easy," she says, putting two plates of food in front of us.

"It's not too easy," I protest. "How can Grandpa tell? All the smells mix together in the air."

"Close your eyes, John," says Nana. "Tell me what breakfast is."

"I smell the eggs. I smell the toast," I say, my eyes closed. "And something else. The something else doesn't smell good."

155

Vocabulary Strategy Have students use context clues to figure out the meanings of the words *banister, violets, peonies,* and *carnations*. Point out that *violet* also names a color, and ask students how knowing this can help them picture what the flower called a violet looks like. (It helps them to picture a violet as a purple or deep-blue flower.) STRATEGY: CONTEXT CLUES/MULTIPLE-MEANING WORDS

PAGES 156–157 THROUGH GRANDPA'S EYES

"*That* something else," says Nana smiling, "is the marigolds."

When he eats, Grandpa's plate of food is a clock.

"Two eggs at nine o'clock and toast at two o'clock," says Nana to Grandpa. "And a dollop of jam."

"A dollop of jam," I tell Grandpa, "at six o'clock."

I make my plate of food a clock, too, and eat through Grandpa's eyes.

After breakfast, I follow Grandpa's path through the dining room to the living room, to the window that he opens to feel the weather outside, to the table where he finds his pipe, and to his cello in the corner.

"Will you play with me, John?" he asks.

He tunes our cellos without looking. I play with a music stand and music before me. I know all about sharps and flats. I see them on the music. But Grandpa plays them. They are in his fingers. For a moment I close my eyes and play through Grandpa's eyes. My fingering hand slides up and down the cello neck—toward the pegs for flats, toward the bridge for sharps. But with my eyes closed my bow falls from the strings.

"Listen," says Grandpa. "I'll play a piece I learned when I was your age. It was my favorite."

He plays the tune while I listen. That is the way Grandpa learns new pieces. By listening.

Second-Language Support Students may not understand the terms *sharps, flats, neck, pegs, bridge, bow,* and *strings* in the context of musical instruments. Use the picture on page 156 to point out the cello's neck, pegs, bridge, bow, and strings. Explain that sounds are created by moving the bow across the strings. If possible, play some pairs of notes to illustrate *flat* and *sharp*.

MEETING INDIVIDUAL NEEDS

Expanding the Literature When Nana puts "two eggs at nine o'clock and toast at two o'clock," where on the plate does she put the food? Have a volunteer draw a circle on the board and show where the eggs and toast would be on the plate. CREATIVE: VISUALIZING

"Now," says Grandpa. "Let's do it together."

"That's fine," says Grandpa as we play. "But C sharp, John," he calls to me. "C sharp!"

Later, Nana brings out her clay to sculpt my Grandpa's head.

"Sit still," she grumbles.

"I won't," he says, imitating her grumbly voice, making us laugh.

While she works, Grandpa takes out his piece of wood. He holds it when he's thinking. His fingers move back and forth across the wood, making smooth paths like the ones on the stair banister.

"Can I have a piece of thinking wood, too?" I ask.

Grandpa reaches in his shirt pocket and tosses a small bit of wood in my direction. I catch it. It is smooth with no splinters.

"The river is up," says Nana.

Grandpa nods a short nod. "It rained again last night. Did you hear the gurgling in the rain gutter?"

As they talk, my fingers begin a river on my thinking wood. The wood will winter in my pocket so when I am not at Grandpa's house I can still think about Nana, Grandpa, and the river.

When Nana is finished working, Grandpa runs his hand over the sculpture, his fingers soft and quick like butterflies.

"It looks like me," he says, surprised.

Social Studies Connection Ask students why they think John's grandmother is making a sculpture of his grandfather. (Accept reasonable responses: She loves her husband and enjoys sculpting.) Tell students that people who study the past believe that sculpture tells a lot about the values of the people who create it. For example, the ancient Greeks greatly admired physical strength and mental ability. To show their admiration, the Greeks made numerous statues of strong, athletic, powerful, and thoughtful-looking people. Since the sculptors often worked in durable materials such as bronze, the statues can tell us today about an ancient culture.

PAGES 160–161 THROUGH GRANDPA'S EYES

My eyes have already told me that it looks like Grandpa. But he shows me how to feel his face with my three middle fingers, and then the clay face.

"Pretend your fingers are water," he tells me.

My waterfall fingers flow down his clay head, filling in the spaces beneath the eyes like little pools before they flow down over the cheeks. It does feel like Grandpa. This time my fingers tell me.

Grandpa and I walk outside, through the front yard and across the field to the river. Grandpa has not been blind forever. He remembers in his mind the gleam of the sun on the river, the Queen Anne's lace in the meadow, and every dahlia in his garden. But he gently takes my elbow as we walk so that I can help show him the path.

"I feel a south wind," says Grandpa.

I can tell which way the wind is blowing because I see the way the tops of the trees lean. Grandpa tells by the feel of the meadow grasses and by the way his hair blows against his face.

When we come to the riverbank, I see that Nana was right. The water is high and has cut in by the willow tree. It flows around and among the roots of the tree, making paths. Paths like Grandpa's on the stair banister and on the thinking wood. I see a blackbird with a red patch on its wing sitting on a cattail. Without thinking, I point my finger.

"What is that bird, Grandpa?" I ask excitedly.

Strategic Reading

MODELING A STRATEGY: PAGES 150–161 What kind of a person would you say John's grandpa is? How do you know?

THINK ALOUD You may want to model with this think-aloud: *I think Grandpa is a caring person. I know by the way he tries to teach John things. He is also a kind and gentle person. He shows that by the way he talks to John.* ANALYZING CHARACTERS

SET PURPOSE/PREDICT: PAGES 162–167 Ask students what other things they think John might learn from Grandpa. Have them read the rest of the story to confirm their predictions.

T256 / A PLACE TO DREAM, UNIT 2

"*Conk-a-ree,*" the bird calls to us.

"A red-winged blackbird," says Grandpa promptly.

He can't see my finger pointing. But he hears the song of the bird.

"And somewhere behind the blackbird," he says, listening, "a song sparrow."

I hear a scratchy song, and I look and look until I see the earth-colored bird that Grandpa knows is here.

Nana calls from the front porch of the house.

"Nana's made hot bread for lunch," he tells me happily. "And spice tea." Spice tea is his favorite.

I close my eyes, but all I can smell is the wet earth by the river.

As we walk back to the house, Grandpa stops suddenly. He bends his head to one side, listening. He points his finger upward.

"Honkers," he whispers.

I look up and see a flock of geese, high in the clouds, flying in a *V*.

"Canada geese," I tell him.

"Honkers," he insists. And we both laugh.

We walk up the path again and to the yard where Nana is painting the porch chairs. Grandpa smells the paint.

"What color, Nana?" he asks. "I cannot smell the color."

"Blue," I tell him, smiling. "Blue like the sky."

"Blue like the color of Grandpa's eyes," Nana says.

163

Science Connection Tell students that geese are migratory birds. Some geese fly as far north as the Arctic coast of North America and as far south as Mexico. When they fly long distances, they adopt the great V-shape formation used by all large birds that migrate in groups. They fly at high speeds—one mile per minute or faster—making loud, honking noises. The birds are excellent navigators, often returning to the same spot they left the previous season.

See page T272 for information found on Project Card 21A.

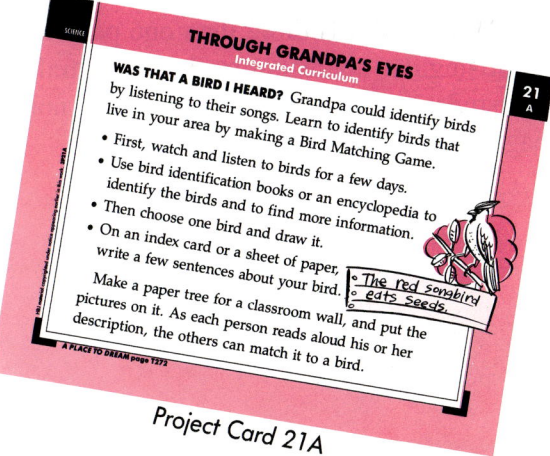

Project Card 21A

THROUGH GRANDPA'S EYES / T257

PAGES 164–165 THROUGH GRANDPA'S EYES

When he was younger, before I can remember, before he was blind, Grandpa did things the way I do. Now, when we drink tea and eat lunch on the porch, Grandpa pours his own cup of tea by putting his finger just inside the rim of the cup to tell him when it is full. He never burns his finger. Afterward, when I wash the dishes, he feels them as he dries them. He even sends some back for me to wash again.

"Next time," says Grandpa, pretending to be cross, "I wash, you dry."

In the afternoon, Grandpa, Nana, and I take our books outside to read under the apple tree. Grandpa reads his book with his fingers, feeling the raised Braille dots that tell him the words.

As he reads, Grandpa laughs out loud.

"Tell us what's funny," says Nana. "Read to us, Papa."

And he does.

Nana and I put down our books to listen. A gray squirrel comes down the trunk of the apple tree, tail high, and seems to listen, too. But Grandpa doesn't see him.

After supper, Grandpa turns on the television. I watch, but Grandpa listens, and the music and the words tell him when something is dangerous or funny, happy or sad.

Somehow, Grandpa knows when it is dark, and he takes me upstairs and tucks me into bed. He bends down to kiss me, his hands feeling my head.

"You need a haircut, John," he says.

Before Grandpa leaves, he pulls the light chain above my bed to turn out the light. But, by mistake, he's turned it on instead. I lie for a moment after he's gone, smiling, before I get up to turn off the light.

GRAMMAR CONNECTION

REVIEWING SINGULAR AND PLURAL NOUNS Remind students that plural nouns name more than one person, place, or thing. Review the ways most singular nouns are made into plural nouns. (by adding -s or -es) Then ask students to identify the two plural nouns in the first paragraph on page 165. (things, dishes)

T258 / A PLACE TO DREAM, UNIT 2

THROUGH GRANDPA'S EYES   PAGES 166–167

Then, when it is dark for me the way it is dark for Grandpa, I hear the night noises that Grandpa hears. The house creaking, the birds singing their last songs of the day, the wind rustling the tree outside my window.

Then, all of a sudden, I hear the sounds of geese overhead. They fly low over the house.

"Grandpa," I call softly, hoping he's heard them too.

"Honkers," he calls back.

"Go to sleep, John," says Nana.

Grandpa says her voice smiles to him. I test it.

"What?" I call to her.

"I said go to sleep," she answers.

She says it <u>sternly</u>. But Grandpa is right. Her voice smiles to me. I know. Because I'm looking through Grandpa's eyes.

What did you learn about the way John sees "through Grandpa's eyes"?

What makes John's relationship with his grandfather special?

How are Grandpa's fingers like John's eyes?

WRITE   Write a description of an object for a friend. Use words that will help him or her "see" the object without actually looking at it.

167

Strategic Reading

MODELING A STRATEGY: PAGES 162–167   Have students summarize what they read on these pages.

THINK ALOUD   You might want to model with this think-aloud: *John likes visiting his grandfather because there he learns to "see" the world with senses other than sight. John pays attention to and imitates the way his blind grandfather performs his daily activities.*   SUMMARIZING

Returning to the Predictions/Purpose

PREDICTION CHART   Invite students to discuss the predictions they made before reading and to discuss whether or not these predictions changed as they read. After students complete the chart, ask them what they learned from the selection.

NOTE: Responses to the questions and support for the Write activity appear on page T260.

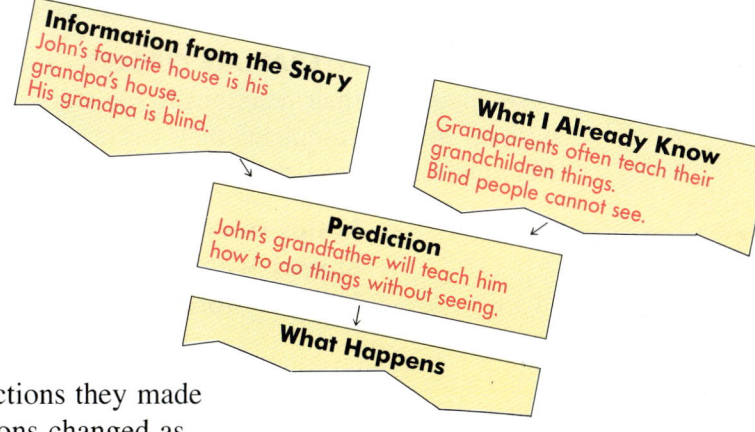

THROUGH GRANDPA'S EYES / T259

PART 2

Responding to the Literature

Personal Response

Encourage critical thinking.

What did you learn about the way John sees "through Grandpa's eyes"? (Responses will vary.) CRITICAL: EXPRESSING PERSONAL OPINIONS

What makes John's relationship with his grandfather special? (Accept reasonable responses: They help each other in special ways—John guides Grandpa on their walk, and Grandpa teaches John to use his five senses.) INFERENTIAL: SYNTHESIZING

How are Grandpa's fingers like John's eyes? (Grandpa can "see" with his fingers much of what John can see with his eyes—for example, Grandpa feels what the sculpture looks like.) INFERENTIAL: MAKING COMPARISONS

Encourage creative written responses.

 **WRITE** Write a description of an object for a friend. Use words that will help him or her "see" the object without actually looking at it. Encourage students to include descriptive details that appeal to the reader's senses. These might include details about the object's size, color, texture, temperature, and aroma. CREATIVE: EXPANDING STORY CONCEPTS

Cooperative Response

Have reader response groups extend their discussions.

LITERATURE CIRCLES Encourage Literature Circles to discuss their reactions to the story. They might begin by sharing any comments they wrote about the theme or mood of the story. Then have them discuss a question such as this one:

Is this story a happy story or a sad one? Support your answer with examples from the story. You might want to look for words and phrases that tell how the characters feel.

STRATEGY CONFERENCE

Ask students how the prediction chart helped them understand the story. (Accept reasonable responses: Making predictions helps readers decide on a purpose for reading. They look forward to finding out how the story turns out and whether they guessed correctly.)

NOTE

An additional writing activity for this story appears on page T263.

Summarizing the Literature

Have students retell the story and write a summary.

Have students summarize the story by charting in order the things John and Grandpa do together and the special way Grandpa experiences each activity. Suggest that students use their sequence chart to retell the story and to write a brief summary. See *Practice Book* page 47 below.

What John and Grandpa Do	Special Way Grandpa "Sees"
1. (Eat breakfast)	(Grandpa knows what's cooking by smell. He can tell there are marigolds in the kitchen.)
2. (Play their cellos)	(Grandpa plays by touch. He learns by listening.)

Critical Thinking Activity

Investigate use of imagery.

CHART MULTIPLE-MEANING WORDS Display the chart for students and have volunteers read the phrases and tell what each one means.

Phrase	What It Means
Do you see?	(Do you understand?)
Wait and see.	(Watch for changes.)

Discuss reasons why the word *see* has so many uses in everyday conversation. Then, have students think of other phrases that use the word *see*. CRITICAL: APPRECIATING LANGUAGE

Writer's Journal

Practice Book

INFORMAL ASSESSMENT

Having students order the details of a selection in this way will help you informally assess how well they understood key relationships. Ask yourself: Did students grasp time relationships? Did students recognize the causes of effects and the effects of causes? Can students tell which details are more important than others?

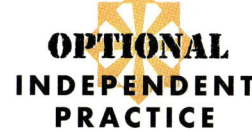

OPTIONAL INDEPENDENT PRACTICE

WRITER'S JOURNAL

page 30: Writing a personal response

PRACTICE BOOK

page 47: Summarizing the selection

THROUGH GRANDPA'S EYES / T261

VOCABULARY WORKSHOP

Reviewing Key Words

Display the Key Words and have students answer the following "Who Am I?" questions orally or in writing.

Who Am I?

1. *dollop*   I put a dollop of jam on Grandpa's plate. (Nana)
2. *promptly*   I promptly named the red-winged blackbird. (Grandpa)
3. *exercises*   I did exercises with Grandpa. (John)
4. *imitating*   I like imitating Grandpa. (John)
5. *sternly*   I sternly told John to go to sleep. (Nana)
6. *Braille*   I read Braille books. (Grandpa)
7. *marigolds*   I knew marigolds were in the kitchen without seeing them. (Grandpa)
8. *sculpt*   I use clay when I sculpt. (Nana)

Extending Vocabulary

INFLECTED ENDING -ING   Write the following words from "Through Grandpa's Eyes" on the board as shown below:

| bending stretching walking | |

Ask students what the words have in common. (All end with *-ing*; all have something to do with exercise.) Have a volunteer go to the board and circle the common ending. Then write the words *bend*, *stretch*, and *walk* in the second column of the chart, and explain to students that these forms of the words can be used as commands, while the inflected *-ing* forms are used to tell what someone is doing. Ask volunteers to use each form of the word in a sentence.

Have students suggest other exercise words to add to the list. Encourage students to use the inflected *-ing* form of each word in a sentence.

Have students work independently to design an exercise program, using at least three of the words from the board as they write their program. You may wish to have volunteers demonstrate their exercise program.

READING	WRITING

Oral Rereading/Drama

Have students form groups of four. Three students will each choose the part of John, Nana, or Grandpa. The fourth student will be the narrator for the sections not in quotation marks. Have groups orally reread the kitchen scene, beginning with "We go into the kitchen" on page 155 and ending with "I make my plate of food a clock, too, and eat through Grandpa's eyes" on page 157, or have students select another scene. Model a few lines to demonstrate how to read with the appropriate pitch, intonation, and expression. Have students rehearse together before presenting their rereading. **LISTENING/SPEAKING/READING**

Writing About the Literature

Available on Project Card 20A

 **WRITE A DESCRIPTION** Have students describe their favorite place. Ask them to begin by brainstorming a list of favorite places, such as the beach. Choose one, and model for students what senses you would use while visiting it. Work with students to create on the board a five-senses web like the following. Encourage individual students to create their own five-senses web before they begin writing. See Writing Model, page R93. **WRITING**

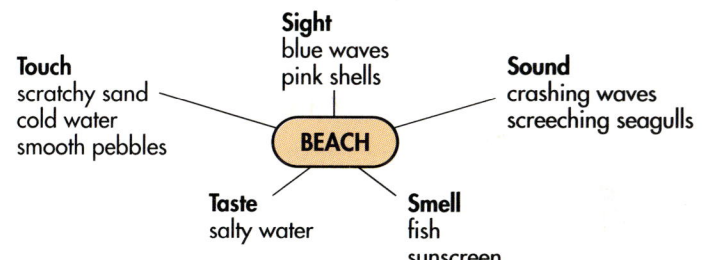

GRAMMAR REVIEW: SINGULAR AND PLURAL NOUNS When students revise remind them to check words they used that name people, places, and things. They should make sure they have used singular nouns and plural nouns correctly. Then, have students work in pairs, and have each student find five nouns in his or her partner's description. Students should circle the nouns and indicate whether each noun is singular or plural. Partners can check that the correct plural ending is used and, if necessary, suggest revisions.

 **LANGUAGE HANDBOOK** *Writing to Describe,* pages 44–46; Singular and Plural Nouns, pages 96–97

 **DAILY LANGUAGE PRACTICE** Oral language exercises are provided on pages R66–R67.

THROUGH GRANDPA'S EYES / T263

Language Arts WORKSHOP

SPELLING

Reviewing Spelling Words

SPELLING WORDS: *choose, fresh, push, sharp, shirt, shook, speech, strange, string, strong, wheat, white*

WORDS TO EXPLORE: *exercises, marigolds, promptly, sternly*

Write the Spelling Words on the board, and ask students to suggest additional words with the consonant clusters and digraphs *ch, sh, str,* and *wh.* Begin a story by writing and saying a sentence. Include one or more words with the consonant clusters and digraphs. Have volunteers suggest sentences that continue the story, including words that contain these elements. Have all students list those words. When the story is finished, post one student's list next to the story. **LISTENING/SPEAKING/WRITING/SPELLING**

Use *Integrated Spelling* Lesson 8 to reinforce the Spelling Words and the Words to Explore. See pages T57–T62 in *Integrated Spelling Teacher's Edition.*

SPELLING POSTTEST You may want to use the Pretest/Posttest Sentences on *Integrated Spelling Teacher's Edition* page T57 to assess students' knowledge of the spelling generalization.

WRITING

Understanding Braille

Explain that the Braille alphabet consists of various arrangements of raised dots, each arrangement standing for a different letter. Make a chart or poster of the Braille alphabet like the one below. Have students create and exchange messages using Braille. Some students may wish to use clay to create Braille raised-dot patterns. You may wish to borrow a Braille book from your local library so that students can gain an understanding of how a nonsighted person reads.
WRITING/VIEWING

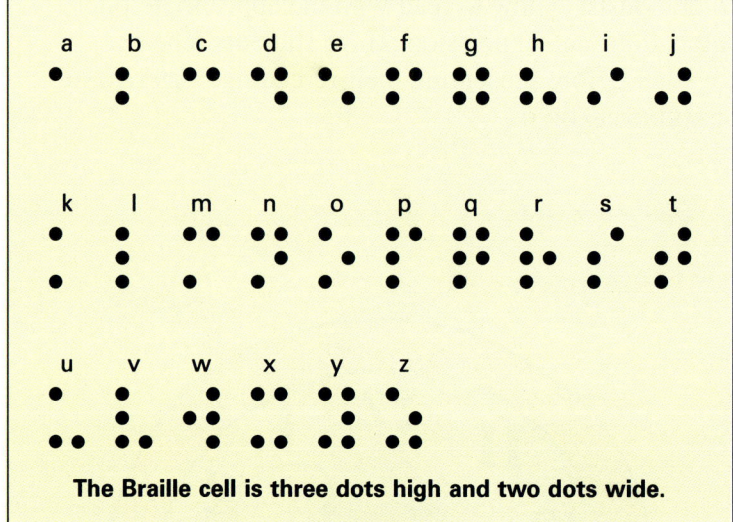

The Braille cell is three dots high and two dots wide.

T264 / A PLACE TO DREAM, UNIT 2

Language Arts WORKSHOP

LISTENING AND SPEAKING

Can You See Through Grandpa's Eyes?

Available on Project Card 20B

COOPERATIVE LEARNING
Have small groups of students take turns closing their eyes for a few minutes and using their other senses to figure out what is going on around them. Then have them write lists of all they heard, smelled, or felt. Suggest that one student act as a Recorder and another as a Reporter who will share the group's description of what was happening in their classroom or school. LISTENING/SPEAKING/WRITING

LISTENING AND SPEAKING

Role-Play a Conversation

Remind students that John does not live with his grandparents; he is staying with them for a while. Ask students to work in pairs to role-play a conversation between John and a friend at home about his visit with his grandparents. Suggest that the student playing John's friend ask questions based on his or her own experience of visits with relatives as well as on what John shared with readers in the selection. LISTENING/SPEAKING

WRITING

Character Features

Tell students that in the story John describes his grandfather this way: "He is tall with dark gray hair. And his eyes are sharp blue even though they are not sharp seeing." Ask students to write a description of John, using similar details about his physical appearance. Ask students also to include in their paragraph a sentence or two about John's other qualities. (caring, thoughtful, playful) Then have pairs of students compare their descriptions. LISTENING/SPEAKING/WRITING

LISTENING AND SPEAKING

Create a Game

COOPERATIVE LEARNING Remind students that Grandpa and John like guessing games. Help students organize their own guessing game. Ask a volunteer to think about something that is in the classroom without telling anyone else what it is. The others should try to guess the object by asking questions that can be answered with *yes* or *no*. Allow students to select a Summarizer, who from time to time should recap what students have learned about the object. Whoever guesses correctly gets to think of something else for the others to guess. LISTENING/SPEAKING

THROUGH GRANDPA'S EYES / T265

Grammar MINI LESSON

More Plural Nouns

OBJECTIVES: *To recognize that nouns that end in a consonant and* y *form the plural by changing the* y *to* i *and adding* -es; *to recognize that some plural noun forms are irregular; to correctly form plural nouns with* -ies *endings and irregular plural forms*

Oral Warm-Up

Display and have students read the following sentences from "Through Grandpa's Eyes":

- **When Nana is finished working, Grandpa runs his hand over the sculpture, his fingers soft and quick like <u>butterflies</u>.**
- **Then, all of a sudden, I hear the sounds of <u>geese</u> overhead.**

Point to the underlined plural noun in each sentence, and help students figure out the word that names just one of the items. Display this information in a diagram similar to the one below.

ONE   **MORE THAN ONE**

butterfly  butterflies

goose  geese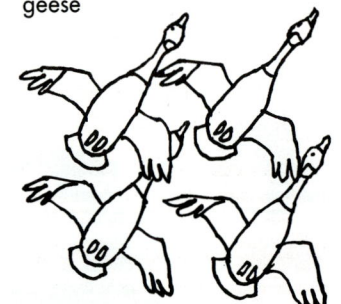

Interactive Teaching

PLURAL NOUNS WITH *-IES* ENDINGS Point to the words *butterfly* and *butterflies* in the Oral Warm-Up diagram, and have a volunteer circle the different spellings at the ends of these two words. Explain to students that for singular nouns that end in a consonant and *y*, the plural is formed by changing *y* to *i* and adding *es*. Write the following list of singular nouns on the board: *fly, baby, fairy, kitty, sky, cry*. Ask volunteers to change each word to the plural form by erasing the *y* and adding *i* + *es*.

IRREGULAR PLURAL NOUNS Point to the words *goose* and *geese* in the Oral Warm-Up diagram. Explain that some nouns have a plural form that does not follow the patterns they have learned. Write the following list of singular nouns on the board and, one at a time, add the plural forms:

foot (feet)
woman (women)
child (children)
mouse (mice)

Help students brainstorm a list of other irregular plural nouns, and have them add these nouns to their personal journals to use for reference.

 **LANGUAGE HANDBOOK**
More Plural Nouns, pages 98–101

T266 / A PLACE TO DREAM, UNIT 2

Practice Activities

One for Me, Two for You

Write the following singular and plural nouns in two separate columns on the board: *baby, babies; mouse, mice; woman, women; child, children; party, parties; berry, berries*. Have students work in pairs. Partners should take turns writing sentences using either a singular or a plural noun from one of the lists. The other partner should respond by writing a sentence using the other form of the noun. As a variation, have partners try to connect the meanings of the sentences to tell a story.   **VISUAL**

Rules Match

Have students copy the singular and plural nouns from the previous activity onto index cards, one singular–plural combination to each card. You may want to add other nouns that fit the patterns below for forming plurals. Collect the cards. Then write these statements about plural nouns on the board:

1. For nouns ending in a consonant and *y*, change the *y* to *i* and add *es*.
2. Some nouns don't follow a regular pattern in the plural form.

Shuffle and distribute the index cards. Have students review their cards and ask them, one at a time, to go to the board, display their card, and identify the rule that applies. Then, ask students to write a sentence using the word on their card.
VISUAL/KINESTHETIC

Practice Book

MEETING INDIVIDUAL NEEDS

SECOND-LANGUAGE SUPPORT   Write each of the following words on an index card: *foot, feet, woman, women, child, children, mouse, mice.* Distribute the cards. Draw on the board simple sketches for each noun form. Ask the student with the appropriate card to write the noun beneath the sketch.

RETEACH   Follow the visual, auditory, and kinesthetic/motor models on page R21.

OPTIONAL INDEPENDENT PRACTICE

PRACTICE BOOK
page 48: Using more plural nouns

GRAMMAR PRACTICE
pages 24–25: Recognizing and writing more plural nouns

THROUGH GRANDPA'S EYES / T267

PART 3

Learning through the Literature

LITERARY APPRECIATION	**Point of View**
INTRODUCE	OBJECTIVE: *To determine whether a story is told from the first- or third-person point of view*

Interactive Teaching

Identify the story's narrator.

LITERATURE CONNECTION Ask students who told the story "Through Grandpa's Eyes." (John) Tell students that knowing who is telling a story will help them understand the characters and events.

Compare different points of view.

MODEL HOW TO RECOGNIZE POINT OF VIEW Explain that the way in which an author chooses to see and tell a story is called *point of view*. Tell students that there are two basic points of view that an author can use to tell a story:

- A story told from the *first-person point of view* is told by a story character who refers to himself or herself as *I*.
- A story told from the *third-person point of view* is told by an outside observer, and all of the characters are called *he* or *she*.

Read aloud the first paragraph of the story on page 151. Then model the thinking:

> **I know this story is written from the first-person point of view because one of the characters is telling the story. He calls himself *I*, and he tells the reader exactly what he is thinking and feeling.**

Now reread the paragraph on page 151, changing the point of view to the third person. (Of all the houses that John knows, he likes his grandpa's best.) Discuss with students how changing the point of view affects the reader's understanding of characters' feelings. (John's emotions don't come across as strongly because they don't come directly from him.)

ADDITIONAL BOOKS FOR APPLYING POINT OF VIEW

Happy Birthday, Grampie by Susan Pearson. Dial, 1987. **EASY**

The True Story of the Three Little Pigs by Jon Scieszka. Viking. 1989. **EASY**

T268 / A PLACE TO DREAM, UNIT 2

Practice Activity

Who Is Telling the Story?

Have students identify point of view. Display the following chart and have pairs of students copy it. Then have partners complete the first two columns of the chart by identifying points of view in previously read stories. **VISUAL**

Story Title	First-Person or Third-Person Point of View	How I Know

Performance Assessment

Ask students to display the charts they completed for the Who Is Telling the Story? activity. Have them fill in the third column, telling how they know from which point of view each story was told. For evaluation guidelines, see *Staff Development Guide*.

Reader ↔ Writer Connection
Point of View

WRITERS can show the thoughts and feelings of one character by using different points of view.

READERS may feel differently about the story, depending on the point of view the writer uses.

WRITE A STORY Have students write a story from an ant's point of view.

MEETING INDIVIDUAL NEEDS

RETEACH Follow the visual, auditory, and kinesthetic/motor models on page R22.

CHALLENGE Have students select a passage from the story and rewrite it, using the third-person point of view.

SECOND-LANGUAGE SUPPORT Students can demonstrate their understanding of this skill by selecting one passage from the story and pointing out the words that identify the point of view. See also the manual *Alternative Teaching Strategies*, pages 10, 62–65.

OPTIONAL INDEPENDENT PRACTICE

WRITER'S JOURNAL
page 31: Writing a story

PRACTICE BOOK
page 49: Determining point of view

Writer's Journal

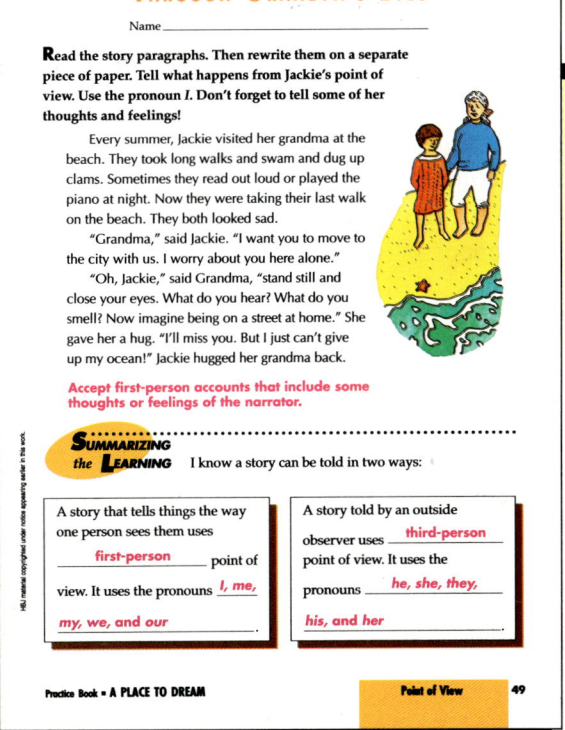

Practice Book

THROUGH GRANDPA'S EYES / T269

COMPREHENSION
REVIEW

Author's Purpose

OBJECTIVE: *To determine authors' purposes for writing*

Review

Discuss Patricia MacLachlan's purpose.

REVIEW PURPOSES FOR WRITING Ask students to recall the reasons an author may have for writing. (to entertain; to inform or teach; to give directions) Remind them that understanding the author's purpose for writing can help them set a purpose for reading. Model the thinking.

> When I previewed "Through Grandpa's Eyes," I thought I might learn something about people who are blind, and I did. I found that the story is mostly about how John and Grandpa do things together. It was also an entertaining story. So, I decided that the author's purposes were to entertain and to inform.

Practice Activity

Have students chart purposes.

COOPERATIVE LEARNING Organize students into groups of three or four, and have each group complete the following chart:

Title	Purpose	How We Know
1.		
2.		

As group members name the selections they have read so far in their Student Anthology and determine each author's purpose (to entertain, to inform or teach, or to give directions), the Recorder should write this information on the chart. Then the Checker should ask the group members how they decided on each author's purpose. The Recorder should write these reasons in the third column.

Encourage the groups to compare their charts and discuss any differences between them. VISUAL

MEETING INDIVIDUAL NEEDS

CHALLENGE Ask students to write a paragraph that informs or gives directions.

T270 / *A PLACE TO DREAM,* UNIT 2

COMPREHENSION STRATEGY
REVIEW

Active Reading Strategies

OBJECTIVE: *To use authors' descriptions and prior knowledge to visualize story events, actions, characters, and setting*

Review

Discuss the strategy.

REVIEW VISUALIZING STORY ELEMENTS Discuss with students some of the things good readers do during reading. (predict, reread, change reading rate, visualize) Ask students what helped them form a picture in their minds of the setting, characters, actions, and events as they read "Through Grandpa's Eyes." (the words the author used; what they already knew) Remind students that forming a mental picture is called *visualizing*. Explain that as they read, they should picture what is happening.

Practice Activity

In Your Mind's Eye

Have students visualize a scene.

Have each student choose a scene in the story that is not illustrated, and ask them to visualize it. Tell them to draw the scene and then to write a paragraph in which they describe the picture they formed in their mind. VISUAL

MEETING INDIVIDUAL NEEDS

CHALLENGE Ask students to pretend that they are professional artists who have the assignment of designing a cover for "Through Grandpa's Eyes." Have them first visualize the cover and then, when they have a clear mental picture, draw it on a piece of paper.

OPTIONAL INDEPENDENT PRACTICE

PRACTICE BOOK
pages 50–51: Visualizing

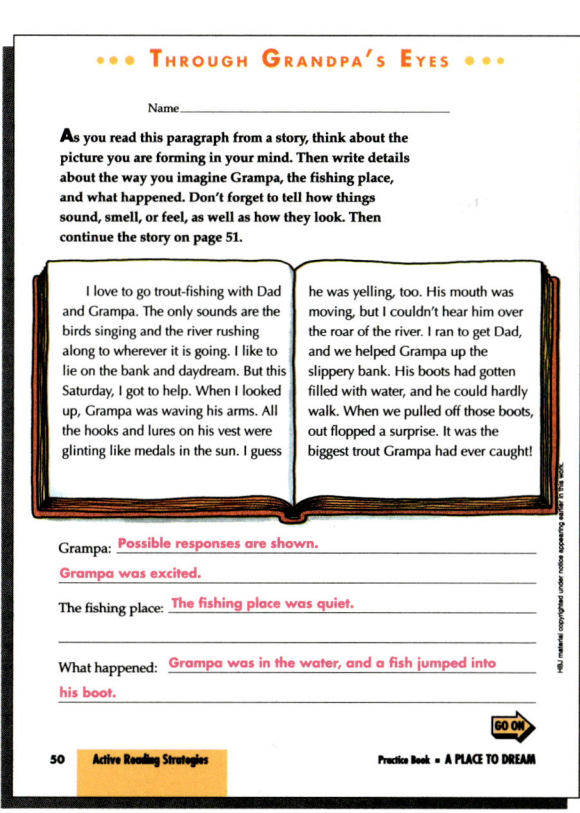

Practice Book

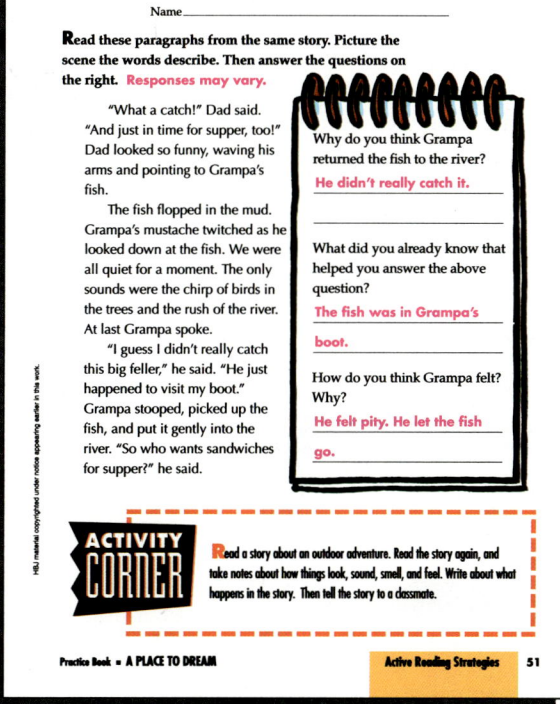

Practice Book

THROUGH GRANDPA'S EYES / T271

Integrated CURRICULUM

ART

Sculpt a Gift

Remind students that Nana was making a clay sculpture of Grandpa's head. Have students discuss the kinds of things they might like to sculpt. Provide students with self-hardening modeling clay or dough, and ask them to sculpt something as a gift for a friend, a relative, or a neighbor. Give each student an opportunity to describe his or her sculpture. **LISTENING/SPEAKING/VIEWING**

SCIENCE

Was That a Bird I Heard?

Available on Project Card 21A

USE REFERENCE SOURCES Students might enjoy identifying birds that live in your area. Give students a few days to look and listen for birds. Help them use bird identification books or an encyclopedia to find information about local birds. Ask each student to draw a picture of a bird he or she has seen or read about and write a few sentences describing it on a separate sheet of paper. Have students cut out their bird pictures and mount them on a large construction-paper tree on the wall. Read each description aloud, and ask students to match it with a bird on the tree. **LISTENING/READING/WRITING/VIEWING**

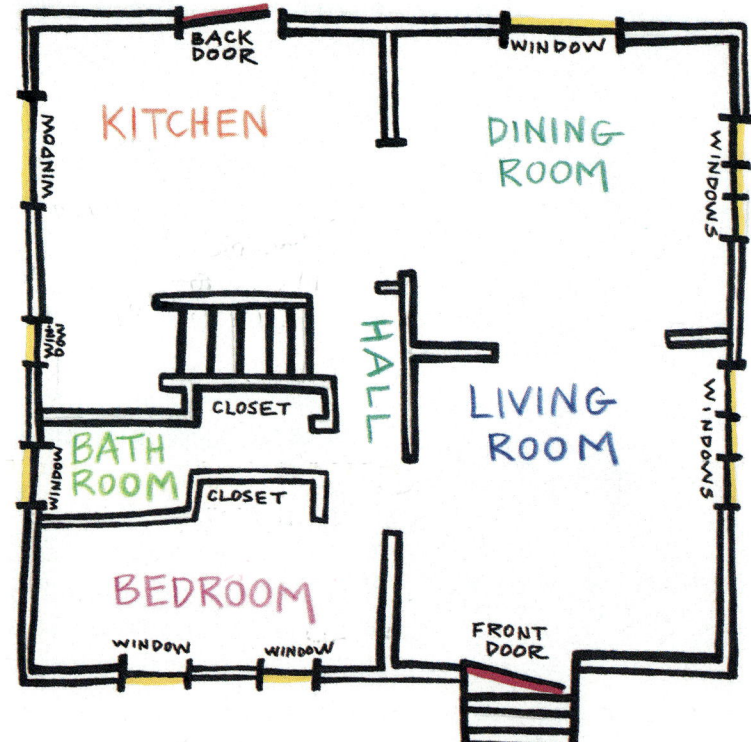

SOCIAL STUDIES

Mapping from Memory

Available on Project Card 21B

Explain that people who are blind must memorize the layout of their home so they know how to get from one room to another safely. Have students visualize the layout of rooms in their own home and draw a map, labeling the rooms and other features such as doorways, windows, closets, and hallways. Demonstrate how to do this by drawing a map of the classroom. Have students take their finished map home, compare it to the actual layout of the rooms, and revise it. (Students who live in two-story homes should choose one level to map.) **WRITING**

SCIENCE

Labeling Flowers

Ask students to recall the flowers mentioned in the story. (marigolds, violets, peonies, carnations, dahlias, Queen Anne's lace) Tell students they can create their own flower garden. On a large piece of paper, have students draw a house with grass around it. Then have them cut out pictures of flowers from old seed packets, magazines, or garden catalogs and paste them around the house to create a garden. Have students write the name of each flower under its picture. **WRITING**

MATH

Determine Time

COOPERATIVE LEARNING Assign students to small groups. Have them work together to draw or paste pictures of food on a paper plate and write the numerals 1–12 around the edge as on a clock. Then have students cut out clock hands and attach them to the plate with a paper fastener. Have one student position the hands of the clock and ask, "What time is [name of the food]?" Another student tells the time indicated by the clock hands. Suggest that a Recorder write down all the questions and a Checker read the information to make sure the answers are correct. **LISTENING/SPEAKING**

MUSIC

Make a Musical Instrument

CULTURAL AWARENESS Remind students that Grandpa and John enjoy playing music together. Bring in recordings of different kinds of music, such as classical, mariachi, and folk music from various countries. Talk about the place where each originated. Then tell students that they will all make and play their own instruments. Provide students with small sticks, small wooden boxes, cans, string, small bells, beans, and seeds. When they are ready, students can present their instruments and tell how they made them. Then they can play along with their favorite recordings. **LISTENING/SPEAKING**

 **BOOKS TO SHARE**
SCIENCE *And Still the Turtle Watched* by Sheila MacGill-Calahan. Dial, 1991. **CHALLENGING**
SOCIAL STUDIES *Loop the Loop* by Barbara Dugan. Puffin, 1993. **AVERAGE**

THROUGH GRANDPA'S EYES / T273

MULTICULTURAL PERSPECTIVES

Overcoming Challenges

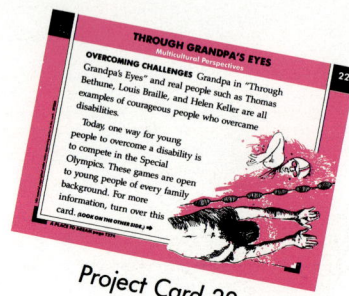

Project Card 22

DISCUSSION STARTER
Do you remember a time when you needed to work very hard to succeed at something?

READ ALOUD
Many people have overcome physical challenges and gone on to achieve greatness.

Thomas Bethune, of African descent, was born blind. From an early age, he was fascinated with sounds, especially classical music played on the piano. He learned to play whatever he heard, and play it with extraordinary skill. By the age of sixteen, this musical genius had played at the White House and had amazed audiences throughout Europe.

Louis Braille, a Frenchman, was blinded in an accident at the age of three. As a young man, he invented a system of printing that replaced type with raised dots. The Braille system allows people to read with their fingertips.

Helen Keller became blind and deaf through illness when she was just two years old. Nevertheless, with the help of her teacher, Annie Sullivan, she learned to read using the Braille system and to write with a special typewriter. After she graduated from college in 1904, she gave lectures and wrote several books. Her achievements give hope to people all over the world.

ACTIVITY CORNER
Available on Project Card 22

- Help students research the Special Olympics and the achievements of its athletes. Include in a general discussion of Special Olympics questions about how children, regardless of disability, are alike in more ways than they are different. Students can share their ideas and information about Special Olympics by working together to create a mural or posters.

- Turn out the lights and close the window blinds. Have students close their eyes and just listen for a full minute. Then have them tell what sounds they heard and discuss whether it was easier or more difficult to identify the sources in the dark.

Successful people such as Helen Keller and Thomas Bethune have given others the courage to meet and overcome their physical challenges.

T274 / A PLACE TO DREAM, UNIT 2

POEM

Writers

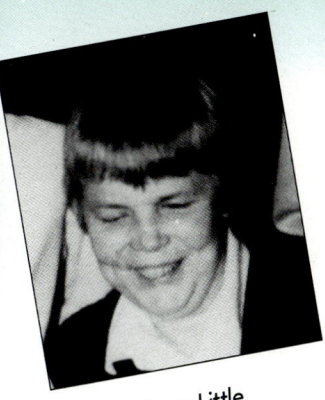
Jean Little

ABOUT THE POET Teased and chased by her schoolmates, visually handicapped Jean Little retreated into the world of books, reading, and daydreaming. Before long, she began to write for her own entertainment. Before becoming a full-time writer, Little taught handicapped children.

ABOUT THE POEM "Writers" is from Jean Little's *Hey World, Here I Am!*—an ALA Notable Book. The poem explores how two children who are different in many ways—including what they write about—can still be good friends.

Reading the Poem

Help students set a purpose for reading.

Tell students that they are going to read about two friends. Then ask them to discuss whether best friends always agree with each other about everything and always see things the same way.

Ask students to predict how differences in likes and dislikes might affect the friendship between two children. Have them read to find out whether their predictions hold true for the narrator of the poem and her friend Emily.

Responding to the Poem

Return to the purpose for reading.

Ask students whether their predictions were confirmed. Encourage them to speculate why the two girls are friends. Read the poem aloud to students. Then have them read it aloud with you.

Encourage students to respond creatively.

You may wish to select one of the following activities for responding to the poem:

WRITING A DESCRIPTION FROM ANOTHER POINT OF VIEW
Ask students to discuss what they think the poet means when she says, "So I can look through Emily's eyes / And she through mine." Then have each student choose an object in the classroom to look at through the eyes of an ant. How does the object look? Does it make noise? How does it feel? Students can take turns reading their descriptions and guessing what each "ant" sees.
LISTENING/SPEAKING/READING/WRITING

PERSONAL JOURNAL: WRITING ABOUT A FRIEND
Ask students to draw a picture of a friend. Then have them write a poem or paragraph that tells about their friendship. **READING/WRITING**

TEACHING TIP

Have students form groups, and assign each group a set of lines or stanzas. Allow students time to practice their lines independently and then together. If a tape recorder is available, you may wish to record and play back their interpretation.

MEETING INDIVIDUAL NEEDS

SECOND-LANGUAGE SUPPORT Students may misunderstand the meaning of *beat* in the third line of the poem. Point out that many words in English have more than one meaning. The word *beat* can mean "to strike," "to mix by stirring rapidly," "to flap (wings)," or "to defeat." In this poem, *beat* is used to mean "to defeat," as in a contest.

WRITERS / T275

Writers

by Jean Little
illustrated by Roberta Ludlow

Emily writes of poetic things
Like crocuses and hummingbirds' wings,
But I think people beat hummingbirds every time.

Emily likes to write of snow
And dawn and candlelight aglow,
But I'd rather write about me and Emily and stuff like that.

The funny thing is, I delight
To read what Emily likes to write,
And Emily says she thinks my poems are okay too.

Also, sometimes, we switch with each other.
Emily writes of a fight with her mother.
I tell about walking alone by the river,
—how still and golden it was.

I know what Emily means, you see,
And, often, Emily's halfway me. . . .
Oh, there's just no way to make anybody else understand.

We're not a bit the same and yet,
We're closer than most people get.
There's no one word for it. We just care about each other
the way we are supposed to.

So I can look through Emily's eyes
And she through mine. It's no surprise,
When you come right down to it, that we're friends.

Expanding the Poem Why does the narrator say it's funny that she and Emily like to read what the other writes? (Accept reasonable responses: *Funny* means *interesting* or *odd* in this usage; it is odd because she and Emily like to write about different things.) INFERENTIAL: DRAWING CONCLUSIONS

Do you think it's odd that two people with different interests can enjoy each other's writing? Why or why not? (Responses will vary.) CRITICAL: EXPRESSING PERSONAL OPINIONS

OPTIONAL INDEPENDENT PRACTICE

WRITER'S JOURNAL
page 32: Writing a creative response

T276 / A PLACE TO DREAM, UNIT 2

A Gift for Tía Rosa

by Karen T. Taha

illustrated by Laura Kelly

A Gift for Tía Rosa
pages 170–184

	READING	LANGUAGE ARTS	CROSS-CURRICULAR CONNECTIONS
PART 1 *Reading the Literature* pages T280–T290	**Building Background** **Vocabulary Strategies** **Prereading Strategies** Story Chart Setting a Purpose **Options for Reading**	**Spelling** Pretest Spelling-Vocabulary Connection Generalization: /ô/ sound **Grammar Connection** Reviewing Plural Nouns	**Cultural Awareness** Spanish-language terms of affection Spanish words for *aunt* and *uncle* **Social Studies** Mourning customs
PART 2 *Responding to the Literature* pages T291–T297	**Personal Response** **Cooperative Response** **Summarizing the Literature** **Critical Thinking Activity** Role-Play **Vocabulary Workshop** Key Words Action Words	**Language Arts Workshop** **Reading** drama **Writing** story, directions, description **Listening and Speaking** onomatopoeic words, oral reports **Reviewing Spelling Words** Posttest **Grammar Review** Plural Nouns **Grammar Minilesson** Singular Possessive Nouns	**Art** "Around, Over, Through, and Pull" The Perfect Gift My Favorite Hobby
PART 3 *Learning Through the Literature* pages T298–T304	**Introduce** Literary Appreciation: Story Elements **Review** Decoding: Structural Analysis (Tested) Study Skills: Following Directions (Tested)	**Reading** Calculating Recipe Amounts **Writing** Volunteer Work **Listening and Speaking** Cross Your Fingers	**Social Studies** Volunteer Work Cross Your Fingers **Health** Five Ways to Stay Healthy **Math** Calculating Recipe Amounts **Art** Ready, Set, Knit! **Social Studies** *Hola* Means "Hello" **Multicultural Perspectives** Remembering Heroes

OPTIONAL MATERIALS
Charts/Transparencies 18–19
Integrated Spelling pp. 42–45; TE pp. T63–T68
Practice Book pp. 52–58
Writer's Journal pp. 33–34
Alternative Teaching Strategies pp. 11, 66–69
Language Handbook pp. 36–39, 98–101, 104
Grammar Practice pp. 26–27
Family Involvement Activities: Unit 2, pp. 1–4
Response Card 3
Project Cards 23A, 23B, 24A, 24B
Literature Cassette

MEETING INDIVIDUAL NEEDS
Second-Language Support pp. T281, T282, T288, T297, T299
Mainstreaming p. T282
Reteach pp. T297, T299
Challenge pp. T299, T300, T301

FAMILY INVOLVEMENT You might suggest that family members have students jot down gift ideas for special people. Students may want to draw or cut out pictures of these ideas and keep them in a place where they can be referred to when needed. See *Family Involvement Activities*.

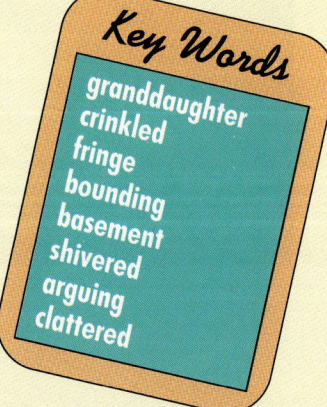

Key Words
granddaughter
crinkled
fringe
bounding
basement
shivered
arguing
clattered

T278 / A PLACE TO DREAM, UNIT 2

Selection Summary

Carmela is overjoyed when her good friend, Tía Rosa, returns from the hospital. Carmela visits Tía Rosa and is surprised to find her in bed. Tía Rosa tells Carmela that she has missed her and presents her with a silver rose necklace. Carmela's father tries to tell her that her friend is very ill, but Carmela refuses to believe him. The friends pass the next few weeks together knitting. Carmela finishes a scarf, and Tía Rosa knits a blanket for an expected grandchild. One day Carmela learns that Tía Rosa has died. She is devastated and does not even want to see Tío Juan, Tía Rosa's husband, because he reminds her of her friend. She is brokenhearted that she didn't get a chance to make a gift for Tía Rosa. With her mother's help, Carmela realizes that the best gift she can give is to pass on Tía Rosa's kindness. Then she remembers the unfinished blanket and realizes that finishing it for Tía Rosa's grandchild will be the perfect gift.

About the Author

Karen Taha has written one novel, *A Gift for Tía Rosa*. She has also co-authored (with Janet Greeson) *Name That Book!* which contains questions and answers about exemplary books for children. Taha has written for the children's magazines *Ebony Jr., Story Friends,* and *Friends*. She works as a library media specialist and has taught in three countries: the United States, Spain, and Egypt. She has lived in Mexico and Kuwait. About traveling, Taha says, "For me, the greatest joy of traveling and living in other countries lies not in seeing monuments and museums, but in getting to know the people and making friendships that enrich one's life."

Additional Reading

OTHER THEME-RELATED BOOKS

Blackberries in the Dark by Mavis Jukes. Alfred A. Knopf, 1993. EASY

Brave Irene by William Steig. Farrar, Straus & Giroux, 1988. AVERAGE

Dora's Book by Michelle Edwards. Carolrhoda, 1990. EASY

Grandmama's Joy by Eloise Greenfield. Philomel, 1980. CHALLENGING

Magical Hands by Marjorie Barker. Picture Book Studio, 1991. EASY

*Mandy by Barbara D. Booth. Lothrop, Lee & Shepard, 1991. AVERAGE

BOOKS FOR APPLYING STRATEGIES: STORY ELEMENTS

Nana Upstairs and Nana Downstairs by Tomie dePaola. Puffin, 1978. EASY

Wilfred Gordon McDonald Partridge by Mem Fox. Kane-Miller, 1989. EASY

*Available as a Harcourt Brace PASSPORTS title

PART 1

Reading the Literature

Building Background

Access prior knowledge and build vocabulary concepts.

Tell students that the next story, "A Gift for Tía Rosa," is about a girl named Carmela who has a close friendship with her neighbor, an older woman named Rosa.

Ask each student to tell about his or her favorite older person, and have students work together to create a web like the one below:

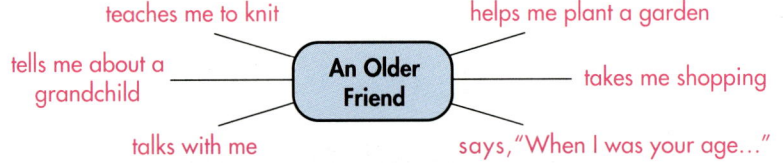

Have students quickwrite.

Have students write one or two sentences telling why they like spending time with that older person.

Vocabulary Strategies

Introduce Key Words and strategies.

Display Chart/Transparency 18, or write the story on the board. Ask students to read the sentences silently, using context clues to figure out the meanings of the underlined words. Suggest that students use picture clues along with the sentence clues "around the edge of the tablecloth" and "helped her fringe" to determine the meaning of the word *fringe*.

Chart/Transparency 18   Key Words

I am Nana's favorite <u>granddaughter</u> because I am the only one! When she saw me yesterday, her face <u>crinkled</u> into a smile. We sewed <u>fringe</u> around the edge of the tablecloth. Then I helped her <u>fringe</u> the napkins. Then her big dog, Bobo, came <u>bounding</u> into the room.

Nana sent me down to the <u>basement</u> for Bobo's food. I <u>shivered</u> because it is cold and dark down there. It was no use <u>arguing</u>, though. Nana wouldn't change her mind. As I <u>clattered</u> noisily down the stairs, I found a surprise from Nana!

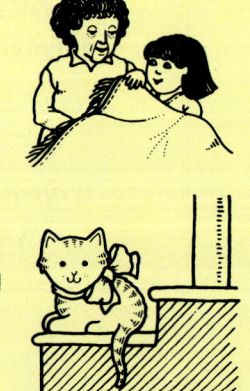

CULTURAL AWARENESS

Students might be interested to learn that Spanish-speaking adults often show affection for children by adding *-ito* to boys' names and *-ita* to girls' names. The name ending means "little."

Key Words

granddaughter
crinkled
fringe
bounding
basement
shivered
arguing
clattered

KEY WORDS DEFINED

granddaughter   daughter of one's son or daughter

crinkled   wrinkled

fringe   *n.* border of hanging threads; *v.* to make a border of hanging threads

bounding   bouncing

basement   part of a building that is underground

shivered   trembled, as with cold or fear

arguing   disagreeing

clattered   made a rattling noise

T280 / A PLACE TO DREAM, UNIT 2

Check all students' understanding.

Display or read aloud each group of words. Have students choose the word in each group that does not belong and explain why it does not belong. The correct responses are underlined.

STRATEGIES: SYNONYMS/CLASSIFYING

• trim	burn	fringe
• bounding	springing	covering
• <u>cousin</u>	neighbor	granddaughter
• crumpled	decorated	crinkled
• roof	basement	cellar
• shivered	straightened	shook
• tiptoed	banged	clattered
• disagreeing	arguing	whispering

Integrate spelling with vocabulary.

SPELLING-VOCABULARY CONNECTION *Integrated Spelling* Lesson 9 reinforces the spelling of the /ô/ sound in words found in the selection such as *soft*. In addition, the Words to Explore help reinforce the concept of family as it relates to the selection.

SPELLING PRETEST You may want to use the Pretest/Posttest Sentences on page T63 in *Integrated Spelling Teacher's Edition* to assess students' knowledge of the spelling generalization.

MEETING INDIVIDUAL NEEDS

SECOND-LANGUAGE SUPPORT Have students discuss English and Spanish words that tell names of relatives, such as *tía* and *tío* and *aunt* and *uncle*. You may wish to have students work together to complete a chart of such words. See also the manual *Alternative Teaching Strategies*, pages 11, 66–69.

Spelling

Spelling Words	Words to Explore
1. almost	arguing
2. also	bounding
3. always	granddaughter
4. cause	knitting
5. draw	
6. fault	Concept Words
7. law	13.
8. lost	14.
9. small	15.
10. soft	16.
11. song	
12. talk	

Spelling generalization: /ô/ sound

Practice Book

OPTIONAL INDEPENDENT PRACTICE

INTEGRATED SPELLING pages 42–45: Words like *draw* and *cause*

PRACTICE BOOK page 52: Reinforcing Key Words

NOTE: This page may be completed now or after students have read the story.

A GIFT FOR TÍA ROSA / T281

Prereading Strategies

Story Chart

Have students preview the story.

Ask students to preview the story by reading the title, looking at the pictures, and reading through page 172.

Encourage students to predict.

Have students think about what the story might be about, and then guide them in completing a story chart like the one below.

Title:	"A Gift for Tía Rosa"
Who?	Carmela, Tía Rosa
When?	in the fall
Where?	Carmela's home, in a neighborhood
What happens?	1. Tía Rosa helps Carmela knit a scarf. 2. Tía Rosa is sick.

PERSONAL JOURNAL Have students use the story chart to make predictions about the story, and then add their predictions about the story to their personal journals.

Setting a Purpose

Encourage students to set purposes.

Ask students to use their predictions to set a purpose for reading. Have volunteers share what they want to find out as they read the story.

If students have difficulty setting a purpose, offer this suggestion:

I'm going to read to find out what the gift for Tía Rosa is.

MEETING INDIVIDUAL NEEDS

SECOND-LANGUAGE SUPPORT Students may benefit from a more detailed discussion of the story characters and their relationships. Students should participate in the Strategic Reading activities under the Student Anthology pages. See also the manual *Alternative Teaching Strategies*, pages 11, 66–69.

SUPPORT FOR MAINSTREAMING Write Spanish terms and names from the story on the board, and help students pronounce them: *Mamá, Papá, Carmela, Carmelita, Tía Rosa, Tío Juan, Pepe, Rosita, hola, tamales.*

Options for Reading

SUSTAINED SILENT READING	STRATEGIC READING	READER RESPONSE GROUPS	TEACHER READ-ALOUD
After students finish reading, encourage them to discuss the questions at the end of the selection with other students who have read independently.	To stimulate discussion, use the suggestions that appear on pages T283, T286, and T290.	Follow the suggestions for Literature Circles on page T283. As students read, they should note any thoughts and feelings about the story problem and solution that they would like to discuss with the group.	You may want to read aloud the first half of the selection and then give students an opportunity to discuss briefly Tía Rosa's condition and Carmela's relationship with Tía Rosa. Then students can read the rest of the selection silently.

T282 / A PLACE TO DREAM, UNIT 2

A GIFT FOR TÍA ROSA PAGES 170–171

A Gift for Tía Rosa

by Karen T. Taha

"AROUND, OVER, THROUGH, AND PULL. Around, over, through, and pull," Carmela repeated as she knitted. A rainbow of red, orange, and gold wool stretched almost to her feet. Now and then she stopped and listened for her father's car. He mustn't see what she was knitting!

The rumble of a motor made her drop the needles and run to the window. In the gray November shadows, she saw a battered brown station wagon turn into the garage next door.

illustrated by Laura Kelly

Reader Response Groups

LITERATURE CIRCLES Have groups of three to five students read the story silently, pausing after page 176 for a brief discussion. You may wish to distribute Response Card 3 (Plot), found on page R81, or provide the following questions:

- What is the problem in the story?
- What main events happen in the story?

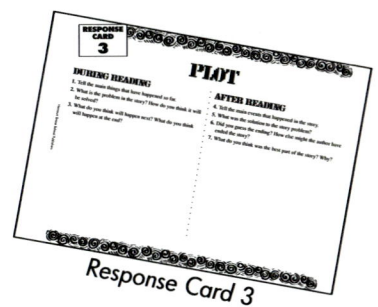

Strategic Reading

SET PURPOSE/PREDICT: PAGES 170–176 Have students read through page 176. Ask them what they will be reading to find out.

A GIFT FOR TÍA ROSA / T283

PAGES 172–173   A GIFT FOR TÍA ROSA

"Mamá, she's home! Tía Rosa is home!" Carmela called. Carmela's mother hurried out of the bedroom. She put her arm around Carmela. They watched as lights flickered on in the windows, bringing the neat white house back to life.

"I know you want to see Tía Rosa, Carmela," said her mother, "but she and Tío Juan have had a long trip. Tía Rosa must be very tired after two weeks in the hospital."

"But can I call her, Mamá?" asked Carmela. "The scarf for Papá is almost done. She promised to help me fringe it when she came home."

"No, Carmela. Not now," her mother replied firmly. "Tía Rosa needs to rest." She smoothed back Carmela's thick black hair from her face.

Carmela tossed her head. "But Mamá . . . !"

"No, Carmela!"

Carmela knew there was no use arguing. But it wasn't fair. Tomorrow she would have to go to school. She couldn't see Tía Rosa until the afternoon. Her mother just didn't understand.

Frowning, Carmela plopped back on the sofa and picked up the silver knitting needles. At least she would finish more of the scarf before Tía Rosa saw it tomorrow. She bent over her knitting and began once more. "Around, over, through, and pull." The phone rang in the kitchen.

172

Informal Assessment

FOLLOWING DIRECTIONS   To assess whether students need instruction in following directions, point out the memory-helper at the beginning of page 170 that Carmela repeats as she knits. Then ask:

- How does the phrase *around, over, through, and pull* help Carmela? (It helps her remember the order of the actions.)
- What might happen if she leaves out one or more of the steps? (She won't knit correctly.)

A review lesson on **following directions** appears on page T301.

Cultural Awareness

Carmela calls her friends "Tía Rosa" and "Tío Juan," which is Spanish for "Aunt Rose" and "Uncle John." Point out that although Tía Rosa and Tío Juan are not really Carmela's aunt and uncle, Carmela uses those terms as a sign of respect and affection.

See page T294 for information found on Project Card 23A.

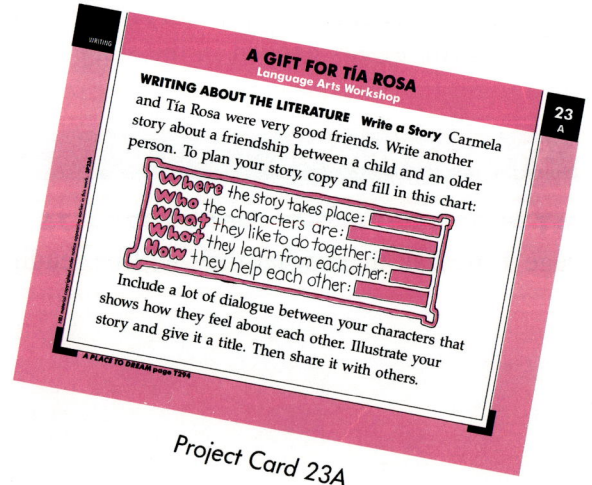

Project Card 23A

T284 / A PLACE TO DREAM, UNIT 2

"I'll get it!" Carmela shouted, bounding into the hall. "Hello?" Her dark eyes sparkled. "Tía Rosa! You must see Papá's scarf. It's almost finished . . . You did? For me? Okay, I'll be right there!"

The phone clattered as Carmela hung up. "Mamá! Tía Rosa wants to see the scarf. She even brought me a surprise!"

Carmela's mother smiled and shook her head. "Tía Rosa is unbelievable."

Carmela stuffed the bright wool into her school bag. "I'm going to make Tía Rosa a surprise after I finish Papá's scarf!" she called as she ran out.

She ran across the yard to Tía Rosa's front door. The door swung open, and there was Tío Juan. He looked taller and thinner than she remembered, and his eyes looked sad.

Tío Juan was as tall as Tía Rosa was short, Carmela thought. He was as thin as Tía Rosa was plump. And he was as good at listening as Tía Rosa was at talking.

"*Hola*, Carmelita," he said, bending to kiss her cheek. He led her down the hall. "Tía Rosa is sitting up in bed. She's tired, but she wanted to see her favorite neighbor."

Tía Rosa in bed! In all her eight years Carmela had never seen Tía Rosa sick. She held her breath and peeked into the bedroom. Tía Rosa's round face crinkled into a smile when she saw Carmela.

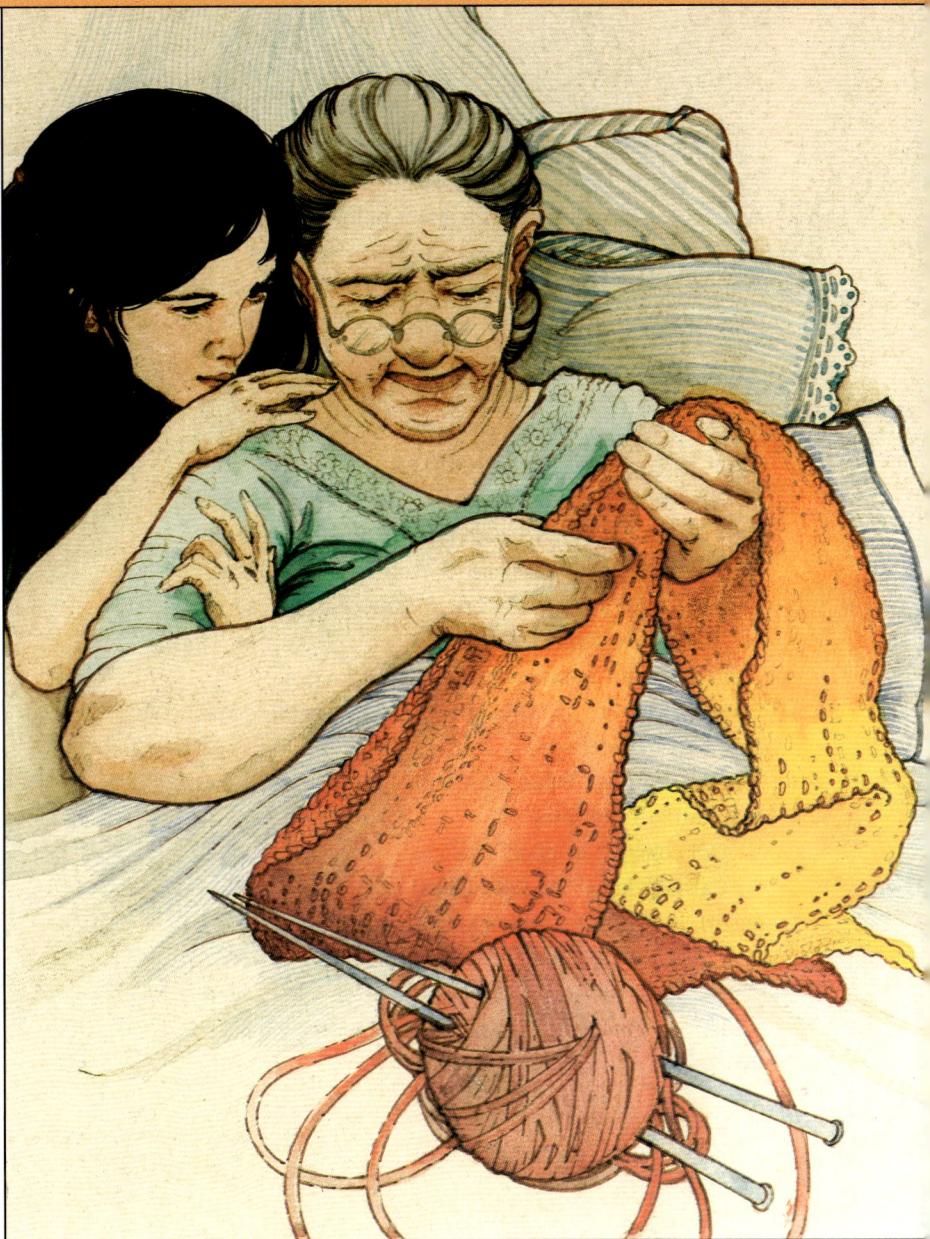

Expanding the Literature What kind of surprise do you think Tía Rosa will have for Carmela? (Accept reasonable responses: possibly something she has knitted.) INFERENTIAL: MAKING PREDICTIONS

In what ways does the author show how ill Tía Rosa is? (by having Carmela's mother shake her head, by describing Tío Juan's sad eyes, and by having Carmela feel great surprise when she finds Tía Rosa in bed)
CRITICAL: AUTHOR'S CRAFT/IDENTIFYING WITH CHARACTERS

PAGES 176–177   A GIFT FOR TÍA ROSA

"Carmelita, come give me a hug!"

Hugging Tía Rosa always made Carmela feel safe and warm. Tía Rosa was like a soft pillow that smelled of soap and bath powder and sometimes of sweet tamales. Now there was another smell, a dentist office smell, Carmela decided.

"Carmelita, I've missed you!" said Tía Rosa. "Let's look at what you have knitted."

Carmela handed her the scarf. Tía Rosa smiled. "Your papá will be proud to wear it," she said. "Tomorrow I'll show you how to fringe it, and I will start on the pink baby blanket for my granddaughter!"

Carmela laughed. "How do you know that Pepe's wife will have a girl?" she asked. Pepe was the oldest of Tía Rosa's six sons.

"Because," answered Tía Rosa with a grin, "anyone who has six sons and no daughters, deserves a granddaughter!"

"But Tía Rosa, what if the baby is a boy? Won't you love him just the same?"

"Of course," laughed Tía Rosa.

Carmela knew Tía Rosa would love the baby, boy or girl, but she crossed her fingers and wished for a girl, too.

"Now for the surprise!" said Tía Rosa. She handed Carmela a small white box. "Go on now. See what's inside."

Carmela opened the box carefully. A snowy ball of cotton lay inside. As she pulled at the cotton, her fingers touched something hard and very small. She heard the "clish" of a chain as she lifted the surprise from under the cotton. In her hand Carmela held a tiny silver rose on a fine chain.

"Oh, Tía Rosa. It's beautiful!" exclaimed Carmela.

"The rose is so you'll remember your old Tía Rosa," she said.

"How could I forget you, Tía Rosa?" asked Carmela. "You're right here!"

Before she went home, Carmela put the rose around her neck. She promised to return the next day after school.

Strategic Reading

MODELING A STRATEGY: PAGES 170–176   How do you know that Tía Rosa likes Carmela very much?

THINK ALOUD   You may want to provide a think-aloud model: *I see that even though Tía Rosa has just returned from the hospital, she asks Carmela to come over; Tío Juan says that Tía Rosa is waiting to see "her favorite neighbor"; and Tía Rosa tells Carmela she missed her.*   **SUMMARIZING**

SET PURPOSE/PREDICT: PAGES 177–184   Have students predict what will happen next. Encourage them to read the rest of the story to confirm their predictions.

A GIFT FOR TÍA ROSA   PAGES 178–179

Carmela returned the next day, and the next, and every day for a whole week. Tía Rosa stayed in her room, and Tío Juan moved a chair by the bed for Carmela. Together the two friends worked on their surprise gifts.

"Why does Tía Rosa stay in bed all the time?" Carmela asked her father at breakfast one day.

Her father looked away for a moment. Then he took Carmela's hands in his. "Tía Rosa is very sick, Carmela. The doctors don't think she can get well," he explained.

"But Papá," said Carmela. "I have been sick lots of times. Remember when Tía Rosa stayed with me when you and Mamá had to go away?"

"Yes," answered her father. "But Tía Rosa . . ."

Carmela didn't listen. "Now I will stay with Tía Rosa until she gets well, too," she said.

Every afternoon Carmela worked on her father's scarf. The fringe was the easiest part. With Tía Rosa's help she would have the scarf finished long before Christmas.

Tía Rosa worked on the pink baby blanket, but the needles didn't fly in her sure brown fingers like they once did. Carmela teased her. "Tía Rosa, are you knitting slowly because you might have to change the pink yarn to blue when the baby is born?"

"No, no," replied Tía Rosa with a grin. "The baby will surely be a girl. We need girls in this family. You're the only one I have!"

Sometimes Tía Rosa fell asleep with her knitting still in her hands. Then Carmela would quietly put the needles and yarn into Tía Rosa's big green knitting bag and tiptoe out of the room.

Carmela liked Saturdays and Sundays best because she could spend more time at Tía Rosa's. Mamá always sent a plate of cookies with her, and Tío Juan made hot chocolate for them.

One Saturday morning when Carmela rang the doorbell, Tío Juan didn't come. Carmela ran to the garage and peeked in the window. The brown station wagon was gone.

179

GRAMMAR CONNECTION

REVIEWING PLURAL NOUNS   You may want to point out the word *baby* on page 179 and write it on the board. Ask a volunteer to write the plural form of *baby*. *(babies)* Ask another volunteer to describe the rule for making this plural form. *(Change the y to i and add -es.)*

Vocabulary Strategy   Explain to students that on page 179 the word *fringe* names something that is part of a scarf, but that on page 172 *fringe* tells what Tía Rosa is going to help Carmela *do* to the scarf—"help me fringe it." Tell students that many words can be used in more than one way and that to figure out how a word is being used in a sentence and what the word means, they need to use context clues.   STRATEGY: CONTEXT CLUES

See page T303 for information on Project Card 24B.

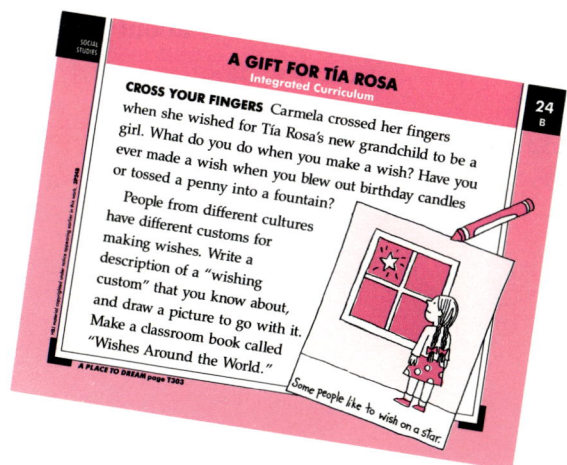

A GIFT FOR TÍA ROSA / T287

PAGES 180–181   A GIFT FOR TÍA ROSA

She returned home and called Tía Rosa's number. The phone rang and rang. Carmela went down the steps to the basement. Her mother was rubbing stain into the freshly sanded wood of an old desk.

"Tía Rosa isn't home," said Carmela sadly. Her mother looked up from her work.

"I thought I heard a car in the night," said her mother. "Surely Tío Juan would have called us if . . ."

Just then the phone rang upstairs. Carmela heard footsteps creak across the floor as her father walked to answer it.

Moments later the footsteps thumped softly towards the basement door. Carmela's father came slowly down the steps. Carmela shivered when she saw his sad face. He put his arms around Carmela and her mother and hugged them close. "Tía Rosa is gone," he whispered. "She died early this morning."

No, her father's words couldn't be true. Carmela didn't believe it. Tía Rosa would come back. She had always come back before.

"It's not true!" cried Carmela. She broke away from her mother and father and raced up the stairs. She ran out the front door and through the yard to Tía Rosa's house. She pushed the doorbell again and again. She pounded on the silent door until her fists hurt. At last she sank down on the steps.

Later her father came. With a soft hanky he brushed the tears from her cheeks. At last they walked quietly home.

180

Second-Language Support   Students may not understand the terms *stain* and *freshly sanded*. Explain with gestures that the first step in refinishing old wooden furniture is to scrape or sand off the old paint or varnish. Carmela's mom has just done this, so the old desk is "freshly sanded." Then explain that stain is a dye or tint, a liquid that colors wood.

Expanding the Literature   What sentences help you predict that Carmela will hear bad news about Tía Rosa? ("Moments later the footsteps thumped softly towards the basement door" and "Carmela shivered when she saw his sad face.")   METACOGNITIVE: MAKING PREDICTIONS

MEETING INDIVIDUAL NEEDS

The next days were long and lonely for Carmela. She didn't care that Papá's finished scarf lay hidden in her closet, bright and beautiful. She didn't want to see it. She didn't want to feel the cool, smooth knitting needles in her hands ever again.

The white house next door was busy with people coming and going. Carmela took over food her mother and father cooked, but she quickly returned home. She didn't like to see Tío Juan. Seeing Tío Juan made her miss Tía Rosa even more.

One day Carmela said to her mother, "Tía Rosa died before I could give her anything, Mamá. She baked me cookies and taught me to knit and brought me surprises. I was going to surprise her. Now it's too late."

"Carmela, Tía Rosa didn't want her kindness returned. She wanted it passed on," said her mother. "That way a part of Tía Rosa will never die."

"But I wanted to give something to her!" shouted Carmela. "Just to Tía Rosa. To show her that I loved her!"

"She knew that, Carmela. Every smile and hug and visit told her that you loved her," said her mother. "Now it's Tío Juan who needs our love."

"I know," answered Carmela in a soft voice, "but it's hard, Mamá. It hurts so much without Tía Rosa."

One night Carmela's mother asked Tío Juan to dinner. Carmela met him at the door. This time Carmela did not turn away when she saw his sad eyes. Instead, she hugged him tightly.

Social Studies Connection Every society has customs and rituals that allow mourners to express their feelings and to receive comfort after a loved one's death. In Hispanic homes, as in many other cultures, it is customary for people to bring food to the mourners' home. Food is also offered as a symbol of comfort to visitors who come to the home.

PAGE 184 A GIFT FOR TÍA ROSA

For the first time in a week, Tío Juan smiled. "Carmelita, tomorrow you must come next door. I would like you to meet my new granddaughter. Her parents have named her Rosita, little Rose, after her grandmother."

Carmela looked down at her silver rose necklace so Tío Juan would not see the tears in her eyes. Tía Rosa knew the baby would be a girl. Then Carmela remembered the unfinished blanket. "Now I know what I can give!" she said.

After dinner Tío Juan went back to the white house. A few minutes later he returned with Tía Rosa's big knitting bag. Very carefully Carmela pulled out the half-finished blanket and wound the soft pink yarn around the needle.

"Around, over, through, and pull. Around, over, through, and pull." Carmela smiled. At last she had a gift for Tía Rosa.

Would you describe this story as a happy one or a sad one? Give reasons for your choice.

Name some of the ways Carmela and Tía Rosa show that they care for one another.

How does Carmela pass on Tía Rosa's kindness?

WRITE Think of a perfect gift for someone. Write a paragraph that tells why the gift is perfect.

184

Strategic Reading

MODELING A STRATEGY: PAGES 177–184 Have students tell what they learned about gifts and gift-giving on these pages.

THINK ALOUD Provide a think-aloud model, if necessary: *I think about all the different gifts in the story: the scarf, the necklace, and the blanket. Gifts like these can show people you care, but I think the best gift was the kindness that Carmela passed on from Tía Rosa to Rosita.* SYNTHESIZING

Returning to the Predictions/Purpose

STORY CHART Have students revise their story charts if necessary, and then discuss them. Encourage students to tell whether they learned what they wanted to find out.

NOTE: Responses to the questions and support for the Write activity appear on page T291.

Title:	"A Gift for Tía Rosa"
Who?	Carmela, Tía Rosa
When?	in the fall
Where?	Carmela's home, in a neighborhood
What happens?	1: Tía Rosa helps Carmela knit a scarf. 2: Tía Rosa is sick.

T290 / A PLACE TO DREAM, UNIT 2

PART 2

Responding to the Literature

Personal Response

Encourage critical thinking.

Would you describe this story as a happy one or a sad one? Give reasons for your choice. (Responses will vary.) CRITICAL: EXPRESSING PERSONAL OPINIONS

Name some of the ways Carmela and Tía Rosa show that they care for one another. (They visit each other; they bring each other cookies; they enjoy talking together.) INFERENTIAL: DRAWING CONCLUSIONS

How does Carmela pass on Tía Rosa's kindness? (She gives Tío Juan a hug; she decides to finish knitting the blanket for Tía Rosa's granddaughter.) INFERENTIAL: DRAWING CONCLUSIONS

Encourage creative written responses.

 **WRITE Think of a perfect gift for someone. Write a paragraph that tells why the gift is perfect.** Encourage students to state their main idea and support it with details and reasons.
CREATIVE: WRITING A PARAGRAPH

Cooperative Response

Have reader response groups extend their discussions.

LITERATURE CIRCLES Encourage the Literature Circles to discuss their reactions to the story. They might begin by sharing thoughts and feelings they may have recorded in their personal journals. Then have them discuss a question such as this:

How might Tío Juan respond when Carmela shows him the finished baby blanket? What leads you to think so?

STRATEGY CONFERENCE

Discuss with students how the story chart helped them understand the selection. (Accept reasonable responses: Keeping a story chart helps readers pay attention to the characters, setting, and plot and stay focused on the story by looking for answers that tell *who, when, where,* and *what happened.*)

NOTE

An additional writing activity for this story appears on page T294.

A GIFT FOR TÍA ROSA / T291

Summarizing the Literature

Have students retell the story and write a summary. Guide students in beginning a story frame for "A Gift for Tía Rosa." Students may use their completed frames to retell the story and write a brief summary. See *Practice Book* page 53 below.

> The two most important characters in the story are ___(Tía Rosa and Carmela)___.
> The story takes place ___(in the homes of Carmela and Tía Rosa)___.
> Everyone is worried because ___(Tía Rosa is very sick)___.
> When Tía Rosa returns from the hospital, she gives Carmela a _____
> _____
> The two main characters spend time _____
> One Saturday, when Carmela goes to see Tía Rosa, she _____
> Tío Juan calls and says that _____
> At first, Carmela feels _____
> Carmela finally sees that _____
> The story ends when _____

Critical Thinking Activity

Suggest other situations. **DISCUSS OR ROLE-PLAY IDEAS** **What does Carmela learn from Tía Rosa? How might she use what she learns in a different situation?** Encourage students to discuss their ideas in small groups or to role-play the situations they suggest. Situations might include teaching a sick or homebound person how to knit or sew, giving a handmade gift to a special person, or visiting and spending time with a younger neighbor. CRITICAL: MAKING GENERALIZATIONS

Writer's Journal

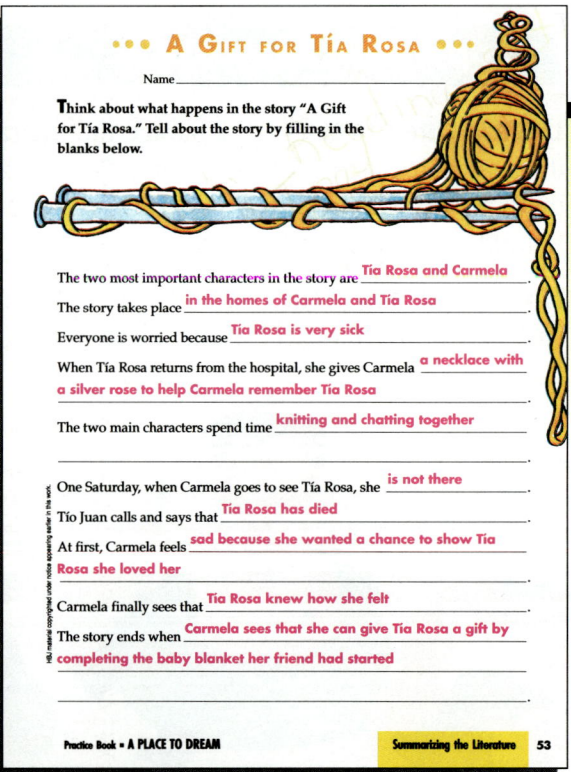
Practice Book

Portfolio

STUDENT SELF-ASSESSMENT

Assist students in self-assessing their story frames by asking them whether they could have filled in any of the blanks differently. Then encourage students to add their summaries to their portfolios.

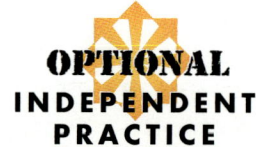
OPTIONAL INDEPENDENT PRACTICE

WRITER'S JOURNAL
page 33: Writing a personal response

PRACTICE BOOK
page 53: Summarizing the selection

VOCABULARY WORKSHOP

Reviewing Key Words

Write the Key Words on the board as shown below, omitting the arrows. Then challenge students to form sentences that incorporate two or more of these words. Each time a sentence is created, draw arrows linking the Key Words in the order they are used. Encourage the students to try different combinations in order to link as many words as possible. Example: *As she knitted the* fringe *on the scarf for her* granddaughter, *her face* crinkled *into a smile.*

shivered   clattered   (crinkled)   bounding   arguing

(fringe) → (granddaughter)   basement

Extending Vocabulary

ACTION WORDS   Write the words *bounding* and *arguing* on the board, and point out that these words tell about actions. Ask students to think of other words that end with *-ing* and that tell about actions. Add those words to the board. Then have students use their action words in shape poems. An example appears below.

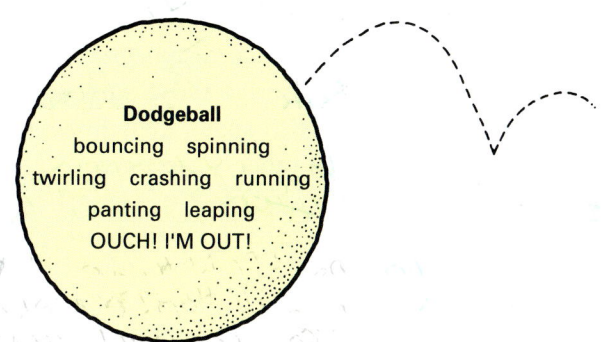

Dodgeball
bouncing spinning
twirling crashing running
panting leaping
OUCH! I'M OUT!

OPTIONAL INDEPENDENT PRACTICE

PRACTICE BOOK
page 54: Writing action words

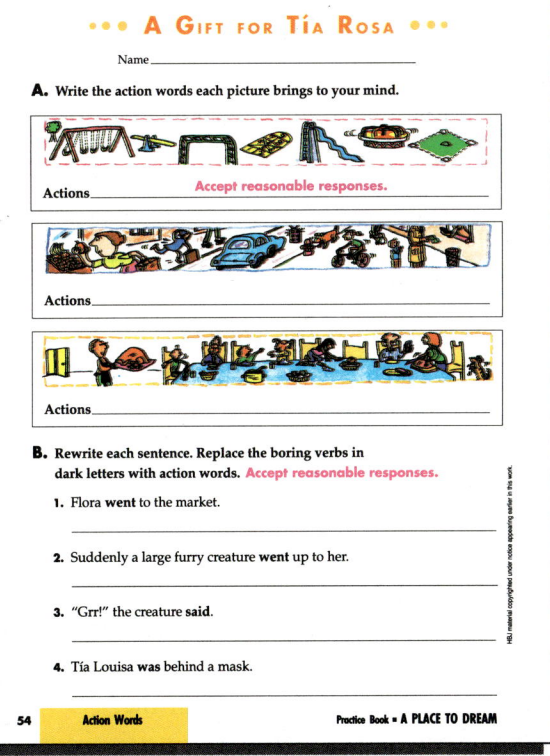

Practice Book

A GIFT FOR TÍA ROSA / T293

Language Arts WORKSHOP

READING

Oral Rereading/Drama

Have groups of three students present a dramatic reading of page 176 or of another passage of their choice. One student in each group should act as the narrator, and the other two should read the dialogue between Tía Rosa and Carmela. Have students begin by rereading the passage silently. Give them a chance to rehearse before they present their reading. Encourage those students taking the two characters' parts to speak their lines as two friends would talk to each other.   LISTENING/ SPEAKING/READING

SPELLING

Reviewing Spelling Words

SPELLING WORDS: *almost, also, always, cause, draw, fault, law, lost, small, soft, song, talk*

WORDS TO EXPLORE: *arguing, bounding, granddaughter, knitting*

Use the Spelling Words and students' own lists to create fifteen to twenty words that fit the spelling pattern (words with the /ô/ sound). Write the words on the board. In groups, have students each write the words on a sheet of paper with the letters scrambled. Erase the words from the board, and have group members unscramble the words within a specified time. Players score one point for each correctly spelled word and five points for being first to finish with all words spelled correctly.   READING/WRITING/SPELLING

Use *Integrated Spelling* Lesson 9 to reinforce the Spelling Words and the Words to Explore. See pages T63–T68 in *Integrated Spelling Teacher's Edition.*

SPELLING POSTTEST   You may want to use the Pretest/Posttest Sentences on *Integrated Spelling Teacher's Edition* page T63 to assess students' knowledge of the spelling generalization.

WRITING

Writing About the Literature
Available on Project Card 23A

WRITE A STORY   Ask students to write their own stories about a friendship between a child and an older relative or neighbor. To begin, have each student complete a planning chart like the one below. Encourage students to create a dialogue between the main characters that shows how they feel about each other. See Writing Model, page R94.   WRITING

Where the story takes place: _____
When the story takes place: _____
Who the two characters are: _____
What they like to do together: _____
How they help each other: _____

GRAMMAR REVIEW: PLURAL NOUNS   When students revise their stories, remind them to check that they have formed plural nouns correctly, particularly those that end with a consonant and *y* or those that change spelling when the plural is formed. To reinforce the skill, have students look up any irregular plural nouns in a dictionary. Suggest that students keep a list of these nouns.

LANGUAGE HANDBOOK   Writing to Entertain and Express, pages 36–39; Plural Nouns, pages 98–101

DAILY LANGUAGE PRACTICE   Oral language exercises are provided on pages R66–R67.

Language Arts WORKSHOP

WRITING

"Around, Over, Through, and Pull"

Ask students what activities besides knitting require a series of actions that must be repeated. (Examples include sewing, tying knots, and swimming.) Have volunteers name some important things to remember when following directions for this kind of activity. Ask students to choose an activity they are familiar with and write directions for completing it. Provide time for pairs of students to try to follow each other's directions.   SPEAKING/READING/WRITING

LISTENING AND SPEAKING

Plop, Boom, Bang, Crash!

Available on Project Card 23B

COOPERATIVE LEARNING   Point out the word *clish* on Student Anthology page 177. Then write the word *onomatopoeia* on the board. Explain to students that this term refers to words like *click*, *buzz*, and *boom*, words that sound like what they represent. Have groups of three students name three onomatopoeic words. Recorders can record both well-known and new sound words that their group names. After a Reader from each group reads aloud the group's words, have students guess the objects that might make those sounds.   LISTENING/SPEAKING

WRITING

The Perfect Gift

Have students draw pictures of the best gifts they have given and received. Ask them to write a description of each of the gifts and tell what made each one special. Display the pictures and sentences.   WRITING/VIEWING

LISTENING AND SPEAKING

My Favorite Hobby

Remind students that Carmela and Tía Rosa liked to knit. Have students give oral reports about their hobbies. Encourage them to bring in materials related to their hobbies, such as sticker collections, roller skates, or models they have built, and demonstrate or teach others how to get started on or how to do that hobby.   LISTENING/SPEAKING

A GIFT FOR TÍA ROSA / T295

Grammar MINI LESSON

Singular Possessive Nouns

OBJECTIVES: *To recognize that a possessive noun shows ownership and that a singular possessive noun shows ownership by one person or thing; to understand that singular possessive nouns are formed by adding an apostrophe + s to the end of singular nouns*

Oral Warm-Up

Ask students to follow along as you display and read aloud the following sentences from "A Gift for Tía Rosa."

- **Now and then she stopped and listened for her father's car.**
- **Then he took Carmela's hands in his.**
- **A few minutes later he returned with Tía Rosa's big knitting bag.**

Then write the lists below on the board, and have volunteers draw a line between each person and the thing that belongs to that person. Ask these questions to guide students: Whose car is Carmela listening for? (her father's) Whose hands are being held? (Carmela's) Whose knitting bag is being carried? (Tía Rosa's) Circle the *'s* after each noun.

Interactive Teaching

SINGULAR POSSESSIVE NOUNS Have students think about something they once borrowed from a friend. Model how to describe such an item using the following sentence format: *I borrowed (friend name)'s (item)*. Ask volunteers to tell about the items they borrowed, and record their responses on the board. Ask students to identify whom each object belongs to.

Point to the name in each sentence. Then ask students what all these words have in common. (There is an apostrophe + *s* at the end.) Explain that these words are singular possessive nouns, or nouns that show ownership by one person. Explain that to make a singular noun possessive, an apostrophe + *s* is added to the end. Point to an item in the room and describe it using this format: *John's hat is red*.

Ask students to use a similar format to describe other items in the room. Write the sentences on the board. Have volunteers circle the part of the word in each sentence that shows ownership.

 **LANGUAGE HANDBOOK** *Singular Possessive Nouns, page 104*

T296 / A PLACE TO DREAM, UNIT 2

Practice Activities

Picture Possessives

Display a reproduction of a painting by Grandma Moses, Norman Rockwell, or Currier and Ives, a mural by Diego Rivera, or a work by another artist whose paintings contain many people and objects. Describe the elements of the painting, using sentences that contain singular possessive nouns. Then have students make their own paintings or drawings. Have them exchange their work with a partner, who should write sentences with singular possessive nouns to describe the elements in the painting and whom or what they belong to. Have partners check each other's work for proper punctuation of singular possessives. Ask them to display their artwork and sentences and to read the sentences aloud.   VISUAL/AUDITORY

Hidden Treasures

Have students think about the attic, the basement, or a closet in their home where there are lots of family belongings. Tell students to make a list of five or six items they might find there. Have students write a sentence about each item and whom it belongs to. (For example: *I found my sister's old rocking chair in the attic.*) Ask volunteers to write their sentences on the board. Ask other volunteers to circle the part of each possessive noun that shows it is possessive.   VISUAL/KINESTHETIC

MEETING INDIVIDUAL NEEDS

SECOND-LANGUAGE SUPPORT   Have each student write a list of three objects in the room and the names of the three people to whom these objects belong. (for example: *coat, hat, pencil; Jack, Marta, Elisa*) Have students switch lists and write three sentences, using the names and objects in the lists to show ownership.

RETEACH   Follow the visual, auditory, and kinesthetic/motor models on page R23.

OPTIONAL INDEPENDENT PRACTICE

PRACTICE BOOK
page 55: Identifying and using singular possessive nouns

GRAMMAR PRACTICE
pages 26–27: Using singular possessive nouns

Practice Book

A GIFT FOR TÍA ROSA / T297

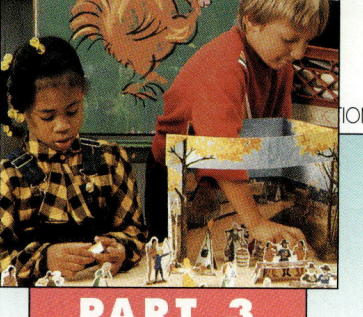

PART 3

Learning through the Literature

LITERARY APPRECIATION
INTRODUCE

Story Elements

OBJECTIVE: *To use details to gain information about setting, characters, and plot*

Interactive Teaching

Use details from the literature.

LITERATURE CONNECTION Write the following details on the board: *gray November shadow, Tía Rosa's front door, garage next door*. Ask students what these details show about *where* and *when* the story takes place. (in fall, in a neighborhood) Tell students that being able to use details to figure out important parts of a story will help them understand what they read.

Use a story map to analyze story elements.

MODEL HOW TO IDENTIFY ELEMENTS If students completed a story chart before and after reading, display it again. Then display a story map like the one below, or distribute copies of the story map on page R105.

Model how you can use the questions *Who?*, *When?*, *Where?*, and *What Happened?* to identify the story elements.

> To identify the characters, I ask myself *who* are the people in the story. For the setting, I ask myself *when* and *where* the story takes place.

Have students to help you complete the story map. If necessary, have them look back in the story for important details they can use as clues.

ADDITIONAL BOOKS FOR APPLYING STORY ELEMENTS

Nana Upstairs and Nana Downstairs by Tomie dePaola. Putnam, 1973. **EASY**

Wilfred Gordon McDonald Partridge by Mem Fox. Kane/Miller, 1985. **EASY**

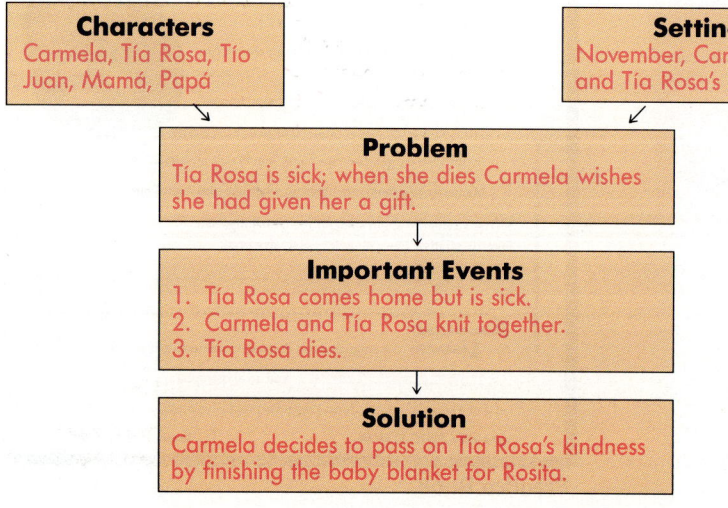

T298 / A PLACE TO DREAM, UNIT 2

Practice Activity

The Plot Thickens

Extend the lesson by having students create a group story.

COOPERATIVE LEARNING Provide each student with three slips of paper, labeled *Character, Setting,* and *Event.* Then have Recorders write ideas that students suggest for each heading. Label a paper bag with each heading. Have students place slips of paper into the correct bags. Then have students form small groups, draw two slips from the *Character* bag, one from the *Setting* bag, and two from the *Event* bag to create group stories.
KINESTHETIC

Performance Assessment

Have volunteers tell whether each story detail from The Plot Thickens reveals something about plot, setting, or a character. For evaluation guidelines, see *Staff Development Guide.*

Reader ↔ Writer Connection
Story Elements

WRITERS must provide helpful details so the reader can understand the important parts of a story.

READERS need to understand how story details tell what is happening and why.

WRITE A STORY Have students choose two characters and a setting as a basis for a story idea and then write the main events in the plot.

Writer's Journal

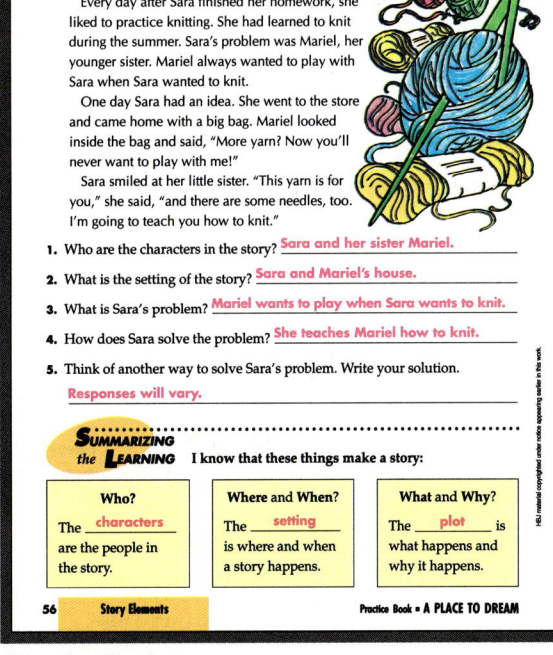

Practice Book

MEETING INDIVIDUAL NEEDS

RETEACH Follow the visual, auditory, and kinesthetic/motor models on page R24.

CHALLENGE Suggest that students make an outline that includes details of plot, setting, and characters for an extension story about Carmela, her parents, and Tío Juan.

SECOND-LANGUAGE SUPPORT Encourage students to keep a list of terms related to story elements, such as *character, setting,* and *plot.* See also the manual *Alternative Teaching Strategies,* pages 11, 66–69.

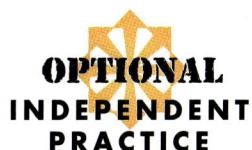

OPTIONAL INDEPENDENT PRACTICE

WRITER'S JOURNAL
page 34: Writing a story

PRACTICE BOOK
page 56: Using story elements

DECODING

REVIEW

Structural Analysis

OBJECTIVE: *To use base words, prefixes, and suffixes for independent decoding of words*

Review

Have students explain prefixes and suffixes.

REVIEW DECODING WITH WORD PARTS Ask students to explain what a *prefix* and a *suffix* are, and give examples of each. Help them recall the meanings of the affixes *un-, non-, -ly,* and *-less*. Then write the following sentence on the board and ask a volunteer to decode the word *happily*: Carmela *happily* knitted. (*happy* + *-ly* means "in a happy way")

Practice Activity

Words and Word Parts

Have students identify and use prefixes and suffixes.

Write the following sentences on the board. Have students identify the base word, the prefix, and/or the suffix in each underlined word and then write another sentence using each word.

1. Tía Rosa is <u>unbelievable</u>! (*un-* + *believe* + *-able*)
2. She seemed to talk <u>nonstop</u>. (*non-* + *stop*)
3. She was never <u>careless</u> when she knitted. (*care* + *-less*)

Ask volunteers to read their sentences aloud. Have other volunteers tell what the underlined words and the sentences mean.   VISUAL/KINESTHETIC

MEETING INDIVIDUAL NEEDS

CHALLENGE Have students make a list of new words by adding the prefixes and the suffixes from the lesson to words in the story. Students can demonstrate their understanding of the new words by using them in oral sentences.

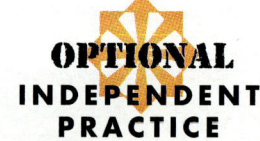

OPTIONAL INDEPENDENT PRACTICE

PRACTICE BOOK
page 57: Using base words, prefixes, and suffixes to decode words

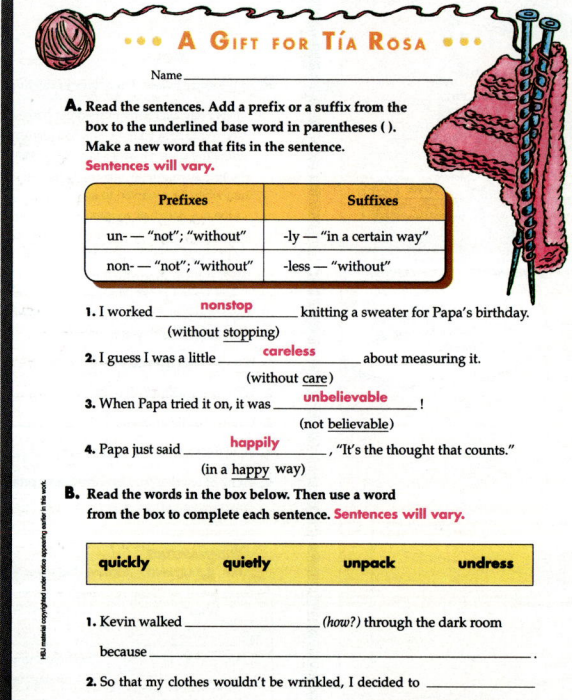

Practice Book

T300 / A PLACE TO DREAM, UNIT 2

STUDY SKILLS
REVIEW

Following Directions

OBJECTIVE: *To follow written directions*

Review

Have students recall ways to follow directions.

CONNECT TO DIRECTIONS IN THE STORY Ask students what directions Carmela followed and how she remembered to follow them. (directions for knitting; she repeated the steps to herself) Then review with students how to follow directions: read all steps; gather materials; look at pictures; follow steps in order.

Practice Activity

Have students follow simple directions.

Display Chart/Transparency 19 or the information on it. Have students follow the directions. When they have finished, have students display their pictures and explain how they completed the activity. VISUAL/AUDITORY/KINESTHETIC

> **Chart/Transparency 19   Following Directions**
> 1. Draw a square that is 4 inches on each side.
> 2. Put a dot in the middle of each line.
> 3. Connect the dots that are across from each other.
> 4. Add a cat on the windowsill and a bee flying by.

MEETING INDIVIDUAL NEEDS

CHALLENGE Have students write directions for another simple drawing. Encourage them to trade directions with a partner, follow the directions, and make suggestions for how to clarify the directions, if necessary.

OPTIONAL INDEPENDENT PRACTICE

PRACTICE BOOK
page 58: Following directions

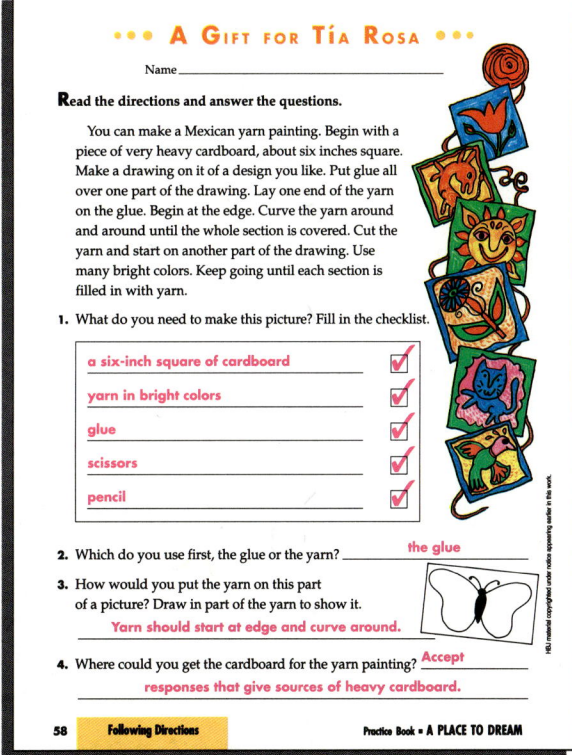

Practice Book

A GIFT FOR TÍA ROSA / **T301**

Integrated CURRICULUM

SOCIAL STUDIES

Volunteer Work

Guide students in finding ways to help patients at a nearby convalescent home or hospital. Students can use the yellow pages of the phone book to locate a facility; you may wish to call the appropriate administrator. Have the group write a letter requesting information on ways students can help. Students might be able to do such things as collecting recent magazines to be dropped off on a regular basis, spending time visiting, or sending letters and art work to be displayed.   WRITING

HEALTH

Five Ways to Stay Healthy

Available on Project Card 24A

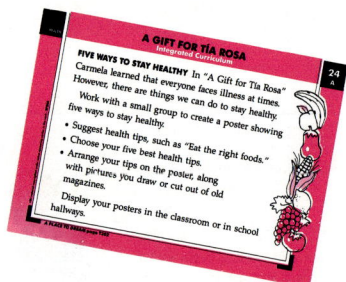

COOPERATIVE LEARNING
Have students form small groups and create posters showing five ways to stay healthy. Have each group choose a Materials Manager and a Checker, who should proofread the "tips."

Groups should first brainstorm lists of health tips (for example, eat the right foods) and then decide how to arrange their tips and art on the poster. You may wish to provide students with magazines and have them cut out pictures that illustrate their tips. Display the posters in the classroom or in school hallways.   LISTENING/SPEAKING/WRITING

MATH

Calculating Recipe Amounts

COOPERATIVE LEARNING   Remind students that Tío Juan and Tía Rosa made cookies and hot chocolate for Carmela. Have students work in groups of four. Copy ingredients from the recipe below on the board, and tell students that these amounts will make four mugs of hot chocolate. Tell students to figure out how much of each ingredient is needed to make the exact amount of hot chocolate for each of the following situations:

- Each group member drinks two mugs.
- Only half of the group members have a second mug.
- Each group member invites a family member to have hot chocolate with the group. Everyone has one mug.

After the groups have discussed each situation and completed their calculations, ask volunteers to tell how the amounts changed for each situation.   LISTENING/SPEAKING/READING/WRITING

T302 / A PLACE TO DREAM, UNIT 2

SOCIAL STUDIES

Cross Your Fingers

Available on Project Card 24B

CULTURAL AWARENESS Have students recall that Carmela crossed her fingers when she echoed Tía Rosa's wish that the new grandchild be a girl. Tell students that people from different cultures have different customs associated with making a wish. Have students share customs they know about. Suggest that they make a "Wishes Around the World" book in which such customs are described and illustrated. LISTENING/SPEAKING/WRITING

ART

Ready, Set, Knit!

Have students start a group knitting project. Suggest that they begin by inviting an adult who is an accomplished knitter to visit the group and teach them to knit. Students might also want to challenge another group to a "knit-off" in which both groups try to knit the longest scarf by a certain date. LISTENING/SPEAKING

SOCIAL STUDIES

Hola Means "Hello"

CULTURAL AWARENESS Point out that in "A Gift for Tía Rosa," the author used several Spanish words, including *tía, tío, tamales,* and *hola.* Have students make illustrated "foreign language" dictionaries with five to ten entries. Students may get ideas for words from ethnic foods they've eaten, movies they've seen, or books they've read. Encourage students who are not native English speakers to use words from their native language for their dictionaries. Each dictionary page should contain one word, its English translation, and a picture. Students should staple their pages between construction paper covers titled with the names of the two languages. Each morning, have one student teach the class a few of the words in his or her dictionary. LISTENING/SPEAKING/WRITING

BOOKS TO SHARE

SOCIAL STUDIES *Chicken Sunday* by Patricia Polacco. Philomel, 1992. AVERAGE

Here Comes the Mystery Man by Scott Russell Sanders. Bradbury, 1993. CHALLENGING

MULTICULTURAL PERSPECTIVES

Remembering Heroes

DISCUSSION STARTER
Why do people everywhere treasure keepsakes, or gifts to remember friends by?

READ ALOUD
People everywhere treasure keepsakes. Some people have photographs or letters that they can look at from time to time. But what can be done if a whole community or nation wants to remember people who have died?

Sometimes a statue or a monument is put in a place that all people can visit. On a hillside in Washington, D.C., there is a special wall with more than 50,000 names carved on it. These are the names of the Americans who died in the Vietnam War. This memorial was designed in 1981 by Maya Lin, a Chinese American architect. In 1989, she designed another special monument in Montgomery, Alabama. Many people visit these memorials every year, and most find it an emotional experience.

ACTIVITY CORNER
• Invite students to imagine that they, like Maya Lin, were asked to design a monument. Suggest that they might design a monument to honor a particular group of Americans they may have heard or read about, or to which they may belong. Encourage students to discuss the kinds of feelings such a monument should reflect, such as strength, pride, and achievement. Then have them work in small groups to draw designs for monuments.

• Ask students whether they have something that they associate with a particular person—perhaps a favorite toy or book. Have them pick one object that is dear to them and write a brief description of it, explaining its importance.

The Vietnam Memorial in Washington, D.C., designed by Maya Lin, attracts thousands of visitors every year.

THEME WRAP-UP

Discussing the Theme

Remind students that the selections in this theme told about ways in which people show they care.

Discussion Question

PAGE 185 The selections you have just finished reading are about caring for someone and sharing with that person. How can *you* show someone you care? How can you share part of yourself with that person? (Responses will vary.)
CRITICAL: AUTHOR'S CRAFT/IDENTIFYING WITH CHARACTERS

Theme Wrap-Up

Caring and Sharing

The selections you have just read are about caring for someone and sharing with that person. How can *you* show someone you care? How can you share part of yourself with that person?

WRITER'S WORKSHOP
Think about something you know how to do, and write a paragraph to tell someone else how to do it. Write each step in order.

Writer's Choice: You might like to write about a very special gift you gave or were given. Choose what you will write. After you are finished, share your writing.

185

Writer's Workshop

See pages T306–T307 for suggestions for guiding students through the writing process as they respond to the literature. WRITING PROCESS: HOW-TO PARAGRAPH

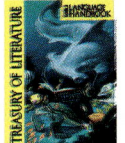

Writer's Choice
Before writing, have students brainstorm a list of topics and choose a topic they wish to write about. You may wish to refer students to the *Language Handbook* as they write.

When students are ready to revise and proofread, have them exchange papers with a partner. Tell them to note descriptive phrases that they especially liked.

Writer's Workshop

How-to Paragraph

Theme Wrap-Up

Students write a how-to paragraph giving instructions for something that they know how to do.

To prepare students for writing a how-to paragraph, ask them to recall the story "A Gift for Tía Rosa." Ask what Tía Rosa taught Carmela how to do. Explain that showing someone how to do something is a good way to teach. Mention that written instructions also work well if they are clear and complete. Elicit examples of written how-to instructions, such as recipes in cookbooks, instructions for assembling or operating a toy, and directions for taking a test.

Use the Writer's Workshop assignment on page 185 as you work through the writing process with students.

ALTERNATIVE TOPICS If you wish, allow students to choose their own topics for writing. Suggest that they refer to the *Language Handbook* for an explanation of the writing process for how-to paragraphs. See Writing Model, page R96.

 **LANGUAGE HANDBOOK** *Writing to Inform,* pages 48–49; How-to Paragraph, page 52

Prewriting

Have students work in pairs to brainstorm things that they know how to do. When they have selected their topics, encourage students to organize their information by making and filling in a chart like the one below.

How to _____
Materials
Step 1
Step 2
Step 3
Step 4

Drafting

- Have students write a draft of their how-to paragraph. Suggest that they
  - begin with a sentence describing what will be accomplished if the directions are followed.
  - include exact measurements or quantities of materials when appropriate.
  - use their charts to make sure that they present steps in the right order.

COMPUTER TIP

 DRAFTING Word processing programs usually include more than one way of representing fractions. Students whose how-to paragraphs require fractions might explore these options.

Responding and Revising

To check their writing before sharing it with others, students should ask themselves these questions:

- Is there a topic sentence at the beginning of my how-to paragraph that tells what I am going to explain?
- Have I listed all materials needed for the project?
- Have I clearly explained all the steps and presented them in the right order?
- Have I used time-order words such as *first, next, then,* and *last* to show correct order?

Have students read their how-to paragraphs to a partner in a peer conference. The partners should then respond to the following questions:

Listener	Writer
Does the how-to paragraph tell what the project will accomplish? When you listen to the steps, do you get a clear picture of what to do? Have any materials been left out?	When you read your how-to paragraph aloud, do any parts seem confusing or unclear? Did you leave out any materials or steps? Jot down ideas for improvements.

T306 / A PLACE TO DREAM, UNIT 2

Proofreading

Offer these tips for students to use as they proofread:

- Check that all your directions are complete sentences.
- Check that abbreviations used to express measurements are written correctly.
- Correct any misspelled words.

MINI-CONFERENCE STRATEGY Help students find and correct sentence fragments by making observations such as this: Is *Without stopping* a complete thought? It looks as if it belongs at the end of the preceding sentence: *Apply the paint without stopping*.

Publishing Options

PROJECT BOOK Encourage students to illustrate their how-to paragraphs. Have them copy the directions neatly and draw illustrations where useful. Place their illustrated paragraphs in a binder in the class library for other students to examine and select projects to do.

DEMONSTRATION Ask for volunteers to select a how-to paragraph other than their own that they would like to demonstrate. Have volunteers present the information in the paragraph or, whenever possible, demonstrate the steps.

Assessment Options

STUDENT SELF-ASSESSMENT Encourage students to summarize the writing experience by responding to this question in their journals:

- **In writing a how-to paragraph, what did I learn about making directions clear?**

You may also want to have students complete the Self-Assessment Checklist in the *Portfolio Assessment Teacher's Guide*.

WRITING OBSERVATION RECORDS Students who at first write too little may be trying to "get it over with." Note each writer's growth in completing the workshop activity.

After students publish, you may want to have them add their how-to paragraphs to their portfolios.

GRAMMAR CONNECTION

Revising: Plural Nouns

Using Transparency E, share the examples below with students to help them determine how using correct forms of plural nouns can help make their directions clearer.

> **Transparency E**
> **Finishing Wood**
>
> **BEFORE**
> You can make a piece of wood have a shiny surface. You will need one square <u>feet</u> of wood, two <u>rages</u>, medium sandpaper, fine sandpaper, stain, and varnish. First, sand the <u>woods</u> with medium sandpaper. Wipe off the <u>dusts</u>. Then sand the wood again with fine sandpaper. Dust it again. Next, rub on stain with a rag, and let it dry. Then brush on the <u>varnishes</u>, and let it dry.
>
> **AFTER**
> You can make a piece of wood have a shiny surface. You will need one square <u>foot</u> of wood, two <u>rags</u>, medium sandpaper, fine sandpaper, stain, and varnish. First, sand the <u>wood</u> with medium sandpaper. Wipe off the <u>dust</u>. Then sand the wood again with fine sandpaper. Dust it again. Next, rub on stain with a rag, and let it dry. Then brush on the <u>varnish</u>, and let it dry.

Have small groups of students share their writing and check that they have used plural nouns correctly in their directions.

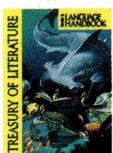

LANGUAGE HANDBOOK *Plural Nouns, pages 96–101*

Unit 2 FRIENDSHIPS

THEME OPENER

Learning About Yourself

Justin and the Best Biscuits in the World

T311   A REALISTIC FICTION STORY by Mildred Pitts Walter
While visiting his grandfather's ranch in Missouri, Justin learns many things about himself, his family, and some famous African American cowboys of the past.

Words About the Author: Mildred Pitts Walter

T329   AN ARTICLE
Mildred Pitts Walter's characters often make difficult choices. Read about why she challenges them.

Versos sencillos (Simple Verses)

T345   A POEM by José Martí
What is the greatest treasure of all? The poet's answer is "friendship."

For pacing suggestions, see page T310.

THEME

Learning About Yourself

Spending time with other people can help you learn about yourself. It can also help you learn to do new things. The story, the words from the author, and the poem you are about to read may help you learn new things. Maybe you can share what you learn with a friend.

CONTENTS

JUSTIN AND THE BEST BISCUITS IN THE WORLD
by Mildred Pitts Walter

WORDS ABOUT THE AUTHOR: MILDRED PITTS WALTER

VERSOS SENCILLOS/ SIMPLE VERSES
by José Martí

Discussing the Theme

Have students look at the illustration, read the information on Student Anthology page 187, and then restate the theme focus in their own words. Encourage students to predict from the selection titles what new things they will learn.

Portfolio Assessment

Remind students to keep their writing responses for the selections in "Learning About Yourself" in their portfolios. Suggest that they also add to their personal journals thoughts about books they have read independently.

 When you see this symbol, you may want to suggest that students save a piece of their work in their portfolios.

Harcourt Brace Big Book
The poems in *Best Friends* may be shared after "Justin and the Best Biscuits in the World" and at other appropriate times throughout the unit.

THEME OPENER

Managing the Literature-Based Classroom

New Students

Plan with your class how new students can be welcomed into the group. Brainstorm what would be helpful to a new student and set up procedures such as having a buddy a day for a week. Consider having students create a welcome packet of student-written introductions to the class members and the school.

Group Guidelines

To help groups keep to their assigned tasks and to make sure that each member participates, provide each student with an evaluation sheet such as the one below to fill in.

Name: _____

Group Assignment: _____

Tell what you gained from the experience:
_____
_____

What went especially well?
_____
_____

What could be improved next time?
_____
_____

Pacing

This theme has been designed to take about two weeks to complete, depending on your students' needs.

MEETING INDIVIDUAL NEEDS

LOW-ACHIEVING STUDENTS   Students may benefit from shared reading experiences. Read aloud "Justin and the Best Biscuits in the World" a section at a time. Invite students to reread each section with you. Afterward, discuss with students the questions at the end of the selection.

GIFTED AND TALENTED   After they read all the selections in Unit 2, challenge students to create business cards for the main characters in their favorite stories. Each card should include the character's name, his or her address, and an occupation or a service. *Challenge Cards* provide additional activities to challenge students. Challenge notes throughout the lesson plans suggest additional activities to stimulate critical and creative thinking.

SPECIAL-EDUCATION STUDENTS   If a student has difficulty comprehending or remembering oral instructions, you may wish to appoint a "listening partner" who will review oral material with that student and help him or her make brief notes in a special notebook or on color-coded cards to serve as convenient memory aids.

STUDENTS ACQUIRING ENGLISH   Students may have difficulty remembering the rules of punctuation and capitalization when writing in English. For example, in Spanish the months of the year are not capitalized and the question mark and exclamation mark are placed not only at the end of a sentence but upside down at the beginning of the sentence as well. Have students make individual punctuation and capitalization charts. Second-Language Support notes throughout the lesson plans offer strategies to help students acquiring English to understand the selection.

Justin and the Best Biscuits in the World

by Mildred Pitts Walter

illustrated by Brian Deines

Integrated Lesson Planner

Justin and the Best Biscuits in the World

pages 188–213

	READING	LANGUAGE ARTS	CROSS-CURRICULAR CONNECTIONS
PART 1 *Reading the Literature* pages T314–T329	**Building Background** **Vocabulary Strategies** **Prereading Strategies** Story Impressions Setting a Purpose **Options for Reading**	**Spelling** Pretest Spelling-Vocabulary Connection Generalization: /o͞o/, /o͝o/ **Grammar Connection** Reviewing Singular Possessive Nouns	**Cultural Awareness** Spanish influence in the New World Mexican and South American cowboys **Social Studies** Ranching terms
PART 2 *Responding to the Literature* pages T330–T337	**Personal Response** **Cooperative Response** **Summarizing the Literature** **Critical Thinking Activity** Discussion **Vocabulary Workshop** Key Words Inflected Endings	**Language Arts Workshop** **Reading** drama **Writing** story ending, new scene, story, recipe **Listening and Speaking** storytelling, personal experience, description **Reviewing Spelling Words** Posttest **Grammar Review** Singular Possessive Nouns **Grammar Minilesson** Plural Possessive Nouns	**Social Studies** Stories from the Past
PART 3 *Learning Through the Literature* pages T338–T344	**Introduce** Literary Appreciation: Figurative Language **Review** Decoding: Structural Analysis (Tested) Comprehension: Main Idea and Details (Tested)	**Reading** Ranches and Rodeos Home, Sweet Home **Writing** Git Along, Little Dogies Wilderness Survival Scenes of the West **Listening and Speaking** Compute Food Amounts	**Social Studies** Ranches and Rodeos Home, Sweet Home **Music** Git Along, Little Dogies **Science** Wilderness Survival **Math** Compute Food Amounts **Art** Scenes of the West **Multicultural Perspectives** Mexico's Vaqueros

OPTIONAL MATERIALS
Chart/Transparencies 20–21
Integrated Spelling pp. 46–49; TE pp. T69–T74
Practice Book pp. 59–64
Writer's Journal pp. 35–36
Alternative Teaching Strategies pp. 12, 70–73
Language Handbook pp. 38–39, 102–106, 192–197
Grammar Practice pp. 28–29
Family Involvement Activities: Unit 2, pp. 1–4
Response Card 6
Project Cards 25A, 25B, 26A, 26B

 MEETING INDIVIDUAL NEEDS
Second-Language Support pp. T315, T316, T320, T337, T339
Mainstreaming p. T316
Reteach p. T339
Challenge pp. T339, T340, T341

FAMILY INVOLVEMENT Suggest that family members show students how to do simple tasks that might interest them. See *Family Involvement Activities*.

Key Words
plains
prairie
skillets
scrape
rodeo
impress
mimicking

Selection Summary

Justin is tired of being asked to make his bed and help with the dishes, and he is frustrated with his inability to do "women's work." In this excerpt from the novel, Justin spends time on his grandfather's ranch. Grandpa, a kind and gentle man, teaches Justin domestic and ranching skills: how to feed the animals, how to clean fish, how to make a bed, and how to repair fences. In the process, Justin learns about his family history and about famous African American cowboys of long ago. Justin learns that he can do many things right. He also finds out that his grandfather loves him just as he is.

In 1987 *Justin and the Best Biscuits in the World* won the Coretta Scott King Award for fiction.

About the Author

Mildred Pitts Walter lives in Colorado, but for many years she taught elementary school in Los Angeles. She started writing while she was still a teacher there. In 1977 she was a delegate to the Second World Black and African Festival of the Arts and Culture, in Lagos, Nigeria. Mildred Pitts Walter has written a number of books for children and young adults. In 1984 *Because We Are* won an honorable mention from the Coretta Scott King Award committee.

Additional Reading

OTHER THEME-RELATED BOOKS

Different Dragons by Jean Little. Puffin, 1989.
CHALLENGING

Harry in Trouble by Barbara Ann Porte. Greenwillow, 1989.   **EASY**

*Julian's Glorious Summer by Ann Cameron. Random House, 1987.   **AVERAGE**

Mariah Loves Rock by Mildred Pitts Walter. Troll, 1989.   **CHALLENGING**

Masai and I by Virginia Kroll. Four Winds Press, 1992.   **EASY**

BOOKS FOR APPLYING STRATEGIES: FIGURATIVE LANGUAGE

The Cowboy and the Blackeyed Pea by Tony Johnston. G. P. Putnam's Sons, 1992.
AVERAGE

Pecos Bill by Steven Kellogg. William Morrow, 1986.   **AVERAGE**

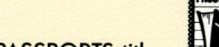

*Available as a Harcourt Brace PASSPORTS title

PART 1

Reading the Literature

Building Background

Access prior knowledge and build vocabulary concepts.

Tell students that the next story, "Justin and the Best Biscuits in the World," takes place on a ranch. Have students discuss what ranches look like, what kinds of animals live on ranches, and what kinds of work ranchers do. Point out that ranchers and cowhands do a variety of chores around the ranch house and out on the range. Work with students to complete a chart of the various chores on a ranch.

Ranch Chores					
On the Range			**Around the House and Barn**		
fixing fences	rounding up cattle	branding cattle	fixing saddles	cleaning boots	cooking

Vocabulary Strategies

Introduce Key Words and strategies.

Display Chart/Transparency 20 or write the story on the board. Have students read the sentences silently, using context clues. For instance, students might use *wide, flat,* and *seem endless* to figure out what plains are like. Point out that *plains* and *prairie* are synonyms.

Chart/Transparency 20   Key Words

The wide, flat <u>plains</u> of America seem endless. Long ago many cowboys lived on the <u>prairie</u>. They carried all they needed on their horses.

<u>Skillets</u> were used for cooking.

A knife was used to <u>scrape</u> animal hides.

Cowboys held a public contest called a <u>rodeo</u>, where they tried to show who was the best bronco rider. They tried to <u>impress</u> one another with fancy riding and roping tricks. Rodeo clowns had fun <u>mimicking</u>, or copying, some of the cowboys' roping tricks.

CULTURAL AWARENESS

Students may be surprised to learn that cattle and horses were introduced to North America by the Spanish in the 1400s and 1500s.

Key Words

plains
prairie
skillets
scrape
rodeo
impress
mimicking

KEY WORDS DEFINED

- **plains**   areas of almost level land that are nearly treeless; prairies
- **prairie**   a plain
- **skillets**   shallow cooking pans used for frying foods
- **scrape**   to remove by rubbing with something sharp
- **rodeo**   public contest of various cowboy skills, such as riding broncos
- **impress**   to affect someone's mind or feelings
- **mimicking**   imitating

Check all students' understanding.

Display or read aloud the words and phrases below. Have students identify the word or phrase in each row that does not belong. Encourage students to tell why they think the word or phrase does not belong. Correct responses are underlined.
STRATEGY: SYNONYMS/EXAMPLE

• <u>rodeo</u>	singing and dancing	riding and roping
• <u>tricking</u>	mimicking	copying
• <u>scrape</u>	remove	cover
• earn respect	<u>disappoint</u>	impress
• <u>skillets</u>	pans	bowls
• <u>mountains</u>	plains	prairie

Integrate spelling with vocabulary.

SPELLING-VOCABULARY CONNECTION *Integrated Spelling* Lesson 10 reinforces the spelling of words with the sounds /o͝o/ and /o͞o/, such as *cook*, found in the selection. In addition, the Words to Explore help reinforce the concept of ranching as it relates to the selection.

SPELLING PRETEST You may want to use the Pretest/Posttest Sentences on page T69 in *Integrated Spelling Teacher's Edition* to assess students' knowledge of the spelling generalization.

Spelling

Spelling Words	Words to Explore
1. cook	cattle
2. cool	mustang
3. foot	prairie
4. good	rodeo
5. moon	
6. noon	Your Own Words
7. pool	13.
8. roof	14.
9. shoe	15.
10. soup	16.
11. wood	
12. zoo	

Spelling generalization: /o͝o/ and /o͞o/ sounds

Practice Book

MEETING INDIVIDUAL NEEDS

SECOND-LANGUAGE SUPPORT Have students use as many Key Words as they can in oral sentences about ranch hands or ranches. See also the manual *Alternative Teaching Strategies*, pages 12, 70–73.

OPTIONAL INDEPENDENT PRACTICE

INTEGRATED SPELLING pages 46–49: Words Like *moon* and *foot*

PRACTICE BOOK page 59: Reinforcing Key Words

NOTE: This page may be completed now or after students have read the story.

JUSTIN AND THE BEST BISCUITS IN THE WORLD / T315

Prereading Strategies

Story Impressions

Have students preview the story.

Have students preview the story by thinking about the title, looking at the illustrations, and reading the introduction.

Have students use story impressions to make predictions.

Tell students that they are going to use selected words and phrases from the story to write their own version of what might happen in "Justin and the Best Biscuits in the World." Write on the board the headings of the chart below and the first two phrases shown in the "Story Impressions" column. Encourage students to identify and add interesting words and phrases from the story to the left-hand column of the chart, based on their preview. Then help students write a brief story such as the one shown in the right-hand column.

Story Impressions	Story
—Grandpa's house ↓ —Justin would do fine ↓ —how to clean fish ↓ —how much he loved him	(Justin felt a little homesick when he was staying at Grandpa's house. But Grandpa knew Justin would do fine after a while. Grandpa taught Justin how to clean fish. When Justin lay in bed that night, he thought about all the things he had learned from his grandpa. He also thought about how much he loved him.)

 **PERSONAL JOURNAL** Have students use their story impressions to predict what might happen in "Justin and the Best Biscuits in the World." Have them add their predictions to their personal journals.

Setting a Purpose

Encourage students to set purposes.

Have students set a purpose for reading. Invite them to share what they would like to find out as they read.

If students have difficulty setting a purpose, offer this suggestion:

I'm going to read to find out how Justin "begins to think differently" about himself.

MEETING INDIVIDUAL NEEDS

SECOND-LANGUAGE SUPPORT Students may benefit from a more detailed discussion about the information in the introduction and about the characters in the story. You may also want to have students complete the Strategic Reading activities under the Student Anthology pages. See also the manual *Alternative Teaching Strategies,* pages 12, 70–73.

SUPPORT FOR MAINSTREAMING Generate interest in Justin's experiences with household chores by asking volunteers to talk about chores they are responsible for completing.

Options for Reading

SUSTAINED SILENT READING	STRATEGIC READING	READER RESPONSE GROUPS
Tell students who are reading independently to keep a record of interesting or challenging words in a vocabulary notebook.	To stimulate discussion, use the suggestions that appear on pages T317, T319, T324, and T328.	Follow the suggestions for Collaborative Response on page T317. As students read, suggest they think about how the events in the story relate to their own lives.

Justin and the Best Biscuits in the World

by Mildred Pitts Walter

illustrated by Brian Deines

Justin lives in the city and is usually surrounded by women—his mother and his two older sisters. Justin's sisters, Evelyn and Hadiya, often complain that he can't do anything right. He starts to believe he can't do "women's work," and the shame of it brings him to tears when his grandfather visits his family. When Justin stays on his grandpa's ranch for a while, he begins to look at things differently.

CORETTA SCOTT KING AWARD

Reader Response Groups

COLLABORATIVE RESPONSE Have each group of four students read the story silently, stopping at page 193 for a brief discussion. Assign group members the following roles: Predictor, Questioner, Summarizer, and Clarifier. You may wish to distribute Response Card 6 (Author's Craft), found on page R84, or provide the following questions:

- What kind of person do you think the author is? Tell why.
- Would you like to read something else by this author? Why, or why not?

Response Card 6

Strategic Reading

SET PURPOSE/PREDICT: PAGES 188–193 Have students read through page 193. Ask students what they will be reading to find out.

PAGES 190–191   JUSTIN AND THE BEST BISCUITS IN THE WORLD

GRANDPA'S HOUSE SAT about a mile in from the road. Between that road and the house lay a large meadow with a small stream. Everything seemed in order when Justin and Grandpa arrived.

Justin got out and opened the gate to the winding road that led toward the house. The meadow below shimmered in waves of tall green grass. The horses grazed calmly there. Justin was so excited to see them again that he waved his grandpa on. "I'll walk up, Grandpa." He ran down into the meadow.

Pink prairie roses blossomed near the fence. Goldenrod, sweet william, and black-eyed susans added color here and there. Justin waded through the lush green grass.

The horses, drinking at the stream, paid no attention as he raced across the meadow toward them. *Cropper looks so old,* he thought as he came closer. But Black Lightning's coat shone, as beautiful as ever. Justin gave a familiar whistle. The horses lifted their heads and their ears went back, but only Black moved toward him on the run.

Justin reached up and Black lowered his head. Justin rubbed him behind the ear. Softly he said, "Good boy, Black. I've missed you. You glad to see me?"

Then Pal nosed in, wanting to be petted, too. Cropper didn't bother. Justin wondered if Cropper's eyesight was fading.

The sun had moved well toward the west. Long shadows from the rolling hills reached across the plains. "Want to take me home, boy?" Justin asked Black.

Black lowered his head and pawed with one foot as he shook his mane. Justin led him to a large rock. From the rock, Justin straddled Black's back, without a saddle. Black walked him home.

Grandpa's house stood on a hill surrounded by plains, near the rolling hills. Over many years, trees standing close by the house had grown tall and strong. The house, more than a hundred years old, was made of logs. The sun and rain had turned the logs on the outside an iron gray. Flecks of green showed in some of the logs.

Expanding the Literature   Does Grandpa's ranch sound like a pleasant place to be? How does the author's description help you know that? (Accept reasonable responses: The description of the meadow grass, the flowers, the rolling hills, and the log house makes the ranch sound pretty and peaceful.)   CRITICAL: AUTHOR'S CRAFT/APPRECIATING LANGUAGE

GRAMMAR CONNECTION
REVIEWING SINGULAR POSSESSIVE NOUNS   Point out the apostrophes in the words *Cropper's, Black's,* and *Grandpa's* on page 191. Remind students that the apostrophes followed by *s* stand for ownership by one person or thing—*Cropper's* eyesight, *Black's* back, and *Grandpa's* house.

When Justin went inside, Grandpa had already changed his clothes. Now he busily measured food for the animals. While Grandpa was away, a neighbor had come to feed the pigs and chickens. The horses took care of themselves, eating and drinking in the meadow. Today the horses would have some oats, too.

"Let's feed the animals first," Grandpa said. "Then we'll cook those fish for dinner. You can clean them when we get back."

Justin sighed deeply. How could he tell Grandpa he didn't know how to clean fish? He was sure to make a mess of it. Worriedly, he helped Grandpa load the truck with the food and water for the chickens and pigs. They put in oats for the horses, too. Then they drove to the chicken yard.

As they rode along the dusty road, Justin remembered Grandpa telling him that long, long ago they had raised hundreds of cattle on Q-T Ranch. Then when Justin's mama was a little girl, they had raised only chickens on the ranch, selling many eggs to people in the cities. Now Grandpa had only a few chickens, three pigs, and three horses.

At the chicken yard, chickens rushed around to get the bright yellow corn that Justin threw to them. They fell over each other, fluttering and clucking. While Justin fed them, Grandpa gathered the eggs.

The pigs lazily dozed in their pens. They had been wallowing in the mud pond nearby. Now cakes of dried mud dotted their bodies. The floor where they slept had mud on it, too. Many flies buzzed around. *My room surely doesn't look like this*, Justin thought.

The pigs ran to the trough when Grandpa came with the pail of grain mixed with water. They grunted and snorted. The smallest one squealed with delight. *He's cute*, Justin thought.

By the time they had fed the horses oats and returned home, it was dark and cooler. Justin was glad it was so late. Maybe now Grandpa would clean the fish so that they could eat sooner. He was hungry.

Grandpa had not changed the plan. He gave Justin

Strategic Reading

MODELING A STRATEGY: PAGES 188–193 What was your purpose for reading these pages?

THINK ALOUD You may wish to provide a think-aloud model: *I wanted to learn more about Justin. He seems to feel excited and happy about being back on the ranch. I can tell this from the way he runs to see the horses.*
RETURNING TO THE PURPOSE

SET PURPOSE/PREDICT: PAGES 194–203 Invite students to predict whether Justin cleans the fish and what he learns from this experience. Encourage them to read through page 203 to confirm their predictions.

PAGES 194–195   JUSTIN AND THE BEST BISCUITS IN THE WORLD

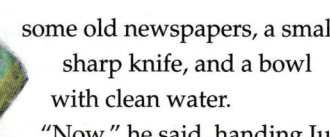

some old newspapers, a small sharp knife, and a bowl with clean water.

"Now," he said, handing Justin the pail that held the fish, "you can clean these."

Justin looked at the slimy fish in the water. How could he tell his grandpa that he didn't want to touch those fish? He still didn't want Grandpa to know that he had never cleaned fish before. Evelyn's words crowded him: *Can't do anything right.* He dropped his shoulders and sighed. "Do I have to, Grandpa?"

"We have to eat, don't we?"

"But—but I don't know how," Justin cried.

"Oh, it's not hard. I'll show you." Grandpa placed a fish on the newspaper. "Be careful now and keep it on this paper. When you're all done, just fold the paper and all the mess is inside."

Justin watched Grandpa scrape the fish upward from the tail toward the head. Little shiny scales came off easily. Then he cut the fish's belly upward from a little vent hole and scraped all the stuff inside onto the paper. "Now see how easy that is. You try," Grandpa said. "Be very careful with the knife." He watched Justin to see if he knew what to do.

Justin scraped the tiny scales off confidently. Then he hesitated. Screwing up his face, he shuddered as he cut, then pulled the insides out. Finally he got the knack of it.

Grandpa, satisfied that Justin would do fine, went into the kitchen to make a fire in the big stove.

194

Second-Language Support   Students may not understand the meanings of the expression *screwing up his face* and the word *shuddered*. To explain the meanings, have a volunteer act them out. Tell students that people sometimes make these kinds of facial expressions and body movements when something makes them feel uncomfortable.

MEETING INDIVIDUAL NEEDS

Expanding the Literature   **Why doesn't Justin want to clean the fish at first?** (He doesn't know how, and he doesn't really want to touch them.) **Why do you think Justin cleans the fish anyway?** (He probably wants to show his grandpa and himself that he *can* do things right.)
INFERENTIAL: DRAWING CONCLUSIONS

T320 / A PLACE TO DREAM, UNIT 2

JUSTIN AND THE BEST BISCUITS IN THE WORLD PAGES 196–197

Later that evening, Justin felt proud when Grandpa let him put the fish on the table.

After dinner, they sat in the living room near the huge fireplace. Great-Great-Grandma Ward had used that same fireplace to cook her family's meals.

Justin looked at the fireplace, trying to imagine how it must have been then. *How did people cook without a stove?* He knew Grandpa's stove was nothing like his mama's. Once that big iron stove got hot there was no way to turn it off or to low or to simmer. You just set the pots in a cooler place on the back of Grandpa's stove.

"Grandpa, how did your grandma cook bread in this fireplace?" he asked.

"Cooking bread in this fireplace was easy for my grandma. She once had to bake her bread on a hoe."

"But a hoe is for making a garden, Grandpa."

"Yes, I know, and it was that kind of hoe that she used. She chopped cotton with her hoe down in Tennessee. There was no fireplace in the family's little one-room house, so she cooked with a fire outside. She had no nice iron pots and skillets like I have now in the kitchen.

"At night when the family came in from the cotton fields, Grandma made a simple bread with cornmeal and a little flour. She patted it and dusted it with more flour. Then she put it on the iron hoe and stuck it in the ashes. When it was nice and brown the ashes brushed off easily."

"How did they ever get from Tennessee to Missouri?"

"Justin, I've told you that so many times."

"I know, Grandpa. But I like to hear it. Tell me again."

"As a boy, my grandpa was a slave. Right after slavery my grandpa worked on a ranch in Tennessee. He rode wild mustangs and tamed them to become good riding horses. He cared so much about horses, he became a cowboy.

"He got married and had a family. Still he left home for many weeks, sometimes months, driving thousands of cattle over long trails. Then he heard about the government giving away land in the West through the Homestead Act. You only had to build a house and live in it to keep the land."

"So my great-great-grandpa built this house." Justin stretched out on the floor. He looked around at the walls that were now dark brown from many years of smoke from the fireplace.

"Just the room we're in now," Grandpa said.

Vocabulary Strategy Ask students to identify the context clues that helped them figure out the meaning of the word *simmer* on page 196. (Justin is explaining that when Grandpa's stove gets hot, there is no way to turn it off or turn it down. So *simmer* must describe cooking at a temperature lower than *hot*. Since *low* is also mentioned, *simmer* probably means "to cook at a very low temperature.") **STRATEGY: CONTEXT CLUES**

PAGES 198–199 JUSTIN AND THE BEST BISCUITS IN THE WORLD

"I guess every generation of Wards has added something. Now, my daddy, Phillip, added on the kitchen and the room right next to this one that is the dining room.

"I built the bathroom and the rooms upstairs. Once we had a high loft. I guess you'd call it an attic. I made that into those rooms upstairs. So you see, over the years this house has grown and grown. Maybe when you're a man, you'll bring your family here," Grandpa said.

"I don't know. Maybe. But I'd have to have an electric kitchen."

"As I had to have a bathroom with a shower. Guess that's progress," Grandpa said, and laughed.

"Go on, Grandpa. Tell me what it was like when Great-Great-Grandpa first came to Missouri."

"I think it's time for us to go to bed."

"It's not that late," Justin protested.

"For me it is. We'll have to get up early. I'll have to ride fence tomorrow. You know, in winter Q-T Ranch becomes a feeder ranch for other people's cattle. In spring, summer, and early fall cattle roam and graze in the high country. In winter when the heavy frosts come and it's bitter cold, they return to the plains. Many of those cattle feed at Q-T.

198

I have to have my fences mended before fall so the cattle can't get out."

"Can I ride fence with you?" Justin asked.

"Sure you can. Maybe you'll like riding fence. That's a man's work." Grandpa laughed.

Justin remembered that conversation in his room about women's work, and the tears. He burned with shame. He didn't laugh.

Upstairs, Grandpa gave Justin sheets and a blanket for his bed. "It'll be cool before morning," he told Justin. "You'll need this blanket. Can you make your bed?"

Justin frowned. He hated making his bed. But he looked at Grandpa and said, "I'm no baby." Justin joined Grandpa in laughter.

Grandpa went to his room. When he was all ready for bed, he came and found Justin still struggling to make his bed. Those sheets had to be made nice and smooth to impress Grandpa, Justin thought, but it wasn't easy.

Grandpa watched. "Want to see how a man makes a bed?" Grandpa asked.

Justin didn't answer. Grandpa waited. Finally, Justin, giving up, said, "Well, all right."

Expanding the Literature What is the main idea of the first two paragraphs on page 198? (Accept reasonable responses: Different people made changes to the house.)
INFERENTIAL: DETERMINING MAIN IDEA

See page T343 for information found on Project Card 26B.

"Let's do it together," Grandpa said. "You on the other side."

Grandpa helped him smooth the bottom sheet and tuck it under the mattress at the head and foot of the bed. Then he put on the top sheet and blanket and smoothed them carefully.

"Now, let's tuck those under the mattress only at the foot of the bed," he said.

"That's really neat, Grandpa," Justin said, impressed.

"That's not it, yet. We want it to stay neat, don't we? Now watch." Grandpa carefully folded the covers in equal triangles and tucked them so that they made a neat corner at the end of the mattress. "Now do your side exactly the way I did mine."

Soon Justin was in bed. When Grandpa tucked him in, he asked, "How does it feel?"

Justin flexed his toes and ankles. "Nice. Snug."

"Like a bug in a rug?"

Justin laughed. Then Grandpa said, "That's how a man makes a bed."

Still laughing, Justin asked, "Who taught *you* how to make a bed? Your grandpa?"

"No. My grandma." Grandpa grinned and winked at Justin. "Good night."

Justin lay listening to the winds whispering in the trees. Out of his window in the darkness he saw lightning bugs flashing, heard crickets chirping. But before the first hoot of an owl, he was fast asleep.

THE SUN BEAMED down and sweat rolled off Justin as he rode on with Grandpa, looking for broken wires in the fence. They were well away from the house, on the far side of the ranch. Flies buzzed around the horses and now gnats swarmed in clouds just above their heads. The prairie resounded with songs of the bluebirds, the bobwhite quails, and the mockingbirds mimicking them all. The cardinal's song, as lovely as any, included a whistle.

Justin thought of Anthony and how Anthony whistled for Pepper, his dog.

It was well past noon and Justin was hungry. Soon they came upon a small, well-built shed, securely locked. Nearby was a small stream. Grandpa reined in his horse. When he and Justin dismounted, they hitched the horses, and unsaddled them.

Vocabulary Strategy Ask students to identify the base word and the suffixes of the word *carefully*, which appears in the fifth paragraph on page 200. (*care* + *-ful* + *-ly*) Then ask them how they can figure out the meaning of *carefully*. (*-ful* often means "full of"; *-ly* often means "in a way that is"; so *carefully* must mean "done with great care." Context clues such as *neat corner* and *exactly* also help readers figure out the meaning of *carefully*.) **STRATEGY: STRUCTURAL ANALYSIS/CONTEXT CLUES**

PAGES 202–203 JUSTIN AND THE BEST BISCUITS IN THE WORLD

"We'll have our lunch here," Grandpa said. Justin was surprised when Grandpa took black iron pots, other cooking utensils, and a table from the shed. Justin helped him remove some iron rods that Grandpa carefully placed over a shallow pit. These would hold the pots. Now Justin understood why Grandpa had brought uncooked food. They were going to cook outside.

First they collected twigs and cow dung. Grandpa called it cowchips. "These," Grandpa said, holding up a dried brown pad, "make the best fuel. Gather them up."

There were plenty of chips left from the cattle that had fed there in winter. Soon they had a hot fire.

Justin watched as Grandpa carefully washed his hands and then began to cook their lunch.

"When I was a boy about your age, I used to go with my father on short runs with cattle. "We'd bring them down from the high country onto the plains."

"Did you stay out all night?"

"Sometimes. And that was the time I liked most. The cook often made for supper what I am going to make for lunch."

Grandpa put raisins into a pot with a little water and placed them over the fire. Justin was surprised when Grandpa put flour in a separate pan. He used his fist to make a hole right in the middle of the flour. In that hole he placed some shortening. Then he added water. With his long delicate fingers he mixed the flour, water, and shortening until he had a nice round mound of dough.

Soon smooth circles of biscuits sat in an iron skillet with a lid on top. Grandpa put the skillet on the fire with some of the red-hot chips scattered over the lid.

Justin was amazed. How could only those ingredients make good bread? But he said nothing as Grandpa put the chunks of smoked pork in a skillet and started them cooking. Soon the smell was so delicious, Justin could hardly wait.

Finally Grandpa suggested that Justin take the horses to drink at the stream. "Keep your eyes open and don't step on any snakes."

Justin knew that diamondback rattlers sometimes lurked around. They were dangerous. He must be careful. He watered Black first.

While watering Pal, he heard rustling in the grass. His heart pounded. He heard the noise again. He wanted to run, but was too afraid. He looked around carefully. There were two black eyes staring at him. He tried to pull Pal away from the water, but Pal refused to stop drinking. Then Justin saw the animal. It had a long tail like a rat's. But it was as big as a cat. Then he saw something crawling on its back. They were little babies, hanging on as the animal ran.

A mama opossum and her babies, he thought, and was no longer afraid.

202

Strategic Reading

MODELING A STRATEGY: PAGES 194–203 Based on what you've read so far, what do you think the author is trying to tell readers?

THINK ALOUD You may wish to model with this think-aloud: *Grandpa has taught Justin to do two things that Justin was afraid he would not be able to do: clean fish and make a bed. I think the author is telling readers that with kind, patient help, people can become more and more sure of themselves.* SYNTHESIZING

SET PURPOSE/PREDICT: PAGES 204–211 Invite students to predict whether Justin will stop feeling ashamed about the time he cried in front of his grandpa. Have them read the rest of the story to confirm their predictions.

T324 / A PLACE TO DREAM, UNIT 2

JUSTIN AND THE BEST BISCUITS IN THE WORLD PAGES 204–205

By the time the horses were watered, lunch was ready. *"M-mm-m,"* Justin said as he reached for a plate. The biscuits were golden brown, yet fluffy inside. And the sizzling pork was now crisp. Never had he eaten stewed raisins before.

"Grandpa, I didn't know you could cook like this," Justin said when he had tasted the food. "I didn't know men could cook so good."

"Why, Justin, some of the best cooks in the world are men."

Justin remembered the egg on the floor and his rice burning. The look he gave Grandpa revealed his doubts.

"It's true," Grandpa said. "All the cooks on the cattle trail were men. In hotels and restaurants they call them chefs."

"How did you make these biscuits?"

"That's a secret. One day I'll let you make some."

"Were you a cowboy, Grandpa?"

"I'm still a cowboy."

"No, you're not."

"Yes, I am. I work with cattle, so I'm a cowboy."

"You know what I mean. The kind who rides bulls, broncobusters. That kind of cowboy."

"No, I'm not that kind. But I know some."

"Are they famous?"

"No, but I did meet a real famous Black cowboy once. When I was eight years old, my grandpa took me to meet his friend Bill Pickett. Bill Pickett was an old man then. He had a ranch in Oklahoma."

"Were there lots of Black cowboys?"

"Yes. Lots of them. They were hard workers, too. They busted broncos, branded calves, and drove cattle. My grandpa tamed wild mustangs."

"Bet they were famous."

"Oh, no. Some were. Bill Pickett created the sport of bulldogging. You'll see that at the rodeo. One cowboy named Williams taught Rough Rider Teddy Roosevelt how to break horses; and another one named Clay taught Will Rogers, the comedian, the art of roping." Grandpa offered Justin the last biscuit.

205

Social Studies Connection A number of students may not fully understand the following expressions: *broncos, branded calves, drove cattle, break horses,* and *bulldogging.* Explain that *broncos* are wild horses, and *calves* are young cows or bulls. They are *branded*, or marked, with a hot iron to show to whom they belong. To *drive cattle* is to make cattle move along. To *bulldog* is to make a steer fall by grabbing it by the horns and twisting its neck.

See page T342 for information found on Project Card 26A.

Project Card 26A

PAGES 206–207 JUSTIN AND THE BEST BISCUITS IN THE WORLD

Jessie Stahl

Nate Love

When they had finished their lunch they led the horses away from the shed to graze. As they watched the horses, Grandpa went on, "Now, there were some more very famous Black cowboys. Jessie Stahl. They say he was the best rider of wild horses in the West."

"How could he be? Nobody ever heard about him. I didn't."

"Oh, there're lots of famous Blacks you never hear or read about. You ever hear about Deadwood Dick?"

Justin laughed. "No."

"There's another one. His real name was Nate Love. He could outride, outshoot anyone. In Deadwood City in the Dakota Territory, he roped, tied, saddled, mounted, and rode a wild horse faster than anyone. Then in the shooting match, he hit the bull's-eye every time. The people named him Deadwood Dick right on the spot. Enough about cowboys, now. While the horses graze, let's clean up here and get back to our men's work."

Justin felt that Grandpa was still teasing him, the way he had in Justin's room when he had placed his hand on Justin's shoulder. There was still the sense of shame whenever the outburst about

---

Cultural Awareness You may want to tell students that the western part of the United States is not the only place where cowboys are found. Explain that there are also cowboys in Mexico, called *vaqueros,* and in South America, called *gauchos.* Point out that cowhands in the United States were sometimes called *cowpokes* or *cowpunchers.*

women's work and the tears were remembered.

As they cleaned the utensils and dishes, Justin asked, "Grandpa, you think housework is women's work?"

"Do you?" Grandpa asked quickly.

"I asked you first, Grandpa."

"I guess asking you that before I answer is unfair. No, I don't. Do you?"

"Well, it seems easier for them," Justin said as he splashed water all over, glad he was outside.

"Easier than for me?"

"Well, not for you, I guess, but for me, yeah."

"Could it be because you don't know how?"

"You mean like making the bed and folding the clothes."

"Yes." Grandpa stopped and looked at Justin. "Making the bed is easy now, isn't it? All work is that way. It doesn't matter who does the work, man or woman, when it needs to be done. What matters is that we try to learn how to do it the best we can in the most enjoyable way."

"I don't think I'll ever like housework," Justin said, drying a big iron pot.

"It's like any other kind of work. The better you do it, the easier it becomes, and we seem not to mind doing things that are easy."

With the cooking rods and all the utensils put away, they locked the shed and went for their horses.

"Now, I'm going to let you do the cinches again. You'll like that."

There's that teasing again, Justin thought. "Yeah. That's a man's work," he said, and mounted Black.

"There are some good horsewomen. You'll see them at the rodeo." Grandpa mounted Pal. They went on their way, riding along silently, scanning the fence.

Finally Justin said, "I was just kidding, Grandpa." Then without planning to, he said, "I bet you don't like boys who cry like babies."

Informal Assessment

STRUCTURAL ANALYSIS To assess whether students need instruction in structural analysis, ask them to identify the base word and the prefix in the word *unfair*, which appears in the fourth paragraph on page 208. *(fair; un-)* Then ask what the prefix *un-* often means. ("not") Based on this meaning, have students figure out the meaning of the word *unfair*. ("not fair")

A review lesson on **structural analysis** appears on page T340.

PAGES 210–211 JUSTIN AND THE BEST BISCUITS IN THE WORLD

"Do I know any boys who cry like babies?"

"Aw, Grandpa, you saw me crying."

"Oh, I didn't think you were crying like a baby. In your room, you mean? We all cry sometime."

"You? Cry, Grandpa?"

"Sure."

They rode on, with Grandpa marking his map. Justin remained quiet, wondering what could make a man like Grandpa cry.

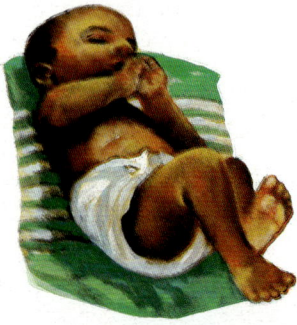

As if knowing Justin's thoughts, Grandpa said, "I remember crying when you were born."

"Why? Didn't you want me?"

"Oh, yes. You were the most beautiful baby. But, you see, your grandma, Beth, had just died. When I held you I was flooded with joy. Then I thought, *Grandma will never see this beautiful boy.* I cried."

The horses wading through the grass made the only sound in the silence. Then Grandpa said, "There's an old saying, son. 'The brave hide their fears, but share their tears.' Tears bathe the soul."

Justin looked at his grandpa. Their eyes caught. A warmth spread over Justin and he lowered his eyes. He wished he could tell his grandpa all he felt, how much he loved him.

210

Justin's grandfather told him that the better you do something, the easier it is to do it. Tell why you agree or disagree.

By the end of the story, how do you think Justin feels about household chores? Explain your answer.

Do you think Justin will be able to go home and make a batch of biscuits? Why or why not?

WRITE Does any character in this story remind you of someone you know? Write a paragraph comparing the character and the person who is like the character.

Strategic Reading

MODELING A STRATEGY: PAGES 204–211 Have students compare their predictions with the events described on these pages.

THINK ALOUD Provide a think-aloud model if necessary: *I predicted that Justin would stop feeling ashamed about the time he cried—and he did. But I didn't know that Grandpa would tell Justin that he cried sometimes, too. This was what really helped Justin feel better.* **CONFIRMING PREDICTIONS**

Returning to the Predictions/Purpose

STORY IMPRESSIONS Have students review the story they wrote based on words and phrases from the selection. Ask them to compare their story with what really happened in "Justin and the Best Biscuits in the World."

NOTE: Responses to the questions and support for the Write activity appear on page T330.

Story Impressions
- Grandpa's house
- Justin would do fine
- how to clean fish
- how much he loved him

Story
(Justin felt a little homesick when he was staying at Grandpa's house. But Grandpa knew Justin would do fine after a while. Grandpa taught Justin how to clean fish. When Justin lay in bed that night, he thought about all the things he had learned from his grandpa. He also thought about how much he loved him.)

T328 / A PLACE TO DREAM, UNIT 2

Words about the Author: Mildred Pitts Walter

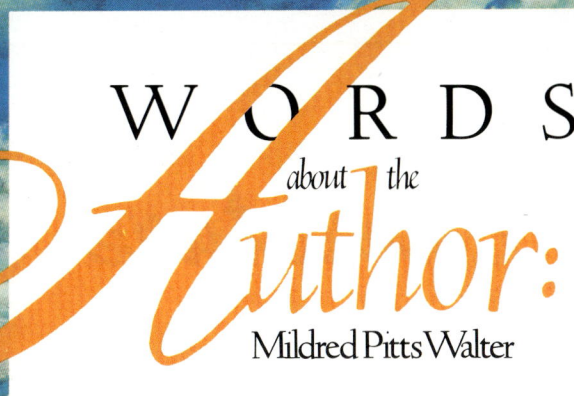

AWARD-WINNING AUTHOR

Mildred Pitts Walter was born in Louisiana, the youngest of seven children. Her father was a log cutter, and the family lived in two small houses owned by the lumber company. They used one house for sleeping and the other for daytime activities such as cooking and washing. The yards of the two houses were used as a community meeting place. On Saturday nights, the neighbors gathered there for food, games, singing, storytelling, and dancing.

Young Mildred was eager for school to start each fall so she could read the school's library books. She spent the summers of her school years working to earn money for college. She was graduated from Southern University in Scotlandville, Louisiana.

After graduation, Mildred taught kindergarten and elementary grades. She also helped organize a program called Head Start. This program prepares young children for school so that they will do well once they start.

Ms. Walter wanted better books for the students in her classes. Someone suggested that she write the books herself, so she did!

Mildred Walter writes about what she knows well—family life, problems at school, and the struggles of black people. Her years spent as a teacher help her write about the characters in her stories. She tries to understand her characters just as she tried to understand her students. She feels that an author needs to notice details that other people may miss.

As a child, Mildred was allowed to make choices, and learned to live with the results. Now she uses this idea in her stories. The characters in her books often face difficult choices, as Justin did in "Spending Time with Grandpa." When her characters use courage to make a choice, they are able to make changes in their lives.

Words About the Author

AUTHOR'S CRAFT Invite students to read pages 212–213 to find out why Mildred Pitts Walter began to write books for young people. When they have finished reading, ask volunteers to explain why in their own words. (Accept reasonable responses: Mildred Pitts Walter always loved to read. When she became a teacher and wanted to find good books for her students, she decided to write them herself.) Discuss with students whether reading about the author helps them think about "Justin and the Best Biscuits in the World" differently.

PART 2

Responding to the Literature

Personal Response

Encourage critical thinking.

Justin's grandfather told him that the better you do something, the easier it is to do it. Tell why you agree or disagree. (Responses will vary.) CRITICAL: EXPRESSING PERSONAL OPINIONS

By the end of the story, how do you think Justin feels about household chores? Explain your answer. (Accept reasonable responses: He feels more sure of his own ability to do household chores. He still admits, though, that he'll probably never like housework.) INFERENTIAL: DETERMINING CHARACTERS' EMOTIONS

Encourage creative written responses.

 **WRITE** Does any character in this story remind you of someone you know? Write a paragraph comparing the character and the person who is like the character. Encourage students to compare the character's and the real person's ages, the things they say and do, their relationships with others, and how they seem to feel about things. CREATIVE: WRITING A PARAGRAPH

Cooperative Response

Have reader response groups extend their discussions.

COLLABORATIVE RESPONSE Suggest that group members share their reactions to the story. Then have them hold a discussion based on a question such as this:

Do any ideas or events in this story remind you of your own life or something that happened to you? Explain your answer.

STRATEGY CONFERENCE

Ask students how using the story impressions strategy helped them understand, remember, and appreciate the story. (Accept reasonable responses: This strategy makes readers pay close attention to story events.)

NOTE

An additional writing activity for this selection appears on page T333.

T330 / A PLACE TO DREAM, UNIT 2

Summarizing the Literature

Have students retell the story and write a summary.

Have students imagine they are Justin and summarize the story by recalling its important events. Help students begin the journal entry below and have them finish it independently. See *Practice Book* page 60 below.

Justin's Journal

These are things that happened during my visit with Grandpa.

Grandpa taught me (how to clean fish) .
Grandpa taught me _____ .
Grandpa taught me _____ .
Grandpa told me _____ .
At the end of my visit, I felt _____
because _____ .

This is what I learned about "women's work": _____

This is what I learned about "men's work": _____

Critical Thinking Activity

Imagine Justin in his grandfather's role.

VISUALIZE THE FUTURE Imagine that Justin is now a grandfather. He is living on the ranch and his grandson visits. How might the ranch be different? What skills might Justin teach his grandson? What problems might Justin's grandson have? Have students form groups to discuss their ideas and record them on webs to share with their classmates. CREATIVE: INVENTING NEW SCENES

- Justin is a grandfather.
  - adds a video room to ranch
  - teaches grandson to cook
  - grandson afraid of horses

Writer's Journal

Practice Book

Portfolio

STUDENT SELF-ASSESSMENT

Ask students to tell how well they think they understood Justin's problem in the story and the way it was solved. Encourage them to answer orally first. Then have them write a paragraph explaining the problem and solution. Suggest that they add their paragraph to their portfolios.

OPTIONAL INDEPENDENT PRACTICE

WRITER'S JOURNAL
page 35: Writing a personal response

PRACTICE BOOK
page 60: Summarizing the selection

JUSTIN AND THE BEST BISCUITS IN THE WORLD / T331

VOCABULARY WORKSHOP

Reviewing Key Words

Display the following groups of words. Then read the descriptions below, one at a time. Ask students to match each description to the appropriate word group by pointing to the letter or by holding up an index card with the letter printed on it.

A. bulldogging
   busting broncos
   roping

B. bluebirds
   quails
   cardinals

C. grass
   roses
   black-eyed Susans

D. very flat
   no hills
   wide open

E. cooks outdoors
   makes a bed
   shares feelings

F. pots
   stove
   iron rods

G. newspaper
   knife
   water

1. the *plains* where Grandpa's ranch is ____(D)____
2. what Grandpa and Justin see growing on the *prairie* ____(C)____
3. things Grandpa might use at the same time he uses *skillets* ____(F)____
4. what the mockingbirds are *mimicking* ____(B)____
5. things Justin uses when he has to *scrape* fish ____(G)____
6. what Justin might see if he went to a *rodeo* ____(A)____
7. things Grandpa does that *impress* Justin ____(E)____

Extending the Vocabulary

INFLECTED ENDINGS Write on the board the words *worked, branded,* and *lived.* Remind students that the story "Justin and the Best Biscuits in the World" tells about some things that cowboys did. For example, they *worked* hard; they *branded* cattle; they often *lived* on ranches. Point out that the ending *-ed* can be added to an action word to mean that something happened in the past. Encourage students to think of more words with *-ed* endings that they could use to write a story about things a cowboy might have done. Have them use an organizer such as the following:

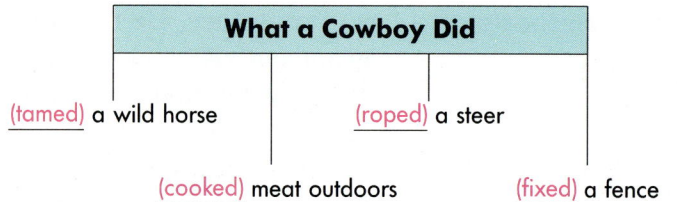

Have students suggest other verbs with *-ed* endings that would fit under each action listed. They can be words from the story or any other words students think of. Add their suggestions where appropriate.

Also encourage students to write sentences or phrases with *-ed* words that tell about things they did this past month.

T332 / A PLACE TO DREAM, UNIT 2

Language Arts WORKSHOP

READING

Oral Rereading/Drama

Have pairs of students reread the dialogue between Justin and Grandpa on pages 196–198, beginning with Justin's question, "Grandpa, how did your grandma cook bread in this fireplace?" and ending with Grandpa's statement, "Maybe when you're a man, you'll bring your family here." Or tell students to select another passage they would like to reread. Suggest that students begin by rereading the passage silently. Give them an opportunity to rehearse before they present their readings. **LISTENING/READING**

WRITING

Writing About the Literature

Available on Project Card 25A

 **WRITE A STORY ENDING** Have students reread the introduction on page 188 of the Student Anthology. Ask them to imagine what will happen when Justin goes home. Suggest that students think of a situation where Justin can show off what he has learned, surprising his family. Before students begin writing, they might work in groups to create a chart such as the one below. **LISTENING/SPEAKING/WRITING**

Situation	What Evelyn and Hadiya Expect	What Will Really Happen
The family buys some fresh fish that needs to be cleaned.	They will have to clean the slimy fish without help because Justin is "no good at women's work."	The girls will fail at cleaning the fish. Justin will say, "Allow me!" and do an expert job of cleaning the fish.

GRAMMAR REVIEW: SINGULAR POSSESSIVE NOUNS
As students revise their story endings, remind them to be sure to include an apostrophe and an *s* at the end of each singular noun that shows ownership. To reinforce this skill, on strips of paper write phrases like *the hat that belongs to Dad* and *the book that belongs to Sue*. Give the strips to pairs of students and have them revise each phrase so that it includes a singular possessive noun.
(*Dad's hat; Sue's book*)

 **LANGUAGE HANDBOOK** Writing to Entertain and Express, pages 36–39; Singular Possessive Nouns, pages 104–105.

 **DAILY LANGUAGE PRACTICE** Oral language exercises are provided on pages R68–R69.

JUSTIN AND THE BEST BISCUITS IN THE WORLD / T333

Language Arts WORKSHOP

WRITING

Creating a New Scene

Remind students that the introduction to "Justin and the Best Biscuits in the World" explains what happens in the book before the excerpt begins. Have students work together to use the information in the introduction and their imagination to write a scene in which Justin's sisters tease him. Then have students compare their version with the information in the actual book.
READING/WRITING

LISTENING AND SPEAKING

What's in a Name?

COOPERATIVE LEARNING Remind students that Grandpa's horses are named Cropper, Black Lightning, and Pal. Have students form three groups. Assign each group one of the horses, and have the group make up a story about how the horse got its name. A Reporter from each group should then tell its story to the other groups. Finally, have students combine their stories into one and record it on an audiocassette. A class Facilitator can direct this process.   LISTENING/SPEAKING

LISTENING AND SPEAKING

Scary Times

Remind students that Justin thinks he hears a snake in the grass, but it turns out to be a family of opossums. Encourage students to tell about situations they have experienced in which something that seemed scary turned out to be harmless.   LISTENING/SPEAKING

SPELLING

Reviewing Spelling Words

SPELLING WORDS: cook, cool, foot, good, moon, noon, pool, roof, shoe, soup, wood, zoo

WORDS TO EXPLORE: cattle, mustang, prairie, rodeo

Have students work independently to create drawings based on two or more of the Spelling Words. For instance, they might draw a *cook* preparing a pot of *good soup*. Below their drawing they should write an incomplete caption with blanks for the Spelling Words: "The _____ is preparing a pot of _____ _____." Have students exchange drawings with a partner and use the Spelling Words to complete their partner's caption. Then they should exchange papers with different partners who will check their spelling and make sure the completed caption makes sense with the drawing it describes.   READING/SPELLING

Use *Integrated Spelling* Lesson 10 to reinforce the Spelling Words and the Words to Explore. See pages T69–T74 in *Integrated Spelling Teacher's Edition*.

SPELLING POSTTEST   You may want to use the Pretest/Posttest Sentences on page T69 of *Integrated Spelling Teacher's Edition* to assess students' knowledge of the spelling generalization.

T334 / A PLACE TO DREAM, UNIT 2

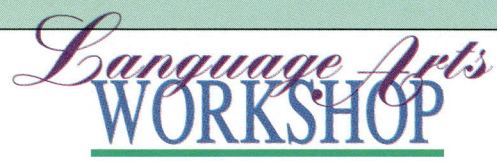

WRITING

Stories from the Past

Remind students that Justin's grandfather tells stories about his past, his family history, and the famous Black, or African American, cowboys of long ago. Have students interview an older family member or relative to find out about a colorful story or event which that person recalls. Encourage students to write an account of the story. Before students begin, develop a list like the following to help them consider possible topics to discuss.

Things to Ask About
1. a historic event
2. an important journey
3. an important event in our family history
4. heroes—both famous ones and "everyday" ones

Suggest that each student begin the interview by telling a little about the story, especially Grandpa's description of his family history and the African American cowboys he knew.   LISTENING/SPEAKING/WRITING

LISTENING AND SPEAKING

A Building like No Other

Available on Project Card 25B

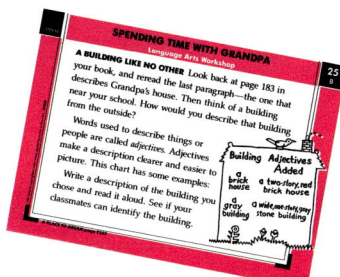

Have students reread the paragraph at the end of page 191 that describes Grandpa's house from the outside ("Grandpa's house stood on a hill. . . .") Then have them each choose a building that is near the school and write a description of how it looks from the outside. Before students begin, remind them that words used to describe people or things are called *adjectives*. Use the following examples to demonstrate how adding adjectives to a description makes it more specific and easier to picture.

Building	More Adjectives Added
• a big house	• a two-story, red brick house
• a gray building	• a wide, one-story, gray stone building

Have each student read aloud his or her description as classmates listen and try to identify the building being described.   LISTENING/SPEAKING/READING/WRITING

WRITING

Tasty Recipes

Remind students that Grandpa made "the best biscuits in the world" for Justin the day they were riding fences together. Encourage students to list tasty dishes that various members of their families are "famous" for. Have them choose their favorite dish and interview the family member who cooks it. Students might ask for the recipe and then ask specific questions to make sure they understand the cooking process. Students can report their findings to classmates in oral reports, or they may write a simple version of their family member's recipe to bind into a book and distribute to classmates.   LISTENING/SPEAKING/WRITING

Grammar MINI LESSON

Plural Possessive Nouns

OBJECTIVES: *To recognize that a plural possessive noun shows ownership by more than one person or thing; to recognize that the possessive form of a plural noun that ends in s is formed by adding an apostrophe (') to the end*

Oral Warm-Up

Display the following sentences from "Justin and the Best Biscuits in the World."

- There was no fireplace in the <u>family's</u> little one-room house, so she cooked with a fire outside.
- The <u>cardinal's</u> song, as lovely as any, included a whistle.

Read aloud the sentences. Ask students these questions: *Is the little one-room house owned by one or more than one family? Does the song belong to one cardinal or more than one?* Write students' responses on the board in a diagram similar to the following:

Interactive Teaching

PLURAL POSSESSIVE NOUNS Point to the word *family's*. Ask students what the plural form of the word *family* is. Write *families* on the board. Ask students to imagine that many families owned the little one-room house. Write this phrase on the board: *the families' little one-room house*. Circle the *s'* in *families'*, and explain that to make plural nouns that end in *s* show ownership, an apostrophe is added to the end of the word.

Have a volunteer make the word *cardinal's* in the second sentence into a plural possessive noun (*cardinals'*) and rewrite the sentence on the board. Then write the following words on the board: *cowboy__ ranch, sister__ horses,* and *horse__ range*. Ask volunteers to fill in the blanks to make the nouns plural and then add an apostrophe to make each one show ownership.

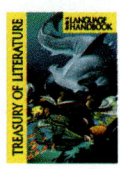 **LANGUAGE HANDBOOK** *Plural Possessive Nouns, page 106*

Practice Activities

Nouns' Display

Have students work in pairs to locate and cut out from old magazines six photographs showing groups of people, animals, or things found on a ranch or farm. Next, have partners paste the photographs on a piece of paper and work together to write sentences that describe the items in each one. Provide examples such as these: *The cowboys' hats are tall. The horses' tails are long and black.* Have partners exchange their sentences with another pair and check each other's use of possessive plural nouns. Have students collect their work in a bulletin board display.   VISUAL/KINESTHETIC

Possessive Collectives

Display and read aloud the following "animal collective" phrases:

team of horses
herd of cows
swarm of bees
litter of pigs

colony of ants
clutch of chicks
pack of wolves

Ask students if they are familiar with any of these phrases. Explain that the first word in each phrase is a name for an animal group. Have each student draw a picture of one animal group. Next, have each student write a sentence describing the animals in the picture. Students should use the plural possessive form of the animal name to tell something about the group. Model this process by writing the following examples on the board: *The chicks' feathers are white; The pigs' feet are muddy.* Ask volunteers to share their pictures and sentences.   VISUAL/KINESTHETIC

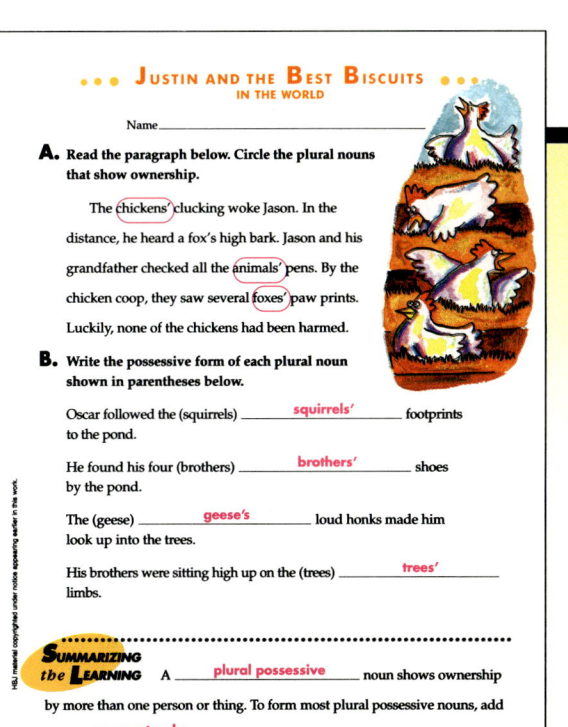

Practice Book

MEETING INDIVIDUAL NEEDS

- **SECOND-LANGUAGE SUPPORT** Write sentences such as these on the board: *The boy's shoes were dirty. The dog's bark is loud.* Model changing the first noun in each sentence from the singular possessive form to the plural possessive form. Have students repeat the procedure.

- **RETEACH** Follow the visual, auditory, and kinesthetic/motor models on page R25.

OPTIONAL INDEPENDENT PRACTICE

- **PRACTICE BOOK**
  page 61: Writing plural possessive nouns

- **GRAMMAR PRACTICE**
  pages 28–29: Using plural possessive nouns

JUSTIN AND THE BEST BISCUITS IN THE WORLD / T337

PART 3

Learning through the Literature

LITERARY APPRECIATION
INTRODUCE

Figurative Language

OBJECTIVE: *To appreciate idioms, similes, and metaphors as they contribute to meaning*

Interactive Teaching

Use the literature to discuss lively expressions.

LITERATURE CONNECTION Write on the board the sentence *Justin's heart was in his mouth.* Ask students what it means. (that Justin was afraid) Point out that authors often use special expressions to make their writing livelier and that figuring out their meanings will help students understand what they read.

Teach/Model

Teach and model using figurative language.

EXPLAIN FIGURATIVE LANGUAGE Tell students that expressions such as *his heart was in his mouth* are called *figurative language* and do not mean exactly what the words say. Explain that sometimes authors use figurative language to make comparisons. Display Chart/Transparency 21 or the following sentences, and have students read them aloud.

Chart/Transparency 21 Figurative Language

1. Justin gave Grandpa a hand by cleaning the fish.
2. The horse's coat was as smooth as silk.
3. Grandpa was an encyclopedia of knowledge about cowboys.

MODEL INTERPRETING FIGURATIVE LANGUAGE Explain what the first sentence means by using a think-aloud. Then discuss idioms, similes, and metaphors.

> **I don't think that the expression in sentence 1 means that Justin actually gave his hand to Grandpa. Using the context, I can tell that it means "helped Grandpa."**

(1) An idiom is an expression that has a meaning different from the words it uses. (2) A simile is a comparison of unlike things, using the word *like* or *as*. (3) A metaphor is another kind of comparison. It states that one thing *is* another thing.

ADDITIONAL BOOKS FOR APPLYING FIGURATIVE LANGUAGE

The Cowboy and the Blackeyed Pea by Tony Johnston. G. P. Putnam's Sons, 1992.
AVERAGE

Pecos Bill by Steven Kellogg. William Morrow, 1986.
AVERAGE

T338 / A PLACE TO DREAM, UNIT 2

Practice Activity

Simile or Metaphor?

Have students identify similes and metaphors. Have students determine what types of figurative language appear in the second and third sentences on the Chart/Transparency. (Sentence 2—simile; Sentence 3—metaphor) Then have them scan fantasy, fairy tale, and folktale books to collect as many similes and metaphors as they can. VISUAL

Performance Assessment

Have students share the similes and metaphors they located in the Simile or Metaphor? activity. Ask volunteers whether they agree with the examples and whether they can visualize what is being described. For evaluation guidelines, see *Staff Development Guide*.

Reader ↔ Writer Connection
Figurative Language

WRITERS make stories and poems more lively and imaginative by including figurative language.

READERS need to understand figurative language to determine events and appreciate characters' actions.

WRITE A PARAGRAPH Have students use figurative language to write a description of a person.

Writer's Journal

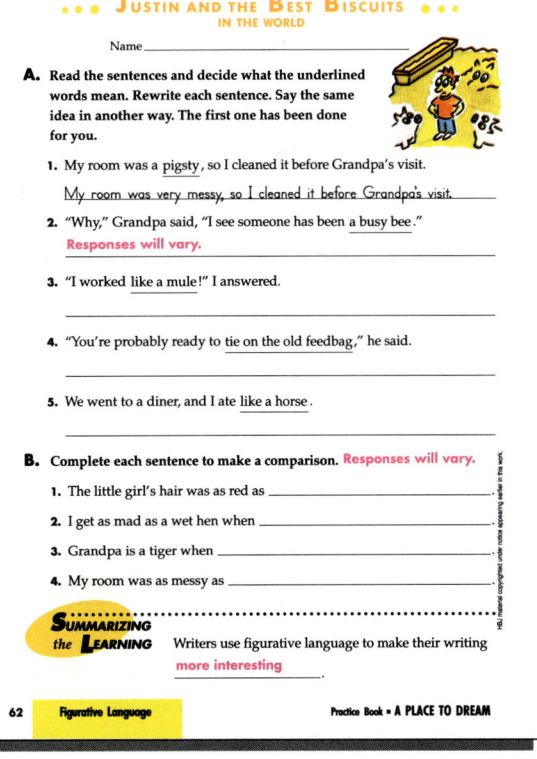

Practice Book

MEETING INDIVIDUAL NEEDS

RETEACH Follow the visual, auditory, and kinesthetic models on page R26.

CHALLENGE Ask students to write a paragraph about an event in the story, using figurative language. Challenge them to include one simile, one metaphor, and one idiom.

SECOND-LANGUAGE SUPPORT Display several illustrations and write captions containing an idiom, simile, or metaphor for each. Call on students to match each caption with its illustration. See also the manual *Alternative Teaching Strategies*, pages 12, 70–73.

OPTIONAL INDEPENDENT PRACTICE

WRITER'S JOURNAL
page 36: Using figurative language

PRACTICE BOOK
page 62: Understanding figurative language

JUSTIN AND THE BEST BISCUITS IN THE WORLD / **T339**

DECODING

REVIEW

Structural Analysis

OBJECTIVE: *To decode unfamiliar words*

Review

Have students identify affixes.

REVIEW PREFIXES AND SUFFIXES Remind students that a prefix or suffix added to a base word changes the word's meaning, and a suffix added to a base word changes the way the word is used.

Display the following sentences: "I was calm when I saw the snake. I calmly walked away from it." "He will tell a joke. He will retell the joke." Have students read the sentences aloud, circle the affixes in the underlined words, and tell how the meanings and usage of the words change when affixes are added.

Practice Activity

Affix Analysis

Have students use words with affixes.

Ask students to use each of the following words in a sentence: *write, rewrite, cook, precook, exact, exactly, thought, thoughtful.* Have students read aloud their sentences and explain how the meaning and usage of each word changed. AUDITORY

MEETING INDIVIDUAL NEEDS

CHALLENGE Ask students to identify words in the story to which they can add the prefix *pre-* or *re-* or the suffix *-ful* or *-ly*. Have them explain the meaning of each new word that they create. Suggest that students refer to a dictionary to be sure the words they create are actual words.

OPTIONAL INDEPENDENT PRACTICE

PRACTICE BOOK
page 63: Understanding prefixes, suffixes, and base words

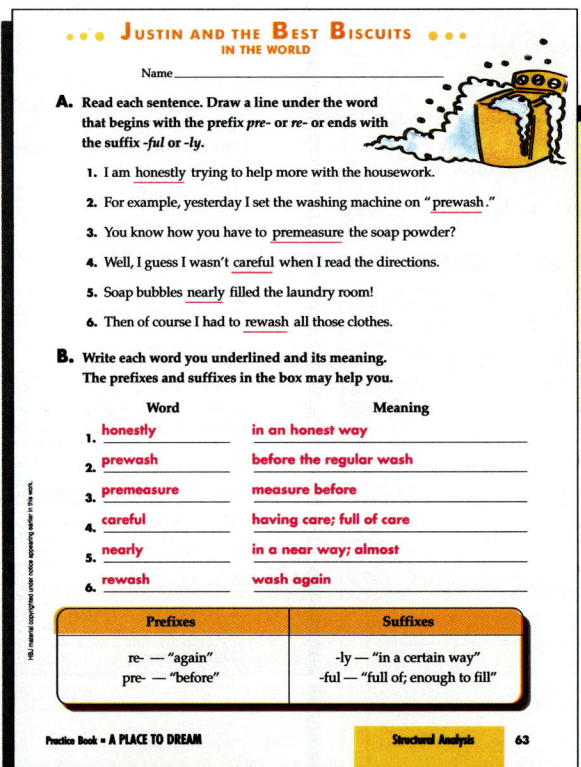

Practice Book

COMPREHENSION REVIEW

Main Idea and Details

OBJECTIVE: *To identify a main idea and its supporting details*

Review

Help students identify main idea and supporting details.

REVIEW IDENTIFYING THE MAIN IDEA Remind students that often they may need to figure out the main idea of a passage. Ask them to identify the details and main idea for the second complete paragraph on page 193. Use their suggestions to complete a chart such as the one below.

Supporting Details	Main Idea
• pigs wallowing in mud • flies buzzed around	The pigpens were very dirty.

Practice Activity

Round Up the Main Idea

Have students find the main idea and details.

Have students reread the passage on pages 204–207 in which Grandpa describes the African American cowboys of long ago. Ask students to write the main idea and three supporting details. Have volunteers share their work.

MEETING INDIVIDUAL NEEDS

CHALLENGE Ask students to state the main idea of "Justin and the Best Biscuits in the World" in one sentence and to point out three supporting details.

OPTIONAL INDEPENDENT PRACTICE

PRACTICE BOOK

page 64: Identifying main idea and details

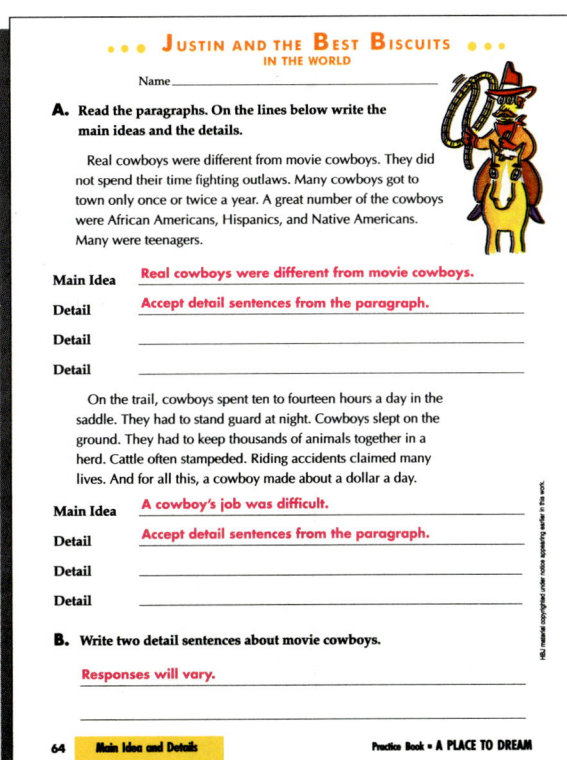

Practice Book

JUSTIN AND THE BEST BISCUITS IN THE WORLD / **T341**

Integrated CURRICULUM

MUSIC

Git Along, Little Dogies

Available on Project Card 26A

Read or sing to students the following lyrics from the old cowboy song "Git Along, Little Dogies." Have students listen for cowboy-related terms and add them to a chart similar to the one below. Then have students add other categories and words related to ranching and cowhands to the chart.

As I was a-walking one morning for pleasure,
I spied a cow-puncher a-riding along;
His hat was thrown back and his spurs were
   a-jinglin',
As he approached me a-singin' this song:

> Whoopee ti yi yo, git along, little dogies,
> It's your misfortune and none of my own;
> Whoopee ti yi yo, git along, little dogies,
> For you know Wyoming will be your new home.

Words of the Wild West			
people	animals	verbs	yells
cow-puncher (cowhand)	dogies (cows)	a-walking a-riding a-jinglin'	whoopee ti yi yo

Have students write their own Wild West poems or songs, using the words on the chart. LISTENING/SPEAKING/WRITING

SOCIAL STUDIES

Ranches and Rodeos

COOPERATIVE LEARNING Have interested students learn more about the cowboys, cowgirls, rodeos, and ranches of today. You might suggest the following books:

- *Round-Up* and *Rodeo* by Cheryl Walsh Bellville
- *Rodeo, America's Number One Sport* by Thomas A. Bryant

Suggest that students work in small groups to prepare oral reports, written reports, or displays about modern-day ranch life or rodeos. Encourage each group to appoint a Facilitator and Materials Manager as well as Reporter(s) to present the group's work.
LISTENING/SPEAKING/READING/WRITING

SCIENCE

Wilderness Survival

COOPERATIVE LEARNING Remind students that Grandpa knows a lot about the natural world and probably would be able to survive for a long time in the wilderness. Have students, working in groups of three, discuss how they might be able to survive if they were lost or stranded in the wilderness. Have each member of the group consider where they would sleep, what they would eat, and how they would know where to go. Guide students in combining their information to create a survival guide for wilderness travelers. Have a Reporter from each group share its guide. LISTENING/SPEAKING/WRITING

MATH

Compute Food Amounts

Recall with students that Justin helps Grandpa feed the three horses. Suggest that one day soon Grandpa might ask Justin to take care of the horses by himself and Justin will have to know how much to feed them. Students might enjoy figuring out the following problems. **LISTENING/SPEAKING**

- **Suppose each horse is to get 10 quarts of oats that day. How many quarts in all will Justin need to feed the 3 horses?** *(30 quarts)*
- **Each horse will drink about 12 gallons of water in a day. Luckily for Justin, the horses can find water on their own! But if Justin had to take 12 gallons of water to each of the 3 horses, how many gallons of water would that be in all?** *(36 gallons)*

SOCIAL STUDIES

Home, Sweet Home

Available on Project Card 26B

CULTURAL AWARENESS Remind students that Grandpa lives in a log cabin that has been expanded over time. Then guide students in using encyclopedias or books to research other types of interesting, unusual houses from different parts of the world and different times in history. These might include igloos, tepees, high-rises, hogans, houseboats, sod houses, and cliff dwellings. Have each student choose one kind of house and draw a labeled diagram of it. Encourage students to write one or two sentences describing their diagram and the people who live in the house. Create a bulletin board display of the various types of dwellings. **READING/WRITING/VIEWING**

ART

Scenes of the West

If possible, share with students pictures of some of the famous paintings and sculptures of cowboys and life in the West done by Charles M. Russell and Frederic Remington. Then ask students to imagine Grandpa in his younger days, on one of the nights he would camp out with his father. He might be tending their horses or having supper with other cowboys. Have students draw the scene they visualize. Then ask them to write a brief poem to go with the scene. Display students' work.
WRITING/VIEWING

BOOKS TO SHARE
SCIENCE *Everyday Things and How They Work* by Steve Parker. Random House, 1991. **AVERAGE**
SOCIAL STUDIES *Yonder* by Tony Johnston. Puffin, 1991. **AVERAGE**

JUSTIN AND THE BEST BISCUITS IN THE WORLD / T343

MULTICULTURAL PERSPECTIVES

Mexico's Vaqueros

DISCUSSION STARTER *What do we know from stories and songs about the first cowhands on the American frontier?*

READ ALOUD The legend of the cowboy is slowly changing as historians uncover new information about the American frontier. All North American cowhands, both men and women, owe much to the Mexican vaqueros [vä·kā′rōs] of the 1800s. The *vaqueros* rounded up wild cattle from the grasslands of Texas, at the time a territory of Mexico. They roped these longhorns from horseback—a dangerous business.

The *vaqueros* wore boots and spurs and wide-brimmed hats to block the sun. Later, North American cowhands would use similar clothing and equipment, with slight name changes. Their word *lariat* came from the Spanish *la reata* [lä rā·ä′tə], or rope. Their *chaps* were really *chaparejos* [chä·pə·rā′hōs], or leather leggings worn over regular pants.

ACTIVITY CORNER

• Point out that cowhands were of African and European, as well as Mexican, descent. Ask students to imagine what might happen at a cattle round-up if cowhands of various backgrounds could not work cooperatively. Have two groups of students prepare and present brief skits. One skit may show what might happen if cowhands didn't cooperate. The other may show cowhands working with mutual respect to get a job done.

• Have groups of students research the cattle drive, from the ranches in Texas to destinations such as Cheyenne, Dodge City, and Topeka. The Cowboy Museum in Oklahoma may be a good resource for information. Based on their findings, have students create maps to show the various routes of the cattle drives.

Three generations of Mexican American cowboys

POEM

Versos sencillos
(Simple Verses)

José Martí

ABOUT THE POET José Martí was a Cuban patriot, author, and lawyer who devoted his life to Cuba's struggle for independence from Spain. He wrote essays, plays, and novels as well as poetry.

ABOUT THE POEM "Versos sencillos" ("Simple Verses") is part of a long poem of the same name. These verses express Martí's belief that true friendship is more important than even life's most basic necessities or its grandest riches.

Reading the Poem

Help students set a purpose for reading.

Discuss with students how Grandpa helps Justin feel better in "Justin and the Best Biscuits in the World." Remind students that friends can be family members, neighbors, classmates, and others with whom people have things in common. Invite volunteers to share their views about friendship. Tell students you are going to read aloud a poem about friendship called "Versos sencillos" [ver'sôs sen·sē'yōs]. Have students listen for the poet's message about friendship. Then have students reread the poem silently. Invite a Spanish-speaking student to read aloud the Spanish version.

Responding to the Poem

Return to the purpose for reading.

Ask students to explain what they think the poet's views about friendship are. (Accept reasonable responses: Friendship is more important than shelter and riches.) Encourage volunteers to read aloud lines that illustrate the poet's feelings.

Encourage students to respond creatively.

You may want to select one of the following activities:

MORE "SIMPLE VERSES" Have students work in pairs to write a new poem about friendship. Have partners brainstorm things they could compare friendship with to show its value. Then have them choose one and write a four-line stanza using the original poem as a model. Have pairs rewrite their stanzas on butcher paper, add illustrations, and display them. LISTENING/SPEAKING/WRITING

FRIENDSHIP MURAL Have students make a friendship mural on butcher paper. Tell students to draw pictures that show how they feel about friendship. Suggest that students draw pictures of themselves and friends doing things they like to do together. They may also want to add captions to the mural. Write the title "I Have a Friend" on the mural and display it. WRITING

MEETING INDIVIDUAL NEEDS

SECOND-LANGUAGE SUPPORT Explain to students that *shelter* means "protection, as from danger or exposure to the weather." Encourage any Spanish-speaking students to read the verses aloud so that others can hear the sounds of the poet's language.

VERSOS SENCILLOS (SIMPLE VERSES) / T345

PAGE 214   VERSOS SENCILLOS (SIMPLE VERSES)

Versos sencillos
by José Martí
illustrated by Edward Martinez

*Tiene el leopardo un abrigo
en su monte seco y pardo:
Y yo tengo más que el leopardo
porque tengo un buen amigo.*

*Tiene el señor presidente
un jardín con una fuente,
y un tesoro en oro y trigo:
tengo más, tengo un amigo.*

Simple Verses
(English version by María Elena Calderón)

The leopard has shelter
In the mountain dry and brown:
I have more than the leopard—
I have a good friend.

The president
Has a garden with a fountain,
And a treasure of wheat and gold:
I have more, I have a friend.

Expanding the Poem   In the first stanza of the poem, the poet describes a leopard's shelter. In the second stanza, he describes the president's "garden with a fountain, / And a treasure of wheat and gold." What do you think these things stand for in the poem? (Accept reasonable responses: The leopard's shelter stands for a basic necessity of life. The president's garden and gold stand for beauty, wealth, and power, while wheat stands for food, also a necessity of life.)   CRITICAL: APPRECIATING IMAGERY

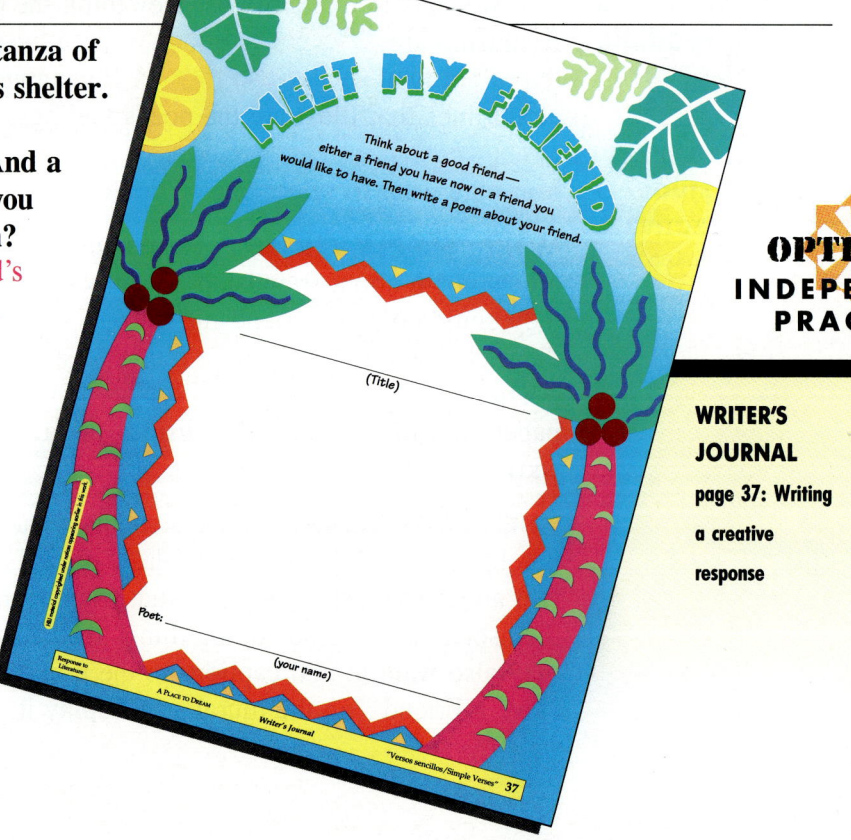

OPTIONAL INDEPENDENT PRACTICE

WRITER'S JOURNAL
page 37: Writing a creative response

T346 / A PLACE TO DREAM, UNIT 2

THEME WRAP-UP

Discussing the Theme

Remind students that the selections in this theme showed how people learn from others and learn about themselves.

Discussion Question

PAGE 215 The title of the theme you have just read is "Learning About Yourself." Think about Justin, and think about the poem. What did you learn about yourself from reading these selections? (Responses will vary.) CRITICAL: IDENTIFYING WITH CHARACTERS

Theme Wrap-Up

Learning About Yourself

The title of the theme you have just read is "Learning About Yourself." Think about Justin, and think about the poem. What did you learn about yourself from reading these selections?

WRITER'S WORKSHOP

In "Justin and the Best Biscuits in the World," you read about real-life cowboys. Choose one of the cowboys mentioned. Write a friendly letter to him, asking questions about what his life is like.

Writer's Choice: Write one or two paragraphs about something you have learned with the help of a friend. Or write about things you think older people can teach you. Organize your ideas, write, and then share your writing.

215

Writer's Workshop

See pages T348–T349 for suggestions for guiding students through the writing process as they respond to the literature. WRITING PROCESS: FRIENDLY LETTER

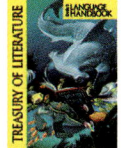

Writer's Choice

You may want to have students refer to the *Language Handbook* for help as they write. Suggest that students organize their paragraphs by writing a main idea statement followed by details that tell more about the main idea.

When students are ready to publish their work, you may wish to arrange a time for students to share with partners or small groups.

Writer's Workshop

Friendly Letter

Theme Wrap-Up

Students choose a cowboy to write to from "Justin and the Best Biscuits in the World" and ask questions about his life.

To prepare students for the writing task and form, ask them how Justin in "Justin and the Best Biscuits in the World" might keep in touch with Grandpa after he returns to the city. Discuss with them the kinds of questions Justin might ask in a letter to gather more information from Grandpa about his ancestors.

Use the Writer's Workshop assignment on page 215 as you work through the writing process with students.

ALTERNATIVE TOPICS If you wish, allow students to choose their own topics for writing. Suggest that they refer to the *Language Handbook* for an explanation of the writing process for friendly letters. See Writing Model, page R97.

LANGUAGE HANDBOOK *Everyday Writing, pages 66–67; Friendly Letter, page 70*

Prewriting

Discuss the five basic parts of a friendly letter shown below. Then have students meet in small groups to discuss the cowboy each of them has selected and to brainstorm a list of two or more questions to ask.

- Heading
- Greeting
- Body
- Closing
- Signature

Drafting

Have students write a draft of their friendly letter. As they do so, remind them to include this necessary information.

- The heading should contain their address and the date.
- The greeting should begin with the word *Dear* and end with a comma.
- The body of the letter should be clear, friendly, and interesting to the person receiving it.
- The closing should use words such as *Your Friend* or *Sincerely* and is followed by a comma.
- Their first and last names should make up the signature.

COMPUTER TIP

DRAFTING Students may want to keyboard and then save their friendly letter to use it again as the basic shell for future letters. Students will need only to substitute a new date, greeting, and body each time.

Responding and Revising

Before students read their friendly letters to a partner, suggest that they read their drafts and ask themselves these questions:

- Does the letter contain all five parts of a friendly letter?
- Does the letter sound friendly and polite?

Then have students read their work aloud in a peer conference and respond to the following questions:

Listener	Writer
Does the letter give enough information for a reader to understand what the writer wants to know? Are the questions clear? Is the letter friendly and polite?	When you read your letter aloud, does it sound clear? Will the person who receives it understand what you would like to know? If some parts of the letter seem weaker than others, think of ways you can make them stronger.

T348 / A PLACE TO DREAM, UNIT 2

Proofreading

Offer these tips for students to use as they proofread:

- Check that the appearance of the letter is neat.
- Check that commas are used correctly in the address, date, greeting, and closing of the letter.
- Correct any misspelled words.

MINI-CONFERENCE STRATEGY If some students have forgotten to use commas in the heading, greeting, or closing, make observations such as this: "In the date, you have written *January 81995*. Is this what you mean, or do you need a comma to separate the day from the year?"

Publishing Options

BINDER BOOKS Have students put their letters in a binder. At a later date, students may want to use the questions in the letters to find topics for paragraphs of information or research reports.

ORAL READING Have students or a classroom guest who has knowledge of western life read the letters and discuss possible answers.

Assessment Options

STUDENT SELF-ASSESSMENT Encourage students to summarize the writing experience by responding to this question in their journals:

- **What words did I use in my letter to make it sound friendly and polite?**

You may also wish to have students complete the Self-Assessment Checklist in the *Portfolio Assessment Teacher's Guide*.

WRITING OBSERVATION RECORDS Record instances in which students evaluate and use the reactions of others to improve their letters.

You may want to have students make copies of their letters to add to their portfolios.

GRAMMAR CONNECTION

Proofreading: Apostrophes in Possessive Nouns

Using the examples on Transparency F, focus attention on correct use of the apostrophe in possessive nouns. Point out that the apostrophe tells the reader whether the noun is singular or plural.

> **Transparency F**
> **"Gallop" Poll**
>
> **BEFORE**
> I would like to know what the building where the horses were kept was like. My <u>horses</u> home is a large heated shed. How did you keep your <u>horses</u> barn warm in winter? Where did you keep the <u>animals</u> food so that it would not freeze?
>
> **AFTER**
> I would like to know what the building where the horses were kept was like. My <u>horse's</u> home is a large heated shed. How did you keep your <u>horses'</u> barn warm in winter? Where did you keep the <u>animals'</u> food so that it would not freeze?

Have small groups of students share their writing to check that apostrophes are used correctly in possessive nouns.

LANGUAGE HANDBOOK *Possessive Nouns, pages 102–106*

WRITER'S WORKSHOP / T349

UNIT 2

CONNECTIONS

The Connections activities on Student Anthology pages 216–217 guide students to link multicultural and content-area information to the unit theme. Invite students to tell which selections in the unit were their favorites and to suggest why they think each was included in a unit entitled "Friendships."

To prepare students for the Multicultural Connection, write *Antonia Novello* on the board and pronounce the name for students. Explain that until recently she held a very important position in the United States. Ask students if they have ever heard her name or know what she did.

Explain that Antonia Novello is from Puerto Rico, an island about 1,000 miles to the southeast of Florida. Ask a volunteer to locate Puerto Rico on a map. Then have students share what they know about the island. You may wish to begin a web to record students' responses. The web can be used for the Social Studies Connection.

CONNECTIONS

Multicultural Connection

Friends Are People Who Care

When Antonia Novello was a child in Puerto Rico, she had a health problem. Every summer, she spent time in the hospital. She came to think of her kind doctors as friends.

Antonia decided to be a doctor herself. Her parents encouraged her through years of hard study. She became a doctor and began running health care programs that helped millions of people.

Dr. Novello then became the surgeon general of the United States. Like the doctors who were her childhood friends, she cared for others through her work.

Write a paragraph about a person who helps others. Publish your work in a class book titled "A Friend Is Someone Who Cares."

Dr. Antonia Novello

Puerto Rico

Social Studies Connection

Special People—Special Places

Antonia Novello came from Puerto Rico. With your classmates, find out some interesting facts about this island. Use the facts to make a collage of pictures and words that tell about this special place.

Health Connection

Staying Healthy

Think about how Antonia Novello helped people stay healthy. Then make a poster that shows some tips for staying healthy. Share your poster with your classmates.

Multicultural Connection

FRIENDS ARE PEOPLE WHO CARE Have students brainstorm a list of people who help others and ask each student to write a paragraph about one of the people. Encourage students to draw a picture of that person. Then help them compile their paragraphs and drawings into a book about helpful people.

Social Studies Connection

SPECIAL PEOPLE—SPECIAL PLACES Provide students with books and magazines containing photographs and facts about Puerto Rico. You may also wish to show a filmstrip or travel video about the island. Have students add the facts they learn to their webs.

Health Connection

STAYING HEALTHY Have students form small groups to discuss how Antonia Novello might answer the question, "What can young people do to help themselves stay healthy?" Then provide students with poster board, markers, and crayons. You may wish to refer students to their health textbooks for ideas. After students tell about their posters, display them on a bulletin board.

UNIT 2 WRAP-UP

Language Arts REVIEW

Reviewing Vocabulary

- Write the following letter grid on the board and explain to students that it contains ten Key Words from Unit 2:

```
a f s c r a p e
c p r a i r i e
u r l i x y z c
r o i a n x y h
a d x n i g z o
a e y z k n e r
c o x y z l s u
y g i g g l e s
s h i v e r e d
```

- Have students form teams. Explain that each team will gain one point when they find and circle a word in the grid. Point out that the words can be found in the following positions: down, across, and diagonal. Tell students that they may win two extra points by using the word in a sentence. When all the words have been found, the team with the most points wins.

Reviewing Grammar

Assign players to two teams and explain that they are going to go on a "noun hunt" through a selection of their choice in Unit 2. Have the members of each team list and identify all the types of nouns they found in the selection. Points are awarded as follows:

Singular Nouns	1 point
Regular Plural Nouns	2 points
Irregular Plural Nouns	3 points
Singular Possessive Nouns	4 points
Plural Possessive Nouns	5 points

The team that accumulates the most points wins.

Reviewing Spelling Words

Integrated Spelling pages 50–51 provide a Unit review of the spelling words. *Integrated Spelling* pages 52–53 provide practice with frequently misspelled words in writing and vocabulary activities.

Writing a Story

- You may wish to have students respond to the unit focus by writing a story to add to the magazines in their *Writer's Journals*. Provide them with copies of different kinds of stories to use as examples. See *Writer's Journal* pages 38–39.

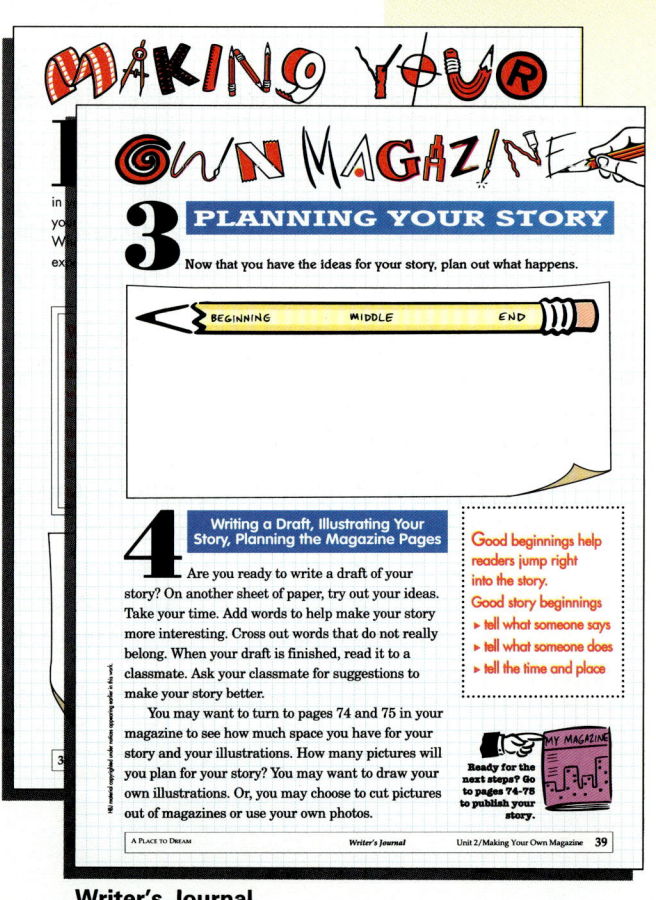

WRITER'S JOURNAL
pages 38–39: Making Your Own Magazine

Writer's Journal

T352 / A PLACE TO DREAM, UNIT 2

UNIT 2 WRAP-UP

Assessment Options

Informal Assessment

See the following suggestions to informally assess students' progress in Unit 2.

INFORMAL ASSESSMENT NOTES AND CHECKLISTS If you used the informal assessment notes in the lesson plans to evaluate students' reading and writing behaviors, you may now want to add to your Running Records. You may also wish to have students complete the Self-Assessment Checklist in the *Portfolio Assessment Teacher's Guide*.

PORTFOLIO CONFERENCE A portfolio conference provides you with an opportunity to learn about each student's

- interest in reading realistic fiction.
- general writing development.
- awareness of main idea and details.

Discuss the realistic fiction stories that were read in Unit 2, focusing on whether the students enjoyed them. Ask students to identify similar stories they have read. Discuss the student's feelings about reading realistic fiction.

Ask the student to select a favorite piece of writing from the portfolio. Perhaps the student may want to share the advertisement book report written in response to "Ramona Quimby, Age 8" or the letter written from Justin's point of view after "Justin and the Best Biscuits in the World." Ask the student to share what he or she liked about the piece. Provide positive feedback and encouragement.

Formal Assessment

The following formal assessment tools are available to meet your assessment needs.

UNIT READING SKILLS ASSESSMENT
The *Unit Reading Skills Assessment* for Unit 2 provides feedback about students' proficiency at the specific skills and strategies taught in Learning Through the Literature. Skills tested in this unit are Structural Analysis, Main Idea and Details, and Following Directions. If students had difficulty, refer to pages R19, R13, and R7 for visual, auditory, and kinesthetic/motor models that can be used to reteach the tested skills.

UNIT HOLISTIC READING ASSESSMENT The *Unit Holistic Reading Assessment* for Unit 2 may be used to assess a student's understanding of passages written at the same level as the selections in the Student Anthology. If students have difficulty, use the Reteach Lesson for Active Reading Strategies. Use the modeling suggestions from the *Teacher's Edition* to assist students as they read the selections in Unit 3.

UNIT INTEGRATED PERFORMANCE ASSESSMENT
The *Unit Integrated Performance Assessment* for Unit 2 gives you a profile of how well each student uses reading, writing, listening, and speaking strategies to read and respond to a piece of literature. Assessment results show how well students employ the strategies modeled and practiced in the classroom.

UNIT LANGUAGE AND WRITING ASSESSMENT
The *Unit Language and Writing Assessment* for Unit 2 includes a Skills Inventory to assess students' knowledge of nouns and a Writing Test, which contains a writing prompt, evaluation rubrics, and scoring guidelines for a how-to paragraph. Corresponding lessons and practice in the *Language Handbook* may be used with students who have difficulty on the assessment instrument.

Break Time!

WAYS TO SAY "YOU'RE TERRIFIC!"

For children and adults, the first step to feeling smart is feeling good—especially feeling good about themselves. What's also clear is that self-esteem doesn't come from a book, box, or kit, but grows out of the many different ways people interact daily. Here are some ideas to help sow the seeds of self-esteem in your classroom today.

1. Demonstrate unconditional acceptance: "I may not like what you just did, but that doesn't mean I don't like you. I do."
2. Express anger responsibly. Don't let your *feelings* be the message.
3. Really listen. Take seriously a student's fears or negative feelings.
4. Allow students opportunities to do things for themselves.
5. Respect and value students' opinions and choices.
6. Help students accept themselves.
7. Help each student celebrate her or his strengths.
8. When students fail, help them recall earlier occasions of success.

While suggestions for building self-esteem are generally aimed at students, teachers can benefit as well by remembering these strategies:

- Acknowledge your own abilities and strengths. Ask, "What am *I* good at?"
- Don't be afraid to ask for what you need.
- Forgive yourself when you make mistakes.
- Remember to schedule activities that make you happy.

TEACHER TEAMS

Often we ask our students to work cooperatively to complete projects. From grade-level meetings to school action committees, teachers are also working cooperatively more than ever.

Here are a few tips to help make collaboration with colleagues a smooth and productive process:

Get to know your colleagues. Early in the process, take some time to get to know the people you're working with. Find out about what they believe and about what they can bring to the team's goal.

Make everyone an active member. Be sure that everyone has a chance to air opinions. Ask questions of the quiet ones to bring their ideas to light.

Resolve conflicts early. Every team is bound to have its conflicts, but be sure to get them out in the open and address them right away. Think of conflict resolution as a positive step in your team's progress.

PEANUTS cartoon by Charles M. Schulz. Reprinted by permission of UFS, Inc.

TEACHERS LEARNING FROM TEACHERS

Working behind closed doors is not only lonely but also bars you from opportunities for learning from colleagues. Some teachers have begun looking for ways to change this situation.

One strategy, mentoring, teams seasoned teachers with beginners. The result? New teachers feel more confident, and veterans get satisfaction from having their abilities recognized.

Of course, mentor programs are never trouble-free: newer teachers may feel vulnerable, and experienced teachers may feel awkward about their roles. *The Mentor Teacher Casebook*, a collection of personal reflections from veteran and novice teachers who have taken part in mentoring programs, offers a clear window on what this rewarding relationship can be like. For information, write: *The Mentor Teacher Casebook*, Far West Laboratory for Educational Research and Development, 730 Harrison Street, San Francisco, CA 94107.

UNIT 3

Adventures

THEME:
Picture This!
T362–T431

THEME:
Mysteries to Solve
T432–T471

THEME:
The Great Outdoors
T472–T509

UNIT 3 OPENER

Planning Center — ADVENTURES

What's Ahead in "Adventures"?

PICTURE THIS!: PAGES T362–T431 Invite your students to meet the characters in a legend and a play and join them in their unusual adventures. The selections are guaranteed to make readers smile.

MYSTERIES TO SOLVE: PAGES T432–T471 Can your students determine who stole the necklace before Piggins the butler does, and can they figure out the answer to a riddle? Challenge students to find the clues and solve the mysteries in the selections.

THE GREAT OUTDOORS: PAGES T472–T509 As your students go on an adventure outdoors with a father and his son and meet the people in the poems, they may find that some adventures sound very familiar to them.

Audiovisual Materials

All I See by Cynthia Rylant. Facets Multimedia, 1990. A shy boy and the artist who paints by the lake become friends. VIDEO

A Bear Called Paddington by Michael Bond. LETRFS, 1983. These three filmstrips include Paddington's Visit to the Theater. FILMSTRIP

Legend of the Indian Paintbrush by Tomie dePaola. Listening Library, 1988. DePaola's story is presented in one short filmstrip (48 frames) and one audiocassette (9 minutes). FILMSTRIP/AUDIOCASSETTE

Piggins and Picnic with Piggins by Jane Yolen. Caedmon, 1988. The butler-sleuth solves two mysteries. Narrated by Roddy McDowell. AUDIOCASSETTE

Runaway Ralph by Beverly Cleary. Warner Home Video, 1988. Live action and animation reconstruct the summer camp adventures of the motorcycling mouse. FILM/VIDEO

Three Days on a River in a Red Canoe by Vera Williams. Reading Rainbow (Great Plains National Instructional Television Library), 1982. LeVar Burton encounters fun and challenges on a camping trip with a group of youngsters. VIDEO

Harcourt Brace Literature Cassette

Recordings of some of the selections in "Adventures" may be used for instruction or for students' listening enjoyment:

- "Paddington Paints a Picture"
- "Piggins"

Daily Language Practice

Proofreading activities for daily use are available on pages R70–R75.

Family Involvement

The *Family Involvement Activities* offer a variety of options for extending each theme and expanding the unit focus. A Read-at-Home piece of literature is also provided for family members to read together.

Pacing

This unit is designed to take approximately five to six weeks to complete, depending on your students' needs.

Bulletin Board Idea

Invite students to help create a bulletin board display entitled "And then . . ." Provide students with index cards and have them write adventure-story starters that introduce a character, describe a setting, and hint at something that is about to happen. You may wish to give this example: *While exploring Grandpa's attic, Lisa found a dusty box with an old photograph inside. Suddenly it brought to mind the story of . . .* Post the story starters. Then have each student choose a story to complete. Encourage students to illustrate their stories and display their work.

Assessment and Evaluation Options

	READING	INTEGRATED LANGUAGE ARTS	LANGUAGE
Throughout the Unit  *Informal Assessment*	**INFORMAL ASSESSMENT NOTES** Record observations of students, using anecdotal records or behavioral checklists in a notebook or on forms provided in the *Portfolio Assessment Teacher's Guide*. Indicates opportunities for teachable moments throughout the lessons.	**READING/WRITING PORTFOLIO** Have students collect samples of reading and writing activities, including finished work, work-in-progress, and plans/ideas for future work; reading and writing logs; and self-assessment checklists. See the *Portfolio Assessment Teacher's Guide* for implementing a portfolio system.	**STUDENT SELF-ASSESSMENT NOTES** Encourage students to monitor and reflect about their writing so that they can begin to take responsibility for their own improvement. Notes at point of use in the lesson plans may be used to monitor growth.
	STUDENT SELF-ASSESSMENT NOTES Follow point-of-use suggestions in the lesson to have students monitor their own learning, attitudes, and interests.	**PORTFOLIO CONFERENCES** Schedule a conference with each student to learn about the student's reading and writing interests, habits, and attitudes and to help the student reflect about his or her reading and writing.	**WRITTEN RETELLINGS** A student's written retellings can help you analyze how well a student organizes ideas, develops ideas, and applies knowledge of conventions of writing. See the Retelling Analysis Summary form in the *Individual Inventory for Reading and Writing*.
	RUNNING RECORDS Gain insights into students' application of reading strategies by tracking oral reading errors, or miscues. See the *Individual Inventory for Reading and Writing* for administering and interpreting results.	**STUDENT LOGS AND JOURNALS** Encourage students to keep a collection of thoughts, ideas, and opinions to use for reflecting on their reading, writing, and learning.	
	ORAL RETELLINGS Retelling may be used as an alternative to questioning to assess students' comprehension of text: recall of major points and relevant/irrelevant details, what the reader adds to or infers from the text, insights into how the reader constructs meaning.		
End-of-Unit *Formal Assessment Tools*	**READING SKILLS TEST** Multiple-choice diagnostic tests, administered at end of unit, assess **lesson vocabulary, making predictions** and **context clues**.	**INTEGRATED PERFORMANCE ASSESSMENT** A structured reading-writing task that provides a natural holistic assessment of realistic literary activities. Administered at end of unit, this task will determine whether students can use reading to write and whether they can accomplish a specific writing task.	**LANGUAGE SKILLS AND WRITING TEST** Administer at end of unit to assess students' knowledge of **pronouns** and **adjectives** and their ability to write a **story** in response to a prompt.
	HOLISTIC READING TEST This test, administered at end of unit, includes theme-related passages accompanied by multiple-choice questions that focus on application of literal, inferential, and critical thinking, major comprehension objectives, and students' ability to construct meaning.		

PLANNING CENTER / T357

PAGES 218–219 Unit Opener

UNIT THREE 3
Adventures

Adventure and mystery may be as far away as Peru or as near as a picture you paint. As you read the selections in this unit, look for the different ways the authors and illustrators share adventure. What does Allen Say tell about an Asian American family's camping adventure? How does Paul Sierra use paint to create mystery? This unit will give you a chance to find out.

THEMES

Picture This! 222

Mysteries to Solve 272

The Great Outdoors 296

218

Introducing "Adventures"

Think of an adventure you've had, and describe it to students. Then invite them to share some of their adventures or unusual and exciting experiences. Have students read the unit introduction and theme titles to help them set a purpose for reading the unit.

Ask students to discuss the faraway places and the different countries they would like to visit. Encourage students to talk about any current or historical events they know of that may have taken place in any of the countries mentioned.
CULTURAL AWARENESS

Writer's Journal pages 40–42: Reading and writing about "Adventures"

T358 / A PLACE TO DREAM, UNIT 3

Unit Opener PAGES 220–221

BOOKSHELF

Picnic with Piggins
by Jane Yolen
The picnic with Piggins has been delightful until . . . CRASH! SPLASH! Rexy, one of the Reynard kits, disappears, leaving baffling clues. Only Piggins can decode the curious note and unravel the mystery.
Award-Winning Author
Harcourt Brace Library Book

Mush!
Across Alaska in the World's Longest Sled-Dog Race
by Patricia Seibert
This is the true story of the Iditarod Trail Sled-Dog Race. The book describes the history of the race and the challenges the racers and the dog teams face.
Notable Children's Trade Book in Social Studies
Harcourt Brace Library Book

Hail to Mail
by Samuel Yakovlevich Marshak
This poem salutes travel, adventure, and mail. Join a letter as it follows John Peck from New York City to the ends of the earth.
Parents' Choice Honor

On the Day You Were Born
by Debra Frasier
This book celebrates the relationship between the earth and its people. It's a song about the moon, the ocean, and all human life.
Parents' Choice Book
Notable Children's Trade Book in Social Studies

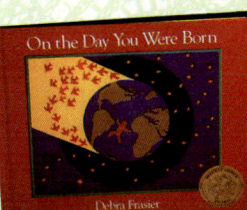

Blast Off to Earth!
by Loreen Leedy
This book takes you to a place where there are four oceans, seven continents, and countless mountains, deserts, and forests—our own planet.
Parents' Choice Honor

From the Harcourt Brace Library

In *Picnic with Piggins,* Jane Yolen and Jane Dyer team up once again to present Piggins with further adventures.

- Encourage students who enjoy "Piggins" to extend their reading with *Picnic with Piggins.* Students may want to perform their own British-style mystery in response.

Mush! chronicles the adventure and danger entailed in the Iditarod Trail Sled-Dog Race, held each year in Alaska.

- You may want to suggest that students read *Mush!* after reading "The Lost Lake." Have partners meet to compare the settings and the authors' purposes for writing.
- You might discuss nonfiction writing with students before reading aloud the first few pages of *Mush!* Have students set a purpose for reading the rest of *Mush!* independently.

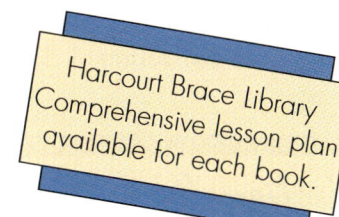

Harcourt Brace Library Comprehensive lesson plan available for each book.

Bookshelf selections *Hail to Mail, On the Day You Were Born,* and *Blast Off to Earth! A Look at Geography* are also available as Harcourt Brace PASSPORTS titles.

UNIT OPENER / T359

Listening to Literature

Read aloud to students.

The Case of the Earthenware Pig
by Donald J. Sobol

"The cops are after me!"

The words came out of a blur. Something that looked like Charlie Stewart in fast motion sped through the Brown Detective Agency and disappeared into the tool closet.

Encyclopedia glanced up and down the street.

"There isn't a policeman in sight," he announced. "You gave them the slip."

The news failed to cheer Charlie. Opening the closet door a crack, he moaned, "I'm a wanted man!"

"Wanted for what?" asked Encyclopedia.

"How should I know?" said Charlie. "Five minutes ago I was walking down Locust Street. I came to the outdoor telephone booth at the corner of Locust and Beech, and there stood Bugs Meany and Officer Carlson. Bugs pointed at me and hollered, 'Arrest that kid!' I got scared and ran."

Charlie tiptoed out of the tool closet.

"I think this has something to do with my tooth collection," he said.

Charlie's tooth collection was the pride of Idaville. No boy anywhere in the state had collected more interesting uppers and lowers than Charlie. He kept them in a flowered cookie jar.

"Bugs owns an earthenware teapot shaped like a pig," Charlie continued thoughtfully. "He wanted to trade it for my tooth collection. I don't drink tea. So I told him no soap."

"What could Bugs want with your tooth collection?" asked Encyclopedia.

"Bugs was going to string the teeth behind the Tiger clubhouse," answered Charlie. "If anybody tried to sneak upon the clubhouse from the rear, he'd trip over the string. The string would shake, and the teeth would start chattering and warn the Tigers."

"Wow, dental detectors!" exclaimed Encyclopedia. "Pretty neat. I have to hand it to Bugs—"

Encyclopedia's voice trailed off. A police car had pulled into the Brown driveway. Bugs Meany hopped out, followed by Officer Carlson.

"I told you we'd find the little thief here!" sang Bugs. "I always knew this detective business was just a cover for a den of crooks!"

Officer Carlson motioned Bugs to be quiet. Then he said to Charlie, "Why were you walking on Locust Street about five minutes ago?"

"I got a telephone call to come there," replied Charlie. "A boy's voice asked me to meet him at the telephone booth right away. He said he had two grizzly bear teeth to sell. He wouldn't give his name."

"Yah, yah, yah!" jeered Bugs. "You were on your way to buy grizzly bear teeth! So how come the second you saw Officer Carlson you made like a drum and beat it?"

"B-because y-you hollered for him to arrest me," Charlie said. "I got plain scared."

"Stop it, you two," said Officer Carlson. "Bugs says you stole an earthenware teapot shaped like a pig, Charlie. Did you?"

Selection Background

Charlie is accused of stealing an earthenware pig from Bugs Meany, the leader of the Tigers. But as Encyclopedia Brown listens to the story, it becomes clear that Charlie is innocent. When Encyclopedia points out the flaw in the story, Bugs admits he made it up.

Donald Sobol writes mysteries for children. His most famous character is Encyclopedia Brown. Encyclopedia is the boy Sobol dreamed about being when he was young. Sobol's books about Encyclopedia have won the Young Readers Choice Award and the Edgar Award.

Strategies for Listening

LISTENING/THINKING STRATEGY—NOTING DETAILS
Remind students that writers use details to tell about an idea, a person, a place, or a thing. Explain that listening for details will help them better understand the mystery.

SET A PURPOSE FOR LISTENING Remind students of the theme, "Adventures." Explain that this story is a mystery. Have students share other mysterious adventures they have read. Then suggest that they listen carefully to the details in this mystery so they may solve the case.

"I did not!" said Charlie. And looking hard at Bugs he added, "I don't like pigs!"

As Bugs turned a lovely shade of purple, Officer Carlson held up his hand. "Let's all go to Bugs's house and try to find out what really happened."

Walking toward the police car, Charlie slipped Encyclopedia twenty-five cents. "I'll need you," he whispered. "I've never been in trouble with the police before."

At his house, Bugs stopped in the entrance hall.

"My folks have gone for the day," he said. He pointed to the staircase on his left. "I'd just come home when Charlie raced down the stairs. He had my teapot pig under his arm. I chased him out the front door, but he got away."

"Why couldn't you catch him?" inquired Encyclopedia. "You're bigger, older, and faster."

"Why?" said Bugs. "I'll tell you why, Mr. Brains. I obey the law. There was a green light over at Locust Street, and I don't cross against the green. I'm no jaywalker!"

"He's lying like a tiger skin," muttered Charlie.

Officer Carlson said, "Let's say Charlie did cross against the light and got away. What did you do next, Bugs?"

"I went straight to the telephone booth on the corner and called the police station," said Bugs. "I waited there till you arrived."

"You told me," said Officer Carlson, "that the cabinet in which you keep the teapot pig is always locked. You said the thief removed the hinges of the cabinet door to get inside it."

"Yeah," said Bugs. "It was a slick job. Charlie sure knew what he was doing." He led the way upstairs to his room.

The cabinet stood in a corner. The glass door, lifted off its hinges, was leaning against the wall.

"There," said Bugs. "Just like I said."

"But Charlie wasn't carrying the teapot pig when we saw him coming toward the telephone booth," pointed out Officer Carlson.

"He had plenty of time to hide it," said Bugs. "Then he tried to bluff you with that nutty story about buying grizzly bear teeth at the telephone booth. He had his alibi all ready!"

Officer Carlson regarded Charlie sternly. "I better call your parents," he said.

"Aw, I don't want him sent to prison or nothing," said Bugs. "I'm the kind that's always ready to forgive and forget. Charlie's been after me for weeks to swap my teapot pig for his tooth collection. I'll tell you what. If he's so crazy for my teapot, he can keep it. I'll take his crumby old tooth collection in trade."

"You won't take anything of Charlie's," said Encyclopedia. "He never stole your teapot pig!"

WHAT MADE ENCYCLOPEDIA SO SURE?

Solution to *The Case of the Earthenware Pig*

According to his own story, Bugs chased Charlie out of the house. Furthermore, he did not go upstairs to his room where the cabinet was until he brought back Officer Carlson, Charlie, and Encyclopedia.

Yet he knew how the cabinet had been opened!

He could not have known whether the lock had been forced, or the glass door broken, or the hinges removed—unless he had been the "thief" himself!

When Encyclopedia pointed out his mistake, Bugs confessed. He had tried to make it look as if Charlie were the thief in order to get Charlie's tooth collection.

The Tiger leader admitted he had been the boy who had lured Charlie to the telephone booth with the offer of selling him grizzly bear teeth. He had wanted Charlie to tell a story so unbelievable that Officer Carlson would think Charlie was guilty.

Responding to Literature

1. **Why do you think Encyclopedia was so sure that Charlie had not stolen the earthenware pig?** (Accept reasonable responses: Charlie didn't have the teapot pig when he was running; Bugs turned purple.) METACOGNITIVE: NOTING IMPORTANT DETAILS

2. **What traits does Encyclopedia have that make him a good detective?** (Accept reasonable responses: He is a good listener.) CRITICAL: MAKING JUDGMENTS

SPEAKING Have students play the part of a newspaper reporter. Ask them to plan and present a telephone conversation they've had with the editor of their newspaper in which they explain the mystery of the stolen pig. CREATIVE: ORAL COMPOSITION

LISTENING TO LITERATURE / T361

Unit 3 ADVENTURES

THEME OPENER

Picture This!

The Legend of the Indian Paintbrush

T365   A LEGEND retold by Tomie dePaola
This retelling of a Native American legend describes how Little Gopher brings the sunset to Earth.

A Note from the Author: Tomie dePaola

T386   AN ARTICLE
Tomie dePaola talks about the Indian paintbrush, a vibrant flower of the Texas high plains.

Paddington Paints a Picture

T401   A PLAY adapted by Alfred Bradley and Michael Bond
Paddington touches up Mr. Brown's painting, with surprising results.

For pacing suggestions, see page T364.

Theme Opener: Picture This! PAGES 222–223

THEME

Picture This!

Each day, you face adventures, although you usually don't think about them. They can be adventures that you experience alone or with others. The unusual adventures in the legend, play, and poem that follow should make you smile and laugh.

CONTENTS

THE LEGEND OF THE INDIAN PAINTBRUSH
retold and illustrated by Tomie dePaola

A NOTE FROM THE AUTHOR: TOMIE dePAOLA

PADDINGTON PAINTS A PICTURE
adapted by Alfred Bradley and Michael Bond

223

Discussing the Theme

Ask students to look at the illustration and discuss how they think it relates to the theme, "Picture This!" Next, have students read the paragraph on Student Anthology page 223 and share some of their own humorous adventures. Then have students read the selection titles and speculate about the kinds of adventures that might await the characters they are about to meet.

Portfolio Assessment

Tell students to keep their writing responses for the selections in "Picture This!" in their portfolios. Remind them also to add to their personal journals thoughts and ideas about books they have read independently.

When you come across this symbol, you may offer students the opportunity to save a piece of their work in their portfolios.

THEME OPENER: PICTURE THIS! / T363

THEME OPENER

Managing the Literature-Based Classroom

Reading Logs

Ask students to record the title, author, number of pages, and their own reactions to the books they are reading in their spare time.

Substitute Folder

To ensure that minimal instruction time is lost if you happen to be absent, create a folder that contains information that a substitute can use to quickly learn about the class. Include a roster of the class, seating chart, name tags, schedule, special notes about student needs, the name of a helpful colleague, explanation of the class routines, and a few tasks that can be used productively if any of the day's plans are not possible without your presence.

Pacing

This theme has been designed to take about two weeks to complete, depending on your students' needs.

MEETING INDIVIDUAL NEEDS

LOW-ACHIEVING STUDENTS Have students work in small groups to complete the Writer's Workshop activity on Student Anthology page 271. Provide positive feedback as the group completes each step of the writing process.

GIFTED AND TALENTED Have students discuss how they might judge Little Gopher's and Paddington's paintings if they were art critics. Then provide art books depicting the paintings of actual artists. Have students study the paintings, select the one they like best, and discuss the reasons for their choice. You may also have students research the artist who created the painting and share their findings in a brief oral report. *Challenge Cards* provide additional activities to challenge students. Challenge notes throughout the lesson plans suggest additional activities to stimulate critical and creative thinking.

SPECIAL-EDUCATION STUDENTS To help students keep their places as they read the play "Paddington Paints a Picture," have them identify certain characters' lines with self-stick notes, a different color for each character.

STUDENTS ACQUIRING ENGLISH Have students point to different items in the illustrations and tell and write the equivalent for the English word in their first language. Second-Language Support notes throughout the lesson plans offer strategies to help students acquiring English to understand the selection.

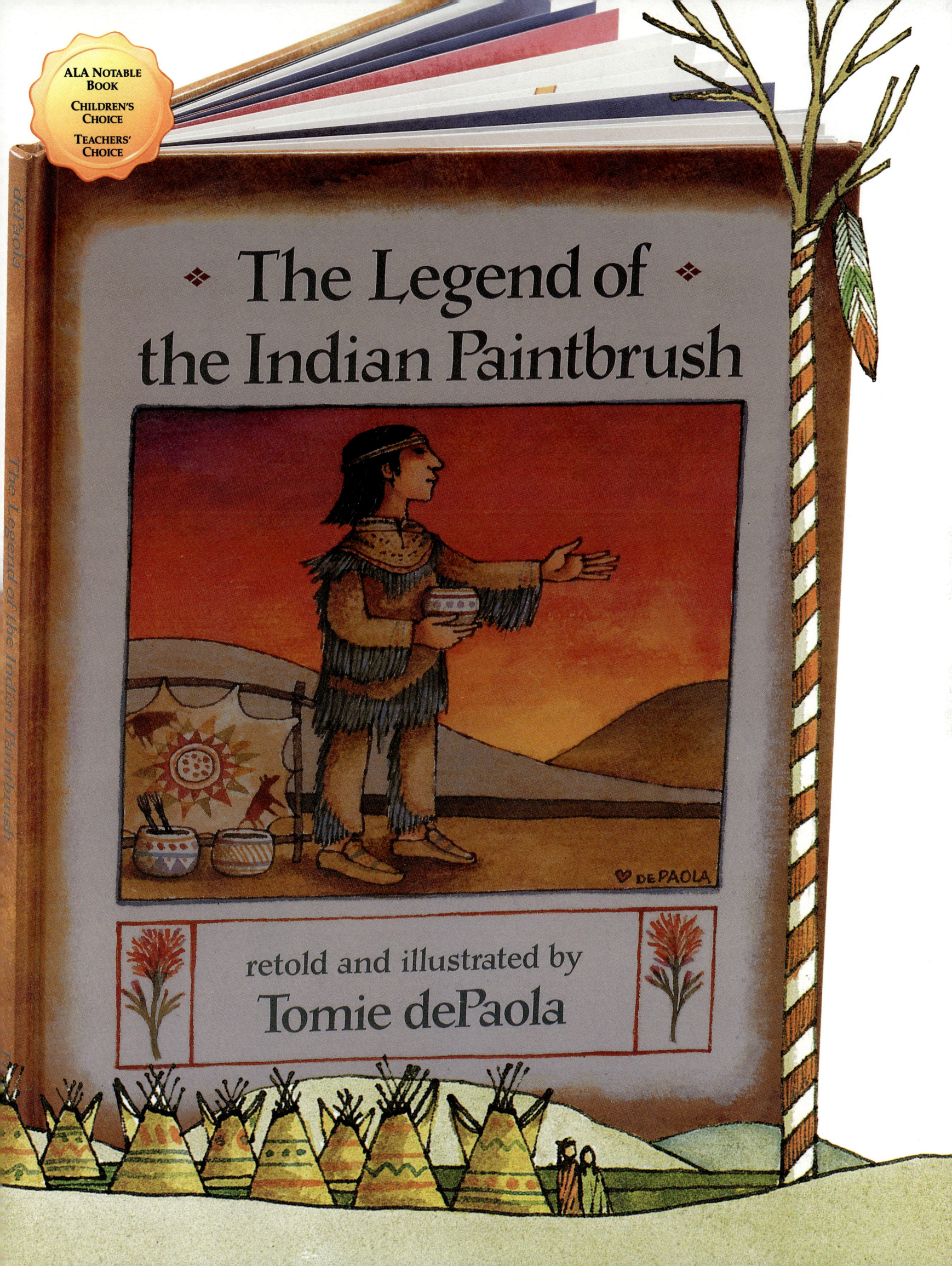

The Legend of the Indian Paintbrush
pages 224–255

	READING	LANGUAGE ARTS	CROSS-CURRICULAR CONNECTIONS
PART 1 *Reading the Literature* pages T368–T386	**Building Background** **Vocabulary Strategies** **Prereading Strategies** Story Impressions Setting a Purpose **Options for Reading**	**Spelling** Pretest Spelling-Vocabulary Connection Generalization: /oi/ and /ou/ sounds **Grammar Connection** Reviewing Plural Possessive Nouns	**Cultural Awareness** Specialization The role of the shaman Natural paints **Science** Red sunsets **Social Studies** Fall and rise of the bison
PART 2 *Responding to the Literature* pages T387–T393	**Personal Response** **Cooperative Response** **Summarizing the Literature** **Critical Thinking Activity** Hold a Discussion **Vocabulary Workshop** Key Words Color Words	**Language Arts Workshop** **Reading** oral rereading **Writing** friendly letter, personal narrative **Listening and Speaking** oral report **Reviewing Spelling Words** Posttest **Grammar Review** Plural Possessive Nouns **Grammar Minilesson** Singular and Plural Pronouns	**Social Studies** Native American Traditions A Special Gift
PART 3 *Learning Through the Literature* pages T394–T400	**Introduce** Comprehension: Making Predictions (Tested) **Review** Literature Appreciation: Story Elements **Maintain** Decoding: Structural Analysis (Tested)	**Reading** Wild and Beautiful Flowers **Writing** Wild and Beautiful Flowers **Listening and Speaking** Coats of Arms Colors and Emotions Singing About Great Deeds	**Social Studies** Coats of Arms **Science** Wild and Beautiful Flowers **Math** A Village in Scale **Music** Singing About Great Deeds **Art** Colors and Emotions **Multicultural Perspectives** Who Needs the Arts? We All Do!

OPTIONAL MATERIALS
Charts/Transparencies 22–23
Integrated Spelling pp. 54–57; TE pp. T81–T86
Practice Book pp. 65–71
Writer's Journal pp. 43–45
Alternative Teaching Strategies pp. 13, 74–77
Language Handbook pp. 66–67, 70, 106, 108–111
Grammar Practice pp. 30–31
Family Involvement Activities: Unit 3, pp. 1–4
Response Card 5
Project Cards 29A, 29B, 30A, 30B

MEETING INDIVIDUAL NEEDS
Second-Language Support pp. T369, T370, T380, T383, T393, T395
Mainstreaming p. T370
Reteach pp. T393, T395
Challenge pp. T395, T396, T397

FAMILY INVOLVEMENT Encourage students to discuss with family members things they dream of doing when they are older. See *Family Involvement Activities*.

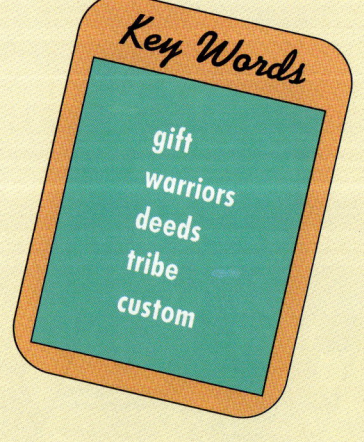

Key Words

gift
warriors
deeds
tribe
custom

T366 / A PLACE TO DREAM, UNIT 3

Selection Summary

As the smallest child in his tribe, Little Gopher is unhappy about his inability to keep up with the other boys. The wise shaman assures him that he will be remembered for a different reason. As custom requires, Little Gopher goes alone to the hills to think about becoming a man. In his Dream-Vision, a maiden and grandfather display a white buckskin, paints, and a paintbrush, telling him that these tools will help him become great. Little Gopher paints for his people but is dissatisfied with his colors. One night a voice tells him he will find what he needs on the hilltop. When he goes there at sunset, he finds brushes dipped in beautiful bright colors. He paints a picture of a sunset in these colors and leaves the brushes behind. The brushes take root and turn into the flowers we call Indian Paintbrushes. From then on, Little Gopher is called He-Who-Brought-the-Sunset-to-the-Earth.

About the Author and Illustrator

Tomie dePaola is no stranger to dreams coming true. As early as first grade he developed a love for books and told his teacher that he was going to be an artist when he grew up.

Throughout his school career, dePaola was involved in many of the arts. He sang, he danced, he made scenery for school plays, and he wrote and edited. After attending art school, dePaola tried many different forms of art. Finally, he had the opportunity to illustrate a science book. This was the beginning of his career as a children's author and illustrator.

Tomie dePaola has written and illustrated dozens of books, and has won many awards, including the Caldecott Honor Medal in 1975 for *Strega Nona*. He talks about "a dream that I expressed as a child, that when I grew up, I would write and draw pictures for books; a dream that people I've never met would get to know me a little better."

Additional Reading

OTHER BOOKS WRITTEN OR ILLUSTRATED BY TOMIE DEPAOLA

The Art Lesson by Tomie dePaola. Putnam, 1989.   **AVERAGE**

The Popcorn Book. Holiday House, 1978.   **AVERAGE**

OTHER THEME-RELATED BOOKS

Eyes of the Dragon by Margaret Leaf. Lothrop, Lee & Shepard, 1987.   **AVERAGE**

On the Day You Were Born by Debra Frasier. Harcourt Brace, 1991.   **CHALLENGING**

BOOKS FOR APPLYING STRATEGIES: MAKING PREDICTIONS

The Girl Who Loved Wild Horses by Paul Goble. Bradbury, 1978.   **AVERAGE**

The Hole in the Dike by Norma Green. Scholastic, 1993.   **EASY**

*Available as a Harcourt Brace PASSPORTS title

PART 1

Reading the Literature

Building Background

Access prior knowledge and build vocabulary concepts.

Tell students that "The Legend of the Indian Paintbrush" is about a Native American boy who thinks he is not strong enough to meet a certain challenge. Ask students to think about a time when they were unable to do something and had to search for a solution. Have volunteers share their ideas as you record their responses in a diagram like the one shown here.

What I Wanted to Do	Challenge	Solution
be on the basketball team	→ needed to learn to shoot baskets better	→ asked a friend to help me practice

Have students quickwrite.

Have students use the diagram as a springboard for writing some sentences about a challenge they faced and how they met it.

Vocabulary Strategies

Introduce Key Words and strategies.

Display Chart/Transparency 22 or the paragraph on it. Encourage students to read the sentences silently and to use context clues to figure out the meanings of the underlined words. For example, they might figure out that the phrase *a long time* is a clue to the meaning of *custom*.

Chart/Transparency 22   Key Words

Red Bird's singing was outstanding. He had a beautiful voice and a <u>gift</u> for choosing words. Brave hunters were pleased to hear their <u>deeds</u> described in one of Red Bird's songs. All the members of his <u>tribe</u> knew Red Bird. He would ride with the other <u>warriors</u> when they went off to hunt buffalo. Before they headed out, they sang Red Bird's hunting songs. This had been their <u>custom</u> for a long time.

CULTURAL AWARENESS

Point out that *specialization* is a sign of an advanced society; people are able to do the work they enjoy and are good at, instead of just struggling to survive. Scientists date the first specialized societies to the Middle East, about 10,000 years ago.

Key Words

gift
warriors
deeds
tribe
custom

KEY WORDS DEFINED

gift   a talent

warriors   people trained in fighting and hunting skills

deeds   things that are done; acts

tribe   a group of people with the same customs united under the same leader

custom   a long-standing tradition

Check all students' understanding.

Display the Key Words. Encourage students to use these words to develop a web, such as the one below, on which they record other words and phrases associated with the Key Words.
STRATEGY: EXAMPLES/PRIOR KNOWLEDGE

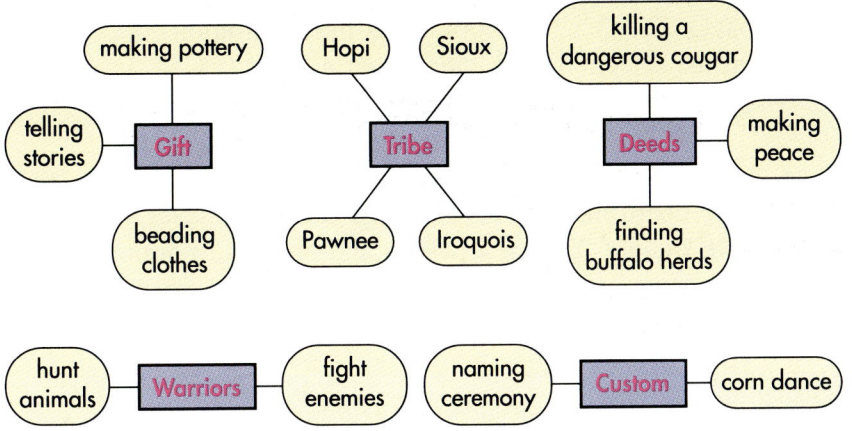

Integrate spelling with vocabulary.

SPELLING-VOCABULARY CONNECTION *Integrated Spelling* Lesson 12 reinforces the spelling of words that contain the /oi/ and /ou/ sounds, such as *enjoy* and *cloud* from the selection. In addition, the Words to Explore help reinforce the concept of legends as it relates to the selection.

 **SPELLING PRETEST** You may want to use the Pretest/Posttest Sentences on page T81 in *Integrated Spelling Teacher's Edition* to assess students' knowledge of the spelling generalization.

MEETING INDIVIDUAL NEEDS

SECOND-LANGUAGE SUPPORT Provide students with a heavily-illustrated book about Native American life. Encourage the students to work in small groups to discuss the pictures, using as many of the Key Words as they can. Prompt them as needed. See also the manual *Alternative Teaching Strategies,* pages 13, 74–77.

Spelling

Spelling Words	Words to Explore
1. brown	buckskin
2. cloud	custom
3. cow	tribe
4. enjoy	warrior
5. flower	
6. house	*Your Own Words*
7. joy	13.
8. loud	14.
9. oil	15.
10. point	16.
11. soil	
12. town	

Spelling generalization:
/oi/ and /ou/ sounds

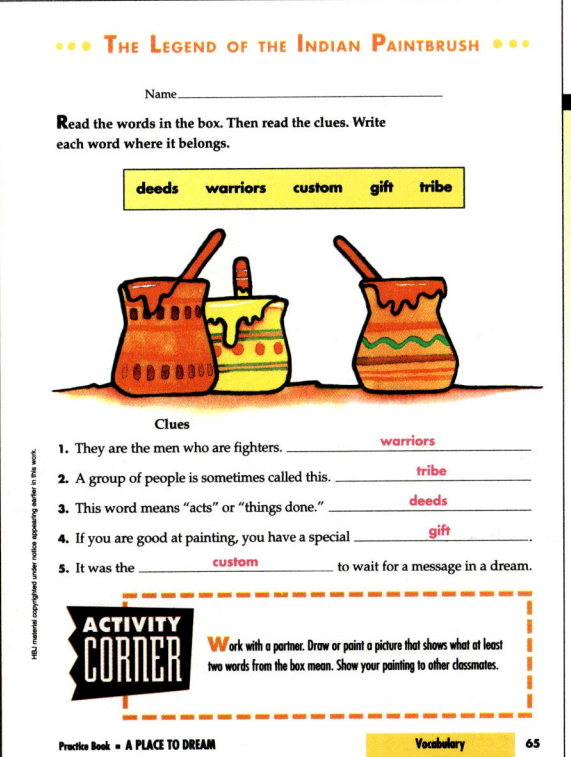

Practice Book

OPTIONAL INDEPENDENT PRACTICE

INTEGRATED SPELLING
pages 54–57: Words Like *point* and *cloud*

PRACTICE BOOK
page 65: Reinforcing Key Words
NOTE: This page may be completed now or after students have read the story.

THE LEGEND OF THE INDIAN PAINTBRUSH / T369

Prereading Strategies

Story Impressions

Encourage students to preview the literature.

Have students preview the selection by thinking about the title, reading pages 224–227, and looking at the illustrations throughout the selection. Ask them what a legend is. (A legend is a story that has been handed down for generations. Some legends tell why something came to be.)

Have students use story impressions to make predictions.

Write on the board the column headings and the phrases shown below. Have students use these words and phrases to brainstorm predictions about the story. Encourage students to develop a group story like the one shown here.

Story Impressions	Story
—the Plains ↓ —tribe ↓ —boy who was smaller ↓ —gift of his own ↓ —Dream-Vision ↓ —brushes filled with paint ↓ —colors of the sunset	(A boy lived on the Plains with his tribe. He was smaller than the other boys, but he had a gift of his own. In a Dream-Vision, he saw many brushes filled with paint. The paints were the colors of the sunset. The boy used the brushes to paint a picture of the flower called the Indian Paintbrush.)

PERSONAL JOURNAL Have students use the story impressions strategy to predict what "The Legend of the Indian Paintbrush" might be about. Encourage them to write their own version of the story in their personal journals.

Setting a Purpose

Encourage students to set purposes.

Have students use their predictions to set their purposes for reading.

If students have difficulty setting a purpose, offer this suggestion:

I'm going to read to find out what the boy's gift is and the part it plays in the story.

MEETING INDIVIDUAL NEEDS

SECOND-LANGUAGE SUPPORT Students may benefit from the Strategic Reading activities and the additional guidance under the Student Anthology pages. See also the manual *Alternative Teaching Strategies,* pages 13, 74–77.

SUPPORT FOR MAINSTREAMING Discuss the idea that each person has his or her own special talents, or gifts, and that people who use their gifts well often feel happy and fulfilled. Encourage students to name a talent they might pursue.

Options for Reading

SUSTAINED SILENT READING	STRATEGIC READING	READER RESPONSE GROUPS
Tell students who are reading independently to think about the predictions they wrote based on their story impressions. Suggest that they pause at intervals to confirm or revise their predictions.	To stimulate discussion, use the suggestions that appear on pages T371, T376, T381, and T385.	Follow the suggestions for Collaborative Response on page T371. As they read, students might record words and phrases from the story that they think are important.

T370 / A PLACE TO DREAM, UNIT 3

THE LEGEND OF THE INDIAN PAINTBRUSH PAGES 224–225

Many years ago
when the People traveled the Plains
and lived in a circle of teepees,
there was a boy who was smaller
than the rest of the children in the tribe.
No matter how hard he tried,
he couldn't keep up with the other boys
who were always riding, running, shooting their bows,
and wrestling to prove their strength.
Sometimes his mother and father worried for him.

Reader Response Groups

COLLABORATIVE RESPONSE For each group, appoint a Predictor, a Questioner, and a Clarifier. Have groups read to the end of page 235 and then pause for discussion. You may want to distribute Response Card 5 (Author's Viewpoint), found on page R83, or provide the following questions:

- Do you think that Little Gopher will be satisfied with the future he has been promised? Why or why not?
- What do you think Tomie dePaola wants you to learn from this story? Explain how you know.

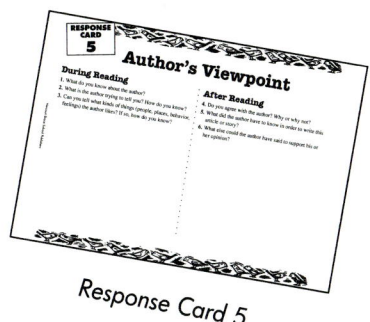

Response Card 5

Strategic Reading

SET PURPOSE/PREDICT: PAGES 225–235 Have students read through page 235. Ask them what they will be reading to find out.

THE LEGEND OF THE INDIAN PAINTBRUSH / T371

PAGES 226–227 **THE LEGEND OF THE INDIAN PAINTBRUSH**

But the boy, who was called Little Gopher,
was not without a gift of his own.
From an early age, he made toy warriors
from scraps of leather and pieces of wood
and he loved to decorate smooth stones
with the red juices from berries
he found in the hills.
The wise shaman of the tribe understood
that Little Gopher had a gift that was special.
"Do not struggle, Little Gopher.
Your path will not be the same as the others.
They will grow up to be warriors.
Your place among the People will be remembered
for a different reason."

Cultural Awareness Explain that a *shaman* is the spiritual leader and doctor of a Native American community and has almost as much status as the chief. The shaman's visions are thought to reveal truths or appropriate courses of action for the tribe.

Teaching Tip Point out that this story is written as if it is a long poem: each important phrase has a line of its own, and each sentence starts on a new line. Suggest that perhaps the author wanted this story to seem like an oral legend, passed down in spoken words rather than in writing. Explain that legends are often told in a poetic or musical way.

THE LEGEND OF THE INDIAN PAINTBRUSH PAGES 228–229

The sky filled with clouds and out of them
came a young Indian maiden and an old grandfather.
She carried a rolled-up animal skin
and he carried a brush made of fine animal hairs
and pots of paints.

And in a few years
when Little Gopher was older,
he went out to the hills alone
to think about becoming a man,
for this was the custom of the tribe.
And it was there that a Dream-Vision came to him.

Expanding the Literature What do you think was on Little Gopher's mind as he went into the hills for his Dream-Vision? (Accept reasonable responses: Because he was not good at physical activities and because the shaman had told him he would follow a different path, he must have been hoping that his Dream-Vision would reveal to him the path he was to take.) INFERENTIAL: DETERMINING CHARACTERS' EMOTIONS

PAGES 230–231   THE LEGEND OF THE INDIAN PAINTBRUSH

The grandfather spoke.
"My son, these are the tools
by which you shall become great among your People.
You will paint pictures of the <u>deeds</u> of the warriors
and the visions of the shaman,
and the People shall see them and remember them forever."

The maiden unrolled a pure white buckskin
and placed it on the ground.
"Find a buckskin as white as this," she told him.
"Keep it and one day you will paint a picture
that is as pure as the colors
in the evening sky."

Vocabulary Strategy   Discuss how using picture clues and structural clues can help students figure out the meaning of the compound word *buckskin* on page 231. Help students identify the clues that tell them the word *buckskin* is a noun. (It is pictured as an object.) Have students break the word into its two parts, *buck* and *skin*, and help them conclude that *buckskin* must be the skin of a buck, or a male deer.   STRATEGIES: PICTURE CLUES/STRUCTURAL ANALYSIS

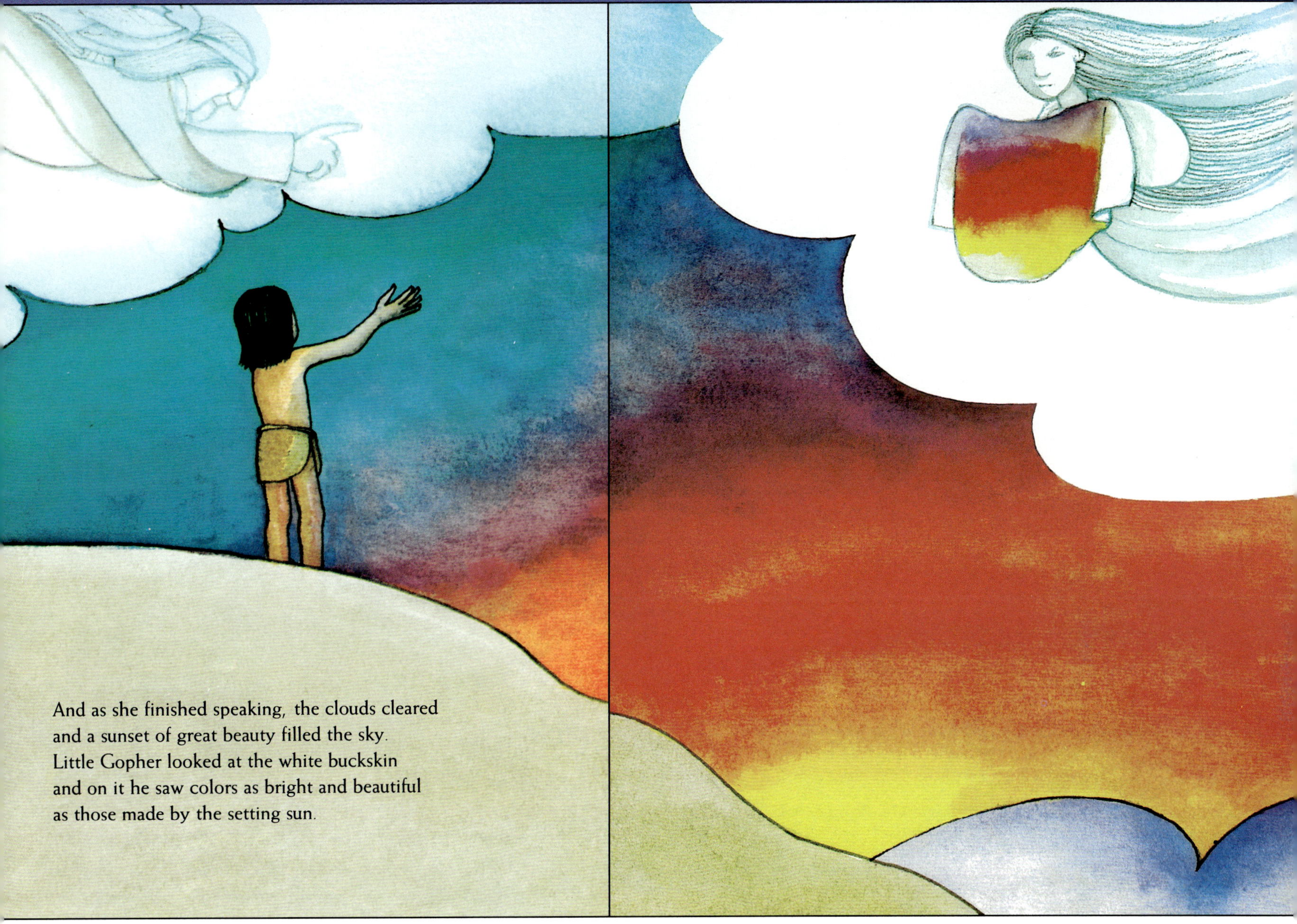

THE LEGEND OF THE INDIAN PAINTBRUSH   **PAGES 232–233**

And as she finished speaking, the clouds cleared and a sunset of great beauty filled the sky. Little Gopher looked at the white buckskin and on it he saw colors as bright and beautiful as those made by the setting sun.

Science Connection   Why do you think the sky can look red when the sun sets? Encourage students to share their speculations and knowledge. Then explain that tiny particles of dust or moisture are always in the air. Light coming through dust is much redder than light coming through moisture, so a very red sunset means that the air to the west is dry.

See page T399 for information found on Project Card 30B.

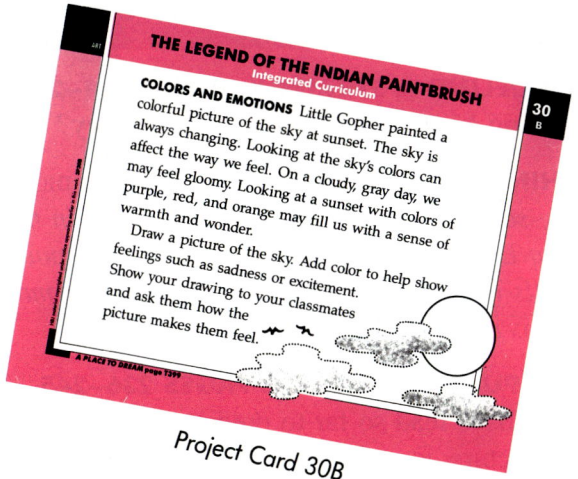

Project Card 30B

THE LEGEND OF THE INDIAN PAINTBRUSH / T375

PAGES 234–235 THE LEGEND OF THE INDIAN PAINTBRUSH

Then the sun slowly sank behind the hills,
the sky grew dark,
and the Dream-Vision was over.
Little Gopher returned to the circle of the People.

Strategic Reading

MODELING A STRATEGY: PAGES 224–235 What effects does the setting have on the action of the story?

THINK ALOUD Provide a think-aloud model, if necessary: *I think that the setting greatly affects what happens in the story. For example, I know that Little Gopher would not be so disappointed in his lack of physical skills if he were not living in a place that made hunting skills important.*
ANALYZING SETTING

SET PURPOSE/PREDICT: PAGES 236–245 Invite students to use what they have read so far to predict whether Little Gopher will be able to paint "a picture as pure as the colors in the evening sky" on white buckskin, and what might happen if he does.

THE LEGEND OF THE INDIAN PAINTBRUSH PAGES 236–237

The next day he began to make soft brushes
from the hairs of different animals
and stiff brushes from the hair of the horses' tails.
He gathered berries and flowers
and rocks of different colors
and crushed them to make his paints.

He collected the skins of animals,
which the warriors brought home from their hunts.
He stretched the skins on wooden frames
and pulled them until they were tight.

Cultural Awareness Ask students how Little Gopher knew what to use for paints. Explain that for many centuries, Plains artists used natural paints and dyes made mostly from pulverized clay and charcoal. The main colors they used were brown, red, yellow, black, blue, and green. The people of the Plains used art to decorate useful objects and to record important events. Painted hides were used for clothing, pouches, drums, shields, tepee covers and linings, and medicine bundles.

See page T391 for information on Project Card 29B.

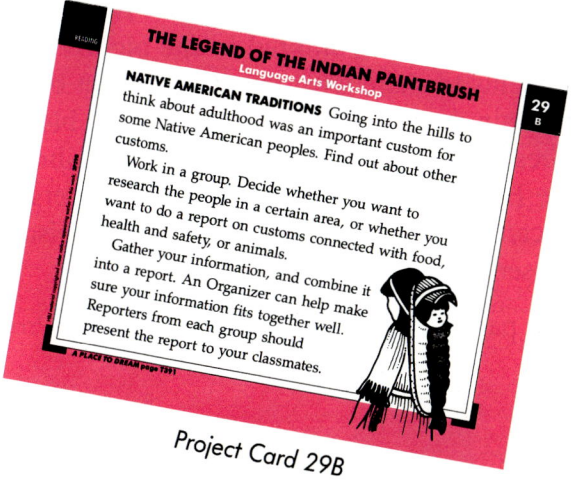

Project Card 29B

THE LEGEND OF THE INDIAN PAINTBRUSH / T377

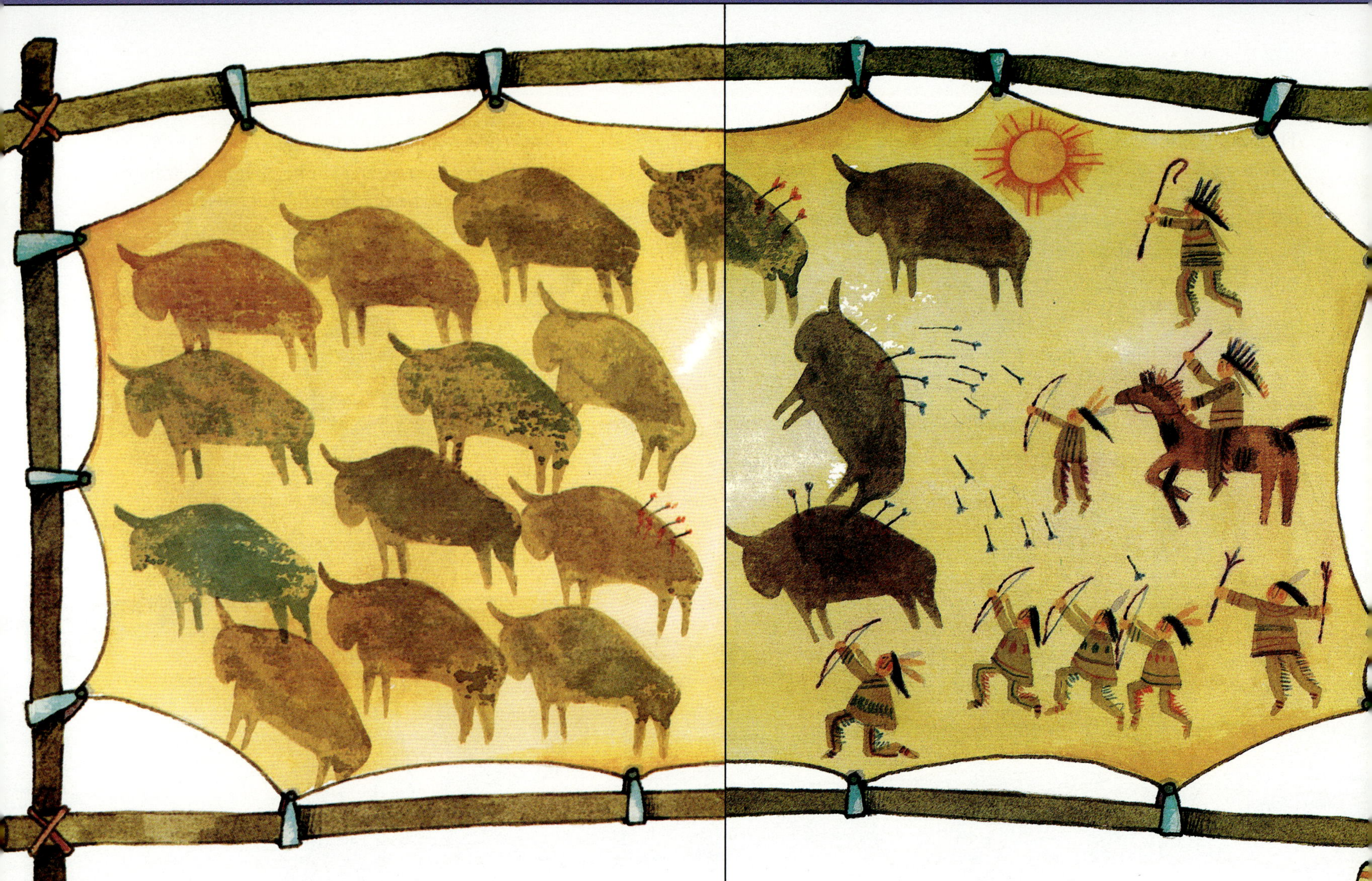

And he began to paint pictures . . .

Of great hunts . . .

238

Social Studies Connection **What do you know about the animal being hunted in the picture?** Encourage students to share what they know about bison, or buffalo. Explain that 150 years ago, 60 million bison roamed the Great Plains. With the coming of the railroads, hunters from the East killed bison in such huge numbers that they almost became extinct. Today, most American bison live on game preserves or in national parks.

See page T398 for information found on Project Card 30A.

SOCIAL STUDIES

THE LEGEND OF THE INDIAN PAINTBRUSH

Integrated Curriculum

30 A

COATS OF ARMS The pictures that Little Gopher drew told a story about his people. A coat of arms also tells something about a family or nation.

A coat of arms is a shield or plaque that has pictures or symbols on it to stand for ideas. For example, a picture of a sword may mean some of the family were soldiers. Similarly, sports teams are often named for animals such as bulls, broncos, and tigers, as symbols of the teams' strength.

Draw a coat of arms that describes your family or your school. Share your work with your classmates.

A PLACE TO DREAM page T398

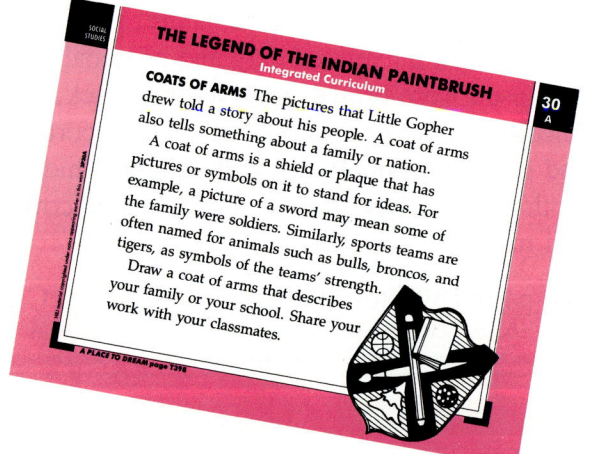

THE LEGEND OF THE INDIAN PAINTBRUSH   PAGES 240–241

Of great deeds . . .

Of great Dream-Visions . . .
So that the People would always remember.

 Informal Assessment

STORY ELEMENTS To assess whether students need instruction in identifying story elements, ask questions such as the following:

- Who is the main character in this story? Name some other characters, and tell how they affect the story events.
- What is the problem in this story?
- What is the setting of this story? If the setting was entirely different, could the events in the story be the same? Explain your answer.

A review lesson on **story elements** appears later in this lesson, on page T396.

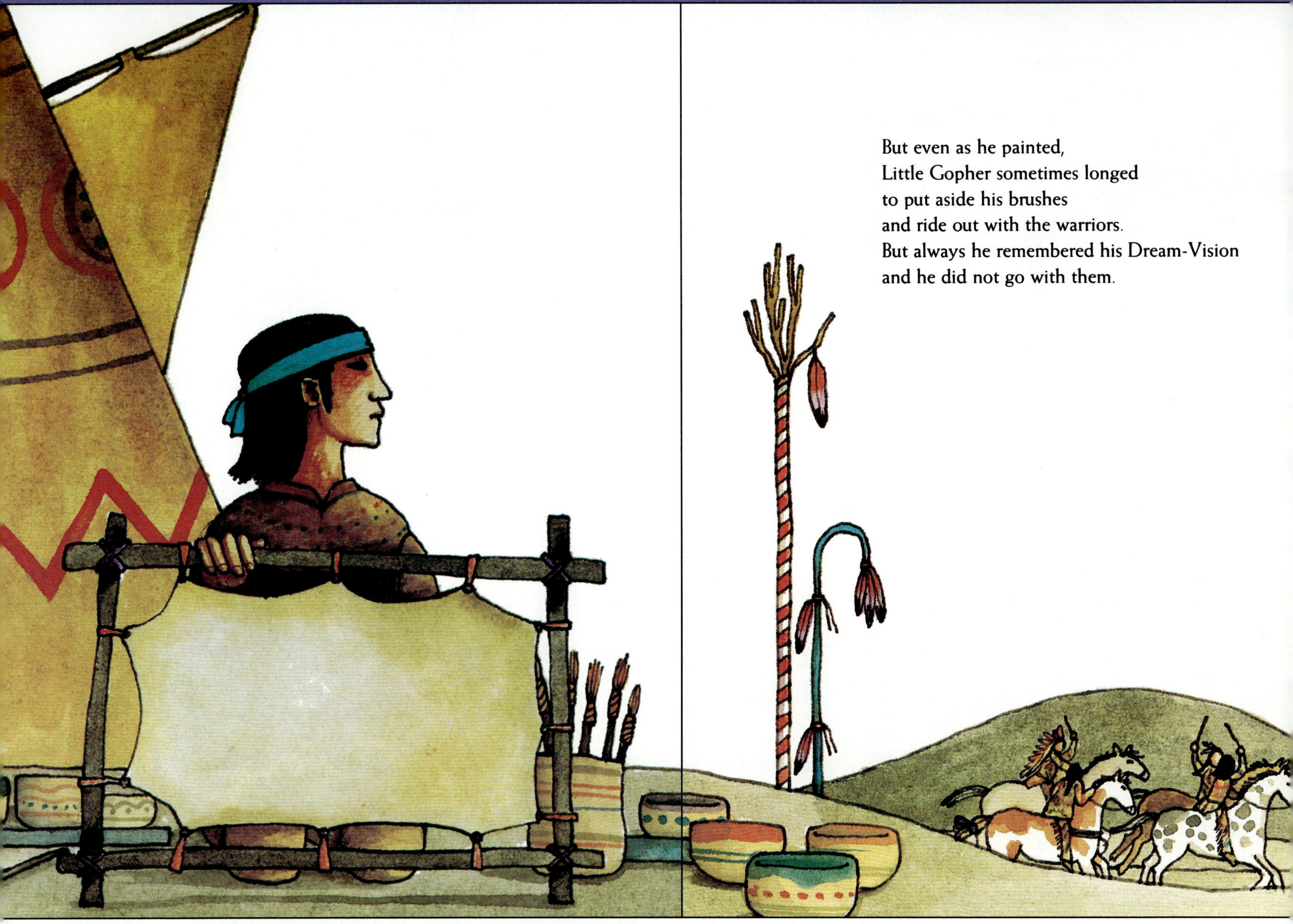

PAGES 242–243 THE LEGEND OF THE INDIAN PAINTBRUSH

But even as he painted,
Little Gopher sometimes longed
to put aside his brushes
and ride out with the warriors.
But always he remembered his Dream-Vision
and he did not go with them.

Second-Language Support Students may have difficulty with the meaning of the word *longed* and of the phrase *put aside* on page 243. Tell them that *longing for something* means "wanting something very much." Discuss whether Little Gopher has an expression of longing, and why that might be so. You might also explain that *put aside* means "put away for awhile."

MEETING INDIVIDUAL NEEDS

THE LEGEND OF THE INDIAN PAINTBRUSH　PAGES 244–245

Many months ago,
he had found his pure white buckskin,
but it remained empty
because he could not find the colors of the sunset.
He used the brightest flowers,
the reddest berries,
and the deepest purples from the rocks,
and still his paintings never satisfied him.
They looked dull and dark.

Strategic Reading

MODELING A STRATEGY: PAGES 236–245 Which of your predictions have been confirmed by the story so far? Did you revise any predictions?

THINK ALOUD Model checking a prediction with this think-aloud, if necessary: *When the maiden told Little Gopher about the picture he should paint on white buckskin, I predicted that it would not be easy for him to find this skin and paint on it. On page 244 it says that he had found the buckskin "many months ago," so it seems that part was easy. It turns out that the hard part is finding paints that are not "dull and dark."* REVISING PREDICTIONS

SET PURPOSE/PREDICT: PAGES 246–253 Suggest that students use what they have learned so far to predict what might happen to enable Little Gopher to make a painting that will not be "dull and dark." Encourage students to read the rest of the story to confirm their predictions.

PAGES 246–247 THE LEGEND OF THE INDIAN PAINTBRUSH

He began to go to the top of a hill each evening
and look at the colors that filled the sky
to try and understand how to make them.
He longed to share the beauty of his Dream-Vision
with the People.

But he never gave up trying,
and every morning when he awoke
he took out his brushes and his pots of paints
and created the stories of the People
with the tools he had.

Expanding the Literature Why do you think it was important to Little Gopher to share his Dream-Vision? (Accept reasonable responses: He probably felt that sharing it was a way of giving his people pleasure; he wanted to do what he had been told to do.) CRITICAL: IDENTIFYING WITH CHARACTERS

THE LEGEND OF THE INDIAN PAINTBRUSH   PAGES 248–249

One night as he lay awake,
he heard a voice calling to him.
"Because you have been faithful to the People
and true to your gift,
you shall find the colors you are seeking.
Tomorrow take the white buckskin
and go to the place
where you watch the sun in the evening.
There on the ground you will find what you need."

The next evening as the sun began to go down,
Little Gopher put aside his brushes
and went to the top of the hill
as the colors of the sunset spread across the sky.

249

Second-Language Support   Point out the phrase *true to your gift* in the fourth line on page 248. Ask students what they think of when they hear the word *true*. (correct; not false) Tell students that *true* also means "loyal." Prompt them to give examples of things that a loyal friend might do. Then ask them what it might mean to have a talent and to be true, or loyal, to that talent. (To be true to a talent is to put hard work into getting better at it and to put the talent to good uses.)

MEETING INDIVIDUAL NEEDS

THE LEGEND OF THE INDIAN PAINTBRUSH / T383

PAGES 250–251 THE LEGEND OF THE INDIAN PAINTBRUSH

And there, on the ground all around him,
were brushes filled with paint,
each one a color of the sunset.
Little Gopher began to paint quickly and surely,
using one brush, then another.

And as the colors in the sky began to fade,
Little Gopher gazed at the white buckskin
and he was happy.

He had found the colors of the sunset.
He carried his painting down
to the circle of the People,
leaving the brushes on the hillside.

GRAMMAR CONNECTION

REVIEWING PLURAL POSSESSIVE NOUNS Point out the phrase *the colors of the sunset* on page 251. Ask students how they might use fewer words to write this phrase. *(the sunset's colors)* Repeat the activity with the phrase *the colors of the sunsets*. *(the sunsets' colors)* Point out that the apostrophe in *sunsets'*, which is a plural possessive noun, is placed after the *s*, while the one in *sunset's*, a singular possessive noun, is placed before the *s*.

THE LEGEND OF THE INDIAN PAINTBRUSH   PAGES 252–253

And the next day, when the People awoke,
the hill was ablaze with color,
for the brushes had taken root in the earth
and multiplied into plants
of brilliant reds, oranges and yellows.

And every spring from that time,
the hills and meadows burst into bloom.

And every spring,
the People danced and sang the praises
of Little Gopher who had painted for the People.

And the People no longer called him Little Gopher,
but He-Who-Brought-the-Sunset-to-the-Earth.

What does Tomie dePaola want you to learn from Little Gopher?

How does the Dream-Vision change Little Gopher's life?

WRITE   Little Gopher has a special talent. Write a paragraph telling about someone's special talents. Your paragraph can be about you or about someone you know.

Strategic Reading

MODELING A STRATEGY: PAGES 246–253   Ask students if their purposes for reading were met.

THINK ALOUD   You may wish to model returning to the purpose: *I read this story to find out what part Little Gopher's gift plays and now I know—he used his gift to "bring the sunset to earth" in his beautiful painting. And according to the legend, the paintbrushes he used took root and bloomed as flowers on the hillside.*   RETURNING TO THE PURPOSE

Returning to the Predictions/Purpose

STORY IMPRESSIONS   Have students look over the group story they wrote before reading. Have them compare their story with what actually happens in "The Legend of the Indian Paintbrush." Encourage volunteers to share their purposes for reading and to tell what they learned as they read.

NOTE: Responses to the questions and support for the Write activity appear on page T387.

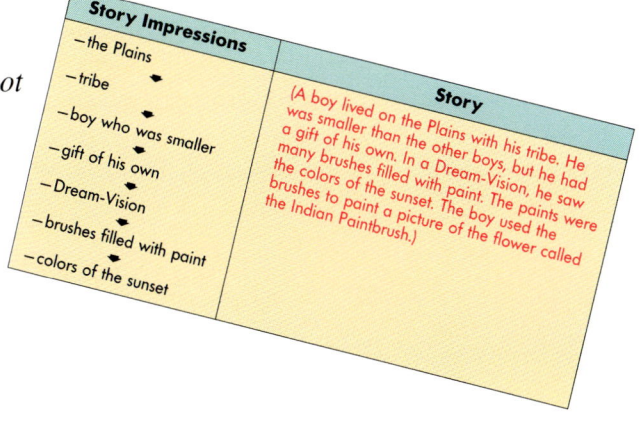

THE LEGEND OF THE INDIAN PAINTBRUSH / T385

Words About the Author and Illustrator

AUTHOR'S CRAFT Invite students to read pages 254–255 to find out how Tomie dePaola's interest in wildflowers and his love of bright colors helped him create "The Legend of the Indian Paintbrush." (He came across this account of how the Indian Paintbrush got its name in a book about wildflowers. The legend of a Native American artist who was searching for just the right colors was meaningful for him, because he is an artist too.)

PART 2

Responding to the Literature

Personal Response

Encourage critical thinking.

What does Tomie dePaola want you to learn from Little Gopher? (Responses will vary.) CRITICAL: SYNTHESIZING/EXPRESSING PERSONAL OPINIONS

How does the Dream-Vision change Little Gopher's life? (It encourages him to identify his own natural gift and to use it rather than worrying about his small size and lack of strength.) INFERENTIAL: DETERMINING CAUSE/EFFECT

Encourage creative written responses.

 **WRITE** Little Gopher has a special talent. Write a paragraph telling about someone's special talents. Your paragraph can be about you or someone you know. Encourage students to think about the ways in which the special talents give pleasure to others. Also suggest that they consider what someone needs to do in order to develop a special talent. CREATIVE: WRITING A PARAGRAPH

Cooperative Response

Have reader response groups extend their discussions.

COLLABORATIVE READING GROUPS Have the groups meet to discuss their reactions to the story and to the author. Encourage them to tell what they learned about Little Gopher and about themselves from reading the story. You might want to have the groups discuss questions such as these:

What do you think Tomie dePaola believes about talent? Do you agree with him? Why or why not?

STRATEGY CONFERENCE

Ask how writing a story based on story impressions helped students read the story. (Accept reasonable responses: Using this strategy encourages readers to keep reading to find out whether the conclusions they drew match what actually happens in the story.)

NOTE

An additional writing activity for this selection appears on page T390.

THE LEGEND OF THE INDIAN PAINTBRUSH / T387

Summarizing the Literature

Have students use a story map to summarize the story.

Guide students in completing a story map for "The Legend of the Indian Paintbrush." Then have them use the map to retell the story and write a summary. See *Practice Book* page 66 below.

Main Character (Little Gopher)

Setting (many years ago on the Plains)

Problem
Little Gopher's special gift is (painting the deeds and visions of his people). But he is not satisfied with his paintings because (he cannot find the colors of the sunset).

Important Events
1. ___
2. ___

Solution

Portfolio

STUDENT SELF-ASSESSMENT

Ask students to identify a word, passage, or event that confused them as they were reading. Ask them to tell what they did to clarify that word or passage. Encourage students to name or demonstrate the strategy or strategies they used.

Critical Thinking Activity

Consider the pros and cons of specialization.

HOLD A DISCUSSION Is it wise to focus on finding your own particular gift? Assign students to small groups to talk about whether devoting one's energies to developing a particular talent is desirable. CRITICAL: MAKING JUDGMENTS

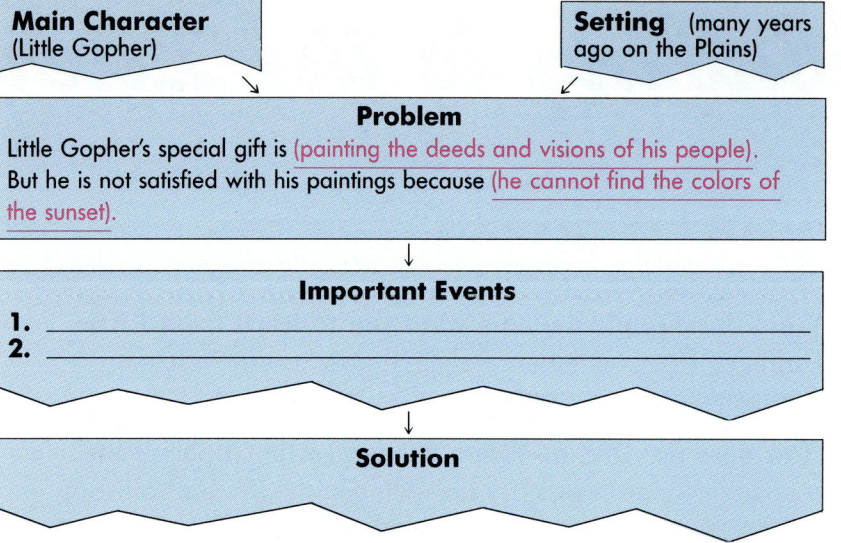

Question: Should people focus on one talent?

Yes, because...	No, because...
To become good at something, you need to spend a lot of time on it.	Learning about new things helps you understand the world and other people

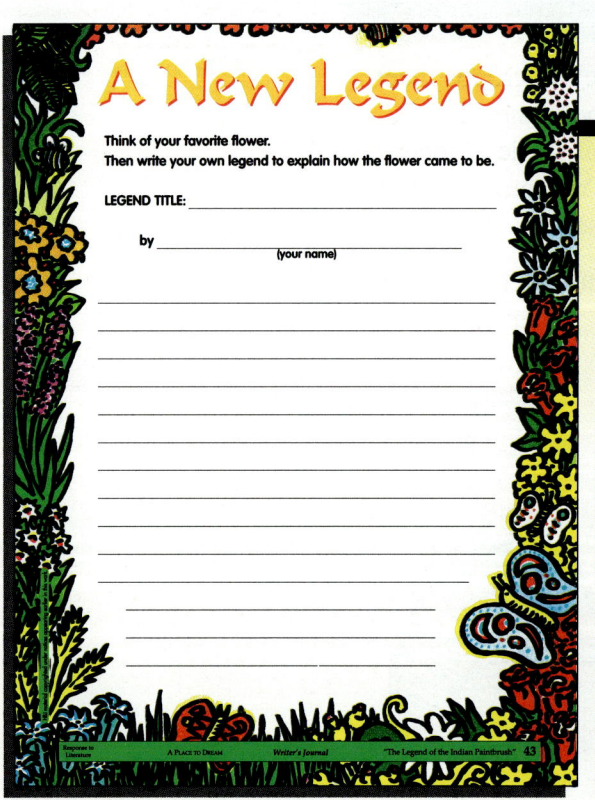
Writer's Journal

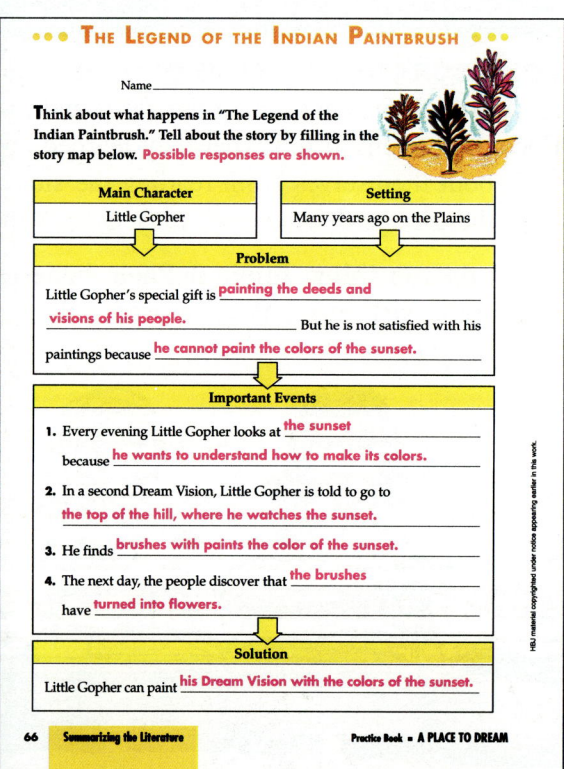
Practice Book

OPTIONAL INDEPENDENT PRACTICE

WRITER'S JOURNAL
page 43: Writing a personal response

PRACTICE BOOK
page 66: Summarizing the literature

T388 / A PLACE TO DREAM, UNIT 3

VOCABULARY WORKSHOP

Reviewing Key Words

On the board, draw a web like the one below, but do not link any of the ovals. Encourage students to write sentences in which the subject is one of the words in bold type and which also includes one of the Key Words. Each time students create such a sentence, draw a line linking the subject to the Key Word, as shown.

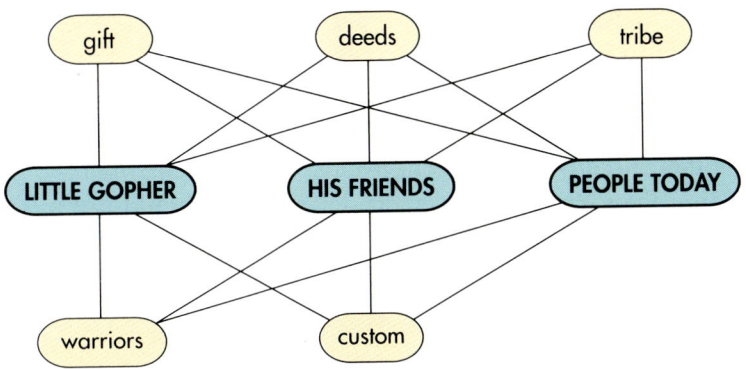

OPTIONAL INDEPENDENT PRACTICE

PRACTICE BOOK page 67: Using a variety of color words

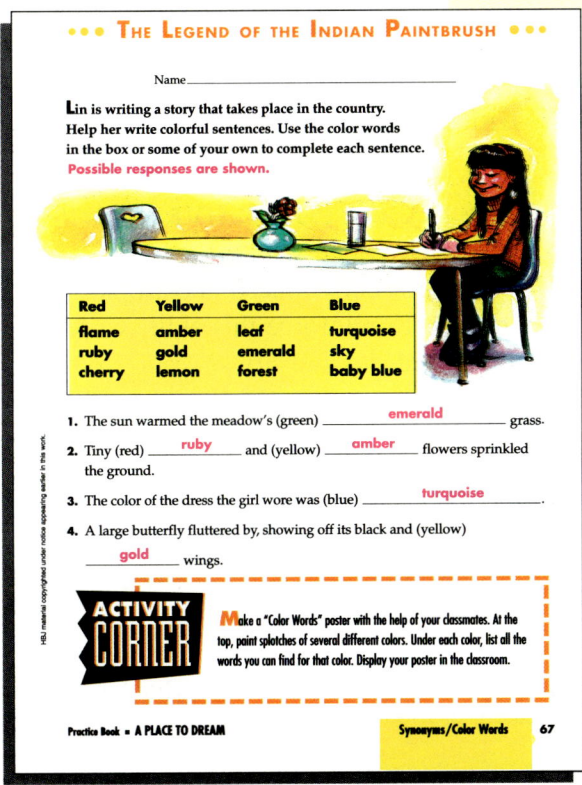

Practice Book

Extending Vocabulary

COLOR WORDS Remind students that Little Gopher longed to capture the vivid colors of the sunset in his painting. Explain that writers must try to capture vivid colors in words. On the board, begin a chart to record words and phrases that precisely name colors.

Colors	
red	(scarlet, crimson, ruby, cardinal red, cherry red, maroon)
orange	(tangerine, copper, apricot, peach, marigold, salmon)
yellow	(lemon, buttercup, gold, straw, sandy yellow, canary yellow)
purple	(lilac, lavender, pansy, plum, burgundy, violet)
blue	(navy blue, baby blue, sky blue, teal, turquoise, sapphire)
green	(apple green, pea green, forest green, emerald, olive, sea green)

Have students suggest words to add to each category. You might encourage them to look at the labels in a large box of crayons or to consult a thesaurus. Suggest that students use the vivid and exact color words to describe an outdoor scene, such as the changing sky at sunset or a city street at dusk.

THE LEGEND OF THE INDIAN PAINTBRUSH / T389

Language Arts WORKSHOP

READING

Oral Rereading

Remind students that one of the purposes of a legend is to entertain. Then have students work in pairs to prepare an oral rereading of "The Legend of the Indian Paintbrush." Suggest that they read the story as they would read poetry. Also encourage them to use the tone of their voices to make their reading entertaining. You might model using a sympathetic voice to read the beginning of the story in which Little Gopher is unable to keep up with the other boys. Have students reread the story silently before they begin to rehearse reading it aloud. If possible, some pairs might perform their readings for younger students in another class.

READING/LISTENING/SPEAKING

WRITING

Writing About the Literature

Available on Project Card 29A

 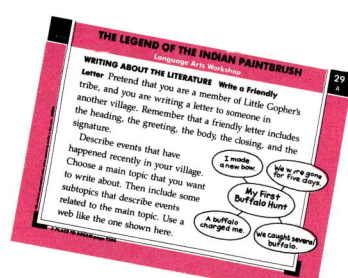

WRITE A FRIENDLY LETTER
Ask students to pretend to be a boy or girl from Little Gopher's tribe, writing to someone in another village about recent events. Tell students that before they write their friendly letter, they should use a web to help them choose a topic and organize subtopics.

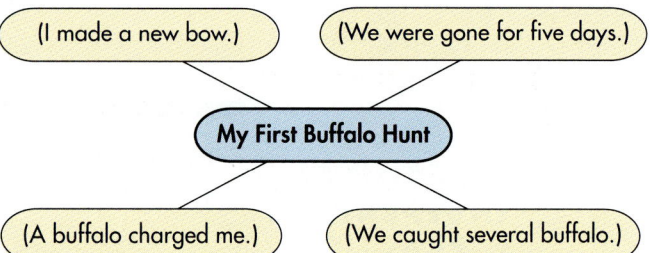

When students are finished, allow them to read one another's letters silently, as though they were the recipients. See Writing Model, page R97. READING/WRITING

GRAMMAR REVIEW: PLURAL POSSESSIVE NOUNS
When students revise their friendly letters, remind them to make sure they have correctly placed apostrophes in plural possessive nouns. To reinforce this skill, write these phrases on the board: *his parents, the other boys.* Have students use each phrase in a written sentence that includes a plural possessive noun.

LANGUAGE HANDBOOK Everyday Writing, pages 66–67, 70; Plural Possessive Nouns, page 106

DAILY LANGUAGE PRACTICE Oral language exercises are provided on pages R70–R71.

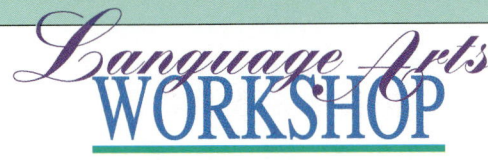
Language Arts WORKSHOP

READING

Native American Traditions

Available on Project Card 29B

COOPERATIVE LEARNING Remind students that going into solitude to think about adulthood was one important custom for some Native American peoples of the Plains. Have students form research groups to create an oral report on the customs of several different Native American peoples. Ask the groups to decide whether they want to focus on people of a certain region or on a category such as customs connected with food, customs having to do with animals, and so on. Once the groups have chosen their topics, they can do their research independently and then meet, under the direction of a Facilitator, to pool what they have learned and to create an oral report. A Reporter from each group can share its findings. Afterward, the whole class can discuss the benefits that the customs might have provided for those who followed them. LISTENING/SPEAKING/READING

WRITING

A Special Gift

Remind students that Little Gopher got a lot of satisfaction out of using his special gift. Ask each student to identify something that he or she does especially well. Have them write a personal narrative telling how they have used their special gift in the past for their own enjoyment and what they plan to do to develop it in the future. Afterward, they can read what they wrote to their classmates. LISTENING/SPEAKING/WRITING

SPELLING

Reviewing Spelling Words

SPELLING WORDS: brown, cloud, cow, enjoy, flower, house, joy, loud, oil, point, soil, town

WORDS TO EXPLORE: buckskin, custom, tribe, warrior

COOPERATIVE LEARNING Have students sit in a circle and use the Spelling Words and other words with the /oi/ and /ou/ sounds to talk about the Old West. One student asks a question such as, "What did you do in the Old West?" A second student responds using one of the Spelling Words, and a third student records the response. The second student then becomes the Questioner, the third student the Responder, and so on. They continue until all of the Spelling Words have been used and no one can think of any new words with the /oi/ and /ou/ sounds. LISTENING/SPEAKING/SPELLING

Use *Integrated Spelling* Lesson 12 to reinforce the Spelling Words and the Words to Explore. See pages T81–T86 in *Integrated Spelling Teacher's Edition*.

 **SPELLING POSTTEST** You may want to use the Pretest/Posttest Sentences on *Integrated Spelling Teacher's Edition* page T81 to assess students' knowledge of the spelling generalization.

THE LEGEND OF THE INDIAN PAINTBRUSH / T391

Grammar MINI**LESSON**

Singular and Plural Pronouns

OBJECTIVES: *To recognize that a pronoun is a word that takes the place of one or more nouns; to recognize that the singular pronouns* I, me, you, he, she, him, her, *and* it *replace singular nouns and that the plural nouns* we, us, you, they, *and* them *replace plural nouns; to always capitalize the pronoun* I

Oral Warm-Up

Copy onto the board and read aloud the following passage from "The Legend of the Indian Paintbrush":

The sky filled with clouds and out of them came a young Indian maiden and an old grandfather. She carried a rolled-up animal skin and he carried a brush made of fine animal hairs and pots of paints.

Ask students to look at the illustration on page 229 in their books. Reread the first sentence of the passage above, circle the word *them*, and ask students to tell what the Indian maiden and the old grandfather came out of. (the clouds) Write *the clouds* above the word *them*. Circle the words *she* and *he* in the second sentence. Ask students who carried a rolled-up animal skin (a young Indian maiden) and who carried a brush made of fine animal hairs and pots of paints. (an old grandfather) Write each answer above the appropriate pronoun.

Interactive Teaching

SINGULAR PRONOUNS Explain that a word such as *them, she,* or *he* that takes the place of one or more nouns is called a **pronoun**. Write *I, me, you, he, she, him, her,* and *it* on the board, and tell students that these words are called **singular pronouns** because they can take the place of singular nouns. Circle the pronoun *I*, and tell students that this pronoun is always capitalized. Then write the following sentence pairs on the board:

- Aunt Gloria hung Geoffrey's <u>painting</u> on the wall.
  Aunt Gloria hung <u>it</u> on the wall.
- Uncle Jessie gave an <u>easel</u> to Maggie.
  Uncle Jessie gave an easel to <u>her</u>.
- Ask <u>Marlow</u> to come for a drive.
  Ask <u>him</u> to come for a drive.

Read the first pair of sentences aloud. Ask students what word replaces *painting*. (it) Circle the word *it*. Repeat the process for the remaining sentence pairs. Point out that using pronouns can help make writing less repetitious. Encourage volunteers to write their own sentence pairs.

PLURAL PRONOUNS Write *we, us, you, they,* and *them* on the board. Explain that these are **plural pronouns** that can take the place of plural nouns or more than one noun. Next, write the following sentences on the board:

- My brothers made a colorful painting.
  <u>They</u> made a colorful painting.
- Dave and I saw the painting.
  <u>We</u> saw the painting.
- The art prize went to Jeb and Doug.
  The art prize went to <u>them</u>.

Have volunteers read aloud each pair of sentences, and explain which words are replaced by the underlined pronoun in the second sentence. As before, encourage students to make up their own sentence pairs.

LANGUAGE HANDBOOK *Singular and Plural Pronouns, pages 108–111*

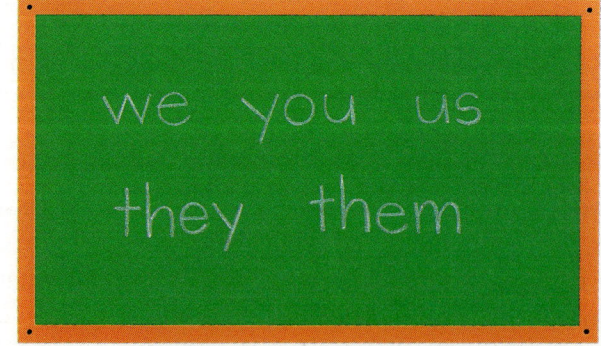

Practice Activities

Pronoun Actors

Model the following exercise for students: Pantomime an easily recognizable activity, such as getting a book and giving it to a student. On the board, write a descriptive sentence similar to the following about what you are doing: *Ms. Jacobs gets a book for David.* Then perform a second related activity, and write another descriptive sentence such as, *Now she is reading to him.* Have students work in groups of two or three to plan pairs of related activities to pantomime. As each group performs, the audience provides descriptive sentences. Write these sentences on the board. Ask students to use pronouns in the second sentence as you did in the model. Then have volunteers reread the pairs of sentences and explain which words are replaced by the pronoun(s) in the second sentence. **AUDITORY/KINESTHETIC**

Legendary Pronouns

Have students write summaries of "The Legend of the Indian Paintbrush" or another legend or folktale they have read recently. Encourage them to use pronouns in their summaries. Then have students exchange their summaries with a partner. Ask partners to read each other's work, circle the pronouns, and identify the noun or nouns each pronoun replaces.
VISUAL/KINESTHETIC

MEETING INDIVIDUAL NEEDS

SECOND-LANGUAGE SUPPORT On the board, write these pronouns: *they, she, he, them, us, you, me.* Have students point to each other to illustrate their meaning.

RETEACH Follow the visual, auditory, and kinesthetic/motor models on page R27.

Practice Book

OPTIONAL INDEPENDENT PRACTICE

PRACTICE BOOK
page 68: Identifying and using singular and plural pronouns

GRAMMAR PRACTICE
pages 30–31: Reviewing singular and plural pronouns

PART 3

Learning through the Literature

COMPREHENSION
INTRODUCE

Making Predictions

OBJECTIVE: *To use text and personal experience to predict story events*

Interactive Teaching

Focus on "The Legend of the Indian Paintbrush."

LITERATURE CONNECTION Point out to students that by using events from the story and their own knowledge, they were able to make reasonable predictions about what was going to happen in "The Legend of the Indian Paintbrush." Invite volunteers to briefly share some predictions they made.

Strategy: Use prior knowledge.

MODEL MAKING PREDICTIONS Remind students that "The Legend of the Indian Paintbrush" contained clues about what would happen. Explain to students that part of making a prediction is using what they already know. Then model how to make a prediction:

> I know that in Little Gopher's Dream-Vision, the maiden tells him that his picture on the white buckskin will be painted in pure bright colors. So I predict that when he can't find the colors, an extraordinary event will occur to help him.

Display Chart/Transparency 23, or write the following paragraphs on the board. Have students make predictions about what might happen to Yahto.

Chart/Transparency 23 Making Predictions

Long ago, a chief had four young sons who were fine hunters. They moved swiftly and quietly through the tall grasses. Their arrows flew as straight as hawks.

The chief had a fifth son, Yahto, who had none of his brothers' skills although he was every bit as big and strong. Yahto tripped and fell on flat ground. His arrows went crooked as snakes. He always came home empty-handed from the hunts. As hard as he tried, he never seemed to get any better. Finally, the day came when it was time for Yahto to go into the hills to hunt alone.

ADDITIONAL BOOKS FOR MAKING PREDICTIONS

The Hole in the Dike by Norma Green. Scholastic, 1993. **EASY**

The Girl Who Loved Wild Horses by Paul Goble. Bradbury, 1978. **AVERAGE**

T394 / A PLACE TO DREAM, UNIT 3

Practice Activity

One Step Further

Have students synthesize clues. Have student partners create a diagram like the one shown, in which they combine story clues with personal experience to come up with a prediction for the rest of the story. **VISUAL**

Story Clues	+	Experience Clues	=	Our Prediction
Yahto's problem is that he's not a good hunter. He is about to go out to hunt alone.		Usually, people who are not good at something can improve with practice.		Because Yahto never practiced, he did badly on the hunt.

Performance Assessment

Have the students display their own diagrams to analyze predictions they made for the "One Step Further" activity. For evaluation guidelines, see *Staff Development Guide*.

Reader ↔ Writer Connection
Making Predictions

WRITERS try to include evidence to help readers make predictions.

READERS use story events and their knowledge to make predictions.

WRITE A STORY Have students write two alternative ideas for a story ending, based on clues in a story beginning.

MEETING INDIVIDUAL NEEDS

RETEACH Follow the visual, auditory, and kinesthetic/motor models on page R28.

CHALLENGE Have students write all but the ending of a short story on one side of a sheet of paper and the ending on the other. Have them exchange papers and predict the endings.

SECOND-LANGUAGE SUPPORT Have students meet in a group to read a story. Have them pause frequently to make predictions. See also the manual *Alternative Teaching Strategies*, pages 13, 74–77.

OPTIONAL INDEPENDENT PRACTICE

WRITER'S JOURNAL pages 44–45: Writing predictions

PRACTICE BOOK page 69: Making predictions

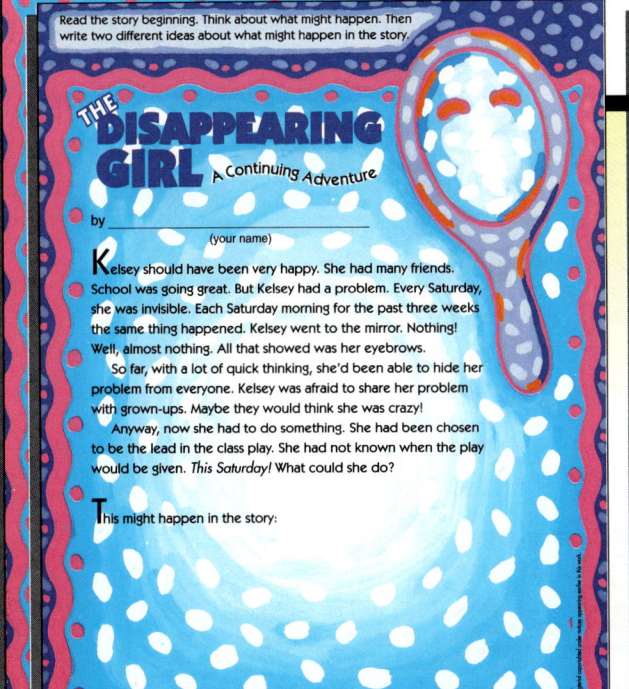
Writer's Journal

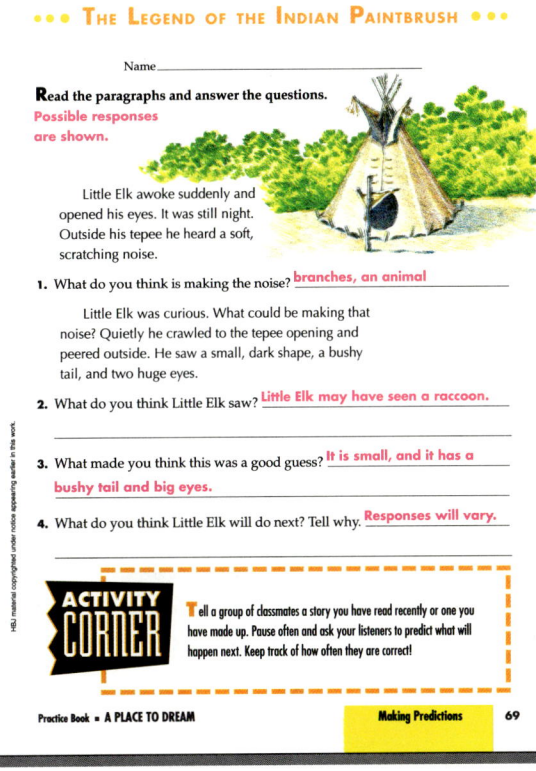
Practice Book

THE LEGEND OF THE INDIAN PAINTBRUSH / T395

LITERATURE APPRECIATION
REVIEW

Story Elements

OBJECTIVE: *To analyze how setting, characters, and plot work together in a story*

Review

Use a diagram to analyze story elements.

REVIEW THROUGH THE LITERATURE Tell students that understanding how important details all work together in the story will help them to better appreciate "The Legend of the Indian Paintbrush." Write the following diagram on the board.

Setting: A village on the Great Plains, many years ago

↓ ↓

Effects on the Main Character's Actions: Little Gopher feels bad because he doesn't have necessary skills for surviving on the Plains; he uses local plants and minerals to make his paints.

Effects on the Story's Plot: The paintbrushes Little Gopher is given take root. The next day the hillside is covered with flowering plants.

Practice Activity

Setting Switch

Have students apply the learning.

Discuss how the story might be different if it were set in modern times. Encourage the class to suggest new plot events based on the new settings. **AUDITORY**

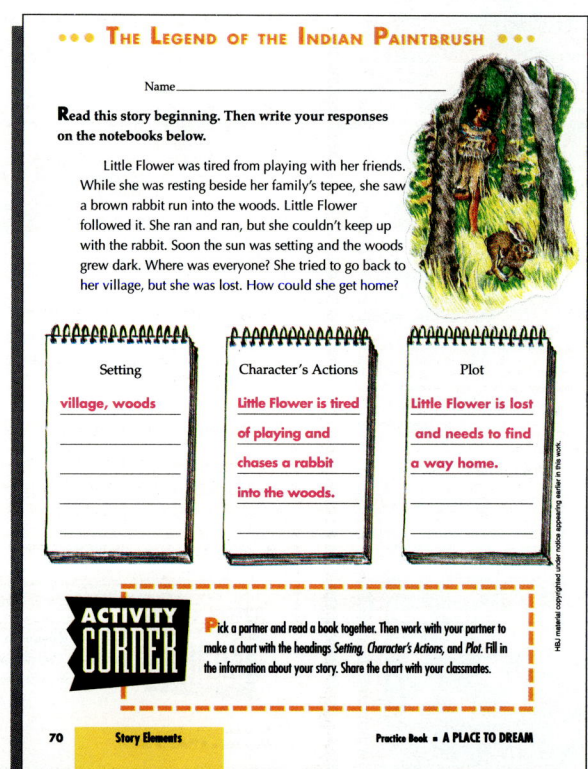

Practice Book

MEETING INDIVIDUAL NEEDS

CHALLENGE Have several students write on an index card either a plot, a setting, or a character trait. Challenge students to pick up one card from each category, and write a short story based on the information.

OPTIONAL INDEPENDENT PRACTICE

PRACTICE BOOK
page 70: Understanding story elements

DECODING

MAINTAIN

Structural Analysis

OBJECTIVE: *To use prefixes, base words, and suffixes to decode words*

Review

Explore the skill in the context of literature.

REVIEW THROUGH THE LITERATURE   Have students read the first sentence on page 231 of "The Legend of the Indian Paintbrush." Ask a volunteer to act out or state in other words what happened to the buckskin. Point out that in order to understand the meaning of the word *unrolled*, they had to know how the prefix *un-* changed the meaning of the verb *rolled*. Ask students what a prefix is and what a suffix is. (Prefixes and suffixes are word parts added to a base word to change its meaning. A suffix also changes the way the word is used.)

Practice Activity

Hunting Affixes

Use the literature for further practice.

Write on the board the following chart. Have students read aloud the entries. Then ask them to scan "The Legend of the Indian Paintbrush" to find other prefixes and suffixes to add to the chart.

Word	Prefix	Suffix	Meaning
surely		-ly	"in a way that is"
unrolled	un-		"did the opposite"

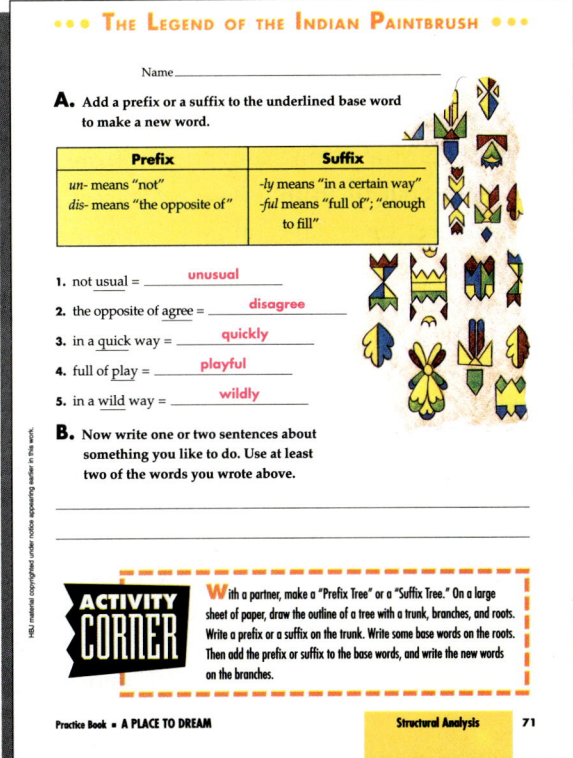

Practice Book

MEETING INDIVIDUAL NEEDS

CHALLENGE   Have students write sentences containing familiar words that have prefixes and/or suffixes. Have them trade papers with a partner, who underlines the words that have prefixes and/or suffixes and then figures out their meanings.

OPTIONAL INDEPENDENT PRACTICE

PRACTICE BOOK
page 71: Using structural analysis

THE LEGEND OF THE INDIAN PAINTBRUSH / T397

Integrated CURRICULUM

MATH/ART

A Village in Scale

Tell students that a tepee that served as a home for a Plains dweller might have been about 20 feet high and 30 feet across. Ask students to work in groups to draw a mural or create a model of a tepee village, trying to keep everything in scale. Have them use reference books to figure out the sizes of horses, tools, and rivers that might have been in or near a Plains village. READING/VIEWING

SOCIAL STUDIES

Coats of Arms

Available on Project Card 30A

Remind students that Little Gopher drew pictures to tell some important things about his people. Explain that the symbol of a nation or of a family is sometimes found on a shield or plaque and is known as a *coat of arms*. Discuss with students how symbols are used on coats of arms to stand for ideas. You might point out that sports teams are often named for powerful animals such as bulls, broncos, and tigers to symbolize how strong and tough they are. Have students draw a coat of arms for their own family or for your school. Let them take turns displaying their work and inviting their classmates to infer the significance of the symbols and pictures found on the coats of arms. LISTENING/SPEAKING/VIEWING

SCIENCE

Wild and Beautiful Flowers

Have a large group work together to create a bulletin board display that shows the wildflowers of your region. To begin, the whole class can scan wildlife guides to create a master list of plants and wildflowers found in your area. Then prompt each student or pair of students to research one or more of the flowers on the list. Suggest that they answer questions such as these:

- What does it look like?
- What are its common and scientific names?
- Where is it found?
- At what time of the year does it appear or bloom?
- Are there any interesting stories or legends about it?

Students might make illustrations to accompany their reports. They can share their work before adding it to the display. If possible, invite students to go for a walk and try to identify any wildflowers in the vicinity of your school. LISTENING/SPEAKING/WRITING

T398 / A PLACE TO DREAM, UNIT 3

CHOICES

MUSIC

Singing About Great Deeds

Remind students that Little Gopher painted some of the great deeds of his People. Then point out that people also write songs about great deeds; for example, "The Star-Spangled Banner" tells about a battle. Encourage groups of interested students to create original lyrics for popular melodies to tell about events and "great deeds" that are important to them. Then have students perform their songs.
LISTENING/WRITING

ART

Colors and Emotions
Available on Project Card 30B

Remind students of the magnificent painting Little Gopher created on his white buckskin. His people loved it because they reacted with their emotions to the beautiful colors of the sunset sky. Discuss with students how the colors used in paintings can affect viewers' emotions. Then discuss how the sky changes in appearance at different times of the day and during different kinds of weather conditions. Ask students to create a picture in which the sky is the dominant feature and to use color to try to create a specific mood such as sadness or excitement. Afterward, let them take turns displaying their paintings and asking their classmates how the pictures make them feel. **LISTENING/SPEAKING/VIEWING**

BOOKS TO SHARE

SOCIAL STUDIES/ART *Colors* by Philip Yenawine. Delacorte, 1991. EASY

Lines by Philip Yenawine. Delacorte, 1991. EASY

Shapes by Philip Yenawine. Delacorte, 1991. EASY

Stories by Philip Yenawine. Delacorte, 1991. EASY

The Young Artist by Thomas Locker. Dial, 1989. AVERAGE

THE LEGEND OF THE INDIAN PAINTBRUSH / T399

MULTICULTURAL PERSPECTIVES

Who Needs the Arts? We All Do!

DISCUSSION STARTER
What would you say if principals, teachers, and parents joined you in class for lessons in singing, dancing, and acting?

READ ALOUD
Victor Kendall has made this happen through his belief that learning about the arts and sharing them with others helps students stay in school, master reading and math, and understand science better.

Kendall has been involved in the arts for years, playing piano and flute, managing the Dance Theatre of Harlem, and developing art education programs in New York. He says he believes strongly in teaching the arts to young people because knowledge of the arts makes them feel good about themselves and helps them realize that "you can't achieve success without the long process of learning and training."

Dance, which is very popular nowadays, is as old as humankind. Did you know that it was used in early times to celebrate birth, to try to cure illness, and to mourn the dead? It was also believed that dancing could inspire good hunting and victory in battle. Dance may be an expression of emotions, an outlet for extra energy, or simply a source of joy.

ACTIVITY CORNER
• Have students work in small groups to research the history of dance. Assign to each group one of the following countries or another country: Spain, France, China, and the United States. Ask students to find information about how a specific dance is performed, what its origin is, what kind of music accompanies it, and what costume is worn during its performance.

• Give students the opportunity to hear music from all over the world. As you play tapes and records of music from various countries, ask students to discuss the mood and feeling the music creates. Then have students work in small groups to plan some dance steps to accompany the music. Give groups time to rehearse, and then have them perform for each other.

Victor Kendall stresses the importance of art education programs in schools.

Children creating a mural

PADDINGTON PAINTS A PICTURE

from PADDINGTON ON STAGE
adapted by Alfred Bradley and Michael Bond • illustrated by Peggy Fortnum

AWARD-WINNING AUTHOR AND ILLUSTRATOR

Integrated Lesson Planner

Paddington Paints a Picture
pages 256–270

	READING	**LANGUAGE ARTS**	**CROSS-CURRICULAR CONNECTIONS**
PART 1 *Reading the Literature* pages T404–T414	**Building Background** **Vocabulary Strategies** **Prereading Strategies** Prediction Chart Setting a Purpose **Options for Reading**	**Spelling** Pretest Spelling-Vocabulary Connection Generalization: /är/, /âr/ **Grammar Connection** Reviewing Singular and Plural Pronouns	**Social Studies** Information about Peru **Cultural Awareness** Women artists
PART 2 *Responding to the Literature* pages T415–T421	**Personal Response** **Cooperative Response** **Summarizing the Literature** **Critical Thinking Activity** Pro-and-Con Chart **Vocabulary Workshop** Key Words Footnoted Words	**Language Arts Workshop** **Reading** drama, about bears **Writing** personal narrative, comparison **Listening and Speaking** role-play **Reviewing Spelling Words** Posttest **Grammar Review** Singular and Plural Pronouns **Grammar Minilesson** Subject Pronouns	**Science** Bears, Bears, Bears
PART 3 *Learning Through the Literature* pages T422–T428	**Introduce** Vocabulary: Context Clues (Tested) Literary Appreciation: Play	**Reading** Earthquakes **Writing** On Holiday **Listening and Speaking** An English Visitor	**Art** Create a Work of Art **Math** Shopping Spree **Social Studies** On Holiday An English Visitor How Nice **Science** Earthquakes **Multicultural Perspectives** Beauty in Art

OPTIONAL MATERIALS
Charts/Transparencies 24, 25
Integrated Spelling pp. 58–61; TE pp. T87–T92
Practice Book pp. 72–78
Writer's Journal pp. 46–47
Alternative Teaching Strategies pp. 14, 78–81
Language Handbook pp. 48–50, 108–113
Grammar Practice pp. 34–35
Literature Cassette
Family Involvement Activities: Unit 3
Response Card 1
Project Cards 31A, 31B, 32A, 32B, 33

MEETING INDIVIDUAL NEEDS
Second-Language Support pp. T405, T406, T409, T421, T423, T425
Mainstreaming p. T406
Reteach pp. T421, T423, T425
Challenge pp. T423, T425

FAMILY INVOLVEMENT Encourage family members to work together to create a painting or collage. See *Family Involvement Activities*.

Key Words
marmalade
cocoa
vacuum
easel
handkerchief
retired
exhibition
antiques

T402 / A PLACE TO DREAM, UNIT 3

Selection Summary

In Scene One of the play, Mr. Brown leaves for work, having completed his painting for an exhibition. Paddington decides that painting looks like fun. Scene Two takes place in Mr. Gruber's antique shop. Mr. Gruber explains to Paddington that he is cleaning a painting and has found another painting underneath that could be an "old master." Paddington rushes home and rubs Mr. Brown's painting with paint remover, hoping to find an "old master." Horrified by the mess, Paddington tries to touch up the painting by smearing it with paints, marmalade, mustard, liquid soap, and ketchup. Soon after, Miss Black from the Art Society picks up the painting. Later that day the president of the Art Society informs Mr. Brown that he has won first prize for his "unusual" painting. Paddington, who has been worried, is relieved and proud.

About the Author

Michael Bond wrote the first Paddington book, *A Bear Called Paddington,* which was published in 1958. It was inspired by a stuffed bear he had bought his wife for Christmas. He named the bear Paddington after the railway station in London, England. Bond has written more than seventy Paddington books. Bond also wrote *The Tales of Olga da Polga,* named by the Child Study Association of America as one of its books of the year in 1973. As Bond explains, he doesn't sit around waiting for inspiration: "Ideas come by living life normally and developing a sense of observing."

About the Illustrator

Alfred Bradley collaborated with Michael Bond to write *Paddington on Stage,* a play adapted from Bond's *The Adventures of Paddington Bear* (1965). The play was first produced in England in 1973.

Additional Reading

OTHER BOOKS BY MICHAEL BOND

A Bear Called Paddington. Houghton Mifflin, 1960.   AVERAGE

The Tales of Olga da Polga. Macmillan, 1989.   CHALLENGING

OTHER THEME-RELATED BOOKS

All I See by Cynthia Rylant. Orchard, 1988.   EASY

The Perfect Spot by Robert J. Blake. Philomel, 1992.   AVERAGE

BOOKS FOR APPLYING STRATEGIES: CONTEXT CLUES, PLAY

Harold and the Purple Crayon by Crockett Johnson. HarperCollins, 1955.   EASY

The Bunny Play by Loreen Leedy. Holiday House, 1988.   EASY

PADDINGTON PAINTS A PICTURE / T403

PART 1

Reading the Literature

Building Background

Access prior knowledge and build vocabulary concepts.

Tell students that the next selection, a play called "Paddington Paints a Picture," is about a bear who tries to paint. Have students discuss what they know about painting, including information about museums, or the names of famous painters or paintings. Have students create a web like the following to record words about painting.

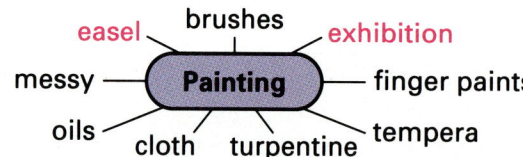

Vocabulary Strategies

Introduce Key Words and strategies.

Display Chart/Transparency 24 or these paragraphs on it. Have students read the paragraphs silently, using context clues to figure out the meanings of the underlined words. For example, students might notice that *spreads, orange,* and *toast* are clues to the meaning of *marmalade.*

Chart/Transparency 24   Key Words

Every morning Grandpa spreads orange <u>marmalade</u> on his toast. Then he mixes milk, chocolate, and sugar to make <u>cocoa</u>. To keep the cocoa warm all morning, Grandpa puts it in a thermos, or a <u>vacuum</u> bottle.

Grandpa then goes to a special room upstairs to work on his painting, which is on the wooden <u>easel</u>. If he can't find a rag, he uses his <u>handkerchief</u> to wipe the paints that drip.

Now that Grandpa is <u>retired</u>, he has more time to paint than when he worked. But he will have to paint very fast to have this picture ready to show at the spring <u>exhibition</u>. Many people bring beautiful <u>antiques</u> that have been in their families for years. But Grandpa always likes to bring a new creation.

TEACHING TIP

Tell students that in the play they are about to read, Paddington Bear comes from Peru, South America. Locate Peru on a map or globe.

Key Words

marmalade
cocoa
vacuum
easel
handkerchief
retired
exhibition
antiques

KEY WORDS DEFINED

marmalade   jam made from fruit, usually citrus fruit

cocoa   hot drink made with powdered chocolate

vacuum   container that keeps liquids hot or cold

easel   three-legged stand for holding a painting

handkerchief   small piece of cloth

retired   no longer working, usually because of age

exhibition   public showing

antiques   things made very long ago

Check all students' understanding.

Display the Key Words. Have students write each Key Word on a separate index card. Read the following related words or phrases. Have students hold up the correct Key Word card. Encourage students to discuss how the words in both columns are alike and to think of additional related words or phrases for each Key Word. STRATEGY: SYNONYMS

Key Words	Related Words
vacuum	thermos
cocoa	hot drink
retired	no longer working
easel	art stand
handkerchief	small cloth
marmalade	orange jam
antiques	old things
exhibition	show

Integrate spelling with vocabulary.

SPELLING-VOCABULARY CONNECTION *Integrated Spelling* Lesson 13 reinforces the spelling words with /är/ and /âr/, such as *chair* and *large*, found in the selection. In addition, the Words to Explore help reinforce the concept of art as it relates to the selection.

SPELLING PRETEST You may want to use the Pretest/Posttest Sentences on page T87 in *Integrated Spelling Teacher's Edition* to assess students' knowledge of the spelling generalization.

Spelling

Spelling Words	Words to Explore
1. air	antiques
2. bear	easel
3. chair	exhibition
4. guard	painting
5. large	
6. mark	Your Own Words
7. dare	13.
8. rare	14.
9. scare	15.
10. square	16.
11. wear	
12. yard	

Spelling generalization: /är/ and /âr/ sounds

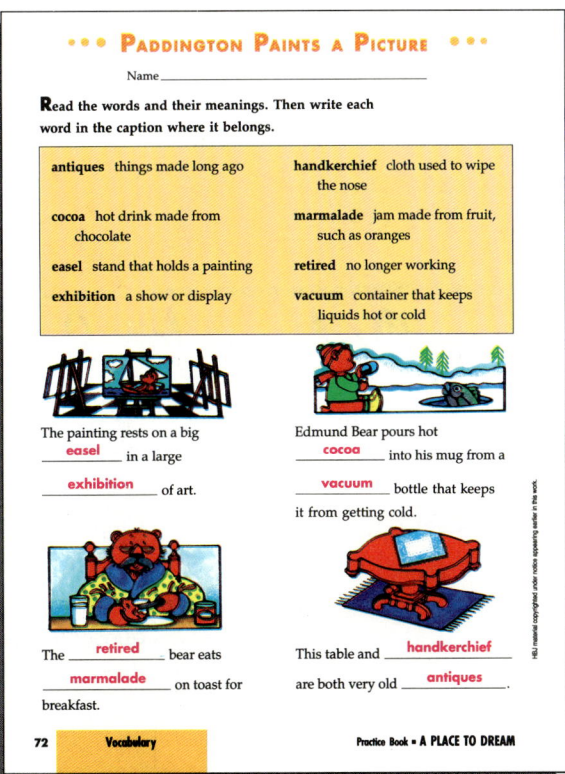

Practice Book

MEETING INDIVIDUAL NEEDS

SECOND-LANGUAGE SUPPORT Encourage students to add a third column to the chart, in which they can list related words in their first language. See also the manual *Alternative Teaching Strategies*, pages 14, 78–81.

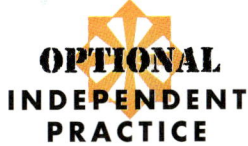

OPTIONAL INDEPENDENT PRACTICE

INTEGRATED SPELLING pages 58–61: Words like *chair* and *large*

PRACTICE BOOK page 72: Reinforcing Key Words

NOTE: This page may be completed now or after students have read the story.

PADDINGTON PAINTS A PICTURE / T405

Prereading Strategies

Prediction Chart

Help students preview the literature.

Review how to preview a selection. (read and think about the title, look at the pictures, and read the first few paragraphs or pages) Then have students preview the selection, stopping at the bottom of page 259.

Encourage students to make predictions.

Briefly discuss the format of a play and the setting, the characters, and the events students discovered in their preview. On the board, create a chart similar to the one below. Or you may want to distribute copies of the prediction chart found on page R102. Help students predict what might happen in the story.

What I Predict Will Happen	What Actually Happens
Paddington paints an unusual picture.	
He uses paint remover, ketchup, and mustard on his painting.	

PERSONAL JOURNAL Have students add their predictions to their personal journals. Ask students to support their predictions.

Setting a Purpose

Have students set purposes.

Encourage students to discuss what will happen in the play, based on their preview and what they know about painting. Then have students use their predictions to set a purpose for reading.

If students have difficulty setting a purpose, offer this suggestion:

I'm going to read to find out what kind of painting Paddington paints, and how everyone likes it.

MEETING INDIVIDUAL NEEDS

SECOND-LANGUAGE SUPPORT Explain to students that as they read, they can sometimes guess the meaning of an unknown word because it looks like a word in their first language. For example, the words *opinion* and *famous* have Spanish equivalents: *opinión* and *famoso*. See also the manual *Alternative Teaching Strategies*, pages 14, 78–81.

SUPPORT FOR MAINSTREAMING Help students sustain the focus needed to appreciate this play by suggesting that as they read silently, they imagine each character having a voice suited to his or her personality.

Options for Reading

SUSTAINED SILENT READING	STRATEGIC READING	READER RESPONSE GROUPS	TEACHER READ-ALOUD
Encourage students to record interesting words in a vocabulary notebook and talk with a partner about British expressions and other words they are unsure of when they finish reading.	Use the suggestions that appear on pages T407, T411, and T413 to generate discussion.	Follow the suggestions for Literature Circles on page T407. As they read, students should note questions they would like to discuss with the group.	You may want to read Scenes One and Two aloud so students can hear you pronounce words with British spellings, such as *centre*, as well as other words that may be unfamiliar to them. Have students read the rest of the play silently.

T406 / A PLACE TO DREAM, UNIT 3

PADDINGTON PAINTS A PICTURE   PAGES 256–257

PADDINGTON PAINTS A PICTURE

from PADDINGTON ON STAGE
adapted by Alfred Bradley and Michael Bond • illustrated by Peggy Fortnum

AWARD-WINNING AUTHOR

CAST OF CHARACTERS

MR. BROWN	MRS. BIRD	MRS. BROWN	JUDY
PADDINGTON	MISS BLACK	JONATHAN	MAN
MR. GRUBER			

PROPS

In the Browns' sitting room:
  A few chairs
  Table
  Easel

For scene II:
  Suitcase

In Mr. Gruber's shop:
  Chair
  Sign saying "Antiques"
  Thermos flask, two mugs and a bun
  Pile of bric-a-brac, china, books, toys
  Half-restored "painting"

In the sitting room, for scenes III and IV:
  Very messy painting
  Paintbrush
  Paints—red and green
  Marmalade jar
  Spoon
  Palette (can be made from cardboard)
  Three empty bottles, painted to look as if they contain paint remover, ketchup and mustard
  Handkerchief
  Washing-up liquid
  Slip of paper for cheque

257

Reader Response Groups

LITERATURE CIRCLES Have groups of four or five students first read the play silently, stopping at page 265 for a brief discussion. Then suggest that groups read the play aloud with each student taking one or more roles. You may want to distribute Response Card 1 (Characters), found on page R79, or provide the following questions:

- Who are the main characters?
- Which character do you like best? Why?

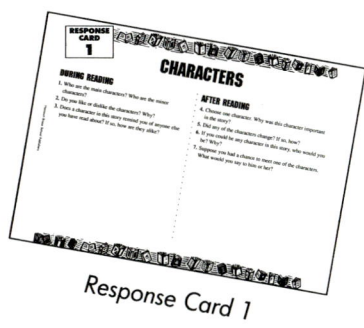

Response Card 1

Strategic Reading

SET PURPOSE/PREDICT: PAGES 256–265 Have students read through page 265. Encourage them to tell what they will be reading to find out.

PADDINGTON PAINTS A PICTURE / T407

PAGES 258–259 PADDINGTON PAINTS A PICTURE

In this play the easel with Mr. Brown's painting should be placed near the centre of the stage so that Paddington has plenty of room to work on it. We don't need to see the painting, as it will be facing away from us until Miss Black brings it back at the end of the play. Of course, the tomato ketchup and mustard and paint remover should not be real (use empty bottles painted to look full), and the painting should be done beforehand so that it is dry for the performance. The painting should look as messy as you can make it.

When we get to Mr. Gruber's shop, all that we need to see is a pile of oddments with a notice saying "Antiques." Mr. Gruber should have a chair to sit on, a half-cleaned picture with a boat on one side and part of a lady's face on the other, a Thermos flask and two mugs.

Scene One

[*The Browns' sitting room.* MR. BROWN *is getting ready to go to work as* PADDINGTON *comes in. The easel is standing with its back to the audience.*]

MR. BROWN   Hello, Paddington. What are your p for today?

PADDINGTON   I think I might do some shopping, Brown. I like shopping.

MR. BROWN   You won't get lost?

PADDINGTON   No, I won't be going very far. Is yo painting finished, Mr. Brown?

MR. BROWN   Yes. [*He looks at it.*] You know, I rea think it's the best I've ever done.

PADDINGTON   I hope you win a prize.

MR. BROWN   Oh, I don't expect I shall. But it's fu That's the important thing, I suppose. I must be now. I'm late for work already. [*He goes to the do* Goodbye, Paddington. I'll see you tonight.

PADDINGTON   Goodbye, Mr. Brown.

[MR. BROWN *goes, and* PADDINGTON *takes a closer lo at the painting.*]

I think I would enjoy painting. It looks *very* interesting.

Expanding the Literature   Is this play realistic or is it a fantasy? **How do you know?** (Fantasy; animals cannot talk and do not go shopping.)   CRITICAL: DISTINGUISHING BETWEEN FANTASY AND REALITY

Teaching Tip   You may want to remind students that the setting of this story is London, England, and that some British expressions and word spellings may be unfamiliar to them. Discuss how students can use context clues to figure out unfamiliar words. Point out the footnotes that appear on pages 260, 261, 267, and 269, and explain how students can use them to understand some of the words.

See page T426 for information found on Project Card 32A.

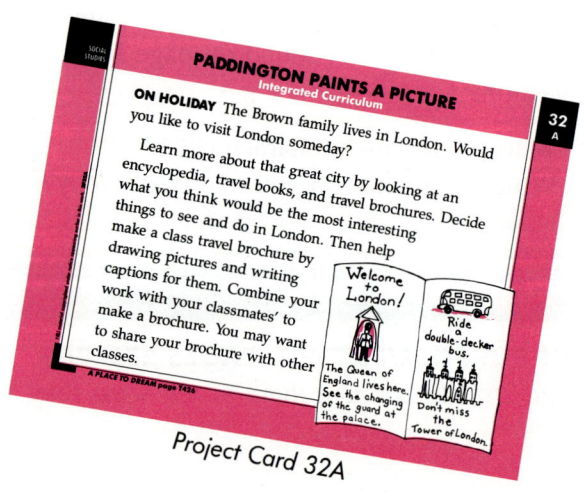

Project Card 32A

T408 / A PLACE TO DREAM, UNIT 3

Scene Two

[*Mr. Gruber's bric-a-brac shop in the Portobello Road. He is cleaning an oil painting when* PADDINGTON *arrives.*]

MR. GRUBER Good morning. Can I help you?

PADDINGTON [*putting down his suitcase*] I don't know really. I was out for a walk and your shop looked so nice, I thought I would like to see inside.

MR. GRUBER Please have a look round, Mr. . . . er . . .

PADDINGTON Brown. Paddington Brown. I come from Darkest Peru.

MR. GRUBER Darkest Peru? How strange. I know Peru quite well. I spent a lot of my early life in South America.

PADDINGTON Fancy that, Mr. . . . er . . .

MR. GRUBER Gruber. Look . . . I've just made some cocoa, Mr. Brown. Would you care for a cup?

PADDINGTON Ooh, yes, please.

MR. GRUBER It's quite hot. I keep it in a vacuum.

PADDINGTON [*amazed*] You keep your cocoa in a vacuum cleaner?

MR. GRUBER No, Mr. Brown, a vacuum flask. [*He pours some cocoa and hands it to* PADDINGTON.] There's nothing like a chat over a bun and a cup of cocoa.

PADDINGTON A bun as well! [*They sit down to enjoy their elevenses.*[1]] What were you doing when I came into the shop, Mr. Gruber?

MR. GRUBER I was cleaning a painting. [*He picks it up.*] Now, what do you think of that?

PADDINGTON [*looking at it*] It's a puzzle, Mr. Gruber. One half is a boat and the other half is a lady in a large hat.

MR. GRUBER There you are. I'd like your opinion on it, Mr. Brown.

PADDINGTON It doesn't seem to be one thing or the other.

MR. GRUBER Ah! It isn't at the moment. But just you wait until I've cleaned it! I gave five shillings[2] for that painting years and years ago, when it was just a picture of a sailing ship. And what do you think? When I started to clean it the other day, all the paint began to come off and I discovered that there was another painting underneath. [*confidentially*] It could be an old master.

[1] elevenses: a snack taken in the middle of the morning

[2] five shillings: British money, worth less than fifty cents

---

Social Studies Connection Tell students that Peru is a large country in South America. It is one of the world's leading producers of copper, lead, silver, and zinc and also ranks among the world's leading fishing countries. Students might also be interested to know that soccer is the most popular sport in Peru and basketball is also enjoyed.

Second-Language Support Point out the word *puzzle* in the first line on page 261 and ask students to name some kinds of puzzles. (jigsaw puzzles, crossword puzzles, word puzzles) Help them conclude that anything that's hard to figure out or understand can be called a puzzle.

MEETING INDIVIDUAL NEEDS

PAGES 262–263 PADDINGTON PAINTS A PICTURE

PADDINGTON An old master? It looks like an old lady to me.
MR. GRUBER [*laughs*] What I mean is, it could be very valuable. It could be by a famous painter.
PADDINGTON That sounds interesting. Very interesting indeed. [*He gets up, his mind obviously elsewhere.*] I'll have to be going now, Mr. Gruber. Thank you for the elevenses.
MR. GRUBER Is anything the matter, Mr. Brown?
PADDINGTON No, Mr. Gruber. I've had an idea, that's all. [*mysteriously, as he makes to leave*] I may come into some money soon.
MR. GRUBER Good day, Mr. Brown. I shall look forward to that. [*He watches* PADDINGTON *go.*] Come into some money! I wonder what he meant by that?

Scene Three

[*The Browns' sitting room.* PADDINGTON *comes in, looks round carefully. He takes a bottle of paint remover from his coat pocket. He soaks a handkerchief in paint remover and rubs it over the painting. He stands back to look and, horrified by what he sees, decides to have another try. He is giving the painting a vigorous scrub when* MRS. BIRD *enters.*]

MRS. BIRD Now, Paddington, what are you up to? I thought you were out shopping.
PADDINGTON I was. But I'm not any more. [*gloomily*] I wish I still was.

MRS. BIRD Whatever's the matter? [*She sees the picture.*] What *have* you been doing? That's the painting Mr. Brown did specially for the exhibition.
PADDINGTON I know. I thought there might be an old master underneath.
MRS. BIRD An old master? [*She looks at the painting.*] It used to be some boats on a lake. It looks more like a storm at sea now. He'll be most upset when he sees it.
PADDINGTON I know, Mrs. Bird. What can I do?
MRS. BIRD They're coming to collect it today. There's only one hope. Perhaps you could touch it up before they get here.
PADDINGTON That's a good idea, Mrs. Bird. Except I haven't any paints.
MRS. BIRD There's an old box under the stairs. I'll get them for you. [*She goes.*]
PADDINGTON I wonder if it will work. [*He gets a jar of marmalade, takes a spoonful, and then puts it on the table near the easel.*]
MRS. BIRD [*coming in with a paintbox and palette*] Here we are. It's very old, but it's the best I can do.
PADDINGTON Thank you, Mrs. Bird.
MRS. BIRD I hope you manage something. I don't know, I'm sure . . .
[*She goes to the kitchen.*]

Cultural Awareness Students might enjoy finding out about famous painters who were women and who learned their craft rather late in life. Two painters you might mention are Grandma Moses, who started painting in her seventies, and Clementine Hunter, an African American artist who discovered her talent when she was in her fifties.

See page T428 for information found on Project Card 33.

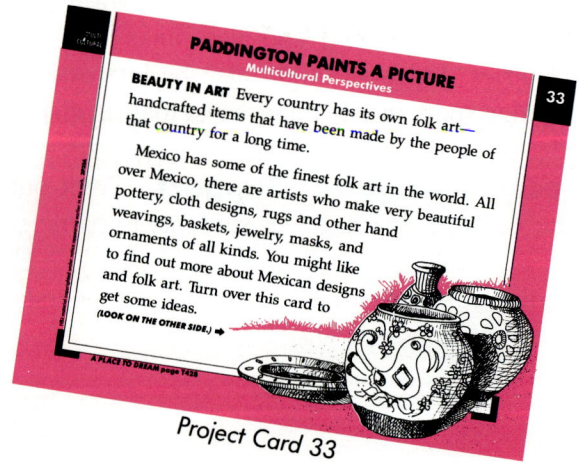
Project Card 33

T410 / A PLACE TO DREAM, UNIT 3

PADDINGTON PAINTS A PICTURE PAGES 264–265

DINGTON [*Holding the brush at arm's length, he ...iders the canvas.*] Uh, huh. [*He squeezes a tube of ...aint on the palette, then he does the same with a ...n tube. He begins to paint boldly. Although we can't ...he painting, it is obvious that he is making a mess.*] ...t looks better! [*Throughout this painting scene ...DINGTON occasionally touches the brush to his face, ...out realizing he is giving himself red and green spots. ...dabs at the painting, absent-mindedly dipping his ...h into the marmalade, and then decides to experiment. ... he adds some mustard, and then the contents of a ...ing-up liquid squeezer and a bottle of tomato ketchup.*] ...re's one thing about painting, it's fun. [*He makes a ... mess of it.* MISS BLACK *arrives to collect the picture ...knocks at the front door.* PADDINGTON *puts down his ...h and goes to the door.*]

...BLACK Good afternoon. I believe Mr. Brown has ...ainting for our exhibition.

...DINGTON Oh, yes. That's right. I'll get it for you. ...goes back, gives the painting a finishing dab, wipes the ...h on his hat, and takes the painting to the front door.]

...BLACK Thank you very much. The final judging ...s place this afternoon.

...DINGTON The *final* judging?

...BLACK Yes, we shall be awarding the prizes ...ay. I expect you will hear the results later this ...ning. Goodbye. [*She goes.*]

...DINGTON Goodbye. There's something else about ...ting—it's fun while it lasts, but it's much more ...icult than it looks. I can't think what Mr. Brown ... say . . .

Strategic Reading

MODELING A STRATEGY: PAGES 256–265 What did you find out in these pages? Was there anything you didn't understand?

THINK ALOUD You may want to model using a fix-up strategy: *So far I know who the characters are, but all of a sudden Mrs. Bird appears in Scene Three. Who is Mrs. Bird? I reread pages 262 to 264 to see if I missed something, but I didn't. If she's important to this story, I'll probably find out in the next part, so I'll keep reading.* USING FIX-UP STRATEGIES

SET PURPOSE/PREDICT: PAGES 266–270 Have students predict what might happen when Mr. Brown comes home. Have them read the rest of the play to confirm their predictions.

PADDINGTON PAINTS A PICTURE / T411

PAGES 266–267 PADDINGTON PAINTS A PICTURE

Scene Four

[*Later that day. The* BROWN *family is in the sitting room after dinner.*]

MRS. BROWN   Would you like a cup of cocoa, Paddington?

PADDINGTON   No, thank you.

MRS. BROWN   Are you all right?

PADDINGTON   Yes, I thank so, think you. I mean, I think so, thank you.

MRS. BROWN   Nothing on your mind?

PADDINGTON   No.

JONATHAN   How about a bull's-eye?³

PADDINGTON   No, thank you. I think I'll just go and have a rest for a bit. [*He goes out of the room.*]

MRS. BROWN   I do hope he's all right, Henry. He hardly touched his dinner, and that's not like him at all. And he seemed to have some funny red spots all over his face.

JONATHAN   Red spots! I wonder if it's measles. I hope he's given it to me, whatever it is. Then I will be able to stay away from school.

JUDY   Well, he's got green ones as well. I distinctly saw them.

MR. BROWN   Green ones! I wonder if he's sickening for something? If they're not gone in the morning, we'd better send for the doctor.

JONATHAN   They're judging the paintings today, aren't they, Dad?

MR. BROWN   Yes, they took mine away this afternoon.

JONATHAN   Do you think you'll win a prize?

MRS. BROWN   No one will be more surprised than your father if he does. He's never won a prize yet.

MR. BROWN   It took me a long while but I don't suppose I'll be any luckier than last time. The lady who collected it this afternoon told Paddington that the resu would be made known today, so we'll soon know.

³bull's-eye: very hard round candy

266

Expanding the Literature   What kind of mood do you think Paddington is in? (He's worried and upset.) How can you tell? (He doesn't want any cocoa. Mrs. Brown asks if he is all right.)
METACOGNITIVE: DRAWING CONCLUSIONS

GRAMMAR CONNECTION
REVIEWING SINGULAR AND PLURAL PRONOUNS   You may wish to point out these pronouns in the lines of dialogue on page 267: *I, he('s), it, me, them, they('re), we('d), you.* Remind students that a pronoun is used in place of a noun to make writing less repetitious. Ask students to identify the noun that each pronoun replaces.

T412 / A PLACE TO DREAM, UNIT 3

JUDY I wonder if he's feeling any better? [*She goes out.*]

NATHAN Perhaps they have been measles in Darkest Peru.

[*There is a knock at the front door. MRS. BIRD goes to answer it.*]

MRS. BIRD Who can that be?

[*MRS. BIRD opens the door. MISS BLACK is waiting outside. She has a MAN with her. He is carrying Mr. Brown's painting, still with its back to the audience.*]

MISS BLACK Good evening. Is Mr. Brown in?

MAN We've come about the painting he entered for our competition.

MRS. BIRD Oh, dear. Will you come this way, please? [*She ushers them into the room.*]

MAN Mr. Brown?

MR. BROWN That's right.

MAN I'm the President of the Art Society, and this is Miss Black, who was one of the judges of the competition.

MR. BROWN How do you do.

MAN I've some news for you, Mr. Brown.

PADDINGTON [*offstage*] Oooooh!

MISS BLACK Good gracious! What was that?

MAN It sounded like a cow mooing somewhere.

MRS. BROWN I think it's only a bear oooohing.

MAN Oh! Er . . . Mr. Brown, as I was saying, the judges decided that your painting was most unusual . . .

MRS. BIRD It certainly was.

MAN And they have all agreed to award you the first prize.

MR. BROWN The *first* prize?

MISS BLACK Yes, they thought your painting showed great imagination.

MR. BROWN [*pleased*] Did they now?

MAN It made great use of marmalade chunks.

THE BROWNS [*chorus*] Marmalade chunks!

MAN Yes, indeed. I don't think I've ever come across anything quite like it before. [*He places the painting on the easel facing the audience. It is, to say the least, unusual, and there are several real marmalade chunks sticking to it.*]

MRS. BROWN I didn't know you were interested in abstract art, Henry.

MR. BROWN Nor did I!

[*PADDINGTON and JUDY put their heads round the door.*]

MAN [*He removes a marmalade chunk with a flourish and swallows it.*] It not only looks good—it tastes good!

MISS BLACK What are you calling it?

MR. BROWN Where's Paddington?

MISS BLACK Where's Paddington? What a funny title!

MAN Well, sir, my congratulations! We'll be wanting the painting back in a day or so to put into the exhibition, but I'll leave it with you for the moment. Just one more thing . . . your prize. [*He hands over a cheque.*] £10.[4]

---

[4] £10: 10 pounds; about fifteen American dollars

PAGE 270 PADDINGTON PAINTS A PICTURE

MISS BLACK   May I ask what you will do with it, Mr. Brown?

MR. BROWN   [*wearily*] I think perhaps I'd better give it to a certain Home for Retired Bears in South America.

MAN   Oh, really? Well, we must be getting along.

[*As they leave,* PADDINGTON *falls into the room.* JUDY *follows him in.*]

MRS. BIRD   Well, Paddington. The secret's out. Now, what have you got to say for yourself?

PADDINGTON   [*Crosses to the painting. He removes a marmalade chunk and goes to eat it.*] I think it looks good enough to eat, Mr. Brown! [*He turns it up the other way.*] But I think they might have put it the right way up. After all, it's not every day a bear wins first prize in a painting competition.

CURTAIN

If you were one of the judges, how would you rate Paddington's painting? Explain why.

Why does Paddington change Mr. Brown's painting? How does he try to correct his mistake?

How does the Brown family feel about Paddington? How do you know?

WRITE   Make up a new ending for this play. List your characters and props first. Then tell what the characters do and say.

Returning to the Predictions/Purpose

PREDICTION CHART   After students complete the second half of their chart, encourage them to talk about how their predictions changed as they read and to tell whether they learned what they wanted to find out.

NOTE: Responses to the questions and support for the Write activity appear on page T415.

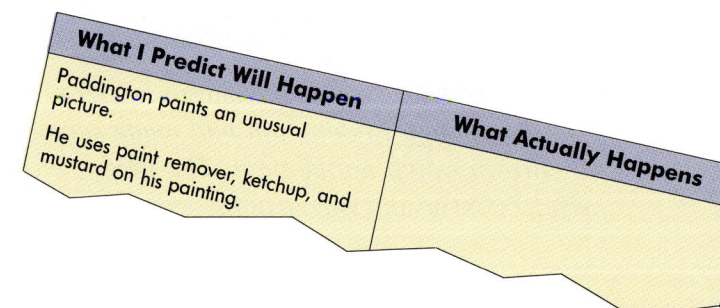

PART 2

Responding to the Literature

Personal Response

Encourage critical thinking.

If you were one of the judges, how would you rate Paddington's painting? Explain why. (Responses will vary.)
CRITICAL: EXPRESSING PERSONAL OPINIONS

Why does Paddington change Mr. Brown's painting? How does he try to correct his mistake? (He hopes to find another painting, an "old master," underneath; he tries to touch it up by smearing it with paint and food.) METACOGNITIVE: NOTING IMPORTANT DETAILS

How does the Brown family feel about Paddington? How do you know? (They care about him; Mrs. Brown worries that he might be sick; Mr. Brown wishes Paddington would retire, but doesn't get angry at him for causing trouble.) METACOGNITIVE: DRAWING CONCLUSIONS

Encourage creative written responses.

 **WRITE** Make up a new ending for this play. List your characters and props first. Then tell what the characters do and say. Encourage students to include humorous ideas. CREATIVE: INVENTING NEW ENDINGS

Cooperative Response

Have reader response groups extend their discussions.

LITERATURE CIRCLES Encourage students to share their reactions to the play. Then have them hold a discussion based on a question such as the following:

Choose one of the characters, and describe him or her. Support your description with details from the play.

STRATEGY CONFERENCE

Discuss with students how using a prediction chart helped them understand the play. (Accept reasonable responses: This strategy helps a reader stay focused on the story line.)

NOTE

An additional writing activity for this selection appears on page T418.

PADDINGTON PAINTS A PICTURE / T415

Summarizing the Literature

Have students retell the story and write a summary.

Encourage students to summarize the play by completing the map below. Then have them use the completed map to retell the play and write a brief summary. See *Practice Book* page 73 below.

Title	Paddington Paints a Picture
Setting	Browns' house and Mr. Gruber's shop
Characters	
Problem	
Event 1	
Solution	

Critical Thinking Activity

Make inferences from character traits.

BRAINSTORM Would you like to live with a bear like Paddington? What are some problems Paddington might cause for you? Have students work in small groups to brainstorm and discuss their ideas. Students can organize their ideas in a pro-and-con chart. CRITICAL: MAKING JUDGMENTS

Pro	Con
He is lively and would cause excitement. My friends would like him.	He would need to be watched all the time.

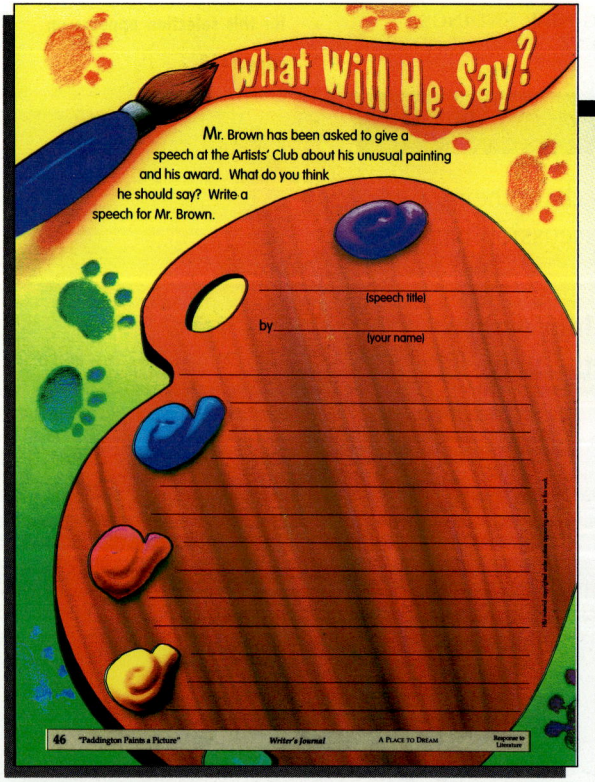
Writer's Journal

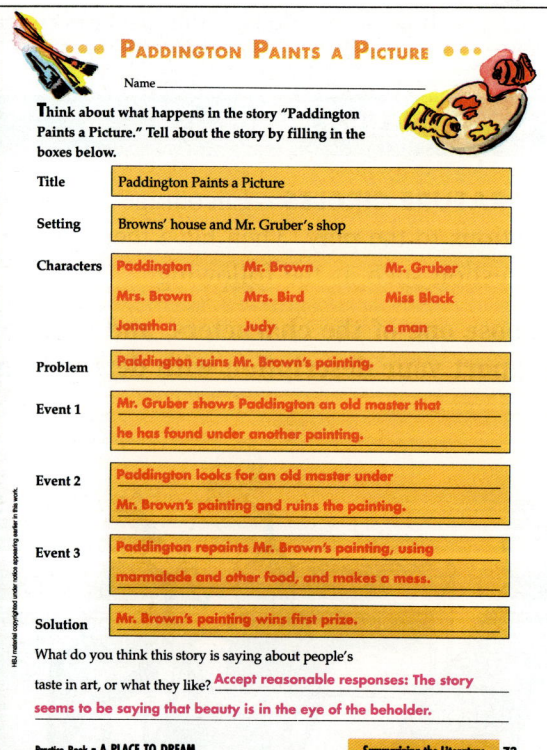
Practice Book

INFORMAL ASSESSMENT

Critical thinking activities provide opportunities to assess important reading behaviors. Judgments, opinions, and conclusions involve using story details to draw high-level inferences.

OPTIONAL INDEPENDENT PRACTICE

WRITER'S JOURNAL
page 46: Writing a personal response

PRACTICE BOOK
page 73: Summarizing the selection

T416 / A PLACE TO DREAM, UNIT 3

VOCABULARY WORKSHOP

Reviewing Key Words

On the board, display the two lists below, but omit the lines. Have each student copy the lists. Have students draw a line from the Key Word in the left-hand column to the character's name that applies in the right-hand column on their paper. Explain that a character can be used more than once.

Key Word	Character
easel	Paddington
antiques	Mr. Brown
vacuum	Mrs. Brown
handkerchief	Mr. Gruber
cocoa	Miss Black
exhibition	Man
marmalade	
retired	

Extending Vocabulary

FOOTNOTED WORDS Point out that the footnotes in "Paddington Paints a Picture" give the meanings of British words that are probably unfamiliar to the reader. Have students turn to page 260 and locate the footnoted word *elevenses* and its definition at the bottom of the page. Ask students to read the definition. ("a snack taken in the middle of the morning")

Have students form small groups, and assign each group one page in the selection. Groups should write helpful footnotes for unfamiliar words on the page. Suggest that students include the Key Words and British idioms and spellings of words such as *cheque, flask, washing-up liquid, bun, bric-a-brac,* and *centre*. Encourage them to use reference materials. Remind students to number their footnotes in sequence. Have students share their footnotes.

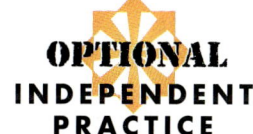

OPTIONAL INDEPENDENT PRACTICE

PRACTICE BOOK page 74: Using footnotes for word meaning

Practice Book

Language Arts WORKSHOP

READING

Oral Rereading/Drama

COOPERATIVE LEARNING To prepare students for putting on the play "Paddington Paints a Picture," encourage them to take turns reading sections of the play aloud, giving them time to rehearse their readings. Then have groups produce the play. Have students choose a Materials Manager to gather props and a Facilitator to act as director. The Facilitator can work with you to assign students to paint scenery, stage manage, act out the play, design posters announcing it, and make play programs. Allow students to perform the play for other classes. **LISTENING/READING/VIEWING**

WRITING

Writing About the Literature

WRITE A PERSONAL NARRATIVE Remind students that this play is about one adventure in Paddington's life. Have students brainstorm adventures in their lives. Ask them to write about one of their adventures. Remind them to use the words *I*, *me*, and *my* to tell about themselves. Have students use the following chart to gather and organize their details. Encourage them to include humorous details. Provide time for students to share their work. See Writing Model, page R91. **LISTENING/SPEAKING/WRITING**

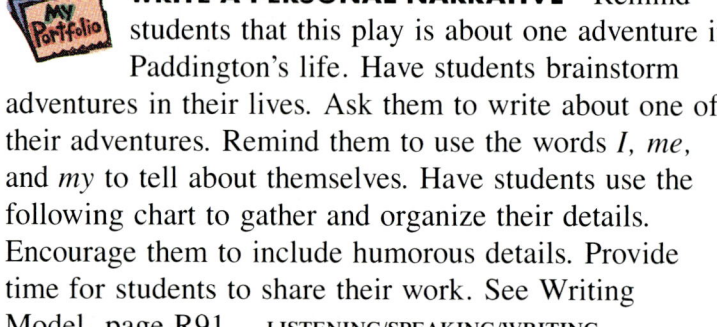

Adventure
1. Detail
2. Detail
3. Detail

GRAMMAR REVIEW: SINGULAR AND PLURAL PRONOUNS When students revise their personal narratives, remind them to check their use of pronouns. They should make sure that singular pronouns replace singular nouns, plural pronouns replace plural nouns, and that they have used the appropriate pronoun for each noun. You might reinforce the skill by having pairs of students choose a passage, find the pronouns, and tell what each refers to.

LANGUAGE HANDBOOK *Writing to Inform, pages 48–50; Singular and Plural Pronouns, pages 108–111*

DAILY LANGUAGE PRACTICE *Oral language exercises are provided on pages R70–R71.*

SPELLING

Reviewing Spelling Words

SPELLING WORDS: *air, bear, chair, guard, large, mark, dare, rare, scare, square, wear, yard*

WORDS TO EXPLORE: *antiques, easel, exhibition, painting*

Have pairs of students create word puzzles using the Spelling Words and words from their own lists that follow the generalization. On the board, draw a grid, and demonstrate placing words so that the letters that spell /är/ and /âr/ are aligned. After partners have arranged their words, have them write clues and prepare a second grid without the letters. Have pairs exchange their grids and clues and solve each other's puzzles.
LISTENING/SPEAKING/SPELLING

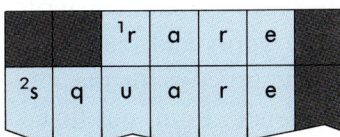
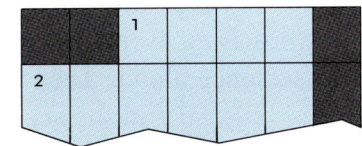

Use *Integrated Spelling* Lesson 13 to reinforce the Spelling Words and the Words to Explore. See pages T87–T92 in *Integrated Spelling Teacher's Edition*.

 **SPELLING POSTTEST** You may want to use the Pretest/Posttest Sentences on *Integrated Spelling Teacher's Edition* page T87 to assess students' knowledge of the spelling generalization.

LISTENING AND SPEAKING

Thoughts on the Matter

Available on Project Card 31A

Have students role-play Mr. and Mrs. Brown, Judy, and Jonathan as they discuss what to do about Paddington's misbehavior. Opinions could run from doing nothing (because Paddington is a young bear who is just getting used to the ways of a different culture) to devising ways to teach him to show respect for another's property. **LISTENING/SPEAKING**

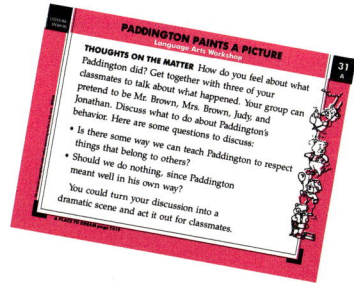

READING

Bears, Bears, Bears

Available on Project Card 31B

COOPERATIVE LEARNING
Have students work in small groups to research information about real bears. Each group could research one type of bear. They may use encyclopedias and other reference sources gathered by the Materials Manager. Suggest that each member look for a different piece of information—for example, where bears live, what bears eat, or how long they live. Suggest that one student illustrate the information. Provide time for group members to combine their information into a pamphlet. The group Recorder can direct this activity. Display the completed pamphlets on a bulletin board in the classroom and ask the group Reporters to briefly describe the contents.   **READING/WRITING/VIEWING**

WRITING

Comparing Paddingtons

Read aloud another Paddington story by Michael Bond. Encourage students to discuss how "Paddington Paints a Picture" is like the other story and how it is different. You may wish to use a Venn diagram like the one below to help students record their information. Then have students use the diagram to write a paragraph comparing the two selections. Suggest that students read their paragraphs aloud.   **LISTENING/SPEAKING/READING/WRITING**

"Paddington Paints a Picture"	Both	"Paddington at the Seaside"
■ play	■ characters—Paddington, Mr. and Mrs. Brown, Judy, Jonathan	■ story
■ takes place at Mr. Brown's house		■ takes place at the seaside
■ Paddington ruins a painting.	■ Paddington ruins something.	■ Paddington ruins a puppet show.

PADDINGTON PAINTS A PICTURE / T419

Grammar MINI LESSON

Subject Pronouns

OBJECTIVES: *To recognize that a* subject pronoun *takes the place of one or more nouns in the subject of a sentence; to recognize that the words* I, you, he, she, it, we, *and* they *are subject pronouns*

Oral Warm-Up

Display and have students read aloud the following lines of dialogue from "Paddington Paints a Picture":

MAN Oh! Er . . . Mr. Brown, as <u>I</u> was saying, the judges decided that your painting was most unusual . . .
MRS. BIRD <u>It</u> certainly was.
MAN And <u>they</u> have all agreed to award you the first prize.

Draw students' attention to the underlined words, and ask them what words each underlined word replaces or refers to. *(I—Man; It—your painting; they—the judges)* Have volunteers record the answers.

Interactive Teaching

SUBJECT PRONOUNS Explain that words such as *it, I,* and *they* that replace or refer to the subject of a sentence are called **subject pronouns**. Write the words *I, you, he, she,* and *it* on the board. Ask a volunteer to describe something Paddington did in the play, and record the sentence on the board. *(Possible response: Paddington painted a picture.)* Then ask students how they could restate this sentence using one of the subject pronouns from the board. *(He painted a picture.)* Ask students to identify which word the word *he* replaces. *(Paddington)* Point out that this subject pronoun takes the place of a singular noun. Help students understand that writers use subject pronouns instead of repeating the names of people, animals, places, and things in every sentence in order to make a story sound better.

Next, give each student a sheet of paper. Have students write the word *We* in large letters on the front and *They* on the back. Then write the following sentences on the board:

- **Paddington and Mr. Brown like to paint.**
- **You and I will go shopping this morning.**

Cross out the words *Paddington and Mr. Brown* in the first sentence, and ask students to hold up their sheet of paper showing the plural subject pronoun that can be used to replace the words. *(They)* Have a volunteer write the word *They* over the crossed-out words and read the new sentence aloud. Then repeat the process for the words *You and I* in the second sentence. Point out that the words *we* and *they* take the place of nouns or pronouns that name more than one subject. Explain also that the word *you* can replace either a singular or a plural subject.

LANGUAGE HANDBOOK
Subject Pronouns, pages 112–113

T420 / A PLACE TO DREAM, UNIT 3

Practice Activities

Picture Perfect Subjects

Have students look through magazines for interesting pictures. Encourage each student to cut out a picture and write a caption explaining what is going on in the scene. (For example: *The polar bear is sleeping in the sun.*) Write all the subject pronouns on the board. Then have each student go to the front of the group and share his or her picture and caption. Ask volunteers from the audience to make another statement about the scene, replacing the noun in the subject with an appropriate subject pronoun. (For example: *It has a pool to swim in.*) Record students' responses on the board.   VISUAL/AUDITORY

What's Your Hobby?

Remind students that Mr. Brown likes to paint as a hobby. Ask them to name their hobbies. Write these on the board. Name a hobby, and ask students to raise their hands if it is something they like to do. Write on the board two of these students' names in a sentence similar to the following: *José and Linda like to roller-skate*. Then ask a volunteer to go to the board, cross out the names of the students, and replace them with a subject pronoun that makes sense. (*They*) Ask students what subject pronoun they would use if they were talking about themselves (*we*) or if they were talking about the person or people they were addressing (*you*). Repeat the procedure several times using one, two, or more students' names in the sentence frame.
VISUAL/KINESTHETIC

Practice Book

MEETING INDIVIDUAL NEEDS

SECOND-LANGUAGE SUPPORT Some students may have difficulty with pronoun–verb agreement. Have students take turns pairing each pronoun below with an appropriate verb and orally composing a sentence.

he	jump
she	laughs
we	sing
they	walks

RETEACH Follow the visual, auditory, and kinesthetic/motor models on page R29.

OPTIONAL INDEPENDENT PRACTICE

PRACTICE BOOK
page 75: Identifying and using subject pronouns

GRAMMAR PRACTICE
pages 34–35: Writing with subject pronouns

PADDINGTON PAINTS A PICTURE / T421

PART 3

Learning through the Literature

VOCABULARY	
INTRODUCE	

Context Clues

OBJECTIVE: *To use context clues to determine word meanings*

Interactive Teaching

Discuss unfamiliar words in the play.

LITERATURE CONNECTION Point out to students that "Paddington Paints a Picture" contains words that may be unfamiliar. Ask them to identify and tell how they figured out the meanings of some of the unfamiliar words they encountered. Explain that *context clues,* or clues in the words and sentences around an unfamiliar word, can help them figure out what the word means.

Model the thinking.

THINK ALOUD ABOUT USING CONTEXT CLUES Write the following sentence on the board, and circle *somber*.

> **Mr. Brown felt very happy, but Paddington was somber.**

Then model how to use context clues:

> **I can figure out the meaning of *somber* by the words around it. The word *but* tells me that Paddington felt the opposite of how Mr. Brown felt. Mr. Brown felt happy. The opposite of *happy* is *sad*, so *somber* must mean "sad."**

Display Chart/Transparency 25 or these sentences. Have students read each sentence and then tell what clue word(s) in the sentence will help them determine the meaning of the unfamiliar word. (Clue words are underlined. Unfamiliar words are circled.)

AN ADDITIONAL BOOK FOR APPLYING CONTEXT CLUES

Harold and the Purple Crayon by Crockett Johnson. HarperCollins, 1955. **EASY**

Chart/Transparency 25 Context Clues

1. The judges liked the painting, but Mr. Brown thought it was repulsive.
2. You could see that Mr. Brown was astonished, or surprised, when he won the contest.
3. Although Jonathan and Judy are twins, they are very different. Jonathan is noisy, but Judy is tranquil.
4. Mr. Brown was angry with Paddington, and Mrs. Brown was just as irritated as he was.

T422 / A PLACE TO DREAM, UNIT 3

Practice Activity

Use the Clues

Have students determine meaning through context.

Have students look through magazines or newspapers for unfamiliar words. Ask them to write the words in a chart like the one below, listing nearby clue words in the second column. In the third column, students should write the possible meanings of the words based on the clue words. VISUAL

Unfamiliar Word	Clue Words	Meaning

Performance Assessment

Have students use the unfamiliar words from the activity in sentences. Encourage volunteers to determine whether the words are used correctly. For evaluation guidelines, see *Staff Development Guide*.

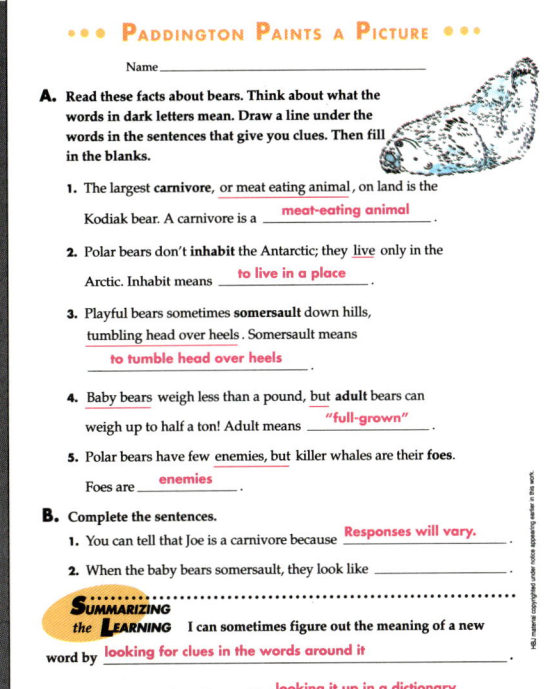

Practice Book

MEETING INDIVIDUAL NEEDS

RETEACH Follow the visual, auditory, and kinesthetic/motor models on page R30.

CHALLENGE Have students locate the words *horrified*, *gloomily* (p. 262) and *ushers* (p. 268). Encourage students to use one of the words in a sentence with context clues and explain the meaning of the word.

SECOND-LANGUAGE SUPPORT Ask students to find clues to the meanings of: *beforehand* (p. 258), and *measles* (p. 267). See also the manual *Alternative Teaching Strategies*, pages 14, 78–81.

OPTIONAL INDEPENDENT PRACTICE

PRACTICE BOOK
page 76: Using context clues

PADDINGTON PAINTS A PICTURE / **T423**

LITERARY APPRECIATION

INTRODUCE

Play

OBJECTIVE: *To understand and appreciate the elements of a play*

Interactive Teaching

Have students compare selections.

LITERATURE CONNECTION Have students compare "Paddington Paints a Picture" with a previously read selection. Discuss the specific elements that make this selection a play. Point out that being able to recognize these elements will help them better understand and enjoy the selection.

Help students identify play elements.

CREATE A LIST Ask students what a play is. (a story written for the purpose of being performed) Have them turn to the beginning of the selection, and use the first few pages to model how to identify the elements of a play.

With students, create a list telling the important parts of a play. The list may look like the following:

Play Elements

Characters: The characters' names are written each time they speak.
Stage Directions: The author's directions are included in brackets.
Scenes: The story is divided into scenes.

Help students deduce that the character's name is given first so actors always know whose turn it is to speak, that directions may include actions as well as tone of voice, and that scenes may take place at a different time (minutes, days, weeks, or even years later) or in a different place, or both.

THINK ALOUD ABOUT USING STAGE DIRECTIONS Model how to identify and use the authors' directions. Display the following excerpt, or have students turn to it on page 263:

PADDINGTON   I wonder if it will work. [*He gets a jar of marmalade, takes a spoonful, and then puts it on the table near the easel.*]

Use this think-aloud to help students understand:

I notice that there are directions for the character in brackets. They tell me what Paddington is supposed to do: take a spoonful of marmalade and then place the jar near the easel. The directions help me visualize the play as I read. They also would help me if I were acting the part.

AN ADDITIONAL BOOK FOR APPLYING PLAY ELEMENTS

The Bunny Play by Loreen Leedy. Holiday House, 1988.   EASY

Practice Activity

Elements on a Page

Have students identify play elements. Have pairs of students refer to a page in "Paddington Paints a Picture" and identify the elements shown on their Play Elements lists. Encourage them to find and discuss as many play elements as possible. If students have performed the play, they may recall additional actions they used that are not in the authors' directions. VISUAL/AUDITORY

Performance Assessment

Ask students to read a section of the page they used for the Elements on a Page activity, following the directions that the authors included. For evaluation guidelines, see *Staff Development Guide*.

Reader ↔ Writer Connection
Play Elements

WRITERS include play elements to make their writing easier to visualize and perform.

READERS look for play elements to help them enjoy and understand the selection.

WRITE SCENE DIRECTIONS Have students write directions for a short scene in a play.

MEETING INDIVIDUAL NEEDS

RETEACH Follow the visual, auditory, and kinesthetic/motor models on page R31.

CHALLENGE Have students add a short scene showing what Mr. Brown does with his prize money. Remind them to include stage directions.

SECOND-LANGUAGE SUPPORT Students can demonstrate their understanding by role-playing the last part of Scene Four, beginning where Miss Black and the Man arrive. See also the manual *Alternative Teaching Strategies*, pages 14, 78–81.

OPTIONAL INDEPENDENT PRACTICE

WRITER'S JOURNAL
page 47: Writing scene directions

PRACTICE BOOK
pages 77–78: Understanding play elements

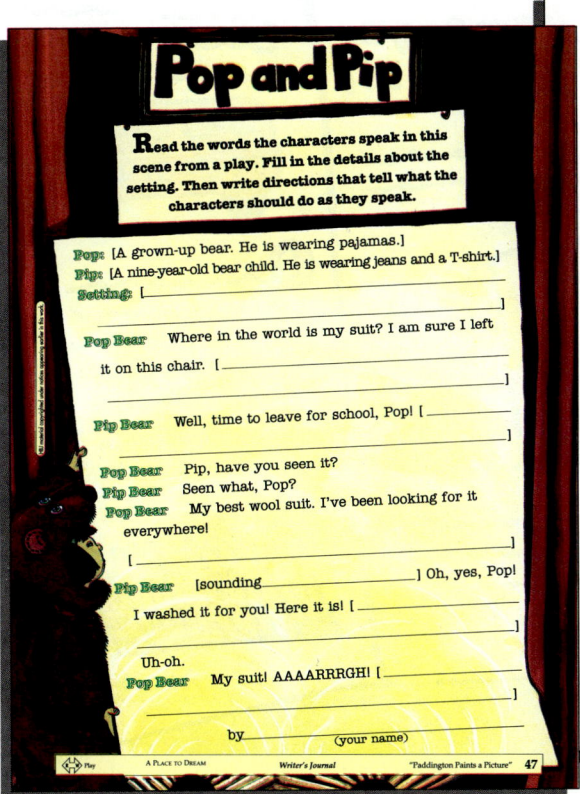

Writer's Journal

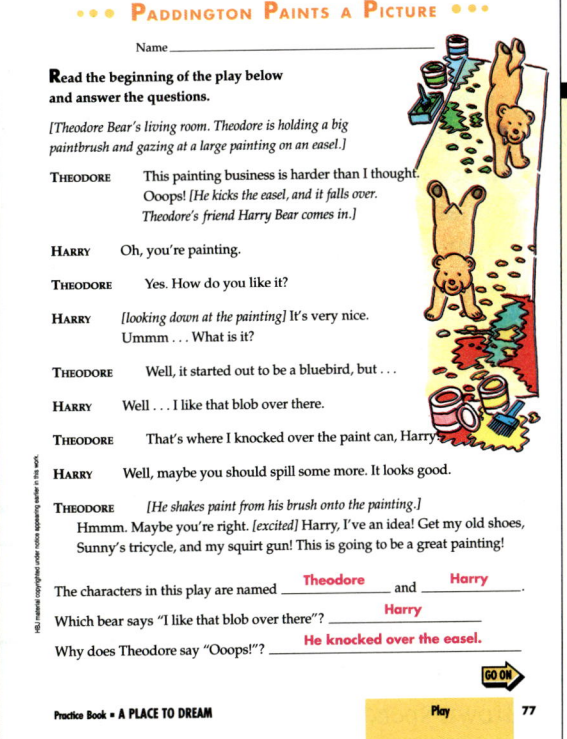

Practice Book

PADDINGTON PAINTS A PICTURE / T425

Integrated CURRICULUM

ART

Create a Work of Art

USE REFERENCE SOURCES Have students look through art books for reproductions of both abstract and realistic paintings. Encourage them to express and explain their opinions about the art. Then ask each student to create a work of art. This could be a collage, a painting, a drawing, a sculpture, or a work in any other medium. Some students may choose to imitate the style of an artist whose work is pictured in a reference. When students have finished, their art may be displayed.
LISTENING/SPEAKING/READING/VIEWING

MATH

Shopping Spree

Tell students to suppose that Mr. Brown wants to spend his £10 ($15) prize money on presents for his wife, Judy, and Paddington. If Mr. Brown spends the same amount of money for each present, how much can he spend on each? ($15 ÷ 3 = $5)   LISTENING/SPEAKING

SOCIAL STUDIES

On Holiday

Available on Project Card 32A

COOPERATIVE LEARNING Have groups of students prepare a brochure showing London's tourist attractions. You may want to display travel brochures that could serve as models. Ask each group to research one London attraction, prepare the artwork, and write a few sentences aimed at making people want to visit it. Have each group assign a Materials Manager to gather art supplies and a Facilitator to oversee the work. Combine the work of all groups into a finished brochure.
READING/WRITING

SOCIAL STUDIES

How Nice

Available on Project Card 32B

The characters in "Paddington Paints a Picture" are very polite to one another. They always say "please," "thank you," and "good-bye," and they share things with one another. Brainstorm ways to act and be polite in school. Then have students work in groups to design a poster with some hints on how to be a polite student. Students can illustrate their posters if they like. WRITING/VIEWING

SOCIAL STUDIES

An English Visitor

To give students a better idea about how the Browns speak, invite someone from England to visit the classroom and talk with the students about the language differences. Suggest that the visitor explore pronunciation differences as well as words that have different meanings in each country, such as *bonnet* (hat; hood of a car) and *lift* (raise; elevator). LISTENING

SCIENCE

Earthquakes

USE REFERENCE SOURCES Remind students that Paddington came from Peru. Point out that earthquakes occur frequently in coastal and mountainous areas of Peru. Have students read about earthquakes and what causes them. Encourage interested students to work together to prepare and present to the others an illustrated report on earthquakes. LISTENING/SPEAKING/READING/WRITING

BOOKS TO SHARE

SOCIAL STUDIES *Michael the Angel* by Laura Fischetto. Doubleday, 1993. CHALLENGING

Visiting the Art Museum by Laurene Krasny Brown and Marc Brown. E. P. Dutton, 1986. AVERAGE

SCIENCE *The Perfect Spot* by Robert J. Blake. Philomel, 1992. AVERAGE

PADDINGTON PAINTS A PICTURE / T427

MULTICULTURAL PERSPECTIVES

Beauty in Art

DISCUSSION STARTER
Why don't paintings all look realistic? Why do some paintings look confusing?

READ ALOUD
Abstract art does not show objects or people as they really look. Some abstract paintings suggest real-life objects, but the images take strange shapes or are oddly positioned on the canvas.

Rufino Tamayo's paintings are abstract. He experimented with painting natural scenes using squares and triangles and other geometric shapes. Tamayo moved from Mexico to New York City, but he continued to use the yellows, browns, and reds of traditional Mexican art.

Some abstract paintings seem to be no more than splotches of paint on the canvas. Jackson Pollock often painted without using an easel. He would roll out a large canvas on the floor and then splatter and drip paint as he moved quickly all around the canvas. Many people found this new style of painting fresh and exciting.

Others prefer folk art. Many folk artists, such as Horace Pippin, taught themselves how to paint. The beauty of their art comes from its simple reflection of the artist's world. Although severely wounded as a soldier in World War I, Pippin continued to work. His paintings are admired for their bold designs and their simplicity.

ACTIVITY CORNER
Available on Project Card 33
• If possible, provide students with pictures of traditional Mexican folk art, such as pottery, textiles, wickerwork, and masks. Encourage students to identify colors and shapes as they talk about what they like. Then give students a chance to draw their own designs, incorporating those elements that especially appeal to them.

• Students may visit the school library to find books with art that they like. Alert them to the fact that sometimes the jacket copy or a page at the front or the back of the book may tell about the medium or the technique the artist used. Have students write a brief critique of the art they find, describing it and telling why they think the artist chose that medium or that technique.

Folk art, such as these paintings by the African American artist Horace Pippin, is usually colorful and realistic.

Rufino Tamayo standing next to his work entitled The Mockers.

THEME WRAP-UP

Discussing the Theme

Remind students that the selections in this theme focused on legendary and humorous adventures involving art.

Discussion Question

PAGE 271 In the selections in this theme, the painters use unusual materials as their paint. In each case, these "paints" help make the paintings special. What do you think is more important—the painter or the paints? Why? (Accept reasonable responses: The artist is more important—for example, because Little Gopher had seen the Dream Vision and had creative talent, he was able to paint beautiful images and bring the sunset to Earth.) CRITICAL: EXPRESSING PERSONAL OPINIONS/JUDGMENTS

Theme Wrap-Up

Picture This!

In the selections in this theme, the painters use unusual materials as their paints. In each case, these "paints" help make the paintings special. Which do you think is more important—the painter or the paints? Why?

WRITER'S WORKSHOP

Picture in your mind your favorite story character. Imagine that he or she has come into your world. Write a story about an experience or adventure the character might have.

Writer's Choice:
Imagine that you want to paint a picture but have no paints. Describe what you might use to paint a landscape. Or write about something else that interests you. Plan how to share your writing.

271

Writer's Workshop

See pages T430–T431 for suggestions for guiding students through the writing process as they respond to the literature.   WRITING PROCESS: STORY

Writer's Choice
You may want to suggest that students use the *Language Handbook* as they write. If students are having difficulty choosing a topic, encourage them to brainstorm a number of ideas and then choose one.

Suggest that students work with a partner to revise and proofread their writing.

THEME WRAP-UP / T429

Writer's Workshop
Story

Theme Wrap-Up

Students write a story about an adventure that a favorite story character might have in their world.

To prepare students for the writing task and form, ask them to imagine that the boy in "The Legend of the Indian Paintbrush" appears one day at the front door of their home. Discuss the kinds of adventures a character might have if he or she stepped from the pages of a book into a student's life. Remind students that a story has a beginning, a middle, and an ending.

Use the Writer's Workshop assignment on page 271 as you work through the writing process with students.

ALTERNATIVE TOPICS If you wish, allow students to choose their own topics for writing. Suggest that they refer to the *Language Handbook* for an explanation of the writing process for stories. See Writing Model, page R94.

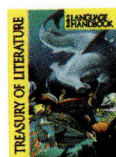

LANGUAGE HANDBOOK *Writing to Entertain or Express,* pages 36–37; *Story,* pages 38–39

Prewriting

Have students meet with partners to brainstorm ideas. Suggest that students use a story map like the one below.

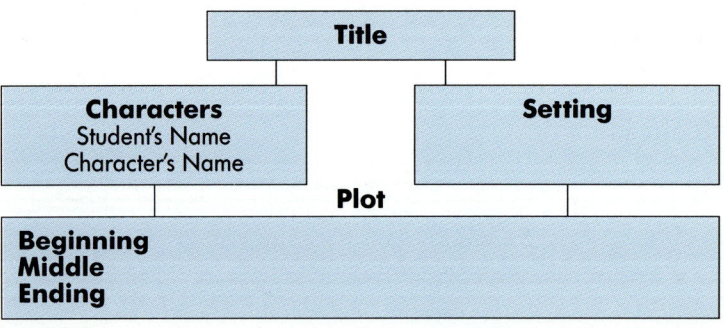

Drafting

Have students write a draft of their story. Suggest that students

- use both dialogue and narration in their stories.
- use their story map or other prewriting notes to help keep the events in order.
- remember to include a problem that must be solved by the end of the story.

If students are having trouble getting started, encourage them to draw the story scenes and then write what they "see."

Responding and Revising

To check their own writing before sharing it with others, students should

- check that they have a title for their story.
- check that they tell what happens in order.
- make sure they have an ending that solves the problem of the story.

Then have student writers read aloud their work to listeners in a peer conference. Have writers and listeners respond to the following questions and complete the following task:

Listener	Writer
Is the story interesting and understandable? Are the characters vividly described? Is the problem in the story solved in the ending?	When you read your story aloud, which part is best—the plot, setting, or characters? If some parts seem weak, think of ways to make them stronger.

COMPUTER TIP

REVISING Students can easily rearrange story elements using the cut-and-paste feature that is part of most word processing programs.

Proofreading

Provide these tips for students as they proofread:

- Look for the difference between sentences with combined subjects or predicates and sentences that are really two sentences joined without correct punctuation.
- Check that proper nouns are capitalized.
- Correct any misspelled words.

MINI-CONFERENCE STRATEGY Point out sentences that students have combined incorrectly by making observations such as "You wrote *The boy skipped the boy hopped*. What punctuation mark is missing here? What might be a shorter, better way to say this?"

Publishing Options

CLASSROOM BOOKS Have students copy their stories neatly onto white paper, decorating them with outline drawings. Make copies of each story on a copier. Then have each student color in the illustrations for all copies of his or her story. Bind the stories into books, and allow them to circulate from a class library.

STORYTELLING CIRCLES Have groups of students sit in circles and take turns reading their stories aloud. Suggest that students spend some time rehearsing their storytelling techniques, varying the speed and pitch with which they read different parts of the story.

Assessment Options

STUDENT SELF-ASSESSMENT Encourage students to summarize their writing experience by responding to this question in their journals:

- **How is writing about a fictional character in my world different from reading about the character?**

You may also wish to have students complete the Self-Assessment Checklist in the *Portfolio Assessment Teacher's Guide*.

WRITING OBSERVATION RECORDS Record instances in which students demonstrated confidence and creativity in writing their stories.

After students publish, you may want to have them add their stories to their portfolios.

GRAMMAR CONNECTION

Revising: Repeating Nouns

Use the examples on Transparency G to help students focus on the importance of using pronouns in their writing. Point out that pronouns replace nouns so that nouns do not have to be repeated throughout the writing.

> **Transparency G**
> **Alexandria to the Vet**
>
> **BEFORE**
> Matilda Bumber took her cat named Alexandria to the pet doctor. Alexandria was Matilda Bumber's only cat, and Matilda Bumber was worried about Alexandria. The pet doctor said Matilda was feeding the cat too much of Matilda Bumber's good cooking. Matilda said Alexandria loved Matilda Bumber's peach pies. Since Matilda Bumber felt Matilda Bumber knew Alexandria best, Matilda Bumber would feed Alexandria what Matilda Bumber knew Alexandria liked.
>
> **AFTER**
> Matilda Bumber took her cat named Alexandria to the pet doctor. Alexandria was her only cat, and she was worried about her. The pet doctor said Matilda was feeding the cat too much of her good cooking. Matilda said Alexandria loved her peach pies. Since she felt she knew Alexandria best, she would feed her what she knew she liked.

Have students work in small groups to share their writing and to check that pronouns are used to avoid repetition of nouns.

LANGUAGE HANDBOOK
Pronouns, pages 107–114

WRITER'S WORKSHOP / T431

Unit 3 ADVENTURES

THEME OPENER

Mysteries to Solve

Piggins

T435   A MYSTERY by Jane Yolen
When Mrs. Reynard's diamond necklace disappears during a dinner party, Piggins, the butler, assembles some clues and solves the mystery.

Words from the Author and the Illustrator: Jane Yolen and Jane Dyer

T448   AN ARTICLE
Meet two women who work together to create wonderful books.

Closed, I am a mystery

T465   A RIDDLE by Myra Cohn Livingston
Read the clues to solve a riddle.

Hello Book!

T465   A POEM by N. M. Bodecker
A book is like a prisoner on a shelf until a reader sets it free.

Would you like

T465   A POEM by Lillian Morrison
What books can surprise you, hypnotize you, advise you, and take you to faraway places? Read this poem to find out.

For pacing suggestions, see page T434.

Theme Opener: Mysteries to Solve PAGES 272–273

THEME

Mysteries to Solve

Some adventures involve a mystery. Sometimes a problem has to be solved or something lost must be found. Read the following story, riddle, and poems. Can you solve the mysteries in them?

CONTENTS

PIGGINS
by Jane Yolen
illustrated by Jane Dyer

WORDS FROM THE AUTHOR AND THE ILLUSTRATOR: JANE YOLEN AND JANE DYER

CLOSED, I AM A MYSTERY
by Myra Cohn Livingston

HELLO BOOK!
by N. M. Bodecker

WOULD YOU LIKE
by Lillian Morrison

273

Discussing the Theme

Have students look at the illustration and read the paragraph on Student Anthology page 273 and then restate the theme focus in their own words. Ask students if they have ever solved a mystery, and invite them to share their experiences. Finally, have students read the selection titles and predict what kinds of mysteries they will encounter in the story and poems they are about to read.

Portfolio Assessment

Remind students to keep their writing responses for the selections in "Mysteries to Solve" in their portfolios. Remind them also to add to their personal journals thoughts and ideas about books they have read independently.

 When you see this symbol, you may want to provide students the opportunity to save some of their work in their portfolios.

THEME OPENER: MYSTERIES TO SOLVE / T433

THEME OPENER

Managing the Literature-Based Classroom

Personalized Spelling Routines

Have students create personal spelling dictionaries in which they record words they have had difficulty spelling in the past. Periodically arrange for students to add to a class list words they choose from the spelling dictionary. Pair students for practice and pronunciation of the personalized spelling words.

Options in Grouping

Though there are often advantages to having students form their own small groups, you may find that certain groups of students choose to work together every time. To expand their horizons, you may wish to vary the methods by which groups are formed. For example, draw names at random or group alphabetically or on a rotating basis.

Pacing

This theme has been designed to take about two weeks to complete, depending on your students' needs.

MEETING INDIVIDUAL NEEDS

LOW-ACHIEVING STUDENTS Evaluate students' prior knowledge of the theme by asking if they have ever read a mystery or seen one on television. Discuss what a mystery is and what makes a mystery different from other types of stories that students have read. You may wish to provide several "two-minute mysteries" for the group to discuss and solve.

GIFTED AND TALENTED Challenge students to develop their own secret codes and then write messages to classmates, using the codes. A student who receives a message must break the code. The writer can provide clues as needed. Suggest that students use numbers, letters, symbols, and rebuses to create their codes. *Challenge Cards* provide additional activities to challenge students. Challenge notes throughout the lesson plans suggest additional activities to stimulate critical and creative thinking.

SPECIAL-EDUCATION STUDENTS Suggest that students who have difficulty focusing on the lines of print and keeping them separate use a strip of oaktag or construction paper to guide their eyes along each line.

STUDENTS ACQUIRING ENGLISH Some students may have difficulty remembering where to place adjectives in their paragraphs for the Writer's Workshop on Student Anthology page 295. For example, students who speak Spanish may write "the story believable" instead of "the believable story." Review the use and placement of adjectives in English. Second-Language Support notes throughout the lesson plans offer strategies to help students acquiring English to understand the selection.

Piggins
pages 274–291

	READING	LANGUAGE ARTS	CROSS-CURRICULAR CONNECTIONS
PART 1 *Reading the Literature* pages T438–T449	**Building Background** **Vocabulary Strategies** **Prereading Strategies** Sequence Diagram Setting a Purpose **Options for Reading**	**Spelling** Pretest Spelling-Vocabulary Connection Generalization: /ôr/ **Grammar Connection** Reviewing Subject Pronouns	**Science** Inventors **Social Studies** Job Duties
PART 2 *Responding to the Literature* pages T450–T457	**Personal Response** **Cooperative Response** **Summarizing the Literature** **Critical Thinking Activity** Discussion **Vocabulary Workshop** Key Words Onomatopoeia	**Language Arts Workshop** **Writing** dialogue, advertisements **Reading** drama, mysteries, animal stories **Listening and Speaking** interview, trial **Reviewing Spelling Words** Posttest **Grammar Review** Subject Pronouns **Grammar Minilesson** Object Pronouns	**Social Studies** Ratsbys in Court **Art** Detective Ads
PART 3 *Learning Through the Literature* pages T458–T464	**Introduce** Literary Appreciation: Fiction and Nonfiction **Review** Comprehension: Making Predictions (Tested) Vocabulary: Context Clues (Tested)	**Reading** Law Enforcers **Writing** A Dog's Life **Listening and Speaking** Festive Foods Great Inventions	**Science** A Dog's Life Great Inventions **Social Studies** Law Enforcers Festive Foods **Art** Tortoise Characters **Math** Going Shopping **Multicultural Perspectives** The Supreme Court

OPTIONAL MATERIALS
Chart/Transparency 26
Integrated Spelling pp. 62–65; TE pp. T93–T98
Practice Book pp. 79–85
Writer's Journal pp. 48–49
Alternative Teaching Strategies pp. 15, 82–85
Language Handbook pp. 36–37, 40, 114
Grammar Practice pp. 34–35
Literature Cassette
Family Involvement Activities: Unit 3, pp. 1–4
Response Card 6
Project Cards 34A, 34B, 35A, 35B

MEETING INDIVIDUAL NEEDS
Second-Language Support pp. T439, T440, T443, T457, T459
Mainstreaming p. T440
Reteach pp. T457, T459
Challenge pp. T459, T460, T461

FAMILY INVOLVEMENT Encourage family members to play "Detective." One person hides an object. The others take turns asking "yes/no" questions. The one to correctly guess the location hides it next. See *Family Involvement Activities*.

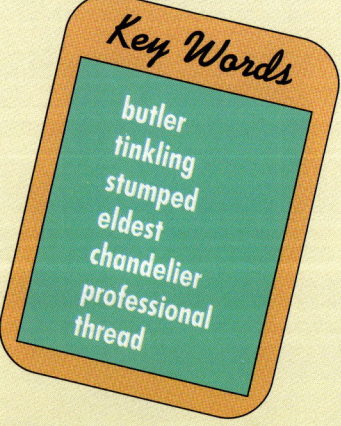

Key Words
butler
tinkling
stumped
eldest
chandelier
professional
thread

T436 / A PLACE TO DREAM, UNIT 3

Selection Summary

Piggins, the butler, supervises at an elegant dinner party at the home of Mr. and Mrs. Reynard. During dinner the Reynards announce that they wish to sell the beautiful diamond lavaliere that Mrs. Reynard is wearing. It seems that the lavaliere brings disaster to all those who have it. Shortly after the Reynards announce their intention, the lights go out. When the lights come on, Mrs. Reynard finds that her necklace is gone. Piggins assembles some clues—a piece of red thread, a trail of cheese crumbs, a tinkling sound, and a scream—and then accuses Lord and Lady Ratsby. As Piggins retrieves the necklace from the chandelier, the Ratsbys try to escape. They are tackled by the Lapin sisters and are taken away by the police.

About the Author

Jane Yolen is the author of more than one hundred books for children and young adults. She spent her early years in New York City, moving to Westport, Connecticut, when she was thirteen. Westport, she says, "was a hotbed of writers and artists, so I just assumed that when you grew up, you became a writer. . . . That seemed a logical explanation for all the writers around." Now living in western Massachusetts, Yolen has been a full-time writer since 1965. She also teaches writing. Yolen's *The Transfigured Hart* and *The Moon Ribbon and Other Tales* were both named Golden Kite Honor books. She also received a Garden State Children's Book Award in 1983 for *Commander Toad in Space*.

About the Illustrator

Jane Dyer is a former kindergarten teacher. Since 1984 she has exclusively illustrated children's books, several of them by Jane Yolen. She still has a drawing, called "Sleep, Mr. Bean," from her own kindergarten year. Dyer and Yolen live near each other in Massachusetts.

Additional Reading

OTHER BOOKS BY JANE YOLEN

All Those Secrets of the World. Little, Brown, 1991. AVERAGE

Commander Toad and the Intergalactic Spy. Coward, McCann, 1986. AVERAGE

Welcome to the Greenhouse. G. P. Putnam's Sons, 1993. EASY

ANOTHER THEME-RELATED BOOK

My Dog and the Green Sock Mystery by David A. Adler. Holiday House, 1986. EASY

A BOOK FOR APPLYING STRATEGIES: FICTION AND NONFICTION

If You Were a Writer by Joan Lowery Nixon. Four Winds, 1988. EASY

PART 1

Reading the Literature

Building Background

Access prior knowledge and build vocabulary concepts.

Tell students that the next story, "Piggins," is a mystery that takes place at a fancy dinner party. Have students describe popular movies or books about mysteries. Encourage them to recount the important events in the stories.

Have students quickwrite events in a mystery.

Then tell students to list on paper some things that might happen in a mystery set at a fancy dinner party. Encourage them to compare their lists. The lists might include the following:

Things That Might Happen
1. The butler did it.
2. A professional detective is called.
3. A chandelier falls.

Vocabulary Strategies

Introduce Key Words and strategies.

Display Chart/Transparency 26 or the story on it. Have students read the story silently, using context clues and phonetic analysis to figure out the meanings of the underlined words. For example, they can use other words in the first sentence to figure out *butler*. If necessary, help with pronunciation.

Chart/Transparency 26   Key Words

The <u>butler</u> was busy with his household duties. Suddenly, he heard a <u>tinkling</u> sound like the ringing of a glass bell. He tried to figure out what was making the sound, but he was <u>stumped</u>. Then the children came into the room. The <u>eldest</u> was in the lead, and the younger children followed.

One child held out a piece of glass. "A piece of the <u>chandelier</u> has fallen. Can you fix it?" They all looked up at the huge light hanging overhead.

The butler said, "I am a <u>professional</u> butler, not a chandelier fixer, but I'll try." He broke off a <u>thread</u> that was hanging from one of his buttons, climbed up a ladder, and tied the piece back on.

Key Words

butler
tinkling
stumped
eldest
chandelier
professional
thread

KEY WORDS DEFINED

butler   servant who supervises other servants

tinkling   series of light, ringing sounds

stumped   unable to figure something out

eldest   oldest

chandelier   light fixture that hangs from the ceiling

professional   having to do with an occupation that requires special training

thread   very thin cord used for sewing

T438 / A PLACE TO DREAM, UNIT 3

Check all students' understanding.

Have students tell whether each of the following statements is true or false. If it is false, have them explain why.

1. **Thread is most often used to tie packages.** (False. Thread is most often used for sewing.) STRATEGY: PRIOR KNOWLEDGE
2. **A small bell makes a tinkling sound.** (true) STRATEGY: EXAMPLE
3. **A butler is a servant who usually washes dishes.** (False. A butler supervises other servants.) STRATEGY: DEFINITION
4. **A chandelier is a small desk lamp.** (False. It is a large light that hangs from the ceiling.) STRATEGY: DEFINITION
5. **A person who knows the answer is stumped.** (False. One who does *not* know is stumped.) STRATEGY: EXAMPLE
6. **A professional librarian has had special training for his or her profession or job.** (true) STRATEGY: EXAMPLE
7. **A word that means the same as *eldest* is *oldest*.** (true) STRATEGY: SYNONYMS

PROPER NOUNS Display the following characters' names and model their pronunciations, as needed: Reynard [rā′nərd], Bayswater [bāz′wô·tər], Ortoise [ôr′təs], Ratsby [ratz′bē], Pierre Lapin [pē·âr′ lap′ən].

Integrate spelling with vocabulary.

SPELLING-VOCABULARY CONNECTION *Integrated Spelling* Lesson 14 reinforces the spelling of words with the /ôr/ sound, such as *your*, found in the selection. In addition, the Words to Explore reinforce the concept of mystery as it relates to the selection.

SPELLING PRETEST You may want to use the Pretest/Posttest Sentences on page T93 in *Integrated Spelling Teacher's Edition* to assess students' knowledge of the spelling generalization.

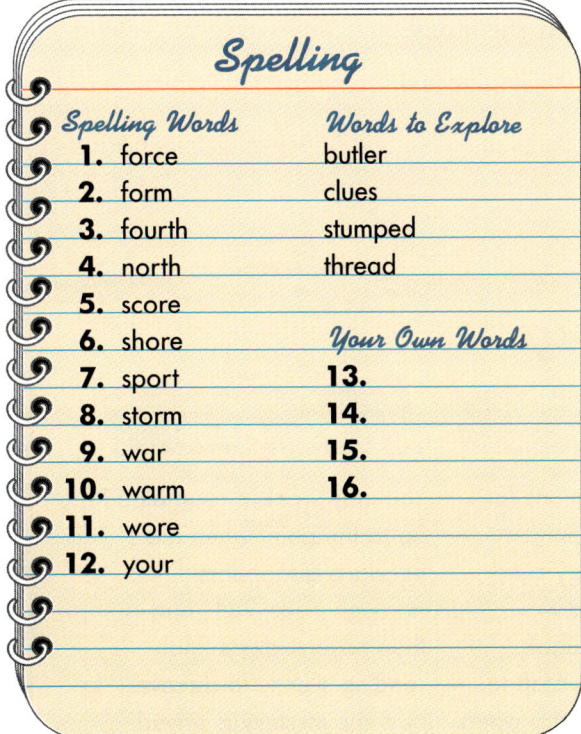

Practice Book

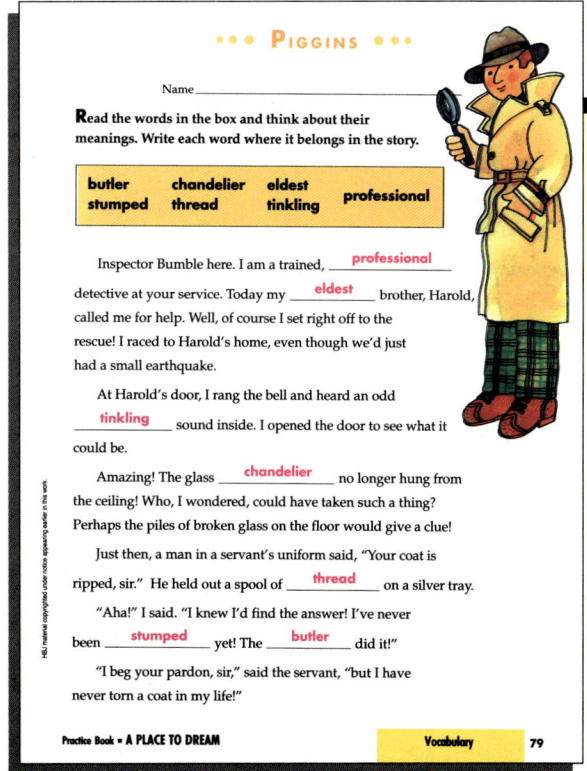

Spelling generalization:
/ôr/ sound

MEETING INDIVIDUAL NEEDS

SECOND-LANGUAGE SUPPORT Display the following checklist to guide students in using context clues:
1. Read the complete sentence.
2. Think of a word that makes sense in the sentence.
3. Reread the sentences that come before and after.

See also the manual *Alternative Teaching Strategies*, pages 15, 82–85.

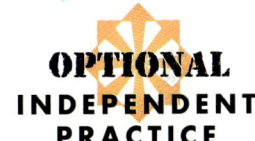

OPTIONAL INDEPENDENT PRACTICE

INTEGRATED SPELLING pages 62–65: Spelling words with the /ôr/ sound

PRACTICE BOOK page 79: Reinforcing Key Words

NOTE: This page may be completed now or after students have read the story.

Prereading Strategies

Sequence Diagram

Have students preview the literature.
Have students recall the steps involved in previewing a selection. (read and think about the title, look at the illustrations, and read the introduction and the first few paragraphs) Encourage students to preview the selection through page 277. Tell them not to preview too much of the mystery because it may spoil the suspense. In addition, you may want to explain that a lavaliere is a necklace.

Begin a sequence diagram with students.
Draw a sequence diagram on the board, and have students use their prior knowledge, along with the information they gained from previewing, to fill in the first box.

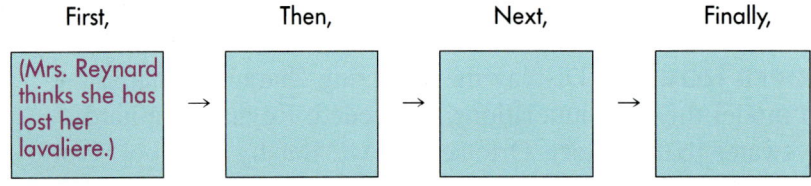

 **PERSONAL JOURNAL** Have students use their sequence diagrams to predict what problem might arise in the story. Suggest that they add their predictions to their personal journals. Ask students to support their predictions.

Setting a Purpose

Encourage students to set purposes.
Have students use their predictions to set a purpose for reading.

If students have difficulty setting a purpose, offer this suggestion:

I'm going to read to find out whether Mrs. Reynard loses her lavaliere again and whether this is the mystery in the story.

MEETING INDIVIDUAL NEEDS

SECOND-LANGUAGE SUPPORT Students may benefit from an explanation of the British terms used in the selection. For example, the expression *balderdash and poppycock* means "nonsense." See also the manual *Alternative Teaching Strategies* pages 15, 82–85.

SUPPORT FOR MAINSTREAMING Some students may be better motivated to read if you point out that detective stories are in some ways similar to detective TV shows and movies. Ask students to explain why detective shows are suspenseful.

Options for Reading

SUSTAINED SILENT READING	STRATEGIC READING	READER RESPONSE GROUPS	TEACHER READ-ALOUD
Remind students who are reading independently to keep their purpose for reading in mind.	To stimulate discussion, use the suggestions that appear on pages T441, T444, and T448.	Follow the suggestions for Literature Circles on page T441. As they read, have students jot down questions and thoughts about the author's craft to discuss with the group when they finish.	You may want to read aloud up to the point when the necklace disappears (through page 281) and then have students finish reading silently to discover how the mystery is solved.

T440 / A PLACE TO DREAM, UNIT 3

PIGGINS PAGES 274–275

WRITTEN BY JANE YOLEN

AWARD-WINNING AUTHOR

Trit-trot, trit-trot.
That is the sound of Piggins, the butler at 47 The Meadows, going up the stairs. He has shined the silver teapot so well he can see his snout in it.

UPSTAIRS Mrs. Reynard is in a terrible dither.

"I cannot find my diamond lavaliere," she says to her husband.

"Is it missing again?" Mr. Reynard asks. "Perhaps one of the servants took it." His whiskers twitch.

"*Our* Cook? *Our* Sara? *Our* Jane? Not possible," says Mrs. Reynard.

Mr. Reynard smiles widely enough so that his teeth show. "Perhaps the butler did it."

"*Our* Piggins?" Mrs. Reynard is clearly shocked. "He *finds* things. He does not *take* things."

"I know, my dear," says Mr. Reynard. "I was making a little joke. Look again and I will help you." He gets up from his chair.

They look and look. At last they find the necklace right where it belongs—in Mrs. Reynard's jewelry box.

ILLUSTRATED BY JANE DYER

275

Reader Response Groups

LITERATURE CIRCLES Form groups of three to five students, and have each group read the selection silently, stopping at page 281 for a brief discussion. You may want to distribute Response Card 6 (Author's Craft), found on page R84, or provide the following questions:

- What pictures has the author left in your mind?
- What is your favorite word, line, or paragraph in the story?

Response Card 6

Strategic Reading

SET PURPOSE/PREDICT: PAGES 274–281 Encourage students to look at the illustrations on these pages and predict what might happen at the party. Have students read through page 281 to confirm their predictions.

PIGGINS / T441

PAGES 276–277 PIGGINS

276

BELOW STAIRS Cook has just removed the cake from the oven. The kitchen is sweet with its smell. Sara, the scullery maid, has scrubbed the pots and pans. She looks as if she needs a scrubbing herself. Upstairs Jane has finished setting the table. Everything is in its proper place.

IN THE DINING ROOM Piggins is pleased. The glasses sparkle. The silver gleams. Even the chandelier glitters like a thousand diamonds.

Ding-dong. That is the front door bell. Piggins goes to answer it. The dinner guests have started to arrive.

Inspector Bayswater and his friend Professor T. Ortoise are on the steps. The professor is telling a joke. Lord and Lady Ratsby alight from a carriage. They are arguing with the driver over the fare. Down the street comes the motorcar of the world-famous explorer Pierre Lapin and his three unmarried sisters. He honks the horn. *Aaaa-OOOO-ga. Aaaa-OOOO-ga.* His sisters scream with delight.

"Lovely weather," says the professor in the living room. He is famous for his conversation. His students all say proudly, "Professor T. Ortoise taught us."

Teaching Tip The story is presented much like a play, with the action set in different parts of Mr. and Mrs. Reynard's house. Point out the "stage directions" on pages 275 and 277. *(Upstairs, Below Stairs, In the Dining Room)* Explain to students that these phrases tell readers where in the house each scene takes place. Suggest that students use these phrases, together with the diagram of the house on page 276, to visualize the story events.

See page T453 for information found on Project Card 34A.

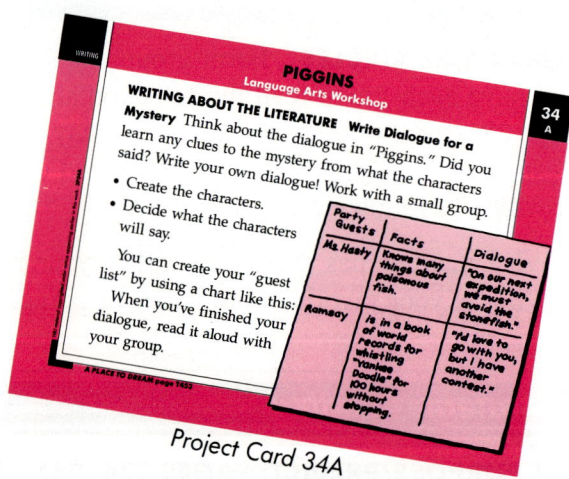

Project Card 34A

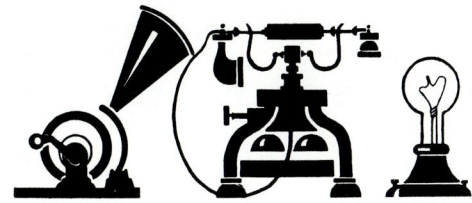

Lord and Lady Ratsby eye the cheeses hungrily. They sample every cheese and even slip a few pieces into their pockets.

Inspector Bayswater takes out his pipe. He does not light it. The doctors have advised him not to smoke.

Pierre Lapin settles his sisters. "Do you want something to drink?" he asks them.

"Anything but tea," the eldest says. The other two giggle.

Mr. and Mrs. Reynard come into the room and smile warmly at their friends. They greet each of them by name. Everyone admires Mrs. Reynard's diamond lavaliere.

"You may wonder why I have asked you here this evening," says Mr. Reynard.

But no one *really* wonders. Mr. Reynard is a tinkerer. He loves to invite friends over to show off his latest invention.

Mr. Reynard surprises them. "Tonight I will say nothing about my inventions, though I do have one or two small new things." He waves his paw toward several strange contraptions in the corner of the room. "Tonight I want to tell you about—"

"Dinner is served," announces Piggins.

So two by two they go in to dinner. Lord and Lady Ratsby are so hungry they scamper on ahead. Slow but steady, the professor brings up the rear, the eldest Miss Lapin on his arm. It would simply not do to let Cook's wonderful food get cold.

When the shrimp soup has been served, Mr. Reynard smiles. "I have invited you to dinner tonight so that you can admire my wife's brand-new diamond necklace. And so you can hear the story of why we must sell it."

"Sell it?" The eldest Miss Lapin leans forward. "But it is so beautiful. How can you bear to part with it?"

"It must be worth a great deal of money," says Lady Ratsby. She fingers her own necklace, a simple gold chain.

"Yes, it *is* beautiful," says Mrs. Reynard. "And quite expensive. But . . . "

"But what?" asks the inspector. His professional interest has been aroused.

"There is a curse on the diamond!" says Mr. Reynard.

"*A curse!*" Everyone talks at once.

Mr. Reynard silences them by holding up his right paw. "Yes—a curse! The miner who found the diamond broke his arm. The cutter who shaped it broke all his tools. The store that sold the necklace burned down right after the sale."

279

Second-Language Support Students may need help understanding the first two sentences on page 278. To help them, reread the sentences using synonyms for the multiple-meaning words *eye* ("look at"), *sample* ("try"), and *slip* ("put").

MEETING INDIVIDUAL NEEDS

Science Connection Why do you think inventors like Mr. Reynard are called "tinkerers"? Do you think serious inventors like being called this? (Accept reasonable responses: They are called tinkerers because they adjust and "toy with" machines and other items, trying to make them work better. They probably do not like the name because it makes them seem silly.) CRITICAL: APPRECIATING AUTHOR'S CRAFT

See page T463 for information found on Project Card 35B.

Project Card 35B

PIGGINS / T443

PAGES 280–281 PIGGINS

280

"And you?" asks the professor, keeping the conversation going.

"Yes," says Pierre Lapin. "What has happened to you?"

Mrs. Reynard looks sad. "I have lost the lavaliere three times already. Sara broke a bowl and a glass. Cook's first cake flopped. The children have the fox pox. And—"

"Nothing serious has happened . . . yet," says Mr. Reynard. "But just in case, we have decided to sell the lavaliere as soon as possible. I know all of you are interested in gems, so I called you together tonight."

"We are interested indeed," says Lord Ratsby. *"What good timing!"*

Suddenly the lights go out.

A strange tinkling sound is heard.

There is a scramble of feet.

Several objects thud to the floor.

There is a high, squeaky scream.

In comes Piggins with a candle.

Lord Ratsby finds the light switch and turns on the glittering chandelier.

Professor T. Ortoise stands up.

Pierre Lapin sets the table aright.

Just then Mrs. Reynard clutches her throat. She screams.

"My diamond lavaliere. It is gone." She falls back in a faint.

Strategic Reading

MODELING A STRATEGY: PAGES 274–281 Was there anything you did not understand as you read these pages?

THINK ALOUD You may want to model using a fix-up strategy: *I wasn't sure why the Reynards wanted to sell the diamond necklace. I looked back at Mr. Reynard's explanation, and I saw that he believes there is a curse on the diamond. He describes all the bad things that happened to the miner, the jeweler, the store, and to the Reynards themselves. They must want to sell the necklace because they think it causes bad things to happen.*
USING FIX-UP STRATEGIES

SET PURPOSE/PREDICT: PAGES 282–288 Ask students what new bad thing has happened to the owners of the diamond necklace. (The necklace has been stolen.) Have students predict whether the necklace will be found. If they think so, have them predict who will find it and where. Encourage them to read the rest of the story to confirm their predictions.

T444 / A PLACE TO DREAM, UNIT 3

Lady Ratsby points her finger at Piggins. "Perhaps the butler did it."

"Balderdash and poppycock," says Mr. Reynard. He turns to the inspector. "I cannot believe *our* Piggins did it. Can you find any clues to the real thief?"

The inspector examines the room. He searches everywhere. He finds a red thread near the door, crumbs on the table, and a little bit of dirt on the floor. He cannot find the diamond lavaliere.

"I am stumped," he says at last.

"*Hummmmph!*" snorts Lady Ratsby.

Professor T. Ortoise is at a loss for words for the first time in his life.

Pierre Lapin comforts his three sisters, who sniffle into their lace handkerchiefs.

Mrs. Reynard comes out of her faint.

Piggins smiles. "I, on the other hand, am not stumped. I know who has done it."

"Good show, Piggins," says Mr. Reynard. "Tell us everything. And I will record it with my latest invention."

"First there are the clues," says Piggins. "A piece of red thread near the door. A trail of cheese crumbs on the table. The tinkling sound we all heard. The scream."

"And the dirt on the floor?" asks the inspector.

Expanding the Literature Why do you think Lady Ratsby accuses Piggins of taking the necklace? (Accept reasonable responses: perhaps to try to keep suspicion away from herself.) CRITICAL: AUTHOR'S CRAFT/IDENTIFYING WITH CHARACTERS

This is the second time that Piggins is accused of taking the necklace. When was the first time? (when Mrs. Reynard misplaced the necklace earlier) **What is the difference between Mr. Reynard's and Lady Ratsby's accusations?** (Mr. Reynard is joking; Lady Ratsby is not.) INFERENTIAL: MAKING COMPARISONS

PAGES 284–285 PIGGINS

"For that I shall have to speak sharply to Upstairs Jane," says Piggins, frowning. "There should be *no* dirt in this house."

"I do not understand the clues," says the professor. "Thread, crumbs, a tinkling sound, a scream."

"There is not one thief—but two," explains Piggins. "One to turn off the lights and make a commotion, and one to steal the diamond lavaliere."

"Oh," says Pierre Lapin. "I know all about making commotions. In my youth, I stole into a farmer's garden and made much too much noise."

"The clues," remind the Misses Lapin together.

Piggins continues. "Before everyone came into dinner, someone tied the red thread to the light switch. At a signal, the thread was pulled and the lights turned off. But the thread was pulled so hard, it broke. In the dark someone grabbed the necklace and stepped up onto the table, leaving a trail of cheese crumbs where no cheese had been served. The tinkling sound was the chandelier being disturbed. The scream was the signal that all was clear."

"Then that means . . . " says Inspector Bayswater.

"That the thieves are . . . " says the professor.

"None other than . . . " says Mr. Reynard.

"Lord and Lady Ratsby," finishes Piggins. "They knew about the diamond all along and planned to steal it at their very first chance."

Teaching Tip You may want to call attention here to the name Pierre Lapin (French for "Peter Rabbit") and the reference to Pierre's sneaking into the farmer's garden. Explain that authors sometimes put humorous references like this in a story.

Social Studies Connection How do you know that Piggins's responsibilities as a butler are to supervise the other servants and make sure everything gets done? (The author mentions how pleased Piggins is that the preparations for the dinner are going well and that Piggins will have to speak sharply to the upstairs maid about the dirt on the floor.) METACOGNITIVE: DRAWING CONCLUSIONS

See page T454 for information found on Project Card 34B.

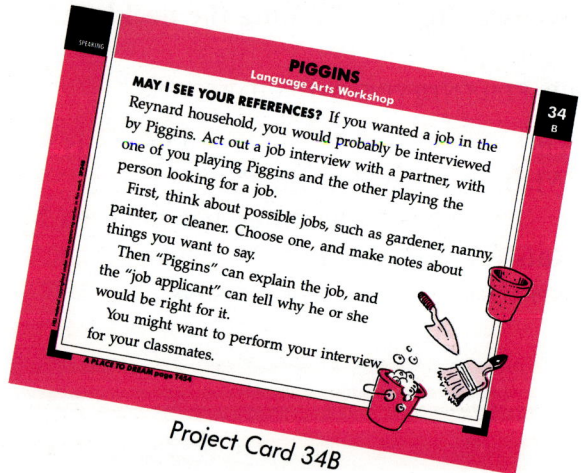

Project Card 34B

T446 / A PLACE TO DREAM, UNIT 3

PIGGINS PAGES 286–287

"But where *is* the diamond?" asks the professor. "Inspector Bayswater looked everywhere."

"Yes," sneers Lord Ratsby. "Where is your precious diamond?"

Piggins smiles. "In plain sight." He steps on one of the chairs and reaches up into the glittering chandelier. He finds the necklace.

"I suspected the Ratsbys were broke," says the eldest Miss Lapin. "Lady Ratsby is wearing a simple gold chain. Usually she drips jewels."

"Catch them!" Mrs. Reynard cries, for the Ratsbys are trying to escape.

The eldest Miss Lapin sticks out her foot. She trips Lord Ratsby. The younger Misses Lapin jump on top of Lady Ratsby.

"Well done, Piggins," says Mr. Reynard.

"Well done, girls!" cries Mrs. Reynard.

"Curses!" says Lord Ratsby.

Professor T. Ortoise laughs. "Curses indeed! Perhaps, Reynard, the curse on your lavaliere is at its end."

The police are summoned and they take the Ratsbys away.

UPSTAIRS Mr. and Mrs. Reynard get ready for bed. Mrs. Reynard carefully wraps the diamond lavaliere in a velvet cloth. She puts it away in her jewelry box. "I hope the curse *is* ended," she says. "I would hate to part with my beautiful necklace."

Informal Assessment

MAKING PREDICTIONS To informally assess whether students make predictions as they read, what information they base their predictions on, and how effectively they check their predictions, you might ask the following questions:

- Where do you think the diamond necklace might be hidden?
- What are some clues in the story?
- What are some clues in the pictures?

A review lesson on **making predictions** appears on page T460.

GRAMMAR CONNECTION

REVIEWING SUBJECT PRONOUNS Remind students that writers use subject pronouns like *I, he,* and *we* so that they don't have to repeat the names of people over and over again. Direct students' attention to the fourth paragraph on page 287. Ask them to whom the subject pronouns *I* and *she* refer. (to the eldest Miss Lapin; to Lady Ratsby)

PAGES 288–289 PIGGINS

Mr. Reynard nods and takes off his tie. "I knew the butler did not do it," he says.

"Not *our* Piggins," says Mrs. Reynard.

BELOW STAIRS Sara has cleaned the last of the dishes. She could do with a cleaning herself. Cook snoozes in her chair. And Jane, having swept up the dirt on the dining room floor, has set the kettle on the stove for one last cup of tea.

IN THE DINING ROOM Everything is quiet and clean. Piggins locks the front door at 47 The Meadows. He hears the kettle whistling.

It has been a long and interesting evening. Piggins is tired. Teapot in hand, he goes back down the stairs. *Trit-trot, trit-trot, trit-trot.*

Would you like to read more mystery stories about Piggins? Why or why not?

Is Piggins a real detective? What makes you think he is or isn't?

How does Piggins solve the mystery?

Would you want to be a member of the Reynards' staff? Give reasons for your answer.

WRITE What do you like or dislike about mystery stories? Write a paragraph telling how you feel.

288

WORDS FROM THE AUTHOR And The ILLUSTRATOR

Jane Yolen and Jane Dyer

AWARD-WINNING AUTHOR

Every story has a starting place, but it is often difficult to guess it. You may think that *Piggins* began with *Trit-trot, trit-trot* but actually it began with a series of mystery books, a television show, and an illustration of three bears.

Strategic Reading

MODELING A STRATEGY: PAGES 282–288 Ask students if what they read on pages 282–288 confirmed their predictions.

THINK ALOUD You may want to model confirming predictions: *I predicted that Piggins would find the necklace somewhere in the dining room. I based my prediction on the fact that Piggins is the main character of the story and that he discovered several clues as soon as the necklace disappeared.* CONFIRMING PREDICTIONS

Returning to the Predictions/Purpose
SEQUENCE DIAGRAM Have students complete and share their sequence diagrams. Ask students to discuss the role the lavaliere plays in the mystery. (The Ratsbys steal it, and Piggins catches them.)
NOTE: Responses to the questions and support for the Write activity appear on page T450.

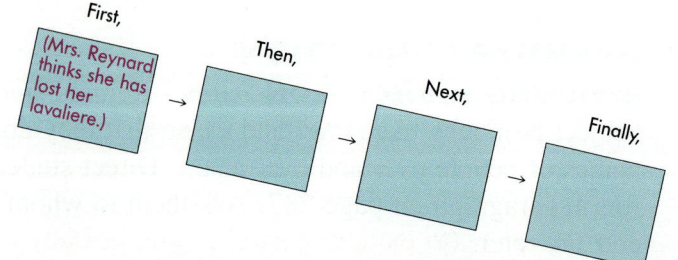

T448 / A PLACE TO DREAM, UNIT 3

The series of mystery books I mean were from England and star a detective named Lord Peter Wimsey. His butler, Bunter, assists him in every mystery he solves. Written in the 1930s and 1940s by British author Dorothy Sayers, these books are particular favorites of mine, and I have read each of them many times.

The television show is a long-running series called *Upstairs, Downstairs*. It's about a British family in the late 1800s and early 1900s. The family has a butler, a cook, a messy young kitchen maid, an upstairs maid, and a house with a great many rooms. They are always holding formal dinner parties.

The illustration was shown to me during a writing class I was teaching. The young artist, Jane Dyer, had done work for textbooks and sticker books, but she had never illustrated a picture book before. I fell in love with one illustration showing three bears sitting down to a breakfast of porridge. They were elegantly dressed in their cozy little forest cottage.

Without really meaning to, I came up with an idea for a book: What about a . . . a pig butler named Piggins, dressed in a tuxedo, who works for a family in a fancy house and solves mysteries? When I asked Jane Dyer if she would like to try the illustrations she looked at me as if I were crazy.

"Would I?" she whispered in a soft voice. Then she almost shouted, "Oh, boy, WOULD I!"

And she did.

P.S. Here is a funny ending to the story. Four years after the first of the three PIGGINS books came out, I got a letter from a lady named Mrs. Ethel Piggins. She wondered if I had heard of her and if her name had given me the idea for my books. She said that I had met her daughter once years before. I didn't remember meeting her daughter and told her so. Several months later a young woman named Ms. Reynard asked me the same question. I hadn't ever met her before either. But sometimes the things you make up come true—in an odd sort of way.

Words from the Author and the Illustrator

AUTHOR'S/ILLUSTRATOR'S PURPOSE Invite students to read pages 289–291 to find out why Jane Yolen wanted to write "Piggins" and how Jane Dyer came to illustrate the book. When students have finished reading, ask volunteers to name some of the works that influenced Jane Yolen. (Lord Peter Wimsey mysteries by Dorothy Sayers; the television series *Upstairs, Downstairs*) Then ask students whether they think "Piggins" would have been created if Jane Yolen had not seen Jane Dyer's illustration of the three bears. (Responses will vary.)

PART 2

Responding to the Literature

Personal Response

Encourage critical thinking.

Would you like to read more mystery stories about Piggins? Why or why not? (Responses will vary.) CRITICAL: EXPRESSING PERSONAL OPINIONS

Is Piggins a real detective? What makes you think he is or isn't? (Accept reasonable responses: Piggins is a make-believe detective, but he looks for clues like a real detective.) CRITICAL: MAKING JUDGMENTS

How does Piggins solve the mystery? (He figures out from the clues of the red thread, the trail of cheese crumbs, the tinkling sound, and the squeaky scream that it was Lord and Lady Ratsby who took the necklace.) INFERENTIAL: SUMMARIZING

Would you want to be a member of the Reynards' staff? Give reasons for your answer. (Responses will vary. Tell students to give details from the story to support their answers.) CRITICAL: AUTHOR'S CRAFT/IDENTIFYING WITH CHARACTERS

Encourage creative written responses.

 **WRITE** **What do you like or dislike about mystery stories? Write a paragraph telling how you feel.** Suggest that students first think about what makes a story a mystery story. If students choose to write about the elements of a mystery they dislike, you may want to extend the activity by asking them to write a second paragraph about the elements they like. CREATIVE: WRITING A PARAGRAPH OF OPINION

Cooperative Response

Have reader response groups extend their discussions.

LITERATURE CIRCLES Encourage Literature Circles to discuss their reactions to the selection. They might begin by sharing any questions or comments about author's craft that they wrote in their personal journals. Then have them discuss a question such as this:

Why do you think the author chose the names she did for the characters in the story?

STRATEGY CONFERENCE

Ask students whether the sequence diagram helped them follow the chain of events. Together, brainstorm strategies such as visualizing the scene when the lights went out (page 281) to help students reconstruct the sequence.

NOTE

An additional writing activity for this selection appears on page T453.

T450 / A PLACE TO DREAM, UNIT 3

Summarizing the Literature

Have students retell the story and write a summary.

Encourage students to summarize the story by completing a story frame. (See *Practice Book* page 80 below.) Students may then use their completed frames to retell the story and write a brief summary.

The story takes place (at Mr. and Mrs. Reynard's house). (Piggins, Mrs. Reynard), and (Lady Ratsby) are important characters in the story. A problem happens when (Mrs. Reynard's diamond lavaliere is stolen). The problem is solved when (Piggins figures out who stole the necklace and finds it). At the end of the story, Mrs. Reynard (wants to keep the lavaliere and hopes the trouble is over).

Critical Thinking Activity

Discuss an old saying.

PRESENT OPINIONS When the Ratsbys hid the diamond necklace in the sparkling chandelier, they were following the old saying "the best place to hide something is in plain sight." Do you think the old saying is true? Explain your answer. Have students work in small groups to discuss their opinions. Encourage them to make a chart showing whether their personal experiences and what they read in the story support the saying. CRITICAL: EXPRESSING PERSONAL OPINIONS

Saying	Experience	Story

INFORMAL ASSESSMENT

Asking students to identify *setting*, *characters*, and *plot* creates opportunities to assess how well they understand important story elements.

OPTIONAL INDEPENDENT PRACTICE

WRITER'S JOURNAL
page 48: Writing a personal response

PRACTICE BOOK
page 80: Summarizing the selection

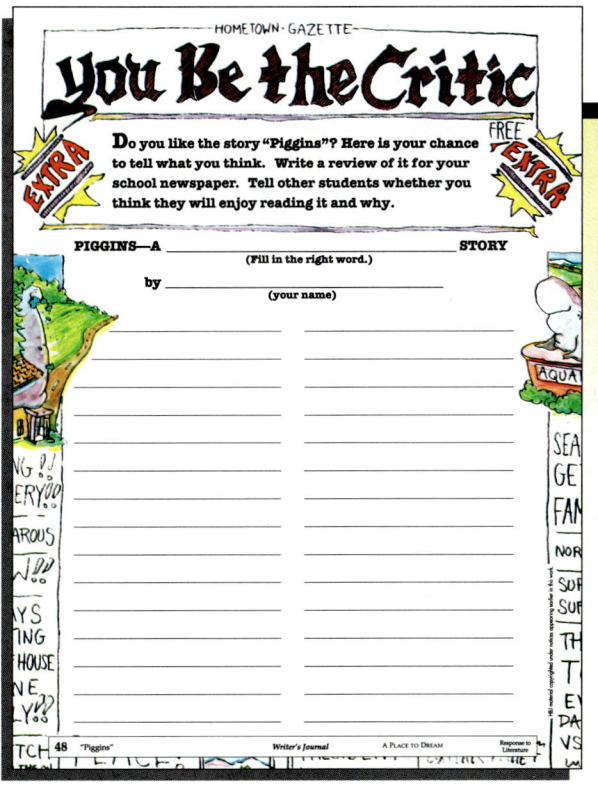
Writer's Journal

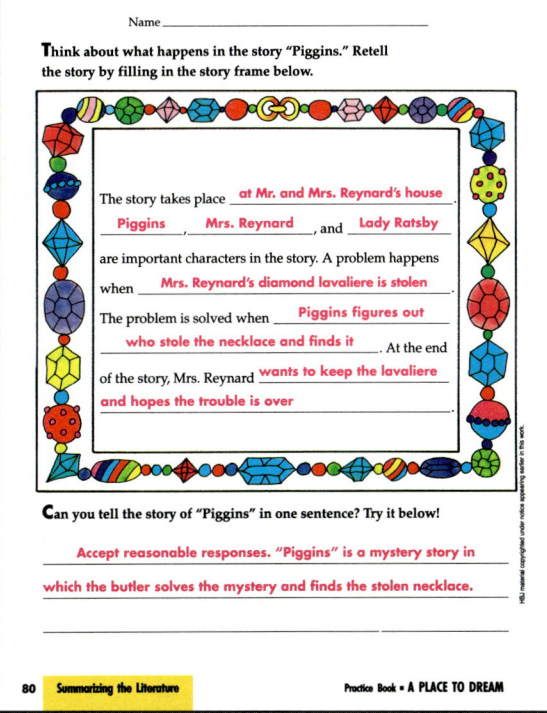
Practice Book

PIGGINS / T451

VOCABULARY WORKSHOP

Reviewing Key Words

Display the Key Words, and have students write them on index cards or slips of paper. Then read aloud the following series of words. Have students hold up the card or slip with the Key Word associated with each series of words.

- servant, supervise, Piggins (butler)
- ceiling, light, sparkle (chandelier)
- oldest, Miss Lapin, age (eldest)
- work, job, special training (professional)
- sound, ringing, bell (tinkling)
- needle, sew, cloth (thread)
- puzzled, mystery, don't know (stumped)

OPTIONAL INDEPENDENT PRACTICE

PRACTICE BOOK
page 81: Writing onomatopoeic words

Practice Book

Extending Vocabulary

ONOMATOPOEIA Write the words *trit-trot*, *ding-dong*, and *aaaa-OOOO-ga* on the board, and have a volunteer read them. Ask students to explain what made each of these sounds in the story. (Piggins' footsteps, the front door bell, the horn in Pierre Lapin's car) Discuss with students what makes these words different from words like *walk* and *door bell*. If necessary, lead them to conclude that the words on the board represent the sounds different things make. Tell students that the use of such words is called *onomatopoeia*. Then have students name some other onomatopoeic words. (Accept reasonable responses: *meow, grrrr, tweet, boom, crunch*.)

Have pairs of students scan the story "Piggins" to locate the following words: *tinkling, thud, squeak, scream, snorts,* and *snoozes*. Encourage them to invent new spellings for the sounds these words suggest. Invite students to read aloud and compare their onomatopoeic words.

T452 / A PLACE TO DREAM, UNIT 3

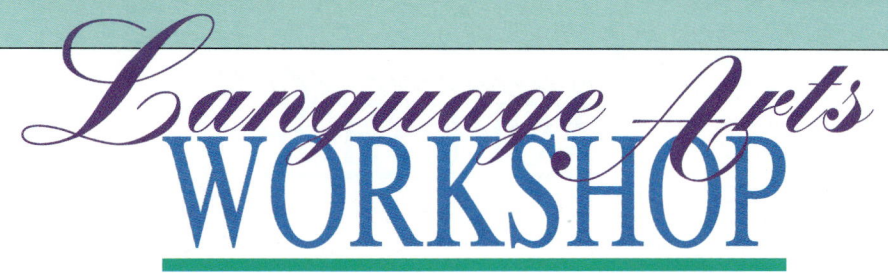

READING

Oral Rereading/Drama

Have pairs of students choose parts of the story to read aloud. Read the first four paragraphs to model how to read narrative with the dialogue. Model how to change your voice to show that a different character is speaking. Give students time to rehearse before they present their readings. Some students may want to prepare to read the entire story to a younger audience. **LISTENING/READING**

WRITING

Writing About the Literature

Available on Project Card 34A

WRITE DIALOGUE Have students write dialogue for mystery stories set at a party. Encourage small groups to make a chart like the one below, including the guests' names, some interesting facts about each guest, and something the guest might say. Use examples from the story to model the correct capitalization and punctuation of dialogue. Then have students use the information on the chart to write their mystery stories. Encourage them to read their stories aloud. **LISTENING/SPEAKING/WRITING**

Party Guests	Facts	What They Might Say
Ms. Hasty	has extensive knowledge of poisonous fish	"The fish have been biting this year."
Ramsay	holds a world record: whistling "Yankee Doodle" for 100 hours without stopping	"I love to whistle."

GRAMMAR REVIEW: SUBJECT PRONOUNS Have pairs of students exchange stories during revising and check that subject pronouns are used correctly. First, help them create a list of points to keep in mind when using subject pronouns. These might include:

- *He* replaces the name of one male.
- *She* replaces the name of one female.
- *They* replaces the names of two or more persons.
- *I* refers to myself or the person telling the story.
- Subject pronouns must agree with verbs in number.

LANGUAGE HANDBOOK Writing Dialogue for a Story, pages 36–37, 40; Subject Pronouns, pages 112–113

DAILY LANGUAGE PRACTICE Oral language exercises are provided on pages R72–R73.

CHOICES

Language Arts WORKSHOP

LISTENING AND SPEAKING

May I See Your References?

Available on Project Card 34B

Have students take turns role-playing an interview between Piggins and someone who wants a job in the Reynard household. Have students begin by brainstorming a list of jobs that might exist. **(gardener, painter, nanny, cleaner)** Have pairs of students choose a job and then rehearse an interview in which Piggins explains the job and the applicant describes his or her qualifications and experience. Each student may want to write notes first. LISTENING/SPEAKING/WRITING

READING

Mystery Readers' Circle

Encourage students who enjoyed "Piggins" to form a Mystery Readers' Circle. They can choose one or more mystery stories to read, meeting on a regular basis to share their responses and predictions. When they have finished reading and discussing a mystery, the circle members may want to share it with other students by creating a poster or by performing a "book commercial." LISTENING/SPEAKING/READING

LISTENING AND SPEAKING

Ratsbys in Court

COOPERATIVE LEARNING Point out that in real life, Lord and Lady Ratsby would have to stand trial for stealing the diamond necklace. Have students work together to create and present that trial. Assign one group of students the task of preparing the Ratsbys' defense and another group the prosecution's case. A third group could act as the jury. Ask other students to play the roles of the Ratsbys, the witnesses, and the judge. Before the trial begins, allow the Ratsbys to confer with their defense team in order to prepare the defense case. The teams may also want to prepare speeches for the summation at the end of the trial. This is when each side sums up its case for the jury. Remind students that the purpose of the speech will be to sway the jury. Ask a Recorder to write down the jury's comments and a Reporter to read aloud the verdict. LISTENING/SPEAKING

T454 / A PLACE TO DREAM, UNIT 3

Language Arts WORKSHOP

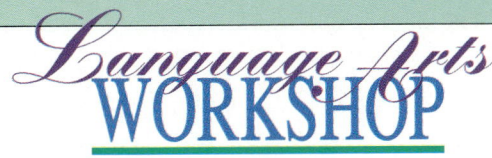

READING

Animal Stories

Ask students to imagine that they were going to write a story about two rats. What kind of characters would they be? Would they be dangerous and sly, or kind and lovable? When students finish sharing their ideas, read aloud or have volunteers read *Dr. De Soto* by William Steig. Encourage students to compare the animal characters with those in "Piggins."

Students should begin by creating a list of character traits for four main characters: Dr. De Soto, Mr. Fox, Lady Ratsby, and Mr. Reynard. Lead them to conclude that the "good" and "bad" animal characters are switched in the two stories. Ask students to think of other stories they know about mice or rats and foxes and to describe what these characters were like. LISTENING/SPEAKING/READING

SPELLING

Reviewing Spelling Words

SPELLING WORDS: *force, form, fourth, north, score, shore, sport, storm, war, warm, wore, your*

WORDS TO EXPLORE: *butter, clues, stumped, thread*

Dictate the Spelling Words to students. Then write these spellings for the sound /ôr/ on the board: *or, ore, ar, our*. Have students take turns writing a Spelling Word in the correct group. As an added challenge, have students brainstorm other words with the sound /ôr/ that are spelled with the letters listed on the board. LISTENING/SPEAKING/SPELLING

Use *Integrated Spelling* Lesson 14 to reinforce the Spelling Words and the Words to Explore. See pages T93–T98 in *Integrated Spelling Teacher's Edition*.

 **SPELLING POSTTEST** You may want to use the Pretest/Posttest Sentences on *Integrated Spelling Teacher's Edition* page T93 to assess students' knowledge of the spelling generalization.

WRITING

Detective Ads

Ask students to imagine that they are setting up their own detective agency. Have them work in pairs to write and illustrate newspaper advertisements describing their services and highlighting their special detective skills. Point out that successful ads use words and pictures to persuade readers. Before students begin, lead them in brainstorming words and phrases that might convince people that they are the best at solving mysteries. You may want to copy the following web and have students expand it with their own ideas. WRITING/VIEWING

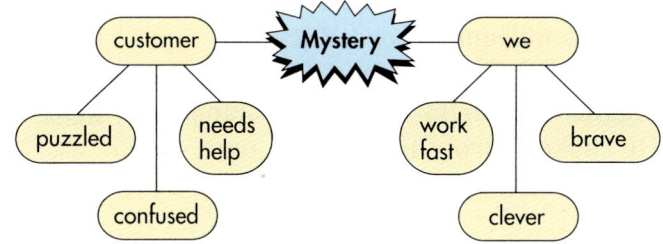

PIGGINS / T455

Grammar MINI LESSON

Object Pronouns

OBJECTIVES: *To recognize that an object pronoun follows an action verb or a word such as* about, at, for, from, near, of, to, *or* with; *that the words* me, you, him, her, it, us, *and* them *are object pronouns; to use object pronouns correctly*

Oral Warm-Up

Display the following sentences from "Piggins":

- **He has shined the silver teapot so well he can see his snout in <u>it</u>.**
- **Inspector Bayswater takes out his pipe. He does not light <u>it</u>. The doctors have advised <u>him</u> not to smoke.**
- **His students all say proudly, "Professor T. Ortoise taught <u>us</u>."**

Ask volunteers to read each bulleted item aloud and tell what or whom each underlined word refers to. Record their answers in a chart like the one below:

Word	What the word replaces or refers to
it	the silver teapot
it	his pipe
him	Inspector Bayswater
us	His students

Reinforce students' responses by having volunteers read the items aloud, replacing the underlined words with the words they refer to. (For example, *He does not light his pipe*.)

Interactive Teaching

OBJECT PRONOUNS Write the following sentence pairs and word list on the board:

- **Piggins cleaned the silver forks.
  Then he polished the silver forks.**
- **Piggins welcomed Lord Ratsby.
  He opened the door for Lord Ratsby.**
- **Piggins was angry at Upstairs Jane.
  He spoke sharply to Upstairs Jane.**

> it
> him
> her
> us
> them

Cross out the phrase *the silver forks* in the second sentence of the first pair, and ask students which word from the list would make sense there. *(them)* Have a volunteer draw a line between *them* and the sentence. Then ask students to identify the word that describes an action in the sentence *(polished)* and underline it. Explain that object pronouns replace nouns after an action verb or a word such as *to, with, for,* or *at*.

Repeat the procedure for the next two pairs of sentences. (*Him* replaces *Mr. Ratsby; her* replaces *Upstairs Jane*.) Write the other object pronouns, *me* and *you*, on the board. Help students identify the singular object pronouns and the plural object pronouns. (singular: *me, you, him, her, it;* plural: *us, you, them*) Point out to students that the word *you* can refer to one person or to more than one. If necessary, reinforce this idea by handing rulers to one student and then to more than one student as you model the sentence *I give the rulers to you*.

LANGUAGE HANDBOOK
Object Pronouns, page 114

T456 / A PLACE TO DREAM, UNIT 3

Practice Activities

Summarize It!

Discuss with students the major events in "Piggins." Then encourage pairs of students to write a summary paragraph similar to the following, underlining the words that could be replaced with object pronouns.

Mr. and Mrs. Reynard invite guests to dinner. Piggins lets the guests in. Mr. Reynard says that he is going to sell his wife's necklace. The lights go out, and someone steals the necklace. Inspector Bayswater looks for clues. The case stumps Inspector Bayswater. Piggins solves the case. He says that the thieves are Lord and Lady Ratsby. The guests help to catch Lord and Lady Ratsby.

Then have pairs rewrite their summaries, replacing each underlined noun or nouns with the appropriate object pronoun. Have volunteers read their summaries aloud and discuss why they used the object pronouns they did. **VISUAL/AUDITORY**

Solve the Mystery

Have students form small groups, and tell them they are going to play Solve the Mystery. Each group chooses a detective. The detectives leave the room while the other members of each group select a small object, such as a book or a pencil, and decide who in the group it "belongs" to. It can belong to one group member or to more than one, including the detective. The group members move their desks into a circle and place the object on the floor in the middle of the circle. The detectives return. Each detective begins the game by picking up the object and asking a group member, "Does this belong to *you*?" The group member responds yes or no. If the object does not belong to that person, he or she responds with a clue in the following format while pointing to the appropriate group member or members: "No, this [object] does not belong to me, but it might belong to [her/him/them]." The detective then repeats the inquiry with another member of the group.
VISUAL/AUDITORY/KINESTHETIC

Practice Book

MEETING INDIVIDUAL NEEDS

SECOND-LANGUAGE SUPPORT Students who translate directly from their first language often make awkward constructions when using object pronouns. Model correct usage using the following commands. Then have students suggest others.

- Show *me* the book.
- Show *them* the answers.

RETEACH Follow the visual, auditory, and kinesthetic/motor models on page R32.

OPTIONAL INDEPENDENT PRACTICE

- **PRACTICE BOOK**
  page 82: Identifying and using object pronouns

- **GRAMMAR PRACTICE**
  pages 34–35: Writing sentences with object pronouns

PART 3

Learning through the Literature

LITERARY APPRECIATION
INTRODUCE

Fiction and Nonfiction

OBJECTIVE: *To distinguish fiction from nonfiction, and mystery stories from other types of fiction*

Interactive Teaching

Help students determine that "Piggins" is fiction.

DISCUSS FICTION AND NONFICTION Write the words *fiction* and *nonfiction* on the board. Explain that fiction is make-believe, created from a writer's imagination. Nonfiction tells about real people, places, things, or events. Point out that being able to identify fiction and nonfiction elements will help students understand and appreciate what they read. Ask students what kind of writing "Piggins" is and how they can tell. (It is fiction. It's about make-believe animal characters.)

Discuss mystery as a type of fiction.

THINK ALOUD ABOUT RECOGNIZING A MYSTERY Tell students that "Piggins" is a type of fiction called a *mystery*. Explain that mystery stories have special elements that make them different from other fiction. Then model how to tell whether a story is a mystery.

> When I'm reading a story which describes a puzzle that the characters try to solve, I know I'm reading a mystery. The characters use clues to solve the puzzle. And until the puzzle is solved, I am in suspense, which is a feeling of not knowing what is going to happen next.

Begin a chart such as the one below. Encourage students to use it to summarize the puzzle, the clues, and the solution of "Piggins." Tell students that while some mystery stories, like "Piggins," are based on crimes such as stealing, others are not: A mystery story can be about any puzzle that requires the characters to use clues to find the solution.

AN ADDITIONAL BOOK FOR REINFORCING FICTION AND NONFICTION

If You Were a Writer by Joan Lowery Nixon. Four Winds, 1988. EASY

Title	Puzzle	Clues	Solution
Piggins	What happened to the diamond lavaliere?	Ratsbys need money. red thread cheese crumbs squeaky scream tinkling sound	The Ratsbys stole it.

T458 / A PLACE TO DREAM, UNIT 3

Practice Activity

Who Dunnit?

Have students analyze mysteries. Have students use the chart on page T458 to summarize the puzzles, clues, and solutions of other mysteries they have read or seen. VISUAL

Performance Assessment

Encourage students to compare the mystery stories they described on their charts in the Who Dunnit? activity. How are the mysteries alike? How are they different? Which of the mysteries did students solve before the characters did? Which clues helped them solve the mysteries? For evaluation guidelines, see *Staff Development Guide*.

Reader ↔ Writer Connection
Fiction and Nonfiction

WRITERS supply clues that enable the reader to try to solve the mystery along with the story characters.

READERS use the elements of a mystery to become involved and to enjoy the story more.

WRITE A MYSTERY STORY Have students write a first-person account of a mystery and its solution.

MEETING INDIVIDUAL NEEDS

RETEACH Follow the visual, auditory, and kinesthetic/motor models on page R33.

CHALLENGE Have students write two possible clues and a solution for a mystery involving a missing lunchbox. Encourage them to compare their writing.

SECOND-LANGUAGE SUPPORT Students may demonstrate their understanding of the lesson by recalling the clues the author used in "Piggins." See also the manual *Alternative Teaching Strategies*, pages 15, 82–85.

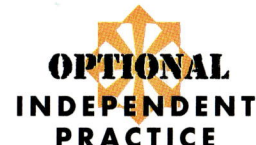

OPTIONAL INDEPENDENT PRACTICE

WRITER'S JOURNAL
page 49: Writing a mystery

PRACTICE BOOK
page 83: Identifying fiction and nonfiction

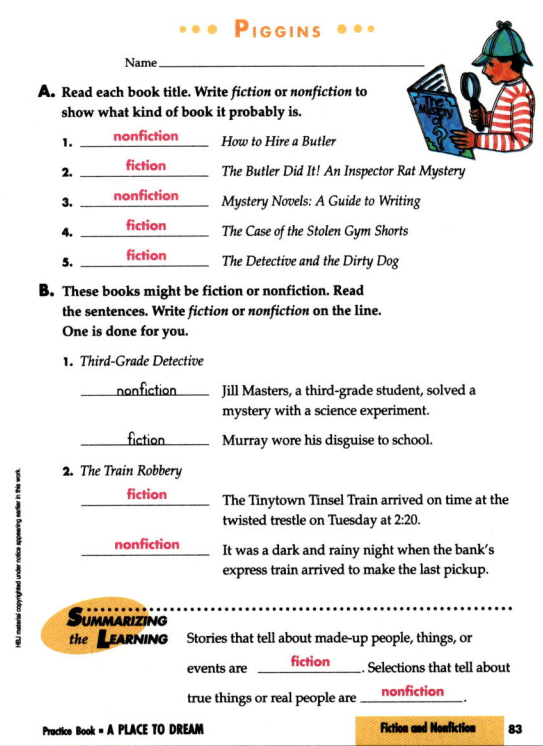

PIGGINS / **T459**

COMPREHENSION REVIEW

Making Predictions

OBJECTIVE: *To make predictions using story evidence and real-life experience*

Review

Have students use story evidence plus prior knowledge.

REVIEW HOW TO MAKE PREDICTIONS Have students recall how to make a prediction about what will happen in a story. (Readers should use evidence from what was read plus their own knowledge to predict what might happen.) Model making a prediction about the characters in "Piggins."

Story Evidence		Knowledge		Prediction
The Ratsbys stole the necklace.	+	If you commit a crime, you can be punished.	=	Lord and Lady Ratsby will be sent to jail.

Practice Activity

What Will She Do?

Encourage students to make other predictions.

Have students make diagrams like the one above and predict what Mrs. Reynard will do with the lavaliere. Have students share their predictions, explaining how they combined prior knowledge with story evidence to lead to their predictions.
VISUAL/AUDITORY

MEETING INDIVIDUAL NEEDS

CHALLENGE Encourage students to choose one of the story characters and make predictions about what might happen to him or her. Have students who chose the same character compare their predictions.

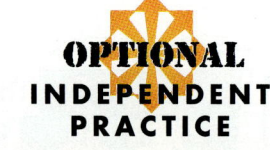

OPTIONAL INDEPENDENT PRACTICE

PRACTICE BOOK
page 84: Making predictions

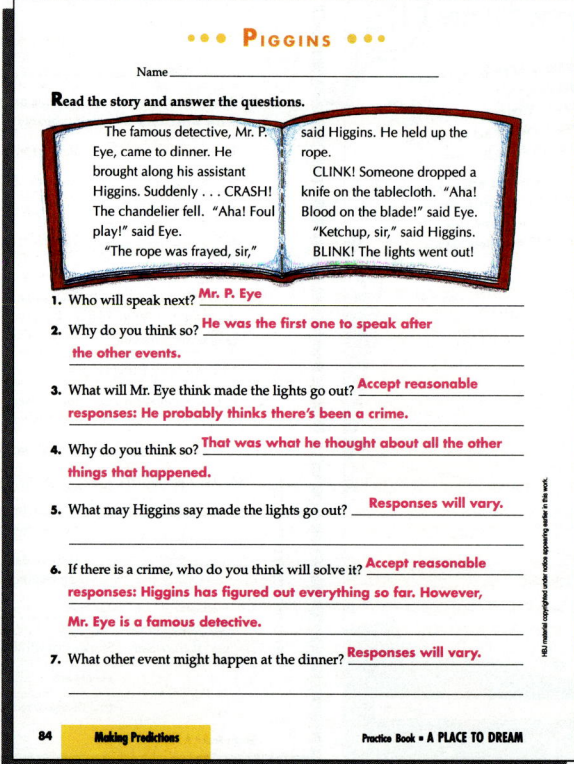

Practice Book

T460 / A PLACE TO DREAM, UNIT 3

VOCABULARY REVIEW

Context Clues

OBJECTIVE: *To use context clues to determine word meanings*

Review

Help students determine the meaning of *lavaliere*.

MODEL USING CONTEXT CLUES Remind students that the story "Piggins" contains several words that may have been unfamiliar. Then model how to figure out the meaning of the word *lavaliere* on page 275.

> When I read, I use context clues and visualize what is happening. I know that Mrs. Reynard is upset about losing something that has diamonds in it. If I can't figure out the meaning from the clues in the sentence, I read a little further. I discover that Mrs. Reynard finds what she is looking for—a necklace. A lavaliere must be jewelry worn around the neck.

Practice Activity

What's That Word?

Have pairs of students determine other meanings.

Ask students to work in pairs to figure out the meanings of these words from the story: *scullery* (page 277), *contraptions* (page 278), and *commotion* (page 285). Have students share the clues they used to determine what the words mean and then tell the meanings or demonstrate them by using the words in original sentences. **VISUAL/AUDITORY**

MEETING INDIVIDUAL NEEDS

CHALLENGE Have students locate the word *alight* on page 277. Ask them to write one or two sentences that use context clues to help a reader figure out the meaning of *alight*. Provide time for students to share their work.

OPTIONAL INDEPENDENT PRACTICE

PRACTICE BOOK

page 85: Using context clues

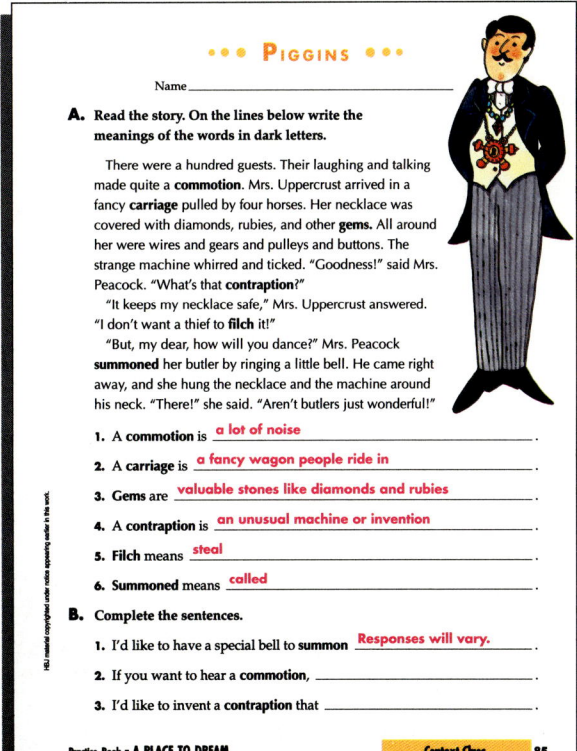

Practice Book

Integrated CURRICULUM

SOCIAL STUDIES

Law Enforcers

COOPERATIVE LEARNING Have students work together in groups to complete a project on law enforcement. Let them begin by consulting an encyclopedia to find some of the different careers in this field, such as police officer, detective, and undercover agent. Encourage each group to research several different careers. Have group members combine their work to make posters. Appoint a Materials Manager and a Recorder, who will write the final copy. Display the completed projects. If possible, invite a professional in law enforcement to speak to the class about his or her work. **LISTENING/READING/WRITING/VIEWING**

ART

Tortoise Characters

Tell students that the character Professor T. Ortoise in "Piggins" may have been inspired by a character in *Alice in Wonderland* by Lewis Carroll. Read aloud the chapter "The Mock Turtle's Story," which includes the line "We called him Tortoise because he taught us." Students may enjoy drawing a scene from the chapter and sharing their drawings. **LISTENING**

SCIENCE

A Dog's Life

Available on Project Card 35A

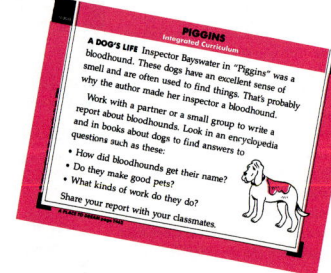

USE AN ENCYCLOPEDIA
Point out to students that Inspector Bayswater in "Piggins" is a bloodhound. Tell them that bloodhounds have an excellent sense of smell and are often used to find things, which is probably why the author made the inspector a bloodhound. Encourage students to do research for a report about bloodhounds. Have them include information such as how did bloodhounds get their name? Where and when did they originate? Do they make good pets? What kinds of work do they do? Encourage students to illustrate their reports and present them to the others. **LISTENING/SPEAKING/READING/WRITING**

MATH

Going Shopping

Tell students that the Reynards have prepared the shopping list shown above for a party they are giving in honor of Piggins. If possible, take students to a nearby store or bring in store circulars. Ask students to record the price that the Reynards would have to pay for each item. When students have determined the price for each item, have them figure out the total cost.   LISTENING/ READING/WRITING

SOCIAL STUDIES

Festive Foods

Remind students that the meal at the Reynards' house began with shrimp soup. Encourage students to describe foods that might be found on the table of a festive meal at their homes. Have them describe as much as they know about the origins of the foods, the ingredients, and the preparation of the dishes.   LISTENING/SPEAKING

SCIENCE

Great Inventions

Available on Project Card 35B

USE REFERENCE SOURCES   Remind students that Mr. Reynard is a "tinkerer" who likes to invent "contraptions." Point out that possibly every invention looks like a contraption at first. Then ask students to research the history of an entertaining or useful object in their lives, such as the bicycle, the television set, or the skateboard. Encourage students to give brief summaries of their findings. Have them accompany their talks with an illustration of the original invention.   LISTENING/ SPEAKING/READING/WRITING/VIEWING

BOOKS TO SHARE

SCIENCE   *Dreamplace* by George Ella Lyon. Orchard, 1993.   EASY
Nature Detective: How to Solve Outdoor Mysteries by Eileen M. Docekal. Sterling, 1989.
CHALLENGING

PIGGINS / T463

MULTICULTURAL PERSPECTIVES

o The Supreme Court

DISCUSSION STARTER
What do you think a lawyer does in his or her job? What different kinds of lawyers can you think of?

READ ALOUD
There are many different kinds of lawyers in the United States today. Some lawyers defend people who are accused of serious crimes. Others work for businesses. Still others devote their lives to public issues. Some dedicated lawyers go on to become judges. The pinnacle of success for a judge is a position on the Supreme Court of the United States. Few judges ever receive this honor. Two who did—Thurgood Marshall and Sandra Day O'Connor— serve as important role models for all of us.

Thurgood Marshall was the first African American appointed to the Supreme Court. After a brilliant career as a lawyer who fought hard for the rights of all Americans, he spent twenty-four years as a justice of the Supreme Court, retiring in 1991.

President Reagan appointed Sandra Day O'Connor to the Supreme Court in 1981. O'Connor, the first woman on the Court, was a lawyer and a state senator in Arizona and then a judge for seven years before being chosen for the Supreme Court.

ACTIVITY CORNER
● Explain that Supreme Court decisions affect the lives of all citizens. Discuss the kinds of personal qualities that a good United States Supreme Court justice might have. Have students draw pictures to show how they imagine a Supreme Court justice might look. Display combined groups of pictures to make diverse nine-member "Supreme Courts."

Lawyers may spend many years gaining the experience and wisdom needed to become a judge, like Thurgood Marshall or Sandra Day O'Connor.

POEMS

Closed, I am a mystery
Hello Book!
Would you like

*Myra Cohn Livingston
Lillian Morrison*

ABOUT THE POETS ALA Notable Book author N. M. Bodecker said he writes and draws because "that is what I was meant to do." In 1980 Myra Cohn Livingston won the NCTE Award for Excellence in Poetry for Children. Some of Lillian Morrison's poetry was inspired by her work with children in a library.

ABOUT THE POEMS All three poems explore the value of books. "Closed, I am a mystery" is a riddle rhyme told from the point of view of a book. "Would you like" is a rhyming poem telling readers why they should "get into books." In "Hello Book!" a child engages in a delightful conversation with a book.

Reading the Poems

Help students set a purpose for reading.

Invite students to tell why they like to read, and the kinds of books they enjoy most.

Read aloud the titles of the three poems, and explain to students that Myra Cohn Livingston, Lillian Morrison, and N. M. Bodecker have each written about books. Then ask students how they think the poets might feel about books and reading. Have them listen to find out as you read the poems aloud.

Responding to the Poems

Return to the purpose for reading.

Ask students if their predictions about how the poets feel about books were confirmed. Have them discuss how or why books are special to the poets.

Encourage students to respond creatively.

You may wish to use the following activity for responding to the poems:

PERSONAL JOURNAL: WRITING A POEM Students can write a riddle rhyme about a favorite book or write a poem about why books are special to them. Invite students to share their verses with their classmates.

LISTENING/SPEAKING/WRITING

TEACHING TIP

You may want to read aloud the three poems and then have students compare the rhythms by tapping or clapping as they read each one aloud.

MEETING INDIVIDUAL NEEDS

SECOND-LANGUAGE SUPPORT Students may need help understanding that the "mystery" involved in these three poems is that readers don't really know what a book contains until they begin reading it. Have students name some "mysteries" that books might contain.

POEMS / T465

PAGES 292–293 POEMS

Closed, I am a mystery
by Myra Cohn Livingston

Closed, I am a mystery.
Open, I will always be
a friend with whom you think and see.

Closed, there's nothing I can say.
Open, we can dream and stray
to other worlds, far and away.

(A BOOK)

Hello Book!
by N. M. Bodecker
illustrated by Merle Nacht

Hello book!
What are you up to?
Keeping yourself to yourself,
shut in between your covers,
a prisoner high on a shelf.
Come in book!
What is your story?
Haven't you ever been read?
Did you think
    I would just pass by you,
And pick me a comic instead?
No way book!
I'm your reader.
I open you up. Set you free.
Listen, I know a secret!
Will you share
    your secrets with me?

Expanding the Poems What clues helped you figure out the answer to the riddle? (Responses will vary.) METACOGNITIVE: DRAWING CONCLUSIONS

How is a book "like a prisoner"? (Accept reasonable responses: A prisoner is someone who is shut in and not free to leave; a book on a shelf is like a prisoner unless someone takes it down, opens it, and reads it.) INFERENTIAL: MAKING COMPARISONS

POEMS PAGE 294

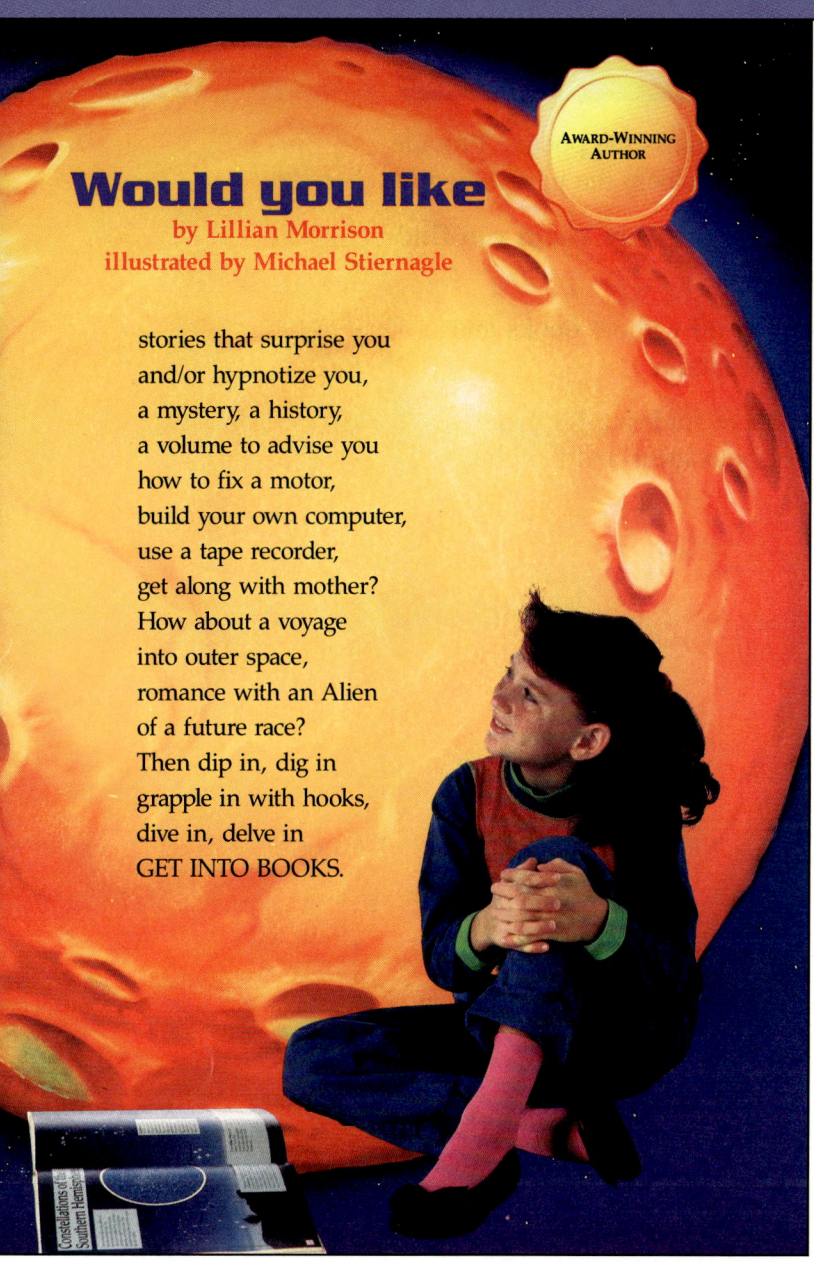

Would you like

by Lillian Morrison
illustrated by Michael Stiernagle

AWARD-WINNING AUTHOR

stories that surprise you
and/or hypnotize you,
a mystery, a history,
a volume to advise you
how to fix a motor,
build your own computer,
use a tape recorder,
get along with mother?
How about a voyage
into outer space,
romance with an Alien
of a future race?
Then dip in, dig in
grapple in with hooks,
dive in, delve in
GET INTO BOOKS.

Expanding the Poems   Why do you think the poet has capitalized all the letters in the words of the last line of the poem? (Accept reasonable responses: She wants to emphasize the importance of books and reading.)   CRITICAL: AUTHOR'S CRAFT/DETERMINING AUTHOR'S PURPOSE

POEMS / T467

Appreciating Literature

Have students share personal responses.

Have students work in small groups to discuss the poems. Provide a general question such as the following to help the groups begin:

Suppose there weren't any books to read. How could you find information you wanted or needed?

Have students discuss what they would do without books and how they would go about getting information.

PERSONAL JOURNAL Have students use their personal journals to write about ideas and feelings discussed in the groups.

Writer's Journal

OPTIONAL INDEPENDENT PRACTICE

WRITER'S JOURNAL

page 50: Writing a creative response

THEME WRAP-UP

Discussing the Theme

Remind students that they were challenged to solve the mysteries in the selections and poems they read in this theme.

Discussion Question

PAGE 295 **The story, riddle, and poems you have just read all contain a mystery. A mystery can be solved by paying careful attention to the clues. Piggins points out things that he sees or hears. What are some other ways to find clues? Describe one.** Encourage creative responses. (Accept reasonable responses: You could find clues by noticing a change; by looking at small details such as footprints, fingerprints, and objects; by using your other senses such as touch, smell, and taste; or by putting together several bits of evidence and drawing a conclusion.) **CREATIVE: SOLVING PROBLEMS**

Theme Wrap-Up

Mysteries to Solve

The story, riddle, and poems you have just read all contain mysteries. A mystery can be solved by paying careful attention to the clues. Piggins points out things that he sees or hears. What are some other ways to find clues? Describe one.

WRITER'S WORKSHOP
Everyone seemed to be sure that Piggins had not stolen the necklace, because he could be trusted. Write a paragraph explaining why it is important to be trusted.

Writer's Choice: Write a paragraph about a favorite mystery. Or write a riddle or a mystery of your own. Choose an idea, write, and then share what you wrote.

295

Writer's Workshop

See pages T470–T471 for suggestions for guiding students through the writing process as they respond to the literature. **WRITING PROCESS: PERSUASIVE PARAGRAPH**

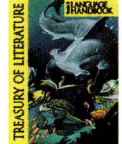

Writer's Choice
You may want to suggest that students use the *Language Handbook* for reference as they write. Students may need help planning their response.

As students revise and proofread their paragraphs, they may benefit from participating in peer conferences. If you wish, provide questions such as these to help student partners evaluate each other's work:

- Is the writer's opinion clear?
- Is it supported with reasons or examples? If not, how could the paragraph be improved?

Writer's Workshop

Persuasive Paragraph

Theme Wrap-Up

Students write a persuasive paragraph explaining why they think it is important to be trusted.

Prepare students for the writing task and form by asking them to recall the story "Piggins." Have a volunteer tell what the story was about. Discuss how the story relates to the task of writing a persuasive paragraph in two ways. One way is through the theme of the story, which is about trust. Mr. and Mrs. Reynard trust their butler Piggins. Another way is through the reasons Piggins gives to support his statement that Lord and Lady Ratsby stole the diamond necklace.

Use the Writer's Workshop assignment on page 295 as you work through the writing process with students.

ALTERNATIVE TOPICS If you wish, allow students to choose their own topics for writing. Suggest that they refer to the *Language Handbook* for an explanation of the writing process for persuasive paragraphs. See Writing Model, page R98.

LANGUAGE HANDBOOK *Writing to Persuade, pages 60–61; Persuasive Paragraph, page 62*

Prewriting

Have students brainstorm and discuss with partners ideas they have for their paragraphs. Encourage them to use a chart like the one below to organize their thoughts.

Opinion
Reason
Reason
Strongest Reason
Request for Action (when possible)

Drafting

Have students write a draft of their persuasive paragraph. Suggest that they

- begin with a sentence stating their opinion that it is important to be trusted.
- include at least three reasons that will convince their audience to agree with their opinion.
- tell their feeling again at the end of the paragraph and ask the audience to agree with the opinion and, when possible, to take action.

Responding and Revising

To check their own writing before sharing it with others, students should ask themselves these questions:

- Is there a clear topic sentence that tells the writer's opinion at the beginning of the persuasive paragraph?
- Are the reasons stated clearly?
- Is the strongest reason given last?

Have students exchange persuasive paragraphs in a peer conference. The writer should read the paragraph aloud to the partner. Then each partner should respond to the following questions and complete the following task:

Listener	Writer
Does the persuasive paragraph have a topic sentence that states the writer's opinion? Do you think the writer presents the reasons in a good order? Does the paragraph persuade you to believe what the writer believes?	When you read your persuasive paragraph aloud, do any parts seem confusing or unclear? Have you left out any reasons? Jot down any ideas for improvements that occur to you.

T470 / A PLACE TO DREAM, UNIT 3

Proofreading

Offer these tips as students proofread:

- Check your pronouns to be sure they are correct.
- Check capitalization and punctuation.
- Correct any misspelled words.

MINI-CONFERENCE STRATEGY Help students find errors in noun-pronoun agreement by making observations such as "At the beginning of this sentence you talk about *the students,* but then you refer to *his habits.* If you are going to write about more than one student, shouldn't you refer to *their habits?*"

Publishing Options

VISUAL SHOW Students might want to use their paragraphs to make different presentations on the theme of trust. Have students prepare neat copies of their paragraphs to distribute. Encourage them to combine them with graphics or other arts, such as dance.

TAPE RECORDING Have students practice and record their persuasive paragraphs. Students can use the recordings to discuss effective ways to use speed, voice, and pauses in oral presentations.

COMPUTER TIP

PUBLISHING Suggest that students explore their desktop publishing features to make the presentation of their final paragraph visually interesting.

Assessment Options

STUDENT SELF-ASSESSMENT Encourage students to summarize the writing experience by responding to this question in their journals:

- **What words did I use to help me be persuasive?**

You may also wish to have students complete the Self-Assessment Checklist in the *Portfolio Assessment Teacher's Guide*.

WRITING OBSERVATION RECORDS Note when a student effectively evaluates strengths and weaknesses of the finished paragraph.

After students publish, you may want to have them add their persuasive paragraphs to their portfolios.

GRAMMAR CONNECTION

Revising: Unclear Pronouns

Using Transparency H, share the examples below with students to show how using pronouns correctly to replace nouns is essential to clear writing.

> **Transparency H**
> **Trash in Public Parks**
>
> **BEFORE**
> People should be careful about leaving picnic trash in a public park. <u>It</u> is something we should care about. A park supervisor gave my friend Harold a lecture about littering. Then <u>he</u> left a paper plate under a bench! <u>He</u> was upset that <u>he</u> let this happen.
>
> **AFTER**
> People should be careful about leaving picnic trash in a public park. <u>A park</u> is something we should care about. A park supervisor gave my friend Harold a lecture about littering. Then <u>Harold</u> left a paper plate under a bench! <u>The park supervisor</u> was upset that <u>he</u> let this happen.

Have students work in small groups to share their writing and to check that any pronouns used refer clearly to nouns.

LANGUAGE HANDBOOK
Pronouns, pages 107–114

WRITER'S WORKSHOP / T471

Unit 3 ADVENTURES

THEME OPENER

The Great Outdoors

The Lost Lake

T475   A REALISTIC FICTION STORY by Allen Say
Disappointed by what they discover when they reach Lost Lake, Luke and his father set out to find their own "lost lake."

Words from the Author and Illustrator: Allen Say

T487   AN ARTICLE
Allen Say tells about how real people and a lake he visited helped spark an idea for a book.

People

T503   A POEM by Charlotte Zolotow
Some people seem to be able to make the birds sing or to fill the sky with music with only a look or a touch.

Some People

T503   A POEM by Rachel Field
It's strange how some people can make you feel inside.

For pacing suggestions, see page T474.

Theme Opener: The Great Outdoors PAGES 296–297

THEME

The Great Outdoors

How does it feel to be outdoors with just nature around you? How does it feel to explore the outdoors with other people? Think about your own feelings as you read the story and the poems.

CONTENTS

THE LOST LAKE
written and illustrated by Allen Say

WORDS FROM THE AUTHOR AND ILLUSTRATOR: ALLEN SAY

PEOPLE
by Charlotte Zolotow

SOME PEOPLE
by Rachel Field

297

Discussing the Theme

Direct students' attention to the illustration as you read aloud the theme title, "The Great Outdoors." Then have students read the paragraph on Student Anthology page 297. Ask students to describe what is happening in the photograph. Then invite students to read the selection titles and speculate about how each one might relate to the theme.

Portfolio Assessment

Remind students to keep their writing responses for the selections in "The Great Outdoors" in their portfolios. Suggest that they also add to their personal journals thoughts and ideas about any books they have read independently.

 When you come across this symbol, you may encourage students to save some of their work in their portfolios.

THEME OPENER: THE GREAT OUTDOORS / T473

THEME OPENER

Managing the Literature-Based Classroom

Mechanical Errors

Use the margins of student papers to denote with the CUPS code the mechanical errors that exist in the paper. *C* denotes capitalization errors, *U* denotes usage errors, *P* denotes punctuation errors, and *S* denotes spelling errors. The number of letters in the margin will match the number of errors in the line. Students will locate and correct the errors, giving them needed practice.

Cooperative Groups

To keep track of groups and the members in each, create and post a chart like the one below. Make a name card for each student. Designate each group by using a different number, letter, or name. As each student joins a group, move his or her name card into the appropriate column. You may want to color-code cards for each group.

Group Assignment Chart

Group 1	Group 2	Group 3	Group 4	Group 5
Jack	Heather	Dennis	Sid	Kisha
Luis	Jeannie	Barb	Andrea	Martin
Molly	Jelani	Jenna	Joan	Rose
Ann	Mike		Robert	Andy
Tina			Dave	

Pacing

This theme has been designed to take about two weeks to complete, depending on your students' needs.

MEETING INDIVIDUAL NEEDS

LOW-ACHIEVING STUDENTS You may wish to meet with students before they read the selection to discuss the theme, "The Great Outdoors." Students may tell what they expect to read about in a selection on camping, the kinds of places where people might camp, and the kinds of items campers might need to take with them. You might list their ideas briefly. Then, after students read the selection, they can review the list and tell what new information they have learned from their reading.

GIFTED AND TALENTED Invite students to form groups to research camping. Suggest that each group member choose one aspect to research and write about, such as how to plan a camping trip, camping equipment and food, how to select a campsite and build a fire, and camping safety. Students can draw posters, create a camper's guide, and put on demonstrations to share what they learn. *Challenge Cards* provide additional activities to challenge students. Challenge notes throughout the lesson plans suggest additional activities to stimulate critical and creative thinking.

SPECIAL-EDUCATION STUDENTS For the student who has difficulty writing, provide alternative means of publishing. A typewriter, computer, or tape recorder can be useful. Be sure to consult with the student, family members, and a therapist to determine specific needs.

STUDENTS ACQUIRING ENGLISH Some students may have difficulty recalling the correct subject-verb-object word order in sentences. Have students play sentence games and unscramble sentences. Second-Language Support notes throughout the lesson plans offer strategies to help students acquiring English.

THE LOST LAKE

written and illustrated by

ALLEN SAY

The Lost Lake
pages 298–312

	READING	LANGUAGE ARTS	CROSS-CURRICULAR CONNECTIONS
PART 1 *Reading the Literature* pages T478–T488	**Building Background** **Vocabulary Strategies** **Prereading Strategies** Sentence Starters Setting a Purpose **Options for Reading**	**Spelling** Pretest Spelling-Vocabulary Connection Generalization: /ûr/ sound **Grammar Connection** Reviewing Object Pronouns	**Cultural Awareness** Comic Books in Japan **Social Studies** Camping Out
PART 2 *Responding to the Literature* pages T489–T495	**Personal Response** **Cooperative Response** **Summarizing the Literature** **Critical Thinking Activity** Role-Play Ideas **Vocabulary Workshop** Key Words English Words from Other Languages	**Language Arts Workshop** **Rereading** drama **Writing** realistic story, poem **Listening and Speaking** speech, interviewing **Reviewing Spelling Words** Posttest **Grammar Review** Object Pronouns **Grammar Minilesson** Adjectives	**Social Studies** Those Were the Days
PART 3 *Learning Through the Literature* pages T496–T502	**Introduce** Vocabulary: Synonyms/Antonyms/ Analogies **Review** Comprehension: Making Predictions (Tested) Vocabulary: Context Clues (Tested)	**Reading** Stargazers In My Part of the World **Writing** On Vacation Stargazers **Listening and Speaking** My Dream Vacation	**Social Studies** On Vacation Determining Distances In My Part of the World **Science** Stargazers **Math** Take a Hike **Art** My Dream Vacation **Multicultural Perspectives** Travelers Get There

OPTIONAL MATERIALS
Chart/Transparency 27
Integrated Spelling pp. 66–69; TE pp. T99–T104
Practice Book pp. 86–92
Writer's Journal p. 51
Alternative Teaching Strategies pp. 16, 86–89
Language Handbook pp. 36–39, 114, 116–121
Grammar Practice pp. 36–37
Family Involvement Activities: Unit 3, pp. 1–4
Response Card 7
Project Cards 36A, 36B, 37A, 37B, 38

 MEETING INDIVIDUAL NEEDS
Second-Language Support pp. T479, T480, T484, T495, T497
Mainstreaming p. T480
Reteach pp. T495, T497
Challenge pp. T497, T498, T499

FAMILY INVOLVEMENT Encourage family members to help students locate lakes featured on their state map and determine which lake is closest to their home. See *Family Involvement Activities*.

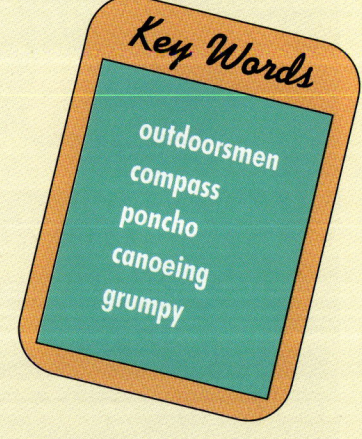

Key Words
outdoorsmen
compass
poncho
canoeing
grumpy

T476 / A PLACE TO DREAM, UNIT 3

Selection Summary

Luke goes to live with his father in the city. Having no friends there, Luke becomes lonely and bored. In search of something to do, he cuts out pictures of lakes and mountains and hangs them on his bedroom wall. One morning, Luke's father tells him that they are going on a camping trip to the Lost Lake, a place where he used to go with his own father. Luke is delighted that his father is a little more cheerful and talkative than usual. When they get to the lake, they see that the "lost lake" has been found and is crowded with people. Luke's father refuses to stay and wants to find another campsite. When they stop that night, Luke suggests that they look for their own lake. The next day they leave the trail and set off to look for a lake. Leaving the woods after dark, they make camp for the night. When they get up the next morning, they see a beautiful lake before them. Luke is happy to be with his father beside their own "lost lake."

About the Author/Illustrator

Allen Say was born in Yokohama, Japan, in 1937 and now lives in San Francisco. When he was twelve years old, he became an apprentice to a well-known Japanese cartoonist. He has also studied at art schools in Japan and in the United States. His first book to attract recognition was *The Bicycle Man*, published in 1982. Say's *A River Dream* was selected by the *New York Times* as the Best Illustrated Children's Book of the Year in 1988. His illustrations for *The Boy of the Three-Year Nap* won a Caldecott Honor in 1989. *Grandfather's Journey* won the Caldecott Medal in 1993.

Additional Reading

OTHER BOOKS BY ALLEN SAY

The Bicycle Man. Houghton Mifflin, 1989. AVERAGE

Grandfather's Journey. Houghton Mifflin, 1993. EASY

Tree of Cranes. Houghton Mifflin, 1991. AVERAGE

OTHER THEME-RELATED BOOKS

Another Celebrated Dancing Bear by Gladys Scheffrin-Falk. Macmillan, 1991. AVERAGE

Kate Heads West by Pat Brisson. Macmillan, 1990. AVERAGE

Making Friends by Margaret Mahy. Macmillan, 1990. AVERAGE

ANOTHER BOOK FOR APPLYING STRATEGIES: SYNONYMS/ANTONYMS/ANALOGIES

The Great Ideas of Lila Fenwick by Kate Hall McMullan. Puffin, 1988. CHALLENGING

PART 1

Reading the Literature

Building Background

Access prior knowledge and build vocabulary concepts.

Tell students that the next story, "The Lost Lake," describes an adventure that takes place on a camping trip. Encourage students to think about places where they might enjoy camping and to complete a chart such as the following.

Camping	
Where I would like to camp	
What I would need for the trip	
What I might see and do	

Have students quickwrite.

Ask students to write briefly what they like and dislike (or think they would like or dislike) about camping. When they have finished, have volunteers read aloud their responses.

Vocabulary Strategies

Introduce Key Words and strategies.

Display Chart/Transparency 27 or the paragraphs on it. Have students read silently, using context clues to figure out the meanings of the underlined words. For example, students can use *in what direction they were walking* as a clue for *compass*.

Chart/Transparency 27   Key Words

Because they loved hiking and being outside, Keith and his father considered themselves great <u>outdoorsmen</u>. Before leaving on a hike, they always checked their equipment. Since they would need to know in what direction they were walking, Keith took a <u>compass</u>.

Each took a plastic <u>poncho</u> to slip over his head if it rained. But even their ponchos did not keep them dry when they tipped over their boat while <u>canoeing</u>! Walking five miles back to camp in wet boots made them <u>grumpy</u>, but later they cheered up and said they had a wonderful time.

CULTURAL AWARENESS

Share with students the fact that Allen Say studied art with a famous Japanese cartoonist. Explain that comic books are very popular in Japan.

Key Words

outdoorsmen
compass
poncho
canoeing
grumpy

KEY WORDS DEFINED

outdoorsmen people who love outdoor activities such as camping, hiking, and fishing

compass instrument that shows directions

poncho garment with a slit in the center for the head

canoeing riding in a light, narrow boat, pointed at both ends

grumpy grouchy

T478 / A PLACE TO DREAM, UNIT 3

Check all students' understanding.

Provide students with index cards with the numbers 1, 2, and 3 printed on them. Write the words below on the board. Have students pick out the word in each group that does not belong and hold up the card to signal in which column the word appears. Encourage them to explain why the word does not belong. The correct responses are underlined.

- <u>happy</u>   angry   grumpy
  (STRATEGY: SYNONYMS)
- canoeing   sailing   <u>walking</u>
  (STRATEGY: CLASSIFYING)
- hikers   <u>drivers</u>   outdoorsmen
  (STRATEGY: CLASSIFYING)
- compass   binoculars   <u>earring</u>
  (STRATEGY: CLASSIFYING)
- raincoat   <u>skirt</u>   poncho
  (STRATEGY: CLASSIFYING)

Integrate spelling with vocabulary.

SPELLING-VOCABULARY CONNECTION *Integrated Spelling* Lesson 15 reinforces the spelling of the /ûr/ sound in words from the selection such as *person, turn, word,* and *work*. In addition, the Words to Explore help reinforce the concept of nature and the outdoors as it relates to the selection.

SPELLING PRETEST You may want to use the Pretest/Posttest Sentences on page T99 in *Integrated Spelling Teacher's Edition* to assess students' knowledge of the spelling generalization.

Spelling

Spelling Words	Words to Explore
1. bird	canoeing
2. church	compass
3. desert	poncho
4. first	trail
5. her	
6. hurt	*Your Own Words*
7. nurse	13.
8. person	14.
9. third	15.
10. turn	16.
11. word	
12. work	

Spelling generalization: /ûr/ sound

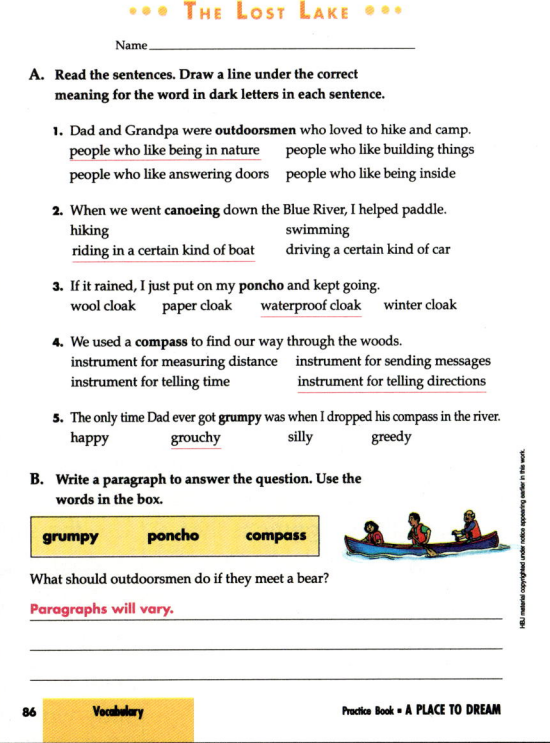

Practice Book

MEETING INDIVIDUAL NEEDS

SECOND-LANGUAGE SUPPORT Help students find pictures in the story that illustrate the meanings of some of the Key Words. See also the manual *Alternative Teaching Strategies,* pages 16, 86–89.

OPTIONAL INDEPENDENT PRACTICE

INTEGRATED SPELLING pages 66–69: Words Like *turn* and *third*

PRACTICE BOOK page 86: Reinforcing Key Words

NOTE: This page may be completed now or after students have read the story.

THE LOST LAKE / T479

Prereading Strategies

Sentence Starters

Help students preview the literature.

Have students read the story title and look at the illustrations. Inform students that the boy in the story is named Luke, and then invite them to tell what the selection will be about.

Have students make predictions.

To help students make predictions about the story, copy on the board sentence starters like the ones below. Ask students to orally complete the sentences. Write the Key Words on the board, and encourage students to use them in their responses.

> **The main characters in the story are**
> (Luke and his father).
>
> **Something they might do in the story is**
> (go hiking and canoeing).

 **PERSONAL JOURNAL** Encourage students to use the sentence starters to predict what will happen in "The Lost Lake." Have students add their predictions about the selection to their personal journals. Ask students to support their predictions.

Setting a Purpose

Encourage students to set purposes.

Discuss with students what they want to find out when they read this story. Have students use their predictions to set a purpose for reading.

If students have difficulty setting a purpose, offer this suggestion:

I'm going to read to find out what happens as a result of Luke's camping trip.

MEETING INDIVIDUAL NEEDS

SECOND-LANGUAGE SUPPORT If students keep word logs, encourage them to mark each word they look up with a small dot. When they find that they have put a dot by the same word several times, they will know that it is a frequently used word and they should learn the word. See also the manual *Alternative Teaching Strategies,* pages 16, 86–89.

SUPPORT FOR MAINSTREAMING If any students are experienced campers, invite them to share their experiences.

Options for Reading

SUSTAINED SILENT READING	STRATEGIC READING	READER RESPONSE GROUPS	TEACHER READ-ALOUD
Remind students who are reading silently to keep their purpose for reading in mind. Suggest that they pause after several pages to confirm or change their predictions.	Follow the suggestions that appear on pages T481, T483, and T486 to stimulate discussion.	Use the suggestions for Partner Reading on page T481. As students read, they might want to write down questions about things they may want to discuss with their partners.	You may wish to read the entire selection aloud before students read it silently. Encourage students to decide if they need to revise their predictions.

T480 / A PLACE TO DREAM, UNIT 3

THE LOST LAKE PAGES 298–299

299

Reader Response Groups

PARTNER READING Ask each pair to decide whether they will read silently or aloud and how frequently they will stop. Suggest that at designated stopping points, each member of the pair should respond freely to what they have read so far. Response Card 7 (Free Response), found on page R85, gives complete directions for using this strategy. You might distribute this card, or provide the following questions for discussion:

- What was your favorite part of the story? Tell why.
- Did you enjoy the author's way of writing? What did you like about it?

Response Card 7

Strategic Reading

SET PURPOSE/PREDICT: PAGES 298–303 Have students read through page 303. Have them recall the illustrations they previewed. Encourage them to tell what they will be reading to find out.

THE LOST LAKE / T481

PAGES 300–301 THE LOST LAKE

I went to live with Dad last summer.

Every day he worked in his room from morning to night, sometimes on weekends, too. Dad wasn't much of a talker, but when he was busy he didn't talk at all.

I didn't know anybody in the city, so I stayed home most of the time. It was too hot to play outside anyway. In one month I finished all the books I'd brought and grew tired of watching TV.

One morning I started cutting pictures out of old magazines, just to be doing something. They were pictures of mountains and rivers and lakes, and some showed people fishing and canoeing. Looking at them made me feel cool, so I pinned them up in my room.

Dad didn't notice them for two days. When he did, he looked at them one by one.

"Nice pictures," he said.

"Are you angry with me, Dad?" I asked, because he saved old magazines for his work.

"It's all right, Luke," he said. "I'm having this place painted soon anyway."

He thought I was talking about the marks I'd made on the wall.

That Saturday Dad woke me up early in the morning and told me we were going camping! I was wide awake in a second. He gave me a pair of brand-new hiking boots to try out. They were perfect.

In the hallway I saw a big backpack and a knapsack all packed and ready to go.

"What's in them, Dad?" I asked.

"Later," he said. "We have a long drive ahead of us."

In the car I didn't ask any more questions because Dad was so grumpy in the morning.

"Want a sip?" he said, handing me his mug. He'd never let me drink coffee before. It had lots of sugar in it.

"Where are we going?" I finally asked.

300

Teaching Tip Page 301 offers an excellent opportunity to understand characters' emotions through dialogue. Discuss with students the tone of voice a character might use for specific statements of dialogue.

Social Studies Connection Luke and his dad will have to take a "long drive" to reach the camping area. Why do you think camping areas are usually far away from cities, where most people live? (Accept reasonable responses: People like to camp in natural areas; cities are too crowded to have large natural areas for camping.)

T482 / A PLACE TO DREAM, UNIT 3

THE LOST LAKE PAGES 302–303

"We're off to the Lost Lake, my lad."
"How can you lose a lake?"
"No one's found it, that's how." Dad was smiling! "Grandpa and I used to go there a long time ago. It was our special place, so don't tell any of your friends."
"I'll never tell," I promised. "How long are we going to stay there?"

"Five days, maybe a week."
"We're going to sleep outside for a whole week?"
"That's the idea."
"Oh, boy!"
We got to the mountains in the afternoon.
"It's a bit of a hike to the lake, son," Dad said.
"I don't mind," I told him. "Are there any fish in the lake?"
"Hope so. We'll have to catch our dinner, you know."
"You didn't bring any food?"
"Of course not. We're going to live like true outdoorsmen."
"Oh . . ."
Dad saw my face and started to laugh. He must have been joking. I didn't think we were going very far anyway, because Dad's pack was so heavy I couldn't even lift it.
Well, Dad was like a mountain goat. He went straight up the trail, whistling all the while. But I was gasping in no time. My knapsack got very heavy and I started to fall behind.
Dad stopped for me often, but he wouldn't let me take off my pack. If I did I'd be too tired to go on, he said.
It was almost suppertime when we got to the lake.
The place reminded me of the park near Dad's apartment. He wasn't whistling or humming anymore.

Strategic Reading

MODELING A STRATEGY: PAGES 298–303 What have you learned about Luke from reading these pages?

THINK ALOUD You may want to provide a think-aloud model, if necessary: *Luke has no friends in the city and has been spending time alone reading and watching TV. His dad is busy and not much of a talker. From these details and other things Luke mentions, I sense that he is feeling lonely and bored. From other comments Luke makes, I can tell that he does not feel close to his father and is careful not to say or do anything that might upset him.* ANALYZING CHARACTERS

SET PURPOSE/PREDICT: PAGES 304–309 Have students predict what has caused Luke's dad to stop humming and whistling. Then have them continue reading to confirm their predictions.

PAGES 304–305 THE LOST LAKE

"Welcome to the *Found* Lake," he muttered from the side of his mouth.

"What's wrong, Dad?"

"Do you want to camp with all these people around us?"

"I don't mind."

"Well, I do!"

"Are we going home?"

"Of course not!"

304

He didn't even take off his pack. He just turned and started to walk away.

Soon the lake was far out of sight.

Then it started to rain. Dad gave me a poncho and it kept me dry, but I wondered where we were going to sleep that night. I wondered what we were going to do for dinner. I wasn't sure about camping anymore.

I was glad when Dad finally stopped and set up the tent. The rain and wind beat against it, but we were warm and cozy inside. And Dad had brought food. For dinner we had salami and dried apricots.

"I'm sorry about the lake, Dad," I said.

He shook his head. "You know something, Luke? There aren't any secret places left in the world anymore."

"What if we go very far up in the mountains? Maybe we can find our own lake."

"There are lots of lakes up here, but that one was special."

"But we've got a whole week, Dad."

"Well, why not? Maybe we'll find a lake that's not on the map."

"Sure, we will!"

We started early in the morning. When the fog cleared we saw other hikers ahead of us. Sure enough, Dad became very glum.

"We're going cross-country, partner," he said.

"Won't we get lost?"

"A wise man never leaves home without his compass."

Second-Language Support Students may need help understanding the meaning of the phrase *I don't mind*. Tell them that it means almost the same as *It's all right with me*.

Vocabulary Strategy Ask how students might use structural analysis to figure out the meaning of the word *cross-country,* which appears near the bottom of page 305. If necessary, suggest that they break this word into two parts, *cross* and *country,* to figure out that going cross-country might mean going "across the [open] country." Guide them as necessary to infer that Dad is suggesting that they leave the trail to get away from the other hikers. STRATEGY: STRUCTURAL ANALYSIS

See page T500 for information found on Project Card 37A.

MEETING INDIVIDUAL NEEDS

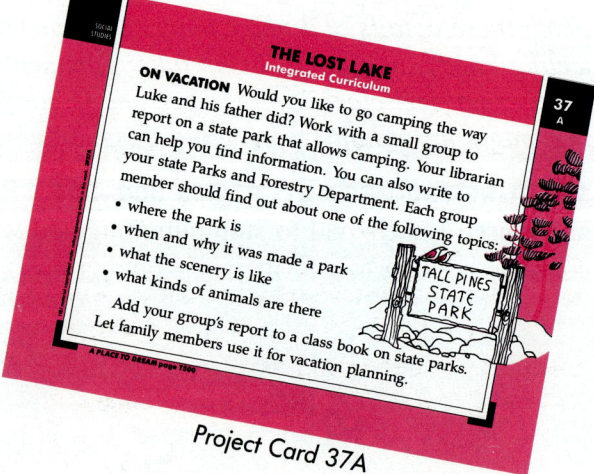

Project Card 37A

T484 / A PLACE TO DREAM, UNIT 3

THE LOST LAKE   PAGES 306–307

So we went off the trail. The hills went on and on. The mountains went on and on. It was kind of lonesome. It seemed as if Dad and I were the only people left in the world.

And then we hiked into a big forest.

At noontime we stopped by a creek and ate lunch and drank ice-cold water straight from the stream. I threw rocks in the water, and fish, like shadows, darted in the pools.

"Isn't this a good place to camp, Dad?"

"I thought we were looking for our lake."

"Yes, right . . ." I mumbled.

The forest went on and on.

"I don't mean to scare you, son," Dad said. "But we're in bear country. We don't want to surprise them, so we have to make a lot of noise. If they hear us, they'll just go away."

What a time to tell me! I started to shout as loudly

307

Informal Assessment

CONTEXT CLUES   To informally assess whether students use context clues and how effectively they use them, you might ask the following questions:

- What context clues on page 306 help you figure out the meaning of *lonesome*? (Luke says that he felt "as if Dad and I were the only people left in the world," which indicates that Luke and his father were alone with no one around for miles.)
- What does *lonesome* mean? ("a feeling of being alone")

A review lesson on **context clues** appears later in this lesson, on page T499.

GRAMMAR CONNECTION

REVIEWING OBJECT PRONOUNS   Read aloud the sentence on page 307 that begins *We don't want to surprise them,* and ask students to reread the paragraph to determine what word or words *them* refers to. (the bears) Point out that *them* is an object pronoun.

THE LOST LAKE / **T485**

PAGES 308–309 THE LOST LAKE

as I could. Even Dad wouldn't be able to beat off bears. I thought about those people having fun back at the lake. I thought about the creek, too, with all those fish in it. That would have been a fine place to camp. The Lost Lake hadn't been so bad either.

It was dark when we got out of the forest. We built a fire and that made me feel better. Wild animals wouldn't come near a fire. Dad cooked beef stroganoff and it was delicious.

308

Later it was bedtime. The sleeping bag felt wonderful. Dad and I started to count the shooting stars, then I worried that maybe we weren't going to find our lake.

"What are you thinking about, Luke?" Dad asked.

"I didn't know you could cook like that," I said.

Dad laughed. "That was only freeze-dried stuff. When we get home, I'll cook you something really special."

"You know something, Dad? You seem like a different person up here."

"Better or worse?"

"A lot better."

"How so?"

"You talk more."

"I'll have to talk more often, then."

That made me smile. Then I slept.

Dad shook me awake. The sun was just coming up, turning everything all gold and orange and yellow. And there was the lake, right in front of us.

For a long time we watched the light change on the water, getting brighter and brighter. Dad didn't say a word the whole time. But then, I didn't have anything to say either.

After breakfast we climbed a mountain and saw our lake below us. There wasn't a sign of people anywhere. It really seemed as if Dad and I were all alone in the world.

I liked it just fine.

Strategic Reading

MODELING A STRATEGY: PAGES 304–309 Encourage students to summarize what they read on these pages.

THINK ALOUD Provide a think-aloud model, if necessary: *Luke's father is disappointed to discover that the "lost lake" he remembers visiting as a child has been "found" by too many people. Luke convinces him to continue searching, and they finally find their own "lost lake" high in the mountains. Most important, as a result of the camping trip, Luke and his father get to better know and understand one another.* SUMMARIZING

See page T493 for information found on Project Card 36A.

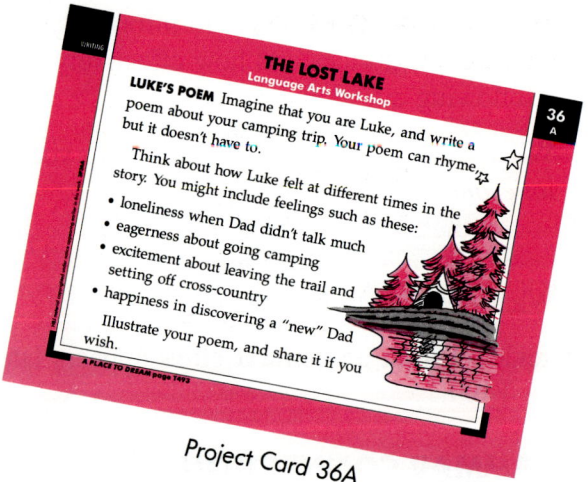

Project Card 36A

T486 / A PLACE TO DREAM, UNIT 3

THE LOST LAKE   PAGES 310–311

Would you have liked to go on the camping trip with Luke and his father? Explain why or why not.

When Luke and his father arrive at the lake, it is crowded with people. How would the story be different if they decided to stay there?

Luke is happy that his father talks more when they go hiking. Why does Luke not mind that they are silent when they look out on the lake at the end of the story?

Write   Imagine that you are on vacation at a "lost" lake. Write a postcard to a friend, telling about the lake.

Words from the AUTHOR and ILLUSTRATOR: Allen Say

AWARD-WINNING AUTHOR AND ILLUSTRATOR

I began *Lost Lake* by painting the pictures. I didn't really know what the story was going to be about until I was halfway through the art. This is how I work. I find my characters through the pictures. When the characters I'm drawing become real to me, then the story starts to take shape.

Returning to the Predictions/Purpose
SENTENCE STARTERS   Invite students to read aloud some of the sentence starters that they completed before reading and any predictions they wrote in their personal journals. Encourage them to tell whether their predictions were confirmed and when they knew to change predictions. Encourage volunteers to share their purposes for reading and tell what they enjoyed about reading this realistic fiction story.
NOTE: Responses to the questions and support for the Write activity appear on page T489.

> The main characters in the story are _(Luke and his father)_.
>
> Something they might do in the story is _(go hiking and canoeing)_.

THE LOST LAKE / **T487**

PAGE 312 ALLEN SAY

I had actually gone to a place called Lost Lake in my twenties when I came out of the army. A friend, who was a very outdoorsy person, took me there. I had done a lot of camping when I was in the army, so I wasn't very keen to go to this place in the Sierra Mountains, but I went with my friend. We had to trek six miles before we got to Lost Lake, and just as in the story, the area was full of people with radios and dirt bikes. It was noisy! I remembered that incident, and it became the kernel of the text.

I also wanted to write about the kind of father I wished I had had, but when I finished the story, I suddenly realized that the father in it is me. Maybe this was my way of apologizing to my daughter, because I didn't feel I was spending enough time with her. So, like my other stories, this one became very personal.

It can take a long time to do a picture book. One book, *El Chino,* took me eleven months to write, and during that period I had only one weekend off.

Although I haven't done it in a while, when I need time off in a quiet place, I go fly-fishing. I've fished in Iceland, Alaska, and Argentina. Now, because I'm so busy, I don't really have an outdoors life. I have to be content with taking walks.

Words from the Author and Illustrator

AUTHOR/ILLUSTRATOR'S CRAFT Invite students to read pages 311–312 to learn about the process Allen Say went through when he was writing and illustrating "The Lost Lake." When they have finished reading, ask volunteers to explain this process in their own words. (Accept reasonable responses: First, Say painted the pictures. He did not figure out what the story was going to be about until he had finished half the illustrations. He based the story on a camping trip he took with a friend. On that trip, as in the story, the place where Say went to camp was filled with noisy people. Say was trying to write a story about the type of dad he wished he had had, but when "The Lost Lake" was done, the author realized he had written about the type of dad he is himself.)

You might also want to share the information about the author on page T477. Ask students whether reading about the author affects how they feel about "The Lost Lake."

PART 2

Responding to the Literature

Personal Response

Encourage critical thinking.

Would you have liked to go on the camping trip with Luke and his father? Explain why or why not. (Responses will vary.) CRITICAL: EXPRESSING PERSONAL OPINIONS

When Luke and his father arrive at the lake, it is crowded with people. How would the story be different if they decided to stay there? (Accept reasonable responses: They would probably not have spent as much time together and not have gotten to know each other better.) INFERENTIAL: DRAWING CONCLUSIONS

Luke was happy that his father talked more when they went hiking. Why didn't Luke mind that they were silent when they looked out on the lake at the end of the story? (Accept reasonable responses: They were both enjoying the beauty of the lake and the quietness together.) INFERENTIAL: DETERMINING CHARACTERS' EMOTIONS

Encourage creative written responses.

 **WRITE** Imagine that you are on vacation at a "lost" lake. Write a postcard to a friend, telling about the lake. Remind students to include parts of a letter needed for a postcard. CREATIVE: WRITING A POSTCARD

Cooperative Response

Have reader response groups extend their discussions.

PARTNER READING Suggest that pairs meet to talk about their favorite part of the story and the postcards they wrote for the Write activity. Then have them discuss a question such as this:

Have you had an experience like Luke's in which you grew closer to someone through a shared adventure? Tell about your experience.

STRATEGY CONFERENCE

Discuss how making predictions based on previewing illustrations and completing sentences about characters and events helped students understand the story. (Accept reasonable responses: Making story predictions helps readers look forward to discovering whether the predictions match what actually happens in the story.)

NOTE

An additional writing activity for this story appears on page T492.

THE LOST LAKE / **T489**

Summarizing the Literature

Have students retell the story and write a summary.

Encourage students to summarize the story by recalling key story elements. Help students in beginning the story map, and have them finish it on their own. Have students use their completed maps to retell the story and write a brief summary. See *Practice Book* page 87 below.

Characters
(Luke and his dad)

Setting
(time: the present; places: city and woods)

↓

Problem
(Luke is lonely and bored.)

↓

Important Events

↓

Solution

Critical Thinking Activity

Create a dialogue chart.

ROLE-PLAY IDEAS What do you think Luke and his father should do to maintain the good relationship they developed during the camping trip? Have students work in small groups to discuss their ideas and then role-play how they would act. You may want to suggest that they plan their role-playing with a chart like the one shown here. CREATIVE: SOLVING PROBLEMS

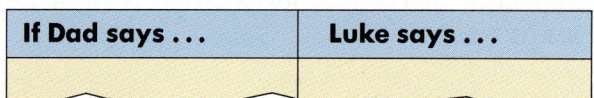

If Dad says . . .	Luke says . . .

Writer's Journal

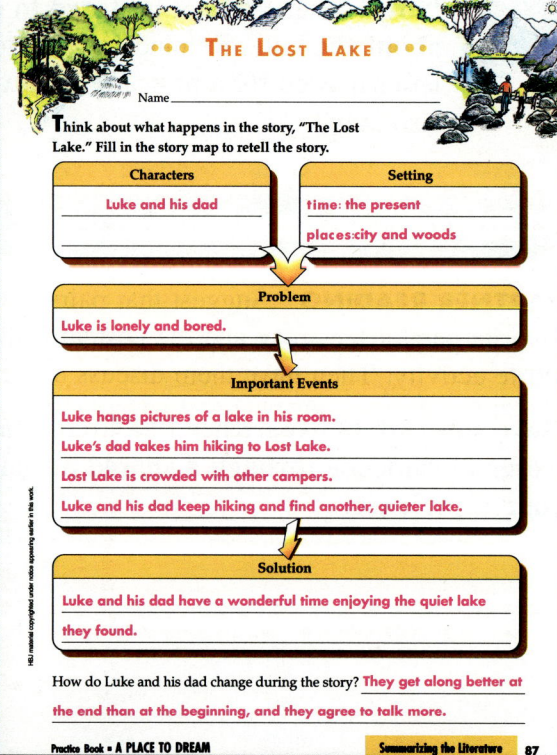

Practice Book

T490 / A PLACE TO DREAM, UNIT 3

Portfolio

STUDENT SELF-ASSESSMENT

Encourage students to self-assess their story maps by checking that they have included all the important events. Ask students to add their summaries to their portfolios.

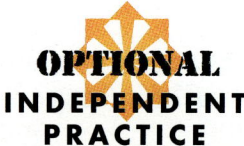

OPTIONAL INDEPENDENT PRACTICE

WRITER'S JOURNAL
page 51: Writing a personal response

PRACTICE BOOK
page 87: Summarizing the selection

VOCABULARY WORKSHOP

Reviewing Key Words

Display the following sentences. List the Key Words alphabetically. Then have students each write on a piece of paper the Key Word that best completes each sentence.

1. Next time we go __(canoeing)__, let's bring some paddles!
2. You __(outdoorsmen)__ certainly know how to rough it!
3. Next time we go camping in the rain, please bring your own __(poncho)__.
4. He needs a __(compass)__ to tell which way is south.
5. Better not speak to Dad right now. He's __(grumpy)__ for some reason.

Extending Vocabulary

WORDS FROM OTHER LANGUAGES Write the words *poncho* and *stroganoff* on the board, and read them. Point out that both words come from other languages: *poncho* is an American Spanish word meaning "woolen fabric"; *beef stroganoff,* which means "a meat dish cooked with onions, mushrooms, and a thick sour-cream sauce," was named after Count Stroganoff, a nineteenth-century Russian. Then begin a chart like the one below, and help students name other words from various languages that fit in these categories.

Clothes	Food
sombrero	tortilla
parka	spaghetti
sari	lasagna

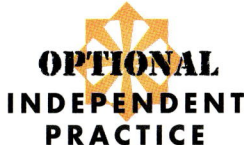

OPTIONAL INDEPENDENT PRACTICE

PRACTICE BOOK
page 88: Identifying words from other languages

Practice Book

THE LOST LAKE / T491

Language Arts WORKSHOP

READING

Oral Rereading/Drama

Have pairs of students choose a section of the story to read aloud. You may wish to read page 301 through the first half of page 303 aloud to demonstrate how to read the dialogue with feeling. Encourage students to read their parts silently before reading them aloud. Ask the pairs to rehearse together before they present their readings to the others. **LISTENING/READING**

SPELLING

Reviewing Spelling Words

SPELLING WORDS: *bird, church, desert, first, her, hurt, nurse, person, third, turn, word, work*

WORDS TO EXPLORE: *canoeing, compass, poncho, trail*

Have students play Guess the Word with one student as Spelling Master. The Spelling Master has 15 or 20 words in a container. He or she pulls out a word, draws lines on the board to indicate the number of letters in the word, and fills in the letters that spell the /ûr/ sound. The other students take turns guessing the other letters in the word until someone has correctly completed the spelling word. The winner gets to be the next Spelling Master. **SPELLING**

Use *Integrated Spelling* Lesson 15 to reinforce the Spelling Words and the Words to Explore. See pages T99–T104 in *Integrated Spelling Teacher's Edition*.

SPELLING POSTTEST You may want to use the Pretest/Posttest Sentences on *Integrated Spelling Teacher's Edition* page T99 to assess students' knowledge of the spelling generalization.

WRITING

Writing About the Literature

WRITE A STORY Point out to students that "The Lost Lake" is an example of realistic fiction, which means that what happens in the story could happen in real life. Have students write their own realistic stories about an adventure that could take place on a trip. Help them get started by making a chart like the following, showing different kinds of trips and some problems that might take place on them. Students may pick one of these situations or make up one of their own. See Writing Model, page R94. **LISTENING/WRITING**

Trip	Problem
• car trip to mall • plane trip to visit grandparents • canoe trip across lake	• car gets flat tire • brother is afraid to get on plane • sudden thunderstorm

GRAMMAR REVIEW: OBJECT PRONOUNS When students revise their stories, remind them to check that object pronouns are used correctly. Write the following object pronouns on the board: *him, her, it, me, us, them.* Then write these sentences: *His aunt took Rajeev on a trip. She took him to San Francisco.* Have partners rewrite this pair of sentences using each of the other object pronouns listed on the board. Example: *Her father took Mary Ellen on a trip. He took her to New York.* When pairs are finished, have them change sentences with another pair to check each other's work.

LANGUAGE HANDBOOK Writing to Entertain and Express, pages 36–39; Object Pronouns, page 114

DAILY LANGUAGE PRACTICE Oral language exercises are provided on pages R74–R75.

T492 / A PLACE TO DREAM, UNIT 3

Language Arts WORKSHOP

WRITING

Luke's Poem

Available on Project Card 36A

Have students pretend that they are Luke and write poems like one he might have written about his camping trip with his dad. Encourage them to begin by brainstorming a list of thoughts and feelings that Luke might want to convey in his poem. The list could include sadness and loneliness because his father does not talk more, eagerness about going on the camping trip, the excitement of setting off cross-country, and the joy at discovering both a "new" lake and a new relationship. Suggest that students illustrate their poems. Have volunteers share their poems.   **LISTENING/SPEAKING/ WRITING**

LISTENING AND SPEAKING

Secret Scenery

Encourage students to think about a special place outdoors that they have visited or seen pictures of. Suggest that they write down some notes about what makes their special place beautiful or peaceful. Then have students develop a speech telling why they would like to keep their special place a secret from others. Encourage them to describe in their speech how being in or seeing a picture of their special place makes them feel. Have students share their speeches with their classmates.   **LISTENING/SPEAKING/WRITING**

LISTENING AND SPEAKING

Those Were the Days

Available on Project Card 36B

COOPERATIVE LEARNING Remind students that Luke's father discovered that Lost Lake was much different from the way it had been when he went there as a child. Encourage students to talk with older family members or neighbors to find out about changes that have taken place. For example, people might remember living without television, or they might recall a favorite movie theater that has closed. Form small groups and have each choose Facilitators and Recorders. Assign each group a task, such as putting the interviewees' remarks into written form, taking or collecting pictures of the people they interviewed, illustrating the remarks, and compiling all the material to make a book. Display the book in the classroom for all to enjoy.   **LISTENING/SPEAKING/ WRITING/VIEWING**

THE LOST LAKE / T493

Grammar MINILESSON

Adjectives

OBJECTIVES: *To understand that an adjective is a word that describes a noun and that adjectives can tell how many or what kind; to correctly use adjectives*

Oral Warm-Up

Display the following sentences from "The Lost Lake":

- In one <u>month</u> I finished all the books I'd brought and grew tired of watching TV.
- One morning I started cutting pictures out of old <u>magazines</u>, just to be doing something.
- Dad didn't notice them for two <u>days</u>.
- Wild <u>animals</u> wouldn't come near a fire.

Have a volunteer go to the board and read aloud the first sentence. Ask the student to circle the word in the sentence that tells how many months it took the speaker to finish all of the books he'd brought. (one) Have the student circle the word *one* and draw an arrow from it to the word *month*. Repeat this procedure with other volunteers for the remaining sentences, asking either a *how many* or a *what kind* question, whichever is appropriate, about each underlined word.

Interactive Teaching

ADJECTIVES Review the third sentence from the Oral Warm-Up with students. On the board, draw a web like the one below. Ask students to suggest other words that a writer could use to describe a certain number of days, and add these to the diagram. (Possible responses are shown in parentheses.)

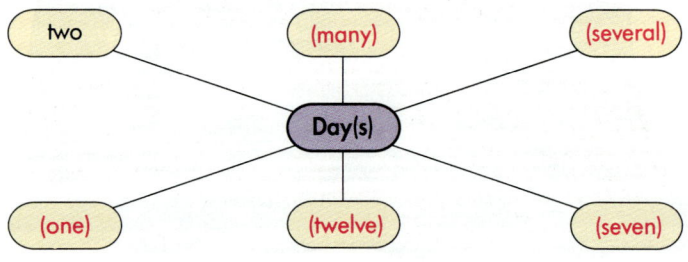

Repeat this procedure to create a similar web for the last sentence in the Oral Warm-Up. Point out that the suggested words should tell what kind of animals the writer is describing.

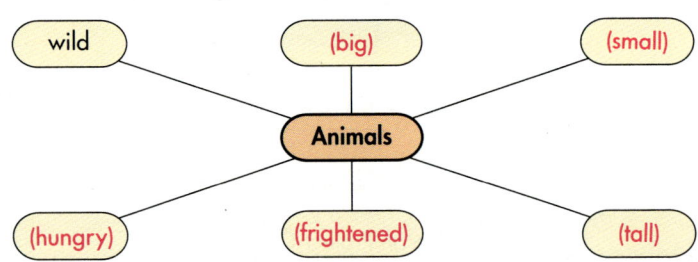

Explain to students that a word that helps describe a noun is called an **adjective** and that adjectives can tell *how many* or *what kind*. Point out that most adjectives come before the nouns they describe. Then have students use the adjectives on the board or ones they think of on their own to write one sentence that tells about the number of days they would like to spend on a trip and one sentence that tells about a kind of animal they like. Have volunteers read their sentences aloud.

LANGUAGE HANDBOOK
Adjectives, pages 116–121

T494 / A PLACE TO DREAM, UNIT 3

Practice Activities

What a Beautiful Scene!

Have students look through magazines for pictures of outdoor scenes. Have each student cut out two pictures and write one sentence for each one that describes what is taking place in the scene. Tell students to use at least one adjective that tells *what kind* or *how many* in each sentence. Have students exchange their work with a partner. Ask partners to read each other's sentences, circle the adjectives, and underline the noun that each adjective helps describe. Then have each student add another sentence describing their partner's picture. Tell students that if their partners used an adjective telling *how many*, they must use one telling *what kind*, and vice versa. Have volunteers share their pictures and sentences with classmates. Have students from the audience identify the adjectives they hear and tell what nouns those adjectives describe. **VISUAL/AUDITORY/KINESTHETIC**

Treasure Hunt

Tell students to each write a paragraph with many adjectives. Group students in pairs. Explain that they are going on a treasure hunt for adjectives. Give each pair a copy of the page. Tell them they have three minutes to circle all the adjectives in the passage. When the time is up, give partners an additional two minutes to create two lists: one of adjectives that tell *what kind* and one of adjectives that tell *how many*. Review the passage with students, helping them identify and classify all the adjectives. Have students check their own work. You might want to extend the lesson by having volunteers act out the meaning of each adjective. **VISUAL/KINESTHETIC**

MEETING INDIVIDUAL NEEDS

SECOND-LANGUAGE SUPPORT Give students added practice by having them take turns describing clothing they are wearing. Model by describing your own clothing, using a sentence frame such as this: *I am wearing a [red scarf].* Record students' sentences on the board.

RETEACH Follow the visual, auditory, and kinesthetic/motor models on page R34.

OPTIONAL INDEPENDENT PRACTICE

PRACTICE BOOK page 89: Identifying and using adjectives

GRAMMAR PRACTICE pages 36–37: Reinforcing adjectives

PART 3

Learning through the Literature

VOCABULARY
INTRODUCE

Synonyms/Antonyms/Analogies

OBJECTIVE: *To understand analogies through the use of synonyms and antonyms*

Interactive Teaching

Use literature to focus on relationships between words.

LITERATURE CONNECTION Have students recall how the lake in "The Lost Lake" has changed and tell what word would describe it. *(crowded)* Then ask them to describe the new lake that is like the one Luke's dad remembers. *(uncrowded)* Point out that they can use words that are related in certain ways to help them understand what they read.

Define and model synonyms, antonyms, and analogies.

DISCUSS SYNONYMS/ANTONYMS/ANALOGIES Ask volunteers to write on the board words that describe Luke's dad at the beginning of the story *(quiet, grumpy)* and words that describe him at the end of the story. *(talkative, happy)* Point out the antonyms and ask students what they notice about the words. (They are opposite in meaning.) Use the information below to discuss synonyms, antonyms, and analogies:

- **Synonyms** are words that are similar in meaning, and **antonyms** are opposites.
- **Analogies** are made up of two pairs of words, both having words related in the same way.

THINK ALOUD ABOUT COMPLETING ANALOGIES Display the following incomplete analogies. Ask volunteers to read them aloud.

Lost is to *found* as *heavy* is to ___*(light)*___ .
Grumpy is to *glum* as ___*(happy)*___ is to *glad*.

Then model how to complete the analogies:

In the first analogy, *lost* and *found* are antonyms. To complete the analogy, I need an antonym for *heavy*. That word is *light*. In the second analogy, *grumpy* and *glum* are synonyms. To complete the analogy, I need a synonym for *glad*, such as *happy*.

AN ADDITIONAL BOOK FOR IDENTIFYING SYNONYMS/ANTONYMS/ANALOGIES

The Great Ideas of Lila Fenwick by Kate Hall McMullan. Puffin, 1988. **CHALLENGING**

T496 / A PLACE TO DREAM, UNIT 3

Practice Activities

This Is to That As...

Have students use synonyms and antonyms to write analogies.

Have students look through "The Lost Lake" to find words for which they could write synonyms or antonyms. Begin a chart such as the one below. Then have students work in pairs to write analogies using the antonyms and synonyms in the chart.

Synonyms	Antonyms
rocks, stones	dry, wet
forest, woods	night, day

Synonym-Antonym Actors

Have students act out analogies.

Have students work in pairs to locate synonym or antonym pairs by identifying objects or physical attributes of things in the classroom (coat, jacket; cap, hat; tall, short; big, small) or by figuring out pantomimes for emotions or actions (happy, sad; laugh, cry). Ask partners to use their synonym and antonym pairs to write down several analogies. Then have them identify or pantomime the elements of each analogy for the rest of the class.
VISUAL/AUDITORY/KINESTHETIC

Performance Assessment

Have pairs rewrite their analogies from the above activities, leaving a blank in place of the last word. Tell pairs to exchange papers and try to complete the analogies. For evaluation guidelines, see *Staff Development Guide*.

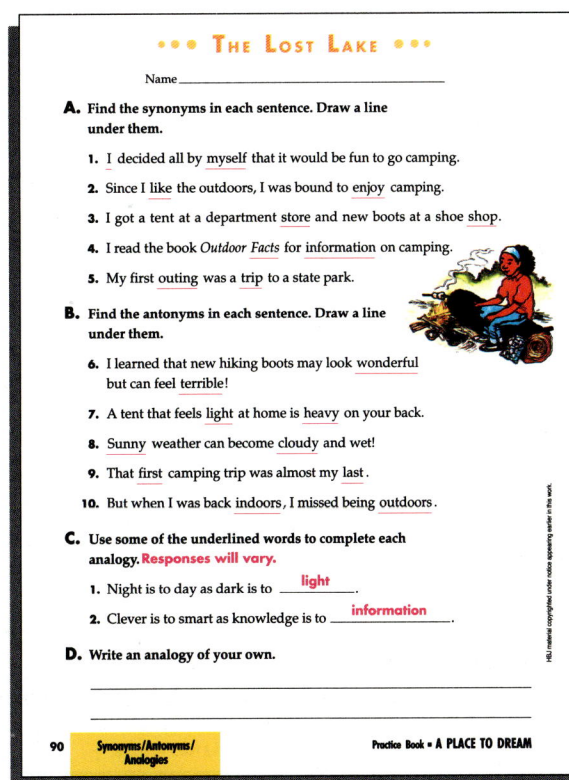

Practice Book

MEETING INDIVIDUAL NEEDS

RETEACH Follow the visual, auditory, and kinesthetic/motor models on page R35.

CHALLENGE Have students generate their own incomplete analogies and give them to a partner for completion.

SECOND-LANGUAGE SUPPORT Show the words *big*, *small*, and *little*. Ask students to demonstrate that they understand synonyms and antonyms by telling which two mean almost the same. (*small* and *little*) Then have them find opposites. (*big* and *small* or *big* and *little*) See also the manual *Alternative Teaching Strategies*, pages 16, 86–89.

OPTIONAL INDEPENDENT PRACTICE

PRACTICE BOOK
page 90: Using synonyms, antonyms, and analogies

THE LOST LAKE / T497

COMPREHENSION REVIEW

Making Predictions

OBJECTIVE: To make predictions using story evidence and real-life experiences

Review

Explain how readers make predictions.

DISCUSS STUDENTS' PREDICTIONS Ask students to share the predictions they made earlier and explain on what information they based their predictions. Point out that readers use information from a story and what they know from real life to predict what will happen in the story. Use the diagram below to model making predictions.

Story Information	Experience	Prediction
Luke and his father have a good time.	+ People repeat things they enjoy doing.	= They will go on trips more often.

MEETING INDIVIDUAL NEEDS

CHALLENGE Encourage students to write predictions about characters from previously read stories. Have them read their predictions aloud, and ask volunteers to give reasons why they agree or disagree.

Practice Activity

In the Future

Predict a future relationship.

Have students make diagrams similar to the one above to predict what Luke and his father's relationship will be like in ten years. Remind them to think about what their relationship was like and how it changed and then to use story evidence plus prior knowledge to make predictions. Have students share their predictions. Encourage them to discuss whether they agree or disagree with each other's predictions.

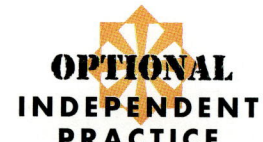

OPTIONAL INDEPENDENT PRACTICE

PRACTICE BOOK
page 91: Making predictions

Practice Book

T498 / A PLACE TO DREAM, UNIT 3

VOCABULARY REVIEW

Context Clues

OBJECTIVE: *To use context clues to determine word meaning*

Review

Use context clues to find word meaning.

MODEL THE STRATEGY Ask students to explain what context clues are and how they can use these clues to determine the meaning of a word. Refer students to the third paragraph on page 305. Model how to use context clues.

> If I don't know the meaning of the word *poncho*, I look at the words around *poncho*. I see the phrases *it started to rain* and *it kept me dry*. I can tell that a *poncho* is probably something you put on to keep dry.

Practice Activity

Use the Clues

Chart context clues. Have students find the words *knapsack*, *stroganoff*, and *creek* in the story, determine meanings based on context clues, and create a chart like the one below. Have them share their work. VISUAL

word	meaning	context clues
knapsack	"a sack or bag for carrying things on the back"	backpack, all packed

MEETING INDIVIDUAL NEEDS

CHALLENGE Invite students to work with a partner and select an unfamiliar word in a story they have recently read. Have them use context clues to figure out the word's meaning.

OPTIONAL INDEPENDENT PRACTICE

PRACTICE BOOK

page 92: Using context clues

Practice Book

THE LOST LAKE / **T499**

Integrated CURRICULUM

SCIENCE

Stargazers

Available on Project Card 37B

USE AN ENCYCLOPEDIA Remind students that Luke and his dad watch shooting stars while they are camping. Have students research and write a report about shooting stars or constellations Luke and his dad might have seen. Have them include illustrations of the constellations and summaries of the myths related to them. Encourage students to share their reports with the others. **LISTENING/SPEAKING/READING/WRITING**

SOCIAL STUDIES

Determining Distances

USE A MAP Encourage students to speculate about how many miles Luke and his dad hike during their camping trip. *(at least ten)* Help them get a sense of such a distance by using a map of your area. Show them how to use the key to determine how far ten miles is from the school or some other familiar spot. **LISTENING/SPEAKING/READING**

SOCIAL STUDIES

On Vacation

Available on Project Card 37A

COOPERATIVE LEARNING Have groups of students prepare reports about state parks that allow camping. Assign a different state park to each group. Each group member should be responsible for finding out about one of the following: the park's location; the reasons it was established; the scenery; the kinds of animals found there; and the recreational possibilities. Before groups illustrate their report, have Checkers make sure that information is recorded accurately. After Recorders from each group have read the reports, have students combine them into a book for the classroom library. Encourage students to share the book with their families.

LISTENING/SPEAKING/READING/WRITING

MATH

Take a Hike

Lead students on a walk to a spot about a quarter of a mile from the school. Have them note the time their walk began and ended. When they return, have them figure out how long it would take them to walk one mile, five miles, and ten miles. Then challenge them to estimate the distance between their home and spots such as the grocery or corner store, the library, or a friend's or relative's home by comparing how long it takes them to walk there to how long it took them to walk the original quarter-mile. **LISTENING/SPEAKING**

ART

My Dream Vacation

Remind students that Luke and his dad find the place of their dreams when they discover the isolated lake. Ask students to draw or paint the place of their dreams, a place where they think they could be very happy. You may want to play a record or audiocassette of "background, mood music" to generate an atmosphere of peace while students are creating their art. When students have finished, display their artwork on the bulletin board. **LISTENING/VIEWING**

SOCIAL STUDIES

In My Part of the World

CULTURAL AWARENESS Encourage students to research natural and scenic wonders in other parts of the world. If possible, invite people from other cultures (either students or adult visitors) with firsthand knowledge of these spots to describe them. For example, people from Asia, South America, or Africa could speak to the class about the Himalayas, the Andes, tropical rain forests, or the African plains and lakes. **LISTENING/READING**

BOOKS TO SHARE

SCIENCE *June Mountain Secret* by Nina Kidd. HarperCollins, 1991. **AVERAGE**

SOCIAL STUDIES *Follow the Water from Brook to Ocean* by Arthur Dorros. HarperCollins, 1991. **AVERAGE**

Snowshoe Thompson by Nancy Smiler Levinson. HarperCollins, 1992. **EASY**

THE LOST LAKE / T501

MULTICULTURAL PERSPECTIVES

Travelers Get There

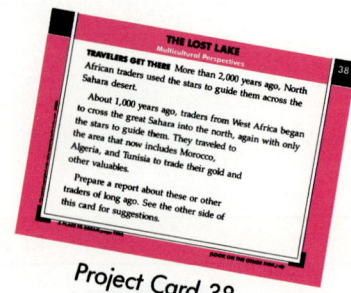

Project Card 38

DISCUSSION STARTER
What did travelers do without a compass to show them the way?

READ ALOUD
More than 2,000 years ago, North African traders regularly crossed the vast Sahara desert, guided only by the stars. Egyptian knowledge of astronomy helped them navigate on water also—their ships traded up and down Africa's east coast without a compass.

Historians believe that the compass originated with the Chinese, who learned that a needle made of a certain kind of metal always pointed in one direction. Arab traders probably carried the idea to Europe in the 1100s. By the 1400s European navigators realized how valuable a compass could be on sea voyages. Columbus and other explorers relied on the compass and other navigational tools when they crossed the Atlantic Ocean. However, they navigated by the stars as well.

ACTIVITY CORNER
Available on Project Card 38

• Have a group of interested students research the kingdoms of western Africa that were involved in trade with North Africa in the 1300s and before. You may also want to have other groups of students find out how the Aztecs, Toltecs, or Mayans in Mexico, Guatemala, or Honduras traded or how the Incas in South America traded.

• Have students think about how ancient travelers were able to cross great distances over land or on the water without a compass. Have them write a paragraph describing a journey and how the traveler knew where to go. Suggest that they include how the travelers probably felt.

• Help students use a compass to figure out where north, east, south, and west are in the classroom. Have volunteers draw, color, and cut out a large *N*, *E*, *S*, and *W* to position appropriately on the walls of the classroom.

In 1324, Mansa Musa, fabulously wealthy ruler of the African state of Mali, traveled across the Sahara on his way to Mecca, in Arabia.

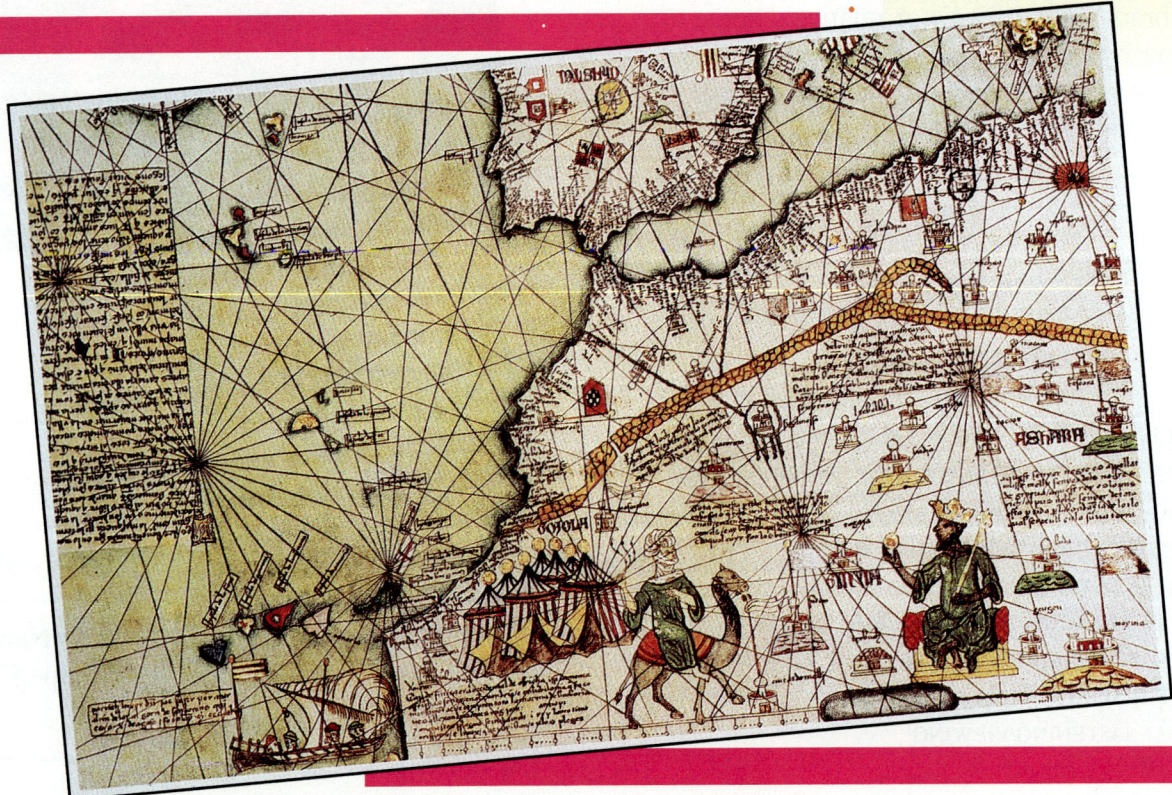

T502 / A PLACE TO DREAM, UNIT 3

POEMS

People
Some People

*Charlotte Zolotow
Rachel Field*

ABOUT THE POETS Charlotte Zolotow has received numerous awards during her career as a children's book editor and writer. Her ability to understand the concerns of children and to express them creatively has made her a favorite with young readers.

Rachel Field—editor, novelist, playwright, poet, illustrator, and children's author—was the first woman to receive the Newbery Medal. She received the award in 1930 for *Hitty: Her First Hundred Years*.

ABOUT THE POEMS Both "People" and "Some People" explore how people affect others.

Reading the Poems

Help students set a purpose for reading.

Remind students that at the beginning of "The Lost Lake," Luke's father seems to be in a bad mood. Invite students to describe how they feel when they are with someone who is in a bad mood, as well as how they feel when they are with someone who is in a good mood.

Read aloud the titles of the two poems, and explain to students that Charlotte Zolotow and Rachel Field have both written about how "some people" affect others. Suggest that students read the poems to find out if they feel the same way the poets do about "some people."

Responding to the Poems

Return to the purpose for reading.

Encourage students to discuss how their feelings are similar to or different from those of the poets. Then read the poems aloud, inviting students to join you.

Encourage students to respond creatively.

You may wish to use the following activity for responding to the poems:

DRAMATIZING A POEM Invite groups of students to dramatize "People." For example, suggest that after saying "Some people" in the first line, students can begin talking in hushed tones to dramatize "talk and talk." **LISTENING/SPEAKING**

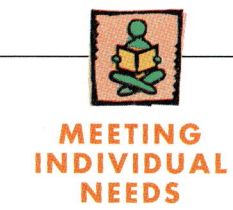

MEETING INDIVIDUAL NEEDS

SECOND-LANGUAGE SUPPORT Students may be unfamiliar with the word *fireflies*. Display a picture of a firefly, and explain that it is a flying insect that produces a glowing light. Point out that fireflies are also known as *lightning bugs* and that there are nearly 1,900 species of fireflies. Invite students to tell the word for *firefly* in their first language.

PEOPLE/SOME PEOPLE / T503

Expanding the Poems Do birds really begin to sing and does music really fill the sky when some people look at you or touch your hand? Explain what you think the poet means. (Accept reasonable responses: The poet is saying how special some people are and how good they can make you feel.) INFERENTIAL: DRAWING CONCLUSIONS

PEOPLE/SOME PEOPLE   PAGE 314

Some PEOPLE

by Rachel Field
illustrated by Andrea Eberbach

AWARD-WINNING AUTHOR

Isn't it strange some people make
　You feel so tired inside,
Your thoughts begin to shrivel up
　Like leaves all brown and dried!

But when you're with some other ones,
　It's stranger still to find
Your thoughts as thick as fireflies
　All shiny in your mind!

Expanding the Poems　How does Rachel Field help you "see" how some people affect your thoughts? (She compares thoughts to dry, brown leaves that shrivel up and also to fireflies that shine.)　CRITICAL: AUTHOR'S CRAFT/APPRECIATING LANGUAGE

Appreciating Literature

Have students work in small groups to discuss the poems. Provide a general question such as the following to help the groups begin:

What are some other words or phrases the poets could have used to indicate how people can make you feel?

 **PERSONAL JOURNAL** Have students use their personal journals to write about ideas and feelings discussed in the groups.

Writer's Journal　　　　　　　　**Writer's Journal**

OPTIONAL INDEPENDENT PRACTICE

WRITER'S JOURNAL

pages 52–53: Writing a creative response

THEME WRAP-UP

Discussing the Theme

Remind students that the selections in this theme are about people like those they see every day—friends, classmates, and family members.

Discussion Question

PAGE 315 In "The Lost Lake" and the poems you read, the writers seem to say that spending time with people you care about can be an adventure. Do you agree? Why or why not? Offer students the opportunity to support their opinions with real-life experience. **(Responses will vary.)** CRITICAL: EXPRESSING PERSONAL OPINIONS

Theme Wrap-Up

The Great Outdoors

In "The Lost Lake" and the poems you read, the writers seem to say that spending time with people you care about can be an adventure. Do you agree? Why or why not?

WRITER'S WORKSHOP
Would you recommend "The Lost Lake" to a friend? Write a review, telling whether you think other people would like it. Give your reasons.

Writer's Choice:
If you have ever gone camping, you might want to write about your camping trip. Or you might want to write about a place you would like to visit. Choose an idea, and write about it. Then share your writing.

315

Writer's Workshop

See pages T508–T509 for suggestions for guiding students through the writing process as they respond to the literature. WRITING PROCESS: BOOK REVIEW

Writer's Choice
Students may benefit from referring to the *Language Handbook* as they write. Encourage students to begin by thinking of all the things they like about the story and all the things they dislike.

When students are ready to publish their work, suggest they illustrate their real or imagined camping trips. They may also work in small groups to compile their writing in a camping booklet.

Writer's Workshop

Book Review

Theme Wrap-Up

Students write a review of "The Lost Lake," telling whether they would recommend it to a friend and why or why not.

To prepare students for the writing task and form, prompt a discussion about the protection of wilderness animals. Then suggest that students recall the story "The Lost Lake." Ask students whether they enjoyed this story, which is also a complete book titled *Lost Lake* that they can find in their library. Tell students that by writing a book review, they can recommend or not recommend the book to others to read.

Use the Writer's Workshop assignment on page 315 as you work through the writing process with students.

ALTERNATIVE TOPICS If you wish, allow students to choose their own topics for writing. Suggest that they refer to the *Language Handbook* for an explanation of the writing process for book reviews.

LANGUAGE HANDBOOK *Writing to Persuade, pages 60–61; Book Review, page 63*

Prewriting

Suggest that students refer to their journals or portfolios for information they may have written previously about the story. Also, encourage students to brainstorm in small groups and use a web like the one below to generate ideas.

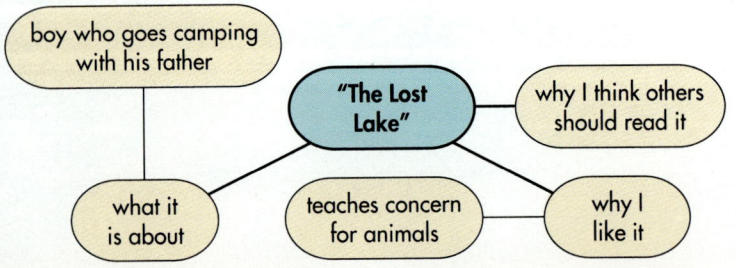

Drafting

Have students write a draft of their book reviews. Suggest that students

- write a topic sentence that briefly introduces the book and names the author.
- write detail sentences that tell what the story is about but don't give away the ending.
- state their opinion about the book and tell reasons others should read it.

Responding and Revising

To check their own writing before sharing it with others, students should ask themselves these questions:

- Have I stated my opinion clearly about this book?
- Does my topic sentence give the book's title and the author's name?
- Is my writing convincing enough to make others want or not want to read the story?

Then have student writers read aloud their work to partners (listeners) and discuss the following questions and complete the following task:

Listener	Writer
Does the review state the writer's opinion clearly? Are reasons given for liking or not liking the story? Does the writing convince you to agree with the writer's opinion?	When you read your book review aloud, are there any parts that seem weaker than other parts? Have you left out any reasons for your opinion? Write down any improvements you should make.

COMPUTER TIP

REVISING Students can use their delete function to highlight and eliminate entire sentences quickly if they've accidentally given away so much of the story that readers who have not read the book will not be surprised or satisfied with the ending.

Proofreading

Offer the following tips as students proofread:

- Check that the title of the book is underlined and that the words are capitalized.
- Check sentences to be sure that subject and object pronouns have been used correctly.
- Correct any misspelled words.

MINI-CONFERENCE STRATEGY Help students locate errors in using subject and object pronouns, especially in sentences using *he* with *him* and *her* with *she,* with observations such as "You begin this sentence with *Her and her friends visited.* Would you say *Her visited* to begin a sentence?"

Publishing Options

CLASS BINDER Suggest that students put the final drafts of their reviews in a binder called *Book Reviews* and add others as the year progresses. Tell the students that the binder will be available for the following year's students to examine.

THUMBS UP/DOWN Ask volunteers to read their book reviews aloud to the other students. Have the group tally the students' opinions for or against the story.

Assessment Options

STUDENT SELF-ASSESSMENT Encourage students to summarize the writing experience by responding to this question in their journals:

- **How did my opinion about the book make me use words to convince my readers?**

You may also wish to have students complete the Self-Assessment Checklist in the *Portfolio Assessment Teacher's Guide*.

WRITING OBSERVATION RECORDS Note when a student uses available resources such as checklists or a language handbook to aid in revision.

After students publish, you may want to have them add their book reviews to their portfolios.

GRAMMAR CONNECTION

Revising: Combining Adjectives

Using Transparency I, share the examples below with students to help them see how combining adjectives can make their writing more interesting and less choppy sounding.

Transparency I
The Hidden Note

BEFORE
The day was cold. The day was windy. Jason headed for the lake anyway. He saw a small spot in the distance. He saw that it was also a black spot. The spot turned out to be a baby squirrel. The squirrel was round. It was fat, too.

AFTER
The day was cold and windy. Jason headed for the lake anyway. He saw a small black spot in the distance. The spot turned out to be a baby squirrel. The squirrel was round and fat.

Have small groups of students share their writing to check for places where adjectives can be combined to make sentences read more smoothly.

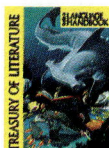
LANGUAGE HANDBOOK *Expanding Your Writing,* page 23; *Adjectives,* pages 116–120

UNIT 3

CONNECTIONS

The Connections activities on Student Anthology pages 316–317 guide students to link multicultural and content-area information to the unit theme. Before students begin, ask them to review quickly the purpose-setting paragraph on page 218. Then invite them to identify their favorite selections in the unit and suggest why they think each was included in a unit entitled "Adventures."

To prepare students for the Multicultural Connection, ask them whether they have ever been to an art museum or an art gallery. Invite them to share their experiences by describing the different kinds of art they observed and by recalling paintings they found interesting. Tell students that they will be reading about a Hispanic artist whose painting is displayed in a Chicago art gallery.

Explain that painting is one of the oldest forms of art, dating back to prehistoric times. Point out that paintings are very important because they are a source of enjoyment and a source of information. Much can be learned from a painting—not only the artist's feelings, but sometimes details about the era in which the painting was completed, such as information about the customs, clothing, interests, and architecture of the period.

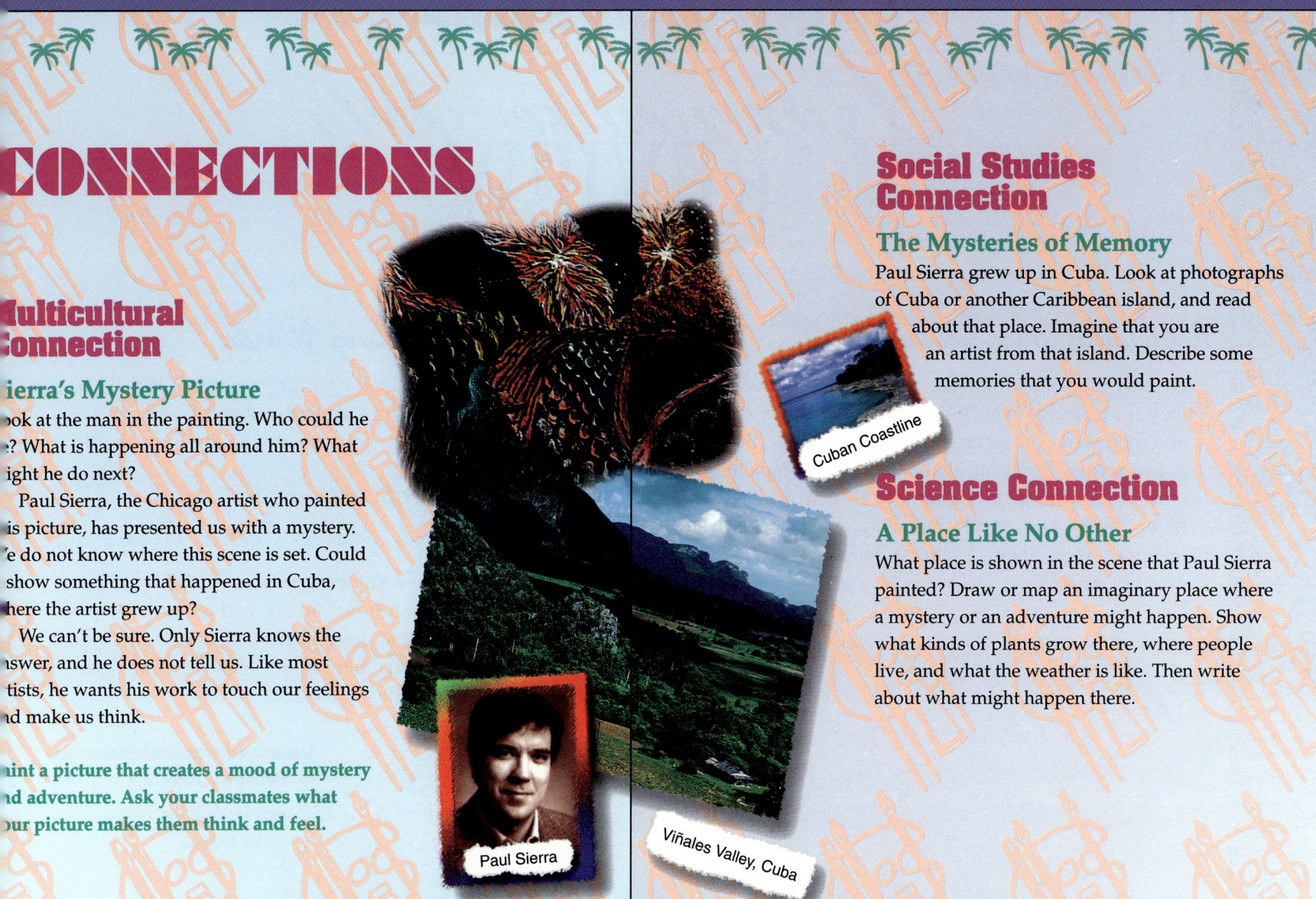

CONNECTIONS

Multicultural Connection

Sierra's Mystery Picture

Look at the man in the painting. Who could he be? What is happening all around him? What might he do next?

Paul Sierra, the Chicago artist who painted this picture, has presented us with a mystery. We do not know where this scene is set. Could it show something that happened in Cuba, where the artist grew up?

We can't be sure. Only Sierra knows the answer, and he does not tell us. Like most artists, he wants his work to touch our feelings and make us think.

Paint a picture that creates a mood of mystery and adventure. Ask your classmates what your picture makes them think and feel.

Social Studies Connection

The Mysteries of Memory

Paul Sierra grew up in Cuba. Look at photographs of Cuba or another Caribbean island, and read about that place. Imagine that you are an artist from that island. Describe some memories that you would paint.

Science Connection

A Place Like No Other

What place is shown in the scene that Paul Sierra painted? Draw or map an imaginary place where a mystery or an adventure might happen. Show what kinds of plants grow there, where people live, and what the weather is like. Then write about what might happen there.

Paul Sierra

Cuban Coastline

Viñales Valley, Cuba

Multicultural Connection

SIERRA'S MYSTERY PICTURE As students read about Paul Sierra, remind them to look at the painting. Encourage them to share their thoughts and feelings about Sierra's painting. Supply students with the necessary materials to paint their own pictures. To help create a mood of mystery and adventure, you may wish to play classical music such as Tchaikovsky's *1812 Overture* or Rossini's *William Tell*.

Social Studies Connection

THE MYSTERIES OF MEMORY Provide students with books and magazines containing photographs and information about Cuba or another Caribbean island. You may also want to show a filmstrip or travel video. Encourage students to close their eyes and visualize what they've seen and what they've read about the island. Then have students describe their "memories" to their classmates.

Science Connection

A PLACE LIKE NO OTHER You may wish to provide students with catalogs, magazines, and books about plants to use as references when planning their imaginary place.

UNIT 3 WRAP-UP

Language Arts REVIEW

Reviewing Vocabulary

- Display the following puzzle. Explain to students that they must decide which Key Word describes each clue and then write the letters in the word on the lines going across. Point out that when they complete all the clues, they will spell out another Key Word using the letters in the box. Have students complete the puzzle independently. Then, discuss a definition for the mystery word.

a. _(c) (o) (c) (o) (a)_
b. _(b) (u) (t) (l) (e) (r)_
c. _(c) (o) (m) (p) (a) (s) (s)_
d. _(e) (l) (d) (e) (s) (t)_
e. _(p) (o) (n) (c) (h) (o)_
f. _(g) (r) (u) (m) (p) (y)_

a. a hot drink made with powdered chocolate
b. a servant
c. an instrument that shows direction
d. oldest
e. a garment with a slit in the center for the head
f. grouchy

The mystery word is (_custom_).

- Have students work in small groups to make similar puzzles using other Key Words they learned. Encourage groups to exchange and complete each other's puzzles.

Reviewing Grammar

Have students write each of the following terms on individual sheets of paper: *singular pronoun, plural pronoun, subject pronoun, object pronoun, adjective*. Spread the sheets face down randomly across a table. Students pick up a sheet and say a sentence that illustrates the term. If the sentence uses the part of speech correctly, the student gets to write his or her name on the back of the sheet. If any sheets have few or no names on the back after fifteen minutes of play, all students should continue playing until they have reviewed that part of speech several times.

Reviewing Spelling Words

Integrated Spelling Teacher's Edition pages T105–T110 contain a practice test in standardized-test format and writing opportunities to help review the Spelling Words.

Writing Directions, an Advertisement, and a Comic Strip

You may wish to have students respond to the unit focus by writing project directions, an ad, and a comic strip to add to the magazines in their *Writer's Journals*. Provide them with copies of ads and comic strips as examples. See *Writer's Journal* pages 54–55.

WRITER'S JOURNAL
pages 54–55: Making Your Own Magazine

Writer's Journal

T512 / A PLACE TO DREAM, UNIT 3

UNIT 3 WRAP-UP

Assessment Options

Informal Assessment

See the suggestions below to informally assess students' progress in Unit 3.

INFORMAL ASSESSMENT NOTES AND CHECKLISTS If you used the informal assessment notes in the lesson plans to evaluate students' reading and writing behaviors, you may now want to update your Running Records. You may also wish to have students complete the Self-Assessment Checklist in *Portfolio Assessment Teacher's Guide*.

PORTFOLIO CONFERENCE The Portfolio Conference provides you with an opportunity to learn about each student's

- understanding of the differences between realistic fiction and fantasy.
- interest in reading mysteries.
- general writing development.
- awareness of context clues and making predictions.

Discuss the realistic fiction and fantasy stories that were read in Unit 3, focusing first on the differences between the two genres and then on the student's reaction to them. Then discuss the mystery story, "Piggins," focusing on whether the student enjoyed it. Ask the student to identify similar stories he or she has read in all three genres. Discuss the student's feelings about reading realistic fiction, fantasy, and mysteries.

Have the student select a favorite piece of writing from the portfolio. The student may want to share the list of Paddington's adventures written in response to "Paddington Paints a Picture" or the postcard Luke might have sent to a friend written in response to "The Lost Lake." Invite the student to share what he or she liked about the piece. Provide positive feedback and encouragement.

Formal Assessment

The formal assessment tools described below are available to meet your assessment needs.

UNIT READING SKILLS ASSESSMENT The *Skills Assessment* for Unit 3 provides feedback about students' mastery of the specific skills and strategies taught in Learning Through the Literature. The tested skills in this unit are Making Predictions and Context Clues. If students need more help, refer to the lessons in the Reteach section for visual, auditory, and kinesthetic/motor models that are available for reteaching the tested skills in this unit.

UNIT HOLISTIC READING ASSESSMENT The *Holistic Reading Assessment* for Unit 3 may be used to evaluate a student's ability to comprehend passages written at the same level as the selections in the Student Anthology. Use the Reteach Lesson for Active Reading Strategies if students need more assistance. You may also refer to the modeling suggestions located throughout the Teacher's Edition to support students while they read the selections in Unit 1 of *Sea of Wonder*.

UNIT INTEGRATED PERFORMANCE ASSESSMENT The *Integrated Performance Assessment* for Unit 3 provides you with a profile of how well each student uses reading, writing, listening, and speaking strategies to read and respond to a piece of literature. Assessment results reflect how well students employ the strategies modeled and practiced in the classroom.

UNIT LANGUAGE AND WRITING ASSESSMENT The *Unit Language and Writing Assessment* for Unit 3 includes a Skills Inventory to assess students' comprehension of pronouns and adjectives and a Writing Test, which includes a writing prompt, evaluation rubrics, and scoring guidelines for a story. You can administer corresponding lessons and practice in the *Language Handbook* with students who have difficulty on the assessment instrument.

Break Time!

CHOOSE YOUR METAPHOR

Metaphors can be dynamic teaching tools, offering the teacher creative ways to express ideas and insights. This seven-step process can assist you in helping students establish meaningful connections as they learn.

Step 1: Decide on the specific objective or concept you want to teach. An objective might be to improve writing skills; a concept might be "change."

Step 2: Choose a metaphor. "Change" might be represented by a tree, the seasons, or a butterfly.

Step 3: Write a "guided fantasy" to involve students in the metaphor. A guided fantasy should include a story line that integrates the concept and the image you have selected using descriptive language that appeals to the senses.

Step 4: Introduce the lesson and its goal. For example, one goal for improving writing skills might be "revising." Ask students to find similarities among trees, change, butterflies, and revising.

Step 5: Read your guided fantasy aloud.

Step 6: Encourage students to express insights regarding ways they have internalized and integrated the metaphor. For example, ask them to explain how change makes them feel.

Step 7: Connect your images to the original lesson objective.

In the days that follow, use metaphoric language in connection with your teaching goals. When learning is metaphor-driven, there's no telling where students' thinking will carry them.

MYSTERIES ADD UP TO COMPREHENSION

Fostering critical thinking is simply no mystery to students who read detective tales. The genre encourages students to pay attention to details, synthesize information, and draw conclusions. Here are some suggestions for using the *Encyclopedia Brown* mystery series by Donald Sobol or a similar collection to help students hone their skills.

1. Read the selection together.
2. List details students remember from the story.
3. With students' help, draw the scene of the crime on the board.
4. List all the clues. Then ask, "What's missing?"
5. Look for red herrings (false clues)!
6. Select the most sensible choice of solutions.

ADVENTURES IN STORYTELLING

Challenge your students' creative thinking and help them sharpen their speaking skills as they have some storytelling fun. You will need a large ball of yarn.

- Have each student bring in or draw an item that might be useful to a character in an adventure story. Students may display their items for classmates to see.

- Read the beginning of an adventure story or book, or make up a story beginning of your own.

- Hold on to the loose end of the yarn, and toss the ball to a student. The student should continue the story, modifying it to include the object he or she is displaying. Once the object is mentioned, the student holds on to the unraveled section of yarn and tosses the ball to another student.

- Students continue the process until each student has had a turn at adding to the story.

"I'd like to dedicate this day to all my students who complain that nothing interesting ever happens in school."

Reprinted by permission of Randy Glasbergen.

Introducing the Glossary

Explain to students that a glossary is often included in a book so that readers can find the meanings of words used in the book. Model looking up one or more words, pointing out how you rely on alphabetical order and the guide words at the top of the Glossary pages to help you locate the entry word. You may also want to demonstrate how to use the pronunciation key on page 319 to determine the correct pronunciation.

As students look over the Glossary, point out that illustrations accompany some definitions. Point out on page 320 that expanded explanations and background information about some words, such as *antique*, are presented in the margin.

Have students look up several words in the Glossary, identifying the correct page and the guide words. Have students tell which words are accompanied by illustrations or additional information in the margin. Students may recall that one vocabulary strategy involves using a dictionary or a glossary.

Glossary

The **pronunciation** of each word in this glossary is shown by a phonetic respelling in brackets; for example, [ə•fek'shən•it•lē]. An accent mark (') follows the syllable with the most stress: [an•tēk']. A secondary, or lighter, accent mark (') follows a syllable with less stress: [fig'yər•hed']. The key to other pronunciation symbols is below. You will find a shortened version of this key on alternate pages of the glossary.

Pronunciation Key*

a	add, map	m	move, seem	u	up, done
ā	ace, rate	n	nice, tin	û(r)	burn, term
â(r)	care, air	ng	ring, song	yōō	fuse, few
ä	palm, father	o	odd, hot	v	vain, eve
b	bat, rub	ō	open, so	w	win, away
ch	check, catch	ô	order, jaw	y	yet, yearn
d	dog, rod	oi	oil, boy	z	zest, muse
e	end, pet	ou	pout, now	zh	vision, pleasure
ē	equal, tree	ŏŏ	took, full	ə	the schwa, an unstressed vowel representing the sound spelled
f	fit, half	ōō	pool, food		
g	go, log	p	pit, stop		a in *above*
h	hope, hate	r	run, poor		e in *sicken*
i	it, give	s	see, pass		i in *possible*
ī	ice, write	sh	sure, rush		o in *melon*
j	joy, ledge	t	talk, sit		u in *circus*
k	cool, take	th	thin, both		
l	look, rule	th	this, bathe		

*Adapted entries, the Pronunciation Key, and the Short Key that appear on the following pages are reprinted from *HBJ School Dictionary*. Copyright © 1990 by Harcourt Brace & Company. Reprinted by permission of Harcourt Brace & Company.

---

absentminded

A

accordion

ab•sent•mind•ed [ab'sənt•mīn'did] *adj.* Forgetful; not paying attention: My *absentminded* uncle forgot my birthday.

ac•cor•di•on [ə•kôr'dē•ən] *n.* A musical instrument that is played by fingering a keyboard on one side and by squeezing large folds or bellows in and out on the opposite side: The *accordion* is so large that the player uses straps to hold it.

antique *Antique* comes from the Latin version of a word meaning "before." The Latin word later became the English word *ancient*. During the last century *antique* has come to mean "made long ago and of value." So some people collect old furniture, jewelry, and dishes in the hope they will one day be worth lots of money.

ac•cu•ra•cy [ak'yər•ə•sē] *n.* Correctness; having no mistakes: Bruno does math with *accuracy*.

ad•ven•ture [ad•ven'chər] *n.* A thrilling experience; an exciting event: Bill's dream was filled with *adventures* at sea.

af•fec•tion•ate•ly [ə•fek'shən•it•lē] *adv.* With love and emotion: Mother hugged us *affectionately* when we came home.

apricot

argue

an•ni•ver•sa•ry [an'ə•vûr'sə•rē] *n.* Usually a celebration of a day of the year to remember something important from the past: Claudia attended a party for her aunt and uncle's wedding *anniversary*.

an•tique [an•tēk'] *n.* Something made long ago and valued for its age: The *antiques* in our house are all over a hundred years old.

a•part•ment [ə•pärt'mənt] *n.* A place someone lives in: Lara lives in an *apartment* that has six rooms.

a•pri•cot [ā'pri•kot or ap'ri•kot] *n.* A small, orange-colored fruit: Sally ate two *apricots* for a snack.

ar•gue [är'gyōō] *v.* **ar•gued, ar•gu•ing** To fight by using words: George and Alice are *arguing* loudly about who will sit in the fror seat. *syn.* disagree

assembly

as•sem•bly [ə•sem'blē] *n.* In school, a gathering of students and teachers for educational or entertainment programs.

as•sign [ə•sīn'] *v.* **as•signed, as•sign•ing** To give someone a job or task to do: The teacher *assigned* homework today.

as•sur•ance [ə•shŏŏr'əns] *n.* Words or actions that make someone feel better or less afraid: The child needed *assurance* that he was safe during the storm.

au•di•ence [ô'dē•əns] *n.* A group of people who listen to and watch a performance: The *audience* must be quiet so that everybody can enjoy the play.

B

band [band] *n.* A group of musicians who get together to play their instruments, usually brass, percussion, and woodwinds.

Braille

base•ment [bās'mənt] *n.* The lowest floor of a house or building, partly below ground level: We ran down into the *basement* when we heard the tornado warning.

bound

beck•on [bek'ən] *v.* **beck•oned, beck•on•ing** To signal or call to come over: The teacher waved and *beckoned* the students into the classroom.

bois•ter•ous [bois'tər•əs] *adj.* Noisy and wild: The *boisterous* children made it hard to hear the TV. *syns.* loud, excited

bound [bound] *v.* **bound•ed, bound•ing** To leap: We saw the playful kitten *bounding* toward the fallen leaf.

Braille [brāl] *n.* A system of writing for people who are blind that uses raised dots as letters and numbers to be read with the fingertips: Instead of using their eyes to read printing, people who are blind use their fingers to read *Braille*.

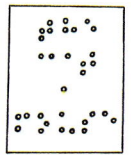

Braille

GLOSSARY PAGES 322–325

brass

burrow

canoe

brass [bras] *n. (pl.)* Musical instruments, such as a trumpet, that are made out of metal and that give a loud sound when blown.

bron·co·bust·er [brong′kō·bus′tər] *n.* A person who rides wild horses or bulls: *Broncobusters* may get hurt when they ride wild horses.

buck·skin [buk′skin′] *n.* A soft material made from the skin of deer or sheep: My uncle has a beautiful jacket made of *buckskin*.

bur·row [bûr′ō] *v.* **bur·rowed, bur·row·ing** To dig or hide in a hole: I watch my hamster *burrow* into the leaves to make a warm nest.

but·ler [but′lər] *n.* A person who works as the head servant of a house.

clatter

C

ca·noe [kə·nōō] *v.* **ca·noed, ca·noe·ing** To ride in a *canoe*, which is a small boat for one or two people.

cat·a·logue [kat′ə·lôg′ or kat′ə·log′] *n.* A book that lists things for sale: Mr. Cortez orders many clothes from *catalogues*.

chan·de·lier [shan′də·lir′] *n.* A lamp that hangs from the ceiling: The *chandelier* over the table lit the room.

chord [kôrd] *n.* In music, three or more sounds (notes) from a musical instrument that are played at one time: Juan plays *chords* on the piano.

cho·rus [kôr′əs] *n.* A group of singers.

clat·ter [klat′ər] *v.* **clat·tered, clat·ter·ing** To make a loud crashing or knocking noise: The falling dishes *clattered*.

cockatoo

cock·a·too [kok′ə·tōō] *n.* A kind of parrot: *Cockatoos* are birds with colorful crests.

co·coa [kō′kō] *n.* A hot chocolate drink: Mrs. Brown gave us a cup of *cocoa*. *syn.* hot chocolate

com·mer·cial [kə·mûr′shəl] *n.* An advertisement on TV or radio for the purpose of selling something.

com·pass [kum′pəs or kom′pəs] *n.* An instrument that always points to the north, so people can figure out in which direction to go.

con·ser·va·to·ry [kən·sûr′və·tôr′ē] *n.* A small greenhouse for growing plants and flowers: Jim worked in the *conservatory*, raising tulips and roses.

creek [krēk *or* krik] *n.* A small river: Every summer we waded in a *creek* by our house. *syns.* stream, brook

dollop

crin·kle [kring′kəl] *v.* **crin·kled, crin·kling** To wrinkle or put ridges into: She *crinkled* her nose at the smelly garbage in the alley.

cu·ri·ous [kyŏŏr′ē·əs] *adj.* Very interested; eager to learn about or do something: The children were *curious* to hear how the story ends.

cus·tom [kus′təm] *n.* Something that has been done by a group of people for a long time so that it becomes part of their ways: A *custom* at our house is to light candles every Friday, before sunset.

D

deed [dēd] *n.* An action taken; something someone has done: Jeff's good *deeds* in helping injured animals were reported in the local newspaper.

dol·lop [däl′əp] *n.* A lump or blob of something: She spread a *dollop* of butter on the toast.

cocoa The people of Mexico gave us our word *cocoa*. Chocolate is made from *cocoa* beans. Mexicans, who first used chocolate, called it chocolatl, their word for "bitter water." Believe it or not, it takes a lot of sugar to make chocolate sweet!

crinkle

dollop

a	add	ŏŏ	took
ā	ace	ōō	pool
â	care	u	up
ä	palm	û	burn
e	end	yōō	fuse
ē	equal	oi	oil
i	it	ou	pout
ī	ice	ng	ring
o	odd	th	thin
ō	open	th	this
ô	order	zh	vision

ə = { a in *above* e in *sicken*; i in *possible*; o in *melon* u in *circus* }

dough

easel Our word *easel* comes from the Dutch word *ezel*, which means "donkey." Why would a stand made to hold paintings be named after a donkey? Because a donkey is a "beast of burden" used to hold and carry loads, just as an *easel* is.

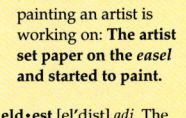
exhibition

dough [dō] *n.* A mix of flour and liquid used to make foods such as bread and muffins: I added raisins to the *dough* before I baked the cookies.

E

ea·sel [ē′zəl] *n.* A frame or stand used to hold the painting an artist is working on: The artist set paper on the *easel* and started to paint.

eld·est [el′dist] *adj.* The oldest: Carlos is the *eldest* child in his family because all his brothers and sisters are younger than he is.

emp·ty [emp′tē] *adj.* Not filled; holding nothing: Waiting for dinner, Ken had an *empty* feeling in his stomach.

en·ter·tain·ment [en′tər·tān′mənt] *n.* Something performed to interest or give pleasure to an audience: Movies are my favorite kind of *entertainment*.

explore

ex·ag·ger·ate [ig·zaj′ə·rāt′] *v.* **ex·ag·ger·at·ed, ex·ag·ger·at·ing** To make something seem greater or more than it really is: My brother *exaggerated* when he said he caught a big fish because it weighed only five pounds.

ex·cit·ing [ik·sī′ting] *adj.* Bringing out strong feelings of interest: The fair was very *exciting* because of the rides.

ex·er·cise [ek′sər·sīz′] *n.* Active movement of the body to improve strength or health: We did *exercises* in gym class to strengthen our arms.

ex·hi·bi·tion [ek′sə·bish′ən] *n.* A showing of art: We liked seeing the paintings at the *exhibition*. *syn.* exhibit

ex·plore [ik·splôr′] *v.* **ex·plored, ex·plor·ing** To look around in order to find new things: Our friends are going to *explore* the caves.

fiddle

F

fid·dle [fid′(ə)l] *n.* Another term for a violin: Country music is often played on a *fiddle*.

fig·ure·head [fig′yər·hed′] *n.* A carved figure set at the front of a sailing ship: The museum's old ships had *figureheads* of beautiful women.

fringe [frinj] 1 *n.* A decorative trimming of threads hanging from an edge. 2 *v.* To attach or border with fringe: Terri helped her mom *fringe* the tablecloth with long, silky threads.

frol·ic [frol′ik] *v.* **frol·icked, frol·ick·ing** To play happily about: The happy children were *frolicking* in the first snow. *syn.* romp

G

gift [gift] *n.* Talent; a person's inborn ability to do something well.

handkerchief

gig·gle [gig′əl] *v.* **gig·gled, gig·gling** To laugh in a silly way: All the children started to *giggle* when Joey's hat fell in the fish tank.

grain [grān] *n.* A tiny bit or piece of something: I can't count every *grain* of sand on this beach. *syns.* particle, speck

grand·daugh·ter [gran(d)′dô′tər] *n.* The daughter of a person's son or daughter: My *granddaughter* has dark hair and blue eyes, just like my son has.

grump·y [grum′pē] *adj.* In a bad mood: I'm *grumpy* because I had a bad day. *syns.* crabby, grouchy

H

hand·ker·chief [hang′kər·chif] *n.* A square piece of cloth used to wipe the nose: He blew his nose with his red *handkerchief*. *syn.* hankie

fiddle Similar to *violin*, *fiddle* comes from the name of a Roman goddess of joy and victory, Vitula. In Latin, *Vitula* means "a stringed instrument." Stringed instruments were played at festivals, thus the meaning "joy." *Vitula* became *violin*. In German, it became *fiedel* and in English, *fiddle*.

figurehead

a	add	ŏŏ	took
ā	ace	ōō	pool
â	care	u	up
ä	palm	û	burn
e	end	yōō	fuse
ē	equal	oi	oil
i	it	ou	pout
ī	ice	ng	ring
o	odd	th	thin
ō	open	th	this
ô	order	zh	vision

ə = { a in *above* e in *sicken*; i in *possible*; o in *melon* u in *circus* }

GLOSSARY / T517

GLOSSARY

hollow — lemming

hol·low [hol′ō] *n.* A small valley: Ferns grow in the low ground of the *hollows*.

I

imitate Imitate is from the Latin word *imitari*, which means "make a copy of." The words *image* and *imitate* share the base *im* meaning "likeness."

im·i·tate [im′ə·tāt′] *v.* **im·i·tat·ed, im·i·tat·ing** To do something the same way as someone or something else: When Matt was *imitating* Jim's laugh, we thought Jim was in the room.

im·press [im·pres′] *v.* **im·pressed, im·press·ing** To affect someone's feelings or mind: Juan hopes his extra work will *impress* his teacher.

in·stru·ment [in′strə·mənt] *n.* A device, such as a trumpet, piano, or drum, used to make musical sounds: Out of the many *instruments* Bo plays, he likes the drums best.

isle [īl] *n.* A small island: We paddled our canoe around the *isle* in the center of Beaver Lake.

knapsack

lemming

J

jew·el [jōō′əl] *n.* A gemstone of great value: The *jewel* in the ring was a ruby.

K

knap·sack [nap′sak′] *n.* A bag with shoulder straps, worn on the back: Joe carried our picnic lunch in his *knapsack*. *syn.* backpack

L

la·va·liere [lăv′ə·li(ə)r′] *n.* A necklace: Her gold *lavaliere* slipped off her neck during dinner and fell into her tomato soup.

lem·ming [lem′ing] *n.* A small ratlike animal that lives in the Arctic: *Lemmings* move from place to place and sometimes drown by rushing blindly into the sea.

library — nuisance

li·brar·y [lī′brer′ē *or* lī′brə·rē] *n.* A place where books are kept for reading and research: I borrowed some books from the public *library*.

lu·pine [lōō′pin] *n.* A kind of plant related to peas and beans that has lovely flowers: We found a blue *lupine* and some other wild flowers growing along the trail.

M

mar·i·gold [mar′ə·gōld′] *n.* A yellow flower: We planted *marigolds* in our flower garden.

mar·ma·lade [mär′mə·lād] *n.* A kind of jam: The orange *marmalade* Aunt June made tasted good spread on biscuits and toast.

mast [mast] *n.* A tall pole that holds up a ship's sail: The storm broke all the ship's *masts*, and the sails crashed into the sea.

mem·o·rize [mem′ə·rīz′] *v.* **mem·o·rized, mem·o·riz·ing** To learn something by heart: Mike is so good at *memorizing* songs that he can sing songs without looking at the words. *syn.* remember

mim·ic [mim′ik] *v.* **mim·icked, mim·ick·ing** To copy or repeat what someone does or says: The parrot was *mimicking* everything we said.

mu·si·cian [myōō·zish′ən] *n.* Someone skilled in playing a musical instrument and performing music: The *musicians* were playing one of their hit songs for the concert.

N

nui·sance [n(y)ōō′səns] *n.* Someone or something that bothers others: Everyone thought Harold was a *nuisance* because he cried a lot.

library In Latin, *book* comes from the word *liber*. It also is related to the Russian word *lub*, which means "bark." Bark was one of the first materials people used to write on. *Liber* eventually became *libraria*, meaning "bookstore." In English, *library* has never meant "bookstore," but "a place where books are kept."

marigold

musician

a	add	ōō	took
ā	ace	ōō	pool
â	care	u	up
ä	palm	û	burn
e	end	yōō	fuse
ē	equal	oi	oil
i	it	ou	pout
ī	ice	ng	ring
o	odd	th	thin
ō	open	th	this
ô	order	zh	vision

ə = { a in *above*, e in *sicken*, i in *possible*, o in *melon*, u in *circus* }

opera — pioneer

orchestra Orchestra comes from the Greek word *orkhēstrā*, which means "a semicircular space at the front of a stage in which the chorus dances." In English it has been used to mean "the part of a theater where the musicians play." Eventually it came to mean the group of musicians itself.

O

op·er·a [op′ər·ə *or* op′rə] *n.* A play set to music in which the lines are sung: When I attend the *opera*, I sit up front so I can better see the singers.

or·chard [ôr′chərd] *n.* A field of trees grown for their fruit or nuts: We went to the *orchard* to pick apples.

or·ches·tra [ôr′kəs·trə] *n.* A group of musicians who play different instruments: The *orchestra* received great applause when it played "The Star-Spangled Banner."

out·doors·man [out·dôrz′mən] *n., pl.* **out·doors·men** A person who enjoys spending time outdoors in nature: We call Pedro and Luis the family *outdoorsmen* because they love to fish and hike in the mountains.

P

per·cus·sion [pər·kush′ən] *n. (pl.)* The group of musical instruments, such as a drum, whose sound is produced by striking or hitting: The timpani, or kettledrums, the bells, the cymbals, the triangle, and the snare drum all belong to the *percussion* section of the orchestra.

per·form·ance [pər·fôr′məns] *n.* A show, play, or concert in front of an audience: The audience clapped loudly at the end of the *performance*. *syn.* act

pi·o·neer [pī′ə·nir′] *adj.* Having to do with one of the first people to settle in a particular area: American *pioneer* families traveled west in wagons and on horseback to find new homes.

percussion

pistil — reed

pis·til [pis′təl] *n.* The part of a flower that produces seeds: If you open the *pistil* of a flower, you will often see the seeds inside.

plain [plān] *n.* A large area of almost level land without trees: We could see for miles across the empty *plains*. *syns.* prairie, field

pol·len [pol′ən] *n.* A powder in plants that helps seeds make new plants: *Pollen* may be carried from one flower to another by bees.

pon·cho [pon′chō] *n.* A rain jacket that is pulled over the head.

prai·rie [prâr′ē] *adj.* Having to do with a large grassy area without trees: *Prairie* dogs are small animals that live in holes in the ground.

pre·his·tor·ic [prē′his·tôr′ik] *adj.* From a time very long ago, before written history began: Dinosaurs were *prehistoric* animals. *syn.* ancient

pro·fes·sion·al [prə·fesh′ən·əl] *adj.* Having to do with a job that requires special training: A mechanic's *professional* skill is needed to fix the car.

prompt·ly [prompt′lē] *adv.* Quickly: We were glad the fire truck arrived *promptly*. *syn.* immediately

prow [prou] *n.* The front end of a boat or ship: Sailors stood at the *prows* of the ships, looking ahead for signs of land. *syn.* bow

R

rec·ol·lec·tion [rek′ə·lek′shən] *n.* Something remembered. *syns.* memory, remembrance

reed [rēd] *n.* A small, thin, flat piece of wood, metal, or plastic used as the mouthpiece or in the mouthpiece of some musical instruments, such as the clarinet: Tracey's *reed* was broken, so no sound came out of her clarinet.

pistil, pollen

prehistoric

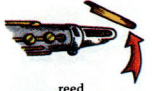
reed

a	add	ōō	took
ā	ace	ōō	pool
â	care	u	up
ä	palm	û	burn
e	end	yōō	fuse
ē	equal	oi	oil
i	it	ou	pout
ī	ice	ng	ring
o	odd	th	thin
ō	open	th	this
ô	order	zh	vision

ə = { a in *above*, e in *sicken*, i in *possible*, o in *melon*, u in *circus* }

GLOSSARY PAGES 330–332

rein

riper

rodeo

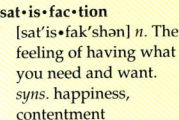
scrape

rein [rān] *v.* **reined, rein·ing** To pull back or control: **Edward *reined* in the ox and stopped plowing.**

re·tired [ri·tīrd′] *adj.* No longer working: **My mother plans to travel now that she is *retired*.**

rhythm [riŧh′əm] *n.* Repetition of a beat played throughout a musical piece: **I tap my feet to the song's *rhythm*.**

rip·er [rīp′ər] *adj.* More ripe; fully grown or ready to eat: **Each day the tomatoes grow *riper*.** *syn.* mature

ro·de·o [rō′dē·ō *or* rō·dā′ō] *n.* A contest for people like cowhands to show their skill: **In the *rodeo*, he rode the wild horse and won a prize.**

S

sat·is·fac·tion [sat′is·fak′shən] *n.* The feeling of having what you need and want. *syns.* happiness, contentment

shiver

sci·en·tist [sī′ən·tist] *n.* A person who finds and studies information about different things: ***Scientists*** try to learn more about dinosaurs.

scrape [skrāp] *v.* **scraped, scrap·ing** To take something off by rubbing it with a sharp edge: ***Scrape*** the food off the plates before washing them.

sculpt [skulpt] *v.* **sculpted, sculpt·ing** To make or shape a statue: **The artist *sculpts* the shapes of faces in clay.** *syn.* form

set·tler [set′lər] *n.* Someone who comes to live in a new area: **Early American *settlers* came mainly from Europe.**

sha·man [shä′mən *or* shā′mən] *n.* A type of priest among Native Americans; a person who gives advice and who is greatly respected in his community.

shiv·er [shiv′ər] *v.* **shiv·ered, shiv·er·ing** To shake because of feeling cold or afraid.

shortening

short·en·ing [shôr′tən·ing] *n.* Butter or oil used in cooking.

shrill [shril] *adj.* Having a high-pitched sound: **The *shrill* sound of the whistle made us jump.**

sin·gle [sing′gəl] *adj.* Only one; one person or thing: **Not a *single* person laughed when I dropped my award.**

skil·let [skil′it] *n.* A frying pan.

splin·ter [splin′tər] *n.* A thin piece of wood split off from a larger piece: ***Splinters*** from the wood got in my fingers.

stern·ly [stûrn′lē] *adv.* Firmly; strictly: **The girl spoke to her brother so *sternly* that he began to cry.** *syn.* harshly

strings [stringz] *n.* (pl.) Musical instruments, such as the violin, that have thin wires and that are played with a bow.

stumped [stumpt] *adj.* *informal* Confused or without an answer: **The problem was so hard, Mom was *stumped*.**

sub·way [sub′wā′] *n.* An underground train.

T

ther·mos [thûr′məs] *n.* A bottle for keeping liquids hot or cold for several hours.

thread [thred] *n.* A very thin string of cloth: **He used *thread* to sew a tear in the old shirt.**

tin·kling [ting′kling] *adj.* Sounding soft and like a small bell.

tran·quil [trang′kwil *or* tran′kwil] *adj.* Calm and quiet: **We easily rowed the boat across the *tranquil* lake.** *syn.* peaceful

treas·ure [trezh′ər] *n.* Valuable items, such as jewels and money, which are kept stored: **The ship set sail in search of *treasure* buried deep at sea.**

tribe [trīb] *n.* A group of people who have a leader and who share beliefs: **The Seminoles are an Indian *tribe*.**

tribe

skillet

tribe *Tribe* comes from the Latin word *tribus*, meaning "division of the Roman people." Since *tri* means "three," it meant the three original tribes of Rome.

a	add	o͞o	took
ā	ace	o͞o	pool
â	care	u	up
ä	palm	û	burn
e	end	yo͞o	fuse
ē	equal	oi	oil
i	it	ou	pout
ī	ice	ng	ring
o	odd	th	thin
ō	open	ŧh	this
ô	order	zh	vision

$$a = \begin{cases} \text{a in } above & \text{e in } sicken \\ \text{i in } possible \\ \text{o in } melon & \text{u in } circus \end{cases}$$

tropical

tropical

wilderness

woodwind

trop·i·cal [trop′i·kəl] *adj.* Like or related to a jungle or warm climate: **We enjoyed the warm weather and delicious fruit on the *tropical* island.**

U

u·ten·sil [yo͞o·ten′səl] *n.* A tool used to do or make something: **We keep our gardening *utensils* in the garage.**

V

vac·u·um [vak′yo͞o·(ə)m] *n.* **vac·u·um flask** A kind of bottle that keeps liquids hot or cold, such as a thermos bottle: **Marie kept the ice water in a tightly closed *vacuum* bottle to keep it cold.**

vi·sion [vizh′ən] *n.* Something imagined, as in a dream; a look into the future: **Kathy had *visions* of becoming a ballet dancer.**

woodwind

W

war·ri·or [wôr′ē·ər *or* wor′ē·ər] *n.* A person who is or has been involved in war: **The brave *warriors* defended their homeland.**

wharf [(h)wôrf] *n., pl.* **wharves** or **wharfs** A dock along a shore, where boats wait to load or unload: **The fishermen steered their boats toward the *wharves* to unload the day's catch.**

wil·der·ness [wil′dər·nis] *n.* An area where people have not settled: **The family happily hiked and camped in the *wilderness* for three weeks.** *syn.* outdoors

wood·wind [wo͝od′wind′] *n.* A musical instrument, usually made of wood or metal, that you blow into or use a reed to play: **The saxophone is one of the popular *woodwinds* used to play jazz.**

Using the Index of Titles and Authors

Explain to students that an index is often found at the back of a book and usually consists of an alphabetical listing of topics covered in that particular book. Tell students that sometimes books have special kinds of indexes, such as the Index of Titles and Authors at the back of their anthologies.

In looking over with students the first page of the Index, Student Anthology page 333, point out that all of the entries are in alphabetical order and that authors are listed with last names first. Ask students how they can tell at a glance which entries are selection titles and which are authors' names. You will also want to call attention to the references to page numbers in light print. Then you may want to select several index entries and have students predict what they will find when they turn to the page or pages listed.

INDEX OF TITLES AND AUTHORS

Page numbers in light printed letters refer to information about the author.

Adventures of Ali Baba Bernstein, The, 56

Bodecker, N. M., 293
Bond, Michael, 256
Bradley, Alfred, 256

Cleary, Beverly, 130, 132, 144
Closed, I am a mystery, 292
Cooney, Barbara, 16, 31

dePaola, Tomie, 224, 254

Field, Rachel, 314

Gift for Tía Rosa, A, 170

Hayes, Ann, 82
Hello Book!, 293
Holman, Felice, 78
Hurwitz, Johanna, 56, 75

Johnny Appleseed, 38
Justin and the Best Biscuits in the World, 188

Kellogg, Steven, 38

Legend of the Indian Paintbrush, The, 224
Lisa's Fingerprints, 76
Little, Jean, 168
Livingston, Myra Cohn, 292
Lost Lake, The, 298

MacLachlan, Patricia, 150
Martí, José, 214

Meet the Orchestra, 82
Merrill, Claire, 32
Miss Rumphius, 16
Morrison, Lillian, 294
Music, Music for Everyone, 94

O'Neill, Mary, 76

Paddington Paints a Picture, 256
People, 313
Piggins, 274

Ramona Quimby, Age 8, 132
Ramona's Neighborhood, 130

Say, Allen, 298, 311
Seed Is a Promise, A, 32
Some People, 314

Taha, Karen T., 170
Through Grandpa's Eyes, 150

Versos sencillos/Simple Verses, 214

Walter, Mildred Pitts, 186, 212
Who Am I?, 78
Williams, Vera B., 94, 120
Would You Like, 294
Writers, 168

Yolen, Jane, 274, 289

Zolotow, Charlotte, 313